# reflective
# teaching
## in early education

# reflective teaching

## in early education

Jennifer Colwell

with Helen Beaumont, Helen Bradford, Julie Canavan, Emma Cook, Denise Kingston, Holly Linklater, Sue Lynch, Catriona McDonald, Sheila Nutkins, Sarah Ottewell, Chris Randall and Tim Waller.

B L O O M S B U R Y

LONDON • NEW DELHI • NEW YORK • SYDNEY

**Bloomsbury Academic**

An imprint of Bloomsbury Publishing Plc

| | |
|---|---|
| 50 Bedford Square | 1385 Broadway |
| London | New York |
| WC1B 3DP | NY 10018 |
| UK | USA |

**www.bloomsbury.com**

**BLOOMSBURY and the Diana logo are trademarks of Bloomsbury Publishing Plc**

First published 2015

**British Library Cataloguing-in-Publication Data**
A catalogue record for this book is available from the British Library.

ISBN: HB: 978-1-4411-7798-8
PB: 978-1-4411-7204-4
ePDF: 978-1-4411-8095-7
ePub: 978-1-4411-8470-2

**Library of Congress Cataloging-in-Publication Data**
A catalog record for this book is available from the Library of Congress.

Series: Reflective Teaching

Typeset by Fakenham Prepress Solutions, Fakenham, Norfolk NR21 8NN
Printed and bound in Great Britain

*In memory of Margaret Hayes, who always thought of others before herself*

# Contents

www. ↻

# Part four  Reflecting on consequences

# Part five  Deepening understanding

# Introduction

This book recognizes that reflective teaching in early education will take place in a broad range of contexts and settings. The term Early Childhood Education and Care (ECEC) is used throughout this text to describe the practice in any of these contexts and in any early years setting. The adults working in the settings are referred to as early years practitioners. This includes all colleagues with expertise in early years who work in a considered way to support babies' and children's learning and development, whatever their context of work or job title.

We believe that caring relationships between practitioners and children must be the bedrock for pedagogy in ECEC settings, and that it is not possible to support children's learning and development without providing an emotionally supportive environment. Thus, the placing of 'care' and 'education' at opposite ends of the spectrum when considering early years provision is recognized as a false dichotomy, with cognitive development, physical development and social and emotional development all being seen as vital aspects of a child's education.

Along with parents, carers and families, early years practitioners can play a highly influential role in children's development in these formative years. A wealth of research literature is available to show the enduring beneficial effect of high-quality ECEC on children's future lives and educational achievement, with particularly strong evidence showing the positive impact of early educational interventions for children living in situations of socio-economic disadvantage.

Practitioners in ECEC may be working with children from birth to seven years within a diverse range of settings. This includes, but is not limited to, maintained schools, private, voluntary and independent sector nurseries, pre-schools and schools, childminding settings, nurseries operating as part of projects such as Children's Centres, academies and free schools. Given this range of settings it is likely that there will be a variety of roles taken on by early years practitioners, including childcare manager, room leader, lead professional, teacher and childminder. This book builds on the belief that whatever the context and in whatever role, children have an entitlement to high-quality ECEC, led by professionals who are committed to reflective practice.

This book offers *two* levels of support:

- Comprehensive, evidence-based guidance on key issues in early years practice, including: child development, building relationships, and learning and teaching strategies.

- Unique, evidence-informed principles and concepts to support a deeper understanding of the theories informing and underpinning early years practice.

There are three key messages presented within this book, the companion Readings book and the website. The first is that it *is* possible to identify practice which is more effective than other forms of practice in most circumstances. Practitioners can, therefore, develop, improve, promote and defend their expertise by gathering evidence and by embedding inquiry and evaluation within their practice. We believe that this is crucial to ensuring that the key role early years practitioners provide is recognized within society, which supports the need to raise awareness of early years practitioner as a high-status profession.

The second message is that evidence about effective practice should be interpreted. As well as having information about teaching strategies, we need to be able to identify the theory behind these strategies, to help us to understand both what we are doing and why we are doing it – we need to *understand* what is going on so we can develop our practice accordingly.

Finally, we need to remember that ECEC has moral purpose and social consequences. The provision we make is connected to our future society, our own personal enjoyment and fulfilment and, crucially, to the life chances of the babies and children with whom we work. These issues require very careful consideration.

Reflective activity is thus of vital importance to developing early years practice as a profession. Being able to consider and understand our own actions:

- allows us to make professional judgements and justify our position and actions;
- provides a vehicle for learning and professional development: when we unpick our actions we can identify our own learning and development needs;
- above all, is a means to improve practice, raise children's achievements and ensure that the experiences of the babies and children in our settings is of the highest quality possible.

We hope that you will find the information and guidance provided in this book helpful. We advocate working collectively whenever possible. We make suggestions that you extend many of the reflective activities provided in the book to work with a colleague or another student to extend your thinking. We have done this as we believe that drawing on the experience, knowledge, ideas and expertise of others helps to extend knowledge and develop thinking. We have mirrored this approach in the production of this book – working together to extend our thinking and combine our knowledge to provide a comprehensive overview of the key issues facing early years practice and provision today. Information about the authors is provided below.

**Jennifer Colwell** is a Fellow at the Education Research Centre, University of Brighton, an educational consultant and a Fellow of the Higher Education Academy. Her research focuses on how practitioners support the development of children's social competencies and how such competencies impact upon children's learning and development. Her teaching centres on researching practice and supporting practitioners through their undergraduate and postgraduate studies. Jen has a PhD in Education (Early Years).

**Helen Beaumont** taught in primary schools in Hackney, Islington and Brighton for 14 years. She has been a local authority Early Years Consultant in Brighton and Hove since 2001, where she leads a team supporting private, voluntary and independent settings and early years classes in maintained schools. She has a Professional Doctorate in Education.

**Helen Bradford** taught in early years education before moving into teacher education at the Faculty of Education, Cambridge University in 2004. She is currently a member of the course management team for the Early Years and Primary PGCE where she co-coordinates the Professional Studies and English courses, with a focus on early years practice. Helen has published extensively in the area of language and communication development.

**Julie Canavan** is a Senior Lecturer in the School of Education at the University of Brighton. As a trained early years teacher she initially worked in south London as a nursery and reception class teacher, with a special interest in providing English as an Additional Language (EAL) support. Julie then moved on to work for a language service, working with families and training staff across East Sussex. Julie's research interests include the role of language development in inclusion in early childhood settings.

**Emma Cook** is Deputy Manager at One World Nursery at the University of Brighton. She also works with students at the Research, Development and Training Base and Leadership Centre at Pen Green, which provides professional training and higher education courses for early years practitioners.

**Denise Kingston** is a Senior Lecturer in the School of Education at the University of Brighton. She is a qualified educational psychologist and trained teacher. She has worked for many different local authorities as a teacher, educational psychologist, portage supervisor, advisor, consultant and Early Years Development and Childcare Partnership senior manager. Her teaching areas include early years care and education, where she enjoys working with work-based students and the emphasis of relating theory to practice. She also works with students who are preparing for and have achieved Early Years Professional Status and Early Years Teacher Status. Denise worked with the Centre for Studies on Inclusive Education on the *Index for Inclusion*: developing play, learning and participation in early years and childcare, which has been well received both nationally and internationally. Currently she is a researcher for the Institute of Education's department of Early Years and Primary Education.

**Holly Linklater** divides her time between teaching in a primary school and lecturing for the Faculty of Education, Cambridge University, particularly the Early Years and Primary PGCE and MEd in Researching Practice. Her research focuses on developing ways to more fully articulate the complexity of pedagogy, or the 'craft' of teaching. She is also deeply committed to writing and teaching about the importance of inclusive education: how educationalists must work in ways that recognize the full humanity of all children, and what we can practically do to enhance the experiences of all learners.

**Sue Lynch** is Senior Lecturer in Education Studies and Physical Education at the University of Brighton. Prior to this she worked as an advisory teacher for a Local Authority, taught in primary schools and managed a nursery that promoted daily motor skill and physical development for all children. She is an educational consultant, specializing in supporting early years practitioners in developing children's physical literacy.

**Catriona McDonald** is a Senior Teaching Fellow at the University of Aberdeen. She is Programme Director for the BA Childhood Practice and for the Post Graduate Certificate in Early Years Education. She also teaches on initial teacher education programmes. She is particularly interested in active learning through play which supports an integrated and holistic approach to learning and development of young children. Catriona worked for around 20 years in Uppsala, Sweden, within the state education system. On her return to Scotland she worked for a number of years in the Further Education sector, in the delivery of programmes for Early Years Professionals in Childcare and Education at HNC level and beyond.

**Sheila Nutkins** is a Teaching Fellow in the School of Education at the University of Aberdeen. She is involved in teaching, developing and supporting students on all Initial Teacher Education courses, BA Childhood Practice (BACP) and the Early Years Postgraduate Certificate in Education (EYPGCE). She taught in London as Deputy Head and has lived and worked in Aberdeen since 1991.

**Sarah Ottewell** is Deputy Manager at One World Nursery at the University of Brighton. She is an Early Years Professional and has over 20 years' experience working with children under the age of five years.

**Chris Randall** is an Early Years Professional working at One World Nursery at the University of Brighton. Chris is particularly interested in inclusion and in developing the role of men in ECEC.

**Tim Waller** is Professor of Child and Family Studies in the Faculty of Health, Social Care and Education at Anglia Ruskin University. Tim is a Convener of the Outdoor Learning SIG in the European Early Childhood Education Research Association (EECERA). Tim taught in nursery, infant and primary schools in London and has also worked in the USA. His research interests include well-being, outdoor learning, pedagogy and social justice in early childhood. Recently, he has edited a special edition of the *European Early Childhood Education Association Journal* on 'Outdoor Play and Learning'.

**PART ONE: BECOMING A REFLECTIVE PROFESSIONAL** We start this book with a chapter focused on ourselves and on the significance of the contribution we can make, as early years practitioners, to children and their families. This is followed by an introduction (Chapter 2) to ways of understanding 'learning', and how children come to know and understand. The chapter on reflective practice (Chapter 3) discusses the process of reflection and how developing this process as an individual and as a staff team can lead to improvements in the quality of practice. Chapter 4 introduces and considers *ten principles of effective teaching and learning* and how they can offer a structure for developing and reviewing practice in the early years. These come from a major UK research and development programme and also draw on accumulated evidence from around the world.

Together, these four chapters support the process of beginning to understand ourselves and our actions, to think about what we do and why we do it, and introduce structure to the process of reflection. Additionally, through consideration of how babies and children learn, and a discussion of the *ten principles of effective teaching and learning,* the chapters support a deeper understanding of the theories informing and underpinning early years practice.

**PART TWO: CREATING CONDITIONS FOR LEARNING** concerns the creation of environments to support high-quality teaching and learning. We begin by thinking about the ways in which people contribute to and challenge such circumstances through their actions. We then move to the heart of life with a focus on relationships (Chapter 6). Chapter 7 builds upon this to illustrate how positive cycles of behaviour can be created. Finally, we consider a range of learning spaces both indoors and outdoors (Chapter 8), and the affordances they offer for formal and informal learning.

**PART THREE: TEACHING FOR LEARNING** supports the development of practice across the three classic dimensions of teaching: curriculum, pedagogy and assessment. Chapter 9 starts us off with a consideration of the benefits and challenges of having a curriculum for the early years, before we review curricular aims and design principles. Chapter 10 puts these ideas into action and supports the development of short-, medium- and long-term planning across the age range. Chapter 11 offers ways of understanding the art, craft and science of pedagogy, and the development of a pedagogic repertoire. 'Communication' (Chapter 12) extends this with an introduction to the vital role of talking, listening, reading and writing across the curriculum. Finally, this part concludes by demonstrating how assessment is an integral aspect of teaching in ECEC (Chapter 13).

**PART FOUR: REFLECTING ON CONSEQUENCES** draws attention the consequences of what we do in ECEC. Chapter 14 reviews big issues in assessment, with particular attention to how we need to work with parents when we are assessing children's needs and progress. 'Inclusion' (Chapter 15) asks us to consider various dimensions of difference and also the ways in which routine processes differentiate between people. The emphasis is on accepting difference as part of the human condition and on how to build more inclusive communities within settings, which in turn will contribute to the development of a more inclusive society.

**PART FIVE: DEEPENING UNDERSTANDING** is the final, synoptic part of the book. It integrates major themes though discussion of expertise and professionalism. 'Expertise' (Chapter 16) harvests and integrates powerful ideas from previous chapters into a holistic conceptual framework of enduring issues in teaching and learning in ECEC. The chapter constructs a framework describing dimensions of expert thinking. In Chapter 17, 'Professionalism', we consider the role of ECEC in our societies and suggest how reflective practitioners can contribute to democratic processes.

In addition, supplementary chapters are available on the website, **reflectiveteaching.co.uk**. These chapters provide an introduction to Inquiry, offering support in researching your practice and the methods and tools you may adopt to do this.

# part one

# Becoming a reflective professional

1. **Identity** Who are we and what do we stand for?
2. **Learning** How can we understand learner development?
3. **Reflection** How can we develop the quality of our practice?
4. **Principles** What are the foundations of effective teaching and learning?

Chapter 1 focuses on ourselves and on the significance of the contribution we can make to children and their families as early years practitioners. This is followed by an introduction (Chapter 2) to ways of understanding 'learning', and how children come to know and understand. The chapter on reflective practice (Chapter 3) discusses the process of reflection and how developing this process as an individual and as a staff team can lead to improvements in the quality of our practice. Chapter 4 introduces and considers *ten principles of effective teaching and learning* and how they can offer a structure for developing and reviewing practice in the early years. These come from a major UK research and development programme and also draw on accumulated evidence from around the world.

Together, these four chapters support the process of beginning to understand ourselves and our actions, to think about what we do and why we do it, and introduces structure to the process of reflection. Additionally, through consideration of how babies and children learn, and a discussion of the *ten principles of effective teaching and learning*, the chapters support a deeper understanding of the theories informing and underpinning early years practice.

# Identity
## Who are we and what do we stand for?

**1**

# Introduction

This chapter is concerned with the practitioners working in Early Childhood Education and Care settings (ECEC), the babies and children attending those settings, and with the feelings and perceptions we hold in relation to ourselves and others.

A key issue we explore in this book is that of 'identity', in a context where the role and status of early years practitioners, as professionals, is continually evolving. We also consider how the identities of adults and children relate to each other and to the cultures and opportunities we encounter. To understand the identities of each other, and crucially of ourselves, we must consider how our individual life experiences shape who we become and how we see the world and others.

The first section of this chapter focuses on the role of early years practitioners, and how this is perceived by ourselves and others. We consider why people choose to work within ECEC and the values that might inform and sustain our practice. We consider the debates surrounding the terminology and meanings of 'professional'. We introduce what is known about the complex role of ECEC practitioners and how practitioners respond to the multiple and complex aspects of their role. This section also reflects the belief that there are always things that we can do to improve the quality of our provision for the benefit of our colleagues, the babies, children and families with whom we work and indeed ourselves.

Section 2 focuses on thinking about babies and young children. We consider how our values and pre-existing understandings may influence how we think about babies, children and their learning, and how we can challenge our expectations to ensure we have the highest aspirations for them all.

Section 3 considers the ways in which early education influences babies and young children as they develop, and how children's early experiences of education influence their lives and future educational achievements. The section concludes with a discussion of the development of the careers of reflective early years practitioners, including the aspiration of matching personal values with practice.

Below we have indicated the evidence-informed 'principles' which are relevant to this chapter. We provide this information at the beginning of each chapter. Chapter 4 provides detail on the origin of the ten principles, their development and how we believe these principles support a deeper understanding of the theories informing and underpinning early years practice.

## TLRP principles

Two principles are of particular relevance to this chapter on identity and values in early education:

**Principle 1: Effective teaching and learning equips learners for life in its broadest sense.** Learning should aim to help people to develop the intellectual, personal and social resources that will enable them to participate as active citizens, contribute to economic development and flourish as individuals in a diverse and changing society. This implies adopting a broad view of learning outcomes and ensuring that equity and social justice are taken seriously.

**Principle 9: Effective teaching and learning depends on teacher learning.**
The need for teachers to learn continuously in order to develop their knowledge and skills, and adapt and develop their roles, especially through classroom inquiry, should be recognized and supported.

## 1 Understanding ourselves as practitioners

## 1.1 Becoming an early years practitioner

*I think I'm very lucky to be working with children of this age because they're very fresh and they're very optimistic, and so they're naturally positive.*

*It's rewarding seeing the progress that individual children make, when you see them coming out of themselves more, making friends, making connections with the world and each other.*

*I'd worked with very young special needs children – all my holidays were based around that kind of work – and I knew that was where I wanted to go.*

*Everybody's just so totally committed and really cares about what they're doing.*
(Practitioners from a Children's Centre nursery; Beaumont, 2008: 142–9)

There are many reasons why people choose to work in ECEC. The diversity of ECEC settings in the UK, ranging from large maintained nurseries and schools to small, private, home-based childminding settings, offers the potential early years practitioner a great deal of variety, and certainly more choice and flexibility than found in the traditional school-based education sector alone.

The range of opportunities in non-maintained settings in the UK is accompanied, however, by considerably lower wages and poorer working conditions than offered in the maintained sector. Unlike their colleagues considering teaching in other phases of education, the early years practitioner considering training for a qualification that does not include Qualified Teacher Status, and where the work is likely to be found in non-maintained settings, may well not enter the sector motivated by the prospect of a stable, lifelong career with recognized status, pay and conditions. This has to date been available to those in mainstream teaching. Despite this there are a great number of reasons why people choose to work in ECEC; indeed, recognition of this role is growing.

The motivations of early years practitioners on entry to the sector include:

- Liking, and wanting to work with, children
- Enjoyment of learning and teaching

- A moral commitment to early education
- The influence of school, college or family

'Liking children' is often a strong motivation for those who choose to work in ECEC, and was the most frequently cited reason in a study of the childcare workforce by Szanto, Banks, Gracethorne and Balloch (2003). This echoes long-standing descriptors of the qualities required of early years practitioners, as identified by McGillivray (2008) and the passion practitioners working with children of this age have for supporting the education of young children described by Moyles in Reading 1.1.

Alongside this, early years practitioners relish the opportunity to share their enthusiasm about learning in its widest sense. People may be particularly attracted by the potential freedom and creativity of the early years phase of education, where a holistic concern for children's development is clearly stated, and where exciting, active and playful learning contexts are encouraged, indoors and out.

Many are attracted to work in the sector because of a principled commitment to the education and care of babies and young children. These may be explicitly stated within the aims of the particular organization or embedded within a particular approach or philosophy, such as Montessori (see O'Donnell, Reading 9.3) or Waldorf-Steiner (see Ullrich, Reading 9.4). People may be looking to work with families and children living in socio-economic disadvantage, wishing to contribute to improving the life chances of these children and the community. The chances to work to support particular aspects of child development and learning may attract others, such as a focus on early communication and language or an interest in Special Educational Needs, seeing the opportunity to intervene early in the child's life and the work with families as particularly important. Whalley has highlighted the political motivation of some practitioners:

> Many of the Pen Green staff team, like early years educators in other settings, first became interested in working with young children because of a passion for social justice and a commitment to children's rights. (2001: 136)

The links between early years practice and wider society are discussed in Chapter 17.

The influence of schools, college and families can also be an important factor in people choosing to work in ECEC. It is important to recognize the impact on the early years sector of the perception of childcare as women's work. Women continue to constitute the vast majority of the early childhood education and care workforce (Nutbrown, 2012). This situation is inextricably linked to the perceived 'naturalness' of the relationship between women, mothering and paid care work (see Spencer-Woodley, Reading 1.3). One practitioner stated:

> I used to love playing with my sister's children – my mum always said I should be a nanny or look after children as a job, because I'm very patient. (Szanto et al., 2003: 20)

## Reflective activity 1.1

*Aim:* To reflect upon your own decision to work in ECEC.

*Evidence and reflection:* Write for yourself a short summary about how you felt when you began to work with young children for the first time. If appropriate, also record you feelings at the point of qualifying/completing your initial training.

*Extension:* Read what you have written and highlight where you have made reference to specific value commitments. List these, and try to identify personal experiences that informed why they were so important. (For example: to ensure children have time to play – because I am concerned young children do not have enough free play opportunities.)

Share your thinking with a colleague or fellow student and discuss the range of motivations which inform 'becoming an early years practitioner'.

You may find that some of the reasons are more practical than others (for example: I took the job as it allowed me to work and still collect my daughter from school). It is important that you are honest with yourself. We all make decisions based upon multiple factors. Think about how, if at all, your motives and values have changed over time.

An enduring perception of ECEC as highly gendered runs throughout the sector at all levels. Many practitioners themselves share this view. A study by Penn and McQuail explored the perception of childcare as 'women's work' through interviewing a number of trainee practitioners (1997: 22). Personal qualities cited by the interviewees as important for the work included 'patience, kindness, understanding, tolerance, flexibility, consistency and reliability'. These were echoed in a study of practitioners' perceptions of their role by Szanto et al., which confirmed the perceived low status of the work and echoed the view of childcare as 'natural' for women (2003: 24).

The promotion of childcare in settings other than schools as a career choice for young women who have struggled academically, as noted by Nutbrown (2012), works to perpetuate the view that practitioners in ECEC rely on inherent qualities which the female students bring with them rather than practice acquired through training (Szanto et al., 2003: 66).

The equation of early childhood practice with a female workforce can be a powerful deterrent to men considering the role:

I never even considered that I could work with children – it was certainly never mentioned as a career option for boys at school or college – I came into it by accident in a way. When I was doing my degree I lived with another student who had a small child, and I helped look after him. I found I really enjoyed this and so decided to make childcare my career. Now I have my own children and work part-time so that I can take a very active part in bringing them up – it has been about lifestyle choices for me – unconventional ones in the eyes of many. (Szanto et al., 2003: 21)

Men working in childcare have described how stereotyped notions of masculinity and various forms of societal prejudice, including a suspicion of men's motives for working with children linked to safeguarding, can discourage men from considering a career in ECEC (Cameron 2001, 2006; Szanto et al., 2003). Other aspects that men in childcare report include perceptions of being excluded from women's conversations in the workplace, and a burdensome pressure to perform better than female colleagues, alongside a feeling that they represent all men in the field. Some men have described ways that they continually try to counteract prejudice.

---

### Reflective activity 1.2

*Aim:* To reflect upon perceptions of the characteristics of men, women and early years practitioners.

*Evidence and reflection:* Think of a woman you admire and a man you admire. They do not have to be ECEC practitioners but should be people you know. List the key characteristics of their personality, e.g. committed to a cause, loyal, consistent.

Now list key characteristics of an effective early years practitioner.
What crossovers are there? What differences?

*Extension:* How does this inform your image of ECEC as a gendered occupation?

---

**www. C**    See **reflectiveteaching.co.uk** for links to Men in Childcare site and campaign.

## 1.2 Values informing early years practice

The values we hold as individuals about the importance and role of early years education are critical to sustaining our motivation and resilience as early years practitioners. This relates to the extent to which these values and motives are allowed to flourish in practice. The report by Szanto et al. considered the match or 'goodness of fit' between early years practitioners' needs and skills (intrinsic sources) and the characteristics of the work environment (extrinsic sources), citing Jorde Bloom's work on job satisfaction, where 'the greater the congruence between the person's needs and skills and their work environment the greater the degree of work satisfaction' (Szanto et al., 2004: 22).

The values that inform our practice are not necessarily explicit, but it is important to try to identify them for at least three further, related reasons. First, being clear about values can help us to assess whether we are consistent, both in what we as individuals believe, and in reconciling differences which may exist between colleagues working together. Second, it can help us to evaluate and respond to external pressures, for example how we respond to changes in government policy. Third, it can help us to assess whether what we believe is consistent with what we actually do. For example, we might state that it is crucial that we listen to young children; when we are busy, do we listen?

## Reflective activity 1.3

*Aim:* To reflect upon whether your practice and your philosophy are always compatible.

*Evidence and reflection:* Think about your value commitments, as defined in the earlier activity (**Reflective activity 1.1**). Think about different times of the day, different times of the year and different children. Do you always follow your value commitments? Are there times when other factors mean that you do not always act as you would wish?

*Extension:* Think about how you might adapt your practice, or act to remove some of the factors which cause you to act outside of your values.

Share your thinking with colleagues and discuss how your practice aligns with your value commitments and times when it may not.

In addition to our personal value commitments working in particular contexts may require us to follow certain codes of conduct, Standards or Guidance documents which state the value commitments of the specific early education service. Examples of these codes of conduct are included in the table over the page (**Table 1.1**). One of the arguments for developing codes and standards for professional practice is that they articulate and make explicit the practice of the early years practitioner, both for the workforce and for a wider audience.

A growing international research literature, particularly since the start of the twenty-first century, has continued to highlight the enduring benefit of high-quality early education on children's later educational achievements. As the qualification levels of staff working in the UK ECEC sector have risen, with more early years practitioners achieving graduate and postgraduate qualifications, there have been increasing calls for ways to develop meaningful career pathways. This has been linked to the formation and rethinking of early years practice as a recognized professional status, as discussed below and in Chapter 5.

Codes or standards of practice are useful as tools to reflect upon, consider and develop our practice and to ensure that parents and other professionals understand the complex and diverse role of the early years practitioner. These professional codes or standards are intended to encourage us to be reflective and responsible, to remind us of professional values, aims and commitments. Gaps between aspirations, values and outcomes are common in many walks of life, but in early education it is particularly important to examine why this may occur. After all, if early years practitioners are working in circumstances where their own well-being is low, this is likely to have a detrimental effect on the lives of young children and their families.

Of course, self-improvement is often based, one way or another, on the collection and analysis of evidence. So the contemporary professional has to be willing to test his or her value positions and beliefs. Indeed, the reflective practitioner, as we will later see, is able to justify his or her practices and provide an explanation or 'warrant' for them.

An important step in developing as reflective practitioners is to identify and start to understand our own personal values and beliefs, how they relate to our practice and how

www.C

**Table 1.1:** Professional values (for updates, see links at **reflectiveteaching.co.uk**)

| National College for Teaching and Leadership | **Early Years Teacher Status Standards – Preamble**<br><br>Early Years Teachers make the education and care of babies and children their first concern. They are accountable for achieving the highest possible standards in their professional practice and conduct. Early Years Teacher Status is awarded to graduates who are leading education and care and who have been judged to have met all of the standards in practice from birth to the end of the Early Years Foundation Stage (EYFS). Early Years Teachers act with integrity and honesty. They have strong early development knowledge, keep their knowledge and skills up-to-date and are self-critical. Early Years Teachers recognize that the Key Stage 1 and Key Stage 2 curricula follow the EYFS in a continuum. They forge positive professional relationships and work with parents and/or carers in the best interests of babies and children. |
|---|---|
| **DfE England** | **Teachers' Standards – Preamble**<br><br>Teachers make the education of their pupils their first concern, and are accountable for achieving the highest possible standards in work and conduct. Teachers act with honesty and integrity; have strong subject knowledge; keep their knowledge and skills as teachers up-to-date and are self-critical; forge positive professional relationships; and work with parents in the best interests of their pupils. |
| **Scottish Government Policy Scotland** | **The Early Years Workforce – Scotland**<br><br>All those who work with children in the early years, whether in the statutory, voluntary or private sectors, are committed to delivering the highest quality provision for children and families. They are outward-looking; confident about working together across organizational and professional boundaries; share information and resources; and have strong interpersonal skills and understanding of relationships.<br><br>Those who work with children and families in the early years are committed to their own continuous professional development to improve their knowledge and skills. |
| **Curricular Guidance for Pre-school Education Northern Ireland** | **The Early Years Workforce – Northern Ireland**<br><br>Staff working in a pre-school setting should enjoy working alongside young children. They should be interested in and concerned about the overall development of each child within the setting. The staff needs to have a clear understanding of how young children learn and develop and should try to understand each child's background and needs. They should consider the children's needs and best interests and put these before any other aspect of their work in the setting. Adults working with young children need to be flexible and ensure that the children's well-being and self-esteem are nurtured. |

**Practising Teacher Standards – Wales**

Teachers must meet the Practising Teacher Standards (PTS) at the end of the induction period and continue to meet them throughout their teaching career. This includes:

- Appreciate the diverse needs of children and young people.
- Value fair, respectful, trusting, supportive and constructive relationships with children and young people.
- Have high expectations of children and young people in order to improve outcomes and well-being for all learners.
- Value the importance of building positive relationships between home and school.
- Value the active involvement of children and young people in their progress, development and well-being.
- Be actively involved in professional networks and learning communities which share and test beliefs and understandings with colleagues and contribute to the wider development of the school and profession.
- Value the improvement of practice through reflection and taking responsibility for continuing professional development.

PACEY – the Professional Association for Childcare and Early Years – works with government, local authorities and others to raise standards in ECEC. They provide a 'code of ethics' for members. This includes:

- The welfare of the child is paramount.
- I contribute to children's care, learning and development and this is reflected in every aspect of my practice.
- I work with parents, carers and families who are partners in the care, learning and development of their children and are the child's first and most enduring educators.
- The needs, rights and views of the child are at the centre of my practice.
- Individuality, difference and diversity are valued and celebrated.
- Children's health and well-being are actively promoted.
- Children's personal and physical safety is safeguarded, while allowing for risk and challenge as appropriate to the capabilities of the child.
- Self-esteem, resilience and a positive self-image are recognized as essential to every child's development.
- Confidentiality and agreements about confidential information are respected as appropriate unless a child's protection and well-being are at stake.
- Professional knowledge, skills and values are shared appropriately in order to enrich the experience of children more widely.
- Best practice requires reflection and a continuous search for improvement.

they have been and continue to be influenced by our experiences, circumstances and understandings. We need to become self-aware and 'reflexive' and thus able to question ourselves, as an important element of our reflective practice. While the latter addresses a wide range of social, organizational, pedagogic and other factors, reflexivity focuses directly on our ability to reflect on ourselves (Moore, 2004). When we begin to examine ourselves and our practice it can be challenging and at times uncomfortable, particularly when we acknowledge that we may not always have acted as we would have liked.

Beliefs, of course, can be particularly difficult to change since they may rest on significant cultural and material foundations. Indeed, we may even feel that our beliefs are representations of 'objective truths' and so that nothing more needs to be considered. Reflective practice requires an interesting combination of moral commitment and open-mindedness. While being fully value-committed, we must still aspire to learn and improve. We will explore this more fully in Chapter 3 where we consider how we can challenge our own preconceptions about babies, children and learning.

## 1.3 Practitioner identities

The concept of 'identity' summarizes the ways in which we think about ourselves. Our sense of personal identity forms through life and is particularly influenced by 'significant others' such as parents, friends and colleagues. Our identities as early years practitioners will be affected by the way the role of settings and the adults working in them are perceived by all those around us, as well as within the wider society, including images in the media. So, how is the role of ECEC envisaged, and how is the role of early year practitioners seen by others and ourselves? (see Heilbronn, Reading 1.4).

As noted above, there is a general consensus among educationalists and policymakers on the impact of early experiences, including those experiences taking place in ECEC settings. A growing body of neuroscientific evidence is now available to show in detail how these experiences impact significantly on brain development of babies and young children (see The Royal Society, Reading 4.3). This adds to evidence from longitudinal studies, such as the Effective Provision of Pre-School Education (EPPE) project, that explores the impact of high-quality early educational experiences on children's later educational outcomes.

It is agreed that the early years are important – and possibly *because* it is agreed that the early years are important – policymakers identify and refer to a number of different reasons to continue to invest in ECEC in the non-maintained sector, and prior to statutory school age. A continuing debate on the role of ECEC is seen at all levels of strategy, spanning education, social care and health. It includes discussion about the primary role of ECEC: whether it is to provide day care to enable parents, particularly women, to access paid work; an intervention to support children's learning and development where needs are identified; to provide the educational grounding for later schooling; or

> ### Expert question
>
> **Society's educational goals**: What vision of 'education and care' is the provision designed to achieve?
>
> This question contributes to a conceptual framework representing enduring issues and expertise (see Chapter 16).

to ensure their development as a learner and a unique child. This inevitably influences views on the practice within ECEC, and our roles as practitioners.

In the public rhetoric surrounding early years pedagogy, much has been made of children becoming 'school ready' (see Whitebread and Bingham, Reading 5.3). This has chimed with the long-standing argument between the polarized positions of those advocating child-led, informal approaches versus those who argue for a structured approach, particularly towards early literacy. Play-based learning is often placed at one end of a continuum, with a more formal approach designed to foster academic skills at the other (Guimaraes and McSherry, 2002). Similarly, in many eyes, especially in public debate, there is a binary divide concerning appropriate practice in the early years, between those who are concerned with the *processes* of teaching and learning and those who are focused on *outcomes and the reaching of specific goals* (see, Mathers, Singler and Karemaker, Reading 1.6).

The Tickell Report (2011, see **reflectiveteaching.co.uk**) made two important and considered advances on this stalemate, by turning the debate on its head to look at 'school unreadiness', and by highlighting three prime areas of learning within the English Early Years Foundation Stage.

---

### Reflective activity 1.4

*Aim:* To reflect upon the ideas of 'school readiness' and 'school unreadiness'.

*Evidence and reflection:* Identify a child you have worked with or known that you would define as school unready. What characteristics did they show? What would have helped this child?

*Extension:* To what extent do you agree with the assertion that schools should be made child-ready?

---

Taking a reflective approach to practice ought to support us to understand the position we take as individuals, consider the basis of that position, consider the evidence and adapt and evolve as we feel is necessary.

## The role of the early years practitioner

The view of the purpose of ECEC will inevitably influence the role of the early years practitioner. Contracts and job descriptions will describe the specific responsibilities of practitioners in whatever context they work. (See **reflectiveteaching.co.uk** for link to Early Years Teacher Standards and Teacher Standards.) However, while contractual conditions are extremely important, the most significant question concerns how we interpret both them and the role more generally. This question needs to be posed because, as we have seen, early years practice is a complex activity and job descriptions and contractual terms, while necessary, are not sufficient to validly represent it.

Moss has identified two widespread ways that early years practitioners are seen, which relate to the underlying assumptions of the role of ECEC. In his model, practitioners (or workers) are seen as 'substitute mothers' or as 'technicians' of early years practice. In this way we can get a sense of the elements of both the affective aspects of the role, and the aspects of the role that can be regarded either as a science or a craft. He identifies a third role of the practitioner as researcher and co-constructor, which he particularly links with early childhood services in the Reggio Emilia region of Italy (Moss, 2006). This framing emphasizes the creative aspects of the role, with the practitioner as a facilitator, artist and co-learner.

However described, and in whatever circumstance or setting, the role of the early years practitioner will encompass a balance of affective and intellectual aspects, in order to support and develop babies' and young children's holistic learning and development. A number of these aspects are, of course, common to all phases of education, whereas the role of key person has a particular relevance for the early years age phase.

The affective role of the early years practitioner will include:

- Demonstrating sensitivity towards children, with a high regard for their wellbeing (Laevers).
- Demonstrating emotional literacy, ensuring that children and families have their emotional needs recognized and met (Goleman).
- Acting as a Key Person and ensure babies and young children are able to form appropriate attachments (Elfer).

In addition, the practitioner in ECEC must:

- Have a high regard for matters of equality and anti-discrimination.
- Have a high regard for the health of children and their physical safety.
- Have a high regard for safeguarding matters.

The role of the early years practitioner as early educator will include:

- Providing stimulation for learning and thinking (Laevers).
- Promoting children's autonomy in learning (Laevers).
- Observing and listening to children (Lancaster, Hutchin).
- Assessing children's progress and planning next steps in learning (Hutchin).
- Raising awareness of learning: making the learning visible and encouraging a growth mindset (Hattie, Dweck).
- Actively engaging in thinking with children, including sustained shared thinking (Siraj-Blatchford et al., EPPE).
- Forming and sustaining positive relationships with parents.

Like teaching in other phases of education, the role of the reflective early years practitioner in reality is likely to be more fluid than any job description, code of practice, model or theory might imply. The personal values and identity of each practitioner will always be significant in our practice, which returns us to the emphasis of this chapter. There are links to National Strategy archive at **reflectiveteaching.co.uk**. The Learning, Playing and Interacting document may be particularly useful.

WWW.C

## 2 Knowing babies and young children

Much of the way that early years teaching is defined rests on the view we have of the child as 'nested' within a family and community. Developing an understanding of babies and children requires a reflective practitioner to empathize with their wider experience as well as develop personal knowledge of and rapport with individual children.

## 2.1 How babies and young children experience early years education

Children's experiences of ECEC will vary considerably due to the child's age, period of time their families require or choose them to attend, and the type of provision selected. An ECEC setting may be the child's first experience of any prolonged period away from their main carer, and as such will be particularly significant for the child and their family. How the transition and induction into the setting is experienced depends very much upon the child and the policy in place for babies or children entering the setting, such as whether they must attend for short periods with their carer. The emotional attachment of children to adults, and the role of the key person in ECEC, is discussed in more depth in Chapter 6 (also see Bowlby, Reading 6.4).

Children entering ECEC become aware of the values held by adults, and what attributes are considered to be desirable. A central strategy in the development of positive self-concepts among the children lies in being clear with ourselves about our purpose, and continually providing opportunities where children can develop the learning attributes and qualities that we want to foster. As reflective early years practitioners we must be aware of the verbal and non-verbal cues which we communicate to children and parents, consciously or unconsciously. For instance, do we ensure that we identify and narrate children's learning and thinking in our feedback to children and parents, valuing all aspects and areas of learning and all contexts for learning, such as learning that has taken place outside the setting?

These early experiences will impact upon the way that children think of themselves, and will directly influence their approach to learning. Dweck's concept of 'mindsets' is particularly relevant here, as discussed further in Chapter 2 (Dweck, 1986; see Reading 2.5). In addition, the characteristics of effective early learning, which were given  a greater emphasis following the Tickell Review, have become a powerful way to focus on aspects of the process of learning, such as play and exploration, active learning and creativity and critical thinking (DfES, 2012; Early Education, 2012). Particularly in school contexts, Hattie's work has been used by early years practitioners to 'make the learning visible' for young children (2012). For example, animal characters have been introduced that exemplify positive learning behaviours such as 'having a go' and 'keeping going'. Practitioners refer to the characters regularly, and articulate the behaviours, which children are then able to understand, identify with and articulate themselves.

> ## Case study 1.1 Whole-school approach to early learning
>
> At Woody Lane Infant and Nursery School the nursery children are introduced to eight toy animal characters at group times. Each animal character is named after a particular characteristic of successful learning, such as the Persevering Penguin, Concentrating Cat and Learning Leopard. Anecdotes are shared with the children that show how the characters display each characteristic using everyday language and familiar situations, for example, the Curious Crocodile noticed that the plants and vegetables in the nursery garden were growing differently, and that some had been eaten by slugs and snails. The Curious Crocodile noticed which plants were being eaten, asked questions and thought about why this happened, and wondered what would happen if the plants were covered over. He also looked at the internet to investigate more about slugs and snails, and which plants they eat the most. The children and adults subsequently highlighted occasions where they saw or demonstrated characteristics of Curious Crocodiles. Parents are told about the characters at a meeting and via the school website, and are encouraged to share times when they notice the characteristics at home. This is part of a whole-school approach, where all adults, children and the wider community are encouraged to use the language of learning, using examples and characters in age appropriate ways.

A further way that we can be explicit about our values, and actively support young children to identify and reflect on their own learning, is through programmes that support group work, where children are encouraged to see themselves as one part of the whole. We will consider these issues again in Chapter 6, which explores relationships, and Chapter 13, which considers assessment for learning.

At the beginning of this chapter we considered the core values that we hold as early years practitioners, which underpin our practice and shape how we work. Many early years practitioners have a high regard for ethical practice in terms of respect for children and a democratic approach within their settings, sometimes linked to the UN Declaration of the Rights of the Child. This may be particularly important for those working for certain areas of the UK or within particular organizations, but it can be highly relevant in any ECEC setting, large or small. For some, this ethical concern runs throughout their practice, creating a pedagogy that incorporates and values children's thoughts and feelings in everyday contexts. These include developing close observation tools for babies and pre-verbal children to enhance practitioner awareness of the unique individual, sharing observations with children, and asking them to comment using their own words based on these observations. Carr's work on narrative and 'stories' can be used particularly effectively to include the child's perception and avoid adult interpretations of children's learning, where the narration from the practitioner may include phrases such as 'I noticed you …' (Hutchin, 2012; Carr, 2001).

Taking a more consultative approach, influential work on listening to children and children's voices by Lancaster has been used to elicit children's thoughts about their provision, through the use of a number of techniques including photography and creative projects. A 'mosaic' approach has been developed, described by Clark et al. (2005), which embeds the use of child-led, multimedia documentation methods into practice, which are selected flexibly to meet the needs of the setting, children and particular project.

# 2.2 Understanding children's needs

Just as we need to consider our personal identities and values, so a similar kind of 'biographical' knowledge about each child is valuable in understanding them as individuals and as learners. We are likely to find that many characteristics are shared in common, but others will be more unique and individual. Records that vary in title, including individual child profiles, *All about me* books and learning journeys, are usually kept for each child in an ECEC setting, sometimes in electronic formats.

The extent to which these individual records focus on assessment of the child's progress and targets, or the degree to which they are a multi-voiced and evolving record of learning and thinking varies across settings and according to external requirements by the inspecting body.

Hutchin (2007), details how children's learning journeys or profiles may include over time:

- information from and about families;
- material reflecting children's home interests;
- information from other groups and significant people, such as bilingual assistants;
- documentation, in the form of photos and annotated drawings and meaningful marks, of the process of thinking, and how the child would like to develop their project;
- if noticed, observations of schematic play.

---

### Reflective activity 1.5

*Aim:* To deepen your understanding of a child.

*Evidence and reflection:* Take an interest in a child's general behaviour. Consider how they interact with other children and how they tackle learning tasks. Refer to the characteristics of effective learning or other materials such as those developed by Hattie or Dweck.

- Where possible, present open-ended opportunities where the child can write, draw, talk or otherwise communicate about herself or himself. Discussions about friends, experiences, family or about favourite books or TV characters can be revealing. Make notes.
- Discuss the child with parents and other practitioners ask them to provide information on the family, photographs of special people, occasions or toys.
- Where possible, discuss the child's own perception of their individual needs with them.
- Summarize what you have learned.

*Follow-up:* Consider what implications your new understanding has for shaping the provision that is appropriate for that child. In addition, consider how this deeper understanding has supported your understanding of the child and their behaviours.

---

As highlighted above, children may also participate in decisions about what to include, and be given support to narrate their own thoughts about items of meaning to them (Hutchin, 2012).

Such records can provide an excellent starting point and continuing record for each child, enhancing the understanding of the individual learner, where children's material, social and cultural circumstances are acknowledged and understood. Home visits can also be offered, which initiate a personal contact for the start of the child's time in ECEC, and which can then be built on throughout their time at the setting. Indeed the early years practitioner role is one which requires a reciprocal relationship with parents/carers to enable both to understand and support the child's development.

It is often argued that the 'needs' of the learner should be seen as the starting point for teaching and learning policies. However, the notion of appropriate needs begs questions about our aims and how we make judgements about what is worthwhile. It may be valuable for us as reflective practitioners to state what we see as the basic 'needs' of every learner which we commit ourselves to trying to meet. In this way we are making our value commitments and how we see our role clear to both ourselves and to others.

The classic work of Maslow (1954) is worth considering here, since he linked the drive to have needs met with motivation in learning. Maslow proposed a hierarchy of basic needs, and proposed that the lower level order of needs must be met before people could fulfil higher level needs. This argument is represented as a pyramid.

**Figure 1.1**
Maslow's hierarchy of needs

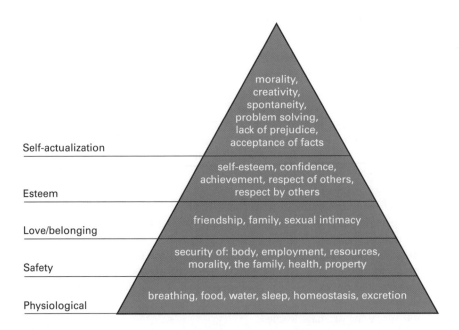

The lowest level (1) expresses our primary biological need for food, shelter, oxygen, water, etc. The second level (2) encompasses the need for security and freedom from anxiety. The third level (3) includes the need to feel that one belongs and to be loved and be able to love in return. The fourth level (4) addresses the need for prestige and status, to be successful and to feel good about oneself. The final level (5) might be seen as the ultimate goal of education – the need of people to fulfil their potential.

Practitioners and children are no different in their humanity, and they therefore share the needs which each of these elements represent. To learn, and to work, physiological needs are basic – and we will explore one dimension of this in Chapter 8 when considering the physical qualities of learning environments. More significantly, if a baby or young child is hungry or distressed, teaching and learning interactions are unlikely to be effective. Successful settings enable both practitioners and children to feel safe, respected and valued.

## 2.3 Examining our perceptions of young children

All of us are likely to have views about what we would like the babies and young children at our settings to be like. These descriptors might include aspects such as happy, healthy, engaged with our provision, at ease with themselves and others, motivated to learn, good at listening, among many others. We will also have ideas about the characteristics which may be less desirable or valued.

It has been found that our assessments and judgements of children can be highly influenced by the gender, ethnicity, socio-economic status of the child's family and even by their names (Meighan and Siraj-Blatchford, 1981). If we hold preconceptions without reflecting on them, it can result in our treating particular individuals or groups of children and/or their families in particular ways which may not be fair or just. Labelling, or stereotyping, can lead to a phenomenon known as the 'self-fulfilling prophecy' and thus result in considerable social injustices (Brophy and Good, 1974; Nash, 1976; Mortimore et al., 1988; Hart, Dixon, Drummond and McIntyre, 2004).

As reflective early years practitioners, we must focus on supporting and enhancing the achievement of *all* children in our care. We therefore need to occasionally step back from our initial or routine reactions, and interrogate our conscious or unconscious processes of categorization. For instance:

1  How do we personally acknowledge, categorize and label the children and families we work with?

2  How can we think about and work with those children and families, moving beyond labels?

Of course, practitioners do have to develop ways of understanding, organizing and grouping children in order to respond effectively to their needs, and to promote the progress of vulnerable groups. However, this should be done with regard for the purposes of each particular situation, and what is known about how contexts can enhance learning (see Chapter 15 for extensive discussion of inclusive practice). For instance, research informs us that opportunities for children of different ages to play and learn together can lead to gains in cognitive development, particularly for the youngest children (Howes and Farver, 1987).

## Reflective activity 1.6

*Aim:* To understand our perceptions of children and their families.

*Evidence and reflection:* First, without referring to the register or any lists, write down the names of the children you work with. Note which order you have listed them in and if you found any children's names hard to remember. What does the order tell you about which children are more memorable than others, and for what reasons?

Second, if the children you work with are older, develop a grid with each child's name along both the top row and down the left-hand side. Moving down the left-hand side, consider each child in turn and indicate across the line which children you think would like to play with that child. Add up each child's 'score'; you will then have a list of which children you think like to play together.

When you have done this, take each child to one side and ask them to select from photographs all of the children they like to play with. Record this in a new grid. Take care to explain that there are no right or wrong answers and not to allow other children to overhear. You need to be aware that this could cause issues if not well managed. If you think the children will become concerned, or discuss their answers, perhaps conduct observations to see who the children engage with for any sustained period. Be aware that this is less reliable than asking the child.

Compare the two grids. What does this tell you about how you perceive children and how they are perceived by their peers? Did you overestimate for some children and underestimate for others? Why do you think this was? What have you learned about your views of these children?

*Extension:* Consider each child and the words you would use to describe them. Note any patterns that might exist – for example, whether some of your ideas relate more to boys than girls, or to children from different class, ethnic or religious backgrounds. There may be some constructs that relate to such things as academic ability, physical attributes or behaviour. How might this be problematic for the identities of those children, or for your expectations of them as learners?

Reflecting on our own thinking and practice helps us to understand the complexity of our choices and decisions that are faced routinely every day. It helps us to ensure that future actions can be justified, and that we continue to be accountable for our work.

There are various 'tools' available to support reflective practice, which will be explored in detail in Chapter 3. Material of particular relevance here is Hart's *Framework for Innovative Thinking* (2000). The essence of this framework is that it invites us to break down, or interrupt, our routine thinking and to try new ideas. The latter are framed in constructive, enabling and inclusive ways. **Table 1.2** summarizes Hart's 'five moves'.

**Table 1.2** A framework for innovative thinking [adapted from Hart, 2000]

| Five moves for innovative thinking | |
|---|---|
| Making connections | This move involves exploring how the specific characteristics of the child's response might be connected to features of the immediate and wider learning environment. |
| Contradicting | This move involves questioning the assumptions underlying a given interpretation by searching out a plausible alternative interpretation which casts the meaning of the situation in a new light. This helps to tease out the norms and expectations underlying the original interpretation so that it can be re-examined. |
| Taking a child's eye view | This move involves trying to enter the child's frame of reference and to see the meaning and logic of the child's response from the child's perspective. |
| Noting the impact of feelings | This move involves examining the part that our own feelings play in the meaning that we bestow on the situation and in leading us to a particular interpretation. |
| Postponing judgement in order to find out more | This move involves recognizing that we may lack information or expertise needed to have confidence in our judgements. It involves holding back from further analysis and the attempt to arrive at judgements about the child's needs while we take steps to acquire further information. |

## Reflective activity 1.7

*Aim:* To review the learning of a child in the light of Susan Hart's *Framework for Innovative Thinking*.

*Evidence and reflection:* Think of a child who is puzzling you, and review an example of their play or learning activities which surprised you.
Write a brief account of what happened.
Now use Hart's framework to reflect on what happened. Does it help in illuminating possible interpretations? What more would it be helpful to know? How might you find this out?

*Extension:* Share what you have written with a colleague who also knows the child. How does their understanding match or contrast with yours? Why do you think this is? What strategies seem most appropriate for the future? Discussing our interpretations of children and their behaviours can be a helpful way of challenging our own preconceptions. We will consider the value of reflecting as a team in Chapter 3.

## 3 Learning and teaching through life

## 3.1 Developing a career in Early Childhood Education and Care

This book on reflective early years teaching is situated in a context of calls for increased professionalism by many leading figures in the ECEC sector in the UK, most notably Nutbrown. We would like to make it clear that our understanding of professionalism in this book goes beyond a vernacular use of the term, used to describe behaviours and features of practice such as confidentiality, towards a deep-level focus on the examined practice ECEC, and the active role that reflective practitioners can take. Ball has defined 'professionalism' as involving 'actions which are derived from a theoretical approach' and 'which reflect explicit and shared professional values' (1994: 59). A 'key term descriptor' for 'professional dimensions' suggested by Moyles, Adams and Musgrove rests on the idea of critically reflective practice in a context of continued learning:

> Professional thinking includes the ability to reflect on practice and to make informed decisions through well-conceived examination and analysis of pedagogy. It involves the thinking practitioner in articulating and evaluating practice and a continuous striving to improve. Professionals have a positive disposition to learn and are capable of extending themselves professionally. (2002: 5)

The chapters that follow rest on this definition. However, there are potential pitfalls which should be considered. It is highly pertinent in the context of this book to consider whether the move to professionalize ECEC and the role of the early years practitioner could establish or reinforce an exclusionary ethos with a reliance on external codes, which potentially devalues, undermines and undervalues the voices and expertise of practitioners as well as children (see Brock, Reading 1.2 and Moss, Reading 1.5).

When considering ECEC as a long-term career, the often challenging material conditions and low financial rewards, particularly of colleagues in non-maintained settings, cannot be ignored. The focus on reflective early years teaching as part of the wider debate on the workforce in the ECEC sector will, we hope, have the potential to support the on-going development of a collective voice in the early years which can be used to influence policymakers and budget-holders (at all levels) to address issues of pay, conditions and public perception of the work – for this will be part of what is needed to ensure that the expertise of early years practitioners are valued, rewarded and kept within the sector.

Chapter 17 considers the place of the ECEC sector in society.

## Conclusion

This opening chapter has considered the identity of early years practitioners, inviting consideration of our motivations, our views of ourselves, of children, of families and of our roles. We believe that reflective early years practitioners must continue to play an active role in shaping and influencing understandings and debate about teaching in early education, based on moral and democratic principles. Our views of children as young citizens of today and tomorrow, whose voices should be respected and valued, and our ways of working with families and each other should exemplify our commitment to these principles.

This book explores and offers a guiding framework for reflection to support this continuing evolution of early years teaching into the twenty-first century.

## Key readings

For an overview of contemporary issues in the early years, see:

Tickell, Dame C. (2011) *The Early Years: Foundations for Life, Health and Learning*. London: Department for Education.

Nutbrown, C. (2012) *Foundations for Quality. The Independent Review of Early Education and Childcare Qualifications. Final Report*. London: Department for Education.

—(2013) *Shaking the Foundations of Quality? Why Childcare Policy Must Not Lead to Poor-quality Early Education and Care*. University of Sheffield. Available from: **shef.ac.uk/polopoly_fs/1.263201!/file/Shakingthefoundationsofquality.pdf** (accessed 12 December 2013).

To help consider aspects of professionalism in ECEC, see:

McGillivray, G. (2008) 'Nannies, nursery nurses and early years professionals: constructions of professional identity in the early years workforce in England', *European Early Childhood Education Research Journal*, 16 (2), 242–54.

Moss, P. (2006) 'Structures, understandings and discourses: possibilities for re-envisioning the early years worker', *Contemporary Issues in Early Childhood*, 7 (1), 30–41.

To further develop ideas and understandings of how socio-economic disadvantage impacts upon children's lives, see:

Allen, G. (2011) *Early Intervention: The Next Steps*. London: Cabinet Office.

Field, F. (2010) 'The Foundation Years: Preventing Poor Children Becoming Poor Adults. The Report of the Independent Review on Poverty and Life Chances'. London: Cabinet Office.

Pascal, C. and Bertram, T. (2013) 'The impact of early education as a strategy in countering socio-economic disadvantage'. CREC, London: Ofsted. **ofsted.gov.uk/ accessandachievement**

For an examination of the role of men in ECEC, see:

Cameron, C. (2001), 'Promise or problem? a review of the literature on men working in early childhood services', *Gender, Work and Organization*, 8 (4), 430–53.
—(2006), 'Male workers and professionalism', *Contemporary Issues in Early Childhood*, 7 (1), 68–79.

For examples of strategies to support children's voices in ECEC, see:

Carr, M. and Lee, W. (2012) *Learning Stories: Constructing Learner Identities in Early Education.* London: Sage Publications Ltd.
Clark, A. and Moss, P. (2001) *Listening to Young Children: The Mosaic Approach.* London: National Children's Bureau Enterprises Ltd.
—(2005) *Spaces to Play: More Listening to Young Children using the Mosaic Approach.* London: National Children's Bureau.
Lancaster, Y. P. and Kirby, P. on behalf of Coram (2010) *Listening to Young Children.* 2nd edn. Buckinghamshire: Open University Press.

***Readings for Reflective Teaching in Early Years Education*** directly complements and extends the chapters in this book. It has been designed to provide convenient access to key texts. It will be of particular help as a compact and portable library.

 The associated website, **reflectiveteaching.co.uk**, offers a wealth of supplementary resources including reflective activities, research briefings, advice on further reading and downloadable diagrams, figures and checklists from the book. It also features a compendium of educational terms, links to useful websites, policy and curriculum documents, and showcases examples of excellent research and practice.

# Learning
## How can we understand learner development?

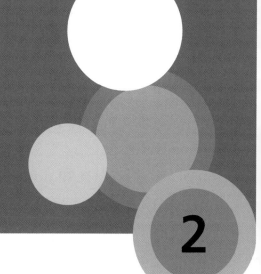

**2**

## Introduction

In this chapter we explore what is meant by *learning* and explore different theories of processes of learning, including learning through play. Following this, we move on to consider how our views of learning and how children's early learning experiences shape children's educational experiences, their feelings towards themselves, towards each other, towards learning itself and, thus, how this impacts upon future learning outcomes.

---

### TLRP principles

Four principles are of particular relevance to this chapter on learning:

**Principle 1: Effective teaching and learning equips learners for life in its broadest sense.** Learning should aim to help people to develop the intellectual, personal and social resources that will enable them to participate as active citizens, contribute to economic development and flourish as individuals in a diverse and changing society. This implies adopting a broad view of learning outcomes and ensuring that equity and social justice are taken seriously.

**Principle 3: Effective teaching and learning recognizes the importance of prior experience and learning.** Teaching and learning should take account of what the learner knows already in order to plan their next steps. This includes building on prior learning but also taking account of the personal and cultural experiences of different groups of learners.

**Principle 6: Effective teaching and learning promotes the active engagement of the learner.** A chief goal of teaching and learning should be the promotion of learners' independence and autonomy. This involves acquiring a repertoire of learning strategies and practices, developing positive attitudes towards learning, and confidence in oneself as a good learner.

**Principle 8: Effective teaching and learning recognizes the significance of informal learning.** Informal learning, such as learning out of school, should be recognized as at least as significant as formal learning and should therefore be valued and used appropriately in formal processes.

---

Learning can be considered as the process by which humans acquire, understand, apply and extend knowledge, concepts, skills and attitudes. How we understand children and their learning affects the choices that we make when planning, facilitating, encouraging and supporting learning. There is a tendency to attribute differences between children's learning and attainment to deficits in the children themselves. However, this deficit approach can be turned around. The 'credit approach' sees all children as rich, strong, powerful learners, as long as environments are conducive to learning and compelling opportunities for learning are provided (Hart et al., 2004; Swann et al., 2012).

Reflective practitioners taking the credit approach focus on what babies and children can do, not on what they cannot do. They are more interested in a child's desire to understand and develop, than in gaps in their knowledge or abilities. If we see all children as rich, strong, powerful learners, then we are inescapably committed to the educability of every child, and to building and using our professional expertise to seek, understand and remove barriers to learning.

## 1 Learning processes

Learning is a highly complex aspect of human activity. For centuries, philosophers and psychologists have analysed learning. As a result there are many theories which attempt to describe the process of learning. We have simplified this complex field by identifying three approaches of learning which have been of particular influence on teaching and learning within education, each of which highlights a particular dimension of learning.

## 1.1 Behaviourism

This approach suggests that living creatures, animal or human, learn by building up associations or 'bonds' between their experience, their thinking and their behaviour. Experience, particularly repeated experience, helps us to develop responses and learn new things. In exploring this approach to learning, Thorndike (1911) formulated two principles. First, the 'law of effect':

> The greater the satisfaction or discomfort, the greater the strengthening or weakening of the bond.

Second, the 'law of exercise':

> The probability of a response occurring in a given situation increases with the number of times that response has occurred in that situation in the past.

Thus, activities which are satisfying, problematic or uncomfortable are more memorable, and likely to lead to new thinking and/or behaviours, as are those which are repeated.

Behaviourist theories provided the dominant perspective on learning until the 1960s. Perhaps the most significant of these theories was proposed by the psychologist B. F. Skinner (e.g. 1968, see Skinner, Reading 2.1). Skinner built upon the work of Thorndike to develop a model of learning which states that behaviours which are reinforced (i.e. lead to positive or successful outcomes) tend to be repeated, and those which are not reinforced tend not to be repeated.

The influence of the behaviourist approach in education has been immense. In the early part of the twentieth century, it provided the foundations of work on a 'science of teaching' based on teacher-led activities through which knowledge and skills were to be taught. This approach places the learner in a relatively passive role, as the teacher selects the activities and leads the discussions and the children are often required to listen. This approach tends to have a more obvious impact in the early years as the child moves towards statutory schooling: we can see the influences of such an approach when we consider the view of some that children need to be prepared for formal schooling. Teaching which has been influenced by behaviourism can be seen throughout our schools. The importance of reinforcing children's work and effort is well established, i.e. the desired behaviours are reinforced.

**Figure 2.1** represents the roles of children and adult in behaviourist-influenced teaching and learning processes.

**Figure 2.1**
A behaviourist model of roles in the teaching–learning process

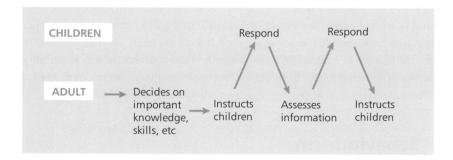

Of particular interest here is the high degree of adult control in the process: deciding on the subject matter, providing instruction, pacing the tasks, correcting, assessing and reinforcing responses. In many ways this makes it easy to plan sessions and ensure all aspects of topics are covered. However, there are also some difficulties with teaching in this way. The most important is the question of connecting with the existing understanding of the learner. What does the child already know and understand? How does new learning connect with the experiences of the child? If the new knowledge does not link with what the child already understands this can lead to a lack of motivation and interest, as the child cannot use the knowledge which is offered to build a meaningful understanding. (For more on this, see Chapter 11, where we consider social learning theory.)

## 1.2 Constructivism

This approach suggests that people learn through an interaction between thinking and experience, and through the sequential development of more complex cognitive structures. The most influential constructivist theorist was Piaget (e.g. 1926, 1950, 1961; see Reading 2.2).

Piaget states that when children encounter a new experience, they both 'accommodate' their existing thinking to it and 'assimilate' aspects of the experience. In so doing they move beyond one state of mental 'equilibration' and restructure their thoughts to create another. Gradually then, children come to construct more detailed, complex and accurate understandings of the phenomena they experience. That is, as their knowledge increases they understand more complex issues and make links between different phenomena.

Piaget proposed that there are characteristic stages in the successive development of these mental structures, stages in which children's learning and understanding grow. These stages are:

- Sensori-motor stage (approximately birth–2 years).
- Pre-operational stage (approximately 2–7 years).
- Concrete operations stage (approximately 7–12 years).
- Formal operations stage (approximately 12 years onwards).

In each of the first three stages, the role of the child's direct experience is deemed to be crucial.

The influence of Piaget's theory on ECEC has been profound. Its influence can be seen in many areas, such as the widespread emphasis on providing challenging environments in which children can explore and learn independently (Parker-Rees, 2010). Perhaps its greatest influence has been the promotion of learning through play. For Piaget, play and practical experimentation have a crucial role in the assimilation process at each stage (Piaget, 1951). Indeed play is recognized by many early years practitioners as crucial for the development of lifelong learning dispositions (Elkind, 2007), for developing young children's self-esteem and ability to become independent learners (Bowman et al., 2001) and for supporting children's social and emotional development (DeVries, 2000). Nevertheless, the emphasis on play as a rich element of early years pedagogy is not always recognized (Whitebread et al., 2012.).

The influence of the constructivist approach in primary education has also been considerable following the report of the Plowden Committee (CACE, 1967) in which it was suggested that:

> Piaget's explanation appears to fit the observed facts of children's learning more satisfactorily than any other. It is in accord with what is generally regarded as the most effective primary school practice, as it has been worked out empirically. (CACE, 1967: para. 522).

The image of the active child as the agent of his/her own learning runs through Plowden. 'Child-centred' teaching approaches, based on interpretations of Piaget's work, were adopted with enormous commitment by many teachers in the late 1960s and 1970s. Great imagination and care was put into providing varied and stimulating classroom environments from which children could derive challenging experiences (e.g. Marsh, 1970). Constructivism has always been particularly influential in work with younger pupils with whom the benefits of working from children's interests, from play and from practical experience are relatively clear-cut (Anning, 1991; Dowling, 1992; Doddington and Hilton, 2007). Yet, despite this, empirical research has shown that constructivist methods were not greatly reflected in the actual practice of teachers of older primary children (Galton, Simon and Croll, 1980). Thus, as the child progresses through school, the influence of constructivist theories on their daily experience may be reduced.

Teaching which has been influenced by constructivism can be seen in all educational establishments. It is reflected in the provision of a rich, varied and stimulating environment, in individualized work and creative arts and in extended projects and investigations. Above all, though, the influence of constructivism is reflected in the ways in which teachers relate with children and work closely with them. This provides many opportunities for practitioners to share in the child's fascination and excitement when encountering new and meaningful experiences.

**Figure 2.2** represents the roles of child and adult in constructivist-influenced teaching and learning processes.

**Figure 2.2**
A constructivist model of roles in the teaching–learning process

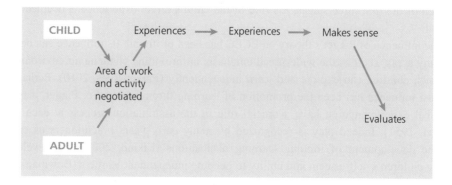

Note here the *negotiation* of the activity and the emphasis placed on direct experience in learning. Together, these have the enormous strength, in principle, of creating high levels of motivation and engagement as the child follows their own interests rather than being led by the practitioner.

However, critics of constructivist approaches note that coverage of a particular task, issue or curriculum is hard to monitor in instances where the child has not received a structured input. Further, the diversity of interests tends to produce relatively complex forms of setting organization, as a range of activities is provided sometimes in different rooms or environments (see Chapter 8 for details on managing the environment). Research shows that practitioners can be drawn into managing this complex environment rather than directly supporting children's learning. In addition this emphasis on self-discovery ignores the social context in which learning takes place. In so doing, the potential of practitioners, other adults and other children to support each child's learning is underestimated. Examples of this can been seen where adults lay out a stimulating play environment for children but do not offer support to the child to extend their learning through play, or support the children to develop the skills to support each other's learning through collaborative play. Bredekamp and Rosegrant (1992) coined the term 'early childhood error' to describe the folly of practitioners laying out stimulating play environments but not supporting children in play and therefore their learning.

Indeed, there are many important critiques of Piaget's work, in particularly the way in which a model of sequential structured stages of development can lead to an underestimation of children's capacities. Psychologists, such as Donaldson (1978) and Tizard and Hughes (1984), have demonstrated that children's intellectual abilities are far greater than those reported by Piaget. Their findings emerged when children were observed in situations that were *meaningful* to them. In such circumstances children show considerably more social competence at younger ages than Piaget's theory allows (Dunn, 1988; Siegler, 1997). Colwell (2012) states that practitioners who do not believe a child is capable of developing social competence are less likely to provide an environment in which children can interact and work on tasks together. As such, the belief that children are not capable may lead to a cyclical process in which children are not expected to have the skills and, as such, are not given the opportunity to develop or practise such skills; thus they are deemed not to have such skills.

## 1.3 Social cognition

This perspective on learning takes two main forms. On the one hand, it draws attention to the language and forms of understanding that are embedded in particular contexts and social practices, and sees these as important 'cultural resources' that are available to a learner. Studies with this emphasis are often referred to as *socio-cultural*. On the other hand, it draws attention to the key role of experienced *others* in supporting less competent learners, and in 'mediating', 'scaffolding' and extending their understanding. Studies with this emphasis are known as *social constructivist*, because they retain the constructivist concern with learner activity, but also recognize the importance of social processes and interactions.

The seminal writer on this approach was Vygotsky (1962, 1978, Reading 2.3) whose publications in Russian date from the 1930s. The increasing availability of Vygotsky's work in English coincided with reappraisals of the strengths and weaknesses of Piagetian theory. Psychologists such as Bruner (1986), Wood (1988) and Wertsch (1985) have been able to demonstrate the considerable relevance of Vygotsky's work to modern education.

The influence of social practices and social contexts starts as soon as a child is born. Babies and young children interact with their parents, carers and families, experiencing the language and forms of behaviour of their culture. They learn, through these interactions and observations, the expected behaviours and what is valued. Mercer (1992), for example, considered how his daughter 'appropriated' new ways of playing from watching an older child. As such, it is proposed that practitioners must consider children's cultures and the child's understanding before they initiate new learning experiences to ensure that the child can give meaning to this knowledge and make connections with what is already known.

The key role of more experienced others is best illustrated through the work of Vygotsky (1978). Vygotskian socio-cultural theory proclaims that children learn in a social context – as a member of a relationship (Vygotsky, 1962), in which the guiding role of more knowledgeable members is key. For Vygotsky, learning is reliant on a more knowledgeable partner. This partner allows a child to move from what they know to what they can know with the support of another. He coined the phrase 'Zone of Proximal Development' to refer to this 'gap' in their understanding. The more knowledgeable partner helps them to bridge this gap. This can been seen as similar to the support of the practitioner or peer partner highlighted in the feature of early years pedagogy known by the term 'sustained shared thinking' (Colwell, 2012). Vygotsky claims that for the full learning potential of a task to be reached, a more knowledgeable partner or guide plays a crucial role, which may be filled by teacher or peer partner (Rogoff, 1990). In either case, the support functions to extend and to 'scaffold' the child's understanding across their ZPD for that issue. An appropriate analogy, suggested by Bruner (Reading 2.4), is that of building a house. Scaffolding is needed to support the process as the house is gradually constructed from its foundations – but when it has been assembled and all the parts have been secured, the scaffolding can be removed. The building – the learner's understanding – will stand independently. In Chapter 6 we will consider how this supporting role in learning can be fostered through the development of relationships.

**Figure 2.3** represents the social cognition model of learning and how that learning can be supported and scaffolded by an experienced other. This model again reinforces that new knowledge is built upon what the child already knows and understands

**Figure 2.3**
A social constructivist model of roles in the teaching–learning process

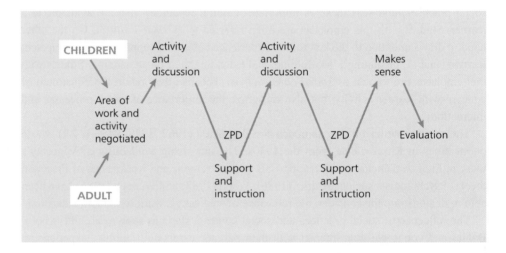

In recent decades, the influence of social constructivism has underpinned the work of curriculum associations (e.g. EYFS, 2012). Where Piagetian theory was criticized for underestimating the potential of practitioners, other adults and children to support the child's learning, Vygotsky highlighted their importance (Penn, 2008).

So far in this chapter, we have considered three major theoretical influences on learning and teaching processes. We now move on to focus more specifically on babies and young children as learners, and on factors which influence individual differences in learning.

## Reflective activity 2.1

*Aim:* To consider the application of behaviourist, constructivist and social constructivist psychology in practice.

*Evidence and reflection:* Review a selection of major learning situations and teaching methods, which you use across the day.

Note each learning situation, each teaching approach and then consider the psychological rationale for its use.

| Learning situation | Teaching approach used | Psychological rationale for the teaching approach |
| --- | --- | --- |
|  |  |  |
|  |  |  |
|  |  |  |
|  |  |  |

Consider if you are drawing effectively on the strengths of each approach. Does this activity have any implications for the repertoire of teaching strategies that you use? Are there changes to be made? Might some of your staff team benefit from gaining a deeper understanding of the theories behind the approaches used?

*Extension:* Consider the influence, strengths and weaknesses of each learning approach on your practice.

# 2 *Nature*, nurture and agency

The following two sections provide an introduction to some of the factors which influence learning. Debate about the relative importance of 'nature' (biological factors) and 'nurture' (environmental factors) has continued for centuries. The first section leads on nature, but shows how nurture is important. The second leads on nurture, but suggests that nature is similarly always present as an influence. So, to be clear, it is our contention, and indeed the contention of many, that nature and nurture are both hugely important and influential factors in learning and development. As such, to support children's learning and development we need to understand them both.

These sections also consider 'agency'. This refers to the capacity of humans to act on the basis of their understanding, their *free will*. Although we are very significantly influenced by our biology and our circumstances and environment, we are not determined by them. Indeed, in all circumstances, actions always make a difference of some sort. While this idea places the responsibility for our actions with us as individuals it also highlights how as practitioners we have a responsibility to support children to exercise their agency.

## 2.1 The developing brain

A baby's brain is a highly capable organ (Huotilainen, 2010). When a child is born, almost all of the neurons they will have are present – that is, all of the information-transmitting cells are in place. As the brain develops and as we learn, connections are made between these neurons. The greater number of connections formed, the better the brain will function (Nutkins, McDonald and Stephen, 2013).

There are two key ways in which these connections (synapses) are developed: in part determined by biology, and in part by each child's experiences. First, in the early stages of development, the brain over-produces synapses but then selectively prunes out those which are not used. As Bransford et al. put it:

> … the nervous system sets up a large number of connections. Experience then plays on these networks, selecting appropriate connections and removing inappropriate ones. What remains is a refined form that constitutes the sensory and cognitive bases for later phases of development. (1999: 104)

The second way in which synapses are added is actually *driven* by experience, when additions occur as a biological consolidation of new learning. This process of adaption and development is known as 'plasticity', and operates throughout life. Such processes have enormous implications for teaching. Practitioners working with babies, and indeed all children, must be aware that the child's interactions with others plays a crucial role in supporting the development of such connections (Zeedyk, 2006; Szalavitz and Perry, 2011; see also Bowlby, Reading 6.4 on attachment) – highlighting one of the ways in which nature and nurture are nature both play a crucial role in a child's development. Research tells us that the greatest period of development for such connections is between the ages of 6 and 12 months and that their brains have reached 80 per cent of the full-grown size at age 3 years and 90 per cent by age 6 years (Lenroot and Giedd, 2006). Thus, this period is crucial for supporting children to learn and develop and reach their full potential to learn (Mustard, 2006; Nutkins, McDonald and Stephen, 2013). The reflective practitioner should therefore be aware of the role they play in supporting babies and young children to develop, to learn, and to develop a brain capable of learning.

Indeed the work of biologists and neurologists has attracted much attention in recent years and new knowledge is beginning to affect our understanding of human development and its implications for learning and teaching (Dowling, 1999). From the educational point of view, we must accept the contribution of genetic variation while also affirming our responsibility with parents and others for helping each child to fulfil their potential. To support our work with young children, it helps to understand a little more about the brain itself.

The brain has three key biological elements:

- **reptilian system**: monitors basic survival needs, such as hunger, thirst, warmth and risk.
- **limbic system**: associated with emotions and long term memory.
- **neocortex**: associated with more advanced mental functions such as language development.

Research
Briefing
# Education and neuroscience

TLRP assembled leading practitioners, neuroscientists, psychologists and educationalists to review the impact of neuroscience on education. There was agreement about its enormous potential significance. There was also agreement that many recent applications were inappropriate and that some 'neuro-myths' in schools needed to be challenged.

Essentially, aspirations to apply 'brain science' too directly to 'practice' are misplaced. The model below represents the relationship between brain, mind and behaviour, and indicates the wide range of mediating environmental and intra-individual factors.

| Examples of environmental factors | Examples of intra-individual factors | Factor affected |
|---|---|---|
| Oxygen<br>Nutrition<br>Toxins | Synaptogenesis<br>Synaptic pruning<br>Neuronal connections | BRAIN |
| Teaching<br>Cultural institutions<br>Social factors | Learning<br>Memory<br>Emotion | MIND |
| Temporary restrictions<br>e.g. teaching tools | Performance<br>Errors<br>Improvement | BEHAVIOUR |

A model of brain, mind and behaviour [from Morton and Frith, 1995]

| Key findings: | Implications: |
|---|---|
| *Nature/nurture:* Biology is not destiny. Biology provides no simple limit to our learning, not least because our learning can influence our biology. | Teaching should aim to enable children's potential and to enrich their experience. |
| *Neuro-myths:* Education has invested an immense amount in 'brain-based' ideas that are not underpinned by recognisable scientific understanding of the brain. Many of these ideas remain untested and others are being revealed as ineffective, such as:<br><br>*The belief that learning can be improved by presenting material to suit an individual's preferred 'learning style' is not supported by high quality evidence (Coffield et al., 2004).*<br><br>*Encouraging teachers to determine whether a child is left or right brained is misplaced. Performance at most everyday tasks, including learning activities, requires both hemispheres to work together in a sophisticated parallel fashion.* | Professional judgement should be applied in respect of commercial 'brain-based' programmes<br><br>Focusing on learning styles too narrowly could actually inhibit learner development more broadly.<br><br>Right brain/left brain beliefs, particularly if linked to gendered assumptions, categorises children inappropriately. |
| *Neuroscience:* Some particular insights from neuroscientists and psychologists have broad implications for teaching and learning strategies which merit further exploration. For example:<br><br>*When we learn new information, the semantic links that form between this new information and our existing knowledge serve to make it meaningful. An area of the left hemisphere is a vital structure in this. (Fletcher et al., 2003).*<br><br>*Mental visualisation of an object engages most of the brain circuitry which is activated by actually seeing it (Kosslyn, 2005).* | There are grounds for 'cautious optimism'.<br><br>The construction of meaning is a key to understanding and remembering information.<br><br>'Visualisation' has considerable power and usefulness as a learning tool. |
| *Cautious optimism:* We are still at an early stage in our understanding of the brain. There are methodological limitations and the transfer of concepts between neuroscience and education requires caution. Nevertheless, the potential is great and there are grounds for optimism that interdisciplinary work will produce important, secure knowledge in years to come. | There is a growing need for research collaborations between neuroscience, psychology and education that embrace insights and understanding from each perspective. |

**Further information:**
Howard-Jones, P. (ed.) (2007) *Neuroscience and Education: Issues and Opportunities.* A TLRP Commentary. London: TLRP. Available at **tlrp.org/pub**
Blakemore, S. J. and Frith, U. (2006) *The Learning Brain: Issues for Education.* Oxford: Blackwell.
Coffield, F., Mosley, D., Hall, E. and Ecclestone, K. (2004) *Learning Styles and Pedagogy: A Systematic and Critical Review.* London: ISRC.
The TLRP seminar series was coordinated by Paul Howard-Jones from the University of Bristol.

For education or teaching to be successful, it is essential that core survival needs, monitored by the reptilian system, are met, and while this is particularly true for babies who rely on us to support almost all of their needs, it is a factor at any age. This is at the heart of care and education in the early years.

In Chapter 6 we will consider the role of emotion and how being part of a trusting relationship is essential for many children to support learning. Indeed, we have already noted that, in part, brain development is supported or hindered by the child's interactions with others. The limbic system is responsible for controlling various functions in the body, including interpreting emotional responses, storing memories, and bodily functions – including the regulation of hormones. It therefore seems apposite to suggest that, as reflective practitioners, we need to ensure that we support this aspect of brain development and that we understand that behaviour and a child's ability to respond to a variety of situations may be due to the level of brain development.

Within the neocortex, parts of the left hemisphere have been found to be particularly significant for analytic capacities such as language, logic, pattern recognition and reflective thought, while much of the right hemisphere is associated with more intuitive and representational capabilities such as visualization, imagination, rhyme, rhythm and expression. There is a danger here of us over-simplifying what is a complex, interacting cognitive system (Hellige, 1993). However, what is important is that as, early years practitioners, we recognize that as the young child's brain develops, many of the skills and functions required for later learning are being developed.

Through this – albeit rather superficial – overview of the human brain, we can see that there is little room for doubt that children's mental capacities are the product of the interaction between both biological and environmental factors. So how do we help children to enhance their learning capacity? One answer to this has been provided by those promoting forms of brain-based learning such as 'brain gym', 'brain-compatible classrooms' and other related programmes. Such initiatives aim to enable practitioners and teachers to consider the implications of recent research so that it can be drawn into practice. However, considerable caution is necessary because, as TLRP demonstrated (see **Research briefing** on the preceding page), much scientific knowledge on the brain is not yet sufficiently robust to underpin the conclusions that are sometimes drawn for practice. There are many neuro-myths in circulation at present and 'brain-based' schemes should be approached with great caution. The Royal Society has published summaries of existing knowledge with explicit warnings on these matters (2011a, 2011b). As they put it: 'much of neuroscience is still "upstream" of application' (2011b: 76).

## 2.2 Health, physical development and disability

A child's development is holistic, with behaviour and learning resulting from interaction between emotional, cognitive and health factors (e.g. Evangalou et al., 2009; Denham et al., 2002; Cowie, 2012). It is our position that physical development acts as a foundation for the optimal development of cognitive skills such as communication and language, and that good physical development is essential for healthy emotional development and well-being, as well as general good health. As such, young children will benefit from activities that support the development and refinement of their fundamental gross and fine motor movement skills. Such experiences should be designed to enhance their knowledge of the body and its potential for movement. The development of such skills will help enable the child to become physically able to engage in many learning tasks. The question for us therefore is not whether a child is ready to learn, but what a child is ready to learn within the context of their development. Observation will again be the key tool in supporting the reflective early years practitioner to plan suitable activities which support and extend the child's skills and offer clear progressive opportunities, which build upon and use that which nature has provided.

For many children, modern-day living has led to reduction in the opportunities and motivation for them to freely run, jump and move their bodies. Indeed there is a growing body of evidence that show a rise in the number of children starting school with immature motor skills and that this is impacting upon their learning experience. For example, Goddard Blythe's research findings (2006), which involved 64 primary schools in Northumberland, showed 40 per cent of 4–6-year-olds and 88.5 per cent of 7–8-year-olds had developmentally immature balance and coordination skills, as defined by the project. Such evidence highlights the importance for young children to engage in physical activities which support physical growth and perceptual motor-skill development. Once again, this highlights that both nature and nurture are crucial to a child's development.

Additional concerns have risen with the rise of childhood obesity, as one in five children are now identified as being overweight as they enter statutory schooling. Research states that children who are overweight in the early years of life risk going on to become obese teenagers and adults (Reilly et al., 2005; Nadar et al., 2006) and developing associated health problems. As such, there has been an increased focus on early years practitioners promoting healthy lifestyles for young children and their families (e.g. the Children's Food Trust: Eat Better, Start Better programme).

Health has always been strongly associated with social conditions (Rutter and Madge, 1976; Wilkinson and Pickett, 2010) and a general rise in average standards of living since the 1970s reduced the prominence of the issue for a time. However, more recently, UK poverty levels have steadily worsened and the conditions in which many children and families live have deteriorated (see the index of poverty and social exclusion provided annually by the Joseph Rowntree Foundation; Ball, 2003; see Green and Janmoat, Reading 5.4). This is of key concern to the reflective early years practitioner, given that poverty has been shown to negatively impact on children's futures: 'poverty in childhood is one of the five most powerful and consistent predictors of subsequent disadvantage' (Lanyard and Dunn, 2009: 133). While we may feel that there is little we can do about certain economic and social problems, we can work to identify the needs of the families and children with whom we work. Where necessary, we can provide links to appropriate support networks and other professionals who can support families in need. In addition, we can develop specific strategies to support these families within the setting.

To assist the identification of health and developmental difficulties, key developmental milestones have been identified to allow practitioners across the fields of health, social care and education to monitor the growth and progress of babies and children. A summary of these can be found at **reflectiveteaching.co.uk.** Such guidance for considering a child's development, and indeed planning developmentally appropriate practice for working with children, can be useful. The reflective practitioner may draw upon these for guidance but, while doing so, must be aware that 'Development does not progress at the same rate in all children – there is a broad variation in "typical" ages of achieving milestones' (Sharma and Cockerall, 2014: 29). As we noted earlier, the limits of strict adherence to age-related developmental stages is one of the key criticisms of Piagetian theory. As such, milestone guides ought not to be used as a checklist. There is concern that young children may, at times, be expected to do things before they are sufficiently physically developed. At all ages, levels of attainment may reflect present development rather than long-term learning capabilities, and this is a vital distinction. We must not judge and assume that the child's current ability is indicative of their future abilities. Yet, this needs to be balanced against the need for the early years practitioner to identify potential developmental issues and identify potential support needs. Such guides can be a useful tool for planning suitable learning opportunities for children.

Here we would like to draw attention to disability as we discuss nature, nurture, and a child's development (see Chapter 15 for a more detailed discussion of inclusion and disability). Understanding disability as a question of rights and opportunities has grown in recent years and as a result people with impairments have articulated a strong voice – rejecting the traditional perception of people who are disabled as 'inadequate', 'damaged', 'less than whole' or 'less than fully human' (see Barton, 2012). This debate has identified that it is 'context' which makes somebody 'disabled'; rather, the person has an impairment. For example, a person may not be able to climb steps as they have an impairment; the context makes them disabled – remove the steps, remove the disability. Thus, it is our duty to spend time coming to understand and identify those needs arising from an impairment, work with the family and other support workers to provide a stable, suitable and consistent way of working with the child and remove barriers which may prevent the child from enjoying and/or accessing learning. We must consider that while the root of disability may be within nature, nurture plays a significant role in the child's experiences and how they may come to see themselves as the strong, capable learners we noted we consider all children to be at the beginning of this chapter.

The concept of intelligence was once taken for granted and has passed into our culture as a generalized term to label a child's abilities as a learner. Psychologists such as Kline (1991) argue that it is possible to measure ability based on inherited attributes. Indeed, practitioners and parents often talk about children in terms of 'brightness' or 'cleverness', and teachers routinely describe pupils and classroom groupings in terms of 'ability'. These terms (*intelligence* and *ability)* and the language used to describe children influences the ways in which we think about them, what we expect of them and what we share with them. It has become routinely assumed that there *is* both a generalized trait of intelligence and that it is possible to measure it objectively and use it to predict future achievement. However, there is a body of work which describes how this is not the case and that measures of intelligence are flawed and potentially harmful to children and young people. For example, research (e.g. Egan and Bunting, 1991) shows us that children can be taught to do intelligence tests and that it is not possible to identify or measure ability with any confidence. That is, children without access to coaching, particular styles of teaching or from particular groups may be classified as having low levels of intelligence based purely upon their experiences rather than their capabilities.

To read more about this, including the work of Howard Gardner on 'multiple intelligence' and Golman on 'emotional intelligence', see **reflectiveteaching.co.uk**.

---

### Reflective activity 2.2

*Aim:* To consider the early years practitioner's duty to identify potential developmental issues in babies and children. Consider the complex role of differentiating between the need to allow the child to develop at their own pace with the need to refer the child for assessment or support from other professionals.

*Evidence and reflection:* We suggest that you work with a colleague and consider times when you have suspected that a child may have Special Educational Needs or developmental issues which needed professional intervention. Consider times when this was the case and the child benefited from the support. Also consider times when this was not the case and that the child's development differed from what you had expected.

*Extension:* Are there children you that you have concerns about now? Discuss with your colleague the developmental differences between the children you currently work with. Do you make assumptions about how these children will progress in the future? Are these assumptions justified?

---

Research by Dweck over many years (e.g. 1986, 1999; see **Reading 2.5**) demonstrates why challenges to fixed-ability thinking or notions of a fixed level of intelligence are so important. Dweck studied, in particular, how children think about, explain and 'attribute' their own capability. Those who adopt an 'entity theory' of intelligence tend to believe that their personal capability is fixed, and that they either 'can' or 'cannot' succeed at the new challenges that they meet. For this reason, they tend to adopt a form of 'learned helplessness' and this disposition tends to continue into adult life. However, those who adopt an 'incremental theory' of their capability believe that they are able to learn and improve. They are thus likely to be more highly motivated, have greater engagement and take risks, exhibit 'resilience' (Claxton, 1999) and act independently. To support the children in our settings to become motivated learners who believe they can succeed, we must lay these foundations in the early years; being mindful of how our actions and comments may lead children to think of themselves using a deficit rather than a credit approach.

As we have seen, while the influence of 'nature' is real, and differences in children's development and capabilities do exist, we have also seen that these are profoundly mitigated by cultural factors and the actions of practitioners and teachers. We do have the power to shape children's futures.

## 3 *Nurture*, nature and agency

In this section, we lead on the social and cultural factors which contribute to 'nurture' and the learning environment, while remaining aware of 'nature'. We draw attention to the opportunities for practitioners and parents and carers to enhance learning opportunities.

The development of social constructivist and sociocultural psychology has led to a much greater understanding of how culture, experience and language impact upon learning (see section 1.3 of this chapter). The major sources of such cultural influence are commonly seen as family and community, peers, educational environments, and the media and new technologies. We will consider each in turn.

It is useful to note how many of these issues are discussed in other chapters, sometimes in greater detail and sometimes from a slightly different angle. This is necessary because, as we have noted, the development of the child is holistic, and there are a number of forces at work in any given situation impacting upon experiences and outcomes. This is why the reflective practitioner should seek to consider any incident from multiple perspectives.

## 3.1 Family and community

Family background has been recognized as playing a crucial role in children's educational achievement for many years. There are a number of different ways in which the culture of the family and community impact upon children's learning and development.

### Wealth and future outcomes

While we would acknowledge that material objects are not the most important human need and that a great many families care for and provide for their children on very low incomes, there are issues associated with wealth and outcomes for children. For example, Coghlan et al. state that living in poverty is the greatest influence on children's outcomes in the early years and that it '…can lead to poor health and poor academic progress (especially communication, language and literacy; mathematical development; and personal, social and emotional development) (2010: 1). Such issues continue throughout school life and in to adulthood. Data collected in schools informs us that 'The performance of pupils eligible for free school meals is lower than their non-eligible counterparts at all key stages and in all performance measures' (Statistics for Wales, 2014). As such, children born into poverty are likely to continue to live in poverty. Research has shown that how wealthy a child's family is directly correlates with how wealthy the child is likely to become. Blanden et al. (2004) found that a son from a family which earns twice as much as another family will earn on average 25 per cent more at age 30 than a son from the second family – indicating that potential is not the only determinate for how 'successfully' a child will perform in the education system. As reflective early years practitioners, we must be aware of this and work to alleviate such issues wherever we can.

# Learned behaviours

From birth, babies are learning how to behave by observing and interacting with adults, siblings and peers. Evangalou et al. concluded, following their review of the literature regarding children's learning:

> … babies are learning how to behave by being placed in social settings, surrounded by important adults, siblings and peers. Through these shared interactions children understand their own social realities. One of the most important 'lessons' through these cultural interactions and the use of shared language is the appropriate forms of emotional displays and behaviours. These shared languages are offering enriched discourse and narratives of their social experiences through the individual family's cultural repertoire. It is important for settings to recognise and nurture these different repertoires. (2009: 81–2)

From birth, then, the child is learning appropriate behaviours and what is and is not valued within their family and often in their community. The child will then enter pre-school with behaviours and values rooted in their cultural experience.

## Through cultural capital

Pierre Bourdieu's theory of cultural capital has been highly influential in the field of education. The theory states that the actions, behaviours and values of the most wealthy/upper classes are considered superior to those of the less wealthy and/or lower classes. That includes the learned behaviours discussed above. The cultural capital held by some children 'does not provide them with a system of knowing or ways of doing which will grant them easy access to learning' (Fleer, cited in Parker-Rees and Willan, 2006: 407). Thus, the system itself promotes social inequalities by valuing the cultures of some families over others. The reflective practitioner may take time to consider whether they do indeed favour the behaviours of some children, groups or communities and what can be done to ensure that all children have opportunities to access learning and succeed.

## Through the Home Learning Environment (HLE)

While wealth has been shown to have an impact on children's outcomes, the actions of parents have been shown to have a significant impact on a child's learning. Indeed, the Effective Provision of Pre-school Education Project (EPPE), a large on-going project which follows the progress of children from age 3 years (see, Sylva, Melhuish, Sammons, Siraj-Blatchford and Taggart, Reading 4.2), found that parental involvement in learning makes a significant contribution to children's attainment and social outcomes (Sylva, 2004). Activities that were found to contribute to a positive HLE included reading to the child, teaching the child songs and visiting the library (Sylva et al., 2004). Thus, strategies to support parents to understand the benefits of, and indeed enjoy, learning experiences with their children may support children's learning. This may be one way in which babies and children begin to develop the skills of learning at a young age.

# Supporting the development of dispositions for learning

The fundamental purpose of education for the twenty-first Century, it is argued, is not so much the transmission of particular bodies of knowledge, skill and understanding as facilitating the development of the capacity and the confidence to engage in lifelong learning. Central to this enterprise is the development of positive learning dispositions, such as resilience, playfulness and reciprocity (Claxton and Carr, 2002: 9).

Katz (1993: 2) defines dispositions as 'relatively enduring habits of mind or characteristic ways of responding to experience across types of situations'. Learning dispositions are, then, the ways in which we respond to learning situations. Do we approach a new task with curiosity, a willingness to try and perhaps fail and try again, to problem-solve? Or do we fear failure, find new tasks a chore? Supporting children to develop the dispositions to learn must be a key concern for the early years practitioner. Indeed, the benefits of a positive HLE may be in part due to the skills of curiosity, interest that this instils. Developing a 'can do' curious approach to learning tasks can determine how children will learn as they grow up. We give implicit messages to children when we respond to desirable and undesirable dispositions. Praising curiosity and investigation rather than focusing on the successful completion of tasks may be a useful way to support the development of positive learning dispositions. Again, supporting families to understand the development and impact of positive dispositions may be hugely beneficial for the child and their future learning. For example, families with high expectations of their child may inadvertently discourage the development of the dispositions which support learning.

> ## Expert question
>
> **Inclusion:** Are all children and their families treated respectfully and fairly in both formal and informal interaction? Is information made available and accessible?
>
> This question contributes to a conceptual framework representing enduring issues and practitioner expertise (see Chapter 16).

> ## Case study 2.1 How families and communities impact on children's learning and development
>
> Szymon is four and has been coming to the nursery for three months. He is a bright boy – for example, he can read simple books. His mother is aware he is very bright and is always praising his work. His key person has noticed that, while Szymon is progressing well, his dispositions to learn are not as she would hope. As he is very used to doing well, when he finds something difficult he tends to leave it and get frustrated with himself. She has on occasion seen him hitting his leg with a closed fist.
>
> After reflecting upon these issues in a staff meeting, the staff agreed a two-stepped process. First, they plan activities to undertake with Szymon which will stretch his abilities. They plan to undertaken some of these on a one-to-one and others on a small group basis. His key person states that she will endeavour to enter into sustained discussions with him about challenge and resilience. They agree they will use examples, such as the world's best scientists, and how they succeed by trying and keeping going when

they get things wrong. Secondly, as a team, they decided to be very aware of the praise they give Szymon. They agree to praise his efforts and perseverance over his achievements.

As this plan was put into action, the staff team agreed they would tentatively approach their concerns with his mother. They recommended a book for her to read with him: *Be a Perfect Person in Just Three Days!* by Stephen Manes (1996), so they can discuss that it is neither possible nor necessary to be perfect.

Through consideration of how families and communities impact on children's learning and development, we have noted that their relationships and interactions with others play a significant role in the learning. As babies and children enter early years settings, the number of people they interact with grows. We now turn our attentions to the impact of these interactions on children's learning.

## 3.2 Peer relationships

Children experience two distinct social worlds within pre-schools (Colwell, 2012). These relate to either a child's interactions with the practitioner, or with their peers, with each involving children being in groupings of differing in size, composition and involved in tasks with different foci and purpose (Kutnick et al., 2007). We know that children's peers make a significant contribution to each others' development (Ladd, 2005). Indeed, within pre-school settings children spend more of their time with their peers than they do with practitioners (Wilcox-Herzog and Kontos, 1998; Kutnick et al., 2006). The time spent with peers extends as children progress through education. During this time with their peers, children learn a great deal, both in terms of building understanding and also learning about what is valued, and the language and behaviours that are deemed appropriate. As such, the culture of the group, what they value and what they do not value, can have an impact on what the child begins to value. This can set the tone for learning throughout life.

We explore children's relationships with their peers in greater detail in Chapter 6.

## 3.3 Educational environments

As the sections above have alluded to, children's dispositions to learn are environmentally sensitive. These dispositions are supported or weakened by the environment and children's interactions with others (Bertram and Pascal, 2002). Each educational setting, pre-school or school has its own unique culture, created by those who work in the settings and those associated with them. This may include the owners, local authority staff and people from the local community. This culture must be seen as a learning context which is at least as important as the bricks and mortar and toys and equipment which make up the material environment. The culture of the group implicitly indicates to the child and their families

## Expert question

**Culture:** Does the setting support expansive learning by affirming children contributions, engaging partners and providing attractive opportunities?

This question contributes to a conceptual framework representing enduring issues and practitioner expertise (see Chapter 16).

what is valued and what is important. Indeed, the cultures adults create have been shown to influence children's behaviours. Sheridan (2007) found that where pre-school practitioners asserted dominance and demanded obedience from children, the children themselves demonstrated more antisocial behaviours with peers. Thus, our actions impact upon the actions of the children in our care. A part of the role of the reflective early years practitioner must therefore be to create a culture in which learning, curiosity and respect are fostered.

## 3.4 The media and new technologies

Babies and young children are growing up in a digital world, awash with media input and ever-new technological advances. Marsh et al. concluded from their study into the use of popular culture, media and new technologies that 'young children are immersed in practices relating to popular culture, media and new technologies from birth … [through this immersion] they are developing an understanding of the role of media and technology in society' (2005: 5). Some have been concerned about these developments and how children are targeted by advertisements (for example Palmer, 2010), while others have focused on the new exciting learning potential of such technology (e.g. Beck and Fetherston, 2003; Tancock and Segedy, 2004). There can be issues where some children are unable to access particular technologies at home or in the setting and also instances of early years staff not feeling confident about using technology. Formby (2014) found that the majority of early years practitioners held positive views about the use of technology, with three-quarters of practitioners stating that they feel it is important to learn to use technology from an early age. Technology does indeed provide tools for children to access multiple, often playful, learning opportunities.

Clearly, the impact each of these cultural influences has on a particular child will vary. It is important for the reflective early years practitioner to understand these influences and reflect upon how they may impact upon the babies and children in their care. **Reflective activity 2.3** focuses on this issue.

---

**Reflective activity 2.3**

*Aim:* To consider the influence of culture on the development and the learning disposition of a child.

*Evidence and reflection:* Think of a child in your setting. Consider the way culture and experiences influence the child's understanding, the language he or she uses and the learning disposition he or she adopts. If you have time, it would be valuable to talk to the child, their parents, and your peers to improve the quality of your evidence.

*Extension:* Repeat this exercise with different children, or compare the results of the same activity conducted by a colleague. What insights are produced by comparisons of children of different sex, ethnicity, religion, social class? You can see some examples of this sort of analysis in the final chapters of Pollard and Filer (1996, 1999).

---

# 3.5 Personality, self-esteem and learner identity

Research has indicated that personality is not set and people develop and change (Ardelt, 2000). We must therefore not assume that a child in our care has particular traits which will remain with them for life. A part of our role is to nurture development and support the child to become the strong capable learner we defined at the beginning of this chapter. Psychologists' understanding of personality has, according to Hampson (1988), derived from three contributory strands of analysis.

- *The lay perspective:* the understandings which are implicit in common-sense thinking of most of us about other people. It is a means by which people are able to anticipate the actions of others – ideas about the character and likely actions of others are used for both the prediction and explanation of behaviour.

- *Trait theories:* such theories reflect the attempt to identify personality dimensions and to objectively measure how this leads to individuals having different *learning styles*. However, while a learning style approach is important in recognizing that children, and indeed adults, may learn in different ways, it is not straightforward to translate it into specific classroom provision. Indeed, a systematic review of such research concluded that the scientific basis of 'learning styles' is weak (Coffield et al., 2004; see also the **Research briefing** on neuroscience in this chapter).

- *The self perspective*: this sees the development of personality in close association with that of self-image and identity. Crucially, it draws attention to the capacity of humans to reflect on themselves and to take account of the views of others. The social context in which children grow up, their culture, interaction and experiences with significant people in their lives, is thus seen as being very important in influencing their views of self and consequent patterns of action. As we play a significant role in working with babies and young children, our behaviours can shape how the child grows to see themselves as learners and as individuals and subsequently their motivation to learn.

These three strands all have useful roles in helping us to understand children as individuals with potentially different styles of learning. Yet they also highlight the importance of being wary of inappropriately limiting the expectations that we make of children.

As we consider the impact of nature and nurture, we must also consider that humans are not entirely shaped by nature and/or nurture. We also have agency. Costa and McCrae highlight the role of the individual in the development of their personality. They state: 'personality is not a product of the life course … People are not mere pawns of the environment, but active agents who steadfastly pursue their own style of being throughout life' (1997: 283). We propose that for children and adults to act as active agents in their personal growth, we must support them to develop the skills to become aware of their agency and how they can employ that agency.

## 4 Taking stock of learning

This section offers an overview of the key factors that affect learning and motivation.

# 4.1 Metaphors for learning

Within our cultural history, theories about learning have come and gone. And although, as we have seen, contemporary sciences are gradually accumulating more stable knowledge, the field remains complex. It is helpful therefore to consider the resonance of two metaphors which attempt to make sense of this cultural variability and scientific complexity.

We draw here on the work of Sfard (1998), whose paper was entitled: 'On two metaphors for learning and the dangers of choosing just one'. Sfard suggests that metaphors provide a deceptively simple way of representing our tacit frameworks of understanding. In particular, they reach between culturally embedded intuition – what we feel we know through common sense and experience – and more formal knowledge – that which has been shown to be the case through research.

## Learning as 'acquisition'

'Since the dawn of civilization', human learning has been 'conceived as the acquisition of something', writes Sfard (1998: 5), whether this be knowledge *per se* or conceptual development. In either case, the image is of the 'human mind as a container to be filled with certain materials and of the learner becoming an owner of these materials' (p. 5). This aligns with the idea that the child is an *empty vessel*, ready to be *filled* by curriculum content. This may include knowledge, skills, facts and attitudes. They are to be acquired through remembering, with help of practitioners who guide, support, deliver and explain. Once acquired, the capabilities can be applied, transferred, shared with others, etc. National education systems tend to rest on the foundation of this metaphor, and are designed in systematic ways to provide the conditions, support and instruction which will maximize learner attainment at each stage of development. We will explore alternative approaches to this model throughout this book, for example in chapter 11 which focuses on pedagogic practice.

## Learning as 'participation'

This alternative metaphor is more recent but is rapidly growing in significance in the contemporary world. The emphasis is on the learner as 'a person interested in participation in certain kinds of activities' (Sfard, 1998: 6). So this is learning through activity; through direct, authentic engagement in an applied situation: learning through practice. With the support of parents, family and friends, a child might learn to play games, go shopping, identify with a football team – or become a bit more independent by sleeping over. The possibilities are endless. This metaphor affirms direct experience in real situations.

We may wish to debate the relative advantages and disadvantages of these two metaphors for learning. However, the reflective early years practitioner should carefully note that these metaphors represent two very important ways through which learning occurs. Put another way, the acquisition of capabilities though formal education or a set curriculum is necessary but not sufficient. Some approaches to learning may be more or less appropriate at different stages of a child's development. Acquisition alone risks a formalized education unsuitable for the needs of the young developing child, while as the child grows and develops, participation alone risks contextually bounded thinking and for the child to have gaps in their knowledge which may hinder future learning – specifically, we have discussed new knowledge being built upon knowledge which is already in place.

## 4.2 The characteristics of effective learning

Within this chapter, a number of complex interconnecting issues which impact upon learning have been reviewed. As the evidence of the benefits of high-quality early years education has strengthened, and as our understanding of children's learning and development has grown, so has the guidance, support and advice for early years practitioners. In 2008 the Early Years Foundation Stage (EYFS) was introduced in England as an overarching framework for early years providers. The EYFS provided information on how children learn and develop in the early years of life. A review of the EYFS curriculum was conducted by Dame Clare Tickell. The review identified the need to make explicit the ways in which children learn, labelling these as the *Characteristics of Effective Learning*. Tickell stated:

> All early years practitioners will need to understand the different ways in which children learn, in order to provide effective support. While implicit in the current EYFS, I believe the EYFS would be a better product if these were made explicit. I therefore recommend that playing and exploring, active learning, and creating and thinking critically, are highlighted in the EYFS as three characteristics of effective teaching and learning,

describing how children learn across a wide range of activities. These … describe how children learn rather than what they learn. They begin at birth and are lifelong characteristics which need to be fostered and developed during the early years as they are critical for building children's capacity for future learning. (Tickell, 2011: 27–8)

These characteristics were taken forward in the revised EYFS (see *Development Matters*, Early Education 2012). The table below provides an overview of the elements of these three characteristics.

**Table 2.1** The three Characteristics of Effective Learning

| Playing and exploring | Active learning | Creating and thinking critically |
|---|---|---|
| • finding out and exploring<br>• playing with what they know<br>• being willing to have a go | • being involved and concentrating<br>• keeping on trying<br>• enjoying achieving what they set out to do | • having their own ideas<br>• making links<br>• choosing ways to do things and finding new ways |

Resonance with the topics covered in this chapter are evident. Within *Playing and exploring*, which promotes the child's engagement, there is reference to the child 'having a go', exploring and playing. Within *Active learning* the focus turns to the child's motivation, their involvement in tasks and how adults nurture that involvement. For us all, deep and enduring learning only occurs when new knowledge has relevance and connects meaningfully with the personal narratives through which we make sense of life. Knowing the children in our care, planning appropriate activities and supporting them to see the value of tasks will be a crucial element in supporting active learning. The final element, *Creating and thinking critically*, involves children learning how to learn and includes the building of the confidence and ability for children to make links between knowledge, to have their own ideas and explore new ways of doing things.

This final element is arguably the most vital when looking to support children's learning as they grow and develop into adults. Humans have the unique capacity to reflect on their own thinking processes and to develop new strategies. This capacity for self-awareness regarding one's own mental powers is called 'meta-cognition' (Flavell, 1970, 1979). This has received strong endorsement and extension in recent years through the refinement of practical ways of developing 'thinking skills' (e.g. Fisher, 2008) and specifically in the early years through sustained shared thinking (SST) (Siraj-Blatchford et al., 2004).

Sustained shared thinking occurs when two or more individuals 'work together' in an intellectual way to solve a problem, clarify a concept, evaluate an activity, extend a narrative etc. Both parties must contribute to the thinking and it must develop and extend the understanding. (Siraj-Blatchford et al., 2004: vi)

Engaging in episodes of SST may support children to develop the skills of thinking critically and increase learning, where SST has been closely linked with higher cognitive and linguistic outcomes (Siraj-Blatchford and Sylva, 2004; Sylva et al., 2007). In addition to improving outcomes, Salmon and Lucas (2011) suggest that when thinking is valued, children are more likely to value thinking; thus, SST may contribute to a culture in which learning is valued.

---

### Reflective activity 2.4

*Aim:* To review your planning.

*Evidence and reflection:* Do you plan learning activities which are meaningful to the child, take each child's different experiences and personalities into account, and offer opportunities for each child's learning to be extended?

*Extension:* Consider whether there are further opportunities for observation to be used to plan for particular children and their needs.

---

## Conclusion

In this chapter we reviewed three influential theories on children's learning. Learning is an immensely complex topic and this chapter has simply touched the surface of some of the many issues which are involved. Indeed, much remains to be discovered about human learning. The vocation of teaching will certainly always include an element of intellectual challenge as we seek to understand what children understand, and then to provide them with personalized support to extend their understanding and their abilities.

We have also considered how physical and biological factors in the body and brain interact with the social and cultural factors of family and community – elements of the long-running 'nature–nurture' debate impact on children's learning and how we can seek to increase the learning potential of activities through understanding these issues.

Perhaps most importantly, through this chapter we sought to establish that a commitment to the learning capacity of all children is seen as a professional responsibility and a precondition for enhancing children's lives. Whatever the child's circumstances may be, early years practitioners have the precious opportunity to influence their learning and their lives for the better.

## Key readings

For further information on learning dispositions, see:

Carr, M and Claxton, G. (2002) 'Tracking the development of learning dispositions', *Assessment in Education: Principles, Policy & Practice*, 9 (1), 9–37.

Claxton, G. and Carr, M. (2004) 'A framework for teaching learning: learning dispositions', *Early Years International Journal of Research and Development*, 24 (1), 87–97.

For a good overview of learning in the early years, see:

Nutkins, S., McDonald, C. and Stephen, M. (2013) *Early Childhood Education and Care*. London: Sage Publications Ltd.

Parker-Rees, R., Leeson, C., Savage, J. and Willan, J. (eds) (2010) *Early Childhood Studies*. London: Sage Publications Ltd.

For more on pedagogy and practice, see:

Siraj-Blatchford, I. (2005) *Quality Interactions in the Early Years.* Keynote address at the TACTYC Annual Conference, Cardiff, 5 November – Birth to 8 Matters! Seeking Seamlessness – Continuity? Integration? Creativity? **tactyc.org.uk/ pdfs/2005conf_siraj.pdf**

Siraj-Blatchford, I. and Sylva, K. (2004) 'Researching pedagogy in English pre-schools', *British Educational Research Journal*, 30 (5), 713–30.

Siraj-Blatchford, I., Sylva, K., Muttock, S., Gilden, R. and Bell, D. (2002) *Researching Effective Pedagogy in the Early Years (REPEY)*, DfES Research Report 365. HMSO London: Queen's Printer.

**For more on sustain shared thinking, see:**

Siraj-Blatchford, I. (2007) 'Creativity, communication and collaboration: the identification of pedagogic progression in sustained shared thinking', *Asia-Pacific Journal of Research in Early Childhood Education*, 1 (2), 3–23.

The associated website, **reflectiveteaching.co.uk**, offers a wealth of supplementary resources including reflective activities, research briefings, advice on further reading and downloadable diagrams, figures and checklists from the book. It also features a compendium of educational terms, links to useful websites, policy and curriculum documents, and showcases examples of excellent research and practice.

# Reflection
## How can we develop the quality of our practice?

**3**

## Introduction

This book is based on the belief that effective early years practice is a complex and highly skilled activity which, above all, requires practitioners to exercise judgement in deciding how to act. High-quality practice, and thus children's learning and development, is dependent on the existence of professional expertise.

The process of reflective practice supports the development and maintenance of professional expertise. As we develop as early years practitioners, our professional expertise grows alongside us. What is particularly apparent within the early years sector is that this expertise may develop and be recognized in a number of different ways. Penn (2012) describes three internationally recognized routes through which practitioners within early years develop their expertise: early years specialists, teachers and social pedagogues.

- Early years specialists are typically trained to work with children aged birth to 5 and in the UK they would often engage in work-based degrees such as foundation degrees, or early years-related degrees and Early Years Professional Status/Early Years Teacher Status.

- Teachers tend to cover a broader age range and may work with children from birth to 7. Typically they have completed degrees which incorporate teaching practice and Qualified Teacher Status (QTS), or a degree followed by a postgraduate professional qualification, often with the older age group 3–7 years.

- Social pedagogues have a wider remit than working with young children, as they tend to work across settings. They often teach artistic or practical skills and promote the ideals of positive living and lifelong learning. In the UK we can see elements of this role in some peripatetic teachers, with some Early Years Professionals/Teachers who are responsible for more than one setting and with advisory and support staff.

As a practitioner engages with their learning journey, whichever route they take, they develop their professional expertise. Certain milestones can be identified which mark this growth – for example, gaining a qualification such as a foundation degree, degree or postgraduate qualification, or through recognition in the place of work, such as being promoted to manage practice. Indeed, research has shown us how important the skills and knowledge of early years practitioners are, and government reviews and commitment to having graduate-led early years settings has supported this (Sylva et al., 2004; DfE, 2010). However, this is not the end of the journey, as further expertise is developed over time as we become more experienced and learn more about children, families and working with colleagues.

If our learning is to continue throughout our careers we must engage in the process of reflection, as this feeds a constructive spiral of professional development and capability (see **Figure 3.1**). We note that this model talks about the process of 'teaching', which we understand can be a contentious issue within early years. However, we have interpreted the word 'teaching' as encompassing all activities which bring about learning (Hirst, 1973). In Chapter 11 we discuss this further, but, as we are not suggesting that teaching only

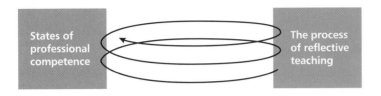

Figure 3.1
The spiral of
professional
development

happens when we follow particular practices, we believe this model is relevant to all early years practitioners whether or not they view themselves as teachers in the traditional sense.

Reflective practice should be personally fulfilling for practitioners, but also lead to a steady increase in the quality of education and care. Indeed, because it is evidence-based, reflective practice supports within setting training, undergraduates in training, practitioners with early years degrees, newly qualified teachers, teaching assistants and experienced professionals in satisfying performance standards and competences. Additionally, as we shall see, the concept of reflective practice draws particular attention to the aims, values and social consequences of education.

## TLRP principles

Two principles are of particular relevance to this chapter on learning:

**Principle 7: Effective teaching and learning fosters both individual and social processes and outcomes.** Learning is a social activity. Learners should be encouraged and helped to work with others, to share ideas and to build knowledge together. Consulting learners about their learning and giving them a voice is both an expectation and a right.

**Principle 9: Effective teaching and learning depends on teacher learning.** The need for teachers to learn continuously in order to develop their knowledge and skills, and adapt and develop their roles, especially through classroom inquiry, should be recognized and supported.

This chapter has three main parts. The first introduces some of the *dilemmas* and challenges which early years practitioners face and key issues surrounding evidence-based practice, professional standards and competences. In the second part, seven major characteristics of reflective teaching are identified and discussed. In exploring these characteristics, particular emphasis is placed on evidence-informed practice and on the ways in which practitioners might support one another's reflective practice. In the final part, we draw some conclusions that might inform the future actions of early years practitioners. Ultimately, this chapter will act as a guide to building the foundations for reflective teaching both for individuals and for those working in teams.

## 1 Dilemmas, reflection, effectiveness and quality

## 1.1 Dilemmas and challenges in early years provision

The complicated nature of children's learning and development and the practical demands of the early years environment ensure that a practitioner's work is never finished. Merely considering the multiple aspects of practice covered in this book gives us a sense of the breadth of professional concerns that are part of early years work. When practicalities, performance standards, personal ideals and wider educational and learning concerns are considered together, the job of reconciling the numerous requirements and possible conflicts may seem to be overwhelming. As a nursery deputy supervisor shared with us:

> Nursery is changing all the time. Since we have been taking the funded two-year-olds in we've all had to change ... yet again! We've had to think about their parents and help them to become part of the nursery community. Which has meant we needed to support our existing parents and children to accept these younger and more demanding children and their families into the nursery. What it has meant really is much more diversity in the setting. So we have had to adapt what we do to suit these much younger children while not detracting from the learning experiences of the older ones. Then we have needed to explain to the rest of the staff that we need to change and learn what these new younger children need rather than expecting them to just 'fit in' with the rest. It has made us completely rethink our key person system, induction procedures, how we observe and report, the learning journeys, nursery routines, staff training and staff meetings ... everything really! It has been a challenge and meant that we've really had to work extra hard. I've made loads of home visits for instance. We have had to think about what works and new ways of doing things and just try things out. And it has been the most satisfying and exciting time I have ever spent in the nursery.

This quote illustrates the complicated nature of being an early years practitioner within a nursery setting. It demonstrates that, among other things, early years practitioners are required to learn a complex set of technical skills and understandings; position themselves within a larger community of practice; manage emotional dimensions of 'personal development'; and connect, integrate and reconcile various sources of theory and experiences of practice.

It also reflects the fact that the expertise needed across the early years workforce is diverse, complex and subject to change, and is partly dependent upon the role of the practitioner and the setting that they work within. For early years professionals/teachers, and for this deputy supervisor, the role includes leading practice and supporting staff and may also include elements of management. For Reception and Key Stage 1 teachers, many elements of management are already in place within the school, but the teachers are required to lead

**Table 3.1** Common dilemmas that occur for early years practitioners

| | |
|---|---|
| Treating each child as a whole person | Treating children as a member of the group or class |
| Organizing the children on an individual basis | Organizing children according to groups |
| Allowing the children free play and choice over the activities they do and how that progresses | Providing adult-led activities, which direct their learning and guide the activities they do |
| Seeking to motivate children through the use of intrinsic involvement and enjoyment of activities | Offering reasons and rewards so that children are extrinsically motivated to complete tasks |
| Developing areas of learning and activities from an appreciation of children's interests and schemas | Providing topics or themes linked to the long term planning of the school/ nursery as a whole or which 'society' expects them to receive |
| Developing activities that support children's learning across the areas of learning | Dealing systematically with each area of learning in a separate and discrete way |
| Aiming for quality experiences in the processes of learning during activities | Aiming for high-quality end products of children's activities |
| Focusing on individual aspects of a child's development and learning | Seeing a child's development and learning in an holistic manner and putting equal emphasis on all areas of development |
| Trying to build up cooperative social skills | Developing self-reliance and self-confidence in individuals |
| Inducting children into a common culture | Affirming the variety of cultures in a multi-ethnic society |
| Allocating practitioner time, attention and resources equally among all children | Paying attention to the special needs of particular children |
| Working with 'professional' application and care for the children | Working with consideration of one's personal needs |
| Using routines to support children's feelings of safety and security and to support staff rotas and ratios | Moving away from routines to support understanding of change and excitement and/or seeing them as times to extend play and learning |
| Supporting and encouraging children to take risks and explore potentially risky activities | Minimizing risks and controlling activities and the environment to support safety |
| Allowing children to choose what they do and whether they will take part in activities | Supporting children to join whole-group activities in order to prepare them for later educational experiences |
| Allowing children private spaces and places to retreat into | Organizing the space so that children can be seen and heard at all times |
| Allowing free-flow for most of the day (both indoors and outside) | Restricting outside play and choice to timetabled times during the day |

practice within their classrooms, and may have a team working with them to lead including teaching assistants and specialist staff working to include children with additional needs. Regardless of role, all early years practitioners, across the four nations within the UK are required to follow an early years framework as legislated by government. These frameworks set some minimum standards and some non-negotiable ground rules about how young children should be treated. However, they are also flexible on how the details are put into practice on a day-to-day basis. They do, however, tend to cover similar ground and offer important guiding principles to follow. Typically, they charge early years practitioners with recognizing the unique child, the importance of establishing positive relationships, providing enabling environments and supporting learning and development (DCSF, 2008; DfE, 2012). These principles lead to expectations and commitments to both the learning and development of the individual child within the setting but also extend expertise beyond the classroom or nursery environment, to consider, for example, the importance given to building partnerships with parents. These principles can clearly be aligned to research (see for example the REPEY findings in Chapter 11). They also give insights into some of the possible dilemmas a practitioner might meet. The resolution of such dilemmas calls for early years practitioners to use professional judgement to assess the most appropriate course of action in any particular situation.

Dilemmas occur at every level of practice and on an everyday basis; consider **Table 3.1** on the previous page, which outlines some commonly occurring dilemmas within the nursery/classroom environment itself. This is not an exhaustive list and does not include more specific leadership related dilemmas, so, as you read through them, reflect on their relevance to you and whether there are other dilemmas which relate to your specific role and context.

## Reflective activity 3.1

*Aim:* To review experienced dilemmas.

*Evidence and reflection:* Think about your own situation and experiences. Look carefully at **Figure 3.1** and see whether any of the identified dilemmas provide a realistic reflection of those you are experiencing. Are there other dilemmas that relate to your specific context?

Having carried out this exercise, try to identify the three most pressing dilemmas that you are facing. Think carefully about each of these and consider whether there are any measures that you might take to help mitigate them (for example, discussions with relevant colleagues about developing approaches to behaviour management; changing assessment practices in line with recent CPD events; changing the routines within the learning environment to ensure a better mix of child-initiated and adult-led activities.)

The important point here is to start with one dilemma and consider what evidence you need to be able to address it effectively, and where that evidence might come from. Progress will often be slow and incremental, but such professional development has powerful potential for change.

*Extension:* Note that this reflective activity may well lead to a more formalized piece of within setting research; this is considered in **Reflective activity 3.2** opposite.

## Reflective activity 3.2

*Aim:* To plan to conduct a small piece of research in your setting.

*Identify an issue to research:* What additional dilemmas does your context/your role
 bring?

Dilemmas can occur at any level. Consider some that face those with leadership
and management responsibilities. How might you resolve issues such as: high staff
turnover; understanding of the need for high-quality staff but concerned that
employing them might make costs so high that the setting is priced out of the market;
ensuring that all staff have a working understanding of complex concepts such as
sustained shared thinking; ensuring that all staff work together as a team; ensuring
that parents' views and voices are taken seriously even when they differ from those of
the staff.

*Evidence:* Plan your research. This book provides a practical guide to ways of
 reflecting on such issues. Indeed, it offers strategies and advice for developing
 the necessary expertise to resolve them. There are also two additional chapters
 at **reflectiveteaching.co.uk.** Resolution of such dilemmas will always be based on
 practitioner judgement. However, in contemporary education, the use of research
 evidence and performance data is now routinely used to augment (and sometimes
 challenge or refine) such judgements.

# 1.2 Reflection and evidence-informed practice

Three main forms of evidence are available to early years practitioners: first, evidence
from research by academics and specialist educational research organizations; second,
practitioner-based research; and finally, performance data. Each will be considered in turn.

There has been considerable discussion in recent years about the use of 'evidence' to
inform early years educational practices (Peeters and Vandenbroeck, 2011; see **Reading 3.1**).
It has led to major changes in early years as both national and international research
evidence clearly demonstrated the importance of the quality of ECEC. It suggested that
early experiences lay the foundation for all learning (Sylva et al., 2004; Allen, 2011),
that they can reduce inequalities linked to parental background and socio-economic
status (West et al., 2010) and that they can have the most profound impact on economic
growth and prosperity generally (Ho et al., 2010; Field, 2010). Both nationally and internationally, such understandings have led to a plethora of government policy documents
and legislation as this stage of life became valued for its definite and pervasive effect on
children's learning and development. Consider, for example, the Early Years Foundation
Stage (DCSF, 2008; DfE, 2012); Pre-birth to Three: Positive outcomes for Scotland's
children and families, the Curriculum for Excellence in Scotland 3–18 (Scottish Executive,
2009). Recognition of the importance of early years also led the English government to
transfer the regulation and monitoring of pre-school settings to the Office for Standards
in Education (Ofsted) in 2000 and away from the social care sector; they saw this as way

to establish a sound universal basis of quality. Ofsted provides some of the performance data discussed later.

Melhuish (2004) reviewed the international research literature on the effects of ECEC. He noted that while high-quality care consistently supported children's educational and social development, low-quality childcare produced no benefit or even negative effects. This type of information, together with notable pieces of research such as the Effective Provision of Pre-school Education (EPPE) project (Sylva et al., 2004; see Reading 4.2) and similar studies in Northern Ireland – the Effective Pre-School Provision in Northern Ireland (EPPNI) project (IDE, 2006) and Wales – the Monitoring and Evaluation of the Effective Implementation of the Foundation Phase (MEEIFP) Project Across Wales (Siraj-Blatchford et al., 2006), together with many other international studies, highlighted the need for high-quality practitioners to support and develop this important stage of development and learning. In particular, they led to the recognition of the need for specialist early years practitioners and leaders within the early years sector (birth to 7 years). They promoted the idea that early years practitioners needed to be highly skilled, knowledgeable and experienced and understand the importance of evidence-based practice, reflection and critical thinking (Siraj-Blatchford and Manni, 2007; Siraj-Blatchford, 2008; Allen, 2011).

The second source of evidence is, arguably, the most important for reflective practitioners. In this case, early years practitioners themselves collect their own evidence. It suggests, in other words, that practitioners take control of their own research and development. Sylva (1999) looked at different research paradigms in the early years, and highlighted how within-setting research could usefully contribute to policy and practice. Goodfellow and Hedges (2007) suggested that engaging in enquiry of their own practice is critical to early years practitioners' professionalism. Solvason (2012) stated that it is imperative early years practitioners feel empowered to become capable researchers who can then add their own voices to what happens in early years. As the number of early years practitioners and specialists has grown, so too has the professionalism of the sector and the opportunities for active involvement in research, through working practices within settings, early years

forums, conferences and continued professional development (see Stenhouse, Reading 3.2).

The model, **Figure 3.2**, summarizes the relationship between practice in the learning environment and enquiry. It suggests that a practical *problem* in the setting can helpfully be considered in terms of the *issues* which might underlie it. Some careful thinking might help! As we saw earlier in the chapter, this foregrounds an appreciation of *dilemmas* within our practice – the challenge of deciding what to do when there are a number of competing possibilities.

The essence of professionalism in early years practice is being able to make high-quality *judgements*, and **Figure 3.2** shows how evidence from action research and other research sources can enhance such judgements. This ability to make such judgements is found in many examples of research which look at high-quality early years practice and

important attributes of continuous professional development (Children in Europe, 2008; NAEYC, 1993; OECD, 2001, 2006; Nutbrown, 2012; see Pring, Reading 3.3). There is a general consensus that higher staff qualifications are correlated with higher quality in early years settings and that reflection is a very important part of this professionalism (Peeters and Vandenbroeck, 2011).

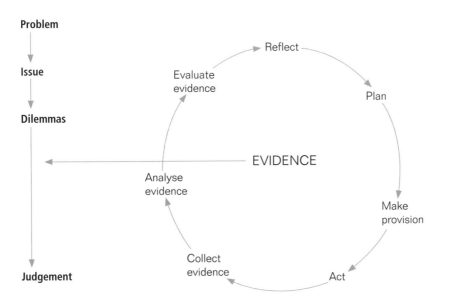

Figure 3.2
Evidence-informed
practice

Take, for example, a child's behaviour which challenges typical practice in the setting and how that might result in an immediate, angry response from a practitioner to assert control. However, later reflection might promote consideration of a number of possible longer-term issues. Are practitioner–child relationships beginning to go awry for some reason? Do the children respect the practitioner's authority and accept his or her actions as fair? Are the environment and activities engaging the children, or causing them to become bored? Are the adult-led activities well planned, offering focus, interest, progression and successful learning experiences? Each of these topics, and others, could merit further investigation through research in the setting.

For many in early years, team working is a fundamental part of practice. While we must understand our own actions and reflect on our own behaviours, research shows that where staff teams work together with shared expectations and outlooks, outcomes improve (e.g. Banergee, 2012). Peeters and Vandenbroeck (2011) extended this work recently and considered the importance of involving whole staff teams and working in collaboration with others during professional enquiry by the practitioners themselves. They summarized their ideas on what early years practitioners required in order to engage successfully in reflection as follows:

*The ability to look for (always provisional) solutions in contexts of dissensus.* By dissensus they meant disagreements, alternative views or dilemmas as above and, as we have already seen, this is often the starting point to reflection. They reported that early years teams who could discuss different ideas and opinions intensely and then come to an agreement which was put into practice showed effective reflective practice.

*The ability to focus on the meeting of the Other, the one we don't know.* By this they meant that the ability to try to understand and put oneself into another person's 'shoes', someone outside of one's own frame of reference, such as a parent, for example. They saw this as a basic competence of working reflectively in early years.

*The ability to co-construct knowledge with others (colleagues, parents, children).* By this they meant the ability to work in collaboration with others (e.g. advisors, outside supporters, researchers, colleagues, parents and children) and together construct new practical knowledge and new ways of working.

*The ability to act with a focus on change.* The ability to engage in experimentation within the setting to try new things, ideas and be creative within their work.

These ideas highlight the importance of both knowing oneself and reflecting upon one's own practice and the practice of the staff team. Dahlberg and Moss (2005) suggested that one practical aspect which they saw as essential to allow reflective practice and professionalism to flourish was 'communicative spaces' or 'islands of democracy', in which staff, policymakers and researchers could work together to develop their knowledge.

The third type of evidence is setting performance or benchmark evidence, generated from assessment, inspection or intake data. It is often made available to early years settings and schools to support improvement strategies. Such data may also be provided to parents to inform choice. It is also now very significant to setting and school managers if trends appear, and for inspection teams and others who make judgements about setting *and* practitioner effectiveness.

Reflective professionals should thus be able to draw on, or contribute to, many sources of evidence, and use them to *inform* their practice. However, we should note and *emphasize* that a simple or direct translation of findings into action is not wise. This is because there are so many variables involved in learning and teaching, and direct 'cause and effect' findings rarely stand up to scrutiny. Simplistic answers to the question 'What works?' are thus unlikely to be secure, and professional judgement will remain a highly significant filter in interpreting the significance of research evidence for particular children or learning contexts.

Of course, the sources of evidence we have reviewed – interpreting educational research, professional enquiry by practitioners themselves and using performance or benchmark data – actually complement each other. Reflective professionals should thus be able to draw on, or contribute to, many sources of evidence, and use them to inform their practice. However, evidence in ECEC must always be critically evaluated, as in other fields of social science, because absolute 'truth' is not available. There are many different perspectives and potential situations which may be found within early years settings. The reflective practitioner must therefore be able to use both personal judgement, based upon experience, and any available sources of evidence to support decision-making.

# 1.3 Standards for effectiveness within early years provision and for career development

In recent years, competency criteria and 'standards' have been set by governments in many countries to provide a framework for those undertaking and seeking training and further professional development. Standards are used to describe the particular sets of attributes, skills, knowledge and understandings that practitioners are expected to demonstrate in order to receive a recognized qualification within a chosen profession (for example EYPS, Early Years Teachers and QTS). Standards set for Scotland, Northern Ireland, Wales and England are set out on their respective agency websites.

The evolution of such standards can take a considerable time and is often predicated on the political perspectives of particular regional or national governments. In most cases, such standards provide a statutory framework for initial training, continuing professional development and performance management.

Broad standards and competences can be helpful in defining goals for students, practitioners, mentors, head teachers, supervisors, managers, tutors and others who are engaged in ECEC and professional development. They can:

- set out clear expectations;
- help practitioners to plan and monitor development, training and performance;
- maintain a focus on improving educational quality;
- provide a basis for the professional recognition of practitioner expertise.

However, we need to be clear about the status of such models and criteria. Those required by a centralized national curriculum and legally defined assessment procedures may well differ from those which are called for where practitioners are more engaged with a greater degree of partnership; for example, there is a substantial difference in the character of the standards in the different countries of the UK, in different states in North America and in various countries of the European Union, in addition to the difference

**Regulations respecting the education of pupil teachers.**
**Minutes of the Committee of Council on Education, 1846.**

*Qualifications of candidates:*

To be at least 13 years of age.

To not be subject to any bodily infirmity likely to impair their usefulness.

To have a certificate of moral character.

To read with fluency, ease and expression.

To write in a neat hand with correct spelling and punctuation, a simple prose narrative read to them.

To write from dictation sums in the first four rules of arithmetic, simple and compound: to work them correctly, and to know the table of weights and measures.

To point out the parts of speech in a simple sentence.

To have an elementary knowledge of geography.

To repeat the Catechism and to show that they understand its meaning and are acquainted with the outline of Scripture history. (Where working in schools connected with the Church of England only.)

To teach a junior class to the satisfaction of the Inspector.

Girls should also be able to sew neatly and to knit.

**Figure 3.3**
Regulations for the education of pupil teachers, 1846

between such as Montessori, Reggio Emilia and Te Whāriki, as discussed in Chapter 9 (see Readings 9.2, 9.3 and 9.6). Those called for where class sizes are high and resources scarce (as in many parts of the world) may vary from those needed when much smaller classes or groups are taught with good access to suitable equipment. Further, it is worth considering that the standards required at any particular period in history are unlikely to remain constant. To illustrate this point, it is interesting to consider the requirements made of apprenticed 'pupil teachers' in England almost 160 years ago (see **Figure 3.3** on p. 61).

We have to remember, then, that officially endorsed standards are historically and contextually specific. Despite the moderating influence of available research, they are likely to be strongly influenced by the cultures, values and the priorities of decision-makers who happen to be in power at the time of their construction. Within the UK, the clear expectations or characteristics of the standards which focus on knowledge and understanding, skills and attributes are often considered to be too confining and limited (see for example Osgood, 2004). They fail to take account of other equally important qualities of the early years practitioner. Cable and Miller (2011) talk about the importance of affective factors, personal histories, views, beliefs and values. They see the views of competence embodied in such documents as narrow and performance-related, part of the political culture of monitoring and accountability, which fails to recognize the complexity and potential creativity of early years practitioners. Emotionality is singularly missing, although it is clear from practitioner accounts and from research that it is a fundamental underpinning competence that requires complex understandings and management by all those working with young children and their parents (Cable and Miller, 2011). While others point to a lack of room for innovation, Greenfield (2001) outlined the importance of new ways of thinking and interacting during her work in multidisciplinary contexts. Peeters and Vandenboerg (2011) extoled the virtues of encompassing the unknown and yet-to-be-known, the willingness to engage in ongoing learning, questioning, discussion and a readiness to respond and act.

During a 40-year career, an early years practitioner is likely to experience many such systems, and historical or comparative reflection will help keep them in perspective. Baldock et al. (2009) advised that for any policy document it is important to determine any values that have informed it, as they may be rooted in a particular time frame which has subsequently changed. In addition, there may be tensions between government policy and the autonomy of local authorities and/or our own personal values.

---

### Reflective activity 3.3

*Aim:* To support critical engagement with policy documents.

*Evidence and reflection:* Consider any of the current policy documents you are working to – they may be standards or frameworks of practice – and ask yourself:

- What is the aim behind this document?
- What values and underlying assumptions does it portray?
- What effects will it have for our individual professional roles and then for the children and families with whom we work?

This, of course, is an important element of reflective and evidence-informed practice.

---

Despite the recognition of the changing and subjective nature of such standards, many early years practitioners, researchers and policymakers still value this approach because of its practical nature. It remains the main way in which we can work to ensure the safety and well-being of the children and families with whom we work (Kingston and Melvin, 2012; see Reading 3.4). This debate regarding standards associated with professionalism and high-quality practice in early years is discussed in more detail in Chapter 11.

**Expert question**

**Principle:** Is our pedagogy consistent with established principles for effective teaching and learning?

This question contributes to a conceptual framework representing enduring issues and practitioner expertise (see Chapter 16).

So, while individual characteristics of the standards may be criticized for their over-prescription and limited nature, the ways in which training and support for professional development is provided remains flexible and up to the early years sector to decide.

## 2 The meaning of reflective practice

The concept of reflective practice stems from Dewey (1933, Reading 3.6) who contrasted 'routine action' with 'reflective action'. According to Dewey, routine action is guided by factors such as tradition, habit and authority and by institutional definitions and expectations. By implication it is relatively static and is thus unresponsive to changing priorities and circumstances. Reflective action, on the other hand, involves a willingness to engage in constant self-appraisal and development. Among other things, it implies flexibility, rigorous analysis and social awareness.

Reflective action, in Dewey's view, involves the active, persistent and careful consideration of any belief or supposed form of knowledge in the light of the grounds that support it. Practitioners who are unreflective about their work tend to accept the *status quo* in their settings and simply 'concentrate on finding the most efficient means to solve problems that have largely been defined for them' by others (Zeichner and Liston, 1996: 9). Of course, routine action based on on-going assumptions is necessary, but Dewey argued that it is insufficient on its own. In Dewey's view, reflection 'enables us to direct our actions with foresight' (1933: 17).

Donald Schön (1983, 1987; see Reading 3.5) extended these ideas, analysing the actions of many different professional occupations: medicine, law, engineering, management, etc. Schön emphasized that most professionals face unique situations that require the use of knowledge and experience to inform action which he called 'professional artistry'. It is the 'kind of professional competence which practitioners display in unique, uncertain and conflicted situations of practice' (1987: 22) – a form of 'knowing-in-action'. Schön thus came to distinguish between 'reflection-on-action', which looks back to evaluate, and 'reflection-in-action', which enables immediate action. Both contribute to the capabilities of a reflective practitioner.

Others, such as Solomon (1987), have made a powerful case for reflection as a social practice, in which the articulation of ideas *to others* is central to the development of an open, critical perspective. The support of colleagues and mentors is thus extremely helpful in building understanding – ideas which have been extended further with concepts such as 'culture of collaboration', 'community of enquiry' and 'network' learning.

Such ideas about what it is to be a reflective professional, when developed and applied to practice, are both challenging and exciting. In this section, we review their implications by identifying and discussing seven key characteristics of reflective practice. These are:

1  Reflective practice implies an active concern with aims and consequences, of our actions.

2  Reflective practice is applied in a cyclical or spiralling process, in which practitioners monitor, evaluate and revise their own practice continuously.

3  Reflective practice requires competence in methods of evidence-informed enquiry, to support the progressive development of higher standards of practice.

4  Reflective practice requires attitudes of open-mindedness, responsibility and wholeheartedness.

5  Reflective practice is based on practitioner judgement, informed by evidence and insights from other research.

6  Reflective practice, professional learning and personal fulfilment are enhanced through collaboration and dialogue with colleagues.

7  Reflective practice enables practitioners to creatively develop the imposed frameworks for learning and teaching.

Each of these characteristics will now be considered more fully.

## 2.1 Aims and consequences

Reflective practice implies an active concern with aims and consequences as well as means and technical competence. This issue relates first to the immediate aims and consequences of practice within the learning environment, for these are any practitioner's prime responsibility. However, such practice cannot be isolated from the influence of the wider society and a reflective practitioner must therefore consider both spheres.

An example from the history of educational policymaking in England will illustrate the way in which changes outside educational settings influence actions within them. In particular we will consider the contested status and value placed on ECEC, its relationship to practice and how policy development has impacted here.

At the end of the last century, early years services in the UK suffered from low levels of public funding compared with their European neighbours. There were numerous different and diverse providers of ECEC, many of whom had different aims and purposes, with a heavy reliance on the private, voluntary and independent (PVI) sector. Despite the diversity, in practice there was little choice for parents within each local area, and little collaboration or coordination between the private, voluntary and the maintained sector. Concern was expressed in a number of prestigious reports, including the Rumbold Report 'Starting with Quality' (DES, 1990), and later by notable researchers such as Sylva et al. (1999), which were largely ignored by government. There was, at this time, a lack of political awareness about the importance of the early years in the UK. The general view was that young children were the private responsibility of their parents and that the care of young children was the natural 'work' of their mothers.

Over the following 20 years, as the government was presented with international and national research showing the potential for change that high-quality early experiences could have on both the economic growth of the country and on children's learning and development, there was an explosion in policy development and funding (Sylva et al., 2004; Melhuish et al., 2004). However, the growth was mainly in the PVI sector and concentrated on increasing the quantity of early years places to meet the demands of parents returning to work over improving their quality. The short-term goal of growth in provision took precedence. This emphasis was severely criticized by many in the sector, who felt that expansion came at the expense of quality, which was essential if the provision was to improve children's education, care and ultimately their life chances. Government appeared to ignore the research regarding children's learning and development which supported the view of young children as active co-constructors of their own learning who needed well-qualified, experienced and knowledgeable early years practitioners in order to thrive.

Although there were some attempts at funding initiatives designed to promote quality, for example through the 'Transformation Fund' in 2006 which supported early years practitioners in gaining qualifications, this didn't significantly change the composition of the workforce, and the majority of early years practitioners in England remain under-qualified (Nutbrown, 2012). The workforce is underpaid and has very few male workers (Miller and Cable, 2008). Early childhood teaching is often considered to be of a lower status than teaching older children (King, 1998) and there remains a deep divide between the PVI sector and the maintained sector (Moss, 2006). In addition, Moss (2008) noted the effect on practice, as he surveyed the views of early years practitioners. First, he discovered the continuing view of young children as immature and incomplete and who consequently had fairly simple developmental needs. Second, he discovered that this deficit construction of children meant that training was devalued and, by many, considered unnecessary for the care of young children, which in turn legitimized low status, qualifications and pay.

Moss (2006) looked at the PVI and maintained sector divide in Northern Ireland. He found that there were differences in material conditions, qualifications, employment terms and conditions, despite both sectors working towards one legislative framework. However, even within the better-resourced maintained sector, views about how young children learn can be equally misconceived and early years practice devalued. In settings where education is valued over care, for example, children may be subjected to overly formalized learning environments in an ill-conceived effort to better prepare them for the work to come as they move through the school (Katz, 2011).

In conclusion, some aspects of research evidence (such as the EPPE project [Sylva et al., 2004]) have played a major part in policy development and change over the past 20 or so years. However, important aspects of the research have been sadly neglected in policy.

The universal quality of provision and the professionalization of the sector, together with the recognition of the importance of early experiences, remains in need of development (Melhuish, 2004). Research suggests that we have not moved far away from a nineteenth-century patriarchal view of care and the oppression of women (Robert-Holmes and Brownhill, 2011). Of additional concern, the messages from the current government do not appear to be moving away from this position or supporting the view of the child as an active agent in their own learning who co-constructs meaning with the support of well-qualified and knowledgeable early years practitioners. Early years practitioners may wish to reflect on these big issues and how they impact on within setting practice.

The varied and changeable political and policy climate in the early years illustrates the need for active involvement of early years practitioners, parents and researchers in policymaking decisions. In order to impact on decisions outside the setting there are three important roles that we can play.

First, we should consider the central importance of early years practitioners developing 'a sense of collective identity' (Adams, 2008: 208). This is particularly important in such a diverse sector, which spans a number of different stages of development. It is worth reflecting on the PVI and maintained sector divide here, as any divide can potentially make the early years 'voice' appear fractured and unconvincing. In order to develop a sense of collective identity we should identify other early years practitioners, both within and outside of our settings, and work together to present a unified voice. Westcott (2004) links this sense of professional identity to standards and quality; unfortunately, this remains problematic in the UK, where different sectors (for example PVI and maintained) typically have different standards to follow. In addition, practitioners from these sectors often follow different training routes, despite research suggesting there are many common indicators of quality between them and they have similar government frameworks and legislation to follow. Another way that we might develop a collective identity would be to consider Oberhuemer's (2005) creation of a shared profession, or democratic profes-sionalism, which rests on the creation of a similar and broad knowledge base, participatory relationships between all staff and parents, quality interactions with children and effective leadership. Developing this broad base of knowledge and participatory relationships could extend to colleagues within as well as across settings.

Second, while accepting a responsibility for translating politically determined aims into practice, practitioners should speak out, as they have done in the past, if they view particular aims and policies as being professionally impracticable, educationally unsound or morally questionable. In such circumstances the professional experience, knowledge and judgements of practitioners should be brought to bear on policymakers directly – whether or not the policymakers wish for or act on the advice which is offered (for interesting developments of this argument, see Thompson, 1997). Indeed, it is important that, within a modern democratic society, practitioners should be entitled to not only a hearing, but also some influence, on educational policy. Professional and subject associations, such as the British Association for Early Childhood Education (Early Education), the Association for Professional Development of Early Years Educators (TACTYC), the Association for the Study of Primary Education (ASPE) and the Geographical Association (GA), together with the General Teaching Councils of each part of the UK, provide collective forms of organization for such voices. However, in recent years, teacher unions such as the NUT, ATL, NAHT and the newer EYP unions such as Aspect have undoubtedly been the most effective in making their voices heard.

The third way would be for practitioners to adopt the role of an 'activist' (White, 1978; Sachs, 2003). This recognizes that early years practitioners are individual members of society who, within normal political processes, have rights to pursue their values and beliefs as guided by their own individual moral and ethical concerns. They should be as active as they wish to be in contributing to the formation of public policy.

The reflective practitioner should thus be aware of the political process and of their legitimate oversight of public educational services. They should also be willing to contribute to it both as a citizen and as a professional.

## 2.2 A cyclical process

Reflective practice is applied in a cyclical or spiralling process, in which practitioners monitor, evaluate and revise their own practice continuously. Reflective practitioners are expected to plan, make provision and act. They also need to monitor, observe and collect data on their own, and the children's, intentions, actions and feelings. This evidence then needs to be critically analysed and evaluated so that it can be shared, judgements made and decisions taken. Finally, this may lead the practitioner to revise their policies, plans and provision before beginning the process again. It is a dynamic process which is intended to lead through successive cycles, or through a spiralling process, towards higher-quality standards of practice. This model is simple, comprehensive and certainly an extremely powerful influence on practice. It is consistent with the notion of reflective practice, as described by both Dewey and Schön, and provides an essential clarification of the procedures for reflective practice. Consider, for example, *Development Matters in the Early Years Foundation Stage*, which was developed to support practice in early years settings in England (Early Education, 2012).

**Figure 3.4** represents the key stages of the reflective process.

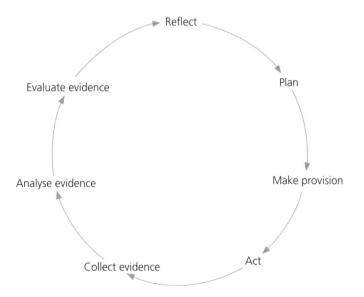

Figure 3.4
The process of
reflective teaching

**Reflective activity 3.4**

*Aim:* To explore how improvement can come from collecting evidence of our practice.

*Evidence and reflection:* The key to this process is to create a focus and to consider what evidence is required in order to make judgements about how to proceed. For example, we may be considering the progress of a particular child in a particular area of learning, or analysing the effectiveness of a method for encouraging group work. Whatever your focus, the stages we will consider are:

1   Which facet of setting life should be investigated and why?
2   What evidence to collect, and how?
3   How can we analyse, interpret and apply the findings?

This may seem rather formal, but these are all things to think about in any situation where practice is being evaluated.

   To start with, pick a small issue or dilemma (see section 1.1 and **Reflective activity 3.1**) and see if you can construct a plan for evidence-gathering, on which you can base subsequent action.

*Extension:* Generally, practitioners focus their setting-based research and development activity on an individual child or group of children. Is there a part of the learning environment that you would like to change? How will the evidence base change for such work?

## 2.3  Gathering and evaluating evidence

Reflective practice requires competence in methods of evidence-informed enquiry, to support the progressive development of higher standards of practice. We can identify four key skills here: reviewing relevant, existing research; gathering new evidence; analysis; and evaluation. Each of these contribute to the cyclical process of reflection (see section 2.2).

*Reviewing relevant, existing research.* The issue here is to learn as much as possible from others. Published research on the issue of concern, from practitioners or from professional researchers and often digested in professional publications, may be reviewed. Internet-based search techniques make this an increasingly straightforward task, as do other resources, such as the *Key readings* which conclude each chapter of this book and materials available at **reflectiveteaching.co.uk**).

WWW.C

*Gathering new evidence.* This relates to the essential issue of knowing what is going on in a room or setting as a means of forming one's own opinion. It is concerned with collecting data, describing situations, processes, causes and effects with care and accuracy. Two sorts of data are particularly relevant. Objective data are important, such as descriptions of what people actually do. Standardized performance data comes into this category of course, but is only part of the picture. Additionally, it is also vital to collect more subjective data which describe how people feel and think – their perceptions. The collection of both types of data calls for considerable skill on the part of any investigator, particularly when they may be enquiring into their own practice.

*Analytical skills.* These skills are needed to address the issue of how to interpret descriptive data. Such 'facts' are not meaningful until they are placed in a framework that enables a reflective practitioner to relate them one with the other and to begin to theorize about them.

*Evaluative skills.* Evaluative skills are involved in making judgements about the educational and care consequences of the results of the practical enquiry. Evaluation, in the light of aims, values and the experience of others, enables the results of an enquiry to be applied to future policy and practice.

---

## Practitioner research

Sylva (1999) discussed the classroom research of Paley in 1992. Paley, a nursery class teacher, introduced a new rule: 'you can't say "you can't play"'. The rule was introduced and discussion was augmented through storytelling and questioning. Paley documented the important discussions of how the children thought and felt together with the changes in attitude and practice that took place over the year of the research. She collected and presented a variety of data including the stories she told, her own thoughts and involvement as well as field notes taken of the class itself.

Sylva recognized her excellent practice and, although she noted some difficulties in terms of generalization, stated that such research could support others looking for inspiration and illuminate and promote good practice. It serves as a vibrant account of the class as a community of learners (Wenger, 2002) which works together and strives towards morality and equality.

---

Increasingly, the early years community is engaged, at a room or setting level, in enquiries into learning and practice, in order to inform subsequent practice and the developmental priorities of a setting. Many of such enquiries exhibit characteristics of case study and action research (Carr and Kemmis, 1986; Hamilton and Corbett-Whittier, 2013). The 'case' is often a room, a year or full setting in which spiral of *action research* develops. (Further details on action research, a cyclical process of research, evaluation and adaptation of practice, can be found at **reflectiveteaching.co.uk**.) A range of data collection methods may be used, focusing on children's perspectives, direct observations, interpretations of development data, among other things. Such work can both develop and legitimize setting, room or classroom policies – and thus provide sound answers to challenges where a practitioner or setting is required to justify their practice.

WWW. C

While researching and evaluating one's practice provides a sound basis for reflective practice to develop, such competence alone is not sufficient. Certain attitudes are also necessary and need to be integrated and applied with enquiry skills. As considered in Chapter 1, we must be able to challenge our own perspectives and feelings.

# 2.4 Attitudes towards practice

Reflective practice requires attitudes of open-mindedness, responsibility and wholeheart-edness. In this section we draw directly on the thinking of Dewey (see Reading 3.6).

*Open-mindedness.* As Dewey put it, open-mindedness is:

> An active desire to listen to more sides than one, to give heed to facts from whatever source they come, to give full attention to alternative possibilities, to recognize the possibility of error even in the beliefs which are dearest to us. (1933: 29)

Open-mindedness is an essential attribute for rigorous reflection, because any sort of enquiry that is consciously based on partial evidence only weakens itself. We thus use the concept in the sense of being willing to reflect upon ourselves and to challenge our own assumptions, prejudices and ideologies, as well as those of others – no easy task. However, to be open-minded regarding evidence and its interpretation is not the same thing as declining to take up a value-position on important social and educational issues. This point brings us to the second attribute which Dewey saw as a prerequisite to reflective action: 'responsibility'.

*Responsibility.* Intellectual responsibility, according to Dewey, means:

> To consider the consequences of a projected step; it means to be willing to adopt these consequences when they follow reasonably … Intellectual responsibility secures integrity. (1933: 30)

The position implied here is clearly related to the question of aims that we discussed in 2.1 above. However, in Dewey's writing the issue is relatively clearly bounded and he seems to be referring to within setting practices only. Tabachnick and Zeichner (1991) take this considerably further. Moral, ethical and political issues will be raised and must, they argue, be considered so that professional and personal judgements can be made about what is worthwhile. It clearly follows that a simple instrumental approach to practice is not consistent with a reflective social awareness.

*Wholeheartedness.* 'Wholeheartedness', the third of Dewey's necessary attitudes, refers essentially to the way in which such consideration takes place. Dewey's suggestion was that reflective practitioners should be dedicated, single-minded, energetic and enthusiastic. As he put it:

> There is no greater enemy of effective thinking than divided interest … A genuine enthusiasm is an attitude that operates as an intellectual force. When a person is absorbed, the subject carries him on. (1933: 30)

Together, these three attitudes are vital ingredients of the professional commitment that needs to be demonstrated by all those who aim to be reflective practitioners. Echoes with the issues discussed in Chapter 1 will be readily apparent.

In modern circumstances, these attitudes of open-mindedness, wholeheartedness and responsibility are often challenged, as a result of continual change from the political centre in many countries. Halpin (2001) argues that maintaining 'intelligent hope' and imagining future possibilities are essential for committed educationalists. Beyond simple optimism, this requires 'a way of thinking about the present and the future that is permeated by critique, particularly of the kind that holds up to external scrutiny taken-for-granted current circumstances' (2001: 117). Maintaining a constructive engagement, a willingness to imagine new futures, and a self-critical spirit are thus all connected to reflective practice.

## 2.5 Practitioner judgement

Reflective practice is based on practitioner judgement, informed by evidence-informed enquiry and insights from other research. Yet, as discussed in Chapter 1, the early years practitioner is often seen as less able and engaged in less challenging work than those working with older children in schools. Indeed, practitioner knowledge has often been criticized for being resistant to change. For instance, Bolster (1983) carried out an analysis of teachers as classroom decision-makers and suggested that, since teacher knowledge is specific and pragmatic, it is resistant to development. Bolster argued that teacher knowledge is based on individual experiences and is simply believed to be of value if it 'works' in practical situations. Similarly, Vincent, Braun and Ball (2008) reported an inability for pre-school practitioners to see the value of developing their practice; they dismissed the need for any academic study as they saw their roles as natural carers who were born with the ability to care. These findings suggest practitioners will stick to routinized or naturally acquired practices. Thus, there is a need to develop an understanding of the potential benefits of developing as a reflective practitioner and indeed the shortcomings of failing to reflect on one's decisions.

For an alternative view we can again draw on Donald Schön's work (1983; Reading 3.5) on the characteristics of 'reflective practitioners'. Schön contrasted 'scientific' professional work, such as laboratory research, with 'caring' professional work, such as education. He called the former 'high hard ground' and saw it as supported by quantitative and 'objective' evidence. On the other hand, the 'swampy lowlands' of the caring professions involve more interpersonal areas and qualitative issues. These complex 'lowlands', according to Schön, tend to become 'confusing messes' of intuitive action. He thus suggested that, although such 'messes' tend to be highly relevant in practical terms, they are not easily amenable to rigorous analysis because they draw, as we have seen, on a type of knowledge-in-action. It is spontaneous, intuitive, tacit and intangible, but it 'works' in practice. Recognizing how we navigate our practice through 'knowledge-in-action' helps us to see how crucial it is to ensure our thoughts are informed by research.

Schön's ideas have received powerful empirical support in recent years, with the sophistication of practitioners' thinking and 'craft knowledge' being increasingly recognized and understood by both researchers (Calderhead, 1987, 1988; Leeson, 2007; Lindon, 2010) and some organizations with an influence on policymakers (OECD, 2005; Barber and Mourshead, 2007). It is clear that effective practitioners make use of judgements all the time, as they adapt their practice to the ever-changing learning challenges which their circumstances and children present to them. There has also been much greater recognition of the role of intuition in the work of experienced practitioners (Atkinson and Claxton, 2000; Tomlinson, 1999) and decision-making. Of course, reflective practitioners need to recognize potential bias in their judgements as a result of their diverse experiences, and this again emphasizes the need for open-mindedness.

Educational researchers' knowledge has often been criticized, although much of it derives from work undertaken by former early years practitioners who have moved into academia. It may be based on comparative, historical or philosophical research, on empirical study with large samples of settings, practitioners, parents and children, on innovative methodologies, or on developing theoretical analyses. Many researchers certainly regard it as their duty to probe, analyse and evaluate – particularly with regard to the impact of policy – even though this is not always popular with governments! Whatever its character, such educational research has the potential to complement, contextualize and enhance the detailed and practical understandings of practising early years staff.

In recent years, considerable effort has been made to improve the relevance, significance and impact of educational research, and to engage with practitioners and policymakers. Indeed, the best work is of very high quality and is an important source of ideas and evidence on pedagogy, learning, policy and practice. A selection of such work, and links to useful sites, can be found at **reflectiveteaching.co.uk.** For ease of use, this material is organized using the chapter headings of the text of this book.

Politicians' knowledge of education has also often been criticized. However, governments have a democratic mandate and are appropriately concerned to ensure that educational services meet national needs. Practitioners would thus be unjustified if they ignored the views of politicians, though independence, experience, judgement and expertise remain the defining characteristics of professionalism. Indeed, where politicians' views appear to be influenced by fashionable whims, media panics or party considerations rather than established educational needs, then a certain amount of 'professional mediation' may be entirely justified (see section 2.7).

Taken as a whole, we strongly advocate attempts to maximize the potential for collaboration between practitioners, researchers and politicians. For such collaboration to be successful it must be based on a frank appreciation of each other's strengths and weaknesses. While recognizing the danger of unjustified generalization, we therefore identify these strengths and weaknesses (see **Figure 3.5**).

We arrive, then, at a position that calls for attempts to draw on the strengths of the knowledge of practitioners, researchers and politicians or policymakers. By doing this, we may overcome the weaknesses which exist in each position. This is what we mean by the statement that reflective practice should be based on 'informed early years practitioner judgement'. The implied collaborative endeavour underpins this whole book.

| | Strengths | Weaknesses |
|---|---|---|
| Teachers' knowledge | Often practically relevant and directly useful<br><br>Often communicated effectively to practitioners<br><br>Often concerned with the wholeness of classroom processes and experiences | May be impressionistic and can lack rigour<br><br>Usually based in particular situations which limits generalization<br><br>Analysis is sometimes over-influenced by existing assumptions |
| Researchers' knowledge | May be based on careful research with large samples and reliable methods<br><br>Often provides a clear and incisive analysis when studied<br><br>May offer novel views of situations and issues | May use jargon unnecessarily<br><br>May seem obscure and difficult to relate to practical issues<br><br>Often fragments educational processes and experiences |
| Politicians' knowledge | Often responsive to issues of public concern.<br><br>May have a democratic mandate<br><br>May be backed by institutional, financial and legal resources | Often over-influenced by short-term political considerations<br><br>Often reflects party political positions rather than educational needs<br><br>Is often imposed and may thus lack legitimacy |

Figure 3.5
A comparison of practitioners', researchers' and politicians' knowledge

## 2.6 Learning with colleagues

Reflective practice, professional learning and personal fulfilment are enhanced through collaboration and dialogue with colleagues. The value of engaging in reflective activity is almost always enhanced if it can be carried out in association with other colleagues, be they trainees, teaching or nursery assistants, early years practitioners, supervisors, managers, mentors or tutors. The circumstances in settings with very high proportions of contact time with children have constrained a great deal of such educational discussion between practitioners in the past – though this is gradually changing as whole-setting professional development assumes a greater priority. On teacher-education and early childhood courses, despite the pressure of other requirements, reflection together in seminars, tutor groups and workshops, at college or in the setting, should bring valuable opportunities to share and compare, support and advise in reciprocal ways. Indeed, early years settings and schools are particular examples of the development of 'communities of practice' which Wenger (2002) analysed. This concept of workplace communities of practice has also been powerfully developed beyond settings and schools through the use of practitioner networks.

Whether professional conversations occur between experienced practitioners or between novice and experienced practitioners consideration of professional ethics and structuring will ensure that the participants derive the maximum benefit from activity. For example:

- agreement about roles and relationships within such arrangements must be clear.
- the central focus of discussions should be on the benefits for children's learning that derive from the joint reflection.
- in cases where the focus is on developing the practice of one person involved in the discussion, clear parameters for any observations and subsequent conversations need to be agreed.
- decisions on future targets should be agreed together before the discussion concludes.

Central here, of course, is the idea that trust between practitioners and others must be really secure – for without this, the sharing of ideas, concerns and challenges can seem threatening. Interestingly, Kettle and Sellars (1996), in looking at the developing reflective practice of trainee teachers, found that the use of peer groups encouraged them to challenge their existing theories and preconceived views of teaching while modelling a collaborative style of professional development.

This sort of work can be very exciting and support development in a number of ways, as the following case study shows.

## Case study 3.1 Using a journal to develop reflective practice

As part of a decision to develop group reflective practice in the setting, a team of early years practitioners embarked on reflective dialogue via a journal. This involved the team agreeing to use a paper journal, stored in the staff room, to continue conversations about issues arising in the setting. The excerpt below illustrates how the staff used the journal to continue conversations following meetings and in-service training – matters which it was felt were often left unexplored as time did not allow for deeper conversations.

Following a meeting with a representative from the Traveller Information Service the following discussion developed.

**Gemma** 'After our meeting with Sara from the Traveller Education Service I began thinking about my reasons for wanting to visit the site and the homes of my contact family. I needed to make sure that it was for the right reasons and not wanting to just satisfy my curiosity. Why am I thinking of doing this – but haven't offered it to my other contact children…It would be good to visit the site and build our understanding of their way of life and to gather some positive images (photos) to share with the traveller children (and all of the other children) at nursery…'

**Craig** '…the inclusive practice we are working at is equalities and anti-bias work and to do that effectively we need to be honest (with ourselves and others) and informed – and so isn't curiosity an OK drive in itself?…'

**Sally** 'I agree with the equity point. I also thought along the same lines of pastoral reasons for a visit. I wondered what the families would feel about being visit too…'

**Beth** 'My immediate reaction was one of personal interest (curiosity) – is that right? I have worked in places where home visits have been part of the initial settling-in period…if we are going to incorporate it as part of our settling policy – fine, but otherwise I would feel uncomfortable – curious but uncomfortable?!'

**Craig** 'Home visits were often impractical in the past …is it time to look again at this?… visiting a traveller site would be hugely beneficial in terms of building partnerships and gaining knowledge … that is free from our assumptions/ preconceptions.'

**EVE** 'I think it would be a good idea to visit the traveller site in terms of building partnership and also to show our support and interest …'

As these thoughts were collected over a couple of weeks, the topic was discussed in a staff meeting. Given the thought that had already gone into the process and the fact that the staff had had time to consider the views of others, they felt that they were able to come to a unanimous decision which they all understood and were comfortable with.

Wherever and whenever it occurs, collaborative, reflective discussion capitalizes on the social nature of learning (Vygotsky, 1978; see Reading 2.3). This is as significant for adults as it is for children and it works through many of the same basic processes. Aims are thus clarified, experiences are shared, language and concepts for analysing practice are refined, the personal insecurities of innovation are reduced, evaluation becomes reciprocal and commitments are affirmed. Moreover, openness, activity and discussion gradually weave the values and self of individuals into the culture and mission of the setting or course. This can be both personally fulfilling and educationally effective.

At a time when the development of coherence and progression in setting policies and practice have become of enormous importance, collaborative work is also a necessity. It is imperative that management work actively and positively with staff to find institutional solutions to dilemmas and challenges. Beyond settings, the development of Networked Learning Communities and other forms of web-supported activity are very exciting, though are not always sustained. Professional and phase-based associations, together with the existing UK General Teaching Councils, often provide important opportunities for collaborative work.

Whatever their circumstances, reflective practitioners are likely to benefit from working, experimenting, talking and reflecting with others (see **Reflective activity 3.3**). Apart from the benefits for learning and professional development, it is usually both more interesting and more fun!

## 2.7 Reflective teaching as creative mediation

Reflective practice enables practitioners to creatively mediate external requirements. 'Creative mediation' involves the interpretation of external requirements in the light of a practitioner's knowledge of their children, values and principles. A study of change in education (Osborn et al., 2000) identified four different kinds of 'creative mediation' deployed by teachers to interpret such situations. We believe they are appropriate for all early years practitioners.

- *Protective mediation* calls for strategies to defend existing practices which are greatly valued (such as the desire to maintain an element of spontaneity in practice in the face of assessment pressure).
- *Innovative mediation* is concerned with practitioners finding strategies to work *within* the spaces and boundaries provided by new requirements – finding opportunities to be creative.
- *Collaborative mediation* refers to practitioners working closely together to provide mutual support in satisfying and adapting new requirements.
- *Conspirational mediation* involves settings adopting more subversive strategies where practitioners resist implementing those aspects of external requirements that they believe to be particularly inappropriate.

Such forms of mediation exemplify major strategies in the exercise of professional judgement. Clearly they need to be carefully justified – but the irony is that creative mediation is often the source of essential forms of innovation for future development. Indeed, innovative settings are often sought out by charities, think tanks, associations and even government agencies in the constant quest for improvement in the quality of early years settings.

All education and care systems need to be able to guarantee consistency in entitlements to provide opportunities for all – but they also require some capacity for innovation and change. In applying principles and evidence through their practice, and making this public when appropriate, reflective practitioners have a significant role in providing such leadership.

## Conclusion

In this chapter we have considered the spiral of professional development and the potential to raise standards of practice through evidence-informed judgement. We have outlined the seven key characteristics of reflective practice.

Some readers may well be wondering if this isn't all just a bit much to ask. How is the time to be found? Isn't it all 'common sense' anyway? These are essentially questions that we asked at the outset, to which two broad responses may be made. First, it is certainly the case that constantly engaging in reflective activities of the sort described in this book would be impossible. The point, however, is to use them as *learning experiences*. Such experiences should lead to conclusions which can be applied in new and more routine circumstances. This is how professional expertise is actively developed. Second, there is certainly a good deal of 'common sense' in the process of reflective practice. However, when reflective practice is used as a means of professional development it is extended far beyond this underpinning. The whole activity is much more rigorous – carefully gathered evidence replaces subjective impressions, open-mindedness replaces prior expectations, insights from reading or constructive and structured critique from colleagues challenge what might previously have been taken for granted. 'Common sense' may well endorse the value of the basic, reflective idea but, ironically, one outcome of reflection is often to produce critique and movement beyond the limitations of common-sense thinking. That, in a sense, is the whole point, the reason why reflection is a necessary part of professional activity. The aim of reflective practice is thus to support a shift from routine actions rooted in common-sense thinking to reflective action stemming from professional understanding and expertise.

In summary, our view is that evidence-informed reflection makes an important contribution throughout professional life. New practitioners, including those undertaking in-setting training or training at an institution such as a university, may use it to improve on specific and immediate elements of practice, while more experienced practitioners may use reflection as a means of self-consciously increasing understanding and capability, thus moving towards a more complete level of professionalism (Lindon, 2010). Expert practitioners will work at a higher level, understanding the various issues concerning children's care and education generally. They use their reflections to support individual understandings, lead others and develop new and creative responses to the complex work of the early years practitioner. Reflective activity makes an important contribution throughout a professional career.

# Key readings

The importance of reflective practice in educational and care decision-making and the notion that reflection is a continually necessary element of practice are discussed in:

Leeson, C (2007) 'In Praise of Reflective Practice'. In J. Willan, R. Parker-Rees and J. Savage (eds) *Early Childhood Studies*. 2nd edn. Exeter: Learning Matters.

The importance of reflection throughout the profession:

Lindon, J. (2012) *Reflective Practice and Early Years Professionalism: Linking Theory and Practice*. London: Hodder Education.

On the potential gains from self-evaluation and enquiry, see:

Miller, L., Cable, C and Devereux, J. (2005) *Developing Early Years Practice*. Oxon: David Fulton.

A classic work by Dewey which has strongly influenced the development of reflective practice is:

Dewey, J. (1933) *How We Think: A Restatement of the Relation of Reflective Thinking to the Educative Process*. Chicago: Henry Regnery.

For analyses on the nature of professional knowledge and its potential to enhance learning, see:

> Schön, D. A. (1983) *The Reflective Practitioner: How Professionals Think in Action.* London: Temple Smith.

For an overview of different forms of research in early years, including the contribution of setting-based action research, see:

> Slyva, K. (1999) 'The Role of Research in Explaining the Past and Shaping the Future'. In L. Abbott and H. Moylett (eds) *Early Education Transformed.* New Millennium Series. London: Falmer Press.

More specific guidance on conducting research is at **reflectiveteaching.co.uk** and includes:

> Menter, I., Elliot, D., Hall, J., Hulme, M., Lewin, J. and Lowden, K. (2010) *A Guide to Practitioner Research in Education.* Maidenhead: Open University Press.
> Mitchell, N. and Pearson, J. (2012) *Inquiring in the Classroom. Asking the Questions that Matter About Teaching and Learning.* London: Continuum.

The significance of learning and developing practice with colleagues is elaborated in:

> Wenger, E. (1999) *Communities of Practice. Learning, Meaning and Identity.* Cambridge: Cambridge University Press.

The associated website, **reflectiveteaching.co.uk**, offers a wealth of supplementary resources including reflective activities, research briefings, advice on further reading and downloadable diagrams, figures and checklists from the book. It also features a compendium of educational terms, links to useful websites, policy and curriculum documents, and showcases examples of excellent research and practice.

# Principles

## What are the foundations of effective teaching and learning?

**4**

## Introduction

This chapter is focused on ten 'evidence-informed educational principles' developed by the UK's Teaching and Learning Research Programme (TLRP) (2000–12). The TLRP was the UK's largest ever coordinated programme of educational research (Pollard, 2007). Spread over a decade, the programme involved over 100 projects and other initiatives including the aforementioned Effective Pre-School and Primary Education (EPPE 3–11, 2003–8) (Sylva et al., 2004). By reviewing the outcomes of these research projects, consulting with UK practitioners in Early Years Education, Primary and Secondary education, and comparing these findings with other research from around the world (James and Pollard, 2012), ten evidence-informed principles were developed. These principles provide a summary of *what we think we know* about effective teaching and learning. The principles will be discussed individually, before drawing them together, to provide a holistic and interrelated picture of the complexities and intricacies involved in working as early years practitioners.

## 1 Evidence-informed principles

Each of the ten principles which are described in this chapter, the principles which we have acknowledged at the beginning of each chapter of this book, has an extensive research base – they are 'evidence-informed'. Emphasis is placed upon the understanding that if we are to educate a child effectively, we have to consider more than the content of any curriculum. They do not, however, seek to tell practitioners what to do. Each principle provides a general overview of a key concept which can be considered by practitioners in the light of his or her knowledge of the needs of the children with whom they work, and the circumstances of the setting in which they work. When challenges arise, the principles will not determine an appropriate course of action, for that is the job of the reflective early years practitioner. They are intended as a guide and support for making the professional judgements which practitioners themselves are uniquely positioned, and required, to make. Having an understanding of these principles will, however, support evidence-informed decisions to be reached. It is important to note that the principles, while separated for this discussion, are not necessarily separated in practice, as they are strands that overlap and threads that are closely woven together.

In the following section, we introduce and illustrate the ten principles. Together they provide valuable information about teaching and learning which, if we are to support babies and young children to learn and develop the skills to learn, we must be aware of. As Euade (2011) states, these principles provide a valuable basis for considering pedagogy in the early years, and what is distinct about this phase of education. Throughout this chapter, and indeed this book, we have demonstrated the links between these principles and key theories of ECEC and theories of child development, including Bruce's ten principles of early childhood education (Bruce, 2011).

# Effective teaching and learning

**10** Effective teaching and learning demands consistent policy frameworks with support for teaching and learning as their primary focus. Policies at national, local and institutional levels need to recognize the fundamental importance of teaching and learning. They should be designed to create effective learning environments in which all learners can thrive. (Chapters 5, 8, 9 and 17)

**1** Effective teaching and learning equips learners for life in its broadest sense. Learning should aim to help people to develop the intellectual, personal and social resources that will enable them to participate as active citizens, contribute to economic development and flourish as individuals in a diverse and changing society. This implies adopting a broad view of learning outcomes and ensuring that equity and social justice are taken seriously. (Chapters 1, 9 and 17)

**9** Effective teaching and learning depends on teacher learning. The need for teachers to learn continuously in order to develop their knowledge and skills, and adapt and develop their roles, especially through classroom inquiry, should be recognized and supported. (Chapters 1, 3 and 16)

**2** Effective teaching and learning engages with valued forms of knowledge. Teaching and learning should engage with the big ideas, facts, processes, language and narratives of subjects so that learners understand what constitutes quality and standards in particular disciplines. (Chapters 9 and 10)

**8** Effective teaching and learning recognizes the significance of informal learning. Informal learning, such as learning out of school, should be recognized as at least as significant as formal learning and should therefore be valued and used appropriately in formal processes. (Chapters 2, 5, 8, 12 and 15)

**3** Effective teaching and learning recognizes the importance of prior experience and learning. Teaching and learning should take account of what the learner knows already in order for them, and those who support their learning, to plan their next steps. This includes building on prior learning but also taking account of the personal and cultural experiences of different groups of learners. (Chapters 2 and 10)

**7** Effective teaching and learning fosters both individual and social processes and outcomes. Learning is a social activity. Learners should be encouraged and helped to work with others, to share ideas and to build knowledge together. Consulting learners about their learning and giving them a voice is both an expectation and a right. (Chapters 3, 6, 7, 12, 15 and 17)

**4** Effective teaching and learning requires teachers to scaffold learning. Teachers should provide activities which support learners as they move forward, not just intellectually, but also socially and emotionally, so that once these supports are removed, the learning is secure. (Chapters 6, 11 and 12)

**6** Effective teaching and learning promotes the active engagement of the learner. A chief goal of teaching and learning should be the promotion of learners' independence and autonomy. This involves acquiring a repertoire of learning strategies and practices, developing positive attitudes towards learning, and confidence in oneself as a good learner. (Chapters 2, 7, 11, 12, 13 and 14)

**5** Effective teaching and learning needs assessment to be congruent with learning. Assessment should help to advance learning as well as determine whether learning has taken place. It should be designed and carried out so that it measures learning outcomes in a dependable way and also provides feedback for future learning. (Chapters 13 and 14)

**Figure 4.1**
Ten evidence-informed educational principles for effective teaching and learning

**Expert question**

**Reflection**: Is our practice based on incremental, evidence-informed and collaborative improvement strategies?

This question contributes to a conceptual framework representing enduring issues and practitioner expertise (see Chapter 16).

In the following sections we will consider each of these ten principles in relation to ECEC provision and practice, first individually, before drawing them together to provide a holistic and interrelated picture of the factors that are necessary for effective teaching and learning. This will then be considered in light of what we can and have learned from those working and researching in ECEC around the world.

## 2 TLRP's principles

## 2.1 Education for life

The commitment to provide broad, rich and inclusive forms of education gave rise to the first of TLRP's ten principles.

> **Principle 1: Effective teaching and learning equips learners for life in its broadest sense.** Learning should aim to help people to develop the intellectual, personal and social resources that will enable them to participate as active citizens, contribute to economic development and flourish as individuals in a diverse and changing society. This implies adopting a broad view of learning outcomes and ensuring that equity and social justice are taken seriously.

Education makes an enormous difference to the people we become. Early years practitioners have the privilege and responsibility to support young learners in what is often their first experience of learning and often *being* outside of the family environment. Research has shown us that early learning experiences shape future outcomes for children. That is why this principle on 'education for life' is so important. Teaching has moral purpose. The learning referred to here includes both the academic skills and the social, emotional and personal skills children will need to participate in the life in and beyond educational

systems (see Swann, Peacock, Hart and Drummond, Reading 4.1).

Having a high-quality pre-school experience has been shown to have significant benefits for children's cognitive and social gains (e.g. Clifford and Bryant, 2003; Magnuson et al., 2004; Sammons et al., 2004). Among the most commonly cited studies are Highscope (Schweinhart et al., 1985), the Carolina Abecedarian Project (Campbell et al., 2002) and the Effective Pre-school and Primary Education project (EPPE) (Sylva et al., 2004a).

Conducted in the USA, with a focus on children living in poverty, the Highscope Perry Pre-school Study and the Carolina Abecedarian Project both

**Expert question**

**Outcomes for certification and the lifecourse:** Does the educational experience equip children for an unknown future?

This question contributes to a conceptual framework representing enduring issues and practitioner expertise (see Chapter 16).

found that high-quality pre-school provision had substantial benefits for children. The Highscope Perry Study found that focused high-quality pre-school education led to increased educational attainment, income and economic status over the life-course (Schweinhart et al., 2005). The research concluded that every dollar spent on the pre-school intervention gained a return on investment of $7.16 (Barnett, 1993). The Carolina Abecedarian Project concluded that attendance at their specifically designed high-quality settings resulted in children outperforming a comparison group on IQ tests at ages 8 and 15 years (Campbell and Ramey, 1995) and being more likely to attend post-compulsory education (Campbell et al., 2002).

In the UK, the ongoing EPPE project (see Reading 4.2) has dominated research in this field. EPPE was the first major European longitudinal study of the effects of pre-school education on children's Primary, Secondary and Post-compulsory education experiences. The initial phase of EPPE followed a sample of approximately 3,000 children (decreasing slightly over the lifetime of the project), across a variety of ECEC providers. Using a range of methods including assessments of cognitive, social and behavioural skills and observation, the research team developed a picture of pre-school education in a range of settings and recorded the impact of these experiences. Significant findings of the phase one pre-school study include:

- Pre-school experience compared to none, enhances all-round development in children.

- Disadvantaged children benefit significantly from good-quality pre-school experiences, especially where they are with a mixture of children from different social backgrounds.

- There are significant differences between individual pre-school settings and their impact on children; some settings are more effective than others in promoting positive child outcomes.

- High-quality pre-schooling is related to better intellectual and social/behavioural development for children.

- Settings that have staff with higher qualifications have higher quality scores and their children make more progress.

  (Sylva et al., 2004b)

Subsequent research phases revealed that children's pre-school experiences continued to remain significant throughout a child's education. For example, throughout primary education:

- The positive benefits of both medium- and high-quality pre-school education persisted to the end of Key Stage 2 for attainment in reading/English and Mathematics and all social/behavioural outcomes.

- High-quality pre-schooling [compared with low-quality or no pre-school experience] was especially beneficial for the most disadvantaged pupils and for those of low qualified parents in promoting better Mathematics outcomes at age 11.

- Children who attended poor-quality/less effective pre-schools generally showed no significant age 11 benefits in improved outcomes compared with those who did not attend any pre-school.

(Sylva et al., 2008)

Each of these studies recognizes high-quality provision as key to children's futures, benefiting both their social and cognitive development. Thus, understanding and defining what constitutes high-quality provision is crucial for early years practitioners, researchers and policymakers alike. Throughout this book we provide an overview of many of the attributes of high-quality provision and provide reflective activities to support ongoing interrogation of these attributes. Yet we note that the concept of quality is value-laden and culturally sensitive (Sheridan, 2001 see Moss, Reading 1.5). As a consequence, what one person considers high-quality provision may differ from the view of another. Those working inside pre-schools may have a different opinion of quality than those external to the setting, e.g. inspectors and parents (Katz, 1993). Given the reported benefits of a high-quality pre-school experience, a number of tools have been created to understand and measure quality within ECEC provision. Such tools often identify both *structural attributes* and *processes* (Howes and Hamilton, 1993; Howes and Smith, 1995; Sylva et al., 2004) as being key dimensions for measures of quality. The structural attributes are the regulatory features of a setting – that is, curriculum guidance, child-practitioner ratios and staff qualifications, and the latter to the process style, or the pedagogical approach, adopted by the practitioner and/or setting. The processes implemented by pre-schools vary more across providers in England given that the former are prescribed and often carry a legal obligation.

A number of tools have been developed to measure quality within ECEC, which include the Caregiver Interaction Scale (CIS) (Arnett, 1989) and the Early Childhood Environment Rating Scale (ECERS) (Harms and Clifford, 1980). ECERS has been revised and developed to produce ECERS-R (Harms, Clifford and Cryer, 1998); the Infant Toddler Environmental Rating Scale (ITERS-R) (Harms, Cryer and Clifford, 2006) and, ECERS-E (Sylva et al., 2010).

As we consider the notion of equipping children for life in their first years of education, it is important to recognize what this does and does not mean for our practice. Bruce notes that 'the best way to prepare children for their adult life is to give them what they need as children' (Bruce, 2011: 40). Many believe that, above all else, for young children this involves freedom to play. Developmental psychologist Peter Grey (2013) states that play with other children is crucial for healthy psychological development; it helps children to learn how to control their emotions, to make decisions and build relationships (see The Royal Society, Reading 4.3, Parker Rees, Reading 4.4. for more on play). Yet, research has shown that despite such recognition of the value of play, it does not always lead to play being embedded in early years practice. Adams et al. (2004) found some early years practitioners felt pressures to perform in tests and related performance tables and targets led to children having less time to play, particularly as they enter statutory schooling. Those practitioners reported feeling a need to justify time to play, rather than for play to be an end in itself. Such findings remind us of the challenges facing early years practitioners. Having a strong knowledge of research can help support us to both justify and be comfortable with the decisions which need to be made on a day-to-day basis.

Providing children with what they need as children also involves careful consideration of subject matter. Children's early learning will provide a basis upon which more complex knowledge can be built in the future. Bruner (1977; see Bruner, Reading 2.4) stated that a key facet of learning was that it ought to allow us to move forwards in our thinking more easily. Learning is seen as a staged and phased process. For the early years practitioner, then, it is necessary to see what the child needs today as both something which interests them and supports their development in the here and now, but also is related to where their learning may take them in the future. This links to Principle 2.

## 2.2  Valued knowledge

**Principle 2: Effective teaching and learning engages with valued forms of knowledge.** Teaching and learning should engage with the big ideas, facts, processes, language and narratives of subjects so that learners understand what constitutes quality and standards in particular disciplines.

Creating a supportive and challenging learning environment for young children (see Chapter 8) requires an examination of what is worth teaching. Over recent years, the examination of what is worth teaching has led to the development and redesign of curricula across early years and schools systems. Within early years education in particular, this has led to the benefits of having a set curriculum being contested. The Steiner-Waldorf Foundation, through the Open EYE campaign, openly criticized the development of a curriculum for the early years in England, stating:

> The very idea that it is appropriate to have a 'curriculum' for young children is absurd and represents a totally inappropriate encroachment of a schooling ideology into the lives of young children. (House, cited by Hofkins, 2008: 1)

A term which has been associated with the development of curricula is 'school readiness'. Reports such as the Tickell report (2011) and the Allen review (2011) have used this term to mean that a function of early years education is to ensure children have developed the skills they will need as they enter statutory schooling, e.g. writing skills, ability to sit still and to listen. There is a possibility that such a philosophy could lead to a child's learning and development being stifled and narrowed by a focus on specific skills (see Field Review, 2010, and Reading 5.3, for more on this). Bruce (2011: 46) draws upon the work of Piaget to emphasize the importance of recognizing that young children do not learn in a 'neat and tidy way', that subject matter cannot be taught separately as 'children learn

**Expert question**

**Connection:** Does the curriculum engage with the cultural resources and funds-of-knowledge of families and the community?

This question contributes to a conceptual framework representing enduring issues and practitioner expertise (see Chapter 16).

in an integrated way'. Thus, while the content of the curriculum is important the ways in which it is implemented and the perceived or intended target of curricula is also of great significance.

Another aspect of engaging with valued forms of knowledge relates to children needing practitioners who see the development of their own knowledge as a part of their responsibility as an educator. Early years practitioners must be enabled to participate in professional dialogue and development opportunities which extend their learning and understanding. They themselves must keep abreast of the big ideas and developments across key areas of learning, such as science. Such understandings support practitioners to engage children in learning which supports their growing understanding of big ideas and concepts for later learning in this field. Where teaching is taking into account new understandings, children are more likely to benefit from a relevant foundation of knowledge which enables them to be secure curious learners.

## 2.3 Prior experience

**Principle 3: Effective teaching and learning recognizes the importance of prior experience and learning.** Teaching and learning should take account of what the learner knows already in order for them, and those who support their learning, to plan their next steps. This includes building on prior learning but also taking account of the personal and cultural experiences of different groups of learners.

Few people now think that children are 'empty vessels' to be filled. Whatever the age of the children you are working with, they will have gained prior knowledge from their experiences at home, with parents, siblings, other carers and possibly within other early years settings. The principle of effective teaching, starting from where a child's thinking currently is and then helping them to move forwards, is widely recognized. The scientific  foundation of this principle lies in the practical philosophy of Dewey and the constructivist psychology of Piaget and Vygotsky (see Chapter 2 and **Readings 2.2 and 2.3**). A famous quote by Ausubel put this clearly:

The most important single factor affecting learning is what the learner already knows. Ascertain this, and teach him accordingly. (1968: vi)

### Expert question

**Dialogue:** Does practitioner–child talk scaffold understanding, build on existing knowledge and strengthen dispositions towards learning to allow children to become active learners?

This question contributes to a conceptual framework representing enduring issues and practitioner expertise (see Chapter 16).

One of the key ways in which children's current learning, understanding and interest can be gauged is through observation. (The use of observation is discussed in detail in Chapter 14.) We must understand the child's current position in order to plan effectively for future learning. Having a curriculum helps us to consider what effective planning should encompass. Observation can also allow us to identify any schemas the child is currently displaying, which can help us to plan to support a child's learning in both a spontaneous and a planned way. Piaget (also see Chapter 2) identified a schema as a pattern of repeated behaviour that children demonstrate when they are exploring the world. For example, a child may display the *rotation schema* by watching the wheels of a toy car as they spin, watching the washing machine and/or rolling around, or perhaps a baby may demonstrate the *trajectory schema* by repeatedly dropping a toy or food from a high chair or cot. Identifying schemas can help us to understand (see Nutbrown, **Reading 4.5**) children's interests and their current levels of understanding. They can help us to plan activities which they will find interesting, which they can link to their current levels of understanding and to their previous experiences.

A second rationale for focusing on prior learning is concerned with motivation and providing appropriate opportunities to learn. Here, it is essential to take account of the knowledge, understandings, skills and attitudes derived from the other worlds that the children inhabit: from their homes, communities and peer groups. In Chapter 2 we noted how we can supplement our understanding of a child's knowledge, and what is valued in their lives, through discussions with children, parents and carers, for example. However difficult it may be to understand each child and their current level of understanding, reflective-committed early years practitioners will seek to understand each child as a learner so that appropriate starting points are identified and practitioners can work to support the child's confidence to grow.

## Case study 4.1 Understanding children's knowledge, learning and experience from outside the setting

Amy (42 months) attends a sessional nursery school three times a week. At home, her mother has always encouraged Amy to take part in physical activities and her gross motor skills are well developed for her age. When at nursery, Amy prefers the outside play environment, and will often find objects to climb. She can confidently jump and land in a stable, controlled position. Other children often join in, with varying degrees of success. Her nursery teacher commented that Amy could be 'dangerous' in the outside environment, and had asked her to stop climbing and jumping. Amy became upset and demotivated, with a noticeable drop in her self-confidence.

Amy's competence with gross motor skills positively impacted upon her personal and social development as the other children joined her games. Yet, once her nursery teacher had decided that she was playing dangerously, Amy's general involvement level in all activities was affected and reduced. The nursery teacher was imposing her views on how Amy should play, based upon a fixed assumption that a child of Amy's age could not safely climb and jump – that the risk of this play was too great.

This reinforces the notion that the knowledge, learning and experience that children bring from outside the setting may go unrecognized at times and how we can possess fixed ideas about what children are capable of. This can mean that learning opportunities that facilitate progression are being missed and possibly for some children, regression in learning or a desire for learning and developing new skills may occur.

A central aspect then of inclusive and reflective practice is knowing and under-standing the children that you work with. This involves active listening – engaging with the views of the individual, noting the invisible questions that are implied through children's actions, combined with effective use of questioning and observation. Assessment of children's development in specific areas and the inter-relatedness of those areas can then be made from a standpoint of informed knowledge and understanding.

## 2.4 Scaffolding understanding

**Principle 4: Effective teaching and learning requires teachers to scaffold learning.** Teachers should provide activities which support learners as they move forward, not just intellectually, but also socially and emotionally, so that once these supports are removed, the learning is secure.

In Chapter 2 we considered Vygotsky's position on children's learning – that for the full learning potential of a task to be reached, a more knowledgeable partner or guide is a crucial role, which may be filled by a practitioner or peer partner (Rogoff, 1990). We noted that this partner supports learning and 'scaffolds' the child's understanding. Bruner's analogy of building a house was noted as particularly useful when developing our understanding of this concept – that is, that scaffolding is needed to support the learning process, as when building a house; as the connections strengthen and all the parts have been secured, the scaffolding can be removed. The building – the learner's understanding – will stand independently. The key ways in which early years practitioners can scaffold learning is through understanding the concept being explored and having an understanding of the different ways in which children learn. It is our belief that at the heart of effective early years practice is an informed and secure knowledge of the many and various ways in which children learn, and an understanding that their learning is not compartmentalized. Indeed, Bruce notes that 'subjects such as mathematics and art cannot be separated: young children learn in an integrated way and not in neat tidy compartments' (2011: 46). Thus, effective early years practice involves practitioners recognizing when children need support to extend their learning.

Providing appropriate learning activities in the early years involves an awareness of children's choices at play, based upon their interests and experiences, knowledge and understanding of where each child is in their social development and therefore readiness to interact in a play-based environment. To be effective, practitioner support must be carefully matched to the current understanding and/or capabilities of the learner. Thus, again, observation (see Willan, Reading 14.2 and Emilson and Pramling Samuelsson, Reading 14.4) is a key tool in the repertoire of the reflective early years practitioner. In addition to observation, engaging with the child will increase practitioner understanding of the child's current understanding and the support they need to extend their knowledge. The aforementioned processes of sustained shared thinking – that is, engaging in an extended interaction with a child around a topic to support and extend a child's thinking – will again support and scaffold a child's learning, while also providing the practitioner with information on the child's current knowledge and understanding. Such information can inform future ways to scaffold the child learning.

Principle 4 highlights how such scaffolding is intellectual, social and emotional. Because learning is an intrinsically personal, intellectual process, it can be enabled or constrained by many factors, including by social expectations and feelings of personal security. In Chapter 6 we will consider how the social and emotional climate can support learning in greater detail.

## 2.5 Assessment for learning

**Principle 5: Effective teaching and learning needs assessment to be congruent with learning.** Assessment should help to advance learning as well as determine whether learning has taken place. It should be designed and carried out so that it measures learning outcomes in a dependable way and also provides feedback for future learning.

While formal assessment of young children's abilities and learning is highly contested, undoubtedly we need to know where children's learning and understanding is positioned in order to plan for and support their future learning; the basis for this argument has been made in our discussions of the previous principles.

We consider these types of assessment and the impact the perspectives of the person conducting the assessment have in Chapters 13 and 14. These chapters are informed by principles which align

> **Expert question**
>
> **Validity:** Are the forms of assessment used to identify next steps based upon individual children's needs and interests?
>
> This question contributes to a conceptual framework representing enduring issues and practitioner expertise (see Chapter 16).

with Education Scotland's 'Key messages' about assessment (see Broadfoot, **Reading 13.2**),  which include: that assessment is an integral part of learning, teaching and planning; that assessment provides an emerging picture of the child, that assessment can help to motivate learning; and that it can also support staff to engage with a wider range of sources and resources to plan for children's learning.

## Case study 4.2 Assessment in the early years

This case illustrates how assessment in the early years must be based upon more than a short observation of a child.

Ben (30 months) is playing happily on the carpet at his pre-school, using and developing his fine motor skills and eye–hand coordination to build a stacking tower. As he builds he counts out loud. His involvement level is high, continuing to try again when the tower tumbles over, banging the pots together before he starts building again. The following day a practitioner is asked to observe Ben and another boy building towers. Ben shows no interest and spends his time banging the pots together directly in front of the practitioner and choosing not to let the other boy, who he does not know, share the pots. Based solely upon this snapshot, the practitioner notes that Ben cannot build a tower and that he 'struggles' to share resources.

The example provided demonstrates a limited observation with too little thought about the process. We must understand that all assessments are only ever partial, they can only ever provide an incomplete picture of a child (Bruce, 2011). It may be useful therefore to share observations among staff teams, to have a more fluid approach to noting children's behaviours, schemas, interests and abilities rather than relying on a fixed time observation. *Learning journeys* and *All about me books,* as discussed in Chapter 2, would provide ways in which this could be achieved. It may also be useful to integrate a range of tools over an extended period to provide a more useful and complete picture of a child's current understanding. At the heart of the matter are concerns about fitness for purpose. Do we want to measure the children or help them to grow? Effective assessment involves a pedagogy of listening and the development of a detailed knowledge of children's capabilities, learning preferences and attainment. Typically this is accomplished through observing, listening and interacting with them and others who know them well, across a range of activities and contexts, ensuring that what children can do and what children can aspire to is at the heart of our pedagogical decisions.

## Reflective activity 4.1

*Aim:* To review TLRP's principles on knowledge, prior learning, pedagogy and assessment (sections 2.2, 2.3, 2.4 and 2.5).

*Evidence and reflection:* This cluster of four principles represents enduring issues in teaching. Take some time to think about any issues you do not feel relate to your practice and why that is. Then take time to think about how these principles relate to effective early years practice and provision. What might they mean for your practice?

*Extension:* If possible, discuss your thoughts with a colleague or fellow student. Do the principles enable you to better understand your own practice? Are there skills or processes on which you and your partner could work together to develop your expertise?

# 2.6 Active engagement

**Principle 6: Effective teaching and learning promotes the active engagement of the learner.** A chief goal of teaching and learning should be the promotion of learners' independence and autonomy. This involves acquiring a repertoire of learning strategies and practices, developing positive attitudes towards learning, and confidence in oneself as a good learner.

The most pragmatic reason for emphasizing active engagement is simply that it is essential for learning. As we saw in Chapter 3, Piaget's constructivist psychology emphasized processes of accommodation and assimilation through which learning takes place, and Vygotskian theory envisages a learner whose capability and confidence are greatly influenced by others. Almost all TLRP research projects affirmed the importance of developing active engagement, positive learning dispositions, self-confidence and learning awareness (see also Chapter 2, section 3).

Within ECEC we are in the midst of negotiating how we can aim for equitable and equal life chances for all children and provide enough guidance to ensure entitlements, while also trying to protect early childhood as a time for freedom to explore and develop without targets. While also trying to provide practitioners with sufficient scope and support for them to respond to the needs of the babies and children for whom they care (see Chapter 9). Recent developments in the UK have emphasized the active engagement of the child in their learning as crucial to effective early years practice. This is exemplified through the development of the three key *characteristics of effective learning* (see Tickell, 2011 and the revised EYFS, 2012 at **reflectiveteaching.co.uk**). These characteristics draw heavily on the findings of the aforementioned EPPE project and the Effective Early Learning (EEL) project of Pascal and Bertram (1998). **Table 4.1** below provides an overview of these characteristics.

Principle 6 encompasses aspects of active learning and playing and exploring. These skills begin at birth and are lifelong characteristics which need to be fostered and

**Table 4.1** Characteristics of Effective Learning

| Characteristics of Effective Learning | |
|---|---|
| **Playing and exploring – engagement** | Finding out and exploring<br>Playing with what they know<br>Being willing to 'have a go' |
| **Active learning – motivation** | Being involved and concentrating<br>Keeping trying<br>Enjoying achieving what they set out to do |
| **Creating and thinking critically – thinking** | Having their own ideas<br>Making links<br>Choosing ways to do things |

developed during the early years as they are critical for building children's capacity for future learning' (Tickell, 2011: 28). We are seeking to support children to be confident to 'have a go', to accept challenges and to enjoy learning. In practice, this means having the patience to allow them to try new things – even if they do spill liquids as they pour themselves a drink!

The promotion of learner independence and autonomy has been seen as essential to the effectiveness of learning. Bruce claims that 'children learn best when they are given appropriate responsibility, allowed to experiment, make errors, decisions and choices, and are respected as autonomous learners' (2011: 47). In the early years of a child's life the independence and confidence needed to experiment and make errors and decisions will often need to be fostered. Where a child feels secure, they often feel more able to explore. Within ECEC this can often be through the development of a relationship with a particular adult or key person. This relationship provides a secure base and a constant in children's learning lives, thereby giving children the confidence and encouragement to try out new activities, explore and experiment with resources, and in doing so realize their abilities and challenge their capabilities. Knowing that an adult is there to support them as they begin to take 'risks' in their learning provides the emotional security that is necessary for learning to occur. This idea is built upon attachment theory. More on attachment can be found in Chapter 6, Bowlby Reading 6.4.

### Case study 4.3 Building relationships through observation

Lydia (31 months) is sitting on the floor, singing to herself, as she happily and carefully tears paper into pieces and places them into a shoebox. Her key person, Sara, is nearby observing her play, at the same time supporting a small group of older children who were using scissors to cut out their hand and foot prints that were going to form a large tree collage. Occasionally Lydia stops what she is doing and watches the children using the scissors. After a while she says to Sara 'Me try'. From previous observations, Sara had noted that Lydia was showing signs of a preferred laterality and showed her the drawer where the right-handed scissors were kept. Lydia's first attempts at cutting frustrated her, as the scissors would not open and close as she tried to manipulate them. After trying with some success with a thumb in each handle, she tried again with one hand. With gentle encouragement and demonstration from Sara, Lydia persevered, until eventually she cut the paper in two. Her sense of achievement was clearly evident from her facial expression and her desire to share her success with Sara.

The relationship that Lydia had built with Sara has enabled her to have the confidence to tackle new things, because she felt safe in doing so, and is stimulated to try, knowing that Sara will be there if she needs help. Such consistency enables young children to become active and independent learners. The knowledge that practitioners have of children as learners, based upon informed observations that have been carefully analysed, provides the means for children to sustain their effort and persevere when they encounter learning which they initially find difficult. Such perseverance facilitates the development of attention and concentration and resilience, and enables children to become autonomous, self-regulated learners and thinkers, capable of making decisions about their own learning and how to progress it.

## 2.7 Social relationships

**Principle 7: Effective teaching and learning fosters both individual and social processes and outcomes.** Learning is a social activity. Learners should be encouraged and helped to work with others, to share ideas and to build knowledge together. Consulting learners about their learning and giving them a voice is both an expectation and a right.

> **Expert question**
>
> **Engagement:** Do our teaching strategies and the organization of the environment allow for planned and unplanned learning experiences both indoors and outdoors?
>
> This question contributes to a conceptual framework representing enduring issues and practitioner expertise (see Chapter 16).

Learning is a social as well as an individual activity. It flourishes through interaction with other minds, when the conditions are right. Good relationships between practitioners and children, children and their peers, staff in the setting, and with children's families underpin such conditions. There are two distinct social worlds that children experience within ECEC: one in which the child interacts with the practitioner, the other in which they interact with their peers (Kutnick et al., 2007). Research has shown us that with the older children in our age range, these interactions with their peers are crucial for social and emotional and cognitive development (e.g. Ladd, 2005).

We have already noted some of the ways in which building relationships between practitioners and children can support learning. By developing understandings of babies and children through speaking with families and conducting observations, for example, practitioners can develop deeper relationships with children and engage more easily in episodes of SST.

TLRP's studies on group work which investigated children learning together – for example, the Social Pedagogic Research into Groupwork (SPRinG) project (Blatchford, Galton, Kutnick and Baines, 2005) – have shown us that when learning is collaborative, both staff and children and young people thrive both collectively and as individuals. The SPRinG project found that Key Stage 1 children who were supported to develop relationships and the skills to work together effectively in groups did measurably better on individual exams in reading and mathematics than those who did not develop collaborative working skills. We will explore these findings in greater detail in Chapter 6, as this research was extended to include babies and children with equally beneficial results.

> **Expert question**
>
> **Relationships:** Are relationships nurtured as the foundation of mutual well-being?
>
> This question contributes to a conceptual framework representing enduring issues and practitioner expertise (see Chapter 16).

# 2.8 Informal learning

**Principle 8: Effective teaching and learning recognizes the significance of informal learning.** Informal learning, such as learning out of school, should be recognized as at least as significant as formal learning and should therefore be valued and used appropriately in formal processes.

The key message of this principle resonates with ECEC practices. Though we would not necessarily engage in any formal processes, particularly with babies and young children, recognizing learning which takes place outside of the setting, particularly inside the home, is an essential aspect of ECEC practice.

---

### Case study 4.4 Observing home learning experiences in the preschool

Paul (41 months) and Matilda (51 months) had recently been camping with their respective families. In the outside area they decided to make a den. They worked well together, first pushing together two low-level climbing stools and then covering them with a blanket. They discussed how they would stop their tent blowing away 'if the wind got up in the night', and used stones from the garden to place around the bottom of the blanket. They independently selected toys and books from inside to put in their tent and then decided to find cooking equipment to make their lunch. At this point they had selected the role of Mum and Dad, with Matilda commenting that 'It was Dad's turn to cook lunch today, and they better use the sausages up, because the ice box isn't cold now.' Neither children had particularly played together before, but their camping experiences had provided a joint interest and the opportunity for child-initiated learning and social interaction. The practitioner realizing the value of this interactive and cooperative experience, observed from a distance without interrupting.

---

In early years, perhaps more so than other sections of the education system, home learning and ongoing discussions with families are seen as fundamental to supporting learning in the setting. A great deal of time and effort is spent on developing relations and processes to support this, many of which are discussed through this book (see for example Chapters 6 and 13). The relationships between the setting and home is reciprocal – that is, both can potentially benefit from engaging with the other to support a child's learning. As part of this relationship there is a need to reflect upon what we value, what may be of value in a child's life and what may be of value to their families, while also recognizing that some of the children with whom we work may not have access to the same experiences as other children.

Explicit home-setting knowledge exchange activities have been shown to lead to positive developments as practitioners develop a deeper

### Expert question

**Congruence**: Is observation and dialogue with families widely used to inform understanding of the child, their needs and their next steps for learning?

This question contributes to a conceptual framework representing enduring issues and practitioner expertise (see Chapter 16).

understanding of children's lives and families are supported to understand and develop rich learning experiences for the child. For example, the EPPE project identified that the quality of the home learning environment (HLE) has the biggest impact on cognitive development, and has three times the impact on literacy than the quality of the pre-school attended (Sylva et al., 2008).

---

### Reflective activity 4.2

*Aim:* To review TLRP's principles on engagement, relationships and informal learning (sections 2.6, 2.7 and 2.8).

*Evidence and reflection:* This group of principles concern how teaching makes *connections* with the learner. Emphasizing the construction of meaning, they acknowledge personal and social influences on children and young people in settings and beyond – as realized through both formal and informal learning processes. Once again, these are enduring issues – they are forever with us.

*Extension:* An excellent development of this activity would be to explore the issues directly through discussion with selected families or other stakeholders in the community. How do families feel that they understand what is being provided in the setting and how this aligns with what happens at home? Would they welcome greater opportunities to discuss/share learning opportunities with you?

---

## 2.9 Teacher learning

**Principle 9: Effective teaching and learning depends on teacher learning.** The need for teachers to learn continuously in order to develop their knowledge and skills, and adapt and develop their roles, especially through classroom inquiry, should be recognized and supported.

This principle provides the rationale for this book as a whole: we need to be reflective, and thus commit to our own learning, because this enhances our effectiveness in supporting children.

Learning is concerned with both what we do *and* how we think. Put another way, the most effective forms of teaching depends not only on behavioural change and the acquisition of new knowledge about pedagogy, but also on the development of values and understanding. With the right leadership and support, such learning is particularly effective in the workplace and through participation in collaborative activities with colleagues.

---

### Expert question

**Repertoire:** Is our pedagogic expertise sufficiently creative, skilled and wide-ranging to support all elements of learning?

This question contributes to a conceptual framework representing enduring issues and practitioner expertise (see Chapter 16).

---

These conclusions began to emerge early in the life of TLRP. A summary of the common themes suggested have been slightly adapted for early years practice below:

1 Learning is both individual and collective and involves the acquisition of knowledge and skills *and* participation in social processes. Thus the development of supportive professional cultures within which practitioners can learn is vitally important. Dynamic and expansive learning environments need to provide opportunities for boundary crossings, which encourage practitioners to learn from others in different networks or communities of practice.

2 Practitioners are most ready to accept ideas for change if they resonate with their existing or previous beliefs and experience. However, this does not necessarily make then 'right' or appropriate. Practitioners need to develop knowledge and skills to evaluate evidence and the confidence to challenge taken-for-granted assumptions, including their own. This is difficult and it is often helpful to involve outsiders, perhaps researchers from universities or visiting professionals, in helping practitioners to see things differently. Practitioners need to be assured that it is acceptable and often fruitful to take risks. Trust is therefore of the essence.

3 Evidence from research about effective practice is not always sufficiently accessible for practitioners to use as a basis for action. Findings often need to be transformed into practical and concrete strategies that can be tried out. This may involve the production of concise and user-friendly materials, although ideas are often mediated best by talk and personal contacts with other Practitioners who have had some success in using them (adapted from James, 2005: 107–8).

## 2.10  Policy frameworks

**Principle 10: Effective teaching and learning demands consistent policy frameworks with support for teaching and learning as their primary focus.**
Policies at national, local and institutional levels need to recognize the fundamental importance of teaching and learning. They should be designed to create effective learning environments in which all learners can thrive.

There is growing international awareness of the significance of the coherence, or otherwise, of national systems. We have noted that ECEC is recognized as a crucial time for children and their learning. We have also recognized the responsibility this places on early years practitioners. As discussed in Chapter 3, there has been some investment in training and support for early years practitioners. New qualifications have been developed and there has been funding for practitioners seeking to attain higher-level qualifications. In addition, curriculum developments in the UK have increasingly recognized the needs of young children and the need to support transitions between ECEC provision and statutory schooling. Yet challenges remain; a global recession has led to cuts in funding and support for training, and the call for early years practitioners to be remunerated in line with other teaching professions has made few inroads. And while there is a wealth of knowledge about high-quality ECEC provision, we have seen increasing pressure, for example from the coalition government in the UK, to impose tests and assessments on young children – for example, the phonics test.

> ### Reflective activity 4.3
> Working with colleagues, consider some recent government policies on education which you know about. Are they coherent with other contemporary national policies? Are they coherent with your views of ECEC and child development? How do they relate to the evidence-informed principles proposed by TLRP?

## Conclusion

It is important that, in accepting these principles for teaching and learning which underpin developmentally appropriate practice, we recognize and reflect upon our own values, as we explore and question those of others. The key for all practitioners is a critical mind which challenges, questions and extends thinking.

## Key readings

The issues covered in this chapter are extended within other chapters; the key readings provided for the corresponding chapters may also be of interest.

For an extended academic review of the principles and international commentaries, see:

James, M. and Pollard, A. (2012) *Principles for Effective Pedagogy. International Responses to Evidence from the UK Teaching and Learning Research Programme.* London: Routledge.

The EPPE research has produced an extensive list of publications; we recommend:

Sylva, K., Melhuish, E., Sammons, P., Siraj-Blatchford, I. and Taggart, B. (2010) *Early Childhood: The Effective Pre-School and Primary Education Project: Early Childhood Matters.* London: Routledge.

**For a review on the experiences of children in schools, see:**

Alexander, R. J. (ed.) (2010) *Children, Their World, Their Education.* Final Report of the Cambridge Primary Review. London: Routledge.

For a consideration of the impact of support in the early years can have on society and a child's life, see:

Allen, G. (2011) *Early Intervention: The Next Steps.* An Independent Report to Her Majesty's Government. London: Cabinet Office. [Online] **dwp.gov.uk/docs/early-intervention-next-steps.pdf**

For more on the Home Learning Environment we recommend:

Siraj-Blatchford, I., Siraj-Blatchford, J., Taggart, B., Sylva, K., Melhuish, M., Sammons, P. and Hunt, S. (2007) 'How low SES families support children's learning in the home: Promoting equality in the early years' (Part 3). London: Report to the Equalities Review.

*Readings for Reflective Teaching in Early Years Education* directly complements and extends the chapters in this book. It has been designed to provide convenient access to key texts. It will be of particular help as a compact and portable library.

 The associated website, **reflectiveteaching.co.uk**, offers a wealth of supplementary resources including reflective activities, research briefings, advice on further reading and downloadable diagrams, figures and checklists from the book. It also features a compendium of educational terms, links to useful websites, policy and curriculum documents, and showcases examples of excellent research and practice.

# part two

# Creating conditions for learning

This section of the book is concerned with the creation of environments to support high-quality teaching and learning; environments in which children can thrive. We begin by considering the circumstances which impinge on families and early years settings (Chapter 5) – and we note the ways in which people contribute to and challenge such circumstances through their actions. We then move to the heart of life within ECEC with a focus on relationships and how positive learning relationships can be forged and maintained (Chapter 6). Chapter 7 considers how we can ensure children are engaged and motivated to learn and how this in turn can support behaviour management. Finally, we consider a range of learning spaces (Chapter 8) and we consider the affordances they offer for formal and informal learning.

# Contexts

## What is, and what might be?

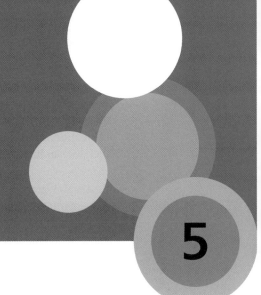

**5**

## Introduction

This chapter provides a brief review of some of the contextual factors which are important in education, and how practitioners, children and families respond. Within this chapter we briefly move away from focusing primarily on ECEC to consider the broader educational contexts in which we operate. We do not operate in a vacuum. The influence of social context pervades everything that happens in education, and awareness of such issues is therefore an important contributing element of reflective teaching. This influence is felt at many levels – from the 'big picture' of government policies in England, Northern Ireland, Scotland, Wales, or elsewhere, to the detail of community, setting and family cultures and particular individual circumstances.

A second purpose of the chapter is to establish some principles concerning the relationships of individuals and society. Indeed, the chapter is very deliberately in two parts. The first, 'social context', emphasizes the ideas, social structures and distribution of resources which *structure* action in various ways. The second part, 'people and agency', is concerned with the factors which, in various senses, *enable* action by individual practitioners and children.

A particular theoretical position underpins this chapter and, indeed, the book as a whole. At its core is the conception of a dialectical relationship between society and individuals. This suggests the existence of a constant interplay of social forces and individual actions (see, for example, Giddens, 1984). On the one hand, the decisions and actions which people make and take in their lives are constrained by social structures and by the historical processes which bring about such structures. On the other hand, each individual has a unique sense of self, derived from his or her personal experiences. Individuals have a degree of free will in acting and in developing understandings with others. Sets of these understandings, which endure over time, form the basis of cultures. Such understandings can also lead to challenges to established social structures and thus to future changes: we must understand why things are the way they are if we wish to challenge them (see Mills, Reading 5.2).

The ways in which these processes play out is significantly influenced by the circumstances of various social groups in terms of power, wealth, status and opportunities (Reid, 1998; Halsey, 1986). Individuals, each with their own background and sense of self, will react to such factors in a variety of ways. Some in powerful positions might wish to close ranks and defend themselves by suggesting that their position is inherited by right or earned by merit. Some among those who are less fortunate may accept the social order or even aspire to success in its terms. Others may try to contest it – for, of course, to be able to question existing social arrangements is a fundamental right in our democratic societies.

The particular historical era in which we happen to live also makes a substantial difference. Following the Second World War, the UK economy was still the third-largest in the world (after the USA and Soviet Union). Since then our living standards have trebled and life expectancy has steadily risen. However, relative to some other countries such as Germany, our growth has been relatively faltering and unbalanced. In the future, competition from countries such as China, India and Brazil seems likely to continue to force structural changes in our economies. In recent decades, these global forces have resulted in increasingly interventionist education policies from governments of both left and right. The form of intervention differs, but intervene they do. Educational provision, in other words, cannot escape its circumstances.

There is thus an enduring ebb and flow in social change – a process of tension and struggle. It is the product of a constant interaction between agency and circumstance, voluntarism and determinism, biography and history (Mills, 1959; see Gu, Reading 5.1). A reflective practitioner has responsibilities within this process which should not be avoided.

The interaction of structure and agency can be seen in education, as in other fields of life. Among the many ways in which this interaction is realized includes their influence both on national policy frameworks and on everyday informal learning. One example of where we see this in ECEC is in the use of the term 'school readiness', the idea that the purpose of ECEC is to prepare children for what comes next (see, Whitebread and Bingham, Reading 5.3).

---

## TLRP principles

Two principles are of particular relevance to this chapter on the broader contexts in which teaching and learning take place:

**Principle 8: Effective teaching and learning recognizes the significance of informal learning.** Informal learning, such as learning out of school, should be recognized as at least as significant as formal learning and should therefore be valued and used appropriately in formal processes.

**Principle 10: Effective teaching and learning demands consistent policy frameworks with support for teaching and learning as their primary focus.** Policies at national, local and institutional levels need to recognize the fundamental importance of teaching and learning. They should be designed to create effective learning environments in which all learners can thrive.

---

## 1 Social context

We now consider four aspects of the social context which are particularly significant for practice in education: ideology, culture, opportunity and accountability. The influence of each can be traced at national, regional, local and at all levels of education; although such issues sometimes seem distant, they shape ECEC provision and activity in very real ways.

## 1.1 Ideology

A dictionary definition of ideology states that it means a 'way of thinking'. However, particular sets of ideas are often used, consciously or unconsciously, to promote and legitimize the interests of specific groups of people. Indeed, if a particular way of thinking about a society is dominant at any point in time, it is likely to be an important influence on education. It may determine the types of pre-schools and schools which are created, produce a particular curriculum emphasis, and even begin to frame the ways in which practitioners think about their work and relate to children and young people. For instance, views of childhood vary across time and across cultures. When comparing childhood experiences in modern-day America with those of the American Colonial period (1600–1775), Ehrenreich and English (1979) comment that while a 4-year-old today who can tie her shoelaces is considered to have advanced and developed fine motor skills, in colonial times a 4-year-old child produced intricate embroidery.

Indeed, views of childhood and the role of ECEC in childhood have changed and continue to do so. The excerpt below demonstrates how changes in ECEC can be driven by changes in policy and how the state has become more involved in ECEC.

> Service development for young children in Ireland was, until the 1990s, largely driven by the voluntary sector, in particular membership groups such as the Irish Preschool Playgroup Association and the Comhchoiste Réamhscolíaochta [Irish medium playgroups]. In addition there had always been a philanthropic interest in developing family supports for disadvantaged children through charitable organizations such as the Civics Institute, the Daughters of Charity and Barnardos. However, while these organizations did receive some state support for their work the developments across the country were ad hoc and unregulated.
>
> The Child Care Act 1991 was a crucial piece of legislation, updating legislation from 1905 to bring Irish law into line with much of the practice in the social and health domain. The Act was significant in that it gave a legal definition of the child as under eighteen and focused on the protection and welfare of children and the responsibility of the state in this regard.
>
> Specifically in relation to ECEC this was the Act, which outlined the context for the regulation of preschool services. This created a national context within which early childhood care and education settings were regulated and standards established. Prior to the implementation of Section VII of the 1991 Act, early years services were unregulated. (Hayes, 2006: 3)

 A study by the LLAKES research centre in London (Green and Janmaat, 2011; see Reading 5.4) analysed the values and assumptions underpinning education policies in the Western world. They identify three main positions:

- **Liberal** – with core beliefs in individual opportunities and rewards based on merit (English-speaking countries, particularly UK and USA).
- **Social Market** – with a core belief in solidarity, depending more on the state and less on civil society (NW continental Europe, including Belgium, France, Germany, Netherlands).
- **Social Democratic** – with egalitarian and solidaristic values and higher levels of social and political trust (Nordic countries, such as Denmark, Finland, Norway, Sweden).

The specific ideologies which influence education in the UK come and go. For example, there have been very different beliefs over the years about what kinds of schools should be provided and who should go to them. After the Second World War, it was thought that the most appropriate way of organizing secondary education was to have different types of school: grammar schools, technical schools and secondary moderns. Pupils would be selected for each of these schools on merit, based on how they performed in 'eleven plus' tests. However, it was not long before this 'tripartite' system came to be criticized for favouring well-off families rather than widening educational opportunities. This led to proposals for the introduction of a system of common secondary schools, which would be 'comprehensive' in that there was to be no selection of students. By the 1960s this view had become the new orthodoxy and, with support from all major political parties, comprehensive schools supported by local education authorities became the norm in most of England, Scotland and Wales. The commitment to the meritocratic ideal of 'opportunities for all' was distinctive, but comprehensives were criticized in the 1990s for being too complacent or, as an English Minister once put it, 'bog standard'. The coalition government in England (2010–15) urged that schools should become responsive to their clientele by breaking free from local authorities and establishing themselves as independent 'academies'. Competition between such schools is expected to improve the performance of the system overall.

While such discussions may seem irrelevant to some ECEC practitioners, it is our contention that this is far from true. Indeed, understanding these systems helps to frame the expectations placed in ECEC staff and children – for example, it helps us to identify where the concept of 'school readiness' originated. Pressure on schools and schools teachers pushes down the system, and ECEC is at the 'bottom' of that system. Understanding such pressures is the beginning of recognizing and, where appropriate, pushing back against pressures we feel are unjust or inappropriate. The chief inspector of the Office for Standards in Education (Ofsted) Sir Michel Wilshaw, speaking on national radio, BBC Radio 4, in 2014 stated:

> The corollary of not preparing children well for school is that they don't do well in reception and, if they don't do well in reception, they don't get on at Key Stage 1, they find it difficult to read at seven, they fail at the end of primary school and that failure continues into secondary school.

Such comments are likely to permeate society.

In recent years politicians have taken to claiming that their policies are 'evidence-based' – though the academic community is sometimes rather sceptical of this assertion. We often see that parts of the evidence are taken forward while other aspects are left behind or modified. However, the commitment in principle to the use of evidence to inform policy and practice is a very important development. Significant work has been done on this though organizations such as the Economic and Social Research Council, the British Academy and, in education, the UK Strategic Forum for Research

> **Expert question**
>
> **Warrant:** Are our teaching strategies evidence-informed, convincing and justifiable?
>
> This question contributes to a conceptual framework underpinning professional expertise (see Chapter 16).

in Education (SFRE), Campaign for Evidence-Based Education (CEBE) and British Educational Research Association (BERA).

Even at national levels, ideologies interact with culture and identity as well as with material interests. For example, in England, as we will see in the discussion of accountability later in this chapter, the big story of the last 30 years has been the growth of centralized control over the education system. No ideology is all-powerful, and countervailing ideas emerge over time, based on their own power bases and social movements.

The Scottish Government ensures that education policy responds to Scottish, rather than English, priorities. Similarly, the National Assembly for Wales and the Northern Ireland Assembly, with more limited powers, act to interpret primary legislation and to develop their own new policy initiatives. However, such measures are influenced by *different* sets of beliefs and power relations. In Wales, for instance, the *Curriculum Cymreig* and the compulsory teaching and learning of the Welsh language are particularly distinctive. This has seen a considerable change in ECEC practice with regards to language and the development of more bilingual ECEC settings.

The relationships between the four major parts of the UK have always been complex and, of course, they will continue to evolve. While such complexity has increased since devolution, the basic educational issues to be tackled remain much the same. Education is inevitably concerned with the future, with opportunities and life chances, with productivity, wealth, community, identity and fulfilment. It is not surprising that it is contested. If possible, reflective practitioners should try to develop their understanding at this enduring level.

In summary, the ideas, perspectives or beliefs which prevail at a particular point of time are likely to be reflected in public debate and education policy. While the basic issues being contested are likely to remain much the same, the settlements reached will change and change again over a teaching career. At some point in time, critique and experience lead to evaluation, counter-proposal, development and change (Bowe, Ball and Gold, 1992). Societies and dominant ideologies are never static, but awareness of the concept of ideology makes it more likely that reflective practitioners will be able to evaluate the values or interests that may lie behind new ideas, policies, practices or other proposals. From this position, the process of looking at new policy initiatives changes. We can approach a new policy with the attitude of 'Should we question this?' or 'How do we work with this to ensure it is suitable for the children in our care?'.

It is important to remember that no one, including ourselves, is immune to the influences of ideologies. For instance, professional ideologies are always likely to remain strong among practitioners: they represent commitments, ideals *and* interests. Reflective practitioners should be open-minded enough to constructively critique their own beliefs, as well as those of others. For many of us, this takes time and practice and can at times be uncomfortable. It is, however, hugely valuable and worthwhile.

# 1.2 Culture

Cultures can be seen as sets of shared perspectives. They often develop from collective activity and from the creative responses of groups to situations. Furthermore, cultures endure over time and thus represent sets of perspectives, values and practices into which individuals are likely to be socialized. The playground cultures of young children provide an example here. In one sense, children in friendship groups develop unique and particular ways of perceiving education. Indeed, they use these as a means of understanding education systems and coping with it (Clarricoates, 1987; Davies, 1982; Pollard, 1987b). Yet at the same time, continuities in children's culture, from generation to generation, provide a context which young children absorb (Opie and Opie, 1959; Sluckin, 1981). Children's cultures are strongly influenced by films, television, games, books, computer tablets and other technologies – but they are played out through collective agency.

The community within the setting provides another cultural context. This will influence and be influenced by the perspectives of parents, children and practitioners. However, few communities can be characterized as single, united entities. Among the many divisions which may exist are those relating to ethnicity, language, religion, social class, gender, sexuality and to political or personal values. The existence of such cultural diversity is particularly important in many inner-city areas defined 'areas of deprivation'. Practitioners, particularly those working in 'areas of deprivation', are likely to explore the relationship between cultures in children's' homes, communities and education very carefully indeed (Vincent, 2000). While this brings with it potential benefits, the reflective practitioner must be aware of how they are viewing particular groups or individuals. A great deal of research has shown problems arising when working-class cultures are regarded as being deficient by those working in education (for example, Lareau, 1989; Sharp and Green, 1975; Ball, 1981). Similarly, institutionalized forms of racism are likely to result if practitioners fail to take appropriate account of the perspectives of ethnic groups (Troyna and Hatcher, 1992; Wright, 1992; Mac and Ghaill, 1988; Gillborn, 1995). We will explore these issues and the potential consequences of such actions in greater detail in Chapter 15 on inclusion.

Stereotypical perceptions of practitioners may also have gender or sexuality dimensions that could impinge in a number of ways on the educational opportunities of both girls and boys (see for example Thorne, 1993; Kehily, 2002; Skelton, 2001; Mac and Ghaill, 1995). This is a particularly pertinent issue within ECEC. Male practitioners account for just 2 per cent of the ECEC workforce, despite general agreement that male practitioners offer a great many benefits to children, not least to boys, and to counteract the negative process of 'feminization' of learning and teaching in settings. Having male practitioners within settings has been shown to raise the academic motivation, engagement and attainment levels of boys, as they act as 'strong male role models' (Parkin, 2009: 6, cited in Brownhill, 2010). Despite such benefits, issues remain with pay and prejudice, meaning many men typically stay away from the field. The practitioner reflection on the following page expresses how such issues are experienced.

**www.** ⟳

## Case study 5.1 Gender and prejudice in the childcare sector

**This is taken from a report written by Sue Learner at National Day Nurseries. See reflectiveteaching.co.uk for a link to the full paper.**

I was the first man ever to have done the NNEB course at the college and for the first six weeks, the course teachers thought it was really funny to call me Jane when they were doing the register. Being the only man on this female-dominated course and the butt of the teachers' jokes was hard in the beginning. I cried every evening for the first few weeks. I had a good friend there who helped get me through it. This did happen many years ago and things have improved since I started out but men still encounter prejudice and men are still very much a minority in childcare as only two per cent of the early years workforce is male and this statistic has remained steady in the past decade, despite national and local recruitment campaigns aimed at men.

I decided to work in the early years after doing a placement at a primary school in the nursery and reception class so I applied to college to an NNEB course. When I told the careers adviser I wanted to work in childcare he said 'why do you want to do that? It is for girls!' But childcare was something I really wanted to do. I did a placement in a primary school and they were very accepting. But I was also expected to do a placement in a special baby unit. But they wouldn't accept me because I was a man. At that time male midwives were a rarity as well.

My first training placement in a nursery was very difficult. Everything I did was wrong. So if I put a jumper on the child the wrong way they would immediately say typical man, he doesn't know what he is doing. Or if I was putting a girl's hair in a ponytail they would say I did it funny. I was lucky though as the room leader was very protective of me.

On finishing the course I applied for 42 nanny jobs and didn't get one interview. Confused as to why I wasn't getting anywhere, I went to the agency and asked them what the problem was and they said the mothers didn't want a man looking after their children.

So I decided to look for work in a nursery. The first interview I had went well until the woman who would be my manager went off track and asked the question 'would I fit in as one of the girls', my response was to stand up and say if you want me to fit in as one of the girls then you need to employ a girl.

In addition to cultures based on religion, race and gender, there are also likely to be cultures among the adults within any setting. For example, primary school staff rooms provide a backstage area where tensions are released, feelings are shared and understandings about school life are developed. This is the territory of the classroom teacher, and the resulting relationships usually provide a source of solidarity and sympathy when facing the daily pressures of classrooms (Southworth et al., 1989). Within ECEC settings such as pre-schools where staff teams work together much more, often ratios must be maintained and there is little opportunity for staff to meet in a designated staff room, as break times are staggered. Adults in pre-schools often have to rely on scheduled meeting times for formal discussions. This particular set of circumstances does, however, mean that cultures are more likely to be played out in front of the children. As discussed in Chapter 6, such cultures must be carefully evaluated, given the propensity they have to influence children.

Cultures have a huge impact on learning and behaviour, as is being demonstrated by the work of cultural psychologists (Wells, 2011; Bruner, 1986, 1990; **Readings 2.4**, and **10.3**; see also Chapter 2). For instance, Wertsch (1991) argues that the thinking of any learner is dependent on the 'cultural tools' they deploy. These tools frame and mediate their understanding and thus shape their development. Similarly, new learning may affect, or even change, the sense of identity of individuals, and such changes may or may not feel worthwhile or valuable to them within their home culture. For instance, a classic study (Jackson and Marsden, 1962) showed the unease of working-class boys on being sent out of their communities to a grammar school, and similar problems may affect the performance of children from minority ethnic groups today. While we may not see the direct influence of such issues on very young children, understanding the issues which they may face can help us to help them prepare for school life in very different ways than an approach which assumes being ready for school is being able to hold a pencil, write one's name or sit still on a carpet. It has been argued that organizations like schools can helpfully be seen as 'communities of practice' (Wenger, 1999) which evolve and maintain strong norms of behaviour and thought. New members, i.e. children entering the setting, must learn how to conduct themselves and there may be a process of 'cognitive apprenticeship' (Rogoff, 1990) as new understanding is acquired. However, depending on the social, cultural and economic background of a child or indeed the practitioner, such induction may or may not be comfortable. Cultures can thus be exclusive as well as inclusive, as we saw in the case of the male practitioner entering ECEC settings.

---

## Reflective activity 5.1

*Aim:* To reflect upon how the current political, social and economic climate is impacting upon ECEC.

*Evidence and Reflection:* Consider the current political, social and economic climate. What impact has this had on your setting? The families in your setting? Can you identify how practitioner practice is being shaped in the current climate?

*Extension:* If possible discuss this with a colleague or fellow student. Consider what, if anything, can or should be done to question current policies and/or pressures.

Consider the current political and social climate and the impact this has had on the policies relevant to your practice. Can you identify how practitioner practice is being shaped by such policy? Can you see the benefits of such policy? Can you also identify any potential issues or problems? Think particularly about children as learners and about our desire to support them as unique, curious independent learners.
If possible discuss this with a colleague or fellow student.

---

There is thus a sense in which cultures can both enable and constrain learning. Indeed, they are likely to afford different opportunities for particular individuals and groups. In the case of educational cultures, it should be remembered that they develop in response to particular conditions – many of which we are unlikely to control. One crucial factor here is the availability and nature of opportunities and resources, and it is to these issues that we now turn.

# 1.3 Opportunity

It has been said that 'education cannot compensate for society' (Bernstein, 1971) – and yet ECEC practitioners and others seek to ensure that all children can thrive and reach their potential, whatever their circumstances. However, the challenge of creating such opportunities through education is not to be underestimated. Although there are substantial differences in Scotland, Wales, Northern Ireland and in England's regions, the UK as a whole is very wealthy in terms of global criteria – but at the same time there is significant inequality in the distribution of income and wealth. For instance, in 2011/12 the bottom 10 per cent of households received just over £10,000 in annual income before tax, while the top 10 per cent received over £100,000 – ten times higher (ONS, 2012). Such differences have existed for many centuries and tangible evidence of this is available in the contrasts of our buildings, estates and landscape in both urban and rural settings. 3.8 million UK children (29 per cent) live in poverty (as defined by the Department for Work and Pensions [2011]). In many instances, these children are concentrated in particular communities  in which 'cycles of disadvantage' (Rutter and Madge, 1976) are remarkably resistant to change (Ball, 2003; see Reading 5.5). In the UK, there was a substantial rise in inequality during the 1980s and in recent years the incomes of top earners have continued to grow (Sibieta, 2011), further increasing inequality. Economists speculate about the causes of these trends and debate factors such as changes in employment opportunities, returns from high-level skills and education, regional differences and demographic patterns. The direct consequences of government policies on tax and benefits may moderate such structural factors, but the UK's recent experience is of a low level of inter-generational mobility (Blanden and Machin, 2008). In other words, the circumstance of parents tends to be reproduced for their children. Children who are born into poverty remain in poverty, as we discussed in Chapter 2 (see Blanden et al., 2004).

International comparison shows that health, social and educational problems are closely related to inequality within wealthy countries (Wilkinson and Pickett, 2009), as illustrated in **Figure 5.1** overleaf. International agencies draw data from within each country on issues such as social relations, life expectancy, mental health, obesity and, not least, educational performance and their relationship to inequality. Thus, inequality becomes a key concern for governments and indeed society. Affluence and poverty are both growing and becoming 'locked in' (Crawford et al., 2011). The social differences in our societies tend to be reproduced from generation to generation. How then does this process of reproduction occur? What place does education have within this?

An illuminative analysis of this has been provided by French sociologist Pierre Bourdieu (1977). While recognizing exceptional cases, he argued that overall social status is significantly affected by three forms of 'capital' – each of which can be transferred from one generation to another. 'Economic capital' concerns access to material assets. 'Social capital' focuses on relationships in the family, community or wider society which offers contacts, networks and support. 'Cultural capital' relates to the understanding, knowledge and capabilities of individuals to act within particular social settings. The seeds of difference are sown in the ways in which young children are brought up. For

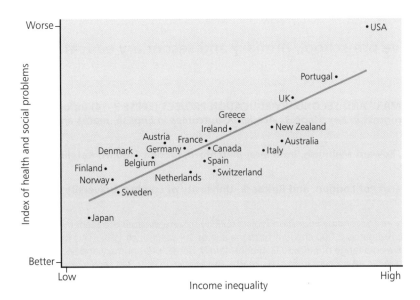

Figure 5.1
Health and
social problems
in relation
to inequality
(Wilkinson and
Pickett, 2009)

instance, Lareau (1989) contrasts the 'concerted cultivation' of middle-class families with the assumption of 'natural growth' which causes less-aware families to interact with their children in quite different ways – with particularly significant consequences for language development. Reay (2000) illuminates how mothers in different circumstances deploy 'emotional capital' to support their children, and she suggests that generational reserves are built up over time. Families thus provide economic, social, cultural, linguistic and emotional resources. These affect the experiences, opportunities and expectations which are made available to the next generation.

Using very large data-sets and innovative statistical techniques, it is now possible to measure the relative influence of neighbourhood, school, family and personal influences on a child's education (Leckie, Pillinger, Jenkins and Rasbash, 2010). This shows that family and personal factors are the most significant, which puts the work of early years practitioners and other educationalist into perspective.

It is clear, then, that it is impossible for education to 'fully compensate for society'. Still, differences can be made, and meeting the particular needs of the children in our care is a moral imperative as well as a professional responsibility. Practitioners must therefore focus on providing the best possible educational opportunities for children. In ECEC this is often considered to be through high-quality provision.

Research which has considered what high-quality provision involves, along with the and the development of programs designed to 'overcome' issues created by inequality, have led to a increased understanding of what 'high-quality' *means* in ECEC. The following research briefings provide an overview of some of the ways in which high quality ECEC provision can support children to reach their potential. As we have noted being aware of research, its findings and the ways in which such work influences policy and practice are crucial for the reflective early years practitioner.

**Research Briefing**

# Effective pre-school, primary and secondary education project

January 2012

**EFFECTIVE PRE-SCHOOL, PRIMARY AND SECONDARY EDUCATION PROJECT (EPPSE 3–14)** *Influences on students' attainment and progress in Key Stage 3: Academic outcomes in English, maths and science in Year 9*

Pam Sammons, Kathy Sylva, Edward Melhuish, Iram Siraj-Blatchford, Brenda Taggart, Katalin Toth, Diana Draghici and Rebecca Smees

Institute of Education, University of London, and Birkbeck, University of London, University of Oxford.

## Introduction

The Effective Pre-school, Primary and Secondary Education Project (EPPSE) has investigated the academic and social-behavioural development of approximately 3,000 children from the age of 3+ years since 1997. This Research Brief focuses on the relationships between a range of individual student, family, home, pre-, primary and secondary school characteristics and students' academic attainment in English, maths and science in Year 9 at secondary school (age 14). It compares the latest findings with those found for students' attainment at younger ages. It also highlights the influences of secondary school on students' attainment in the core curriculum areas and studies their academic progress across Key Stage 3 between the ages of 11 and 14.

## Key Findings
### Individual student, family and home influences

1   Differences in attainment related to background influences which emerged early (at age 3) have remained fairly stable through to the end of Key Stage 3 (KS3; age 14). Both mothers' and fathers' (to a lesser extent) educational level strongly predicted attainment as measured by Teacher Assessment levels (TA) in Year 9 and also progress across KS3.

2   Girls had significantly better attainment in English than boys and also made more progress in English, maths and science over KS3.

3   Older students (autumn-born compared with summer-born) in a year group showed higher attainment and appeared to increase their advantage by making more progress over KS3.

4   Other moderately strong predictors of attainment in all core subjects included the early years home learning environment (HLE), birth weight, family income and free school meal (FSM) status. For English only, a lower family income and FSM status also predicted poorer progress across KS3.

5   Students who lived in disadvantaged neighbourhoods had poorer attainment, over and above child and family characteristics, although these neighbourhood effects are relatively small compared to those of the individual student and family measures.

### Pre-school influences

6   Both pre-school quality and pre-school effectiveness continued to predict students' later academic attainment in Year 9, even after controlling for background characteristics.

7   The early experience of high-quality pre-school predicted better outcomes for maths and science at age 14, but not for English. Pre-school effectiveness1 had a continuing effect on English (for pre-schools effective in promoting pre-reading skills), maths and science (for pre-schools effective in promoting early number concepts). However, these effects were weaker than at younger ages.

8   The continued benefits of pre-school were most evident for students who went on to attend secondary schools of medium or low academic effectiveness (based on the DfE2 contextual value added indicator). This is in line with earlier results which showed that pre-school had a similar 'protective' effect on attainment at the end of Key Stage 2.

### Primary school influences

9   Having attended a more academically effective3 primary school continued to predict significantly better academic attainment for EPPSE students in maths and science, but not English at the end of KS3.

10   Students who had experienced a positive transition from primary school (in terms of gaining familiarity with new routines and continuity in the curriculum) were more likely to have higher attainment in all core subjects and also to make better progress in maths and science at age 14 (controlling for background factors, although the effects were relatively small).

| Research Briefing | The lasting benefits of preschool programs |

**Edited from: Lawrence J. Schweinhart (2000) Lasting Benefits of Preschool Programs, ERIC Research Digest**

More than other educational innovations, high-quality programs for young children living in poverty have demonstrated the promise of lasting benefits. The programs examined served young children living in poverty who were at special risk of school failure. Children entered the programs at some time before age five and remained in them for at least one year. The studies examined a variety of high-quality early childhood programs that included either classes for children or home visits to parents and children or both.

### Effects On School Performance
All of the studies that collected data on early childhood intellectual performance found that those involved in high-quality programs had significantly better intellectual performance than those not involved in such programs during the program and for a year or two thereafter. A comprehensive meta-analysis found evidence of immediate improvements in children's intellectual and socio-emotional performance and health that lasted several years (McKey et al., 1985).

In several studies (Fuerst and Fuerst, 1993; Gotts, 1989; Schweinhart et al., 1993), those involved in such programs had a higher high school graduation rate than the no-program group. In the one study with relevant data for adults (Schweinhart et al., 1993), men who had been program participants had significantly higher monthly earnings, higher rates of home ownership and fewer lifetime arrests than men who had not participated in the program.

### Effects on Community Behavior
One intensive study, the High/Scope study as reported by Schweinhart et al. (1993), found evidence that program participation had positive effects on adult crime, earnings, wealth and welfare dependence. For example, those involved in high-quality programs averaged significantly fewer criminal arrests than those not involved in such programs. Only 7% had ever been arrested for drug dealing compared with 25% of those who did not have access to such programs.

The High/Scope study found that 29% of those who had participated in the program reported monthly earnings at age 27 of $2,000 or more, significantly more than the 7% of nonparticipants who reported such earnings. For men, the difference was due to better paying jobs. For women, the difference was in employment rates: 80% of participants but only 55% of nonparticipants were employed at the time of the age 27 interview. Significantly more of those involved in programs owned their own homes (36% versus 13%). Whilst significantly fewer received welfare assistance or other social services as adults (59% versus 80%).

### Return On Investment
The 1993 Schweinhart et al. study also involved a systematic analysis of the costs and benefits of the preschool program and its effects. The program returned to taxpayers in the following ways:

1  savings in schooling, due primarily to reduced need for special education services, and despite increased college costs for preschool-program participants;
2  higher taxes paid by preschool-program participants because they had higher earnings;
3  savings in welfare assistance; and
4  savings to the criminal justice system and to potential victims of crimes.

The program provided taxpayers a return on investment of $7.16 on the dollar, better than most other public and private investments.

### Only High-Quality Programs Have Lasting Effects
These studies suggest that high-quality programs for young children produce significant long-term benefits because they empower young children, parents, and teachers. Too often, our response to the intractable problems of poverty, crime, drug abuse, unemployment, and welfare dependence is frustration and even despair. Whatever we do, it seems these problems will not go away. Nor will high-quality preschool programs make them go away entirely. But the evidence suggests that providing such programs will significantly reduce the magnitude of these problems; and that is reason enough to provide them.

Available at: **ericdigests.org/1994/lasting.htm** (accessed 24 November 2014).

# 1.4 Accountability

Practitioners are paid to provide professional services. However, the degree of account-ability and external control to which different providers have been subject has varied historically.

Prior to the Second World War it was usual for children under the age of 5 years to be exclusively cared for by the family, often the mother. The majority of children under 5 stayed in the home and would attend school when they reached statutory school age. The playgroup movement, which was established as a self-help organization in the 1960s, worked within the assumption of this role of the mother at home as the childcarer, while the father was assumed to be in the paid workforce as the main breadwinner. Playgroups depended historically on a rota of mothers working on a voluntary basis, with some small payment for the group leaders. The untrained volunteers were often supported to access courses run by the organization (Crowe, 1983), but there was little regulation and no curricular guidance, expectations or accountability.

The Plowden Report of 1967 recommended the expansion of nursery education, although this was envisaged as a part-time facility, with the short hours of the nursery being deemed sufficient time away from the home for young children, and this theme continued up to and including the 1980s, with the place of young children being considered to be at home with the mother. This perspective was, and continues to be, legitimized by psychoanalytical theory (Moss, 2003; May and Nurse, 2007). By the 1990s we had seen a growth in the number of nursery classes attached to schools (Moss and Penn, 1996). Though attached to schools, these nurseries were different from those we see today – for example, the curriculum was unregulated.

During the 1980s and into the 1990s, the move towards paid employment as the government's preferred alternative to state benefits encouraged women to return to the workforce after having children. This was promoted alongside a rise in the attractive rhetoric of 'choice' for affluent families and aligned with long-standing calls for childcare from the feminist movement. However, unlike the feminist vision, this was not seen as a public responsibility. The monetarist economic policies of the Conservative government marked a major shift towards the market and private enterprise in the public sector, including health and education. The growing demand for daycare was, accordingly, met by the private 'for profit' sector. The regulation of these settings was focused on government welfare standards, with inspections carried out by local authority social services. These developments in childcare provision often reinforced a long-standing paradox of women with comparatively high wages depending on a female workforce which was low-skilled and poorly paid – an issue we noted continues to be a concern for the profession today.

With multiple providers offering different ECEC opportunities, children had very different experiences and there was a lack of clarity about what ECEC was and/or its purpose or potential:

> ... should an early years policy be most concerned about preparing children for school or with day care for working parents? Should it provide stimulation for a developing

brain, or equal opportunities for women? Was it about cost savings for employers, able to retain staff when they became parents, or about reducing the benefit bill for single parents, enabling them to return to the workforce? Or was prevention the main driver – whether of developmental delay in children or juvenile crime? (Pugh, 2006: 8)

The introduction in 1996 of government funding for early education places for 3- and 4-year-olds marked a major shift towards the regulation of ECEC. The inspection of providers shifted significantly to be the responsibility of Ofsted teams, who were expected to take into account the 'delivery' of the new curriculum, which began with the Desirable Learning Outcomes in 1996, and evolved into the Foundation Stage and later the Early Years Foundation Stage (DfE, 2012). Although the Ofsted inspection teams for PVI settings continue to differ from the teams inspecting schools, the judgements are made using the same language and similar timings, with an emphasis on regular inspections and re-inspections if settings are 'not yet good'. The inspection teams also regulate all welfare and safeguarding conditions, and issue compliance notices where these are found to be inadequate.

Scotland has taken a very different approach and, in 2011, established Education Scotland, which aims to coordinate almost all of Scotland's provision for curriculum, pedagogy, assessment, leadership, self-improvement, professional development and inspection. It seeks to support quality and improvement by working 'in partnership alongside the full range of bodies and organizations active in Scottish Education'. This includes local authorities, schools, further and higher education, third sector and parent groups. Improvement is thus expected to come from processes of personal and institutional self-development, local collaboration and a collective sense of national purpose.

In 2011 England's General Teaching Council was abolished while GTC Scotland was granted full independence from the government as a self-regulating, professionally led body – the first in the world. The establishment of the GTCS was strongly influenced by the model provided by the General Medical Council. It is thus based, at root, on trust in the teaching profession's capacity to regulate and improve its own professional standards – something we fear is being increasingly eroded in England.

The General Teaching Council for England published a reflective policy paper on these issues just before their abolition (2011). They argued that accountability is by nature 'relational' because it is associated with actions by both the account-holder and the account-giver. Particular forms of accountability thus influence behaviour and provision. A question then arises about the effects of accountability in relation to overarching educational objectives. On this, the GTCE argued that in England there had been insufficient focus on teaching quality and that the foundations of professional collaboration and enduring school improvement had been undermined by fragmentation and short-term expediency. Rather, they suggested, the teaching profession needs to be able to represent its expertise, to demonstrate the ways in which its professional responsibilities are discharged and, ultimately, to regulate itself.

In Wales and Northern Ireland GTCs maintain professional standards of conduct and practice, register teachers and support professional development. Like GTCE, they were established by legislation in the late 1990s and are largely reliant for core functions on income from annual teacher registration. However, since numbers of registered teachers are relatively small in Wales and Northern Ireland, this is challenging. It raises a question about the extent to which teachers should themselves pay for professional regulation or whether it should be funded by governments in the public interest.

The issue of accountability thus crystallizes many issues concerning the relationship between education and society. Should education be a relatively autonomous system or should it be under tight forms of control? Should educators simply carry out centrally determined instructions, or should they develop and exercise professional judgement? What, indeed, is the role of local democratic institutions in this? And who should pay for the accountability system? The history of our education system provides many fascinating instances of attempts to reconcile such dilemmas (Silver, 1980) and there are plenty of related current issues which a reflective practitioner might consider.

In particular, though, and following the dialectical model of social change which we discussed at the beginning of this chapter, the issues of accountability, autonomy and control pose questions of a personal nature for reflective practitioners. How should each individual act? To whom do you feel you should be accountable – to children, parents, colleagues, local or national government, the media, inspectors, or yourself?

---

### Reflective activity 5.2

*Aim:* To review and explore the significance of ideology, culture, opportunity and accountability.

*Evidence and reflection:* Arrange to meet with a small group of work colleagues. In preparation, share out the sections of Chapter 5 we have considered so far, so that ideology, culture, opportunity and accountability are each covered.

In a meeting, each sub-group should explain the issues raised in their section of the chapter, and should relate them to your work context. How, in particular, is your setting affected by the context in which it exists?

*Extension:* What other contextual factors are particularly significant in determining the circumstances of your setting? How does this impact upon provision?

---

## 2 People and agency

We now turn to the individual and personal factors which are the second element in the dialectical model which underpins this book. For instance, setting life can be seen as being created by practitioners and children as they respond to the situations in which they find themselves. Thus, as well as understanding something of the factors affecting the social context, we also need to consider how practitioners and children respond. Such responses reflect subjective perceptions, beliefs, values, commitments, identities, life narratives and imagined futures. This is the exercise of agency and voice – and recognition that our actions are not simply determined by our circumstances. We begin by focusing on practitioners.

# 2.1 Practitioners

Each person is unique, with particular cultural and material experiences making up his or her 'biography' (Sikes, Measor and Woods, 1985). This provides the seedbed for their sense of 'self' and influences their personality, perspectives (Mead, 1934; Gu, 2007) and ultimately the ways in which they behave. The personal qualities of practitioners, such as having the capacity to empathize and the confidence to project and assert oneself, are as important in early years teaching as in any phase of education. Indeed, much of what particular practitioners will be able to offer children and their families will be influenced by them.

Arguably, of even greater importance than the personal qualities of an individual is the capacity to know oneself. We all have strengths and weaknesses. Knowing what these are and how to mediate and regulate the weakness, while utilizing our strengths is a key aspect of reflective teaching.

The particularly human capability of being able to review the relationship of 'what is' and 'what ought to be' is one which practitioners often draw on when considering their aims and examining their educational values and philosophies. While there has always been a good deal of idealism in commitment to providing for babies and young children, there has also always been a concern with practical realism. Indeed, a very important factor which influences practitioners' perceptions is that they have to 'cope', personally as well as professionally. For this reason, we would suggest that a fundamental element of practice is very deeply personal, for it involves people, with a particular image of their self, acting in the challenging situations which settings represent. Working with young children was once described to us as 'exhausting, as it is like having your brain pecked at all day'. When one feels exhausted, are we always as patient as we would like and endeavour to be? Further, the layers of responsibility that come with the role are vast: ranging from caring and nurturing, supporting physical, social, emotional and cognitive development, to supporting families through a multitude of crises – for example, concerns for the child's development. In such circumstances, practitioners face acute dilemmas between their personal and professional concerns and the practical possibilities. They are forced to juggle with their priorities as they manage the stress which is often involved.

In addition to considering the role of the practitioner to be to care and educate, we also need to consider the position of practitioners as employees, for as such they have legitimate legal, contractual and economic interests to maintain, protect and develop (Lawn and Grace, 1987). For example, as we saw in Chapter 1, remuneration for the role is relatively poor and the hours long. Many practitioners also have significant family responsibilities, as well as other interests which may be important to them. Such issues are not inconsequential and can and do impact upon the profession. Notwithstanding such considerations, ECEC attracts people to it who have a sense of moral purpose. There is thus, in general terms across the profession, a principled commitment to providing high-quality education that meets the needs of babies and young children. It is this value commitment which causes practitioners to 'go the extra mile'.

## 2.2 Babies and children

As with the personal factors associated with practitioners, the most important point to make about children is that they are thinking, rational individuals (Corsaro, 2011; James, Jenks and Prout, 1998; Jones, 2009). Each child has a unique 'biography', and unique ways in which they feel about themselves and present themselves. Both will be influenced by their understandings of previous cultural, social and material experience in their families and elsewhere (Bruner, 1986) and by their level of emotional development. From birth and through their educational lives children develop a clear sense of their identity as learners (Warin, 2010; Pollard and Filer, 1996; Reading 13.5). Indeed, pre-school experiences and social processes throughout their schooling lead children to perceive themselves as relative school failures or successes. The work of Dweck and others on the development of growth mindsets and the work of Hattie and others on Visible Learning is of relevance here (see Chapters 1 and 3 of this book).

The foundations of children's 'learning disposition' and stance as a 'lifelong learner' become established early, and there is no doubt that this is the crucial age phase for educational investment (Karoly et al., 1998; Allen, 20011). As children progress further through primary and secondary schools, encountering complex systems of setting, banding, options and 'pathways', their self-perceptions are further reinforced or modified (see Lawrence, 1987; Reading 6.3). At the point of leaving schooling and entering the worlds of college or work, children's life trajectories are thus likely to be well-established. Early years practitioners should not lose sight of the fact that, in their daily work, they are influential in shaping long-term life-chances and identities, as well as working towards immediate goals (Feinstein et al., 2008).

Children in early years settings embody and are influenced by a huge range of circumstances and prior experiences. These include factors such as gender, social class, race, language development, learning disposition, health and types of parental support. As we saw earlier in this chapter in the discussion of opportunities, patterns of advantage and disadvantage are very significant. However, such factors do not determine consequences. The key issue is how children respond to their circumstances – and in this, practitioners can have a crucial role in supporting them to develop the skills which enable them to react and cope in a variety of ways.

Some young children in early years settings may feel particularly uncertain, for instance when encountering messages that differ from those of home (Brooker and Siraj-Blatchford, 2002). Practitioners should be alert to the possibility of differing cultural expectations of the children and families attending their settings. Where a disparity in expectations is particularly marked, young children will, as active individuals, draw on and foster a distinct peer culture within the setting or school – for instance, including specific cultural interests or imaginative games. The early years setting should have many opportunities to include and welcome a range of children's 'voices' as discussed further in Chapters 6 and 8. Children's peer cultures may pose dilemmas in the setting, such as a particular interest in play which challenges the setting's behaviour or inclusion policy. Creative strategies are called for and these may cover a range from conformity through negotiation to rejection – for example, the development and negotiation of a policy on war, weapon and superhero play.

The agency of young children is thus played out in the immediacy of the early years setting. Practitioners have powerful opportunities to influence factors such as motivation and approaches to learning (Rudduck and McIntyre, 2007). Above all, though, we must never forget that children are part of a larger group within early years settings for only part of each day, families, friends, relationships and the media are important to them. A reflective practitioner, therefore, must aim to work with an understanding of the culture of young children. If connections can be made, then children's culture can itself provide an excellent motivational hook into learning.

Parents and carers play a particularly important role in supporting the learning of young children. The EPPE project, among others, highlighted the powerful influence of the home learning environment on children's early educational achievements, with many projects such as the National Children's Bureau 'Raising Early Achievement in Early Literacy', focusing on how all families can support learning.

---

### Reflective activity 5.3

*Aim:* To consider the meaning and significance of 'agency', both for practitioners and for learners.

*Evidence and reflection:* Reflective activity 5.1 reviewed circumstances, and this activity focuses on how people respond and act in relation to these. In particular, it is about the human spirit and the possibilities which always exist, whatever the circumstances.

An interesting way of approaching this is to share one's educational biography with a colleague with whom one feels secure. Taking it in turns, take time to provide a narrative of how you moved through your education, meeting different teachers, growing up, finding some learning difficult but succeeding in others. Identify and focus on some key episodes or turning points which enabled you to progress. Explore, if you can, the actions you took and the encouragement or support you received from others.

Does consideration of such narratives and key moments enable you to see the significance of agency, in the form of your determination to succeed or the judgement by others to encourage you? How your family influenced your education?

*Extension:* You might like to consider the learning of a small number of children you know. To what extent are they able to exercise agency in relation to their circumstances and goals, and might you be able to help?

---

## Conclusion

The intention in this chapter is to discuss the relationship between society as a whole and the people who are centrally involved in education. This is because practice and actions are influenced by the social circumstances within which they occur. However, it has also been argued that individuals can, and will, have effects on future social changes as they exercise their personal agency – though the degree of influence ebbs and flows depending on the roles occupied and at different phases of history.

A theoretical framework of this sort is important for reflective practitioners because it establishes the principle that we can all 'make a difference' within our society. Professional commitment is therefore very important and we should not accept an ascribed position as passive receptors of externally determined prescription. The provision of high-quality education is enhanced when social awareness complements high levels of teaching skills, and when individual responsibilities for professional actions are taken seriously.

This fundamental belief in the commitment, quality and constructive role of practitioners underpins this book. The analysis is optimistic. High-quality education and care depends on the professionalism of practitioners.

## Key readings

We begin with the theoretical framework which informs this book, with its juxtaposition of social context and individual agency.

Mills, C. W. (1959) *The Sociological Imagination*. Oxford: Oxford University Press.

For report on the role of Early Years in society, specifically in reducing social problems, see:

Allen, G. (2011) *Early Intervention: The Next Steps*. An Independent Report to Her Majesty's Government. London: Cabinet Office. [Online] **dwp.gov.uk/docs/early-intervention-next-steps.pdf**

For comprehensive reviews of contemporary issues facing pre-school and primary education in England, see:

Alexander, R. J. (ed.) (2010) 'Children, Their World, Their Education'. Final Report of the Cambridge Primary Review. London: Routledge.

Moss, P. (2014) *Transformative Change and Real Utopias in Early Childhood Education: A Story of Democracy, Experimentation and Potentiality. Contesting Early Childhood*. Oxon: Routledge.

The work of Pierre Bourdieu has influenced ways of understanding different forms of cultural, social and emotional capital, alongside the economic, though which social differences are perpetuated; see:

Bourdieu, P. and Passeron, J. C. (1977) *Reproduction in Education, Society and Culture*. London: Sage Publications Ltd.

An important international study of the consequences of inequality is:

Wilkinson, R. and Pickett, K. (2010) *The Spirit Level. Why Equality is Better for Everyone*. London: Penguin.

To review the contemporary challenges and pleasures of being facing early years practitioners, see:

> Pugh, G. and Duffy, B. (eds) (2010) *Contemporary Issues in The Early Years.*
>    5th edn. London: Sage Publications Ltd.

For an understanding of modern childhoods, take a look at:

> Blundell, D. (2012) *Education and Constructions of Childhood.* London: Continuum.
> Clark, R. (2013) *Childhood in Society for the Early Years.* London: Learning Matters.

Books which focus on parents and practitioners working together in partnership include:

> Lindon, J. (2012) *Parents as Partners (Positive Relationships in the Early Years).*
>    London: Practical Pre-school Books.
> Whalley, M. (2007) *Involving Parents in their Children's Learning* London: Sage
>    Publications Ltd.

***Readings for Reflective Teaching in Early Years Education*** directly complements and extends the chapters in this book. It has been designed to provide convenient access to key texts. It will be of particular help as a compact and portable library.

The associated website, **reflectiveteaching.co.uk**, offers a wealth of supplementary resources including reflective activities, research briefings, advice on further reading and downloadable diagrams, figures and checklists from the book. It also features a compendium of educational terms, links to useful websites, policy and curriculum documents, and showcases examples of excellent research and practice.

# Relationships

## How are we getting on together?

**6**

## Introduction

Relationships in ECEC are extremely important; ultimately the development of secure relationships underpins children's social, emotional, physical and cognitive development (see Evangelou, Sylva, Kyriacou, Wild and Glenny, Reading 6.1). Positive respectful relationships also make working environments more pleasant and fulfilling for both children and adults. Thus, they are at the foundation of a successful, learning environment. In this chapter we explore the importance of relationships between practitioners and children, children and their peers and practitioners and other adults – including colleagues, families and with practitioners working within other agencies.

As we have discussed, for instance in Chapter 1, practitioners working within ECEC often have a strong moral purpose and place great emphasis on establishing good relationships with children and families. However, as we will explore, relationships are at times demanding and large teams can be challenging to work within and manage (see Rankin and Butler, Reading 6.2).

In Chapter 2 we discussed theories of learning. In this chapter we will add to that discussion, giving consideration to how relationships between practitioners and children, and children and their peers can support or hinder learning. Finally, we end the chapter with an overview of the ways in which positive relationships can be developed and managed to create a positive learning environment for all.

---

### TLRP principles

Two principles are of particular relevance to this chapter on relationships as a foundation for learning:

**Principle 4: Effective teaching and learning requires teachers to scaffold learning.** Teachers should provide activities which support learners as they move forward, not just intellectually, but also socially and emotionally, so that once these supports are removed, the learning is secure.

**Principle 7: Effective teaching and learning fosters both individual and social processes and outcomes.** Learning is a social activity. Learners should be encouraged and helped to work with others, to share ideas and to build knowledge together. Consulting learners about their learning and giving them a voice is both an expectation and a right.

---

## 1 Relationships in settings

For many children, their attendance at an ECEC setting is often their first experience of spending any sustained period of time away from their network of close friends and family. Not only do we have a moral obligation to do our best to ensure each and every child feels welcome, cared for, respected and secure, but we must recognize that this represents their first experience of schooling which can impact upon their future educational and life experiences. Many challenges faced by adults, such as mental health issues, criminality, and poor literacy and numeracy, can be traced back to early childhood experiences (World Health Organisation, 2009).

> ### Expert question
>
> **Processes for children's social needs**: Does the educational experience build on social relationships, cultural understandings and children identities?
>
> This question contributes to a conceptual framework representing enduring issues and practitioner expertise (see Chapter 16).

Relationships in settings are the product of particular, complex and subtle personal interactions between children and adults, children and their peers, and how we as adults get along together. These relationships are of such significance that reflective practitioners are likely to have it almost constantly in mind. Reflection can be a useful tool for gaining deeper understanding of these interactions – an understanding which can help us to ensure that the children in our care are being supported to gain the greatest enjoyment and potential from their interactions with both the adults and the children in the setting.

Enduring insights on the foundations of good relationships are provided by the work of Rogers (1961, 1969, 1980) on counselling. He suggests that three basic qualities are required if a warm, 'person-centred' relationship is to be established: acceptance, genuineness and empathy. If we apply this to early years practice, it might suggest that acceptance involves acknowledging and receiving children 'as they are'; genuineness implies that such acceptance is real and heartfelt; while empathy suggests that a practitioner is able to appreciate how events are experienced by children. Rogers introduced the challenging idea of providing 'unconditional positive regard' for his clients and perhaps this can also provide an ideal for what practitioners should offer children and their families. Approaching teaching in this way is likely to feel comfortable for early years practitioners.

Rogers' three qualities have much in common with the three key attitudes of the reflective practitioner discussed in Chapter 1. Being able to demonstrate acceptance and genuinely empathize requires 'open-mindedness' and a 'wholehearted' commitment to children and their families. It also necessitates 'responsibility' when considering the long-term consequences of our actions.

While these qualities provide a useful starting point from which to approach practice in ECEC, there is a need to delve more deeply into the needs of all of those involved in the setting community. For example, there are a number of constraints placed on practitioners who are responsible for relatively large numbers of children, meaning that the challenges of management and discipline must always condition actions. Furthermore, the fact that we ourselves have feelings, concerns and interests means that we, too, need to feel the benefit of a degree of acceptance, genuineness and empathy if we are to give of our best.

# 1.1 Practitioner–child relationships

Perhaps the most important strategy in establishing good relationships with children is to establish some sort of connection with them as people. 'What makes humans so different from the other great apes is not just what individual infants are able to do, but also what adults and infants like to do together' (Parker-Rees, 2007: 3). Each of us welcomes recognition of our individuality and responds to a smile, a kind word, or any other expression of interest – and so it is with children. Many practitioners have these 'soft skills' and an authentic interest in the children for whom they have responsibility. If children feel this open, positive regard (Rogers, 1961) and understand that it has to be framed by the rules and purposes of the setting, then the foundations for good relationships are set. However, within ECEC there is a particular need to forge strong secure relationships to support a child's development. The work of John Bowlby and Mary Ainsworth provides the theoretical basis for this claim and for the key person approached developed for supporting practitioner–child relationships within ECEC settings.

John Bowlby (1969) first identified the importance of the close bond which forms between children and their main carer, usually their parent. Bowlby proposed that 'the infant and young child should experience a warm, intimate, and continuous relationship with his mother (or permanent mother substitute) in which both find satisfaction and enjoyment' (Bowlby, 1951: 13, see Reading 6.4). Bowlby (1944) himself found through his research that many problems in adulthood can be linked to maternal deprivation and a child's separation from their carer at a young age. Ainsworth and Bell (1970) (working with Bowlby) extended this work in part through what has become known as the 'strange situation' experiment. This involved measuring attachment by observing children aged 12 to 18 months and their response to a range of situations, including the parent leaving the room, reunion behaviours and responses to a stranger. Of key interest to us is that the research revealed that a child with a secure attachment feels secure enough to explore their environment and learn without the parent/carer present; conversely, a child who is 'insecurely attached' will not feel confident to explore independently, which may result in the child's learning being hindered.

This recognition of the need for a child to have a secure attachment has led to the role of key person thriving in many ECEC setting around the world. In most cases this involves a practitioner being assigned to a child as they enter the setting, to help them to *settle in* and feel safe enough in the setting to explore their surroundings. It has been referred to as '… an individual and reciprocal commitment between a member of staff and a family' (Elfer et al., 2003: 18). Rather than attempt to forge strong bonds with all families, the practitioner has a smaller number of children whom they can spend time getting to know. This can be rewarding for all involved, as the key person can help build relationships between children, their families and the setting, and those working within the setting (Goldschmied and Jackson, 2004). It can help the child to feel secure, the family can be reassured they have a key point of contact who they know understands their child. While the practitioner has the reward of knowing a child and their family and supporting them through their time in setting. Of course, there are challenges to the approach and it has been contested, for example, for being potentially painful for children when their key worker is not present (e.g. Elfer et al., 2003). In response to this, a *second* key person approach has been developed to support children when their key person is not available – perhaps due to working patterns, holidays, illness, or the child attending long hours at the setting. This approach may also help to widen the community and 'preserve' the parent–child relationship without undermining the original desire to support the child to feel secure in the setting.

---

### Reflective activity 6.1

*Aim:* To consider the 'key person' role in your setting.

*Evidence and reflection:* Think either about a child for whom you are the key person, or, if you have not held this role, ask a colleague or peer about their experience. Think about the purpose of this role. What is the potential value of this role for the child, the family and yourself? What helps practitioners to fulfil this role? For example, procedures in the setting, time to liaise with families. What challenges arise from taking on this role?

*Extension:* Working with a colleague consider how you build close relationships with a child and their family. Are different approaches needed with different children? If relevant how have you managed challenging situations with families, perhaps if you have had a difference of opinion.

---

Another aspect of providing a secure basis for children is to have clear boundaries and expectations. Children often expect adults to set boundaries and make expectations clear, and these may helpfully be expressed in a small number of formal, overt rules – tailored, of course, for the age of the children. (This is discussed in greater detail in Chapter 7 where we explore behaviour management.) Chaplain (2003) considered primary schools, and made the important point that such overarching rules offer children a sense of personal and psychological safety within educational establishments. Such rules also provide a foundational form of moral principles for interpersonal relationships, and should be expressed in a forward-looking, positive way.

Having considered the importance of developing secure respectful relationships with children, it is also useful to consider the issue of power within adult–child relationships. Young children often have little, if any, say in whether they attend ECEC settings. As with much of their lives, the decisions are made by the adults who care for them. In many instances this can be positive, in that the child is being cared for and their needs are being met. But more recently there has been increased recognition of children's rights, particularly since the advocacy of children's rights by the United Nations. (See **reflectiveteaching.co.uk** for more on this and the full list of the *Rights of the Child*.) With this growing understanding that children are holders of full human rights, views of children have also developed. These views have been particularly well documented by childhood sociologists, who have

### Expert question

**Relationships:** Are relationships nurtured as the foundation of mutual well-being?

This question contributes to a conceptual framework representing enduring issues and practitioner expertise (see Chapter 16).

stated that children are seen as competent and knowledgeable actors in society (Mayall, 2000), who are seen as 'being' rather than in a state of 'becoming' and as such are seen as complete (Lee, 2005; Prout, 2011) and having full human value in the present (Mayall, 2000). Viewing young children in this way places a rather different emphasis on their relationships with adults than one may have experienced in the last century. If we are to accept children as competent knowledgeable actors in social situations, and we want them to develop the skills required to participate in discussions about the processes and rules, then one must support them to develop these skills and provide opportunities for them to do so (see Colwell, Reading 6.5).

The issue of children's voice is revisited in Chapter 8 on spaces, which considers how spaces for democratic discussion are needed. At this point we would like to emphasize that, while there is a need for practitioners to fulfil their moral and contractual obligations and shape children's experiences in ECEC appropriately, there is also the possibility for children to be involved in decision-making. Part of building successful relationships with children is allowing them to speak or express their opinions and valuing what they have to say, for what is important in any situation is how a person feels – not how you, the practitioner, think they should feel.

---

### Reflective activity 6.2

*Aim:* To gather information on how children feel about activities which they undertake.

*Evidence and reflection:* You will need to spend some time considering and/or developing an appropriate tool for collecting the information. If possible discuss this with a colleague or peer.

One method suitable for older children is simply to ask them. Initially, if the children are not used to discussing their likes and dislikes or being asked their opinion, they may find this difficult and you will have to spend time modelling the language they will need to participate in such discussions. For younger children, you may have a series of questions and ask them to indicate with a paddle – for example, a happy face or sad face response. With the youngest children and babies you will have to carefully observe their expressions and their interests.

*Extension:* Such activities should yield data of considerable importance for future planning and provision. This data should should be analysed to identify any patterns in the children's perspectives. You may also identify other ways in which these tools could be used to elicit children's views.

---

The specific ways in which practitioners act and the effectiveness of our actions are a focus for professional learning and refinement over many years. Ways of acting convey a great deal to children and families about our views, expectations, confidence and experience. If you ask for a child's opinion, as in the activity above, but then do not listen to their response or take their views seriously, the child will pick up on this. Receiving messages about how their opinion is or is not valued will impact upon how children choose to voice their opinions in the future. (We will consider frustration in young children in Chapter 7.) Such messages can be conveyed in a variety of ways.

Non-verbal behaviours including facial expression, use of eye contact, posture, gesture and movement can reveal much about your feelings to children. It is possible, without saying a word, to convey confidence or anxiety, calmness or tension, satisfaction or displeasure through the ways in which we present ourselves. Thus, a skilful practitioner is aware of, and manages, their non-verbal behaviour as a form of communication. Non-verbal behaviour may have particular significance in our interactions with babies (see for example Parker-Rees, 2007 and Manning-Morton, Reading 12.2).

Verbal communication represents another group of skills. There is the capacity to project one's voice within an ECEC setting. This is not necessarily to do with volume, but is certainly related to clarity in both the form and content of what is said. Pitching one's voice appropriately, so that it is not strained but can be heard, is extremely important and can be developed to improve effectiveness. Through the *ways* in which we speak, we are also able to convey feelings of enthusiasm, confidence or concern, for example, so that the form of the presentation will, hopefully, reinforce the substantive message we intend to communicate.

Listening is an equally important skill, as is the ability to interpret what is said by children. The most important dimension of this is to maintain openness to what is said, rather than 'hearing what we expect to hear'. This is by no means easy. But it is an essential skill if an effective feedback loop from children to practitioners is to be maintained. Without it, we cannot learn from children or their families and the appropriateness of our practice will inevitably be impaired. Listening is a skill. Are you open to what children and others are saying? Are you indicating to them that you are indeed listening and open to hearing their opinions?

## 1.2 Staff teams and relationships

Relationships between members of staff are important for many reasons, not least as positive staff relations create a positive setting environment. In this section we will consider some of the key factors for developing and maintaining a respectful, cohesive staff team, as while colleagues may be stimulating and supportive, they can also become protective of existing practices and inhibit innovation (Pollard, 1987; Sedgwick, 1988), making the job of reflective practice very challenging indeed.

---

### Reflective activity 6.3

*Aim:* Work with one or two colleagues to identify the traits practitioners need to work with young children.

*Evidence and reflection:*

- Consider your own strengths as a practitioner and the traits you have.
- How do the staff you work with complement your traits to ensure that the children in your setting are well supported?
- Conduct a 'needs analysis'; are there areas which you and/or your staff team need to develop? How might you go about this?

*Extension:* Repeat and extend this activity working with the whole staff team.

---

## Interactions

We have mentioned respect in numerous places throughout this book. But what does respect look like and how we do we build staff teams who respect each other and each other's work? As with children, all practitioners are different; we have had different experiences and will have differing views. As such, while some relationships may come easily, others may be more challenging and require greater time, effort and/or understanding to negotiate. We need to find ways of working well together, for both the sake of the children and our own personal satisfaction. Nobody likes to work in an uncomfortable environment.

First and foremost, we must be aware of the ways in which we interact with colleagues, both verbally and non-verbally. We show respect by listening, demonstrating that we are listening (by clarifying what has been said and repeating the key issues) and taking time to listen. Of course, we are not always available to listen to colleagues; we have other commitments inside or outside of work. Explaining why, if we cannot discuss the issue at that moment, is also respectful. Arrange a suitable time for the discussion.

When things go wrong, it is often the case that we avoid the situation. Indeed, many adults find it challenging to explain to others that they are unhappy, that they have found something challenging, but what we sometimes refer to as 'clearing the air' is almost always the best way forward. A reflective practitioner will explain what the issue was, why they felt that way, and will endeavour to find a way to move forward. Tensions, discussing colleagues when they are not around and a general lack of positive interaction is no way to build a respectful team who can work well together. While it may feel that there is not much time, if any, to spare, building good relations will help things to run smoothly in the long term. The old adage of 'treating others how you yourself would wish to be treated' might be the best way to think about working in a team for example, if a colleague works with you on something ensure that you share the credit.

Our own feelings as practitioners are also an important factor in maintaining a positive working consensus. As such, ways of monitoring our feelings may be useful. **Reflective activity 6.4** suggests keeping a personal reflective journal (see Wotton, Collings and Moon, Reading 3.7, for more on reflective writing). Journals have been used by researchers in education for many years (Dadds, 1995) and are a tried-and-tested way of reflexively taking stock of life as it unfolds. Talking with colleagues and friends can also be immensely valuable and supportive. The point is a simple one: to care for others, we must also look after ourselves.

---

### Reflective activity 6.4

*Aim:* To monitor and place in perspective your own feelings about staff relationships.

*Evidence and reflection:* Probably the best way to do this is by keeping a diary. This does not have to be an elaborate, time-consuming one, but simply a personal statement of how things have gone and of how you felt. Be mindful about writing about your own feelings rather than critiquing others, and keeping your journal locked away or password-protected on your computer, etc.

Diary-keeping tends to heighten awareness and, at the same time, it supplies a document which can be of great value in reviewing events.

*Extension:* Once a diary has been kept for a fortnight or so, you might set aside some time to read it carefully and to reflect upon it with a view to drawing reasonably balanced conclusions regarding yourself and how you respond in particular situations. It would be better still to discuss the issues raised with a colleague or friend. Are there ways in which you could seek to develop your responses in particular instances? Are there issues which need to be addressed in the staff team? What might be a positive way forward to address such issues?

## Opportunities

We have noted that staff teams work well if they can interact respectfully, this includes understanding each other's position and working together to common aims. This can only be achieved if staff have time to interact, time to discuss what the values, aims and goals of the setting might be, and agree common aims and shared understandings. We would urge that this time be seen as essential, rather than *nice to have*.

## Management

Managing staff teams is a complex task which takes training and practice. There is a wealth of information about managing staff teams at **reflectiveteaching.co.uk**. Of key concern here is how ECEC managers build relationships with staff and support and enable positive relations to develop across the setting. Daly, Byers and Taylor (2009: 25) draw upon the work of Rodd (1998), Moyles (2007) and Handy (1992) to provide a list of eleven qualities successful managers possess – though perhaps very few people would possess them all, all of the time!

- Confidence in own abilities
- High expectations of both self and staff
- Awareness of current thinking and legislation
- Self-motivation and the ability to motivate others
- Open-mindedness and flexibility
- Experience in their field
- Reliability
- Ability to take initiative
- Vision, innovation and imagination
- Sense of humour
- A reflective thinker

In terms of developing relationships, this list suggests that successful leaders and managers are able to instil confidence in their work through having confidence themselves and up-to-date knowledge. They are able to build relationships with staff by being reliable, having a sense of humour and having high expectations of staff. As we have seen with children, when people expect that you can achieve, you are indeed more likely to have a go and be confident in your abilities. Indeed, a number of these qualities resonate well with the qualities we have been advocating in this book: to be reflective, to be open-minded and flexible. Having such skills as a manager enables one to lead but also to take on the views of others, to be open to hearing alternatives and to changing practice. This again highlights that respect is essential for staff teams to work well together and the value of reflective practice.

## 1.3 Relationships with families

We have already noted the significance of the relationships between practitioners and children's families. Such is the significance of this relationship that it will be continually referred to throughout this book. Here we focus particularly on the relationships parents have with practitioners and how this contributes to children's learning (see Whalley, Reading 13.1).

Building respectful relationships with parents is crucial if we wish to optimize children's learning and create an enjoyable working relationship for children, their families and practitioners. As we have noted children's voice elsewhere, so too should we be mindful of parents' voice. This can be tricky; after all, you may have 60 children in your setting. Should 120 parents have ideas of how the setting should be run and organized, we may not get very far! Hornby (1995) suggests that a successful way of working with parents involves parents being seen as experts on their children, with the practitioner being viewed as the expert on education – both valuing the expertise of the other.

What we strive for is to achieve is a culture of mutual cooperation and respect, where all parties feel they can discuss concerns and challenges, and work together effectively to meet such challenges. Again, we are not suggesting that everybody will always want to be everybody's friend. Indeed, in professional circumstances this may not be a good idea, but there are ways in which even people that would not choose to spend their personal time together can forge respectful working relationships. How can this be achieved?

Communication is a vital aspect of the relationship a practitioner can build with a family. Through our discussions so far in this book we have considered some of the ways in which parents can communicate with practitioners through journals and being asked about the child's preferences and experiences. But how is this achieved on a deeper level, where communication with parents isn't left to a short feedback on the child's day – for example, nappy changes and how much was eaten?

Some of the key aspects of communication to be considered when working with parents include: sharing points of view; taking time to understand each other's perspectives; and being clear that everybody is concerned with the child, what is best for them and their development. We considered some of the ways in which we convey what we mean through our verbal and non-verbal actions in this chapter.

It is also pertinent to note that, while we are concerned with creating learning opportunities for children, our work with parents can at times increase the learning opportunities for children within the home (Sylva et al., 2004). The aforementioned EPPE research clarified that what parents do with their children is much more important than who they are and that support from within the family can support children's learning and development. Activities they might 'do' to achieve this include: reading stories; painting and drawing; talking about and playing with numbers, letters and shapes.

---

### Case study 6.1 Working with families

I was fortunate enough to shadow a Speech Language Therapist as she visited homes in an area where there had been increased instances of children entering school with language delay. Her role was to identify any ways in which parents could be supported to engage in their children's language development. In the initial visits she explained to the parents how, while these young children who were aged between 18 and 36 months had little spoken language, this was the time to engage them in conversations. Being respectful of the busy lives of the parents, she demonstrated how everyday tasks could be turned into opportunities for developing their child's speech. Favoured games included discussing and, where appropriate, asking the child to help pair the socks in the dry washing, or talking and pointing out features of houses, parks or trees to children as they went to the shops. The end result of this programme was a reduction in the number of children entering school with language delay.

What struck me was that it is easy to forget that not everybody has the same ways of being: some families are quiet; some wouldn't be aware of the potential benefits of discussing such issues with their children and so may not engage in such discussions. Most of all, how a simple supportive act can help parents to support their children's learning and development and how this can be achieved in a respectful, friendly supportive way.

---

Alongside the understanding that we can support parents, we must not forget that the original premise for this relationship to work is about seeing parents as partners. It is about working together to share our understanding of children and of learning to ascertain how a particular child may be best supported.

## 1.4 Multi-agency working

So far we have considered relationships between practitioners and children and their families. Here we turn our attention to how we work with other agencies and organizations. While the methods for building relationships with other agencies are similar to those we have already discussed, we want to draw attention to the specific nuances of such relationships, given that when partnerships between agencies fail, the children can be at risk of serious harm, as attested to by a number of inquiries into the deaths of children.

Atkinson, Jones and Lamont (2007) identified four key areas requiring attention if successful multi-agency working is to be achieved:

- **Clarifying roles and responsibilities**: when seeking support from other agencies or when working together, it is useful to begin by identifying the roles and responsibilities of everybody involved and the expertise held by individuals. This can help respect to be built and for each member of the party to understand the responsibilities each member has and, as a consequence, what they will need to do or will not be able to do.

- **Securing commitment at all levels**: when asking for advice or support from another agency or when embarking on case work together, it is important to ensure that you have the support of management. This can help to ensure that time and resources are made available for the work and any meetings, and to allow recommendations to be followed through.

- **Engendering trust and mutual respect**: developing relationships, sharing skills and resources can help a collegiate relationship to develop.

- **Fostering understanding between agencies**: it is very helpful if agencies understand how the other works. Each will have different processes, experiences and expertise; thus, developing shared understandings is essential for developing strong working relationships.

Overall one needs to be thoughtful about how these relationships are developed. When different agencies work well together, the rewards for children and practitioners can be reaped.

## 2 Relationships for learning

In Chapter 2 we considered key theories of human learning including behaviourism, constructivism and social cognition. Through these discussions we identified that, while learning is hugely complex, there are a number of facets to learning, including experience and being supported by another. Following that discussion, we claimed that learning is a social process and that children experience two distinct social worlds within ECEC relating to either their interactions with a practitioner, or with their peers (Kutnick et al., 2007). In this section we will consider how each of these contexts can be valuable sites for learning when supportive respectful relationships are fostered.

## 2.1 Child–peer interactions and learning

In ECEC settings, older children in the age range spend more of their time with their peers than they do with practitioners (Layzer, Goodson and Moss, 1993; Wilcox-Herzog and Kontos, 1998; Kutnick et al., 2006) particularly as children progress through ECEC and adult–child ratios increase. It isn't surprising, then, that research has shown that children's peers make a significant contribution to each others' development (Ladd, 2005) and that children's peer relationships are considered by those working within ECEC to be of great importance. As a consequence there are a number of programmes that exist to support the development of what we will refer to as children's social competencies. Social competencies are defined by the Social Competencies Interpersonal Process (SCIP) model as the skills needed to 'recruit and maintain satisfying and supportive relationships' and the 'trait-like dispositions that govern use of these skills' (Mallinckrodt, 2000: 239); and by Topping et al. (2011) as those skills which allow children to 'integrate thinking, feeling and behaviour to achieve social tasks and outcomes …' (2011: 1). They refer to not only the social skills required for developing relationships but also the traits required to use such skills appropriately.

The work of both Piaget and Vygotsky highlight the significance of interpersonal relationships in the development of young children's knowledge and skills (De Vries, 2000). Vygotskian socio-cultural theory proclaims that children learn in a social context – as a member of a relationship (Vygotsky, 1962), in which the guiding role of more knowledgeable members is key. For Vygotsky, learning is reliant on a more knowledgeable partner. This partner allows a child to move from what they know to what they can know with the support of another. He coined the phrase 'Zone of Proximal Development' to refer to this 'gap' in their understanding. The more knowledgeable partner helps them to bridge this gap, similar to the support of the practitioner or peer partner highlighted in SST. That is not to dismiss the value of play for Vygotsky. He recognizes that the social aspects of play are significant for development, but that for the full learning potential of a task to be reached a more knowledgeable partner or guide is a crucial role, which may be filled by practitioner or peer partner (Rogoff, 1990).

Piagetian socio-cognitive theory, however, purports that social interaction and conflict between individuals leads to higher-order understanding (Piaget, 1928). Piaget recognizes that peer interaction can lead to the advancement of one another's cognitive development through cognitive conflict arising as a result of differing perspectives. Such learning is not dependent on one partner having greater knowledge than the other; here the interaction itself is sufficient to increase the learning potential of the situation (Damon and Phelps, 1989). Piaget did not assume that the peer group was the only context in which children develop (Howes, 2010) but recognized the important role this context plays.

Both Vygotsky and Piaget recognize that children's peer interactions are a key site for both cognitive and social development, a position widely held within education (e.g. Kutnick et al., 2008; Rogoff, 1990; Pellegrini and Blatchford, 2000), and that there are particular dimensions to interactions which support learning. Yet, it is suggested that merely providing children with opportunities to interact is insufficient for supporting the development of a learning environment which supports learning to take place. Of course, many children will learn, but we are concerned with developing an environment which supports all children to learn and for the opportunities of the ECEC context to be maximized. In fact, a child's peer relationships are complex and a number of issues may arise during interactions which hinder learning. Damon and Phelps (1989), drawing upon Piaget's work, state that while interactions are likely to lead to a level of understanding which could not have been reached through working alone, this requires equal power between the individuals. They note that complex understanding is gained through terms such as 'mutuality' and 'connectedness', where both partners are equally participative and they work together (Kutnick and Colwell, 2009). Where power is unequal, a number of issues arise, including that those who fear being mocked may not take the risk of joining the activity and become passive (Galton and Williamson, 1992), and that members of the dyad (pair) or group can become polarized by the group (because of gender or ability, for example) (Cowie and Rudduck, 1990).

Such issues highlight that learning with others can in itself act as an inhibitor to learning, as research has shown that young children with poor peer relationships have an increased risk of school failure (Janes et al., 1979; Kupersmidt and Coie, 1990). Such work suggests that for children to gain the greatest potential benefits from their interactions with their peers, they will need social competencies to benefit from their interactions and for these interactions to be supportive of learning. The reflective early years practitioner must be aware of this and actively seek to support the development of children's peer relationships. At **reflectiveteaching.co.uk** you can find information about some of the programmes which have been designed to support the development of positive relationships and the research which has investigated their use in pre-schools and schools.

## 2.2 Child–practitioner interactions and learning

Interactions between children and practitioners can support learning. We have noted the concept of sustained shared thinking (SST) earlier in this book. We have also discussed how adults can scaffold learning. But what does this mean in practice? A study which underpins our understandings of the role of the practitioner in scaffolding children's learning is the Froebel Block Play Research Group study (Gura et al., 1992), which focused on children's play and on the importance of the role of the practitioner in supporting learning through play with blocks. The study concluded that a number of conditions were required to support or 'scaffold' learning through play activities, including that the practitioner must:

- be involved – listening, discussing extending thinking;
- create an appropriate space for the activity;
- allow children to share the initiative about what is to be learnt;
- use observation to inform future planning.

All of which are activities which we continually refer to throughout this book.

There are also a number of research studies which suggest that the role of practitioner modelling is important in supporting children's learning. Modelling has been shown to be a more effective way of learning than trial and error (Bandura, 1977), or didactic teaching methods (Schunk, 1981). Coltman, Petyaeva and Anghileri's (2002) study found that exploration alone was not sufficient to ensure learning and that modelling, as a form of scaffolding, had a significant impact on children's learning and retention of a new skill. The EPPE research found that adult 'modelling' of skills and appropriate behaviour was often combined with periods of SST, open-ended questioning, and that this was associated with better cognitive achievement (Sylva et al., 2004). Again, the research is indicating to us that interaction between a child and practitioner in learning is complex.

Despite such claims, there is no one generally agreed definition of what modelling is or explanation of its implementation. Orme et al. (1966) use the term *perceptual modelling* to describe an 'expert' demonstrating an action and then allowing time for the 'novice' to trial or imitate the action. Weiss and Klint (1987) have suggested that perceptual modelling may be of particular benefit to early learners as they lack the skills to be able to translate a verbal instruction into a new action. We propose therefore that modelling skills, both social and cognitive, and then providing opportunities for discussion of the action or skill and for the child to 'practise' the skills, is likely to be beneficial for young children's learning. An example of this type of modelling is evidenced in the case below.

---

## Case study 6.2 Modelling behaviour

Ben, a 34-month-old boy, is attempting a jigsaw at pre-school. The practitioner, Beth, scaffolds his learning using modelling as a technique.

First she watches him try to fit the pieces into the spaces, but he is not managing to progress with the task. He is trying every piece in a specific space but he is not turning the pieces.

Beth takes a piece and tries to fit it into an incorrect space. She says 'no, it doesn't fit this way, how about if I turn it and try it now … oh nearly, maybe I could turn it a little bit more. What do you think? Would you like to have a try?'

Ben then tries the piece, turning it, and manages with a little encouragement to place a piece. He is pleased with his achievement and continues with the jigsaw.

In this activity Beth is demonstrating the benefit of modelling her thinking to Ben and allowing him to try the action himself.

---

Another way in which modelling can be used to support learning, which can be particularly useful for discussing challenging behaviours without having to discuss real people, is through the use of story books. Within ECEC practice it is commonplace for story books to be used to facilitate discussions about relationships and how our behaviour impacts upon relationships. This is a practice supported by the neo-Vygotskian concept of using the language of story books to think and communicate (Mercer, 2000) and Bandura's Social Learning Theory (1977). The case below provides an example of how practitioners can model the thinking processes which connect behaviours and underpin relationships.

---

## Case study 6.3 Modelling thinking

Beth has just finished reading a book to Jack, George, Alice and Malachy. The book tells the story of a lady who is very kind and shares all she has with her family, but, because her family takes advantage of her kindness, she becomes angry and stops sharing with them. They begin to discuss the characters.

Beth: Do you think they [her family] were being very kind to her?

Jack: No, they didn't help her; they didn't help with the weeds.

---

George: But she wasn't kind to them at the end …

Beth: You're right, she wouldn't let them have any of the bread. Why do you think that was? [pause] Why do you think she stopped being so kind?

Alice: Because they weren't kind to her.

Beth: I think you're right, she said that they didn't help her make the bread so she didn't feel like sharing it with them … I think if we aren't kind and helpful to other people, then they may not feel like they want to be kind and helpful to us, what do you think?

Malachy: I don't like playing with my brother when he won't share with me …

Beth: No? Oh dear, well perhaps you can talk to him about that and explain how you feel.

So far, then, we have established that it is important for practitioners to consider the nature of their relationships with children while also considering how specific interactions can support children's learning and development.

## 3 Enhancing the setting climate

## 3.1 Climate and emotional security

In this chapter we have focused on specific relationships and the contribution they make to the learning environment. We will now move on to consider the ECEC setting as an environment for learning though the concept of 'climate'. We will review how the climate can support children's self-esteem and inclusive provision for all. We will also consider the ways in which this can be achieved.

Attempts have been made to measure classroom climate by studying the perceptions of teachers and children (see Frieberg, 1999). Indeed, Fraser and Fisher (1984) developed a 'My Classroom Inventory' for teachers to use in their own classrooms. This can give structured feedback on older children's feelings about classroom life and might be used, for example, at the beginning and end of a school year. However, such techniques arguably fail to grasp either the subtleties of the interpersonal relationships or provide us with information about the nuances of early years settings. Asking children to simply 'draw a picture of important things in their setting', such as where they like to play most, can be extremely revealing, and are likely to be more appropriate for those children who are capable of such tasks. However, as reflective practitioners, if we are to take full account of the social and emotional climate in our settings, we need a form of analysis which recognizes this subtlety and allows the children to contribute to this where possible.

> ## Reflective activity 6.5
>
> *Aim:* To evaluate and understand the social and emotional climate of your setting.
>
> *Evidence and reflection:* It is likely that a combination of tools will be required. We recommend a combination of practitioner observations and child-led activities.
>
> In your observations be sure to note how both children and adults are getting on, whether all of the children are engaged, whether the activities offer challenge but that all children feel able to participate and succeed. Try not to dismiss or excuse any child or behaviour; the important aspect here is the overall climate and how children are being supported within that environment. To gain the children's perspective you may feel that for babies your observations are sufficient. However, take some time to think about their capabilities and plan accordingly. Asking young children to draw a picture for you about what is important to them in the setting and their likes and dislikes.
>
> As with the previously suggested activity, it may take time for the children to get used to discussing their thoughts and opinions if they are not used to being asked.
>
> *Extension:* Once you have gathered the perspectives of practitioners and children you may wish to include families. Use this information to consider the positive aspects of the climate and to identify any areas you may wish to develop. Work with a peer to consider how this may be achieved. Do not be disheartened if it takes time. Many things worth doing take time!

## 3.2 Supporting children's confidence and self-esteem

Many of the issues we have considered – children working well together, supporting each other's learning and sharing their opinions with adults – require the child to have confidence and self-esteem. This is a well-recognized aspect of ECEC provision; for example, in England, the EYFS (2012) states that:

Children learn to be strong and independent through positive relationships.
Positive relationships are:
● warm and loving, and foster a sense of belonging;
● sensitive and responsive to the child's needs, feelings and interests;
● supportive of the child's own efforts and independence;
● consistent in setting clear boundaries;
● stimulating;
● built on key person relationships in early years settings.
(Development Matters, 2012: 2)

While in many ways this seems relatively simple and in line with the ideals most ECEC practitioners hold, it has been reported that ECEC practitioners find Personal Social and Emotional Development one of the most challenging aspects of provision to plan for and implement (e.g. Matthieson, 2005). Perhaps one place to start is with how children feel.

Children can feel vulnerable in pre-school settings and classrooms, particularly because of the power held by the adults in the setting. This affects how children experience education and their openness to new learning. Indeed, it is often suggested that children only learn effectively if their self-esteem is positive (Roberts, 2002). A considerable responsibility is thus placed on practitioners to reflect on how they use their power and on how this use affects children, particularly given the vulnerability of the young children we care for.

There are two basic aspects of power which practitioners need to consider in relation to the learning environment. First there is the positive aspect of how practitioners use their power constructively to encourage, to reinforce appropriate child actions and to enhance self-esteem (Lawrence, 1987; see Reading 6.3). Indeed, the importance of maintaining 'high expectations' of children cannot be overemphasized (Gipps and MacGilchrist, 1999). Second, however, there is the potential for the destructive use of such power. This particularly concerns the manner in which practitioners act when 'rules' are broken. This can be negative and damaging, but skilful and aware practitioners will aim to make any necessary *disciplinary* points, ensuring the child is aware of the concern, why this could be problematic and what could be done differently, while remaining calm and preserving the dignity of each child. In Chapter 7 Engagement, we consider behaviour management in greater detail.

'Being positive' involves constant attempts to build on success. The point is to offer suitable challenges and then to make maximum use of the children's achievements to generate still more. This policy assumes that each child will have some successes. Sometimes a child's successes may be difficult to identify. Such difficulties often reveal more about the inability of an adult to understand and diagnose what a child is experiencing. As the psychologist Adler argued many years ago (1927), irrespective of the baseline position, there is always an associated level of challenge – a target for learning achievement – which is appropriate and which can be the subject of genuine praise (Butt, 2011). It may range from being kind to a younger child, building a tower or correctly forming a letter of the alphabet. The appropriateness of the achievement is a matter for the practitioner to judge, but the aim should be to encourage all children to accept challenges and achieve successes (Merrett and Wheldall, 1990).

## 3.3 Developing an inclusive setting

The socio-emotional climate is determined by a number of complex mediating factors. Daily routines, communication, common language challenge creating an environment which is inclusive of all children, particularly where mixed age groups are present (see Chapter 15). An inclusive classroom is one which is consciously designed to enable each child to act as a full participant in activities, to feel themselves and to be a valued member of the group (Kershner, 2009).

One feature which often causes problems is that there are variations in both the quantity and quality of attention that is given to different children. Sadly, this is a clear example of variations in expectation (Gipps and MacGilchrist, 1999). There are many categories around which such differentiation is often found – for example: ability, gender, race and social class (see Chapter 15, section 1). It is very understandable if practitioners tend to deal first with children whose needs press most or whose actions necessitate an immediate response. However, the problem which then arises is that some other children may be consistently passed over (Collins, 1996). While we may have to accept that the needs of all the children in a setting cannot be satisfied simultaneously, where a number of staff are working together plans can be made to ensure that all children, at least some of the time, are receiving some one-to-one engagement with staff. As we discussed earlier in the chapter, these interactions are likely to be crucial in supporting a young child's development.

Differences between children and people must inevitably exist (see Pollard, 1987), but a contrast can be drawn between settings in which the strengths and weaknesses of each child are recognized and in which the particular level of achievement of each child is accepted as a starting point. Where achievements rather than effort or gains are valued, the ethos becomes competitive rather than cooperative, particularly as the children mature. As we have established, children are very astute and will pick up on what is valued and what is not. The overall impact of consistently praising achievements and not providing opportunities for all children to succeed and be motivated is that some children become marginalized. This can have very negative consequences for children's perceptions of themselves as learners (Dweck, 1986, 1999; Reading 2.5).

Praise in itself is also important in the building of positive relationships. Increased attention has been given to the use of praise in recent years, with concerns being raised about praise being given without due care and attention (see for example Henderlong and Lepper, 2002). It has been suggested that praise for ability can reduce motivation (e.g. Mueller and Dweck, 1998). When giving praise we ought to be mindful that it is genuine and that it focuses upon the element of the action that we want to encourage and support – remember we are concerned with supporting children to become independent, motivated life-long learners. Therefore we are less concerned with pointing out the child's achievements; rather, praise is better focused upon the effort, enjoyment and growth. Praise should be given mindfully and take into account a child's age and abilities and be specific. Praising how much a child has shared their love of reading with others, or increased their strength so they can stand alone, might be more supportive in the long term than praising the act itself, as would stating the facts – for example: 'you tried to catch the ball Oscar and you did, you must be very pleased', rather than 'great catching, Oscar'.

We would suggest that an inclusive setting will support children to develop relationships with all of the children in the setting generating understanding and respect for others. Thus, there are some central questions about how children are valued which should be answered by a reflective practitioner. Among them are those which are suggested in **Reflective activity 6.6**. This time they take the form of a checklist.

## Reflective activity 6.6

*Aim:* To evaluate progress towards an inclusive setting.

*Evidence and reflection:* There are many indicators which might be considered – for instance:

1 Are children helped to learn to respect each other? Which is emphasized most, the achievement of children or the learning efforts that are made? Are older children supported to be helpful and play with younger children rather than them always being separated?

2 In decisions about the curriculum, are the interests of each of the children recognized and given appropriate attention? Is the children's previous experience drawn on in your planning?

3 Are the children supported to develop an understanding of their own cultures, religions, communities?

4 Are dimensions of difference (see Chapter 15) recognized and celebrated? Are children supported to understand that others have needs, views, cultures and beliefs different to their own?

5 How wide-ranging are the achievements which are valued? Does every child experience at least some success to reinforce their self-belief and commitment to learning?

*Extension:* Having completed your review, what can you do to increase the sense of inclusion of all children? How could you develop the setting climate to increase children's confidence as learners?

For more extensive elaboration of issues associated with inclusion, see Chapter 15.

## Conclusion

Good relationships are intimately connected to children's well-being and learning. They give pleasure to both children and adults, provide a foundation for learning and pre-empt potential problems. Perhaps, too, an expectation of being caring towards each other may spread among the children and be of longer-term benefit for society more generally.

## Key readings

To further explore how relationships impact upon learning:

Coolahan, K., Fantuzzo, J., Mendez, J. and McDermott, P. (2000) 'Preschool peer interactions and readiness to learn: relationships between classroom peer play and learning behaviors and conduct', *Journal of Educational Psychology*, 92 (3), 458–65.

Mathieson, K. (2005) *Social Skills in the Early Years: Supporting Social and Behavioural Learning.* London: Paul Chapman Publishing.

Papatheodorou, T. and Moyles, J. R. (eds) (2009) *Learning Together in the Early Years: Exploring Relational Pedagogy*. Oxon: Routledge.

Wilcox-Herzog, A. and Kontos, S. (1998) 'The nature of teacher talk in early childhood classrooms and its relationship to children's play with objects and peers', *Journal of Genetic Psychology*, 159 (1): 30–44.

An excellent book for support on gaining young children's perspectives is:

Clark, A. and Moss, P. (2001) *Listening to Young Children: The Mosaic Approach*. London: National Children's Bureau.

One of a number of classic books by Carl Rogers on 'person-centred' theory is:

Rogers, C. (1969) *Freedom to Learn.* New York: Merrill.

On children's confidence and self-esteem:

Roberts, R. (2006) *Self-Esteem and Early Learning: Key People from Birth to School (Zero to Eight).* 3rd edn. London: Paul Chapman.

For more on attachment, see:

Bowlby, J. (2005) *A Secure Base.* Oxon: Routledge.

Elfer, P., Goldschmied, E. and Selleck, D. (2011) (2nd Edition) Key persons in the Nursery and Reception Classes: Building relationships for quality provision, London: David Fulton.

Goldschmied, E. and Jackson, S. (2004) *People Under Three: Young Children in Day Care.* 2nd edn. London: Routledge.

For more on the impact praise can have on young children, see:

Henderlong, J. and Lepper, M. R. (2002) 'The effects of praise on children's intrinsic motivation: a review and synthesis', *Psychological Bulletin*, 128 (5), 774–95.

Mueller, C. M. and Dweck, C. S. (1998) 'Praise for intelligence can undermine children's motivation and performance', *Journal for Personality and Social Psychology*, 75 (1), 33–52.

*Readings for Reflective Teaching in Early Years Education* directly complements and extends the chapters in this book. It has been designed to provide convenient access to key texts. It will be of particular help as a compact and portable library.

The associated website, **reflectiveteaching.co.uk**, offers a wealth of supplementary resources including reflective activities, research briefings, advice on further reading and downloadable diagrams, figures and checklists from the book. It also features a compendium of educational terms, links to useful websites, policy and curriculum documents, and showcases examples of excellent research and practice.

# Engagement
## How are we managing behaviour?

**7**

# Introduction

As we have noted, children's experiences in ECEC settings are likely to be their first experiences away from their families. This new experience is likely to place a number of social demands on them – including, for example, sharing objects and adult attention with a number of other children. This can present challenges for both children and the adults who care for them. 'How to manage behaviour' is an aspect of practice which often assumes enormous significance for student practitioners. We regularly hear such statements as 'We haven't had the lecture on behaviour management yet'. This suggests that perhaps behaviour management is viewed by some students as a series of taught skills which, recipe-like, can be produced and applied to a variety of situations and, if the instructions are followed carefully, then a harmonious situation for both practitioner and child will ensue.

Behaviour management is in fact a much more complex and intricately interwoven series of skills. Although it is certainly the case that in order for effective teaching and learning to take place, behaviour management must already be functioning well, there is no magic wand that can be waved or formula applied in order to produce this desirable state. As you may have inferred from the chapters in this section, our primary focus for behaviour management is creating engaging learning situations (Chapter 8), developing positive relationships (Chapter 6) and supporting children to become inquisitive confident learners, rather than a focus on how to rectify or 'deal with' challenging behaviours.

Children may exhibit behaviours we would like to discourage, but this does not mean they are behaving badly. Gopnik, Meltzoff and Kuhl (1999) explain that a young child's behaviour may arise from a desire to explore and understand; they are, in effect, behaving like scientists, as in the following example, which considers why a child may pull at a lamp cord while they are looking at you.

> A two-year-old doesn't even look at the lamp cord. Instead his hand goes out to touch it as he looks, steadily, gravely, and with great deliberation at you … But this perverse behaviour actually turns out to be quite rational. Two-year-olds have just begun to realise that people have different desires. The grave look is directed at you because you and your reaction are the really interesting thing … The terrible twos reflects a genuine clash between children's need to understand other people and their need to live happily with them … With these two-year-olds, as with scientists, finding the truth is more than a profession – it's a passion.
>
> And of course this passion can overwhelm young children with grief or anger. Learning about expressing emotions appropriately is one of the most complex aspects of understanding ourselves and maintaining relationships with others. The fact that cultures and even individual families differ in their standards for the appropriate display and management of emotions makes this task especially challenging for children … (Gopnik, Meltzoff and Kuhl, 1999: 112)

Thus, supporting children to developing the skills to self-regulate and manage their behaviours – to choose to behave in particular ways – takes time and requires patient guidance.

Two of the TLRP principles are of particular relevance to this chapter.

---

## TLRP principles

**Principle 6: Effective teaching and learning promotes the active engagement of the learner.** A chief goal of teaching and learning should be the promotion of learners' independence and autonomy. This involves acquiring a repertoire of learning strategies and practices, developing positive attitudes towards learning, and confidence in oneself as a good learner.

**Principle 7: Effective teaching and learning fosters both individual and social processes and outcomes.** Learning is a social activity. Learners should be encouraged and helped to work with others, to share ideas and to build knowledge together. Consulting learners about their learning and giving them a voice is both an expectation and a right.

---

# 1 Understanding behaviour

There are a great many explanatory theories about children's behaviour. Three elements are typically posed:

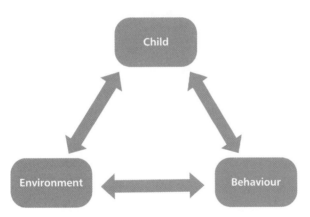

**Figure 7.1**
Elements influencing behaviour

The terminology above is that of Chaplain (2003), who draws on the social learning theory of Bandura (1995, 1997). Bronfenbrenner (1979; Reading 8.4) has a similar conceptualization (see Chapter 8). The key point of each is that the actions taken by anyone relate both to the person they are and to the situation they are in. The role of the reflective practitioner then must initially involve the development of an appreciation of the babies and young children for whom they care; and we must then really think hard about the provision which we make for them, for their behaviour – at least in part – is shaped by the environment within which they are operating.

One aspect of developing this appreciation requires us to take stock of the issues raised in Chapters 1, 2 and 4 of this book and to recognize that children have very different home circumstances. Contemporary societies are seeing extreme differences in wealth and in the associated forms of cultural capital. It is very easy to succumb to stereotypes in seeking to make sense of the complexity of children's lives, but this really should be resisted. Being 'poor' does not denote a lack of commitment to one's children, just as being 'well off' certainly doesn't in itself produce valuable support. Each form of social difference – social class, gender, ethnicity, disability, etc. – is simply a circumstance which needs to be understood. As practitioners we need to do what we can to understand the prior experiences of the babies and young children for whom we care. Some of the ways in which this can be achieved have been touched upon within section 1 of this book.

We ultimately may feel that we have little control over children's lives within their families. Notwithstanding issues of safeguarding. However, by providing a supportive environment and developing positive relationships with children and families, we can influence children's lives. We must believe this, otherwise our belief in our professional roles would diminish. Indeed, children may come into our care with an existing self-concept, formed by the feedback they receive about themselves from others. Many will have a developing self-concept which we have a vital role in nurturing. We need to be able to build on this self-concept by ensuring that the activities we provide encourage the development of confidence and self-esteem. One of the ways in which we can consider whether we are achieving this is to consider whether the needs of the child are being met within the setting.

## 2  Starting from the needs of the child

## 2.1  Well-being and children's behaviour

Babies and children need to feel safe and secure (see Bowlby, Reading 6.4). The well-being of the individual child should always be a central focus of our interactions and we must strive to ensure that all children feel that they are welcome and that they are a valued member of the group. Greig (2001) analyses this from the child's point of view as:

- Am I usually accepted and understood rather than overlooked or scolded by the adults?
- Am I usually glad to be here, rather than eager to leave?

Laevers (2005) describes indicators of emotional well-being in children as:

- Feeling at ease
- Being oneself
- Feeling happy
- Being able to act spontaneously
- Showing vitality
- Showing self-confidence

Placing yourself in the position of the child and using observation to consider the presence of these indicators may be a useful starting point when considering the experiences of the children in your setting. They may help us to understand the extent to which the basic needs of the babies and children in our care are being met.

According to Laevers (2005), the level of well-being in children gives a very good indication of how children are developing emotionally. Good emotional health is a prerequisite for full realization of the child's potential. However, well-being is not only depended on experience in the ECEC setting, it is interdependent on the level of well-being within the family and the wider community. The reflective practitioner must, then, adopt a way of being which promotes an equal and reciprocal dialogue with both children and their families.

## Reflective activity 7.1

*Aim:* To reflect on one child's behaviour and their needs

*Evidence and reflection:* Identify a child within your group to observe. Perhaps you may wish to focus your attention on a child whose behaviour has been causing you concern. Identify:

- The child's initials
- The child's age
- Where the observation took place
- Start and finish time

Carry out short observations, maximum 15 minutes, of the child in the following contexts.

- Alone
- With one other child
- With an adult
- In a group

You could use the observation guides found at **reflectiveteaching.co.uk** and the guidance on observations provided in Chapter 10.

Write down exactly what you see and hear. A useful way to help with this is to imagine that you are describing the situation for someone at the other end of a telephone. This often takes practice so don't be concerned if at first you find this tricky!

Which of the above characteristics of well-being, suggested by Laevers, can you identify within the observations you have made? Are there any causes for concern?

*Extension:* Discuss your findings with a colleague. Do these observations raise any issues which need further consideration? Do the needs of the child, specifically in terms of well-being, appear to be being met? Are further observations required?

By carrying out the above activity on a number of occasions it is possible to get immediate feedback in terms of a child's well-being. If this is deemed low, then, as a responsible professional, we would wish to intervene with a clear aim to improve this state. How this can be achieved may not immediately be apparent. Consideration of particular children, their experiences inside and outside of the setting, perhaps with a colleague, ought to allow for some ways forward to be identified. This may be as simple as introducing some one-to-one support focusing on building confidence, changing routines to better meet the child's needs, or recognition that further support and advice is required. Hopefully, as these developments take shape and the child's needs are being better met, challenging behaviours may decrease or diminish.

## 2.2 Involvement and children's behaviour

How children feel about themselves will affect how they approach activities; this will affect their concentration and their ability to settle and focus and be involved in the tasks of the day (Greig, 2001). Involvement is defined by the Organisation for Economic Co-operation and Development (*OECD*, 2004) as 'a state of being' that can be experienced by any individual of any age, the key characteristics of which are concentration, strong intrinsic motivation, fascination and intensity of functioning. Operating at this level of high involvement contributes to the desirable state referred to by Laevers (2005) as 'deep level learning'. This type of intense mental activity, he states, cannot happen without involvement, the signs of which might include:

- Concentration
- Energy
- Complexity and creativity
- Perseverance
- Precision
- Use of language
- Satisfaction

### Reflective activity 7.2

*Aim:* To consider a child's well-being in relation to their behaviour.

*Evidence and reflection:* Review the observations that you made in **Reflective activity 7.1**. Which of the above characteristics of well-being are visible in these observations?

Now carry out two further observations of the same child, first in an activity of their choice and secondly in an activity led by an adult.

- Analyse these observations with reference to the signs of involvement above.
- Compare and contrast the observations.
- What conclusions can you draw?

Levels of involvement can and will vary: some children will prefer particular tasks over others and children will have different interests at times but, in general, children are more likely to be involved in their learning where they have been able to exercise a certain amount of choice over the activities and, with older children, where there are multiple opportunities for them to be involved in discussion. Large or whole-group activities, even those designed to support social and emotional development can be inappropriate and/or lack interest for young children. We have observed numerous activities, for example circle time, which have children present, seated in the circle, but with minds elsewhere! Thus, when considering behaviour management once the well-being of the children has been considered, looking at session planning, activities and opportunities for child involvement can be extremely useful (see Laevers, Reading 7.1).

---

### Case study 7.1 Reflecting on actions

Staff in a one pre-school setting for children aged 3 to 5 years noted that lunch often started well but ended with children engaging in undesirable activities towards the end of the meal. This included entering the toilets and splashing water on the floor or on each other. The immediate response was to limit access to the bathroom. During a session of reflection the staff team considered the action they had taken. In general, practice at the setting focused on encouraging and supporting the children to develop their independence, i.e. to pour their own drinks and take themselves to the bathroom, yet staff had made a decision to take this away from the children to prevent the challenging behaviours. Noting this tension, they considered why this behaviour was developing. They noted that many of the children were finishing eating and were becoming bored. One practitioner asked why lunch was so long. A member of staff who had worked at the setting for many years stated that lunch had been designed to fit in with staff breaks, rather than being designed based upon the needs of the children. Discussions ensued and the staff team decided to shorten lunch by 15 minutes, with one member of staff staying to clean up so that any child who needed longer would stay and be properly supervised. One member of staff noted that it was strange that we had not thought about this until somebody asked the question 'Why are things this way?'.

This case acts as a reminder of the value of asking questions, reflecting on actions and not just accepting and working within established routines.

---

## 2.3 The Leuven Involvement Scale (LIS)

So far, the suggestions we have made involve observing children for 'general' signs of well-being and involvement. The Leuven Involvement Scale (LIS) allows you to apply a process whereby you can make more detailed judgements about the depth of these states in children. The main focus of this is to be able to look at the educational experience from the point of view of the child. The LIS uses a five-point graded scale, explained in **Table 7.1**.

Table 7.1 Identifying levels of involvement – Leuven Involvement Scale (LIS)

| Level of involvement | Characteristics |
| --- | --- |
| Level 1<br>Low level involvement | The child can appear mentally absent. Any action can appear purely repetitive. |
| Level 2 | The child is engaged in an activity but is open to many distractions and will not necessarily return to the activity voluntarily. |
| Level 3 | The child is engaged in an activity but not really involved in it. Energy and enthusiasm and sustained concentration appear to be lacking. |
| Level 4 | Moments of intense mental activity occur and the motivation is there to sustain this even after interruptions or distractions. |
| Level 5<br>High level involvement | Total involvement expressed by concentration and absolute continuous and sustained involvement. Any interruption would be experienced as a frustrating rupture of a smoothly running activity. The child shows concentration, creativity, energy and perseverance. |

In order to apply this scale to children's behaviours, it is necessary for the adult to try to become the child – that is, to think oneself into the mind of the child, to empathize, in order to be able to assess the observed experience. It may be useful to consider each of these levels in relation to children's behaviour. Are children who are involved in tasks less likely to become involved in disruptive or challenging behaviours? Are children who are struggling to settle less likely to be able to become involved? (see Broadbent, Reading 7.2).

Laevers describes Level 5 of the LIS, the state of total concentration, as a 'state of flow'. This is based on the work of Csikszentmihalyi (1979), who describes this state of flow as where a great deal of mental energy is being used in an efficient way. Thus, when conducting observations of children's levels of involvement, one must consider whether the activity itself is too easy or beyond the present capabilities of the child, as this is likely to impact upon involvement. Katz, in Laevers (1993), frames some questions we can ask of our settings:

- Are most of the activities interesting, rather than frivolous or boring?

- Are most of the activities meaningful, rather than trivial or mindless?

- Are most of the activities engaging and absorbing, rather than just amusing, fun, entertaining or exciting?

The answers to the questions above are likely to have a direct link to the types of behaviour displayed

## Expert question

**Balance:** Does the curriculum-as-experienced offer everything which each child has a right to expect?

This question contributes to a conceptual framework representing enduring issues and practitioner expertise (see Chapter 16).

in any setting. In the following chapters we will consider how we can provide a range of appropriate and engaging activities for all of the children in your setting. Suffice to say not doing so may impact upon the behaviours of the children in our care.

## 2.4 Expectations and encouragement

Children and young people are, just like most of us, extremely good at sensing the beliefs, motivations and dispositions of others. Practitioners who appear to presume that children are 'up to no good' or are unable to manage interactions are likely to engender similarly guarded responses. On the other hand, if a practitioner is able to convey a set of expectations which presumes capability, it is likely that children will try to respond. Most, if not all, of the children we care for will need our support to develop the skills needed to navigate the complexities of social relationships. Chapter 6 provides a detailed discussion of this. In relation to behaviour management, research has shown us that there are more disputes between children, which require adult intervention to resolve, where children are not seen to be capable of managing their relationships and thus are not supported to develop the skills needed. Research conducted by Kutnick et al. (2007) found that pre-school children are able to develop positive relationships with their peers, which involved turn-taking, listening and resolving their own disputes when supported to develop the skills needed to do so. Indeed, the children involved were much more capable of resolving disputes with their peers than staff had anticipated. The work of Cathy Ota and colleagues (n.d.) has shown that babies, when the practitioners support them to develop the skills and have expectations that they will interact, are much more capable of engaging in positive peer interactions than practitioners anticipated. Practitioners therefore need to take control of their own expectations, and to review these carefully – particularly in relation to personal theories about children's capabilities within social situations. The most realistic and effective strategy is to consistently convey presumptions of the best from children, while watching carefully for signs that children need your support.

As we have noted, it helps to 'credit' children with what they do, rather than focus on deficits and failures. It is extremely important to use praise as a motivator for desirable behaviour, but we need to be very sure about what we are praising. Praise too often can be 'empty' – for example, by overuse of 'Well done!' or 'That was really good work!' Praise needs to be specific in terms of what was done well, as this is likely to encourage intrinsic motivation in the child (see Rogers, 2011; Dweck, 2006). Praise attached to children negotiating with each other, playing well together or alongside each other is key here. Praising good listening could be useful. Many children, and adults, find it difficult to really listen to what others say. Pointing out to children what this involves and praising it when it is seen can go a long way to supporting the development of good relationships in any ECEC setting.

## 3 Behaviour management: Practitioner experience

In the previous section we have considered behaviour management from the perspective of the child. In this section we will consider behaviour management from the perspective of the practitioner. Of course, the two are inextricably linked.

# 3.1 Self-presentation

Starting any new job, at any point in one's life, brings with it new challenges and it is not uncommon to feel somewhat deskilled at the start. It does take time to find one's way around a new work environment and build relationships with new colleagues. Children of any age group, will be watching your every move and every response to individuals within the group, analysing your words and actions and relating these to their expected framework for practitioner behaviour. They are forming an opinion of how you present yourself from day one. They will be seeking to determine what responses they are likely to gain from you. Remember the child pulling the light cord? Your responses and actions are likely to be fascinating to young children and some may 'test' your responses. Others may hang back and see what happens. If we think back to the previous section, we considered how children need to feel secure. Initial priorities must therefore involve conveying to children that we care about them, their feelings and their emotions. Only then can a mutual respect begin to develop. Whether new to the role, the job, or experienced, the ways in which we present ourselves to others makes a huge difference to how they see us and, in turn, how they behave (see Sheridan, **Reading 7.2**).

## Confidence

Inexperienced practitioners, in particular, may feel particularly anxious about their first encounter with a new family or group of children. Even if you are not feeling particularly confident, it is extremely important to be able to convey a sense of calm confidence in your initial contact. This can be achieved by remembering to pay attention to a number of actions over which you do have control.

First, do remember to breathe! A few good, deep breaths can steady your voice and help you look more relaxed. Secondly, remember to smile while you are speaking. These are both important as they quickly communicate an expectation that you have confidence. Think about where you have positioned yourself in relation to the children. Consider also your posture. Do you look confident in your appearance? Are you able to make eye contact with the adults and the children? All of these actions are very similar to the advice given to actors or singers about to engage with an audience and indeed there are many similarities between the performing arts and teaching, in terms of communication skills. Each time you meet a new family and child, you will need to rehearse and produce this repertoire of skills again, with the aim of presenting as open and relaxed body language as possible.

Confidence is also about being able to admit to making a mistake or not knowing the answer. We are not infallible and if we can model this aspect for children, where mistakes are equal to a part of learning and asking others is part of a journey of learning, then children too are likely to be more willing to persevere or 'have a go'.

## Communication

The way in which you use your voice will also have an impact on the relationships that you build. Your enthusiasm can influence children in a positive manner. The ability to project one's voice is a learned skill and you may need to practise until it feels comfortable. Children respond well to voices that are pleasant and engaging, but you do also need to be able to convey energy and enthusiasm in your communication. If you are unused to communicating in a way that would encourage children to respond positively, try the following:

---

### Reflective activity 7.3

*Aim:* To reflect upon how adults communicate with babies and/or young children.

*Evidence and reflection:* Observe a range of adults communicating with young children. Analyse this communication in terms of how they use their voices and record your notes.

It would be helpful if you could identify somebody who you feel has a good way of interacting with babies or young children, somebody who the children find engaging. Pay particular attention to the ways in which the adult is communicating with the children.

- Describe how they communicate verbally.
- Describe how they communicate non-verbally.
- Consider the language they use.

Consider the key aspects of their manner. Are they similar to your own? Different? Is there anything you can take from your observations to develop your own practice? Remember, while you may have new ideas to test and trial you don't want to overact. As we said earlier, children are skilled at detecting motivations and dispositions!

---

When adults speak to children they often use a slightly higher pitch of voice than is normal. This is intentional and conveys a friendly and positive communicative tone. Try to emulate this yourself, either by talking to a very young child, or alternatively a domestic pet. Parents, and mothers in particular, use this type of speech intuitively in communicating with babies, where they use a higher than normal pitch and articulate words slowly and clearly. This, combined with somewhat over-exaggerated facial gestures and smiling, forms what is referred to by Trevarthen (2004) and Malloch (1997) respectively as 'motherese' and more recently as 'child-directed speech' (CDS), as it is not only mothers who modify their speech (see Peccei, 2006). The younger the child, the more important it is to develop this skill, as the child's response may well be as much towards the tone in which the communication takes place as the actual words themselves. Sensitivity is extremely important in being able to communicate emotional tone (see Argyle, Reading 7.4).

If you work with large groups of children or in a room or outdoor area which can become noisy, in order to maintain a healthy classroom voice it is really important to work towards being able to maintain your communication with children at an appropriate volume which does not over-tire your voice. If too loud, then the children are likely to copy you and become louder themselves. It is always a better idea to walk across a room, get down to the child's level and speak to a child individually, rather than shout across the room. However, your voice can be put to very good effect by increasing the volume occasionally, in order to raise awareness of a situation. The children will notice this change in volume and it can be very helpful if you need to make the children aware of a danger, for example. The aim is to be able to communicate a sense of calm through your physical and vocal presence which models respectful communication. This will gain the attention of the children and encourage them to engage positively with the learning environment.

While the voice is a useful tool, what is said is also of great significance. Every time we speak to children, for whatever purpose, we have educational opportunities. In relation to behaviour, the aim can be both to keep them focused as effectively as possible as a means to educational ends, and also to support the development of their social skills and competencies. But we must endeavour to use language which is clear to the child, and to use words that they understand.

---

## Case study 7.2 Reflecting on actions and established routines

A recollection from my very first day at school, aged 4 years and 8 months, is that I was very upset because my mother was not in the classroom with me. I do remember that the practitioner spent time trying to convince me that my mother would in fact return and I did calm down. However, for some reason we were then all lined up alphabetically and I was first in the line – a process that I had to resign myself to accommodating throughout my school life, as my surname began with an 'A'. I was asked by the practitioner to go over and *sit on the form,* which provided the cue for me to erupt into floods of tears again. Why? I was unaware of this meaning of the word 'form', where to find it or what to do.

---

It is extremely important that we use language which is accessible to children, remembering that children may speak a different dialect, or language, from the one that we produce. The language also needs to be at the right level for the age and stage of development of the child. The word 'form' can mean a bench without a back support, but is not often used in this context and certainly not by young children.

There were other aspects that might have been considered here. The practitioner was reliant on a verbal message being understood, but the addition of a visual clue would have helped considerably in ensuring understanding, and nowadays is even more important from the point of view of children whose first language is not that spoken within the setting. Rogers and McPherson (2008) remind us that our use of language will determine our ability to enthuse and engage children in their learning. The younger the child, the simpler the language needs to be.

## Humour

Children respond well to the use of humour and to adults who are able to relax enough into their roles in order to be able to make use of this as a motivational tool. It is important to be able to laugh together, and humour can often be put to very good use in order to defuse otherwise tense situations. If we want children to feel relaxed and secure we must also work towards feeling relaxed and secure in our roles so we can engage in fun, enjoyable activities with the children. Where children feel safe, relaxed and are enjoying an activity, behavioural issues are likely to be kept to a minimum.

# 3.2 Practitioner characteristics and beliefs

Chapter 6 considers relationships and how these impact upon children's development. It is pertinent to revisit here how the ways in which adults behave influence the ways in which children behave.

---

### Reflective activity 7.4

*Aim:* To reflect upon the impact practitioners have on children's behaviours.

*Evidence and reflection:* It might be appropriate at this point to reflect on the practitioners you experienced as a child. Though you may have to consider practitioners you experienced when you were older than the children you work with now, this is still potentially a very helpful exercise.

- Think about a practitioner that you liked at school. Why did you like that person? What characteristics did they demonstrate? Record your thoughts.
- Now think about a practitioner that you did not like. Why did you not like that person? What characteristics did they demonstrate? Record your thoughts.
- If possible, share your thoughts with another student or colleague and note the similarities and differences.

What does this tell you about the characteristics you favour? How does this align with how you convey yourself within the setting? Can you recall how these different practitioners impacted upon your behaviours?

---

It is very likely that some of the reasons that you noted above would be in terms of how the practitioner responded to you as a person, how they made you feel, as well as how they managed behaviour.

Practitioner characteristics have a huge impact on children's behaviour. Research conducted by Sheridan (2007) found that practitioners who asserted dominance and demanded obedience from children led to children in these settings having a greater number of conflicts than children attending settings which did not operate in such a way. Conversely, Sheridan found practitioners with a 'democratic style', who fostered trust, respect and reciprocity, promoted much greater cooperation among children and their peers leading to fewer disputes. How practitioners behave can determine how children behave.

## Reflective activity 7.5

*Aim:* To reflect upon how you think children should behave and why.

*Evidence and reflection:* You must be honest with yourself during this activity. This is about what you feel, not what you think you should write!

What are your views on how children should behave?

- What influences this perspective?
- Record your thoughts and make some notes.
- If possible, share your views with other students or colleagues and note the similarities and differences.

*Extension:* Think about how the views you hold about how children should behave influence your behaviours and styles of practice. Look for both the positive and potentially negative outcomes of such behaviours and styles of practice.

Bullock and Brownhill (2011) stress that our own practice in managing behaviour should never be static but needs to be constantly reflected upon, reviewed, analysed and developed through discussion with colleagues, research and taking part in Continuing Professional Development (CPD) opportunities.

## 3.3 Management skills

While we have considered the feelings of anxiety which may arise as we start new jobs, take on new roles or meet families and children for the first time, it is also important to consider managerial responsibilities. Management skills are required in many ECEC positions – for example, room leader, deputy manager, setting manager, classroom teacher. While we have considered some of the key characteristics of a good manager in Chapter 6, we will here consider here some of the managerial skills which may impact upon behaviour management.

### Planning

Planning is extremely important in terms of managing behaviour successfully, both from the point of view of the children, but also in reducing unnecessary stress from the practitioner's point of view. Planning is discussed in depth in Chapter 10. To support cycles of positive behaviour we need to be sure that there are opportunities for children to be engaged, to explore alone, to work with peers and to engage with adults. It is wise to have a backup plan to avoid periods of boredom or disinterest. Having activities and games which can be drawn upon when you sense that there needs to be a change, perhaps when there has been a disruption, the children are unsettled, or a planned activity isn't going well and interest is waning, can be extremely useful. Good practice is not about resolutely seeing a plan through; it is about modifying your plans in line with the needs of the children and the feedback you are receiving from them – be it verbal or non-verbal.

It is common practice in primary schools and some pre-schools settings in the UK to gather the children together on the carpet area for group teaching, but due consideration must be given to the length of time that children are expected to sit, often on a floor. There is a tendency as children approach and enter statutory schooling to keep children sitting for long periods of time, particularly where the practitioner is very articulate and likes to talk. Remember that the group is made up of children with a number of equally important learning styles and we must take all of these into consideration. Some questions about this practice that could be posed in order to promote positive behaviour:

- How comfortable would you be sitting in that position?
- For how long?
- For how long are the children able to remain engaged in this type of task?
- Could this activity be planned in other ways?

Again, remember that sitting with established routines may not be the best way forward. Questioning and reconsidering plans can often be very valuable. If the children are not engaged in the activity, perhaps even with one or two wandering to other parts of the room, they are telling you that this activity is not capturing their interests and isn't appropriate for them. (The learning environment is also important here; we consider this in detail in Chapter 8.)

## Routine

Another aspect of behaviour management worth consideration is the establishment of routines. This can both help children feel secure and develop their independence, as they know what to expect.

Bearing in mind the use of appropriate language, it is a good idea to establish setting rules and routines together with the children from the outset. For example, Rogers and McPherson (2008) suggest the use of an agreed signal to attract the attention of the whole group, rather than having to raise your voice. An example of an audible signal, for older children, would be, for example, to clap a short rhythm and ask the children to clap it back to you. This is also very useful in terms of promoting listening skills in young children. Place yourself in the position of the child: you are enjoying yourself and then you are told to stop. Why? Understanding what comes next and making it part of the expected form of the day can help to minimize frustrations that can lead to undesirable behaviours. For babies and young children, showing what will happen with props can be useful – for example, showing a child that it is snack time by showing them a cup and a piece of fruit, or that it is outdoor time by showing them a coat.

Another routine to consider is how to manage the transition, for older children in the setting, between the 'carpet' to 'work' areas or from free play to story time. If you have large numbers of children sitting in front of you, it is never a good idea to say to all at once, 'Off you go!' Think of creative ways to manage this type of transition, such as 'All those wearing red socks', or 'All those with blue eyes'. The important point here is to vary the criteria – and make it fun and prevent a sudden rush of children through one small door!

Another important routine is how children leave at the end of the day. In Swedish schools, a frequently adopted routine is where the practitioner stands at the door and shakes hands with each child individually as they leave, making eye contact and saying goodbye, using each child's name. At weekends the reciprocal greeting of wishing each other a pleasant weekend is used. This reinforces social norms and promotes a feeling of 'belonging' in that community. Greig (2001: 31) describes this type of experience as 'feeling welcome rather than being captured'. While children may leave your setting at different times, having a routine such as this may still support the child to feel welcome and part of the setting community.

---

## Case study 7.3 Reflecting on our use of language

I was working as a short-term supply practitioner in a nursery setting in a school. On arrival on my first day, I was informed that the class had 'gym time' in the main hall that morning, which would involve finding and setting up equipment in a space with which I was unfamiliar. I decided not to take the class to the hall that day, because of not being prepared for this event. I thought that the children would not notice – but they did! Things ran smoothly until snack time, when a stream of children informed me that snack came after gym, not before, and other children asked when they should get changed for gym.

I had sorely underestimated these young children in terms of the importance of routine as well as the fact that I was obviously denying them access to something for which they were well prepared and were looking forward to. The result was a lot of difficulties in managing the children, but on reflection, I had to admit that I was the cause. I had assumed that they would not notice if we had gym or not and, as a result, had not taken into consideration the views of children.

---

# 4 Behaviour management: Practical guidance

We have made a case for the behaviour management of young children being seen as part of a broader need to consider the experiences of the child, the adults they have contact with and thus the learning environment that they are operating within. We do of course also understand that there will be times when we must manage undesirable or challenging behaviours. In this final section we will explore the benefit of having clear rules, identifying and working with children who give us cause for concern, and approaches to dealing with undesirable behaviours in babies and young children (see Graves and Arbor, Reading 7.5).

## 4.1 Rules

When developing rules, it is important to understand that we are not thinking just about what makes life easy, but about what allows the children to explore, develop and build confidence in a safe environment.

## Reflective activity 7.6

*Aim:* To reflect on how you convey to children the behaviours which are and are not acceptable in particular circumstances.

*Evidence and reflection:* Consider one particular aspect of behaviour – for example,
**Shouting out**

- In what situations do you think is it acceptable to shout out?
- When is it not acceptable to shout out?
- How do children know what is acceptable behaviour?
- How do they learn this?
- How do we teach them?

Record some thoughts on the above questions and share your ideas with another student or colleague. Again, compare and contrast the similarities and differences in your answers.

Reflection on this seemingly simple aspect of behaviour management is a good starting point for a consideration of the ways in which children can be made aware of the rules and the expectations of the adults in the setting. Sometimes when we break things down to their small parts in this way, we realize that the rules and our expectations may not be as clear to the children as we had first thought.

The function of rules is to assist us in controlling situations, as opposed to controlling children, and for all to accept the responsibilities that flow from these. The setting ought to have a Behaviour Management Policy, to which all adults in the setting are expected to subscribe and which will state the overarching philosophy of the setting in relation to this aspect of working with children. If we assume that our intention is indeed to help children internalize pro-social values, then when developing rules we must develop them as part of a process of working towards the promotion of positive behaviour. Yet, it is extremely important to realize that having rules and enforcing them can cause the very behaviours, which stem from frustration and anger, that we are trying to avoid.

In addition to making our expectations clear, it is also crucial that rules are discussed and, where appropriate, developed with the children. Ensuring children have a voice is likely to be a crucial aspect of positive behaviour management. You can find more on this in Chapter 8.

When considering behaviour management and rules, Roffey and O'Reirdan (1997) pose the following questions:

- Do children understand what behaviours are expected?
- Are they able to do what is being asked of them?
- Do they have an understanding of why they need to behave in certain ways?
- Is cooperation in the child's interests?

Rogers (2011) discusses the distinction between negotiable and non-negotiable rules. The non-negotiable rules generally encompass issues of health and safety, for example.

Negotiable rules allow you to agree and establish the rules or norms for behaviour. The most effective way to do this is through discussion with the children. For example, the issue of acceptable noise levels would come into this category. While this represents an individual tolerance level for practitioners, there does need to be a shared understanding of what constitutes a 'good learning environment' and how this can change in different situations and contexts – for example, the need for 'indoor voices' and 'outdoor voices'. The aim of setting rules is to be able to set behaviour within an enabling framework, not to establish a list of rigid commands.

Areas where we may well have to establish rules with young children might include:

- Movement around the setting indoors and outdoors.
- How to get help when it is needed.
- Access to drinks/snacks.
- Toilet visits.
- Consequences of undesirable behaviour.

Once the rules are established, the manner in which we enforce all of the above is extremely important in terms of how successful our management of behaviour will be. Rogers and McPherson (2008) stress the importance of avoiding confrontation with individual children wherever possible, the use of positive corrective language and, in the application of behaviour consequences, the importance of emphasizing the fair, instilling a sense of solutions certainty. Above all, it is extremely important in difficult situations to be seen to be consistent and also to ensure that we do follow through with the expected consequences. It is important the children think that things in the setting are 'fair'.

With babies and young children, we should see disputes as opportunities for learning: opportunities to understand how to share, to develop understandings of other children's feelings and needs, to engage in problem-solving to find solutions – perhaps with adult support. Consistent and calm support from adults using conflict resolution techniques similar to those described as the six steps to conflict resolution would be useful (see HighScope and **reflectiveteaching.co.uk** for more on this).

**WWW. ↺**

Having rules is one thing; being consistent about expectations and about the following of rules is another. We can all imagine scenarios when rules benefit from being adjusted or broken. For young children, and indeed for many adults, seeing rules we are expected to follow being 'bent' can cause confusion and upset. Research has shown that where expectations are clear and consistent and are followed by all adults, the greater the likelihood of the rule having an impact on a child's behaviour.

## 4.2 Children who present as a cause for concern

While we can endeavour to develop an environment which minimizes challenging or undesirable behaviours, there will be times when children give us cause for concern. Establishing what the concern is, why this may have arisen and how to approach the issue requires careful thought. We have a chapter devoted to inclusion in Part Four of this book.

It is pertinent to note here that children with social, emotional and behavioural difficulties may cause concern and may present behaviours which are more complex to manage. However, the majority of children will respond to the general behaviour management strategies described here, and these will also be useful to children who have specific social, emotional and behavioural difficulties.

Initial approaches to identifying the cause for concern would involve observing the child. Such observations can help identify how the child relates to other children and adults and what behaviours they are displaying which may concern you. Such behaviours could include:

- Being withdrawn and not wanting to interact with others.
- Seeming unable to develop communication skills.
- Verbally or physically aggressive behaviours.
- Inappropriate sexual behaviours.

Most children will display a number of behaviours at various times. It is only when they are persistent, troublesome and unusual for a child of that age that there is a cause for concern.

If you are concerned about a child's behaviour, the following approach might be taken to help you to decide what to do next.

1  Conduct several observations and identify the behaviour and what it is about them which concerns you. Discuss this observation with your manager or person responsible for children with behaviour and/or learning difficulties in your setting, to get their perspective and advice.

2  If you remain concerned, following your setting guidelines, discuss these concerns with the family. Tread carefully; the aim is not to upset or worry the family. Find out if they have noticed the behaviour, if they are aware of its origin.

3  If you remain concerned, develop a plan to do more detailed observations of the child. You could use the ABC approach (**Table 7.2**). Use these to develop a plan with all staff to support the child to move past this behaviour. Inform the family of your approach and work with them, so that they can follow a similar approach at home if necessary.

4  If you are concerned about developmental issues, contact the appropriate adviser – e.g. speech therapist. Talk to the family at all points so they are aware, and follow your setting guidelines.

5  If you have issues related to safeguarding, follow the procedure laid out by your setting.

6  Review the child's progress at regular intervals with the family. If the child is progressing, then continue with your plan, adapting as needed.

7  If you do not believe the child is making progress, discuss your concerns with the family and follow your setting guidelines for gaining support from your local advisor.

# 4.3 Practical approaches to managing undesirable behaviours

Ultimately you need to be able to understand a child's behaviour to be in a position to manage the behaviour. The 'ABC' of behaviour management, an overview of which is provided in **Table 7.2**, can be a useful approach to take.

Table 7.2 The ABC approach to behaviour management

| Stage | Undesirable behaviour | Desirable behaviour |
|-------|----------------------|---------------------|
| **A** – Antecedents | What triggers the behaviour? | What could change to make this behaviour less likely? |
| **B** – Behaviour | What is the child doing? | What behaviour would be more appropriate? |
| **C** – Consequences | What happens as a result of the behaviour? What could be done instead? | What could you do to encourage the more desirable behaviour? |

The consequence of what happens to the child as a result of their behaviour can be either negative or positive. If the child takes something from another child, then the outcome is positive unless you (or another) intervene.

As we have discussed, we need to monitor our own behaviours, as these influence the children's behaviours. We need to be mindful of staying calm, as when we are angered we can say things or behave in ways we may later wish we had not. Such uncontrolled use of power is a long way from establishing legitimated authority and respect, and we may see children exerting their power on others in the setting if they observe that this can have the desired outcome – e.g. getting their own way.

Standing back from this a little, the basic point is that to establish our authority we must think carefully about what we say and how we say it. In principle, practitioner language to build good discipline should:

- connect personally with the child;
- identify the behaviour which needs to change;
- encourage re-engagement with the tasks;
- minimize disruption to others;
- follow through to ensure conformity.

Of course, this will play out differently with children of different ages.

## Babies

It is crucial to see a baby's behaviour as their way of giving you messages about what they do and do not like; what they want and do not want. When a baby spits food out they are not misbehaving, they are simply indicating that they do not like the food you have given them. We must remember this is one of the few ways they have of conveying this information. As a baby begins to develop their gross motor movements and they seek to explore their environment, they may grab and pull. If a baby shows an interest in something, support them to explore the object – for example, show them how it moves. However, at times the behaviour may be undesirable – for example, pulling glasses from your face. One of the best ways for managing this is to use distraction. Encouraging the baby to focus on something else can stop the behaviour.

## Toddlers

As we noted earlier in this chapter, young children are exploring the environment and trying to understand human interactions. Distracting a young child can be useful, but you may also want to help build their understanding. If they reach to pull your glasses, you can explain to them very clearly 'I do not like it when you do that, it hurts my ears', 'I won't be able to see if my glasses get broken'. Using these messages can help to build the child's understanding of both their own and others' emotions.

Young children also want to feel they have some control over their lives. Saying 'No' can make them frustrated and increase the likelihood of undesirable behaviours. Offering them a choice and explaining why this is the case can be helpful, as can praising other behaviours.

## Children approaching school age

It can be easy to forget that children approaching school age are still very much in the process of learning about their emotions and how to express them. The methods of offering choice and distracting can still be useful, but you may need to become much clearer that some behaviours are unacceptable. Listening to the child and explaining to them that you hear what they are saying and that you understand how they feel can be helpful. Get down to their level so you have direct eye contact: 'I can see you are cross that the bridge you built has been knocked over; you must be angry as it took you so long to build it.' From this point you can then begin to ask them to consider how to move forward.

## Children in the first years of statutory schooling

Again, get down the level of the child if you are picking up on a particular behaviour. State clearly and concisely what the issue is. Do not allow yourself to get drawn up into a debate and give yourself a way to move on so the issue is not prolonged. The use of phrases such as 'Thank you for putting the book back', 'Thank you for helping Anna' gives the impression that the conversation is complete, that you have high expectations of them and helps to finish on a positive note.

Although audio-recordings never seem flattering, recording yourself interacting with children can be a useful way of considering how you are expressing yourself, whether there are times when children seem to become bored or the day loses its flow. Listening to how often you use reprimands can also be useful. Could you do anything differently? You can also ask yourself whether something matters. Pick your moments. There is little point in repeatedly picking up on a particular behaviour if it does not really matter.

## Conclusion

In this chapter we have considered how children's behaviour is impacted upon by their environment. Specifically, we have considered behaviour management from two positions: that of the child and that of the practitioner. It should now be clear that managing behaviour requires much more than the application of a series of techniques that, if known, would produce an effective practitioner. It requires a combination of personal skills, including 'soft skills', together with effective management techniques on the part of the practitioner. This must be tempered with a responsive awareness to the child's needs and this is modified by what we know about the child as a person and their place in the family and community. Behaviour management is complex.

The discourse in this chapter has been based on the social-constructivist theories of Vygotsky and Bruner, which acknowledge that adults and children co-construct their world through reciprocal dialogue and interaction. For this reason we must never allow our practice to become static and repetitive. What works in one situation may not work within another and in order to be able to meet the very varied needs of the children we are working with, we as adults must be able to reflect on our practice and formulate sensible next steps for ourselves and children as a result.

As practitioners, we must be able to model the type of behaviour that we hope to have reciprocated by the children and should be working towards the promotion of what Roffey (2011) describes as the 'pro-social classroom', which involves the understanding of pro-social and relational skills. If we are prepared to engage with children in this way, the benefits are great in terms of involvement and engagement of children, which also can lead to intrinsic motivation, increased resilience and enhanced achievement.

We must also remember that there is no perfect practitioner and no perfect group of children either. Adults and children are subject to 'off days' through feeling tired or unwell, or being subject to any number of personal circumstances that affect each and every one of us emotionally.

## Key readings

For additional support on identifying the steps to follow to manage behaviour, visit the curriculum section of the HighScope website.

For a helpful discussion of why children display certain behaviours, try:

Mathieson, K. (2012) *Understanding Young Children's Behaviour*. London: Practical Preschool.

Practical guidance on how to encourage positive behaviours in your setting is provided by:

Drifte, C. (2001) *Encouraging Positive Behaviour in the Early Years: A Practical Guide*. London: Paul Chapman.

Rogers, B. (2011) *Classroom Behaviour: A Practical Guide to Effective Teaching, Behaviour Management and Colleague Support*. 3rd edn. London: Sage Publications Ltd.

When thinking about creating environments to support positive behaviour, many of the texts we have recommended will be useful. The following may also be helpful:

Greig, L. (2001) *Supporting Development and Learning 3–5*. Learning Teaching Scotland: Early Education Support.

Jennings, P. and Greenberg, M. (2009) 'The prosocial classroom: Teacher and emotional competence in relation to student and classroom outcomes', *Review of Educational Research*, 79, 491.

Rayna, S. and Laevers, F. (2011) 'Understanding children from 0–3 years of age and its implications for education. what's new on the babies' side? origins and evolutions', *European Early Childhood Education Research Journal*, 19 (2), 161–72.

***Readings for Reflective Teaching in Early Years Education*** directly complements and extends the chapters in this book. It has been designed to provide convenient access to key texts. It will be of particular help as a compact and portable library.

The associated website, **reflectiveteaching.co.uk**, offers a wealth of supplementary resources including reflective activities, research briefings, advice on further reading and downloadable diagrams, figures and checklists from the book. It also features a compendium of educational terms, links to useful websites, policy and curriculum documents, and showcases examples of excellent research and practice.

# Spaces
## How are we creating environments for learning?

**8**

# Introduction

Within ECEC, children normally experience a range of learning environments, both indoors and outdoors, that are often planned in detail by practitioners. This is in addition to the other learning environments they experience in their home and community. In this chapter we discuss the range of factors involved in creating and maintaining effective spaces for children's well-being, development and learning. This includes consideration of both *what* is provided for children and the *way* it is provided (Moyles, Adams and Musgrove, 2002; see Reading 8.1).

In relation to the *way* the environment is established, resourced and organized, the educational *values* of the early years practitioner are seen as a key factor. We therefore begin by considering how cultural values influence the learning spaces that are constructed for children and draw on the typology of learning environments proposed by Claxton and Carr (2004) to reflect on how the environment may afford a variety of educational outcomes.

We then move on to consider the impact of the increasing trend in both public policy and practice in ECEC towards fostering children's participation and voice. The implications of a more 'democratic' and participatory approach for developing children's learning environments are discussed, followed by recent research focused on investigating effective environments for children under 3 years of age in early years settings.

Over the past ten years or so, far greater attention has been paid to the significance of outdoor environments in ECEC. These are discussed in detail, highlighting four particular aspects of outdoor environments: the unique opportunities of outdoor spaces; the particular benefits of 'wild' natural environments; the need for opportunities for 'positive risk-taking'; and the impact on well-being.

Finally, we discuss the impact of digital technologies on learning environments in the early years and the potential of digital spaces in learning environments.

---

## TLRP principles

Two principles are of particular relevance to this chapter on learning environments:

**Principle 8: Effective teaching and learning recognizes the significance of informal learning.** Informal learning, such as learning out of school, should be recognized as at least as significant as formal learning and should therefore be valued and used appropriately in formal processes.

**Principle 10: Effective teaching and learning demands consistent policy frameworks with support for teaching and learning as their primary focus.** Policies at national, local and institutional levels need to recognize the fundamental importance of teaching and learning. They should be designed to create effective learning environments in which all learners can thrive.

---

# 1 Environments for learning

In considering the creation of a learning environment, with the learner at the centre, it is useful to consider the ecological systems theory of Bronfenbrenner (1979, 1993; Reading 8.4). This theory provides a useful way for us to think about the layers which impact upon the child's learning environment. Bronfenbrenner placed the learner at the centre, and represented the layers of environment around the child through a series of expanding concentric circles, as shown in **Figure 8.1** below.

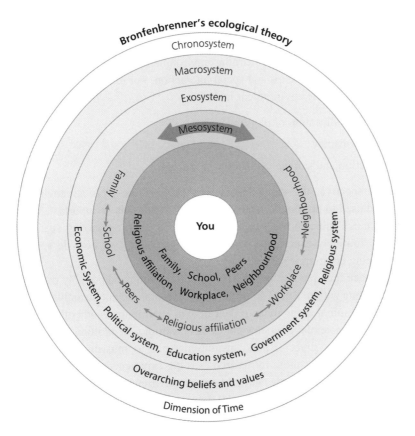

**Figure 8.1**
Bronfenbrenner's ecological theory

Immediately around the learner, Bronfenbrenner defines a layer comprising the learner's own 'biology' and the relationships they have with their immediate surroundings. For example, a child's peers may affect their beliefs and behaviour (and vice versa) and talking to the practitioner may support their learning – for example, through sustained shared thinking (SST).

The next layer is defined as the connections between the components of the previous layer; the relationship between a child's family and the practitioner would be included here. Beyond this lies the larger social system which the child does not directly function within, but which may affect them. Parental work schedules are one example: a child has no role in them, but may be affected by increased pressure in the family home as a result of one, or both, parent(s)/carer(s) being frequently absent. Finally, the outermost layer describes the wider cultural values, customs and laws within which the child is operating.

Thinking about a child's environment in this way makes it clear that no learning space can be considered in isolation. There are connections between the various settings and communities involved in a child's life. Of course, these interconnections change over time, and the ways in which people, resources and space typically interact in early, primary, secondary and further education have some similarities, but are also distinct.

# 1.1  Spaces for children?

Traditionally, a consideration of learning environments within ECEC has focused on physical resources, relationships and social interaction. For example, Dowling (2006: 47) suggests that the learning environment includes:

- The planned allocation of physical space.
- The use of display.
- The selection and storage of material resources.

From this perspective, the key question is: 'How is the physical environment best resourced and used to promote effective learning?' While this is important, we recognize that there is much more to the learning environment than organizing spaces. Children within ECEC routinely experience many 'learning spaces', yet how do spaces become effective learning environments?

The core space for a practitioner is, of course, the setting and possibly particular rooms which they operate within. But of course the setting rooms are not the only spaces in which children learn. Children spend most of their time in environments other than ECEC, many of which have the potential to contribute to their learning. In addition to routine learning spaces such as home, street or park, institutions such as museums, nature reserves or botanic gardens now offer more formalized learning experiences. Television, new media, mobile technologies and specific 'virtual learning environments' often now play a significant role in supporting learning. Above all though, the home remains the most significant influence on children (see for example Siraj-Blatchford, 2010).

All of these learning spaces have 'affordances' for learning. The term, with its origins in Gestalt psychology, was first coined by Gibson (1977) in developing an ecological approach to perception. It has been widely adopted in education, particularly in relation to educational technologies, to express the inherent potential for learning which an environment or tool offers. For such potential to be realized it has to be identified by the user. Thus, for example, a set of bricks may have affordance for building a tower, perhaps as a means of expression of a connection schema – for example, as the child carefully builds a tower – while another child may connect the bricks in such a way as to replicate a gun. The other side of 'affordances' is the idea of constraints – that there are some things about an environment, space or tool that are likely to frame learning potential in particular ways. Such constraints may include when an outdoor space is only available for a short period each day, as other children use the space, or limited resources are available. Reflective practitioners need to be aware of the affordances and constraints of the environments and resources with which they work and the factors which shape these.

## 1.2 Enabling environments

Children learn and develop well in enabling environments, in which their individual needs are met, their learning is valued and there is a strong partnership between practitioners and families (see Whalley, 2012; Reading 13.1). Enabling environments offer 'stimulating resources relevant to all the children's cultures and communities', 'rich learning opportunities through play and playful teaching' and 'support for children to take risks and explore' (Early Education, 2012: 2).

When considering the learning environment, it is easy to focus attention on where resources are placed and the choices that children have. While these things are, of course, important, the concept of 'enabling environments' goes further than just taking into account the organization and provision of resources. Moyles, Adams and Musgrove in the influential SPEEL study (2002), took a wider and more nuanced view when they defined the learning environment to include both the 'physical environment of the setting and the nature of the learning atmosphere within the setting – informed by values, beliefs and understanding of the practitioner' (2002: iv). This is evident in Creating the Learning Environment (CLE) that was developed as a part of the SPEEL project, which identifies the key ways in which practitioners provide for children's learning as follows:

Providing:
    a positive learning environment
    an environment which is conducive to learning
    for children as individuals
    learning opportunities that challenge children appropriately
    opportunities for active exploration
    a balance and variety of activities

Balancing care and education
Grouping children
Positioning adults
Opportunities to promote children's:
    personal, social and emotional development
    communication, language and literacy development
    mathematical development
    knowledge and understanding of the world
    physical development
    creative development

The 'ways' identified by Moyles, Adams and Musgrove above resonate with many of the ideals developed throughout his book, particularly in the previous chapter.

## Case study 8.1 Practitioner reflection: Involving children in organizing spaces

When I first started teaching nursery and infant children in London in the 1970s, the learning environment was set up before the children started school in September to be as stimulating as possible. My colleagues and I would come into the setting several days beforehand to make signs and displays and areas for play and learning. On reflection, over time I realized that one of the problems with this approach was that the children did not feel any ownership of the physical spaces and resources. A much more appropriate approach was to discuss with the children what resources (within reason) we would need and how we might organize and label them. Consequently, because the children were involved in organizing the resources and the space, I felt that they took more responsibility for the management of the physical environment and a more collaborative ethos was fostered through joint ownership. It is not just a question of how the space is organized and why, but what it means to be in that particular place at that particular time.

## Reflective activity 8.1

*Aim:* To reflect upon **Case study 8.1** and what it tells you about values.

*Evidence and reflection:* What values about the organization of the learning environment are demonstrated in the story above? Discuss your answers to this question with a colleague.

Having an understanding of the numerous factors impacting upon the learning environment provides a sound position from which to consider organizing a learning environment, but then how does the reflective early years practitioner go about the task? For MacNaughton (2003: 197), as the practitioner noted above, meaningful content is generated in interaction with children: 'the educator seeks to ground curriculum in children's lived experiences, interests, and concerns and to reflect critically on the consequences, for themselves and for the children.' Gandini (1994) adds to this suggesting that 'the space has to be a sort of aquarium that mirrors the ideas, values, attitudes and culture of the people who live in it' and the child can be found at the centre of all of these influencing factors.

MacNaughton (2003) suggests that reflective practitioners should pose the following questions about how they structure space and materials in their setting:

- Do the everyday objects we use reflect the languages and cultures of the children within this group?
- Do we have everyday objects from diverse cultures?

- Do the materials respect and celebrate cultural diversity?
- Do the materials challenge traditional sex-role stereotypes and understandings?
- To what extent do the materials support and respect diverse abilities and ways of being?

She also suggests that reflective practitioners need to work to create equal access and opportunity for all children through the use of space and materials. She proposes the following additional questions are posed:

- Can children of differing physical abilities move around the space easily?
- Can children of differing physical abilities participate in a range of activities?
- Can children of differing abilities and ages easily touch display areas?
- Can all children in the group – irrespective of their cultural background – recognize their own cultures in the materials and staff they encounter?

(MacNaughton, 2003: 199)

Through consideration of these questions one can begin to organize an environment which provides a range of opportunities to fulfil a variety of needs. Questions such as these are considered in greater detail in Chapter 15 on inclusion.

---

### Reflective activity 8.2

*Aim:* To reflect upon how your values impact upon the provision the children in your care receive.

*Evidence and reflection:* Consider how your (and your colleagues') values and beliefs influence the way you develop and resource the learning environment in your setting.

*Extension:* Discuss with a fellow student or colleague the values and beliefs about educational environments inherent in MacNaughton's questions given above.

---

More recently, greater attention has been given to the socio-cultural perspective on learning. This is concerned with the influence of the contexts in which children learn, how learning varies with social and cultural experiences and the ways in which adults, other children, tools and resources support and shape learning (Stephen, 2010). In addition, work in the field of children's geographies has extended the discussion to include consideration of concepts of space and place – the interrelationship between the physical, cultural and social conditions of young children's lives and how personal identity may be linked to place identity and sense of belonging to a community (Kernan, 2010).

Through such lenses, the learning environment is seen here as a space defined through physical, cultural and social activities, aspects and artefacts. This space is located indoors and outdoors and both within and outside the setting. It does not just concern the built environment, although this is important, but also confirms meaning and belonging (Kernan, 2010) and is a relational space where children and adults engage in mutual and reciprocal activity (Bone, 2008; Moss and Petrie, 2002).

For Sheridan (2007: 211), 'this is an environment that has a message for the child (Rinaldi, 1993), an environment that set frames for learning and development (Bruner, 1996)'. Thus, the way in which we organize environments sends messages about how items can be used, what shall be learnt and what is valued. This notion is further developed in the concepts of 'children's spaces' by Moss and Petrie (2002) and 'living spaces' by Clark (2010). For Clark, the environment is both physical and emotional: 'Early childhood spaces are rich in symbols, rituals and routines, which Cole (1996) describes as artefacts. An environment in which the physical and emotional are bound together' (Clark, 2010: 12–13).

The reflective early years practitioner will need to be aware of the complexities involved in providing and organizing spaces for learning.

## 1.3 Children's voice and democratic spaces

Over the past 20 years or so there has been an increasing trend in both public policy and practice in ECEC towards fostering children's participation and voice. The introduction of the United Nations Convention on the Rights of the Child (UNCRC) in 1989 helped change the dominant image of childhood and bring about a new culture in relation to children's rights and interests in many parts of the world (Smith, 2011). This shifted the debate from deficit models of children's ability, or inability, to contribute to discussions about issues impacting upon their lives, to one which considers *and* strengthens perceptions of children, where children are regarded as competent social actors who are experts on their own lives (James and Prout, 1997; Mayall 2002; Rinaldi 2006).

The implications for developing children's learning environments are inherent in the work of Moss and Petrie (2002), who originally articulated the idea of children's spaces rather than children's services. The concept of 'meeting place' conveys children's spaces as sites of exchange where meanings can be articulated and debated. Their contention is that there should be spaces *for* children, rather than just services which are provided *to* children without any involvement or decision-making. For the reflective early years practitioner, this relates to engaging children in discussions about the organization of the environment and valuing their opinions. To this effect ECEC settings should be established as autonomous and independent sites *'for democratic practice'* where there should be a strong element of local control and it is essential that the voices of parents and local communities should be heard (Moss, 2005, 2006; see also Willoughby, Reading 8.2).

There is much more to democratic practice than the odd or in-passing discussion with children and families. As discussed in Chapter 6, developing the conditions for democratic practice take time and, where successful, will have an impact upon the environment and the learning space. Waller and Bitou (2011) discuss how the concept of children's spaces raises the possibility of enabling both children and adults to be 'governed less by power, to be critical thinkers and to do so in interaction with others' (Moss and Petrie, 2002: 111). Rather than just thinking about engaging children's views, this suggests that we need to rethink children's involvement also in terms of 'spaces for childhood' within which children can exercise their agency to participate in their own decisions, actions and meaning making, which may or may not involve them engaging with adults (Waller, 2006). For example, Titman (1994) identified four places children look for in the outdoor environment: a place for doing; a place for thinking; a place for feeling; and a place for being themselves. Some of the concepts discussed in Chapter 6 will be useful in determining how this can be achieved and perhaps some of the potential benefits of developing such processes are provided by the discussions in both Chapters 6 and 7. A wealth of activities for engaging children in research into issues which impact upon their lives, including methods which use discussions and methods which use the creative arts, can be found at **reflectiveteaching.co.uk** (see for example Johnson, Hart and Colwell, 2014).

---

### Reflective activity 8.3

*Aim:* To reflect upon the spaces provided within the indoor environment in your setting.

*Evidence and reflection:* Reflect on Titman's (1994) four places children look for in the *outdoor* environment: a place for doing; a place for thinking; a place for feeling; and a place for being themselves. Consider whether the *indoor* environment you provide or work within includes such spaces.

*Extension:* Consider how you could adapt the environment to provide these spaces if necessary and how you could include children in the design.

---

**Table 8.1** Learning spaces [adapted from Layers from Clark's (2010) Framework]

| Spaces | Forms |
|---|---|
| **Official spaces** | Controlled spaces, rules, curriculum spaces |
| | Focus formal learning |
| **Informal school** | Personal spaces: self-identity |
| | Personal spaces: family members |
| | Personal spaces: friends |
| | Personal spaces: practitioners |
| | Private spaces |
| | Social places |
| | Imaginary spaces |
| | Caring spaces |
| **Physical landscape of the school** | Outdoor spaces |
| | Lights, ceilings and floors |
| | Beauty and colour |
| | Legibility – the ease with which its parts can be recognized and organized into a coherent pattern (Lynch, 1960: 2–3) |

Clark (2010) notes the physical and emotional aspects of spaces, and recognizes a much wider range of spaces within the learning environment. She draws our attention to the research of Gordon et al. (2000) who identify learning spaces as involving official, informal and physical layers. Clark argues that children's spaces can take a variety of forms, including virtual, imaginary or social functions, but they are not limited to adult-imposed reasoning. She states that we must consider what it means to the child to be in the place. (See **Table 8.1** on p. 177).

---

### Reflective activity 8.4

*Aim:* To reflect upon how you plan the learning environment.

*Evidence and reflection:* Take some time to consider:

- how do you/can you plan for an environment based on the concept of layers?
- the significance of the question posed by Clark (2010: 17): 'What does it mean to be in this place?'
- what some of the spaces in your setting mean to the children in your care.

---

## 2 Organizing spaces for learning

## 2.1 Use of resource, space and time

### Resource

A good supply of appropriate resources is essential, given the importance of direct experience and practical activities to children's learning. Such resources will need to be carefully selected to meet the developmental needs of the children in your care. However, at all levels, resources can:

- motivate, inspire and focus attention;
- provide a basis for discussion;
- be designed to enable children to learn independently;
- explain, instruct, or demonstrate procedures and ideas;
- enable children to access information;
- enable children to learn in manageable steps;
- help children to recall, consolidate and extend their learning;
- support assessment of children's understanding;
- support specific developmental needs, e.g. support fine or gross motor skills development.

Building upon the concepts introduced as we considered the provision of spaces for learning, the selection of resources also requires careful thought and attention to detail. For instance, are there resources which meet the needs of all of the children in your care? Are the resources supporting all children and their cultures to be valued? Are they being well maintained? It is all too easy to discover that the paint has dried out.

When considering employing resources for children's learning, four possible criteria might be considered:

- *Appropriateness.* What resources are needed to support the learning processes which are expected to take place?

- *Availability.* What resources are available? What is in the setting, the community, libraries, museums?

- *Storage.* How are resources stored? Which should be under practitioner control? Which should be openly available to the children? Are they clearly labelled and safely stored?

- *Maintenance.* What maintenance is required? Is there a system for seeing that this is done? In the case of ICT and specialist equipment, where is the expertise and technical support located and how can this be accessed?

---

## Reflective activity 8.5

*Aim:* To plan resources to support specific learning activities.

*Evidence and reflection:* Identify the objective for a proposed learning activity, then consider the resources and organization which are required, using the four criteria listed above as a starting point.

Activity:

Objectives:

Resources required:

Appropriateness:

Availability:

Storage:

Maintenance:

*Extension:* Together with a colleague, consider the resources that you most often have available. Is there a need to invest in further resources to increase the diversity? Is there a need to consider how resources are routinely selected? Are the same toys/ activities always easily accessible with others more difficult to access? Why? Do you have spaces such as the 'role play area' which you change regularly? Who decides what the space 'becomes'?

---

## Space

The way a space is organized has considerable impact on the teaching strategies that can be deployed. Space is always limited, yet what space there is must be utilized in such a way that it allows children to access as many learning opportunities as possible and practitioners to both observe and support the children's play and investigations.

When thinking about the most effective use of classroom space, consider developing a setting or room plan, either on card, by using classroom design software (see **reflectiveteaching.co.uk** for links to websites you could use). Using such a plan, it is possible to explore the affordances and constraints of each possible layout.

---

### Reflective activity 8.6

*Aim:* To produce a room plan.

*Evidence and reflection:* A simple plan should be made of the fixed points in the room: walls, windows, doors, sinks, etc. It is relatively easy to produce a plan 'to scale' on computer or by using squared paper.

Major existing items of furniture should be represented by shapes to the same scale as the room plan.

The furniture can be moved around on the plan to experiment with different layouts.

*Extension:* Careful analysis is needed of the space requirements of each activity and of each activity in relation to the others.

---

## Time

Organizing the day to meet the needs of children requires careful thought, as we noted when we discussed routines (see Chapter 7). Indeed, however well-organized a space is, and however good one's organization of resources, when children start to use that space it can lead to some children becoming frustrated or over-tired, for example, and may also lead to 'evaporated time'. It may therefore be necessary to analyse how the day is planned. For example, in primary schools, Campbell and Neill (1992) showed that almost 10 per cent of the day is lost as 'evaporated time' – time where no learning or necessary procedural tasks are occurring. Minimizing this evaporated time is important to increase opportunities for learning. Furthermore, as we alluded to in Chapter 7, children who are *bored* or *not engaged* are more likely to demonstrate challenging behaviours.

---

### Reflective activity 8.7

*Aim:* To consider the plan for the day.

*Evidence and reflection:* Refer back to **Case study 7.1**, in which the staff considered the length of the lunch break at their pre-school. Consider how sessions are planned out during a typical day in your setting. Consider how movement from one activity to another is managed – e.g. the transition from free play to adult-led activities. Are there points when children are waiting for transitions rather than playing/ engaged in activities? Does the plan meet the needs of all the children in the setting – allowing them time for naps or feeding when needed? Are there changes which could be proposed or trialled to improve the use of time in the setting?

---

Encouraging children to take on more responsibility for organizing themselves and their resources is important. It can support their development, their independence and enhance their learning time. It may be helpful to analyse the amount of time children spend actively learning, in transition and who they are interacting and learning with.

---

### Reflective activity 8.8

*Aim:* To monitor an individual child to estimate active learning time and gain a sense of how they experience a typical day.

*Evidence and reflection:* Observe a child on multiple occasions at different times. Judge the times at which, the child is:

- actively engaged in an activity
- disengaged or waiting
- interacting with their peers
- interacting with an adult

*Extension:* Are there any changes in the planning for the day which could help to maximize active learning time? Did you note anything interesting about the times the child was engaged with their peers, an adult, or playing alone?

---

Through consideration of the procedural aspects of creating environments for learning, we begin to identify some of the ways we can reflect upon how things are done and how they might be changed to increase opportunities for learning. We will now turn our attention to particular spaces within ECEC setting: specifically, the outdoor space and its affordances for learning.

## 2.2 Outdoor spaces

There is a long history of outdoor provision in ECEC (Garrick, 2009) which has recently been influenced and supplemented by outdoor education traditions from Scandinavia and the approach to learning in Reggio Emilia, Italy (Waller and Tovey, 2014, see Nutkins, McDonald and Stephen, Reading 9.2). These developments reflect a growing interest in the use of outdoor spaces for play by young children over the last decade or so. As we have noted in previous chapters, for many parents and early years practitioners outdoor play is seen as a natural and significant part of a child's healthy development (Clements, 2004). Recent interest in the potential of outdoor learning is also evident in policy across the UK. For example, in England, the government launched an 'Learning Outside the Classroom Manifesto' (DfES, 2006). Outdoor play is also seen as significant within the Early Years Foundation Stage in England (DfE, 2012), the Foundation Phase in Wales (Welsh Government, 2012) and the Curriculum for Excellence in Scotland (Education Scotland, 2012).

Waller and Tovey (2014) define outdoor play and learning as an 'umbrella' term used to cover a range of children's experiences in different outdoor locations. As Waite, Davis and Brown (2006a) point out, outdoor learning is not a single entity but comprises many different sorts of activities with distinct purposes. For young children attending an ECEC setting these opportunities may include:

- play in outdoor areas within the setting;
- visits to natural wild environments, community parks and play spaces;
- Forest School experiences.

Recently, many settings and schools in England were able to apply for capital funding to improve the physical resources within their outside area or garden. While this funding opportunity was welcomed by many, Waller and Tovey (2014) strongly argue that whatever the outdoor space in the setting affords, young children also need to benefit from regular visits to a wild natural area (such as a local wood) outside the setting (see below and Hart, 1979).

Wild natural environments are defined as those environments not designed or culti-vated by humans: typically woods, forests, beaches or riverbanks (Fjørtoft, 2004). One educational philosophy which advocates outdoor learning in natural environments is Forest School. Forest Schools provide activities, including traditional games and woodcraft, usually organized and directed by trained Forest School teachers. Forest Schools originated in Scandinavia in the 1950s as a way of teaching about the natural world. By the 1980s they became an integral part of the Danish early years programme, which significantly influenced the development of the Forest School movement in the UK in 1993 (Murray, 2003; Maynard, 2007a). Currently a number of local authorities in the UK organize Forest School programmes for children from the age of 3 onwards (see Knight, 2011).

The changing place of childhood in many countries is widely acknowledged within the sociology of childhood (James and Prout, 1990). A significant aspect of recent changes to childhood in many countries (Fjørtoft, 2004; Holloway and Valentine, 2000) is that facil-ities for outdoor play and opportunities for free play outdoors are declining. Children's participation in the public domain has been restricted in an attempt to keep them *safe from risk*, leading to an erosion of opportunities for independent play in outdoor spaces (Harden, 2000). This is due to rise in traffic, greater institutionalization of childhood (breakfast and after-school clubs) and parents' safety concerns (Burke, 2005). At the same time, access to the outdoors for children has become limited, with far greater use now of adult-controlled and structured space. This risk anxiety and 'culture of fear' (Furedi, 2002) has led to a tendency to protect children 'from situations previously considered to be innocent and risk free' (Sharp, 2004: 91). We can often see that 'culture of fear' has also permeated early years provision. Maynard and Waters (2007) report that reception teachers involved in a study that explored their use of outdoor space with their children stated that concerns about safety were a limiting factor in their provision of outdoor experiences (see Loreman, Reading 8.3).

### Reflective activity 8.9

*Aim:* To consider the opportunities the children in your care have to explore the outdoors.

*Evidence and reflection:* Review your outdoor spaces and any additional outdoor activities which are regularly provided. Reflect on what these opportunities offer and why outdoor play in early years settings is significant for the lives of children under 8.

When organizing spaces to support children's learning, it is pertinent to note that it is proposed that some learning can only happen outdoors and that the outdoor environment provides numerous learning opportunities. Tovey (2007: 37) provides a summary of the opportunities that outdoor learning spaces provide, or particular affordances of the environment:

- space and freedom to try things out;
- an environment that can be acted on, changed and transformed;
- a dynamic, ever-changing environment that invites exploration, curiosity and wonder;
- whole body, multi-sensory experience;
- scope to combine materials in ways that are challenging and problematic;
- opportunity to make connections in their learning;
- a rich context for curiosity, wonder, mastery and 'what if' thinking;
- space to navigate and negotiate the social world of people, friendships, to experience disagreement and resolve conflicts with peers;
- opportunity for giddy, gleeful, dizzy play;
- potential for mastery, willingness to take risks and the skills to be safe;
- a wide range of movement opportunities that are central to learning;
- experience of the natural world and their place within it;
- opportunities for learning in all areas of the curriculum.

It is debated whether these benefits can be can be realized in open, windswept, asphalt-surfaced playgrounds (see Tovey, 2007: 38). Tovey argues that play is about *potential* – what we referred to earlier as affordance: the potential of outdoor spaces to support, enhance and engage children's imagination, curiosity and creativity and foster their health and well-being. Opportunities to play outdoors every day, to engage with the environment in all weather conditions and to build an understanding and appreciation of the natural world are experiences that all young children are entitled to.

## 2.3 'Positive risk-taking' and the limitations of 'staying safe'

We noted in the previous section that growing concerns about children's safety have led to a decline in children's experiences. Attitudes, discourse and practice around safety vary culturally and over time. For example, early years practitioners in Sweden may be happy to encourage 4-year-olds to climb trees several metres high, or play in the forest out of sight of an adult, but many practitioners in the UK would not consider either activity an acceptable risk on the grounds of safety. Also, currently, practitioners in England would be expected to conduct a formal 'risk assessment' exercise (a detailed procedure laid down by the local authority) in order to take children out of a setting. In Sweden this would not be needed and has only recently been deemed necessary in England.

As previously discussed, there is no doubt that the effect of the 'culture of fear' (Furedi, 2002) has been to limit many children's opportunities for outdoor play and as Smith (1998) points out, there appears to be a common assumption that risk is a negative concept that must be avoided and reduced. In the UK, much of the current discourse around children's safety in outdoor spaces is from this perspective. Yet are our fears justified? What does the evidence tell us? In fact, the majority of playground accidents are little more than bruises or cuts and, sadly, children are many times more likely to be seriously injured or killed in a road traffic accident or an accident in the home than in outdoor play (Ball, 2002).

A contrasting view to that of minimizing risk is gathering support. This perspective recognizes the positive benefits of risk-taking behaviour (see for example Tovey, 2007; Waters and Begley, 2007; Little and Wyver, 2011). Tovey argues that a safe environment 'is one where safety is not seen as safety from all possible harm, but offers safety to explore, experiment, try things out and take risks' (2007: 102). This perspective does not seek to be complacent about the possibility of accidents but argues that the danger of creating risk-free environments is that adults' expectations remain low and children do not have the opportunity to develop and demonstrate competence and confidence (Tovey, 2007). How are children expected to develop the skills to manage situations and challenges if they never experience any potentially 'risky' situations? We have to consider the negative consequences if children do not confront and conquer risky physical activities. As Smith (1998) points out, for young children, risk-taking in the physical domain is the starting point for taking risks in other domains (emotional, social, intellectual). Children therefore need the opportunity to take acceptable risks and the question is how we juggle the requirement for safety with the need for children to have physical challenges. As Little (2006) suggests, reflective ECEC practitioners may need to consider how to provide:

> … a safe learning environment in which children feel secure enough to take the risks and make mistakes as necessary for learning. At the same time the environment needs to eliminate opportunities for negative risk-taking behaviours such as misuse of equipment as a result of insufficient challenge or boredom. (2006: 151)

# 2.4 Learning spaces for children under 3 years

Our understanding of the most appropriate educational provision for children under 3 has significantly changed over the last 20 years, so much so that the conception of a birth-to-5 framework for learning (DfE, 2011) is well established. One of the main contributions to this knowledge has come from the extensive work of Trevarthen. His research into the dialogic encounters between babies and mothers has been particularly influential (see Trevarthen, 2013), promoting awareness of the richness and strengths inherent in young children's capacity to 'regulate intimate encounters', the capability to 'share the "communicative musicality"' and 'show aesthetic preferences', the urge 'to learn expressions in dialogue', the demonstration of 'an increasing self-awareness' in infants and how at less than 16 months of age they 'can organise themselves into a working group' (p. 176) – all of which has implications for how the educational space is organized. (The previously mentioned ECERS and ITERS scales would also be helpful here.) Recent research in England (Goouch and Powell), Italy (Musatti and Mayer) and Finland (Rutanen) offers new perspectives for understanding the relationship between learning environments and early sociality in a group situation that may lead to innovative educational practices, which we consider below.

Goouch and Powell (2013) report on 'The Baby Room' research project, where a central space for dialogic encounter between babies and practitioners was created. While they found that many of the practitioners were not 'routinely, incidentally or intuitively' talking to the babies in their care, the study does indicate the rich potential these spaces have for positive talk outcomes in baby room practice.

Musatti and Mayer (2011) illustrate how the practitioners' activities and the spatial arrangement of the setting combine and interact with toddlers' recently acquired independent locomotion in sustaining their cognitive engagement and social encounters during their daily routine in an early childhood setting. They note that in Italy, 'best practice' with children under 3 involves taking special care over the quality and arrangement of the environments, furnishings and play materials (Malaguzzi, 1993) to the extent that it may be claimed that in the Italian early educational approach, 'space and materials made available to children are considered "a third educator"' (Musatti and Mayer, 2011: 207). This is particularly the case in the approach developed in the pre-school centres in Reggio Emilia (Edwards, Gandini and Forman 1993; Rinaldi, 2006; see Nutkins, McDonald and Stephen, see Reading 9.2), which has been internationally renowned for its early childhood programmes for over 40 years. The research by Musatti and Mayer (2011) with children in the second year of their life showed that when activities have a 'spatial', 'material' and 'action' component, 'a framework is created that contributes to episodes with stronger, longer and less interrupted engagement of each child' Rayna and Laevers (2011: 167). They provide a detailed analysis of a particular type of interaction in which 'reciprocal attention' and 'shared engagement' by the children is seen as a mark of success. The research of Musatti and Mayer demonstrates that the spatial arrangement of the setting in a number of distinct areas can specifically promote children's engagement. The article analyses three episodes involving 'exploring sounds', 'exploring objects properties' and

**Expert question**

**Engagement:** Do our teaching strategies and the organization of the environment allow for planned and unplanned learning experiences both indoors and outdoors?

This question contributes to a conceptual framework representing enduring issues and practitioner expertise (see Chapter 16).

'book reading' in a 'toddler room'. Additionally, the demeanour and position of the adult was seen to be significant in drawing children's attention to a potentially interesting activity. The stimulating responses and initiatives of adults in relation to materials and activities were on several occasions reported as instrumental for longer episodes of engagement in children.

Rutanen (2011) analysed the practitioners' role in structuring the physical and symbolic space, and how age is used as a category to construct divergences in spatio-temporal practices (how meanings are constructed in spaces and the practices within them over time). Rutanen showed that it is possible to gain an understanding of the network of powers realized in the production of the institutional space embedded with ideologies, practices and personal, lived experiences (Lefebvre, 2004). First, the power of the adult in indicating the forbidden and allowed areas for children become clear: forbidden areas are separated by rules and boundaries such as closed doors and fences. Specific locations are accessible, yet restricted regarding particular behaviour and interactions ('no running inside'). Furthermore, the interactions might be restricted to a certain time of the day ('no walking about during nap time'). Finally, Rutanen's research showed that the early childhood centre is not a uniform, equal socio-spatial entity for all, but that each actor has a personal (lived) space within, around and aside from the shared through personal experiences and positions. These are complex processes intertwined in the production of social space that is porous and multilayered (Lefebvre, 2004).

Such research reminds us of the complexities of learning spaces and how, as a reflective early years practitioner, it is vital that the possibilities for engaging with children of all ages are considered.

## 3 Using technology in the early years

Recently there has been a growing appreciation of the impact of digital technologies on childhood, children's lives and children's play and communicative practices (Marsh, 2007; Yelland, 2009). For example, *The Digital Beginnings Report* (2005) found that most parents believed that digital technologies would play a significant role in their children's education and future careers, and the majority encouraged and supported their children's early experiences for this reason. Similar findings were reported in the *The Good Child Inquiry* (Children's Society, 2007) and *The Byron Review – Children and New Technology* (2008) which recognized the popularity and range of opportunities for enjoyment, learning and development that digital technologies provide children and young people.

Children now grow up as part of an 'e-society' in which digital connectivity is essential to daily life. Consequently, from birth many children across the world are immersed in a way of life where these digital technologies are used for a range of complex cultural, social and literacy practices (Marsh, 2007). These practices, which are constantly changing, include using a range of hand-held devices such as mobile phones, multimedia players (iPods), tablets and games consoles, playing interactive games on digital and satellite television and accessing the internet to communicate images and text, holding telephone conversations and playing games with participants across the world. Currently, social network websites (shared databases of photographs which facilitate group discussion) and Tweeting (short text messages) and the use of tablet computers are very popular, but as the technology develops new and different communicative possibilities and practices will evolve (Waller, 2010).

Waller (2010) notes that, given the widespread access and use of digital technologies, young children must be recognized as highly competent 'digital natives' (Prensky, 2001) and as 'digitally at home' (Lankshear and Knobel, 2004). Indeed, many children have become experts in using technology and are able to access and use information in different ways as a result (see Facer, 2011). Many young children develop dispositions and competences with and through digital technology in the context of social interaction with their families and peers. For example, Marsh (2007) describes a number of cases which show that mobile phone use was firmly part of some families' communication practices with their young children, including the children's involvement in texting. For some practitioners this is a comfortable place, particularly for those who are themselves competent users of digital technologies. For others, however, this can be challenging and there are often issues around having access and the finance to resource technology within settings (see for example Formby, 2014). As Beastall (2008) notes, although many children are ready for the digital era and e-learning, practitioners may need more strategic and pedagogical support in order to ensure the most appropriate use of technology in the setting. This can be challenging for practitioners given that knowledge of children's home experiences of digital technology is often limited, thus they are not in a position to build on these competences (see for example McPake et al., 2005; Zevenbergen, 2007). The beliefs of many early childhood educators which permeate curricula and pedagogy are based on the view that 'the best conditions for learning are found where there is active learning, inquiry, and problem solving, whereby children are engaged and curious in their explorations' Yelland (2007: 51). Play is seen as a key aspect of learning and fostering positive dispositions, well-being and confidence. This can be linked to the belief that play and explorations are best kept within the real world and 3-D objects.

Waller (2010) argues that three significant implications of this situation are apparent in recent literature. In order to enable young children to participate in 'authentic' forms of social practice and meaning (Lankshear and Knobel, 2004), early years settings and schools need to incorporate children's digital play experiences from home into the curriculum. As children from affluent socio-economic backgrounds usually have greater access to new technologies, it becomes vital that settings equip children, at all levels, with the appropriate experiences and competences in the use of digital technologies (Waller, 2006a). There is a further significant *critical* role for the educational use of digital technology. The 'critical' dimension means that practitioners, and where appropriate children, need to be able to assess and critically evaluate software and other technology resources (Lankshear and Snyder, 2000; McPake et al., 2005).

Given the extent to which digital technologies are impacting upon children's lives, the fact that all children do not have access to modern technology and the range of digital divides the implications for children who are excluded from modern communicative practices should also be acknowledged.

While there is an international recognition of the potential of digital technology, it has been suggested that this potential is '… as yet an untapped resource' (Beastall, 2008: 109). Where digital technologies have been embedded in practice there is a strong argument that the role of the practitioner changes as a result. This new role includes providing opportunities and contexts to exploit the potential of children's experience of digital technology in the wider community. Practitioners need to know their children's capabilities and interests, to understand how to organize their setting and to structure the teaching of their children so that digital resources become an integral part of the learning (Waller, 2006a). Luke (1999) and Yelland (1999, 2007) maintain that the use of digital play opportunities can strengthen everyday teaching and learning in ECEC settings. Long-established play and literacy activities in ECEC settings can now be complemented with different experiences that have been made possible with new digital technologies (Waller, 2006).

 These technologies, and the activities that children may engage in with them, have the potential to extend learning in new and exciting ways and strengthen everyday literacy teaching and learning in early childhood classrooms (Waller, 2010; see Reading 8.5).

Plowman and Stephen (2005, 2007) studied early years settings in Scotland and reported little evidence that computer play acted as a support for learning. Typically, Plowman and Stephen found that children's use of computers usually took place during periods of 'free play', where children could choose from a range of activities. Here children's interactions with the computer were frequently referred to, by adults and children, as 'playing with the computer' in the same way as they would talk about playing with construction or small world toys. There were few examples of adult involvement in computer-based play, although practitioners intervened to ensure turn-taking and were observed occasionally making notes for records and the assessment of children's progress with technology. Noticeably, Plowman and Stephen found that, while there was explicit scaffolding of learning in other curriculum areas, it was absent in relation to children's play with computers. If early years teachers are expected to play alongside children to support their ideas and extend their thinking (Wood, 2009; DfES, 2007), then surely this role also includes play with digital technology?

Zevenbergen (2007) therefore proposes that early childhood education be reconceptualized so as to incorporate notions of digital play in order to sustain and support the habitus of the children now entering the range of early childhood services. As Zevenbergen argues, 'If the emergence of young children into the early childhood settings is to be seen differently as a consequence of their highly digitized home experiences, then the implications for practice are profound' (2007: 20). These issues are summarized within the TLRP research briefing by Plowman opposite.

**Research Briefing**

## Supporting learning with ICT in preschools

| | |
|---|---|
| Children's encounters with ICT are enhanced when practitioners use guided interaction. | → Professional development can help practitioners to find ways of enhancing the value of encounters with ICT whilst balancing child-initiated and adult-led activities. |
| Encounters with ICT accompanied by guided interaction can enhance three key areas of learning: dispositions to learn, knowledge of the world and operational skills. | → Maximising the learning benefits of ICT requires a responsive, reflective pedagogy which values pleasure and engagement as well as operational skills. |
| Providing a broad range of ICT's promotes more opportunities for learning. | → Nurseries should broaden their focus from computers to other forms of ICT, including digital still and video cameras, mobile phones, and electronic keyboards and toys. |

If practitioners are to develop a transformative pedagogy (Larson and Marsh, 2005) then they will need to build on children's digital and online play experiences and involve the children as experts (Waller, 2010). As discussed previously, this will involve the development of democratic spaces in which children have a voice.

---

### Reflective activity 8.10

*Aim:* To review your own practice in relation to digital technologies.

*Evidence and reflection:* What do you feel the role of digital technologies is in young children's lives? Are you able to effectively build on children's digital at-home experiences in your setting? Are you able to provide digital opportunities in the setting for children who do not have them at home?

---

## Conclusion

In this chapter, three major points about learning spaces have been made. First, all contexts and settings (whether directly experienced or virtual) provide conditions which influence learning. Some will enable learning to flourish, while others may inhibit such development. These differences in 'affordance' are similar to the patterns in any ecological context. So, when we organize learning environments, we should consider the likely overall effect on our primary objective of supporting learning and children should have a voice in determining the organizations of such spaces. Second, spaces for learning are contextualized by many other influences on children's lives including economic, technological, political, cultural and social conditions such as the 'fear of risk'. Third, there is a need for ECEC practitioners to consider their role in supporting learning through digital technologies in order that children's digital experiences are supported and built upon in ECEC settings.

Effective organization thus requires consideration of the physical environment – both indoors and outdoors, resources, technologies, structures, routines, processes and people. Awareness of the range of influences on a child's learning and development and appropriate organization of spaces for learning is a hallmark of an expert practitioner.

# Key readings

Understanding of the conditions which enable learning, development and performance have been enhanced by ecological analyses. Classics are:

Baker, R. G. (1968) *Ecological Psychology. Concepts and Methods of Studying the Environment of Human Behaviour.* Stanford: Stanford University Press.

Bronfenbrenner, U. (1979) *The Ecology of Human Development: Experiments by Nature and Design.* Cambridge, MA: Harvard University Press.

—(1993) 'Environments as Contexts of Development, in "Ecological Models of Human Development". In M. Gauvain and M. Cole (eds) *Readings on the Development of Children.* New York: Freeman.

Influences on the development of children and young people have been extensively studied. A good summary is:

Corsaro, W. A. (2011), *The Sociology of Childhood.* London: Sage Publications Ltd.

Mayall, B. (2002) *Towards a Sociology for Childhood: Thinking from Children's Lives.* Milton Keynes: Open University Press.

For a consideration of developing spaces to support relationships, see Chapter 6 and:

Bone, J. (2008) 'Creating relational spaces: everyday spirituality in early childhood settings', *European Early Childhood Education Research Journal [P]*, 16 (3), 343–57. London: Taylor and Francis.

Malguzzi, L. (1993) 'For an education based on relationships', *Young Children*, 49 (1), 9–17.

To include children's voices in decision you need to find innovate ways of gaining their opinions, you may find the following useful:

Burke, C., (2005), 'Play in focus: Children researching their own spaces and places for play', *Children, Youth and Environments*, 15 (1), 27–53.

Johnson, V., Hart, R. and Colwell, J. (2014) *Steps for Engaging Young Children in Research Volume 1: The Guide Bernard van Leer.* **bernardvanleer.org/English/Home/ Publications/Catalogue/Steps-for-Engaging-Young-Children-in-Research-Volume-1-The- Guide.pdf**

For more on outdoor spaces, see:

Clark, A. (2005) 'Ways of Seeing: Using the Mosaic Approach to Listen to Young Children's Perspectives'. In L. Miller, R. Drury and C. Cable (eds) *Extending Professional Practice in the Early Years.* London: Sage Publications Ltd.

Kernan, M. (2010) 'Outdoor affordances in early childhood education and care settings: adults' and children's perspectives', *Children, Youth and Environments,* 20 (1), 153.

Knight, S. (2010) 'Forest Schools: Playing on the Wild Side'. In J. Moyles

(ed.) *The Excellence of Play*. 3rd edn. Maidenhead: Open University Press/
McGraw-Hill.

The associated website, **reflectiveteaching.co.uk**, offers a wealth of supplementary
resources including reflective activities, research briefings, advice on further reading
and downloadable diagrams, figures and checklists from the book. It also features a
compendium of educational terms, links to useful websites, policy and curriculum
documents, and showcases examples of excellent research and practice.

# part three

# Teaching for learning

(9) **Curriculum** What is taught in the early years?

(10) **Planning** How are we implementing the curriculum?

(11) **Pedagogy** How can we develop effective strategies?

(12) **Communication** How does language support learning?

(13) **Assessment** How can assessment enhance learning?

This section supports the development of practice across the three classic dimensions of teaching: curriculum, pedagogy and assessment. Chapter 9 starts us off with a consideration of the benefits and challenges of having a curriculum for the early years before we review curricular aims and design principles. Chapter 10 puts these ideas into action and supports the development of short-, medium- and long-term planning across the age range. Chapter 11 offers ways of understanding the art, craft and science of pedagogy, and the development of a pedagogic repertoire. 'Communication' (Chapter 12) extends this with an introduction to the vital role of talking, listening, reading and writing across the curriculum. Finally, this part concludes by demonstrating how assessment is an integral aspect of teaching in ECEC (Chapter 13).

# Curriculum
## What is taught in the early years?

**9**

## Introduction

The development of a curriculum for the early years is a relatively new phenomenon. Its development can be seen as hugely beneficial, particularly in supporting national aspirations and helping to ensure parity of experience and quality of provision for young children and their families. Yet, developing a curriculum which meets the needs of all young children and supports them to develop as curious, capable, confident individuals is incredibly complex. In this chapter, we will consider how the notion of having an early years curriculum has come into being along with some of the key influences of such policy. We will then move on to consider the different curricula at work in any setting at any one time; how reflection can support the development and implementation of the curriculum in early years settings and, review how the curriculum is experienced in practice. It is our intention that this chapter will support reflective early years practitioners to review the curriculum and its implementation in their setting, both now and in the future.

Pratt (1980) defines the curriculum as a written document which systematically describes planned objectives, session content, learning activities and the procedures for evaluation. Most people working with young children would view this definition alone as too prescriptive for early years practice, not least as there is often a reticence to subject young children to too many planned adult-led activities which lead to evaluations or assessment. As we noted in Chapter 4, the Steiner-Waldorf Foundation, through the Open EYE campaign, openly criticized the development of England's Early Years Foundation Stage curriculum, stating:

> The very idea that it is appropriate to have a 'curriculum' for young children is absurd and represents a totally inappropriate encroachment of a schooling ideology into the lives of young children. (House, cited in Hofkins, 2008: 1)

Indeed there is evidence of conflicting positions which represent opposing pedagogic positions – in other words, those who favour child-centred versus adult-led education, and those who are more concerned with outcomes while others are more concerned about processes (Papatheodorou, 2009). Whichever position is adopted, it seems that latest research findings, including those of the EPPE studies (Sylva et al., 2004, 2010), have led many to believe that it is crucial that all children benefit from high-quality early childhood experiences. One way of supporting this is to ensure that all children have access to the curriculum before they begin statutory schooling.

## TLRP principles

Three principles are of particular relevance to this chapter on the curriculum:

**Principle 1: Effective teaching and learning equips learners for life in its broadest sense.** Learning should aim to help people to develop the intellectual, personal and social resources that will enable them to participate as active citizens, contribute to economic development and flourish as individuals in a diverse and changing society. This implies adopting a broad view of learning outcomes and ensuring that equity and social justice are taken seriously.

**Principle 2: Effective teaching and learning engages with valued forms of knowledge.** Teaching and learning should engage with the big ideas, facts, processes, language and narratives of subjects so that learners understand what constitutes quality and standards in particular disciplines.

**Principle 10: Effective teaching and learning demands consistent policy frameworks with support for teaching and learning as their primary focus.** Policies at national, local and institutional levels need to recognize the fundamental importance of teaching and learning. They should be designed to create effective learning environments in which all learners can thrive.

## 1 Thinking about the curriculum

The National Council for Curriculum and Assessment defines the term curriculum as referring 'to all learning experiences, whether formal or informal, planned or unplanned, which contribute to a child's development' (2004: 2). We propose that to think about all planned and unplanned learning experience it is useful to consider four facets of the curriculum:

- The official curriculum
- The hidden curriculum
- The experienced curriculum
- The global curriculum

## 1.1 The official curriculum and its development in the UK

The curriculum developed in any given society is an exemplar of its time and culture, influenced by theory, practice and political positions. It is designed with both present requirements and the perceived future needs of society in mind. The Organisation for Economic Co-operation and Development (OECD) emphasizes that a society's curriculum cannot be simply copied from elsewhere but 'must be developed in the historical and cultural context of each country' (OEDC, 2004: 28). With this in mind we can look at some of the pioneers, theories and policies which have informed the development of the curriculum for early years practices in the UK.

Historically, concerns for young children centered on childcare, mainly focused on the physical health and welfare of the child, as opposed to their cognitive development.

Table 9.1 Education: The interaction of knowledge, development and curriculum

| 1816 | Robert Owen – opened first known nursery school |
|------|-------------------------------------------------|
| 1826 | Friedrich Froebel published key writings |
| 1870 | The first Education Act in the UK |
| 1889 | The first Children Act in the UK |
| 1897 | John Dewey published key writings |
| 1907 | Maria Montessori opened the first Casa Del Bambini in Rome |
| 1910 | Sigmund Freud formed International Psychoanalytic Movement |
| 1914 | Margaret McMillan opened her first open air nursery |
| 1919 | Rudolf Steiner opened first Stenier Waldorf School |
| 1921 | Jean Piaget became director of studies at the Rousseau Institute |
| 1924 | Susan Isaacs became Head of Malting House School |
| 1926 | Lev Vygotsky began his research |
| 1935 | Burrhus Skinner began his research |
| 1945 | Reggio Emilia – Loris Malaguzzi opened first community run nursery |
| 1960 | Jerome Bruner published key writings |
| 1961 | Belle Tutaev formed the first playgroup |
| 1962 | First High Scope Nursery opened in the USA |
| 1967 | The Plowden Report was published |
| 1969 | John Bowlby published key writings |
| 1984 | OFSTED formed in England |
| 1988 | The introduction of The National Curriculum in the UK |
| 1990 | The Rumbold Report was published |
| 1996 | Te Whāriki introduced in New Zealand |
| 1996 | Desirable Outcomes for Children's Learning on Entering Compulsory Education introduced |
| 1997 | Ferre Laevers published key writings |
| 2000 | Curriculum Guidance for the Foundation Stage introduced in the UK |
| 2001 | The National Standards for Under Eights Day Care and Childminding introduced in England |
| 2002 | *Birth to Three Matters* policy introduced in the UK |
| 2004 | *Every Child Matters* introduced in England and Wales |
| 2008 | Early Years Foundation Stage introduced in England<br>Effective Preschool Provision Findings published |
| 2009 | Aisear introduced in Ireland for children from birth to six years. |
| 2010 | Curriculum for Excellence introduced in Scotland |
| 2011 | The Tickell Review of the Early Years Foundation Stage Published |
| 2012 | The Revised Early Years Foundation Stage launched in England |
| 2014 | Consultation underway for the development of the Curriculum for Wales |

Yet, it came to be understood that such care was complex and that, in order to support a child to reach their potential and have a secure future, education must be a part of that care. 'We need to understand the history of early childhood education because it provides a "rootedness" to our work. It means we are building our work on solid ground and travelling along well-trodden paths' (Nutbrown, 2008: 181). Any historical timeline for early years care and education is peppered with development theories, government policies and practical research, put into action by pioneering educationalists. The table opposite provides an overview of some of the key developments which have influenced ECEC practice in the UK and around the world. Much of this work is referred to throughout this book.

The first known nursery in the UK to consider both care and education was set up by Robert Owen in 1816 in New Lanark, Scotland. The nursery provided a nurturing and stimulating environment for the children while also providing female employees with the opportunity to work. Perhaps the most notable development after this was the opening of McMillan's Froebel-inspired nursery and training centre in London in 1914. The nursery was devoted to improving the physical and intellectual welfare of children living in poverty.

Also championing the concept of child-centered nursery education around this time was psychologist Susan Isaacs. In 1924 she became the Head of Malting House School, an experimental nursery school. Smith writes that '[Isaacs] probably did more than anyone else to integrate the increasing theoretical knowledge of child psychology with practical methodology in both education and child rearing practices' (1985: 17). Isaacs believed that children were competent learners and should have freedom to move around a stimulating environment to enable their development. Self-expression was encouraged and seen as a vital part of the child's personal, social and emotional development. Isaacs' practice and understanding was visionary and her voice echoes nearly 100 years later in ECEC practice, such as the importance of informing our practice through observations of play.

During both World Wars governments supported childcare as a way to free up women for the workforce. After World War II, as male workers returned, women were encouraged back into the home – a move supported by Bowlby's work on infant–mother attachment. Again, the influence of this work can be seen today, particularly in the role of the key person in many ECEC settings.

Possibly the most notable development following this came with the Plowden Report in 1967. Plowden noted the need for some early years provision (though the emphasis was focused upon the need for single mothers to work rather than specific developmental needs). Following this report, much of the childcare in the UK was provided through the voluntary sector and the expansion of full day care – initially with childminders, then eventually private sector day nurseries. The rates at which childcare provision grew differed across the UK.

As provision grew, so too did anxiety surrounding the fluctuating standards of care on offer. Markedly the Rumbold Report *Starting with Quality* (DES, 1990) stressed the importance of a quality early years education. It suggested a new curriculum based on eight main areas of learning and advocated experiential, active learning within a prepared environment. Mainly discounted by the government at the time, it would later become the foundation for good practice within early years settings.

In the 1980s and early 1990s discussions around the reforms needed for early years education consisted of:

> … unclear and conflicting messages about what was required – should an early years policy be most concerned about preparing children for school, or with day care for working parents? Should it provide stimulation for a developing brain, or equal opportunities for women? Was it about cost savings for employers, able to retain staff when they became parents, or about reducing the benefit bill for single parents, enabling them to return to the workforce? Or was prevention the main driver – whether of developmental delay in children or juvenile crime? (Pugh and Duffy, 2009: 8–9).

Such discussions marked the move towards a more universal provision with an overarching curriculum.

In 1996 the School Curriculum and Assessment Authority introduced a set of guidelines to standardize care for pre-school provision. These were linked to the first stage of a nursery voucher scheme affording parents a choice of which early years setting they used. Much criticized for its emphasis on school readiness, the Desirable Outcomes for Children's Learning (SCAA, 1996) stipulated the preferred level of development reached before a child entered school and also informed an inspection framework for the Office for Standards in Education (Ofsted, 1997). The voucher scheme was later abolished with the election of a new government, which introduced direct funding to pre-school settings for part-time places for 3- and 4-year-olds, dependent on meeting the requirements of the regular inspections.

Following the *Qualifications and Curriculum Authority's* (QCA) consultation in 1999 came the introduction of the Curriculum Guidance for the Foundation Stage (DfEE, 2000) for children aged 3–5 (in England, with other approaches being taken in other countries in the UK). Such developments were significant. It gave the early years a more distinct identity as well as a more detailed and focused curriculum which put emphasis on learning through planned play activities. Such guidance was not purely a product of government, but was developed by drawing on the expertise of a variety of early education educationalists. The Curriculum Guidance for the Foundation Stage, devised in England, (DfEE, 2000) revised the Desirable Outcomes for Learning and relabelled them the Early Learning Goals, to be achieved within six areas of learning. It proposed that the child go through stages (or 'stepping stones') to reach their Early Learning Goals and suggested practical ideas for practitioners to help plan play opportunities for children to help them achieve these goals.

Attention then turned towards the development and care of children below the age of 3 years. *Birth to Three Matters* (DfES, 2002) was introduced as a supportive framework of effective practice, though not a curriculum, and was the first time children from birth to 3 had been the focus of an educational review. It aimed to raise quality for young children by focusing on individuality and recognizing that the needs of young children, and the ways in which they learn, differ from those of older children. Following this babies and young children were included in numerous curriculum reviews and guidance, including in the 2009 Aisear in Ireland.

In 2001 Ofsted took over the responsibility for regulating childcare under the Children Act 1989. The National Standards for Under Eights Day Care and Childminding (DfES, 2001) were introduced and embody a set of minimum standards for childcare providers.

In response to the Children Act (2004) and Laming's *The Victoria Climbié Inquiry* (2003), the government announced a restructure for children's services to enable each child to achieve five outcomes to nurture their well-being. The *Every Child Matters* (DfES, 2003) agenda stated that to establish a secure foundation for the future we must enable the child to:

- stay safe;
- be healthy;
- enjoy and achieve;
- make a positive contribution;
- achieve economic well-being.

As early years provision grew, so too did research in the field of ECEC and the role of early years practitioners. In England, this work – much of which has been referred to throughout this book – led to the development of the Early Years Foundation Stage (EYFS) (DCSF, 2008), which, for the first time, fully incorporated all children from birth to 5 years. This combined previous frameworks into one coherent document underpinned by the government's *Every Child Matters* (DfES, 2003) agenda. This framework was the first to recognize and advocate the concept of a play-based curriculum that incorporated notions of education and care (Roberts-Holmes, 2012), as endorsed by the Effective Provision of Pre-School Education project (Sylva et al., 2004).

In 2011, the government commissioned a review of the EYFS (DSCF, 2008) by Dame Clare Tickell. It was feared to be too bureaucratic and needed more emphasis on supporting children's early learning; in addition, criticisms remained that the EYFS placed too greater focus on the reaching of goals and the assessment of these goals, which was not in the child's best interests. The review made 46 recommendations for change, notably suggesting there was an emphasis on how, rather than what, children learn in a way in which is unique to them. Tickell (2011) highlighted three characteristics of effective teaching and learning: playing and exploring; active learning; and creating and thinking critically. She also suggested changes to the previous areas of learning. There should be three prime areas to consider as foundations for learning: personal, social and emotional development; communication and language; and physical development. These underpinning skills can then be applied to a further four more specific areas, namely: literacy; mathematics; understanding the world; and expressive arts and design to deepen the learning experience. Professionals working within the field generally received the reviewed curriculum (EYFS, 2012) favourably, citing the 'reduction in unnecessary paperwork and the encouragement for staff to spend more time with the children' (Kingdon and Gourd, 2013: 88) as an important step to understanding that high-quality practitioners are the most valuable piece of equipment a setting can provide.

Through this, albeit brief, review of the development of the curriculum in the UK, one can begin to understand the influences, pressures and theories which have influenced the development of the curriculum. While the curricular contents differs across countries, the influences – each to varying degrees – have been similar. In addition, what the review shows is that as time has passed, the content of the curriculum has altered. There is a general agreement that a curriculum for the early years is here to stay. For the reflective early years practitioner, this means not only having a solid understanding of the current curriculum and legislation, but also of the forces influencing the developments of such policies, whether they be political, economic or research- and practice-based.

## 1.2 The hidden curriculum

The hidden curriculum includes the things that are learned but are not necessarily explicitly stated. This includes the unwritten social rules and expectations in any setting or school (Martin, 1983). As we noted in Chapters 2 and 6, children learn a great deal from their observations of, and interactions with, adults and their peers in pre-schools. The messages transmitted to children in these ways are every bit as powerful (and often more so) than those contained in any official curriculum. For example, we may have any number of resources depicting women and men working equally together in caring roles in our settings, but the day-to-day reality for the vast majority of children is that there are few men, if any at all, working with them in their setting.

---

### Reflective activity 9.1

*Aim:* To deepen your understanding of the hidden curriculum operating in your setting.

*Evidence and reflection:* Thinking about the images in your setting, what do children, families and visitors to the setting see? Who is represented? Who is absent? For instance, you could think about culture, race, identity, gender roles. What are the underlying messages represented in these images?

Is the uniqueness of every child evident in how and where their work is displayed? What messages do you think the images in your setting are presenting to the children and their families?

*Extension:* Consider your review of the images in the setting. Discuss with a colleague whether there are images which need to be updated, whether there are other ways of representing children's work. Discuss what the changes would be in the 'hidden' messages being given in the images in the setting.

---

Brown recognizes the significance of the hidden curriculum on children's development. She notes that such an awareness can support the everyday decisions and choices we make:

> For instance: What criteria do we use when we select books, toys and other learning resources? How do our attitudes, assumptions and expectations of children and their parents affect the way we relate to them? How do we group children and by what criteria do we choose them to do various activities or tasks? How do we maintain discipline and what reward system do we use? (Brown, 1998: 50)

Such questions are important for the reflective early years practitioner.

One area in which the hidden curriculum can often be easily observed in early years settings is through the unwritten policies on suitable play – for example, whether play is considered to be too loud, too boisterous or too violent. There has been a tendency for war toys and weapon play by children to be seen as unsuitable or negatively in many early years settings. In the past, this often led to a 'zero-tolerance' approach being taken and all weapon play being banned. In our experience, though this was widely practised and was often referred to as 'policy', it was seldom written down. The impact of this was that many children, boys in particular, were receiving message that the setting did not approve of their play or what they enjoyed and, in some cases, that the setting was 'boring'. Research conducted by Penny Holland captured these issues and led many practitioners to reflect upon the messages the children were receiving about certain types of play. The case study below exemplifies this.

## Case study 9.1 Superhero and weapon play

A 'zero tolerance' approach to war play and weapon play was in place in our setting, though it was seldom discussed. Holland's research challenged us to consider this issue through a reflective and questioning process. Thoughtfully guided by the setting manager, the reflection included a series of discussions which were carefully handled to ensure all members of the team felt valued and comfortable with the outcomes.

A staff meeting was given over to very honest discussions, with all being guaranteed time to talk about their feelings on this personal and emotive topic – some team members stressing that they were strongly opposed to any type of play which included enacting acts of violence. Following these discussions, we agreed to observe children who showed an interest in this type of play. Despite the lack of weapons, we found that children made their own from sticks or equipment from the home corner! Through the observations, we found that the ban on weapon play had unwittingly encouraged the children to disguise their play and to be untruthful about what they were doing, creating a hidden or subversive activity and alienating them from the wider nursery culture.

These observations and the following discussion led to a number of changes in the setting. This included the creation of a written policy on play to provide clear guidance for staff. This, in addition to the staff discussions and discussions with parents, enabled us to present a clear and consistent message to the children.

The new policy made clear that we would not provide toy weapons directly but we would not discourage the creation of weapons in a child's play in construction, play dough, mark-making or any other form. We did purchase (cheaply through boot fairs and charity shops) superhero and character-based toys. These have proven to be incredibly popular and have been extended to include TV characters including animals and 'community' figures such as firefighters and doctors. Initially this type of play dominated the sessions and there was a need for increased adult supervision, involvement and scaffolding. However, as the novelty wore off the children went back to selecting a variety of toys and activities.

This reflection on one aspect of the hidden curriculum and its unintended outcomes has allowed a group of children who were previously alienated or given negative messages about their interests or needs to be supported in their choice of play and has reduced the instances of hidden or subversive activity.

Case study 9.1 highlights how those policies which are not written can impact upon children's behaviour and development. There are a great many examples of this, many of which have been discussed in this book – for example, how children with impairments feel in the setting, or what children learn about respected forms of knowledge and behaviour and who does and does not conform to these expectations. On first entering a setting, most parents will not be aware of the official curriculum; more than likely the hidden curriculum will send a number of messages to families about the setting and the values of the staff.

## 1.3 The experienced curriculum

This way of conceptualizing the curriculum draws attention to the parts of the curriculum, both official and hidden, which connect most meaningfully with learners. It is the totality of the substantive provision and experience children have in ECEC settings. Adults can plan all they like, and do so with the best of intentions, but what do children gain from this provision? Arguably, it is this experienced curriculum that has the most impact on young children and their futures.

Education is about the development of individual learners – unique children. There are many dimensions to such development including the personal, social and emotional as well as the physical, neurological and cognitive. For young children in particular, such factors are of great significance because they provide the foundation for learning. The significance of the development of individuals over time has increasingly been recognized in recent years. Longitudinal research has demonstrated the lasting consequences of high-quality early learning experiences (Sylva et al., 2001).

Education can thus be seen, at its simplest, as the product of interaction between socially valued knowledge and individual development. It occurs through learner experience of both of these key elements. Education, through the curriculum, mediates and structures these processes. The core expertise of practitioners is to reach between and facilitate a productive interaction of knowledge and development. As James and Pollard (2012) put it, effective teaching 'engages with valued forms of knowledge' and also 'equips learners for life in its broadest sense' (see the discussion of the TLRP Principles in Chapter 4). This argument is represented in **Figure 9.1** opposite.

Some people emphasize knowledge and skills such as mark making, can children write their names before they enter statutory schooling for example, and discount the significance of more developmental aspects of education such as being curious and resilient and willing to try new things. There are also many who foreground the development of skills, competencies and dispositions while asserting that contemporary knowledge changes so fast that 'learning how to learn' is all that is necessary. But these are unhelpful polarizations, for it is impossible to conceptualize 'learning to learn' except in relation to some substantive purpose. Our position is therefore that *both* elements – knowledge and development – are essential considerations in relation to curricula and thus early years provision. We must therefore consider both curriculum content, the hidden curriculum and, most importantly, the child's experience of these.

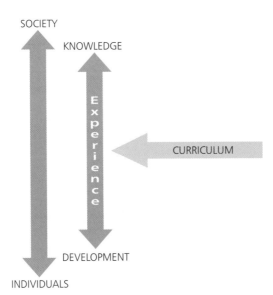

SOCIETY

KNOWLEDGE

Experience

CURRICULUM

DEVELOPMENT

INDIVIDUALS

**Figure 9.1**
Education: The
interaction of
knowledge,
development and
curriculum

# 1.4 The global curriculum

Curricula and the motivations behind them vary from country to country depending on differing social, economic, cultural, religious, political, historical and family contexts, for '[o]ur understanding of what is worth noticing in young children is rooted in our own sociocultural contexts' (Parker-Rees, 2011: 3). For the reflective practitioner they can be points to either reflect on or argue against, using them as a comparative tool to inform practice. It can be helpful to have some understanding of these other curricula and the history and theory behind them to help us to consider our own curriculum and how we can best deliver that curriculum in practice. This knowledge can enhance our reflections, potentially awakening new ways of thinking in ourselves.

As noted earlier, having an early years curriculum at all is a relatively new development, as such early years practices in some parts of the world are as yet poorly researched or are still in the process of development. Among countries where research and investigation have taken place, there are certain aspects of early years practice which are consistent across a range of curricula and approaches. Bertram and Pascal in their review of international practices (2002) found that at some time most countries or states have recognized the importance of an active play-based pedagogy which encourages children to be independent and self-motivated, though they also note that this rhetoric is not always the reality and that educational 'goals' can often hinder children's play in reality.

Our timeline identifies several global movements, approaches and curriculum practices which had varying impacts on modern-day early educational ideas internationally. We have provided brief summaries of five of these approaches.

**Table 9.2** Summary of five international approaches to early years provision

|  | History | Philosophy | Curriculum | Environment | Critique |
|---|---|---|---|---|---|
| **Froebel** see Reading 9.1 | Froebel worked in Germany. In 1837 he developed a programme of early childhood education based upon theories of child development. He believed that children learn through play. | Children are highly capable and adults should act as gardeners to release their potential. Parents are the child's first educator. | Children are taught as a 'whole' person. Plans are built around supporting the child's social, academic, emotional, physical and spiritual development. Children must be allowed to develop at their own pace. | The learning environment is filled with carefully designed activities which the children access through free play. An adult is on hand to support the child's learning. | In the past the approach was criticized for being too rigid and lacking the free play it advocated. There has been some concern that focus is placed too heavily upon the development of fine motor skills at the expense of a focus upon academic skills such as reading and writing. |
| **Montessori** see Reading 9.3 | Montessori worked in Italy. She developed her method of early years education in 1897. She believed that many of the problems that children faced were related to education rather than any medical issues. | Each child is an individual and should be encouraged to work at their own pace. No assessments, tests or grading are undertaken. Children benefit from interacting with children across age ranges: for example, 0 to 3 and 3 to 6 years. | The curriculum is built around the belief that children are natural learners who benefit from being provided with opportunities to choose activities for their own natural path of development. Observations of the child are fundamental to the approach. | Specially designed activities are provided for the children to explore. The activities are selected to be appropriate for the child so they can complete the activities without adult support. The aim is to build positive dispositions to learning. | The activities are carefully designed and are expensive to purchase. Can be rigid and thus not flexible enough to support individual children with differing needs. Concern has been raised that the approach does not foster collaboration and the development of relationships. |

| | History | Philosophy | Curriculum | Environment | Critique |
|---|---|---|---|---|---|
| **HighScope** see Reading 9.5 | Developed in the USA by Weikart in the early 1970s. HighScope was devised to support children living in poverty to prepare for formal schooling. | The approach draws upon theories of childhood, in particular the work of Piaget. The programme is built upon the belief that children can work independently and that they learn from direct experience. | The curriculum is delivered in a way which allows children to develop their individual talents. Hands-on learning is also crucial to the approach to allow children to construct their own knowledge. | The environment is set up with a variety of activities. Routine is the key feature of the environment with a 'plan, do, review' approach taken. | Concerns have been raised that there is the potential for the approach to be replicated too rigidly and as such the emphasis of the day is on teacher-led rather than child-led activities. |
| **The Reggio Emilia approach** see Reading 9.3 | Reggio Emilia is a city in northern Italy. The approach to ECEC was developed by educators and parents after WW2 who wanted to develop a community-based approach to teaching and learning that counteracted fascism. | The child is seen as both an individual and a member of the group. The approach is built upon the belief that cooperation and collaboration lead the child to become a member of the community, which will support their learning. | The child is supported to develop individual projects within the environment. Learning is discussed and questioned in collaborations between adults, children and their peers. A 'documentation' approach is taken. This involves documenting or capturing the child's learning, achievements and connections. | The environment is set up to be attractive, relaxed and homely. This is to ensure the child feels relaxed and comfortable. | As there is no official qualification thus there is concern that the approach lacks consistency and differs across settings. |

| | History | Philosophy | Curriculum | Environment | Critique |
|---|---|---|---|---|---|
| **Steiner-Waldorf** see Reading 9.4 | Developed by Rudolf Steiner in Germany in 1919, the Steiner approach is built upon theories of child development, specifically the work of Piaget. | The approach is built upon the belief that children learn through play and that imagination is a key component of new learning. | The approach encourages participation in 'real-life' activities and skills – for example, sewing and carving. It is thought that creativity and the arts are crucial for children to develop lifelong learning skills. | The environment is aesthetically pleasing, homely, and is set up to encourage group work. | There is concern there is a lack of focus on academic skills such as reading and writing. There have been some concerns over the spiritual teachings of some of the Steiner schools. |
| **Te Whāriki** see Reading 9.6 | Te Whāriki is the New Zealand Government's early childhood curriculum, developed in the 1990s. The approach is built upon a desire to learn in partnership with families. Learning is seen as occurring within a socio-cultural context. | The approach is built upon the assumption that children learn through a combination of interactions and active exploration of the environment. | The curriculum is based upon four key principles: Environment, Holistic Development, Family, and Community and Relationships. There are five strands to the curriculum: Well-being, Belonging, Contribution, Communication, Exploration. The focus is upon the development of knowledge, skills and attitudes. There is no focus on outcomes. | The environment is set up to encourage active exploration. | There is some concern that as the approach is relatively new, there has been little research to establish whether it is beneficial. The approach may be delivered in different ways across settings. |

> **Reflective activity 9.2**
>
> *Aim:* To deepen your understanding of the influences on your practice.
>
> *Evidence and reflection:* Review the table above. Can you see any links with your beliefs and practice? The practice of those you work with? Or your tutors? Are there any aspects which you would like to develop – if so why? Are there aspects you would disagree with – if so why?
>
> *Extension:* Discuss your thoughts with a colleague, and consider potential developments that could be made to the ways in which you deliver the curriculum.

For us to be effective reflective practitioners we must be able to recognize points within the curriculum which we work which are open to interpretation. As you can see, the approaches above, while distinctive, have common threads and all seek to support the child's development. Curricula will always change, and early years curricula in particular are flexible enough that the interpretation and ethos of the practitioner and the staff team are key. Interpretations will differ across settings and you will find that, as and when you move to work in other settings, things will be done differently. Sometimes you may feel that this is for the best and perhaps at other times you will make suggestions for change based upon your experiences. One of the reasons for the differences will be that all children, families, practitioners and settings are unique and so require different approaches. Rigidity in the delivery of the curriculum can lead to some children and families being excluded or feeling that the curriculum, the setting or, indeed, education holds little for them. There are however, we believe, some general principles of curriculum provision which can guide curriculum delivery.

## 1.5 Principles for curriculum provision

The educational role of curricular provision relates to three basic, enduring considerations. They are fundamental to all curricular deliberation:

- the *nature of knowledge*;
- the *needs of learners*; and
- the *interactions* between them.

Consideration of these can help to identify key principles for curricula provision over time and with different children in different settings. These elements were highlighted in the first chapter of an Expert Panel report on England's national curriculum (DfE, 2011). The report noted that:

> *Knowledge* can be seen as representing the accumulated experience of the past and a representation of this for the future. The concepts, facts, processes, language, narratives and conventions of each subject constitute socially refined forms of knowledge – knowledge that is regarded as 'powerful'.

In ECEC we are supporting children to gain the skills to be able to access such knowledge, now and in the future. The significance of the development of individuals over time has increasingly been recognized in recent years. Longitudinal research has demonstrated the lasting consequences of high-quality early learning experiences (Sylva et al., 2001; Reading 4.2), and a Foresight Report (Feinstein et al., 2008) affirms the trajectories of 'learning through life'.

Education can thus be seen, at its simplest, as the product of interaction between socially valued knowledge and individual development. It occurs through learner experience of both of these key elements. The two elements are not, however, equally significant at every age. In particular, developmental aspects and basic skills are more crucial for young children, as we often see emphasized in curricula and approaches to working with children under the age of 7 years. Taking note of these enduring aspects can help to frame delivery of the curriculum. As when creating, adapting or implementing a curriculum, or any element within it, it is crucial to be very clear about the purposes the provision is expected to serve.

At a high level, legislation may define overall educational goals. For example, in Scotland, Curriculum for Excellence 3–18, states that:

> Learners are entitled to a curriculum that includes a range of features at the different stages of learning. The entitlements ensure that children and young people are provided with continuous opportunities to develop skills for learning, skills for life and skills for work. (Education Scotland, **educationscotland.gov.uk/thecurriculum/ whatcanlearnersexpect/**, n.d.)

This is a statement highly influenced by social, economic and political issues:

> We know that children are the future of Scotland and we know that early years experiences provide a gateway to learning and skills that will power Scotland's knowledge economy. Equally importantly, it seeks to address the needs of those children whose lives, opportunities and ambitions are being constrained by Scotland's historic legacies of poverty, poor health, poor attainment and unemployment. (Early Years Framework, 2008: 1)

Thus the curriculum is built upon a clear, aspirational goal to support children to succeed and alleviate issues of poverty. Similar statements set expectations for many curricular frameworks. They are essentially ethical, moral and political statements, which make transparent the values and ambitions to which a nation aspires. A role of the reflective early years practitioner is to consider these aspirations, how they align with their own aspirations and the aspirations of the families with whom they work. Upon doing this, plans for curriculum delivery can be built.

Such principles may help us to consider the purpose of the curriculum and provide a foundation for

---

**Expert question**

**Breadth:** Does the curriculum represent society's educational aspirations for its citizens? Does it support children to develop secure curious dispositions?

This question contributes to a conceptual framework representing enduring issues and practitioner expertise (see Chapter 16).

thinking about planning and the curriculum. We must again turn to consider children as unique learners to further support concepts of how best the curriculum can support children with diverse needs.

## 2 Young children's learning and development, and the curriculum

## 2.1 Development

In earlier chapters we have considered how children learn. In this section we will expand on this to consider learning in relation to the curriculum. We will do this through consideration of what have been termed the 'building blocks of a curriculum for learning' (HMI, 1985). The HMI report identified four building blocks to encourage and refine professional discussions on curricular matters: knowledge, concepts, skills and attitudes. Almost 30 years later the EYFS recognized the development of knowledge, concepts, skills and attitudes as key to ensuring that children have a solid foundation for future learning (DfE, 2012).

*Knowledge:* This includes selections of that which is worth knowing and of interest. Some examples may include numbers and place value or letter sounds and phonics for reading and writing. The content, though guided by curricula, is often flexible enough within ECEC for the practitioner to determine the content. This may of course be shaped by 'goals' or 'indicators' of what the child will be *expected* to have achieved by the time they leave the setting.

*Concepts:* The 'big ideas' which inform a subject, or generalizations which enable children to classify, organize and predict – to understand patterns, relationships and meanings such as temperature, volume and life. For example, practitioners and children may plant seeds, placing one seed in a box and the other in a sunlit window. Looking at the growth of the plants could help the children to understand some of the big concepts about living things and energy.

*Skills:* The capacity or competence to perform a task: e.g. personal/social (listening collaborating), physical/practical (jumping, mark-making, cutting) and intellectual (observing, imagining). The development of such skills is the cornerstone of good ECEC practice. This is one of the reasons the early years have come to be recognized as crucial for children's future development.

*Attitudes:* The overt expression of values and personal qualities: e.g. self-discipline, tolerance, resilience, resourcefulness and dispositions – including dispositions to learning.

## 2.2 Knowledge

Understandings about the nature of knowledge underpin all curricula. Three basic positions are well established, with roots back to the philosophy, psychology and sociology of education.

First, there are those who argue that particular 'forms of knowledge' exist. These are thought to be distinguishable, philosophically, by the different ways of thinking and kinds of evidence which are employed in investigating them (Hirst, 1965; Peters, 1966). Second, there are those who emphasize the ways in which knowledge is socially constructed by individuals and groups in interaction together and with their environment, and by successively restructuring their understanding through these experiences (Berger and Luckman, 1967; Light and Littleton, 1999). This view has resonance with the psychology of Piaget, Vygotsky and Bruner (see Chapter 2). Finally, knowledge can be seen in sociological terms as being defined by powerful groups who define certain types of understanding as being important or of high status. They may attempt to control access to some forms of knowledge, particularly those associated with power (Young, 1971; Bernstein, 1971), but they may also try to insist on the exposure of children and young people to particular forms of knowledge which are deemed appropriate.

Of course, these views of knowledge are not discrete and any one person's perspective may draw on several of them, or even on them all. Such views can be seen in the provision of a curriculum, the idea that children must be educated to allow them to reach their potential and avoid cycles of poverty, and the delivery of the curriculum, for example where the teaching of a particular religion is promoted.

## 2.3 Concepts

Understandings of concepts help children to learn from, organize and explore new knowledge. Piaget proposed that children constantly reframe their knowledge through experience and exploration of their environment. As that knowledge builds, so too do their understandings of key concepts – for example, schemas help children to understand: the trajectory schema helps children to build concepts of what happens when you kick, throw or drop something.

Developing concepts is an important foundation for the development of further knowledge; new situations are rarely entirely novel and we are able to use our store of conceptual understanding to interpret and make sense of new experiences. Concepts illuminate and render accessible the deep structure of subject knowledge. This point has been made by scholars focusing from early years through to higher education (see for example Aubrey, 1994).

Concepts then, to return to HMI's definition, enable learners to classify, organize and predict – and to understand patterns, relationships and meanings within subjects. They are epistemological tools in support of high-quality, authentic learning.

# 2.4 Skills

A skill is 'the capacity or competence to perform a task' (Her Majesty's Inspectors, 1985: 38) but in the context of curriculum planning, use of the term has become more complex. Several uses can be identified:

'Physical skills' normally refers to bodily coordination such as running, catching etc., and to fine motor skills such as writing, sewing or drawing.

'Basic skills' usually refers to communication, literacy and numeracy, and sometimes includes the use of technology.

'Personal skills' is the most fundamental and typically includes capabilities such as self-awareness, thinking and skills of cooperation in working with others.

Systematic and embedded provision for skill development is a vital element of learning within any curriculum. In Wales, the *Skills Framework for 3 to 19-year-olds* (Welsh

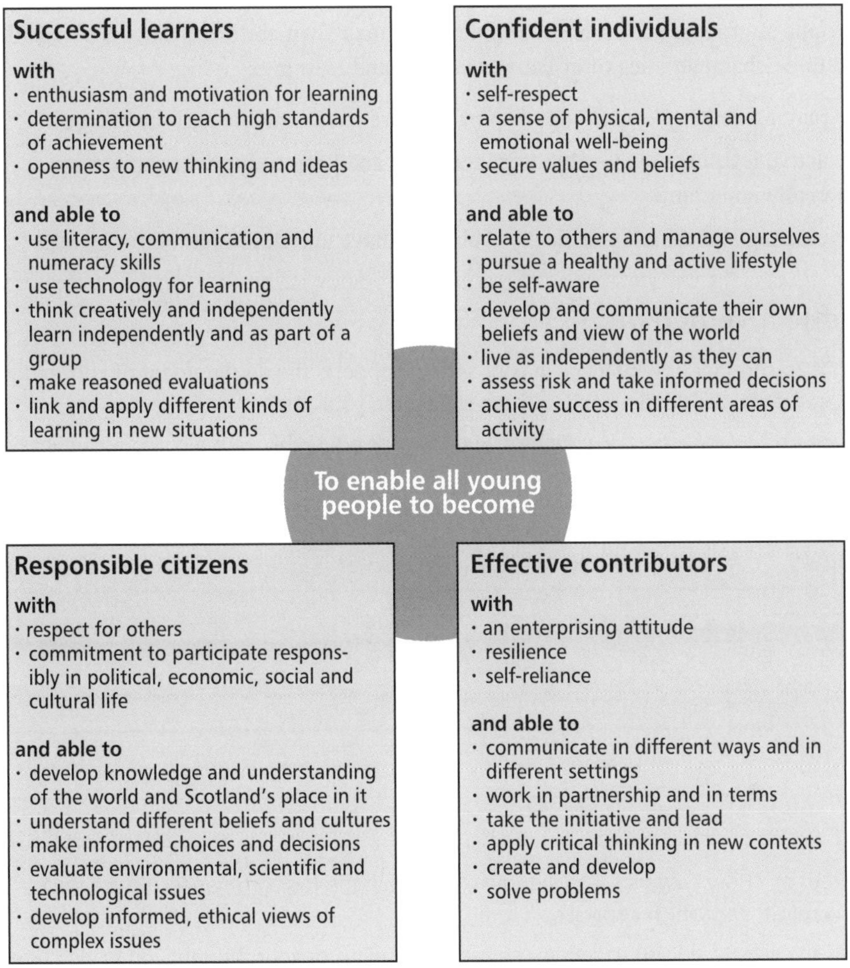

**Successful learners**

**with**
· enthusiasm and motivation for learning
· determination to reach high standards of achievement
· openness to new thinking and ideas

**and able to**
· use literacy, communication and numeracy skills
· use technology for learning
· think creatively and independently learn independently and as part of a group
· make reasoned evaluations
· link and apply different kinds of learning in new situations

**Confident individuals**

**with**
· self-respect
· a sense of physical, mental and emotional well-being
· secure values and beliefs

**and able to**
· relate to others and manage ourselves
· pursue a healthy and active lifestyle
· be self-aware
· develop and communicate their own beliefs and view of the world
· live as independently as they can
· assess risk and take informed decisions
· achieve success in different areas of activity

**To enable all young people to become**

**Responsible citizens**

**with**
· respect for others
· commitment to participate responsibly in political, economic, social and cultural life

**and able to**
· develop knowledge and understanding of the world and Scotland's place in it
· understand different beliefs and cultures
· make informed choices and decisions
· evaluate environmental, scientific and technological issues
· develop informed, ethical views of complex issues

**Effective contributors**

**with**
· an enterprising attitude
· resilience
· self-reliance

**and able to**
· communicate in different ways and in different settings
· work in partnership and in terms
· take the initiative and lead
· apply critical thinking in new contexts
· create and develop
· solve problems

**Figure 9.2** The four capacities of Scotland's Curriculum for Excellence 3–18

Assembly Government, 2008) updates this approach for a twenty-first-century curriculum. Scotland's Curriculum for Excellence 3–18 also provides a carefully developed skills framework offering 'Skills for Learning, Skills for Life and Skills for Work' (Scottish Government, 2009). **Figure 9.2** illustrates the four 'capacities' which have been conceptualized and prioritized in Scotland. There is strong emphasis on the responsibilities of *all* educators to support such learning through all sectors and a framework of National Qualifications offers accreditation.

## 2.5 Attitudes

Attitudes were regarded by HMI as 'the overt expression, in a variety of situations, of values and personal qualities' (1985: 41). Examples they gave were honesty, reliability, initiative, self-discipline and tolerance. Within the area of Personal, Social and Emotional Development, the EYFS (2012: 5) refers to 'helping children to develop a positive sense of themselves, and others; to form positive relationships and develop respect for others; to develop social skills and learn how to manage their feelings; to understand appropriate behaviour in groups; and to have confidence in their own abilities'. This is alongside the noted three characteristics of effective teaching and learning:

- playing and exploring – developing a desire to investigate and 'have a go';
- active learning – to be able to concentrate and keep trying when things are challenging; and
- creating and thinking critically – children have and develop their own ideas.

---

### Reflective activity 9.3

*Aim:* To consider how practice in your setting supports the development of knowledge, concepts, skills and attitudes in the children in your care.

*Evidence and reflection:* Working on your own or preferably with a colleague, identify and list the knowledge, concepts, skills and attitudes which are targeted for development in a specific set of planning materials.

| TOPICS | Knowledge | Concepts | Skills | Attitudes |
|--------|-----------|----------|--------|-----------|
|        |           |          |        |           |
|        |           |          |        |           |
|        |           |          |        |           |
|        |           |          |        |           |
|        |           |          |        |           |

*Extension:* How easy was it to identify elements in the four categories? Which were explicit, and which implicit?

Has the activity led you to refine or extend your plans or your thoughts on your future practice?

---

The discussions so far have led us to conclude that any curriculum for the early years is bound by time and place, that it is complex and has many facets – far more than just what is explicitly written, and that in essence the focus is the building of knowledge, concepts, skills and attitudes which will prepare children well for the future. But how does the reflective early years practitioner deliver a curriculum which meets the needs of the unique child with an awareness of these issues? This brings us to the level of detailed application, where educational aims are chased in everyday provision.

## 3 Delivering a curriculum for the early years in practice

Each member of a staff team brings their own experience and knowledge into the setting. As we have reiterated throughout this book, it is important for a reflective practitioner to seek new knowledge and perspectives continually. Once we embed the knowledge passed on to us from historical pioneers and new research findings and become certain of our own ethos and values, we gain the confidence to interpret the current curriculum accordingly – something that is particularly challenging in the early years of a career. The curriculum comes to be seen as something that is a part of practice rather than the whole of practice. We begin to work with the curriculum in a way that is congruent with our ethos that the curriculum should fit into the child, it is not the child who should fit into the curriculum. The EYFS (2012: 3) states:

Four guiding principles should shape practice in early years settings. These are:

- every child is a **unique child**, who is constantly learning and can be resilient, capable, confident and self-assured;

- children learn to be strong and independent through **positive relationships**;

- children learn and develop well in **enabling environments**, in which their experiences respond to their individual needs and there is a strong partnership between practitioners and families and

- **children develop and learn in different ways and at different rates**.

These principles cover the education and care of all children in early years provision, including children with special educational needs and disabilities.

## Case study 9.2 Supporting the unique child to access the curriculum in practice

A nursery was approached by a Gypsy, Roma and Traveller (GRT) support worker, Helen, and asked to provide a place for a two-and-a-half year-old male, Ed. Helen hoped that this would provide some much-needed respite for his mother, who was caring for Ed and his younger brother who had been diagnosed with disabilities. Ed's family were a part of an Irish Travelling community. Ed's initial visits to the setting were challenging. Ed suffered from significant separation anxiety and did not settle well. After some thought and conversation between setting staff and Helen, it was decided that Ed would benefit from having other children from his community within the setting. Consequently three of Ed's cousins were offered, and accepted, places at the setting.

Having his cousins in the setting eased Ed's separation anxiety. However, the introduction of a new group in the setting, particularly a group that only conferred ethnic minority status in the Race Relations Amendment Act 2000, raised a number of challenges for the staff team and their practice, as they were unclear how best to work with the family and their culture. To address this a number of developments took place. Initially a planned staff meeting was given over to Helen, who provided a workshop on GRT history, culture and customs. Helen also loaned the staff a number of culture-specific resources to supplement what was already available in the setting.

In addition to this meeting, the setting manager and deputy carried out a home visit (not usual practice at the group) during which they and the children took photographs of the family's current site. The mothers chatted candidly about their lifestyle which deepened the practitioners' understanding of their needs. The photographs of trailers, horses, dogs and family members formed the basis of a book which would feature heavily in the next stage of supporting the children within the setting.

The home photographs were used to make a picture book both representing the children's lives and as a way into shared group story times. This book – based on Eric Carle's *Brown Bear, Brown Bear, What Do You See?* – was hugely popular with the children and wider family (the children made a point of sharing it with any member of their wider family circle who came into nursery – and many did). It was also a valuable resource if one of the children was sad at dropping-off time and was a powerful, visible way of showing the children that they, their lifestyle and families were all valued by the setting.

Alongside this process, regular time was given over at staff meetings to reflect on the successes, challenges and failures of various strategies used to work with and support the children in their learning. This also provided staff with a safe space to discuss issues and overcome preconceived ideas or issues they found challenging around the community and their lifestyle.

As understandings of each of the children and their wider community grew, staff were able to undertake observations of the children and use these to plan for future learning activities and curriculum delivery. The children's play was observed and they were supported to develop skills of group working. The more the children felt comfortable and confident, the more they shared about their interests, and as the staff became familiar with their interests they were able to further enrich the children's development (for example, within baking, large-scale collaborative mark-making and ICT).

## Case study 9.3 Supporting a child to access the curriculum

Tom returned to my setting after the summer holiday and was experiencing problems joining in activities and accessing the curriculum. At first we thought it was because most of the other children in his friendship group had attended throughout the summer and the games and social interactions had moved on in his absence. Tom had also had a growth spurt during the holiday. He had grown much taller than his friends and it appeared his spatial awareness and motor skills had not kept pace with this. He appeared to be clumsy compared to his smaller friends who had developed their skills and confidence in outdoor play during his holiday. This had a detrimental effect on his behaviour.

It began in small ways, taking things from others, and then escalated into hitting and, on occasion, biting. He appeared to have lost interest in the activities he had enjoyed before the summer break as he went from area to area disrupting others. A meeting was held with his mother, who was concerned about his behaviour at home, too. It was decided we would give Tom plenty of opportunities to develop his spatial awareness and motor skills. This was easily achieved as it was the year of the London Olympics and all the children were interested in sport and a variety of activities were planned. I felt, though, that this was only a part of the problem.

I was observing him one day as he 'flitted' from one activity to another and it occurred to me that we weren't offering him experiences he was interested in. Reflecting upon this, I noted that Tom had always enjoyed baking. I decided to ask him to help me make dough and he enthusiastically joined in. He paid particular attention to the scales as we weighed the ingredients. We looked at the scales closely and we talked about how they worked. He was engrossed. I decided to combine his love of baking and his apparent interest in how things work by bringing in different kitchen appliances from home. After the usual risk assessments of course! The first thing I brought in was a juicer; this was a great success. Tom was part of a group who cut the fruit into pieces small enough to fit in the juicer. He responded well to working in this small group and following the safety rules regarding the knives. We examined the juicer and thought about how it worked. It made a lot of noise when in use, which made the whole activity even more pleasurable. Tom was one of the children who distributed the juice to the other children for a 'taste test'. Over the coming weeks we extended this. I brought in a variety of equipment; we looked at recipes and 'wrote' shopping lists together and talked about weights. Tom was always given a degree of responsibility and he responded well to this. We had regularly baked before but the introduction of equipment had given these sessions a new interest.

All the children enjoyed these activities; however, for Tom they had a very positive effect. Obviously baking and using and investigating equipment wasn't a magic solution to everything, but it sparked his interest in other activities too. Tom found these experiences interesting and challenging. He became more engaged generally and his behaviour improved as he settled into his friendship group again.

We always endeavour to follow the interests of individual children – not easy when we have over 100 children on the register. Often it can just be in small ways. A key person may just introduce something extra into the role play or share a particular book with a child. In this case the entire cohort became involved and it sparked interests for other children too, helping them access many areas of the curriculum.

Tom is now in school and his mother has sent me note to thank me and say his interest in machinery and how things work has continued.

## Conclusion

National curricula provide a significant means of attempting to fulfil national objectives and of attempting to provide coherence and progression in learning. They also clarify the aims and roles of practitioners within early years provision.

However, by the very act of setting out 'requirements', a 'framework', or a set of 'guidelines', the architects of national curricula select *particular* content for teaching, learning and assessment. This can lead to challenges for early years practitioners – how can one support a child to learn at their own pace while ensuring they reach the expected goals or levels as they enter statutory education?

Indeed, the specification of a national curriculum raises the immediate question: 'Whose curriculum is it?' Any curriculum reflects values, views of knowledge and of learning. Reflective teachers will recognize that dominant opinions and influence can change over time and that they are not always clear-cut or coherent. Ambiguities and dissonances within and between the different agencies that govern education are also commonplace. Thus, they will change over time and reflective practitioners must be able to work within the frameworks provided while delivering what they believe to be best for the children in their care and their families.

In the next chapter we focus on the practical implementation of the curriculum through setting policies, planning and observation.

## Key readings

To delve deeper in to the impact of the hidden curriculum, see:

Martin, J. (1983) 'What Should we do with a Hidden Curriculum when we find one?'. In H. Giroux and D. Purpel (eds) *The Hidden Curriculum and Moral Education*. Berkeley, CA: McCutchan Publishing Corporation, 122–39.

For an overview of curriculum and a great introduction to defining what it is, see:

Lynn, A. (2013) *The Early Years Curriculum: The UK Context and Beyond*. Oxon: Routledge.

For practical support on implementing the curriculum and the importance of starting from the child, see:

Hutchin, V. (2007) *Supporting Every Child's Learning across the Early Years Foundation Stage*. London: Hodder Education.

An excellent discussion on the debate of school readiness is provided by:

Whitebread, D. and Bingham, S. (2011) 'School readiness: A critical review of perspectives and evidence'. Association for the Professional Development of Early Years Educators: Occasional Paper 2. **tactyc.org.uk/occasional-paper/occasional-paper2.pdf**

For extending understandings of curricula development, see:

Hedges, H., Cullen, J. and Jordan, B. (2011) 'Early years curriculum: funds of knowledge as a conceptual framework for children's interests', *Journal of Curriculum Studies*, 43 (2), 185–205.

For sophisticated analysis and proposals on the primary curriculum, see:

Alexander, R. J. (ed.) (2010) *Children, Their World, Their Education.* Final report of the Cambridge Primary Review. London: Routledge.

The classic argument for young children learning through direct experience was expressed in the Plowden Report:

Central Advisory Council for Education (1967) *Children and their Primary Schools.* London: HMSO.

A wonderful book making the point that any curriculum must take full account of learning and developmental process:

Bruner, J. S. (1966) *Towards a Theory of Instruction.* Cambridge, MA: Harvard University Press.

The associated website, **reflectiveteaching.co.uk**, offers a wealth of supplementary resources including reflective activities, research briefings, advice on further reading and downloadable diagrams, figures and checklists from the book. It also features a compendium of educational terms, links to useful websites, policy and curriculum documents, and showcases examples of excellent research and practice.

# Planning
## How are we implementing the curriculum?

**10**

## Introduction

The purpose of this chapter is to think about the practical implementation as well as innovation and personal development of the curriculum in a manner which is appropriate to the children in your care. Planning for groups of very young children is inevitably more complex and fluid than planning for older children or adults, as each child is a unique individual who is growing, developing and learning more rapidly than they ever will again for the rest of their lives (Gerhardt, 2004). It is helpful first to consider what constitutes the curriculum for babies and young children. It encompasses everything that becomes enshrined in curriculum guidelines, which currently apply to children from age 3 in most cases, whether these are early learning goals (DofE, 2012), early level experiences and outcomes (Scottish Government, 2007), or some other current policy document applicable to your setting. In fact curriculum for 0–7, as in any 0–3 setting, includes everything children are doing and therefore learning from. Children will learn from all the routines, such as hanging up their coats or washing hands before snacks, as well as all the one-off events, such as a visit from the local fire-fighters and what might be considered down-time when they are waiting in a line to go into the hall and chat to a friend. This does not mean that we have to plan for every minute of their day, but it is important to recognize that learning – and important learning – is taking place all the time. It helps us realize the importance of planning and creating an environment for learning, developing our skills in interacting with children and remaining responsive to their needs and interests, rather than teaching them in the traditional sense of 'planning lessons'. This also highlights the importance of observation as a key skill for early years practitioners, so that we can identify children's needs, interests and the learning that is taking place all the time.

This chapter is concerned with how we plan to implement the curriculum and it is vital to consider what the curriculum really means in early childhood. The curriculum is more than any national framework and much more than subject content. A curriculum document such as the Statutory Framework for Early Years Foundations Stage, Department of Education (2014) (see **reflectiveteaching.co.uk** for link to the document) can provide, as the title suggests, a framework and guidelines that practitioners can use in their own setting. It cannot and should not be used as a manual or checklist that puts a 'ceiling' on provision and possible learning. Certainly in Scotland, with the introduction of the Curriculum for Excellence 3–18 (Scottish Government, 2010), while the intention was to smooth transitions, build on the good practice enshrined in the 3–5 Curriculum Framework, (SCCC, 1999) that preceded it and move further away from curriculum as content and education as transmission towards process and development (Kelly, 1999, cited in Priestley and Humes, 2010), the reality may be rather different. These curriculum guidelines are now presented as experiences and outcomes under subject headings, e.g. mathematics. This can suggest and lead to coverage of content, transmitting content knowledge and not the importance of the process and an individual child's development – if used as a manual or checklist. Any policy document, such as a curriculum guideline, is only as 'good' as the interpreter (the practitioner) (see Katz, **Reading 10.1**). Early childhood educators such as Katz (1998) argue that the developmental appropriateness of the curriculum is at least as important as rigorous plans for the delivery of subject matter. Smidt (2011) writes:

> ... you may want to think very carefully about the effect of telling children what the learning outcomes are for the activities they are involved in. You are, in effect, determining the outcomes for them and nothing could be less creative than this. (2011: 101)

In early childhood there can often be a disconnect between education and care, with the focus remaining very firmly on care in 0–3 settings, a period of transition between 3–5 where some settings veer towards 'schoolification' and others retain more of an emphasis on care, and then often a very definite, sometimes abrupt, shift to emphasis on education from 5–8. Moss (2006) suggests there are also essentially distinct workforces between 0–3 (care) and 3–8 (education) and that there is 'a clear and deep fault line between the two'. The research of Sylva et al. (2004) indicates that smooth transitions from the start and interaction with specifically qualified adults within a stimulating environment are key to achieving better social and educational outcomes.

## 1 Planning a play-based approach

## 1.1 Why plan?

In the light of this assertion that curriculum includes everything and learning happens all the time, we might also start by considering why we should attempt to plan at all. It is quite possible to provide an exciting, worthwhile experience for young children, from which they will learn as an 'event', with little or no forward planning in terms of identifying prior learning, learning intentions or making assessments. An example might be a picnic organized for a group of children involving games, pond dipping, and provision of diverse and healthy foods taking place in a new environment. Children on such an outing will learn a great deal. However, sustained teaching leading to progression in learning for a large and diverse group of children requires analysis of how the children are learning and how effective the teaching is through assessment, monitoring and evaluation. These are the cornerstones of the planning process or cycle. The purpose of planning is to ensure that the individual needs of children are met and that all children make sustained progress in all aspects of learning and development. This progress needs to be measured against norms and standards in line with curriculum guidelines and policy but with the ultimate aim that each child reaches their full potential. Planning for groups of very young children for whom learning and development is startlingly rapid, highly differentiated and taking place within the context of play, is no small task. It is always a work in progress. Critically, planning should not become a 'straitjacket' or an end in itself that detracts from our ability to respond to children and make the most of those 'magic moments'. Paperwork surrounding the process should not become so burdensome that practitioners spend less and less time interacting with children.

Effective, structured, sustainable plans are needed to capture and share observations, assessments, evaluations and progress to inform the creation of a suitable learning environment, provision of appropriately challenging experiences and ongoing interactions. All plans should be considered as draft or 'plan A' and be open to interpretation in the light of events, change and even wholesale abandonment. Changes made to plans should always be viewed in a positive light if they are justified in terms of enhancing learning experiences for children – *not* giving up on the plan to go outside because it is raining!

---

### Reflective activity 10.1

*Aim:* To consider the value of processes over product.

*Evidence and reflection:* View this short video of the artist Andy Goldsworthy at work in Cumbria at **reflectiveteaching.co.uk** or by putting 'Andy Goldsworthy rainshadow' into your search engine). Consider the possibilities that open up because the focus remains on the process rather than the product and because though plans are made, they remain fluid – literally!

---

Plans need to be structured so that they effectively narrow, focus and become more detailed as they develop from long-term plans to short-term day-to-day plans. There will often be an even narrower focus on planning for individual children. In this chapter we will follow this structure, considering first the long-term plans for a setting which must focus on guidelines and policy with the intention of implementing these for the whole setting. The next phase of planning, which might be labelled medium-term planning, considers the schemes and themes for a particular class or group of children over a period – perhaps a year, a term or a week. Finally the short-term planning for a day, a session or a set period such as 'hall time' provides much more detail to help practitioners provide relevant and purposeful learning experiences. We will move first through these successive levels of detail in the same way in which the ECEC practitioner must when planning their programme.

## 1.2  What are we planning?

Very young children learn from everything they do. They learn very quickly and their learning is affected by their development, their environment and the relationships and interactions they are involved in. Before a child arrives in any ECEC setting, regardless of age, they will have learned a great deal – they are not an 'empty vessel' or a 'blank slate'. It is important to consider our 'image of the child'. Do we hold a 'deficit model' and see them as empty vessels or as unique, competent individuals?

> … we talk about a child who is competent and strong – a child who has the right to hope and the right to be valued, not a predefined child seen as fragile, needy and incapable. Ours is a different way of thinking and approaching the child, whom we view as an active subject with us to explore, to try day by day to understand

something, to find a meaning, a piece of life. (Rinaldi, cited in Clark, Kjorholt and Moss, 2005)

Knowledge and understanding of how children develop and learn is key to our ability as practitioners to plan relevant, stimulating and appropriate learning experiences. It can be very useful to use this term 'learning experiences' when considering planning in the early years, to ensure we do not fall into the trap of thinking in terms of 'lessons'. This can be particularly pertinent to practitioners who may have started their studies and/ or practice with older children. It can be difficult to move away from the structured, teacher-led lesson planning formats without abandoning the whole idea of planning altogether. Equally, it can be difficult for ECEC practitioners who are determined to establish the much-lauded 'routines' that often provide a calm, ordered day that they are comfortable and familiar with themselves, to focus attention on learning experiences that might disrupt this.

Planning an emerging curriculum for a large group of very young children when our view of learning is that it is active and child-initiated requires much detailed observation and monitoring through record-keeping that informs provision. This will allow staff to provide a suitable stimulating environment and offer appropriate experiences. Practitioners require both knowledge and understanding of the content of the curriculum and understanding of the learners. In this way the teaching and learning processes can, as they should, interact. This model is about process not products. It is more about how the child is learning, what they are doing and where, than it is about the end product. For example, while playing at a well-resourced water trolley, children may learn about capacity as intended but may also learn more about sharing than problem-solving and develop their language.

The danger in any discussion on planning is that it quickly becomes prescriptive and it is easy to lose sight of the uniquely enriching role of the creativity and imagination of individual practitioners (Woods and Jeffrey, 1996; Moyles, 2001). It is through dynamic interactions between responsive practitioners and children that high-quality, rich learning experiences really bring the curriculum 'alive' and engage children. Policy documents in England are promoting a more balanced approach and provision of a more responsive curriculum, as it is now acknowledged that the over-prescription of the National Curriculum and Strategies in England made it difficult to engage some children. It is not possible to produce a prescription for engaging and promoting learning for all 3-year-olds or all 5-year-olds. The professional judgement of the ECEC practitioner on the spot is the vital ingredient. Only they can decide on the combination of structure and responsiveness that will be most effective.

Table 10.1 Learning experience plan

| Prior learning/experience: | Learning intentions: |
|---|---|
| identified from observations/investigations – <br><br>What is your starting point or <br>basis for the planned experience? | What do you expect children to learn? <br>Literally what is the intended learning? |
| **Success criteria:** <br>**What** evidence of learning will you be looking for? <br>**When** will you be able to gather this evidence? <br>**How** will you determine what children have learned? | **Curricular links:** <br>Identify aspects of learning and development. <br>Identify criteria from curriculum guidelines that you hope to meet (for example in Scotland, Early Level Experiences and Outcomes from Curriculum for Excellence). |
| **Learning activities:** <br>Describe the learning experience, which may be a whole-class activity over a discrete period of time or the development of a context (e.g. the role-play area) over an extended or open-ended period of time. | **Resources:** <br>Provide details of specific resources required. |
| **Evaluation of learning:** <br>Detailed assessment of children's learning and development which may be individual, groups or whole-group and then identify – <br>**Next steps for the children.** | **Evaluation of teaching:** <br>Detailed assessment of your own actions, communication, interaction, provision and then identify – <br>**Next steps for you.** |

**Table 10.1** provides an example of planning for learning experiences.

---

## Reflective activity 10.2

*Aim:* To consider knowledge and the needs of children.

*Evidence and reflection:* What does a 4-year-old child need to know? For example, does he need to know how to read – right now? Why might we be teaching him to read – is it because he needs this skill now or because he will need it in the future? What skills, knowledge, understanding or informed attitude does this 4-year-old need – right now? What skills, knowledge, understanding or informed attitudes will help this 4-year-old reach his full potential? If this child is becoming interested in books, does this mean he is falling behind? What or who creates this barrier to learning?

---

What we plan for young children depends very much on our view of learning and on our image of the child. A starting point must be defining learning and analysing and identifying our own image of the child. Smidt (2011: 77) asserts that 'we no longer see children as passive learners but as constructors of their own learning'. In stating this, she was drawing on and interpreting the theories of Bruner, who saw learning as a process of constructing knowledge and understanding through interaction with others and the environment; a process of developing skills through activities that use and build on skills already established; a process that takes place within a community through interaction, and a continuing process. Bruner has further developed his theories, particularly his view of narrative. He has systematically developed what might be termed 'a narrative view of culture and mind and has argued that reality is itself narratively constructed' (Smidt, 2001: 93). He sees narrative or storytelling in all its forms, from autobiography to science fiction, as our way of organizing and communicating experience. Very young children as soon as they begin to communicate begin to weave 'proto-narratives' (Bruner, 2002).

Wenger (1998) identified what he called 'communities of practice' to describe groups of people engaged in activities through which they learn together. For a baby, this community would include their parents, other primary carers and siblings, gradually extending to childminder or nursery setting, other children, extended family, neighbours and school. We can all be involved in 'communities of practice' that are flexible and change. For example, a group of adults might be involved in exploring a new technique, perhaps various craft-speople restoring an old house together, and this would constitute a community of practice for a period of time. Young children might be part of such a community as a class or room member or temporarily when engaged in, say, building a 'den' with a group of other children.

## Reflective activity 10.3

*Aim:* To reflect upon the skills children require to participate in shared activities.

*Evidence and reflection:* Observe children engaged in a group activity, perhaps in the home corner or the story corner. Identify children who you would consider core members of the group. Are they deeply involved and fully participating in the activity? Identify children who you would consider peripheral members of the group. Are they on the periphery of the group but perhaps 'legitimate peripheral participants' (Wenger, 1998)? Are they partly involved but lacking in some skills or confidence to fully participate?

You will need to observe closely to determine whether all children are participating fully and if not, why not. Consider the barriers to children becoming fully participant – is it:

- through choice?
- lack of certain skills?
- lack of confidence?
- cultural difference?

Finally, consider whether your organization of the activity has created any barriers to children participating fully. For example, are the resources familiar and relevant to all?

To summarize what practitioners are planning in order to provide a curriculum for very young children, we could say that they:

- create the physical environment to facilitate, structure and contextualize children's learning through play;
- provide resources, models, guidance and feedback to children to support learning;

- provide opportunities for quality interactions between adults, children and children and their peers;
- observe, monitor, assess and record children's progress in order to make useful evaluations and identify next steps.

The role of all adults in an ECEC setting is to enable, instigate and extend children's learning and much of this, certainly for children under 5, happens while children play.

## 1.3 Play

The importance and benefits of adopting a play-based approach to delivering the curriculum and continuing this beyond pre-school is reflected in recent curriculum guidelines across the UK. For example, in Scotland, in an early stage document regarding the Curriculum for Excellence, a Minister wrote:

> The purposes and principles of a Curriculum for Excellence will bring the 3–5 and 5–14 curriculum guidelines together to ensure a smooth transition in what children have learned and also in how they learn. This will mean extending the approaches which are used in pre-school into the early years of primary emphasising the importance of opportunities for children to learn through purposeful, well planned play. (Peter Peacock, 2004: *A Curriculum for Excellence Ministerial Response*, SEED)

The English Early Years Foundation Stage (EYFS) standard demands that learning and development takes place through play and active learning, stating on the 'Play practice cards' that 'Play underpins all development and learning for young children'. Another card states: 'In their play children learn at their highest level' (DCFS, 2008).

The Welsh Assembly Government Play Policy (2002) states their belief that 'Play is the elemental learning process by which humankind has developed' (Curriculum and Assessment Authority for Wales, 1996).

The Department for Education, Northern Ireland (DENI, 2012) states on its website that children should be provided with a rich variety of play activities and other experiences in a stimulating and challenging environment and allowed to learn without experiencing a sense of failure.

Planning for play is a surprisingly complex task. The activities in the setting need to be child-led and meet the individual needs and interests of a number of children. Children need to be able to:

- make choices
- negotiate
- use their own ideas and imagination
- be physically and intellectually active
- experiment, explore and investigate

In order to plan play activities that will provide a broad range of learning opportunities for any group of children, practitioners will need knowledge of:

- normative development, to determine the stage that the child/ren are at and ensure activities are appropriate to their stage of physical, social, emotional, cognitive and language development;

- how children learn, to be able to identify the learning opportunities within play activities;

- the 'lived lives' of the children, to ensure that activities are relevant, attuned to children's interests, stimulating and motivating.

Tassoni and Hucker (2000) identify key points of good practice when planning play that include considering the individual needs of children, hence the need for knowledge of normative child development and where each child fits into this. They also include planning as a team and involving both the children and the parents on the basis that all 'stakeholders' need to take some ownership of the plan, the play and therefore the learning. Parents will be key to understanding the 'lived lives' of children and can extend and integrate learning experiences. Listening to children and involving them in decisions and their own learning is powerful; it enhances learning (Kinney, 2005, also see Moss, Reading 10.2).

The ECEC practitioner needs to determine three key things before planning a play context. These are:

- The children's interests and what is relevant to them.

- What do they need to learn in terms of their current and future needs?

- What stage are they at in terms of their development – what is their 'zone of proximal development? (Vygotsky, 1978, 1987; Reading 2.3).

Sometimes the ECEC practitioner may make a decision based on the above information, and set up a context or activity and introduce it. Sometimes it may be that you simply introduce a resource and see where the children take it. An example of this which is often seen is providing large cardboard boxes and simply leaving them on the carpet, which can lead to a range of imaginative, creative play. It is in such an example that the role of the ECEC practitioner as planner, assessor, indeed as 'teacher', is most challenged and challenging. There is great skill in being able to interact effectively in such a situation to facilitate learning. It is critical when planning to know when and how to introduce such an element. It would not be effective if there were *always* large cardboard boxes on the carpet! There has to be an element of excitement to make this simple resource stimulating. There needs to be a plan in place to provide other resources that might be required, to ensure safety, to allow for as many or as few children who choose to participate to do so, to allow at least one adult in the setting to monitor, observe and interact as children play, and of course a 'plan B' if none of the children choose to participate or there is a 'malfunction' that prevents play continuing.

While having a plan and considering your own involvement is important to enable you to resource play, it is vital that changes are expected. No learning and teaching plans should ever be static. The process of planning should be seen as organic, in the sense that all plans, at whatever level, should be open to modification and change dependent upon their success in aiding the development of learning. It is in the changes, the fluidity, and the flexibility that the children's voices will be heard and where creativity and learning will flourish (Smidt, 2011).

Essentially an adult can do three things to facilitate learning when children are playing: they can interrupt, intervene, or interact. The ECEC practitioner may need to do all three at some point and it is all about getting the balance right. Interruptions should be few but it is sometimes inevitable, particularly in more formal settings – for example, the dreaded routine imposed by the timetable and sometimes for safety. Interventions may occur when:

- individual children need help to 'join in'.
- learning can be extended, for example to add resources.
- asked to by children.
- children are aggressive, but this can often provide an opportunity for sustained shared thinking.
- safety demands it, particularly to reiterate rules for safety; children are distressed.
  (McIntyre, 2012)

Well-planned play activities should not require too much intervention, so this is an excellent guide to assess your planning!

Interacting effectively with children at play is an important aspect of the adult role. ECEC practitioners should *plan* to ensure they have time to observe and, where appropriate, participate and interact with children at play. Supporting and enhancing learning through play is the professional responsibility of an adult in any ECEC setting. The Northern Territory Government (2012) in Australia suggest we can support children's play by:

- allowing for extended periods of time for children to remain in 'the flow' of their play.
- providing resources such as safe household items and materials.
- making enough space to focus on the play activity.
- catering for choices of activity, materials and equipment.
- role-modelling to encourage and extend ideas.
- challenging them with more complex thinking, novel ideas or experience.

This provides a useful, practical summary and encompasses the key elements of the adult role in providing a play-based approach to active learning.

The best way to develop skills in interacting with children at play effectively is to do it, but just doing something over and over does not necessarily enhance skill; you must also be able to reflect and learn from experience. Reflection on interactions should be part of evaluation in the planning cycle. Similarly, you can learn a great deal about what works and what doesn't by observing others interacting with children at play, but again it is the reflection that is so important (see Dewey, 1933, Reading 3.6; Schön, 1983, Reading 3.5).

## 2 The planning process

The planning process is cyclical, beginning with the practitioner planning and preparing tasks, activities or, in the case of early years, play. These are then presented in some way – for example, there may be whole-class discussion, an experiment, singing or playing instruments, or a context for play such as sand or water tray. The children then engage with the activity within a management system set up by the practitioner: for example, four children playing with sand and four with water while the rest engage with a structured adult-led art/craft activity.

While children engage with the activities and/or when they are completed, the practitioner must assess or evaluate learning, giving feedback to children and using the information to inform their next round of planning (Bennett, 1992).

With younger children and babies the ratio allows for more 1:1 interactions and smaller groups. Feedback can be given spontaneously through verbal praise and gestures. Sharing this with parents is important too (see Brodie, Reading 10.4).

## 2.1 Long-term planning

One purpose of long-term planning is essentially to ensure that all aspects of the curriculum receive attention over time. It is a way of ensuring breadth, balance, coherence and consistency for children linking and progressing learning experiences from day-to-day and when transferring to new classes or settings. The long term ECEC practitioners will be concerned with planning over a year to enable them to see and share within the whole team a simple outline over that time. These plans need to be:

- concise – to provide an 'at-a-glance' overview.
- corporate – in the sense that they are developed by the whole team in a setting.
- consistent – so that there is shared understanding and approaches to pedagogy, including assessment, recording, reporting, use of and access to resources.

These plans should take account of policy guidelines and consider what has gone before and what comes after. They could be seen as a 'route planner' providing an outline of starting point, finishing point and major stops on the way. They should help to identify any need for resources and what has to be put in place in advance. On a journey, this might be checking the tyres and refuelling; in this case, it may be purchasing paints or ensuring permissions are granted for outings. An ECEC setting may want to make structural changes, purchase large equipment or some more expensive resources, and these will have to be planned well in advance.

## 2.2 Medium-term planning

Here the practitioner may be considering plans over the next few weeks or at least a week ahead and will have greater control over this part of planning, although there is still a need to fit in with how the whole setting is operating. Of course, these plans should flow from the long-term plans.

There will be a number of fixtures in any setting, such as start and finish times, and children benefit from a structured, stable environment that can enable them to operate independently because they know the boundaries and expectations. However, it may be more helpful to start from the child, asking yourself what their needs and interests are and how you can best accommodate their different needs and interests, rather than *starting* with the constraints of the timetable or 'establishing a routine'. The real purpose of this planning is to look for opportunities for children to make choices, operate independently and develop and learn at their own pace, rather than fitting them into the straitjacket of a timetable, framework or environment.

Most practitioners will plan a theme or topic over a period of a few weeks or sometimes just for a week and this helps contextualize the learning. These themes or contexts can be real or fantastical – for example, a common theme is 'All about me', or a fairy tale such as 'Jack and the Beanstalk' is used. In either case the theme can link past, present and future and help children develop knowledge and understanding, skills and informed attitudes appropriate to their ability. Developing a theme should help to:

- build on the 'lived lives' of children, or their prior learning and experiences.
- make learning relevant.
- provide direct personal, first-hand experiences.
- involve children in problem-solving, questioning and genuine enquiry.
- make best use of the immediate environment and community.
- provide opportunities to develop positive attitudes and relationships as well as a range of skills.
- involve children in sustained shared thinking.
- provide balance across curricular areas.
- provide an appropriate range of challenges for different children.
- make learning enjoyable for adults and children.

It is possible for adults to identify a theme but still provide flexibility to allow the different needs and interests of children to be met. One approach to this that articulates with Bruner's view of narrative discussed in 1.2 above (see Jones, Reading 10.3) is the 'Storyline' approach developed many years ago in Scotland. See reflectiveteaching.co.uk for a link to the Storyline website where you can explore this further. This approach can be used with any age group. Reading and telling stories to children or creating stories with them is a powerful tool in the early years (see Lee, Reading 10.5).

# 2.3 Short-term planning

Short-term or day-to-day planning lies at the heart of the ECEC practitioner's role. Here is the point where the physical environment is actually created, the interactions between adults and children take place, the observations for monitoring and assessment happen and resources have to be found (sometimes quickly) to support children's play and learning. The planning process or 'cycle' for the ECEC practitioner remains the same as that for any teacher of any age group and through each phase of planning. There are eight essential elements, including:

1 Identifying prior learning and experience – what is your starting point?

2 Identifying learning intentions or outcomes – what do you hope children will learn?

3 Identifying success criteria – how will you know what they have learned? How will you monitor and assess the learning?

4 Identifying links to curriculum guidelines – how does this learning fit into the bigger picture?

5 Identifying use of time and space.

6 Identifying required resources, including human resources, materials, time and space.

7 Evaluation of learning – assessing individual's learning and the learning of the whole group and identifying the next steps in learning.

8 Evaluation of teaching – reflecting on your preparation, delivery, interactions, resources, organization and management and identifying the next steps in teaching.

These eight elements should appear on any written planning format, remaining the same no matter what age or stage the learners are at. There might be times when practitioners would wish to add others, such as notes about grouping, differentiation or parental involvement. There will be many times when such detailed planning will not be written down and this is why it is helpful, from time to time, to write up detailed plans showing all eight elements to 'embed' the process. There are a selection of materials at **reflectiveteaching.co.uk** which show how they have been used in a variety of circumstances and with babies and children of different ages.

There are key questions which can help at each stage of the planning process. To support decision-making and planning the practitioner might question:

To identify prior learning and experience –

● How well do I know these children?

● What knowledge and understanding, skills or informed attitudes do the children bring?

● What evidence do I have to support my decisions? (for example, observations, assessment results, conversations with parents or other staff)

- What do I know about the 'lived lives' of these children and what will be relevant to them?
- How does this learning relate to the curriculum guidelines I am working with?

## 3 Evaluating provision

Effective evaluation of learning and teaching is an essential task for the reflective practitioner. A reflective practitioner is one who clearly understands the intimate links between the processes of planning, teaching and assessment (see Brodie, Reading 10.4). Considering the evaluation of provision, it is possible to highlight many of the features of this cycle (see Bennett, 1992).

The following questions are suggested by Scott-Baumann, Bloomfield and Roughton (1997) as a guide:

- What happened?
- What effect did it have?
- Why did it happen?
- How could I make sense of it?
- How could it be different?
- How might I (we) have behaved differently?
- What would I do next time?

> **Expert question**
>
> **Processes for children's affective needs:** Does the educational experience take due account of children's views, feelings and characteristics?
>
> This question contributes to a conceptual framework representing enduring issues and practitioner expertise (see Chapter 16).

These questions have been suggested for secondary school teachers and might be reinterpreted in an ECEC setting under separate headings. For example:

*Learning environment*

- Was the space used effectively?
- Did all the children who wanted to, access the activity?
- Was anything missing?

*Equipment and materials*

- Did children use the equipment/materials provided as intended or differently?
- Did children suggest different equipment/materials or uses?
- Were equipment/materials sufficient and well organized?

*The role of adults*

- Did what adults say make a difference to children's understanding or outcomes?
- Did adults help children who did not understand?
- Did adults interact effectively? Were they involved?

*Responses of individual children*

- Was the group size appropriate?
- Did each child respond or react the same/were they equally engaged? What factors affected this?
- What did each child say or do?
- What interests did individual children express?
- Did children learn or consolidate learning as intended?
- What else did individual children learn?

If any practitioner can answer all these points they will have an extremely effective evaluation!

# 3.1 Identifying learning

It becomes clear when considering the evaluation process that identifying learning, either as intended learning at the planning stage or as part of the assessment and evaluation, is challenging. It is helpful to consider what exactly it is we want young children to learn before we attempt to identify learning intentions or assess the learning that has actually taken place.

This chapter has already highlighted the importance of play and the importance and impact of the environment in terms of supporting children's learning and development. The final piece of the puzzle is relationships and this includes all the relationships children form and engage with, particularly key people in the child's life. This emphasis on social learning and play-based approaches is in line with social-constructivist theories of learning espoused by Lev Vygotsky, Jerome Bruner and Tina Bruce.

A focus on *how* children learn through interaction with their environment and others, coupled with the understanding that these very young children are not 'empty vessels' but competent individuals who are able to build on prior learning to rapidly assimilate new knowledge, skills and informed attitudes, can help us identify *what* children need to learn and are learning.

Vygotsky's theory of the Zone of Proximal Development identified the space between what a child already knows or has mastered and the knowledge that is still beyond their capabilities (Krogh and Slentz, 2011). In this space learning is challenging but not frustrating and with help from a practitioner, parent or more able peer, the child can understand and learn. This is important in terms of planning. This is the 'space' the practitioner needs to identify so that they can plan learning experiences that are challenging but not frustrating and also gauge the level of support required. To do this effectively, practitioners will need to build up a profile of the child involving close observation as well as taking account of their 'lived life', or learning beyond the setting.

> ## Reflective activity 10.4
>
> *Aim:* To consider theory in relation to learning and practice.
>
> *Evidence and reflection:* Consider Vygotsky's theory of learning in relation to children engaging with technology. Observe two or more children using a computer game or other suitable activity. How do they support each other? Is one child more competent? Do they support each other's learning?
>
> *Extension:* We know that technology will be radically different by the time the child reaches adulthood; indeed it is changing at a rapid pace almost from day to day. Consider what the child needs to know about technology (perhaps focus on the use of the computer you have already observed):
>
> - How important is skill development, e.g. use of the 'mouse'? Now? In the future?
> - Is it more important for the child to know *about* technology, what it can and might do for us and how to make good use of whatever is available, but not necessarily practise the use of what will soon become redundant?
> - If they cannot use it, can they learn about it?
> - Look at the video 'A magazine is an iPad that does not work' on Youtube. (See link at **reflectiveteaching.co.uk**)

**www.** ↻

As we have noted in previous chapters, Bruner developed the theory of ZPD and suggested the term 'scaffolding', meaning the process by which others support children in moving from where they are now to where the adults want to take them. Bruce (2005) goes further to point out that there is a subtle difference between this and when 'the adult goes with the child and helps them learn more about what interests and fascinates them' (p. 52). Again, understanding that children learn by being 'scaffolded' in different ways should inform the ECEC practitioner when planning. The practitioner needs to develop the ability of knowing which to use. They need to know when to lead and when to follow, when to lead the child towards the learning intention already determined or simply when to intervene and when to stand back.

Bruner (1960) also identified the 'spiral curriculum'. He suggested the child needs to be introduced to essential elements of learning on any subject at their own level and revisit and build on their understanding. He believes that anything can be 'taught' to anyone at any age 'in some form that is honest' (Bruner, 1977: 108), and also that a useful criterion for any subject taught in primary school should be 'whether, when fully developed, it is worth an adult's knowing, and whether having known it as a child makes a person a better adult' (Bruner, 1960: 52). Again, this is useful understanding for the practitioner in terms of interpreting and implementing curriculum guidelines and planning learning experiences.

The discussion so far, reflecting on elements of learning theory, suggests that there needs to be a clear focus on *how* children are learning throughout the planning cycle rather than simply *what*. This brings us back to the challenge of how we can identify and assess children's learning. Identifying a learning intention to support children to 'know their colours' and assessing this in terms of children telling the adult that the banana is yellow and the T-shirt is blue, for example, will not provide much useful information to inform future planning. If this success is achieved through all colouring in the same worksheet it will not provide much information about each child's individual learning and nothing about what else might have been learned in the process.

---

## Reflective activity 10.5

*Aim:* To reflect upon what children need to learn and when.

*Evidence and reflection:* Work with a colleague or fellow student to consider what children need to learn, for example at age 3.

Is it vital that a 3-year-old is able to identify the colour of objects?

What useful information might a practitioner gain by an exercise that assesses a 3-year-old child's ability to differentiate between colours?

What experience involving 'colour' might a 3-year-old enjoy and learn from? What would they learn?

---

Dweck (2006) has identified what has become known as a positive 'mindset' or disposition towards learning, meaning that individuals are motivated to learn, they are curious, determined and willing and able to concentrate. A 'disposition' simply means 'what you are disposed to do' and, in terms of ECEC, really focuses on maintaining a positive disposition towards learning. The word 'maintaining' is used because all babies start with a positive disposition towards learning (Gopnik et al., 1999). All babies are born with a range of mechanisms at their disposal to learn and the plasticity of the immature human brain allows new pathways to develop through interactions with fellow humans (Zeedyck, 2006; Meltzoff and Moore, 1983). Researchers now believe that as much as 80 per cent of the basic brain architecture is 'wired' by the age of 3 (Kotulak, 1996). Newborn babies search out human faces (Johnson et al., 1991) possibly as an early survival technique; when a close bond is made, the chance of being cared for and protected will be higher. We can see from this research evidence, and indeed by our own close observation of babies, that the human baby is a born 'learner' and certainly does not wait to reach nursery or school to make a start. Sadly, some have already lost or begun to lose this by the time they enter formal education. Perhaps the most important aspect of the role of all adults in a young child's life, particularly ECEC practitioners, is to maintain and nurture these positive dispositions towards learning. Dowling (2010) suggests this may be achieved through:

- secure attachments – key person in the setting.
- models of positive dispositions – particularly from key person.
- opportunities to repeat and practise patterns of behaviour that reinforce these dispositions.
- adults encouraging and extending children's interest – developing autonomy.
- adults explicitly valuing the child's efforts, for example through descriptive praise.

Dispositions are different to attitudes (Katz, 1995); the latter are concerned with a set of beliefs, whereas a disposition demonstrates the attitude in behaviour. The EYFS (2012) identifies excitement, motivation and interest as dispositions for learning. These are three things we need to consider when planning activities. If children are excited, motivated and interested there is more chance they will engage in discussion, be creative, problem-solve, take risks and develop flexible thinking. These three dispositions towards learning correlate with the three domains suggested by Carr (2001). In her work in New Zealand developing 'learning stories' as a means to assess learning and inform planning, she suggests a child needs to be:

- ready – see themselves as a learner;
- willing – because they recognize the environment offers scope for learning; and
- able – because they have sufficient knowledge, skills and understanding to be ready and willing.

Goswami (2008) has identified three types of learning:

1  Learning by imitation

2  The ability to connect cause and effect – explanation

3  Associative learning – analogy

Babies from birth to 3 days have been shown to be able to imitate gestures such as tongue protrusion and mouth opening after watching an adult carry out the same gestures (Meltzoff and Moore, 1983). This ability to learn by imitation supports the development of social cognition. All human contact offers opportunities to imitate. Without this close bond, this type of learning would not occur, as has been shown in children who have been isolated from human contact (Chugani et al., 2001, cited in Gerhardt, 2004).

Babies very quickly demonstrate the ability to connect cause and effect. A baby makes the link that 'if I cry someone will pick me up and soothe me and feed me'. This early example of associative learning is another basic survival technique. As the child develops and is able to ask questions, this process becomes more complex and they begin to explain the cause and effect and 'test' their hypothesis in new situations. This questioning supports the development of early memory and enables young children to learn that certain events co-occur; this is referred to as associative learning.

## Reflective activity 10.6

*Aim:* To consider the learning needs of babies and toddlers.

*Evidence and reflection:* Observe babies and toddlers engaging with technology in the home. Watch how quickly even a very young baby learns to associate pressing buttons with the appearance of their favourite TV show or the ringing of the phone with Mum being occupied and what she does, for example holding the phone to her ear. Initially babies will press any or all buttons before refining their search. These are examples of early associative learning and show us how the brain is making connections and assimilating information.

It is essential to consider exactly what learning we are intending to support when planning experiences for young children. Practitioners should consider how the planned experience supports:

- the development of positive dispositions towards learning.
- the development of knowledge, skills or informed attitudes that are needed now or in the future.
- opportunities for the child to learn through imitation.
- opportunities to make connections with prior learning and experiences.

To do this the practitioner will need to study the children in their care, interact with them and their parents or primary carers and continually modify the provision in terms of the environment they create. Skill in observation will be key to this, as well as the ability to communicate and share information with all stakeholders.

## 3.2 Observation

To make a useful evaluation the practitioner must make assessments and gather evidence. The purpose of the assessment and evaluation is to identify next steps in learning for groups or individuals. In an ECEC setting most of the evidence will be gathered through observation. It is vital to identify what children are actually learning and how they are developing and this cannot be done by examining and assessing what they *produce* – it is essential to examine the *process*. Observing very young children is fascinating and informative. In trying to determine what they are learning the practitioner must observe both formally and informally, recording and sharing information where possible to develop a clearer picture of the complex web of learning that occurs when children go about their activities and play. Consider **Case study 10.1** and what this observation tell us about learning and how this might inform plans to provide learning opportunities.

---

### Case study 10.1 Observing very young children

Roscoe was exactly one year old, as it was his birthday party. He was enjoying a picnic in a small park in a London square with a number of friends and their Mums. His Mum took a range of playthings including a small three-way 'tunnel' which Gran had bought a few weeks ago. For the first hour a few other babies explored this, crawling in and out, sometimes staying in the middle for some time and puzzling about how to work around each other. Roscoe frequently went to one entrance and peered in but never entered. I asked Mum if he had been in before and she said no, he had never actually gone inside yet and seemed quite wary.

At the start of the picnic Roscoe had got his hands on a biro and was waving it about, so Mum wrestled it from his grasp as it seemed a possible hazard. He had 'growled' and held onto it quite determinedly, so she had to be quite firm and then distract him.

About an hour later I noticed Roscoe at an entrance to the tunnel with his head inside. He rocked back and forth a few times, came out, hesitated and then suddenly crawled to

---

the centre. No other child was inside. He emerged quite quickly and went a yard away on the grass. I immediately noticed he had a biro in his grasp. He looked very pleased with himself; when he saw his mother approaching he put the biro under his bottom. I watched closely and he did not go inside the tunnel again during the afternoon.

Observing children, recording these observations and analysing and sharing them so that they are useful involves practise. Developing this core skill is at the heart of good reflective practice. Like cooking, it is part art and part science and certainly some people are much more intuitive and adept from the start, but it is equally certain that it is a skill that can be learned and refined throughout a career. There are a number of techniques used in formal observations, including:

- Written narrative or record
- Time or event sampling
- Checklists
- Graphical diagrammatic recording such as bar or pie charts
- Target child
- Movement or flow charts
- Media such as photographs or video recording

There are others, and techniques can be adapted and combined to essentially form new ways or observing and recording. The reflective practitioner will explore the various techniques and adapt them to suit their own needs. A useful starting point could be to study one child using the written narrative and time sampling approaches and the observation schedules provided at **reflectiveteaching.co.uk**.

**www. C**

A teacher evaluating a discrete lesson for older children can more easily relate this to the objectives set. These are likely to be clearly identified learning intentions and success criteria. These are much less clearly defined with very young children, particularly when adopting a play-based approach. The practitioner must have some idea of intended learning and will be looking for certain behaviours and responses in order to make an assessment, but the learning of a group of children engaged in complex cooperative play is likely to be very varied in every sense. Recorded observations in a variety of formats is the most effective way to capture these rich learning experiences, analyse them, assess learning and development and identify next steps.

## Conclusion

Very young children are learning very rapidly all the time from everything that they do. Adults need to support their learning and development by planning an environment that provides opportunities for learning that are developmentally appropriate. The environment and the play-based learning experiences should be stimulating but provide a sense of security through physical and emotional safety, consistency and relevance. It is important to use policy guidelines and frameworks intelligently and not allow these to become a straitjacket that limits possibilities. Planning should never become prescriptive; it should always remain flexible and responsive to the needs of children as well as circumstances. Planning should always be seen as a cyclical ongoing process, beginning with making an assessment of children's needs and interests and returning to an assessment of progression and achievement to identify the next steps in the process. It is important to remember that the focus should remain on *how* children learn, rather than *what* they learn, and retain and sustain the natural positive disposition and motivation to learn that all babies begin with.

## Key readings

For extending understandings of how we learn with and from others, see:

Bandura, A. (1977) *Social Learning Theory*. New York: General Learning Press.

As we have noted, play is the foundation for a child's learning; see:

Bruce, T. (1991) *Time to Play in Early Childhood Education*. London: Hodder and Stoughton.

McIntyre, C. (2012) *Enhancing Learning Through Play – A Developmental Perspective for Early Years Settings*. London: Routledge.

Tassoni, P. and Hucker, K. (2000) *Planning Play and the Early Years*. Oxford: Heinemann.

Understanding children's development is crucial for successful planning; we recommend:

Bruce, T. (2004) *Developing Learning in Early Childhood 0–8*. London: Sage Publications Ltd.

Doherty, J. and Hughes, M. (2009) *Child Development: Theory and Practice 0–11*. Harlow: Pearson Education Ltd.

Smidt, S. (2011) *Introducing Bruner – A Guide for Practitioners and Students in Early Years Education*. London: Routledge.

The associated website, **reflectiveteaching.co.uk**, offers a wealth of supplementary resources including reflective activities, research briefings, advice on further reading and downloadable diagrams, figures and checklists from the book. It also features a compendium of educational terms, links to useful websites, policy and curriculum documents, and showcases examples of excellent research and practice.

# Pedagogy

## How can we develop effective strategies?

**11**

## Introduction

The term Reflective Teaching has been deliberately used throughout this book despite the controversy which surrounds the word teaching for some early years practitioners. Following intense debate we agreed, while understanding this may cause some consternation, that teaching is an extremely important term that warrants recognition and further exploration. For many early childhood practitioners, particularly in Western societies, the importance of individualized, play-based provisions is well established together with the role of the adult as a co-constructor of knowledge with the child/children. In particular, the adult's role is often seen as non-directive, that of a facilitator of learning rather than the more didactic role often associated with the term teaching. However, we believe this is rather a restricted view of teaching and, further, that teaching is an essential part of pedagogy. We recognize the argument of Freire (1995) and Siraj-Blatchford (2009), among others, that restricting early years practice to facilitation only neglects our civil duty to teach in a society where there is social injustice and inequality.

> ### Expert question
>
> **Principle**: Is our pedagogy consistent with established principles for effective teaching and learning?
>
> This question contributes to a conceptual framework representing enduring issues and practitioner expertise (see Chapter 16).

## Defining pedagogy

The term 'pedagogy' has been defined quite broadly in continental Europe and beyond, which, at times, has led to some confusion between it and the term 'curriculum'. Siraj-Blatchford (2009) argues that they are quite different to each other but also complementary. She explains that curriculum is understood as denoting all of the knowledge, skills and values that children are meant to learn, while pedagogy is the practice (or art, science or craft) of teaching (see The General Teaching Council for England, Reading 11.1). 'To be a pedagogue is therefore essentially, and by definition, to be a teacher' (Siraj-Blatchford, 2009: 148). The facilitation of learning through the provision of educational environments for play and exploration is just one pedagogical strategy that an early years practitioner may employ. Beyond this there are many more strategies, including modelling and demonstration, questioning and direct instruction (see Siraj-Blatchford, Sylva, Muttock, Gilden and Bell, Reading 11.2).

Eadue (2011) draws upon the work of the TLRP (2006) in order to explore different meanings of pedagogy and to emphasize the importance of focusing on how children learn rather than what the adults do. He believes that pedagogy for young children must take account of:

> children's differing backgrounds and prior experience;
> the varied and complex ways in which children learn;
> the multiple, sometimes conflicting aims of education;
> assumptions made about children and learning. (Eaude, 2011: 10)

Thus, pedagogy can be seen as the skilful interplay of practitioners' craft knowledge and

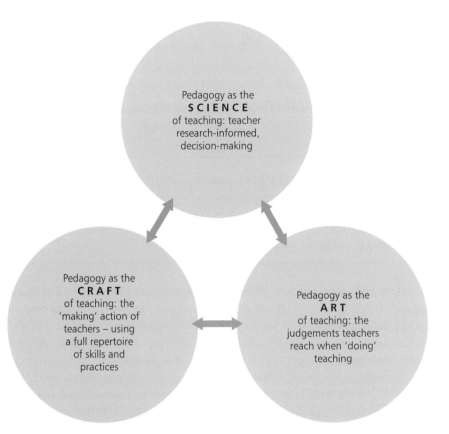

Figure 11.1 The art, craft and science of teaching

their creative responsiveness to specific situations, as informed by theory and research. Practitioners move between these different sources of experience, strategic judgement and understanding, as they take decisions 'in action'. In this chapter, as in others, we use case-study vignettes to represent decision-making in action.

As **Figure 11.1** shows, the art, craft and science of teaching each contribute to the overall concept of pedagogy (GTC-E, 2010). Craft is seen as the repertoire of practitioners' accumulated skills, strategies, methods, approaches and practices from which they select and to which they continue to add through experience. Art is seen as practitioners' moment-by-moment responses to what is happening in the setting in ways that are secure, grounded, creative or innovative, as the occasion demands. Science is seen as practitioners' knowledge, understanding of and engagement in evaluation, reflection and research, in search of evidence to inform the professional choices and decisions they make. This approach to pedagogy can be contrasted with understandings of 'folk pedagogy' which unfortunately still exist in contemporary cultures (Bruner, 1996; Reading 11.3). Indeed, to establish the profession of teaching, it is vital to move beyond folk pedagogy to establish the nature of practitioners' expertise.

Pedagogic judgement enables practitioners to provide both care and education for young children. In particular, practitioners develop a repertoire of skills to 'scaffold' and extend learners' understanding and to support engagement in learning while supporting the development of their personal, social and emotional development.

> ## TLRP principles
>
> Two principles are of particular relevance to this chapter on practitioner strategies and pedagogic repertoire:
>
> **Principle 4: Effective teaching and learning requires teachers to scaffold learning.** Teachers should provide activities which support learners as they move forward, not just intellectually, but also socially and emotionally, so that once these supports are removed, the learning is secure.
>
> **Principle 6: Effective teaching and learning promotes the active engagement of the learner.** A chief goal of teaching and learning should be the promotion of learners' independence and autonomy. This involves acquiring a repertoire of learning strategies and practices, developing positive attitudes towards learning, and confidence in oneself as a good learner.

In discussing pedagogy, we also acknowledge the crucial importance to pedagogy of *subject knowledge*, which we take to mean the concepts, knowledge and understanding, within and between domains of learning, on which practitioners' planning and teaching draws. Of course, this is complemented by the need for understanding about *learning*. Whatever aspirations or expectations may exist, it is essential to take account of the existing knowledge, experience and understanding of children. For a more detailed discussion of learning, see Chapter 2. Pedagogic expertise, as you can see, draws on a wide range of understanding and capabilities – which is what makes it so interesting.

In this chapter, we begin with a case-study vignette enabling us to see the 'pedagogy in action' of a successful practitioner. A short analysis of her pedagogy is then provided, for its significance to the ECEC profession has not been fully established in the UK until recently. Section 3 is focused on pedagogic judgements to support learner development, and we then return to the issue of pedagogic repertoire. This is illustrated through a discussion of the use of talk to 'scaffold' play and understanding through a variety of whole group, small group, individual and play activities. Finally, we look at the way in which pedagogy develops over time.

## 1 Enacting the art, craft and science of pedagogy

## 1.1 Art, craft and science in action

We offer a vignette as a starting point for thinking about how pedagogy, as defined in the previous section, might be enacted in the setting.

# Case study 11.1 Working with water and ice

*A group of six children aged 3 and 4 years are encouraged to join practitioner Clare in one of the small rooms which is set to the side of the main free-flow area of a nursery. Clare invites them to take a seat on the small chairs she has set in circle. She talks to the children about their morning so far, the things they did at the weekend, and there is a relaxed atmosphere. Clare begins by asking the children where they see water and what it used for. She allows the children to speak, she supports their conversations when they struggle or become lost for words. She models listening and questioning techniques to the group, though this is not made explicit. As they talk about drinks and ice in drinks she focuses in one this. 'Why do we have ice in our drinks?' 'What happens to the ice?' She has water in a small container. She and the children take the container to the freezer and Clare says they can look at it tomorrow and see what has happened. Some of the children ask about the freezer and what makes it so cold while others return to the main free-flow area.*

*The following day Clare shows the children the container, which now contains solid ice. Some of the children stay to talk and others quickly move on to their chosen activities. Clare doesn't follow them and the conversations are again relaxed.*

*Later that week Clare has a follow-up session with one male, George. The interaction took place in the nursery garden. Practitioner Clare has a large piece of ice in a box. George looks into the container wide-eyed, he looks up at Clare.*

**Clare***: Do you know what it is, George?*
She looks at him and smiles offering the container so he can see inside more clearly.

**George:** *Ice … and water.*

**Clare***: That's right, we have been talking about ice and water this week haven't we? What do you think is happening to the ice out here in the garden?*

**George:** *Erm … the ice is very cold.*
**Clare:** *It is very cold, George, would you like to have a feel?*
George tentatively strokes the ice, they both laugh.
**Clare:** *How does it feel?*

**George:** *Very cold …and wet …*
He shows Clare the water on his fingers.
**Clare***: It is isn't it, do you remember we talked about this. What happens to water when it gets very, very cold?*
**George:** *Ice, it goes to ice.*
**Clare:** *That's right.* [She smiles encouragingly] *I had to think how I was going to get the ice out of the freezer and into the garden. I put the ice into the container to carry it into the garden, it was too cold for me to carry and too slippery.* [She laughs] *What do you think happens to ice when it gets warm?*

**George:** *Erm, it turns back to water* [claps]*, like there …*

**Clare:** *Excellent George, I think the sun is making it all warm in the garden and so the ice is melting …*

**George:** *Yeah, that's the water in there* [points to the water in the container].
They continue to talk.

## 1.2 Analysing pedagogy

It is interesting to look at case above in the light of the introductory definition of pedagogy we provided. Clare's pedagogy is evident: the ways in which she settles the children, the ways in which she allows them to come back to the topic when they are ready/interested in doing so, the modelling of the skills needed for collaboration: listening and questioning. This does not occur by chance. Both are informed by science, by theories of planning, teaching and learning which Clare has encountered in her prior experience and through her training. The way she relates to individual children and orchestrates small group discussion draws on theories of dialogic teaching and learning – for example, using the power of what Alexander calls 'reciprocal' and 'cumulative' teaching (2008: 113), her plan for the activity is differentiated. She acknowledges that not all children have the same level of understanding that she will be working in the relevant Vygotskyan zone of proximal development (ZPD) with different children (see Chapter 2). For some, the concept of water turning to ice is new learning, for others the discussions around the freezer deepen their understanding of the concept of freezing.

Although the above case study and analysis focus on a very small part of Clare's pedagogy, they show how a seemingly simple activity is multifaceted and planned to support a variety of children. It is no accident that there is an opportunity for George to have the follow-on conversation with Clare.

---

### Reflective activity 11.1

*Aim:* To identify aspects of the craft, art and science of pedagogy in teaching.

*Evidence and reflection:* Think back to a planned activity you have led very recently. On a blank piece of paper, make a rough sketch of the diagram in **Figure 11.1**. In each circle, note down anything from the session you can identify as aspects of the craft, art and science of your pedagogy.

*Extension:* Add to your sketch instances where opportunities arose and your pedagogic repertoire allowed you to make the most of the opportunities presented to you. Also note if there were missed opportunities which you may follow up in the future.

---

## 2 Pedagogy, knowledge and learning

## 2.1 The development of pedagogic principles

As discussed in previous chapters (see Chapter 1), those working in ECEC in the UK were for many years seen as relative amateurs, providing care for children before they enter formal schooling – a history which still leaves a trace today. However, as research has shown the value of ECEC provision, and specifically the need for high-quality provision, debate about the nature of 'quality' and thus pedagogy in ECEC has grown.

In 2000, the House of Commons Select Committee on Education and Employment noted that pedagogy, as teaching, was different to the curriculum. They noted that in ECEC the pedagogic approach is one which should be play-based. But while structuring provision around play may be a key aspect of pedagogy in early years, this alone would not be sufficient to provide a guide to 'high-quality' provision.

The Study of Pedagogical Effectiveness in Early Learning (SPEEL) project sought to identify the key components of effective pedagogy in early years practice (Moyles et al., 2002). The project team devised a framework to highlight the key components of effective pedagogy, as shown in **Figure 11.2**.

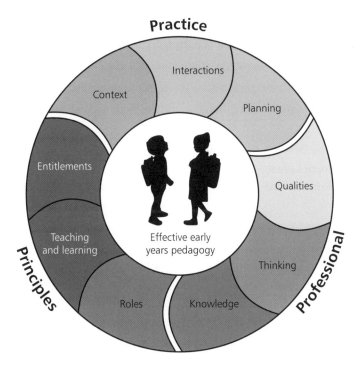

**Figure 11.2**
A framework for effective pedagogy in the early years (Moyles et al., 2002: 49)

The framework clearly identifies the key principles of effective pedagogy in the early years. These sit alongside key components for practice and the professional dimensions of the role. The principles the team identified include the following:

**Effective practitioners believe in, and value, the *entitlement* of all children to, among other things:**

- high-quality education and care;
- quality time with interested adults;
- time to explore and develop friendships with other children and adults;
- be taught by practitioners who:
  - consider children's learning and overall development holistically;
  - build on each child's potential as an individual;

  - differentiate learning experiences;

  - build upon, encourage and extend children's prior learning;

  - ensure children feel secure, included, valued and respected;

  - experience play as a vital process in all areas of development;

  - have opportunities to work and play with practitioners who encourage children's curiosity and exploration, and use praise;

  - provide recognition, respect and equality of opportunity for all.

**Effective practitioners value and believe *in teaching and learning* practices which, among other things:**

- maximize learning and teaching opportunities both indoors and outdoors;

- are well-planned, well-managed, stimulating and visually appealing;

- promote positive learning and socially acceptable behaviour;

- ensure time is available for children to fully explore and extend concepts, ideas and interests;

- promote independence, perseverance and concentration;

- enable children to make choices, take measured risks, talk and think for themselves, have some responsibility for articulating and evaluating their own learning;

- make full use of a range of open-ended, active, hands-on, multisensory learning experiences;

- make full use of collaborative and cooperative ways of learning;

- commit adults and children to having realistic but high expectations of progression, behaviour and self-management;

- use a combination of adult interactions, the learning environment and the assessment of children's responses to inform daily practice and medium- and long-term planning.

**Effective practitioners value and believe in the importance of their own role and capacity to, among other things:**

- engage, intervene and partner children in the learning process;

- establish and build sensitive teaching and learning relationships with children;

- model appropriate social, emotional and intellectual behaviours;

- teach children as well as care for their welfare;

- interact and communicate with children positively, enthusiastically, flexibly and thoughtfully;

- actively seek and promote equality of opportunity for each child, parent, carer and colleague, building positive, supportive and collaborative relationships;

- establish and develop effective teamwork and collaboration within and beyond the setting;

- reflect regularly on current thinking about teaching young children, their learning and development;
- ensure they are up-to-date in their understanding of local and national initiatives and the impact upon their work;
- engage in training and on-going development of professional learning;
- take initiative and trust their own judgements.

(Adapted from Moyles et al., 2002: 53–5)

In Chapter 9 we noted some of the principles underpinning the key approaches that have shaped and influenced ECEC provision around the world. Principles such as those identified by SPEEL, and the key approaches we discussed, have been continually drawn upon and developed by practitioners working in the UK and those responsible for policy development. For example, current policy in England recognizes four guiding principles which should shape practice in early years settings (DoE, 2014: 3). These are:

- every child is a **unique child**, who is constantly learning and can be resilient, capable, confident and self-assured;
- children learn to be strong and independent through **positive relationships**;
- children learn and develop well in **enabling environments**, in which their experiences respond to their individual needs and there is a strong partnership between practitioners and parents and/or carers;
- children develop and learn in **different ways and at different rates**.

The framework covers the education and care of all children in early years provision, including children with special educational needs and disabilities.

And in Ireland, six principles which ought to underpin the planning and delivery of early years education (DENI, 2013: 19–20):

- the early years education and learning needs of all children is the key focus of provision;
- education and learning begins at birth;
- children and their families are entitled to high-quality, age-appropriate early years education and learning services and opportunities;
- the rights of children and their families are respected;
- equality of opportunity and inclusion are essential characteristics of quality early years education and learning;
- collaborative working among the statutory, voluntary, and other relevant sectors and professional bodies will play an important part in securing improved outcomes for young children in their early years.

Thus early years provision is guided by pedagogic principles which, although not identical, have common themes.

---

### Reflective activity 11.2

*Aim:* To reflect upon your pedagogic practice.

*Evidence and reflection:* Consider the key principles of effective pedagogy noted in this chapter. Do they resonate with your personal feelings about effective and high-quality early years provision? Can you identify elements of your practice which sit well with these principles? Do you find any challenging?

*Extension:* If possible, discuss your thoughts with a colleague or fellow student.

---

## 2.2 Perspectives

***Critical pedagogy***: In some parts of the world educators have used the concept of pedagogy to very powerful effect. One of the best-known is the Brazilian educator, Paulo Freire, whose central argument in *Pedagogy of the Oppressed* (2000) is that pedagogy is the means by which the most oppressed people can be taught to reflect critically on their oppression and actively participate in liberation from it. Freire's notion of pedagogy is of teaching through which the oppressed learner becomes literate and gains the power of self-direction, rather than merely adopting the forms of education offered by the oppressor or, indeed, being filled up like an empty vessel. Instead, he views the literacy process as a dynamic one in which 'reading the world always precedes reading the word, and reading the word implies continually reading the world' (Freire, 2000: 37). Education of this kind means making connections between language and life so that each illuminates the other. Freire's pedagogy, often referred to as critical pedagogy to indicate the expectation that some form of action will arise out of the stance being adopted, stems from very particular attitudes and values but resonates with educators in many different parts of the world. In writings about his work it is possible to identify aspects of craft, science and art that he believes practitioners command, integrally related to their subject knowledge.

***Theories of mind***: Meanwhile, other prominent educators, for example Jerome Bruner in the United States, have viewed pedagogy from the perspective of educational psychology, with different consequences. Bruner, strongly influenced by the work of Vygotsky, is interested in how theories of the human mind affect practitioners' practice. He demonstrates that the way in which practitioners perceive learners' minds affects how they teach – a powerful argument for a science of teaching which would enable us to understand the workings of the mind as clearly as possible. Drawing connections between 'models of mind and models of pedagogy' (Bruner, 1996: 53), he demonstrates how a theory of mind which holds that learners acquire knowledge through imitation will lead to very different pedagogy from a theory of mind which privileges learning through conversations and collaboration. Bruner is not arguing for one model over and above another; rather, he suggests that what is needed is the forging of different perspectives on learning into 'some congruent unity, recognised as parts of a common continent' (1996: 65).

*Pedagogical discourse*: Deborah Britzman, an American critical ethnographer with a keen interest in teacher education, likewise argues the need for practitioners to learn how theoretical perspectives inform their pedagogy. In *Practice Makes Practice: A Critical Study of Learning to Teach* (2003), she explores how it is not just important to identify and reflect critically on theoretical perspectives but also on different discourses which can crucially affect the way in which teaching and pedagogy are construed.

Practitioners therefore need to remain aware of the way different perspectives shape their thinking and that of children and their families. Parents' expectations of early years provision will be shaped by such discussions. The following text by Heard (2003, cited in Ang, 2014: 13–14) encapsulates how a parents view on pedagogy and what is to be taught and learned can shape their expectations of practice.

**What did you do at nursery today?**

'Well first I sat at the dough table and rolled the dough in my hands. Lucy said hers was a snake and mine, mine was a worm. Mrs Pitt talked about long ones and short ones, fat ones and thin ones, and Mummy, Katie rolled her dough so long it went right over the end of the table. And nobody said "what are you going to make? A cake would be nice."'

'Yes, but then what did you do?'

'I played on the climbing frame and, do you know Mummy, I climbed to the very top and had great fun sliding down, and Mrs Crompton gave me a clap and said, "Well done!"'

'Yes, but did you do anything today?'

'Megan and I went to the paint table. It was lovely and gooey and we made lots of patterns with our fingers and hands. Megan had yellow paint and I had red, and Mummy, Miss Howard said, "I wonder what would happen if your paint got mixed up?" and Mummy, do you know what, the paint went orange! And no one said, "What a mess you've made."'

'Yes, but what else have you done?'

'At milk time we sat in a circle and talked about our friends. Mummy, I told Mrs Crompton that my best friend is Luke because he came see if I was alright when I fell and hurt my knee outside. And do you know, Mummy, after that Luke smiled at me a lot.'

'And then did you do anything?'

'I made lovely traily patterns in the sand and Daniel and I had a race to see who could make a sand castle the quickest.'

'So, did you do anything today?'

'We sang Happy Birthday to Jack and counted the candles on his cake. Oh, and I helped Hannah to find her coat because it was on the wrong peg so she was a bit upset.'

'But did you do anything today?'

'Well, when Mrs Crompton asked us to tidy up, I quickly painted you a picture 'cos I knew you'd say "what did you do at nursery today?"'

Part of the role of the reflective early years practitioner is to work with parents so both parties can work together to understand the child, their needs and their learning.

*Pedagogical thoughtfulness*: One of the four aspects of pedagogy being discussed in this chapter is the art of pedagogy. Defined in TLRP terms as 'responsive, creative and intuitive capacities' (Pollard, 2010: 5), it is not surprising to find it sometimes characterized as something a practitioner either has or does not have, rather than as an aspect of pedagogy which practitioners can be taught. However, we believe the art of being attentive and responsive is certainly a quality that can be developed. Having an understanding of children, their development and their needs is likely to support such a process; where understanding what you are doing, and why you are doing it, can make work – which can be physically demanding – seem all the more rewarding and worthwhile.

*Learning and experience*: Pedagogy is inextricably linked with learning. John Dewey, the great American philosopher of education working in the early years of the twentieth century, is highly critical of any form of instruction which merely instils facts in learners' minds but does not encourage genuine thinking. Early years practitioners are particularly well placed to understand children's learning holistically. Spending much of each day with the same group of children and getting to know their families always makes for a deep awareness of the children, their needs and the interconnections children may make between ordinary experience and setting learning.

## 3 Enacting learner development

## 3.1 Building from prior learning

### Expert question

**Elements of learning:** What knowledge, concepts, skills, values and attitudes are to be learned?

This question contributes to a conceptual framework representing enduring issues and practitioner expertise (see Chapter 16).

The extent to which ordinary experience may be enriched by learning in ECEC settings is explored in the vignette which follows. It exemplifies TLRP Principle 3, which links teaching to prior experience and learning and 'includes building on prior learning but also taking account of the personal and cultural experiences of different groups of learners' (James and Pollard, 2006: 8). In it, we see an early years practitioner, Tom, carrying out focused observations and analysis of an individual child, Tabitha, and how both of these form part of his pedagogic practice.

## Case study 11.2 Studying a child's reading development

Tom, an early years practitioner, conducting a study into 3-year-old Tabitha's social development. Tom has noticed that Tabitha, who has been attending the setting for eight months, frequently hovers at the side of other children, but rarely engages in any direct conversation with them. She seems to lack the confidence and the skills to engage with the other children as they play. Tom decides he will observe Tabitha to gain some further evidence of whether this is the case, identify any issues Tabitha may have, use the observations to identify ways to support Tabitha to develop any skills needed to engage with the other children – and them with her – and then conduct further observations to note any developments.

The initial observations reveal that Tabitha has very few direct interactions with either her peers or the practitioners. The other children ignore Tabitha and she plays alongside them but not with them.

Following discussions with staff, Tom integrates some additional activities into the session which relate to building relationships. These include:

- Using stories to demonstrate to the children how people feel when they are left out.
- Discussing with children what makes them happy at nursery.
- Asking the children what kind things they have noticed about their friends and the staff at the setting.
- Providing the children with opportunities to work together – for example, ensuring there are activities which require more than one person to complete, for example, asking them to make shapes with their peers during music and movement.

Tom follows up with observations of Tabitha at regular intervals. Tom records that Tabitha has far more positive interactions with staff and her peers after six weeks, that she seems happier in nursery – she smiles more, and that the children are more aware of her when she seeks to join a game.

# 3.2 Analysing pedagogy

Tom's study enables him to make reflective observations about Tabitha's social development. This example demonstrates how focused observations and analysis of an individual child are central to pedagogy. Without observations Tom may not have realized the extent to which Tabitha was isolated during her time at nursery. His experience, pedagogic knowledge and discussions with his peers enabled him to identify a suitable series of activities to support Tabitha, without highlighting the issue.

## Reflective activity 11.3

*Aim:* To reflect from a learner's perspective on aspects of pedagogy.

*Read the following excerpt.*

Mohammed is painting a Mother's day card. Practitioner Katie stands up with Mohammed's picture and begins to walk to the door.

**Katie**: *I'm just going to show this to Sarah.*

**Mohammed:** *I don't want you to.*

**Katie:** *Well I really wanted to show her so she will see how good it is and then she'll do one. OK. Thanks.*

Mohammed nods rather reluctantly as Katie leaves the room.

**Katie:** *Sarah, look at this great picture Mohammed has done for his mum. Would you like to come and do one please, its Mother's day on Sunday and you'll want to give mum a card.*

**Sarah:** *Er, we're just playing.* [points]

**Katie:** *Well if you come and do this now with me you can come and play that again later.*

*Evidence and reflection:* This short excerpt depicts a common issue. Children are experiencing free play and we are working to support their development as independent thinkers and have respect for their wishes. Then, in the rush of a busy day, we ask a child to do something so that every child has a card or picture for a particular occasion. Note how this behaviour fits with or clashes with your pedagogic practice. What action would have been more appropriate? How could similar behaviours be avoided in the future?

*Extension:* Consider the challenges of how you would like to act in practice and when the situation challenges you. Consider how you might go about putting support in place so that you feel enabled to act as you would wish to.

## 4 Pedagogic repertoire

The idea of pedagogy is multifaceted and needs to be constantly refined through practitioners' reflections on their setting experience from their own and others' perspectives. We need to question whether our pedagogic expertise is sufficiently creative, skilled and wide-ranging and whether our teaching strategies are evidence-informed, convincing and justifiable. Some aspects of pedagogy may appear to be more visible and, possibly, more urgent than others, but ultimately all of them need to be in play.

A key step is to link the learning intentions with appropriate strategies. Short-, medium- and long-term planning are discussed extensively in Chapter 10, and particular emphasis is placed on the unique child so that the cognitive and motivational appropriateness of planned activities can be maximized. Being able to draw on a range of strategies complements this by enabling the selection of effective teaching–learning processes.

If we return to the SPEEL framework, we can consider the key components of effective pedagogy which relate to practice and repertoire. For example, that:

**During teaching and learning interactions effective practitioners, among other things:**

- build on children's existing capabilities, interests and experiences, and learning styles
- play alongside children, scaffolding and extending children's learning
- communicate with children at their level, listen to and talk with children, valuing what they say
  - engage and direct children's attention, interest and motivation in focused teaching activities through:
- telling
- describing
- demonstrating
- instructing
- explaining
- pose meaningful, challenging questions and answer children's questions honestly and accurately
- guide and support children through activities and teach children to make connections across learning experiences
  - teach and model:
- language and communication skills
- playful behaviours
- thinking skills
- collaborative working
- positive attitudes
- behavioural/social expectations
- enable children to initiate their own activities, making choices and being responsible for their own learning
- know when (and when not) to intervene in children's learning experiences
- adapt both open-ended and focused activities according to children's abilities, interests and learning styles
- actively seek opportunities to give positive feedback to children, offering praise for stated achievements and celebrating children's genuine successes
- clarify and convey to children learning expectations, intentions, outcomes and targets
- use children's experiences and theories and share own experiences and learning with children

(Adapted from Moyles et al., 2002: 52)

From this detailed analysis, along with other research, we have identified three key components of the pedagogic repertoire of the early years practitioner: scaffolding, modelling and communicating (see Tharp and Gallimore, Reading 11.4).

# 4.1 Scaffolding

Scaffolding is a term that is often used loosely to describe all kinds of support that practitioners may offer (Pea, 2004). However, in the sense that the term was used by Wood, Bruner and Ross (1976) in their seminal paper, the concept offers much more than this. They described scaffolding as the support given to a less experienced learner by a more experienced adult or peer – which Tharp and Gallimore (1988) refer to as assisted performance. In scaffolding learning, practitioners actively, temporarily and contingently provide learners with just the right amount of cognitive support to bring them closer to independence. Over time, an adult, or more experienced other, can reduce the degree of freedom to make a complex task more manageable for the student so that they can achieve independent competence. Their idea of scaffolding can thus be seen to develop the work of Vygotsky and the concept of the Zone of Proximal Development.

Established conceptualizations of scaffolding see it as an interactive process occurring between practitioner and child in which both participate actively and where learners are 'guided by others' (Stone, 1998: 351) to develop understandings that would be problematic for them to achieve unaided. Van de Pol, Volan and Beishuizen (2012) discuss literature around scaffolding and argue that its characteristics are threefold. The first of the characteristics is 'contingency', which suggests that the practitioner's scaffolding approaches are tailored to the specific needs and current levels of performance of the learners. The second characteristic is 'fading', whereby scaffolding is gradually withdrawn according to the learner's developing understanding and competence. Thirdly, transfer of responsibility occurs. The following excerpt provides an example of scaffolding a child's learning during play.

## Case study 11.3

Joe, a 3-year-old, has always enjoyed the art table during free play. He often uses the materials to paint abstract pictures or make collages, for example. Emily notes that Joe has begun to lose interest; he still goes to the art table but there seems to be little challenge for him. He seems to be haphazardly making marks on the page, as if disinterested, and then he looks to move on to something else. Emily discusses her observation with her colleagues. They wonder whether Joe could be supported to engage in new tasks while also providing him with more challenging art-based activities to support his interest.

Two members of the staff team reviewed the resources they made available each day. On reflection they decided that the table looked very similar each day, other than the provision of a different picture to colour. They decide that on two days per week the table would use different materials – for example, they decided to have sessions working with clay. In addition, they felt that Joe was perhaps not being given enough opportunities to be creative. They also considered his love of computers. They decided that they would expand something which was sometimes used in the setting to include the children much more: the use of the digital camera. They purchased two child-friendly cameras.

Emily set about introducing these tasks to Joe. In both cases she introduced the topic to Joe. She allowed him to explore and stayed nearby to answer any questions. Initially she helped with the camera but Joe soon learned to use the camera and connect it to the computer, so he could load the pictures and view them. The conversation below provides some evidence of the scaffolding which took place.

**Emily:** *So now you have turned the camera on, do we know how to take a picture?*
**Joe:** [brief silence as he looks at the camera.] *I think I should press that button.*
**Emily:** *I think so too. So what would you like to take a picture of?*
**Joe:** [looks around] *The trains.*

Joe holds the picture in the general direction of the trains and takes a picture. They look at it in the screen. Joe doesn't seem impressed.

**Emily:** *Great, our first picture. What do you think?*
**Joe:** *You can't see the train's erm the wheels …*
**Emily:** *Ok, so maybe we should get closer. What do you think?*

Joe moves closer and again points in the general direction. He is happier with the picture but still seems a little disappointed.

**Emily**: *I have a camera at home. When I want to take a picture of something I always hold the camera like this [extends her arms] I look at the screen here to see what my picture will look like. If it's not quite right I move until I think it is just right.*
Emily further discusses the picture with Joe, the distance and how to hold it steady.

Joe takes a picture using the techniques demonstrated by Emily. She helps him to hold the camera at first and then moves away. After a short time Joe is taking pictures that he is very pleased with and wants to show to his mum.

Upon review, the staff team felt that they had supported Joe to expand his interests while scaffolding his learning and fostering his creativity.

## 4.2 Modelling

Modelling is considered to be a form of scaffolding. We believe, however, that it ought to be considered separately given the valuable role it plays in ECEC practice (see Colwell, Reading 6.5). There are a number of research studies which suggest that the role of practitioner modelling is important in children's learning. Modelling has been shown to be a more effective way of learning than trial and error (Bandura, 1977), or didactic teaching methods (Schunk, 1981). Coltman, Petyaeva and Anghileri's (2002) study found that exploration alone was not sufficient to ensure learning and that modelling, as a form of scaffolding, had a significant impact on children's learning and retention of a new skill.

The EPPE research found that adult 'modelling' of skills and appropriate behaviour was often combined with periods of SST, open-ended questioning, and that this was associated with better cognitive achievement (Sylva et al., 2004). Despite such claims, there is no one generally agreed definition of what modelling is or explanation of its implementation. Orme et al. (1966) use the term *perceptual modelling* to describe an 'expert' demonstrating an action and then allowing time for the 'novice' to trial or imitate the action. Weiss and Klint (1987) have suggested that perceptual modelling may be of particular benefit to early learners, as they lack the skills to be able to translate a verbal instruction into a new action. Similarly, Tharp and Gallimore (1988) note two distinct approaches to modelling: those of *behavioural modelling* and *cognitive modelling*. The former links to perceptual modelling – the expert demonstrating the action to the novice. The latter, however, refers to a more complex process whereby the expert provides a narrative of their actions, thoughts and decision-making while carrying out the action. They are modelling the cognitive processes to the novice in addition to the act itself.

Making the tacit explicit in this way, and providing a space for the novice to practice the action with help, has been defined by Collins, Brown and Newman (1987) and Dennen (2004) as *cognitive apprenticeship*.

When considering how modelling works as a teaching process, Social Learning Theory (SLT), a model of behavioural transmission developed by Bandura (1977), provides a useful insight. There are three key concepts in SLT:

- **People learn through observation** – Bandura demonstrated in the 'Bobo doll' experiment that children imitate behaviours they have seen in others.

- **Mental states are important to learning** – both environmental reinforcements and our own intrinsic reward systems contribute to the use of a specific behaviour.

- **Learning does not necessarily lead to a change in behaviour**.

Bandura notes that simply having a behaviour modelled is insufficient for learning to take place. He recognizes a number of processes which the expert and novice must be engaged in for learning to occur (Bandura, 1977). Bandura identifies these processes as:

- **Attentional processes** – the novice must be paying attention.

- **Retention processes** – the novice must be able to retain the information gleaned and be able to act on the information as required at a later stage.

- **Moteric reproduction processes** – the novice must have opportunities to practise the behaviour and develop its application.

- **Motivation processes** – for a behaviour to be imitated there must be a motivation to do so, i.e. a reinforcer.

Brophy (2004) supports this, stating that in order to be motivated and to learn pupils need to perceive these activities as worthwhile. Colwell (2012) suggests that recognition of these processes can support early years practitioners to support children's learning, particularly their social and emotional development.

# 4.3 Communicating

A paradox in teaching is that while practitioners use talk as the main tool of their trade, many are not aware of the range of ways they *could* use it when interacting with children. Broadly speaking, as practitioners we use talk to provide information, check understanding and direct children. However, there is much we can also do, such as link present activities to past experience, set up future activities, relate existing ideas to new educational frames of meaning, and model ways of using language (Mercer and Littleton, 2007). Indeed, almost of the cases and examples we have given in this book provide examples of how practitioners use talk to support children's learning and development. Siraj-Blatchford et al. (2002) state that:

> The evidence actually suggests that there is no *one* 'effective' pedagogy. Instead the effective [practitioner] orchestrates pedagogy by making interventions (scaffolding, discussing, monitoring, allocating tasks), which are sensitive to the curriculum concept or skill being 'taught', taking into account the child's 'zone of proximal development', or at least that assumed in the particular social grouping. (2002: 43)

Thus, the reflective early years practitioner must be knowledgeable about the tools and methods available to them, and consider their use in different situations to convey different aspects of learning and in their work with different children.

## 5 Enacting a series of lessons

## 5.1 The art, craft and science of pedagogy over time

The following vignette provides an example of how a specific area of learning is developed over time, in this example numeracy or mathematics. This provides a snapshot of a much larger series of planning documents.

---

### Case study 11.4 Learning to count

*Grace is reviewing how the children in the setting are supported to learn to count. They have a new intake of children aged two-and-a-half years arriving at the setting and the staff team recognized this would be a good time to review the activities. Grace looks at the relevant curriculum; she accesses some new research about numeracy, looks to see what equipment or resources they have and what could be made or purchased, and sets about developing short-, medium- and long-term plans. Grace adds the caveat that these plans will need to be reviewed in light of the needs of the children.*

*Grace recognized that counting is one of the child's first introductions to mathematics and wants to help them gain a secure footing and interest in the topic. She considers the*

---

*ways in which the children can be supported to first recognize numbers, develop oral counting skills and then develop an understanding of place value and more or less. The long-term plans developed by Grace included:*

**Story time:** *the purchase and inclusion of story books which require counting, for example,* Ten Little Monkeys Jumping on the Bed. *Grace notes that it is often the case that books such as this count backwards and so Grace adds a note that the monkeys on each page must be counted. She also notes that this is oral counting and does not necessarily build a child's understanding of place value.*

**Environment:** *Number wall. The children will work together to develop new displays of the numbers 1 to 20. The number wall will be developed over time. Each number will have corresponding pictures – for example, the number 2 will have two objects next to it, e.g. a picture of two bees. Grace noted that it was important that this wall went from left to right to help the children to build the correct number orientation. Grace hoped that this would also support the development of number recognition skills.*

**Tip sheet:** *Thinking about the things she had learned, Grace decided it would be a good idea to have a tip sheet. For example, she placed a notice for practitioners and parents on the number wall which briefly stated the importance of counting from left to right.*

**Example small group activity:** *Grace had a cube-shaped box at home that opened up. She planned a small group activity which would involve the children making a die from the box after carefully looking at dice with Grace. To build upon the activity Grace would fill the box with items and work with the children to guess how many things are in the box. Eventually they open the box and Grace works with them to count the number of objects in the box.*

Grace planned an extension to use if it was seen to be appropriate – for example, if the child guessed there were three in the box and they opened it and there were four items, Grace could encourage them to understand that there were three and one more.

## 5.2 Analysing pedagogy

While only a snapshot of Grace's planning, this vignette offers an insight into how early years practitioners plan for children's learning over time. In this instance, the focus is on continuity and progression. Planning a whole unit of work involved Grace bringing together different opportunities for children to engage with numbers.

### Reflective activity 11.4

*Aim:* To explore how principles about pedagogy relate to our own planning and teaching.

*Evidence and reflection:* Review some medium- or long-term planning. Identify as many different aspects of pedagogy as possible within these plans, explaining and justifying them in the light of what you have just read. What is the balance between the different aspects (science, craft and art)?

# Conclusion

In this chapter we have explored the interconnected aspects of pedagogy: art, craft and science. Pedagogy is a rich and fascinating concept, constantly being shaped and re-shaped by every individual practitioner. At times, some elements of pedagogy will appear more pressing than others. Nevertheless, how we interact with and respond to children will be crucially informed by our understanding of pedagogy as a whole. While some ideas about teaching and learning endure, others change and are transformed, not only as new research is undertaken by practitioners in settings or professional researchers but also because teaching and learning are human enterprises and hence are never static. No two practitioners are the same; no two learning contexts are the same; and, as we know, no two children are the same. We all need, therefore, to reflect on our pedagogy as and when our own understanding is further developed by experience.

# Key readings

TLRP's overall setting findings, including 'ten principles for effective teaching and learning', are discussed in Chapter 4 of this book. For a simple explanation of the idea of pedagogy seen as science, craft and art, and an exposition of 'conceptual tools' for tackling enduring educational issues, see:

> Pollard, A. (ed.) (2010) *Professionalism and Pedagogy: A Contemporary Opportunity.*
> London: TLRP.

A key report to access is:

> Siraj-Blatchford, I., Sylva, K., Muttock, S., Gilden, R. and Bell, D. (2002)
> *Researching Effective Pedagogy in the Early Years (REPEY)*. Nottingham:
> Department for Education and Skills. **ioe.ac.uk/REPEY_research_report.pdf**

For books specifically focused upon practice in early years settings, see:

> Aileen, S. and Whalley, M. (2010) *Supporting Pedagogy and Practice in Early Years*
> *Settings* Exeter: Learning Matters.
> Chilvers, D. (2013) *Creating and Thinking Critically: Learning and Teaching in the*
> *Early Years*. London: Practical Pre-school Books.
> Alexander's comparative analysis of pedagogic issues has generated a strong
> conceptual framework which is applicable to any setting; see:
> Alexander, R. J. (2000) *Culture and Pedagogy. International Comparisons in Primary*
> *Education.* Oxford: Blackwell.

An influential application of a synthesis of global research is:

> Hattie, J. (2012) *Visible Learning for Practitioners*. London: Routledge.

There is a long tradition of thinking about teaching as a creative and organic process. This approach emphasizes how teaching must connect with the learner as a person and with their construction of meaning; see:

Bruner, J. (1996) *The Culture of Education*. Cambridge, MA: Harvard University Press.

Dixon, A., Drummond, M. J., Hart, S. and McIntyre, D. (2004) *Learning Without Limits*. Maidenhead: Open University Press.

For consideration of more radical approaches to pedagogy, try:

Kincheloe, J. L. (2008) *Critical Pedagogy Primer.* New York: Peter Lang.

Leach, J. and Moon, B. (2008) *The Power of Pedagogy.* London: Sage Publications Ltd.

In one way or another, most of Reflective Teaching's chapters are concerned with pedagogy and for readings on more specific issues – such as relationships, engagement, behaviour, assessment, etc. – please consult the relevant chapter.

 The associated website, **reflectiveteaching.co.uk**, offers a wealth of supplementary resources including reflective activities, research briefings, advice on further reading and downloadable diagrams, figures and checklists from the book. It also features a compendium of educational terms, links to useful websites, policy and curriculum documents, and showcases examples of excellent research and practice.

# Communication
## How does language support learning?

**12**

## Introduction

In this chapter we consider important lines of thinking in relation to the prime place of language and communication within early years provision. What can we consider to be best practice? The chapter builds from the premise that young children's successful language acquisition underpins not only the way in which they engage with and make sense of their world, but also their ability to interact with others. Language skills will also impact on access to the curriculum – all things we have identified as crucial to their learning, development and futures. In line with our discussions in Chapter 6, we believe that children's language acquisition is likely to be stronger if they are encouraged to become active participants in conversation, if they are encouraged to be questioning, to hypothesize, imagine, wonder, project and dream out loud, to hear stories and to tell stories to others (Bradford, 2009). Social and cultural aspects of language development are equally important at this time as children learn, through talk, to place themselves within a specific social context. In this way, the development of language and identity are closely linked. The impact of what is happening in the child's home life should never be underestimated and it is important for the early years practitioner to take the time to get to know individual circumstances in order to respond supportively.

Language is central to children's learning and development (see Broadbent, Reading 12.1). Language ability impacts on emergent reading and writing skills – skills that develop alongside language from birth. Ultimately, the ability to manipulate language appropriately and successfully impacts on children's later life chances (Sylva et al., 2010). In this chapter the reflective activities support reflections on the development of spoken language and how to support, plan for and encourage age-appropriate dialogue in settings.

All practitioners need to be aware of the role of modelling, responding to and engaging knowledgeably with children as they scaffold language and modes of communication that are used in settings every day (see Manning-Morton, Reading 12.2). To communicate effectively, children need to develop receptive language skills in order to become increasingly able to understand the language they hear. They also need to develop expressive language skills to convey their own thoughts, feelings and desires.

---

### TLRP principles

The following TLRP principles are of particular relevance to this chapter:

**Principle 4: Effective teaching and learning requires teachers to scaffold learning.** Teachers should provide activities which support learners as they move forward, not just intellectually, but also socially and emotionally, so that once these supports are removed, the learning is secure.

**Principle 6: Effective teaching and learning promotes the active engagement of the learner.** A chief goal of teaching and learning should be the promotion of learners' independence and autonomy. This involves acquiring a repertoire of learning strategies and practices, developing positive attitudes towards learning, and confidence in oneself as a good learner.

Principle 7: **Effective teaching and learning fosters both individual and social processes and outcomes.** Learning is a social activity. Learners should be encouraged and helped to work with others, to share ideas and to build knowledge together. Consulting learners about their learning and giving them a voice is both an expectation and a right.

Principle 8: **Effective teaching and learning recognizes the significance of informal learning.** Informal learning, such as learning out of school, should be recognized as at least as significant as formal learning and should therefore be valued and used appropriately in formal processes.

# 1 Characteristics of effective language development

By the age of 5, provided they do not have language difficulties, all children have *acquired* the adult grammar for the main constructions of their native language (Peccei, 2006). This is true across all cultures and in all languages. All languages have their own sound systems and children tune in to the ones they hear around them from birth. The term 'acquired' is an important one in this context, because linguists make a distinction between *emergent* language constructions and ones which are fully acquired. All children must learn to talk; the development of language must be scaffolded through interaction with more experienced language users. Nature-versus-nurture arguments of language development are worth revisiting briefly before moving on to current thinking.

One of the most influential advocates of the idea that language development is natural was Noam Chomsky. In his early work he hypothesized that children make use of a language acquisition device (LAD). This device, he argued, is a special capacity of the brain that enables children to use the rules systems of their native language. According to Chomsky, language was inherently placed within such an innate internal system and would therefore develop naturally. Jerome Bruner countered that Chomsky's theory correctly identified this innate aspect of the child's capacity, but that this was only part of the process of language acquisition. He argued that the child's LAD could not function without the aid given by an adult who enters with him into a language interaction. Interaction with another individual, Bruner argues, provides a Language Acquisition Support System (LASS). The LASS frames or structures the input of language and interaction to the child's LAD in a manner that teaches the child something about the way in which language works; ultimately 'it is the interaction between the LAD and the LASS that makes it possible for the infant to enter the linguistic community – and, at the same time, the culture to which the language gives access' (Bruner, 1983: 19).

The role of the adult in supporting children's language development using appropriate strategies is well documented in research. Building on Bruner's theories, Vygotsky described the young child as an apprentice for whom cognitive development occurs within social interactions. In other words, as language ability becomes more sophisticated, children are guided into increasingly mature ways of thinking and communicating through interacting with more capable others and through interactions with their surrounding culture. 'More capable others' can include a range of people who are part of the child's immediate social and cultural network such as family members (parents, grandparents, siblings), as well as their playmates and peers.

The role of the adult is a feature of more recent developments in neuroscience which look at both the potential and the vulnerability of a child's brain from birth. Brain development is remarkably rapid and responsive during the first five years of life (see Chapter 2 for a more detailed discussion of this). Neuroscientists have defined the brain's activity in terms of connectionist networks. At birth there are billions of brain cells but they are not 'wired up' together. The brain is therefore a work in progress with early language experiences defining language ability. Evidence from longitudinal development studies and from population studies, for example, provide information that early childhood is the period when the child responds to the environment with a 'tangible malleability that triggers the brain's developing architecture and, through their early experiences, critically shapes who they are as teenagers and adults' (Gammage, 2006: 237). Brain-based research does not in itself introduce new strategies for the early years practitioner, but rather supports connections between what neuroscience tells us and what is already known in relation to good practice for young children, and helps us to justifiably build upon that practice.

## 2 Language and early years practice

An appropriate learning environment for communication and language development is one in which the potential for talk has high status. Children are born with characteristics which predispose them to be successful language learners. It is important to understand, however, that their language experiences from birth play a significant role in their language development, and the significance of the way that adults interact with the child at this time should not be underestimated. Children with fewer opportunities for interaction and for hearing and understanding words and phrases are likely to be delayed in their acquisition of language (Wells, 1986; Harris, 1992). While there are many reasons why children may have problems learning language, a poor linguistic environment in the early years setting should not be one of them. The way early the years practitioner communicates with young children is therefore a very important part of their role. During the early years of life, children are:

- developing their knowledge and understanding about how language works;
- developing a range and variety of vocabulary to use;
- learning to speak coherently and with clarity to make themselves understood;
- learning to speak with confidence.

Adults are usually conscious of the language they are using with children, adapting their own register to accommodate the perceived language ability of the child. Early years practitioners, however, need to be acutely aware of their own language use and to be able to change it as necessary. As we have discussed in Chapters 6, 10 and 11, through taking a reflective approach they can facilitate a range of learning opportunities with all children they care for and teach. This includes the development of language skills.

## 2.1 Communicating with emergent language users

Linguists make a distinction between emergent or preverbal language constructions and ones which are fully acquired; the average vocabulary of a 2-year-old is 200 to 300 words, for example. While a 3-year-old child is capable of speaking using complex sentences, their vocabulary, and sometimes their understanding, is still limited. How should the early years practitioner respond? Of relevance here is research into the ways in which adults speak with young children. One important idea in this area has been the concept of motherese, which is about the impact, appropriateness and helpfulness of language interactions particularly between mothers and their children (Tizard and Hughes, 1984). This is now called 'child-directed speech' (CDS) in recognition of the fact that it is not just mothers who modify their speech when talking to young children, but many key adults involved in a child's life. The early years practitioner is one of those key adults. Peccei (2006) observes that CDS is a natural response to the fact that young children use talk which is semantically and syntactically simple; therefore, if an adult is to communicate effectively with them, they need to use a similar kind of language, a language that the child can understand. Communication between adults and children commensurate with the child's language at different stages is therefore beneficial. The ability of the adult to take into account the limited abilities of the child and adjust their language accordingly so that the child can make sense of it is intuitive for most adults.

## 2.2 Listening and responding to children

A major role of the reflective early years practitioner is to listen and respond appropriately to children's utterances. Through these communications children acquire the cultural 'tools' to aid them in setting and achieving goals and becoming members of communities, exemplified in the following case study.

## Case study 12.1 Acquiring cultural 'tools'

Jemima, a highly articulate child aged 3 years and 6 months old, had recently moved house from one part of the country to another. She was an only child and both her parents worked long hours. She spent most of the day with Sarah, her nanny, and usually saw her parents only briefly each evening. She joined the nursery in September at the beginning of the academic year.

Following detailed observations, it became evident to the practitioner that although Jemima was regularly visiting different areas of the setting, she was doing so as an observer rather than as a participant. She would only play with a resource if no one else was using it. If another child came along and tried to talk to her, she would walk away. Further, if a key adult was focusing on a particular activity with one or more children, Jemima would often try to draw that adult's attention away from them by making a statement such as: 'When I woke up this morning I shouted, "Mummy! Mummy!" but guess what? Mummy didn't come! Sarah came upstairs and helped me get up.'

It became apparent that Jemima had found the house move difficult and was unsettled by it. She talked about the fact that she had lived in a large house before but now she lived in an 'enormous' house. She missed her parents. Jemima was able to express how she was feeling. At the same time, while what she was saying was not inappropriate, the context of the situation was a concern to staff.

As a result of a discussion between key adults in the setting, the following plan of action was agreed. Jemima would be given time to talk with one of the adults about her new routines at home. She would then be helped and supported to understand that these routines were permanent. In addition to addressing the issue, this would give her some of the individual attention she needed. The practitioner would invite Jemima's parents to come in for a progress report. Positives would be discussed, such as their daughter's use of language and her artwork, to provide a balance to the consultation which would also serve to raise her parents' awareness of her insecurity. A series of adult-focused activities involving children working in groups were planned to take place over the period of one month. Jemima would then experience being part of a group with adult support on a regular basis. If Jemima was spending time with one of the key adults in the setting – for example, listening to a story – the adult would invite another child to come and listen too. Jemima would then come to understand that other children needed, and indeed were entitled to, an adult's time and attention as well. Comments would be made by the key adult such as: 'Who can we invite to come and listen to the story with us?' Should Jemima be introduced to another child by a key adult and start to play alongside them, the adult would subtly withdraw and leave them to play together. Names were important to Jemima, so it was agreed that all key adults would introduce Jemima to other children she was with and vice versa.

As a result of the action plan, Jemima gradually needed to talk about home life less and less. Being given the opportunity to talk things through each day with an adult she knew would listen to her helped her to work through her unsettled feelings to ones of understanding and acceptance. Jemima's parents appreciated greatly the practitioners time and obvious care for their daughter. Her mother started to go to work later one day a week so that she could drop Jemima off at the nursery and her father came home early twice a week so that he could pick her up.

Initially Jemima relied on a key adult inviting her to join in with small groups by indicating her willingness to be asked by standing close and trying to make eye contact with the adult. She no longer tried to draw their attention away from other children. Jemima eventually became confident enough to introduce herself to children whose names she was not sure of. One day she wanted to play in the water tray alongside a male peer. 'My name is Jemima,' she said. 'What are you called?' When the boy did not reply she put her hands on her hips, leaned towards him ensuring she made eye contact with him and said: 'You're supposed to tell me your name now!' By the end of her first term, Jemima would greet key adults only briefly when she entered the setting, preferring to seek out the company of her peers straightaway. She started to regularly invite one or two special friends to her home to play and to have tea.

## Reflective activity 12.1

*Aim:* To analyse how listening and responding to children develops them as learners.

*Evidence and reflection:* Read the above case study.

- How were the key adults listening and responding to Jemima?
- Were there any other adults who listened and responded to her?
- How did everyone's communication skills, including Jemina's, support a positive outcome for her?

*Extension:* Undertake a similar series of narrative observations in your setting or classroom, focusing on one child who you believe to be an articulate language user. Review your provision for them in the light of your observations, using the same questions outlined above as a framework for potential response. Repeat the activity with a child for whom you have concerns with regard to language development. What steps will you take to ensure that their language needs will be appropriately addressed? Who will you talk to first?

Listening to children is an integral part of understanding what they are feeling and what it is they need from their early years experiences. For example, most adults enjoy listening to babies and love their reactions as they engage with them. A baby's smile is a great sense of real pleasure to many parents; a gurgle, a laugh, a baby sound, hand wave or kick all have the potential for delight and celebration. If all is well, as children develop and grow physically, so their language skills develop and grow. Being listened to attentively by key adults in their lives will support young children's ability to develop a meta-language with which to successfully communicate and interact with those around them. As children move into primary school classrooms, language skills will be essential in supporting them to successfully access the curriculum – for example, developing relevant vocabulary and reading skills. The frustration for a child who has a limited language repertoire will impact greatly on their ability to achieve, but also on their perception of themselves as a learner. Conversely, ignoring a child who has advanced language skills could likewise impact in similar ways. In summary, children learn language skills from interactions and conversations with adults and their peers.

# 2.3 Scaffolding and modelling language

The early years practitioner is in both an advantageous and privileged position to be able to provide a number of important conditions for young children who are developing language skills, not least of which is that of providing access to a competent user of language. In addition, the practitioner provides opportunities for babies and children to develop their early communication skills through communicating responses which acknowledge the young child as a competent language user. The practitioner models the conventions of language and provides natural feedback on the effectiveness of a child's ability to communicate, thus scaffolding the child's language learning and enabling them to test their current hypotheses about how language works. Specific strategies which can be used to scaffold early language development include: using simple vocabulary; using short phrases or sentences; repeating and emphasizing key words or phrases; and repetition using the same words and phrases for repeated everyday activities.

## Case study 12.2 Different uses of language

Ruby, aged 10 months, cannot reach her teddy bear which she can see sitting on a chair nearby. Her key person, Emma, notices her standing up by herself on her playmat, somewhat precariously, looking at the bear and pointing to it while making noises which Emma interprets as Ruby indicating that she wants her bear.

**Emma:** *Do you want your teddy bear?*
Ruby continues to point and make noises, while making regular eye contact with Emma.

**Emma:** *Shall we go and get your teddy bear?*
Emma holds out her hands to Ruby.

**Emma:** *Would you like Emma to walk with you?*
She takes Ruby's hands to support her balance and walks behind her.

**Emma:** *Let's walk slowly. How many steps do you think we will take before we reach your teddy bear?*
Emma counts every time Ruby places one foot down in front of the other.

**Emma:** *One ... two ... three ... four ... five ...*
They reach the bear. Ruby leans against the chair for support as Emma lets go of her hands and grabs her bear. Emma praises Ruby, clapping and smiling.

**Emma:** *Well done! You did it Ruby! You found teddy!*
Ruby clasps her bear, touching her face with him and smiles back at Emma.

**Emma:** *You love teddy, don't you Ruby?*

Note how Emma uses language in the following three ways:

- breaking the task of reaching the teddy into smaller steps.
- providing motivation to complete the task.
- providing feedback about Ruby's progress using some of the scaffolding techniques outlined above, such as repetitive phrases and words.

## Reflective activity 12.2

*Aim:* To analyse a language episode in your setting or placement – for example, changing a baby's nappy, reading a story, or supporting child-initiated play.

*Evidence and reflection:* You might wish to begin with an audio recording of part of or the entire language episode. You may also wish to ask a colleague to observe your interactions to allow you to obtain another perspective which can support your reflections.

Ask yourself:

- How did you successfully scaffold the child/children's learning through the language that you used?
- What evidence is there to suggest that you were listening to the child/children's utterances?
- What evidence is there to suggest that the child/children were responding to your utterances?

*Extension:* how will undertaking this reflective activity impact on your planning for language activities in your setting/classroom next week?

# 3 Creating an appropriate environment to support communication and early language development

Children's language and communication skills will develop at different speeds. As with all other areas of development we have discussed, each child is unique. In the following section we provide an overview of some of the key areas of development for children across different age ranges and how their learning can be supported in practice.

## 3.1 Birth to three years

It is important to understand that babies are capable communicators from birth, sensitive to the voice levels and tones of adults around them. It is never too early to start talking to a baby because even if they do not understand the words, the sound and tone of spoken language will reassure them and make them feel safe (Dukes and Smith, 2007) and forms the basis for early language learning. The sound of a familiar voice may engender a response in a baby, such as appearing calm and quiet, for example, or by waving their arms and legs around. For reasons such as these, it can be helpful for babies to be allocated a key person. Newborn babies communicate much of the time through crying and it is important to listen to them to understand what they are feeling. In the same way that parents do, the key person will develop a relationship with the baby, and an understanding of the ways in which they communicate – for example, is a cry saying 'I am hungry', 'My nappy needs to be changed', or 'I am tired and I need to sleep'.

By the age of 3 months, babies are able to communicate with adults through facial expressions, slight laughter and new sounds. They learn through imitation (Parker-Rees, 2007). They come to recognize faces, voice and touch. Reading to babies and young children and singing to them, as well as playing imitation games, is therefore valuable. Although not a neuroscientist, Bruner focused on the importance of the social and playful interactions between adults and babies in supporting the development of language. Games involving repetition and rhymes such as 'Peek-a-Boo' and 'Round and Round the Garden' are examples of ways of interacting playfully together. Such games involve actions and consequences that support and reinforce the language of the rhymes, thus creating meaningful, contextualized language experiences for the baby. Stories, songs and rhymes should be drawn from all cultures and babies' home languages.

As babies become toddlers, they will communicate using increasingly sophisticated language structures, beginning with one-word phrases which can sometimes be interpreted by the adult as whole sentences. Context is also important. An example of this might be a child saying *'Milk!'* and holding up their beaker or cup to show the adult. In this case the adult might respond: *'That's right, you are drinking your milk!'* If they do not have milk at the time of the utterance, but the adult hears them say *'Milk!'*, they might interpret this as a request and respond: *'Would you like your milk now?'* Scaffolding language is therefore of great importance at this time of development, in addition to listening and responding. Children will begin to develop preferences such as favourite stories, toys and activities. Building language experiences into their lives that are meaningful and contextualized within their understanding of the world will benefit their developing language expertise.

## 3.2 Three to five years

Language know-how should never be assumed and one of the goals of practice should be to help children develop their language and communication skills. The early years practitioner should continue to model being a listener, both to allow the child opportunities to see what it takes to be a good listener and also in order to be able to respond appropriately to children's utterances. In this way they will develop skills of interaction and appropriate language responses. The development of these skills then supports children to think, understand, and express themselves, as they will have a meta-language or a vocabulary with which to do so. To achieve all this, practitioners must be aware of the language environment they are providing, both physically within the setting, and in terms of their specific role in continuing to scaffold and model language across a wide range of situations, from sharing stories to supporting dispositions such as managing feelings and behaviour.

# 3.3 Five to seven years

As children move into statutory schooling, language ability is crucial in terms of being enabled to access a more structured, subject-based curriculum. Children now have to learn to navigate new situations, such as a playground that may appear more open than the outdoor learning environment they have been used to – for example, it may appear more barren with less equipment and more children, some perhaps older and bigger than themselves. They will need support with the transition into primary school and should be encouraged to use language to express their feelings and concerns. Children build on the foundations of their previous language experiences, listening and responding appropriately to others, for example, and speaking audibly. They develop an increasing sense of audience and should display increasing confidence. At the same time, their vocabulary is still developing. Ultimately they will be able to speak confidently across a range of situations. Mercer and Littleton (2007) have shown that focusing on the quality of spoken dialogue in primary classrooms can significantly improve children's educational attainment. The reflective early years practitioner should therefore be aware that continued development can still never be assumed; language opportunities should be carefully planned within a climate of ongoing concern that children achieve the optimum language experiences. Planning opportunities for talk can broaden and enhance children's command of language by providing them with a range of different contexts in which to use their speaking and listening skills. The use of one-on-one interactions, small group work and large group work, as discussed in Chapter 11, would be examples of different contexts which could support language development.

---

## Reflective activity 12.3

*Aim:* To investigate whether your setting or placement setting provides a stimulating, welcoming, language-rich environment.

*Evidence and reflection:* Undertake an audit of all the language opportunities that the setting provides: display, resources, layout, activities, continuous provision, role-play area, for example. Consider the following:

- How do you know you these are providing language-rich opportunities?
- Now undertake a series of observations on up to four target children:
- How often are children accessing the opportunities you provide?
- How do they respond to the opportunities you provide?
- Do they have the impact you expect them to?

*Extension:* Is there anything that you would now change to enhance the provision?

# 3.4 Non-verbal communication

At various points, for example in Chapter 6, we have noted the importance of non-verbal communication. Here we consider it in relation to the development of children's communication skills.

It is important for early years practitioners to consider their non-verbal communication with children within their personal repertoire of both interpersonal and communication skills. Non-verbal language such as facial expression, effective eye contact, posture, gesture and interpersonal distance or space is usually interpreted by others as a reliable reflection of how we are feeling (Nowicki and Duke, 2000). Mehrabian (1971) devised a series of experiments dealing with the communication of feelings and attitudes, such as like–dislike. The experiments were designed to compare the influence of verbal and non-verbal cues in face-to-face interactions, leading Mehrabian to conclude that there are three elements in any face-to-face communication: visual clues, tone of voice, and actual words. Through Mehrabian's experiments it was found that 55 per cent of the emotional meaning of a message is expressed through visual clues, 38 per cent through tone of voice and only 7 per cent from actual words. For communication to be effective and meaningful these three parts of the message must support each other in meaning; ambiguity occurs when the words spoken are inconsistent with, say, the tone of voice or body language of the speaker.

Similarly, practitioners need to be aware of the messages they are sending out to a child via their use of non-verbal language (see Buckley, Reading 12.3). It is important to remember that whenever we are around others, we are communicating non-verbally, whether we want to or not, and children need to feel comfortable in the presence of the adults around them. According to Chaplain, 'children are able to interpret the meaningfulness of posture from an early age' (2003: 69). Even locations and positions when talking can be important – for example, it is beneficial when speaking with a young child to drop down to their level, sitting, kneeling or dropping down on one's haunches alongside them. This creates a respectful and friendly demeanor and communicates a far more genuine interest in the child and what they are doing than bending over them from on high.

The use of other planned non-verbal forms of communication have increased in recent years to support children with SEN or EAL – for example, Makaton. Makaton uses signs and symbols to support communication. It has become popular as it is very flexible and can be easily adapted to suit individual needs. Case examples and links to Makaton resources can be found at **reflectiveteaching.co.uk**.

# 4 Language and learning

## 4.1 Communication

In addition to understanding how to support children's early developing language skills, the early years practitioner needs to address how children learn through language. There are two important elements of language that must be considered in relation to this line of thinking: those of communication, and representation. Communication is the transmission of meanings, and this chapter has shown how children engage with communication from the moment of birth. Language, however, is also a representational system that emerges with the child's cognitive skills, enabling them to understand and organize their world. Language comprises different elements that are important for effective understanding and communication: these are phonology, vocabulary, grammar and pragmatics. These four basic strands mutually support and influence each other's development; however phonological development is currently a particular focus for study, partly because of its link with learning to read. **Table 12.1** is a summary of Peccei's (2006) introductory chapters on children's language development. It shows the typical ages when significant developmental milestones occur, particularly in relation to:

- *Phonological development:* the development of adult-like organized sounds systems
- *Discourse development*: the developing ability to communicate
- *Vocabulary*: the words the child can understand and use
- *Morphological development*: an understanding of the rules which govern the meaning of words, such as tense and plurals
- *Syntactic development*: the ability to combine words to construct sentences

Table 12.1 Summary of stages of children's language acquisition [based on information from Peccei (2006)]

| Age | Development |
| --- | --- |
| birth to two months | **Phonological development**: vowel-like sounds such as crying and grunting |
| two to four months | **Phonological development**: cooing |
| four to six months | **Phonological development**: vocal play including rudimentary syllables such as /da/ or /goo/ |
| six months | **Phonological Development**: babbling such as /ba/ba/ba/ or /ga/ba/da/do |
| one year | **Phonological Development**: first meaningful words |
| nine months to one year three months | **Discourse development**: prelinguistic directive such as speech sounds and pointing |
| one year six months to one year eight months | **Vocabulary**: first 50 words acquired |
| one year three months to two years | **Discourse development**: telegraphic directives – e.g. 'that mine', 'gimme' |

| Age | Development |
|---|---|
| two years | **Vocabulary**: average vocabulary = 200–300 words <br><br> **Syntactic development**: begin to put words together in sentences. Noun phrases with pre-modification of the noun – e.g. 'more biscuit'. Pronouns appear – e.g. 'me want that' |
| two years three months | **Morphological development**: past tense inflection appears |
| two years to two years four months | **Discourse development**: limited routines – 'where's my X?', 'what's that?' |
| two years six months | **Morphological development**: starting to acquire rules for inflecting nouns and verbs – e.g. 'breaked it' or 'mouses' <br><br> **Syntactic development**: multiple pre-modification of nouns – e.g. 'that red ball' |
| two years eight months | **Syntactic development**: compound sentences – e.g. 'The dog bit the cat and then he ran away' |
| two to three years | **Sense relations**: refer to all members of category as the same – e.g. all flowers as flower |
| two years nine months | **Discourse development**: greater precision of articulation in self-repairs, increased volume and use of contrastive stress – e.g. 'It was on the chair!' (not under it) |
| three years | **Morphological development**: post-modified phrases – e.g. 'the picture of Lego town' <br><br> Complex sentences <br><br> **Discourse development**: can cope with non-situated discourse |
| two years four months to three years eight months | **Discourse development**: embedded requests – 'Can I have big boy shoes?' |
| three years eight months to four years | **Discourse development**: conversation consists largely of initiation/response (I/R) exchanges. |
| four years | **Discourse development**: elaborate oblique strategies – 'We haven't had any sweets for a long time' |
| four years to four years seven months | **Discourse development**: acquisition of auxilliary verbs (might, may, could) and negation. Child's response itself increasingly becomes R/I |
| four years seven months to four years ten months | **Discourse development**: greater ability to encode justifications and causal relationships allows for longer exchanges |
| four to five | **Sense relations**: spontaneously use category names – e.g. rose or daisy |
| four years six months | **Syntactic development**: coordination with ellipsis – e.g. 'The dog bit the cat and ran away' |
| three years eight months to five years seven months | **Discourse development**: advanced embedding – 'Don't forget to buy sweets' |
| six years old | **Vocabulary**: average vocabulary understood = 14,000 words. Average spoken vocabulary = 6,000 words |

# 4.2  Learning through talk: Listening, questioning and responding

Questioning is a powerful tool for teaching because it allows opportunities for supporting, enhancing and extending children's learning. A key question to ask ourselves therefore is how good are we, as reflective early years practitioners, at asking children questions, allowing children time to respond and, listening to their answers. Questions can be used for a wide range of purposes and as a vital tool for teaching and learning. Questioning can be thought of in terms of the level of demand they make on children's thinking. Additionally, they can be broadly divided into two main categories: lower-order and higher-order questions. Lower-order questions are often closed or literal, requiring relatively brief, factual answers which are either 'right' or 'wrong'. Such questions would not support the development of ongoing discussions and therefore do not support episodes of sustained shared thinking (SST), for example. Higher-order questions invite a range of possible answers and require children to apply, reorganize, extend, evaluate or analyse information. Such questions would feature more often in extended discussions where responses provide opportunities for the conversation and/or learning to be extended. It is important to remember that both types of question have their place within effective pedagogy.

> ## Expert question
>
> **Dialogue:** Does practitioner–child talk scaffold understanding, build on existing knowledge and strengthen dispositions towards learning to allow children to become active learners?
>
> This question contributes to a conceptual framework representing enduring issues and practitioner expertise (see Chapter 16).

Questions need to be formulated to match children's learning needs. It is possible for the practitioner to differentiate questions for different abilities and different children,

> ## Reflective activity 12.4
>
> *Aim:* To investigate your use of questioning within your setting.
>
> *Evidence and reflection:* You might wish to use the audio recording from **Reflective activity 12.2**. Alternatively, create another audio-recording where you are working with a child or children, either on a one-to-one basis, in a small group, or during a whole-class episode of teaching and learning. Analyse the recording using the following questions:
>
> 1  What types of questions did I use to support the child's/children's learning?
> 2  What did the children learn; how, and why?
> 3  How did I extend thinking/learning?
> 4  Which specific questioning techniques did I use?
>
> *Extension:* What are the implications for your use of questioning in your future practice? Do you need to focus on the types of question you ask and incorporate them within your planning? How will you target specific children to ensure you are asking them the 'right' questions?

Table 12.2 Different questioning techniques practitioners can use

| Question type | Purpose | Example |
| --- | --- | --- |
| Structuring | To manage the environment. | Does anybody have a question? Does everybody have a space to sit? |
| Probing | To help children to give fuller answers, take their thinking further. | Can you give me an example? Where have you seen that before? |
| Redirecting | To take the focus away from either the practitioner or a child involved in the dialogue. | Can anyone else help? Does anybody have any ideas that could help us? |
| Fact-finding | To check if children were listening, to see what they are able to recall. | Where did Susie go in the story? What happened to Dog? Can anybody remember who came into nursery last week to see us? |
| Higher-order | To encourage children to work out answers for themselves. | If the plant we kept in the dark did not grow, what do you think plants need to grow? Well, if the sand keeps falling into the floor, what could we do to stop that, do you think? |
| Affective | To encourage children to give their opinion and express how they feel. | What did you enjoy about circle time today? Why is monkey so important to you, do you think? |
| Prompting | Answer to support a child in correcting his or her response – for example, simplifying the framing of the question, taking them back to known material, giving hints or clues, accepting what is right and prompting for a more complete answer. | That is an interesting answer. So why do you think that the daddy wanted the children to be quiet? Did you see anything in the pictures that might give us a clue? |

simplifying the questions as necessary. Having a variety of questioning techniques in a pedagogic repertoire will help all children, as different questioning techniques can be used in order to support children's learning. **Table 12.2** provides examples of the types of questions which can be used.

While these questions may not feature in your interactions with babies and very young children, remember that questioning can also be done by looking at things, exploring items. You may also ask yourself questions as you carry out an activity with a baby or child. All of these things contribute to the development of communication skills and in encouraging a child to become a curious learner.

# 4.3 Learning through talk: Dialogic teaching

The term *dialogic teaching* is increasingly used in education discussions and, as such, it is helpful to be aware of its meaning and origins. Alexander (2008b) argues that dialogic teaching demands a balance of talk, reading and writing; management of classroom space and time; a productive relationship between speaker and listener; and attention to the content and dynamics of talk itself. Dialogic teaching, he suggests, is characterized by five key criteria – it is:

- *collective*: practitioners and children address learning tasks together, as a group or as a class.

- *reciprocal*: practitioners and children listen to each other, share ideas and consider alternative viewpoints.

- *supportive*: children articulate their ideas freely, without fear of embarrassment over 'wrong' answers; and they help each other to reach common understandings.

- *cumulative*: practitioners and children build on their own and each other's ideas and chain them into coherent lines of thinking and enquiry.

- *purposeful*: practitioners plan and steer talk with specific educational goals.

  [adapted from Alexander, 2008: 28]

The main pedagogic implication for reflective early years practitioners is an emphasis on the importance of social learning through practitioner–child and child–peer dialogue. Such an approach supports key points which have been made throughout this book, specifically the importance of relationships and collaboration in enhancing learning (Chapter 6) and the use of SST to build upon children's ideas to further their knowledge (Chapter 2). A dialogic approach to teaching and learning requires practitioners and children to build actively on each other's ideas, posing questions and constructing shared interpretations and new knowledge. For practitioners, it involves using open-ended, higher-order questioning, feeding in ideas and reflecting on and interpreting children's contributions. For children as learners, it encourages articulation and justification of personal points of view, appreciating and responding to others' ideas and taking turns in whole-class, group and one-to-one interactions (Mercer and Littleton, 2007). In contrast to a practitioner-led transmission approach, a dialogical pedagogy signals the co-presence of the practitioner as a member of a community of learners, available to guide and coach the learner, modelling the exploratory nature of dialogue. Alexander (2008b) stresses that ensuring the ethos and the conditions of the learning environment are conducive is essential in order for dialogic teaching and learning to take place. Dialogic approaches to teaching in statutory schooling align much more with the pedagogic approaches favoured by early years practitioners.

# 4.4 Exploring dialogue

Mercer and Littleton (2007) have shown that classroom dialogue contributes to children's intellectual development and their educational attainment. Research has further corroborated the fact that both interaction with adults and collaboration with peers can provide opportunities for children's learning and for their cognitive development (Alexander, 2000, 2004; Kutnick, Ota and Berdondini, 2008). Barnes (1971) found that language is a major means of learning and that learners uses of language for learning are strongly influenced by the practitioner's language, which prescribes them their roles as learners. According to Barnes' perspective, children have the potential to learn not only by listening passively to the practitioner, but also by verbalizing, by talking, by discussing and arguing (persuading). Children are capable of developing all of these aspects of language from a very early age, if they are encouraged to participate in two-way dialogue

---

### Reflective activity 12.5

*Aim:* To investigate whether your setting provides a participatory, active, language-rich environment.

*Evidence and reflection:* Undertake observations of three target children during a free-flow child-led play session. The following questions should provide the focus for the observation:

1 Are the children discussing things together?
2 Are there activities which require the children to work together in some capacity?
3 Do practitioners in the setting encourage active dialogue, ask open-ended probing or prompting questions?
4 Do the children demonstrate that they have the skills to engage with each other?

These are four ways of investigating participation in learning, but it is important to note that all are under the control of the practitioner.

*Extension:* Following the observation, consider whether the children's learning could have been supported further through the greater use of effective questioning. Is there anything that you might plan to work on with the children to support their ability to communicate well with each other?

and are treated as able communicators from birth. Mercer and Hodgkinson (2008) have built on the work of Barnes to further explore the centrality of dialogue in the learning process. By studying teacher–pupil interaction it is possible to see how classroom language might offer different possibilities for pupil learning. While some of this may seem complex for the children with whom you work, understanding how children will learn in the future and therefore the skills they need to be observing and practising in the early educational experiences is most helpful. Indeed, while thinking about children's future needs, such an approach also supports the development of the language skills we stressed as being crucial for children's learning and development at the beginning of this chapter.

# 4.5 Dialogic talk and questions

In dialogic talk, the questions asked by children are as important as the questions asked by the practitioner, as are the answers given. The practitioner is not using questions solely for the purpose of 'testing' a child's knowledge, but also to enable them to reflect, develop and extend their thinking. Wragg and Brown (2001) suggest several types of response that can be made to children's answers and comments. Practitioners can:

- ignore the response, moving on to another child, topic or question.
- acknowledge the response, building it into the subsequent discussion.
- repeat the response verbatim to reinforce the point or to bring it to the attention of those that might not have heard it.
- repeat part of the response, to emphasize a particular element of it.
- paraphrase the response for clarity and emphasis, and so that it can be built into the ongoing and subsequent discussion.
- praise the response (either directly or by implication in extending and building on it for the subsequent part of the discussion).
- correct the response.
- prompt the child for further information or clarification.
- probe the child to develop relevant points.

These features indicate the type of response that is possible to make to children's utterances. Decide which you think are most helpful to support learning. It is easy for the practitioner to miss important clues to children's understanding when they are too concerned to lead children towards a predetermined answer, so it is important to give children time to respond and, wherever possible, build further questions from their contributions.

There are other matters to consider. Although it may seem an obvious point to make, the practitioner should allow thinking time (particularly for complex responses). Thinking time will afford children the opportunity to correct, clarify and crystallize their responses once uttered. Avoid 'jumping onto' a response before a child has had time to complete it. The skilled practitioner will build a child's contribution into their own plans for the sequence of the discussion and use a child's contribution to introduce another question to be put to another child. In addition to the practitioner being aware of their own skills and questioning, as we have discussed previously, children spend much more of their time in dialogue with each other than with adults and, as such, it is important to provide them with opportunities to discuss thing together. The account below describes a project in England which was developed to support the development of language and communication skills and the impact this had on one child.

## Reflective activity 12.6

*Supporting dialogic book talk*

*Aim:* To reflect upon how you can use questioning to extend young children's thinking.

*Evidence and reflection:* To effectively plan for the development of language and communication skills for the unique child.

- Choose a picture book that will appeal to the group of children. The main objective is to get children talking and having conversations with you and with each other. It is a good idea to make sure you are very familiar with the story; then think about the kinds of prompts and questions you will use to think and talk about it with the children.
- Which visual aids will you use to support engagement with and comprehension of the text – for example, what would you use with very young children or EAL learners?
- What key questions (story prompts) will you ask? Plan to ask open-ended questions so that you can recast and expand on children's utterances. List the key story prompts on a plan.
- Think about the ways in which children might be able to relate the story to their own lives. What prompts will you ask? List the key prompts on a plan.
- How will you extend the children's vocabulary? Decide the new vocabulary that you will introduce in reading and talking about the story. Decide how it will be introduced.
- Finally, what follow-up experiences and activities will you plan to consolidate this vocabulary?

*Extension:* Ask a colleague to observe the session in light of your planning. Discuss with them the strengths of the session and ideas for enhancing the activity in the future. You may focus on children with particular needs and how well they were supported during the session.

## Case study 12.3 Daisy Chain Nursery: Listening time and the Every Child a Talker project

Every Child a Talker, ECaT, was a national project led by the Early Years National Strategy in England. It aimed to increase the language and communication skills of children from birth to age 4 by:

- providing comprehensive training to settings, specifically in the areas of identifying speech, language and communication needs and supporting children's language development.
- increasing parental understanding of speech and language development.
- facilitating links between the nursery setting and home.
- providing information to help parents support language development at home.

The project was implemented slightly differently in different areas. In the case local authority, a specialist teacher and a speech and language therapist were appointed as Early Language Consultants to lead the project. Over 20 settings took part, including a range of private, voluntary and independent early years settings. Each setting identified an Early Language Lead Practitioner who was responsible for managing the project in their setting and sharing information with their staff team.

During the year, the Early Language Lead Practitioner attended regular cluster meetings and received training on:

- speech and language development
- adult–child interaction
- English as an Additional Language
- using music and songs to support speech and language
- Communication-friendly spaces

Adult–child interaction was a major focus. Each setting was given intensive training on interaction styles and strategies to facilitate language development. They were also provided with a video camera to enable them to capture interactions and reflect back on their practice to help identify areas to change. As a part of this, emphasis was placed on sensitive interventions, giving children time to respond to questions and sometimes asking fewer questions.

Daisy Chain Nursery gave the following account:

*We are paying more attention to each child's language and stopping more to observe and listen rather than question too much. The Observe, Wait and Listen approach and the 'seven second rule', where we count for this length of time after asking a child a question or requesting a child to act, has been very effective. We have been surprised by how much language children do have when we have listened in more carefully and given them to time to respond.*

*It has been noticeable how much all of the children, including those with English as an Additional Language, have progressed due to the staff becoming more knowledgeable about ECaT's principles and practice and language and communication skills. The children's interaction has improved considerably. All the training has given us practical ideas to use within our setting and we have seen the results immediately in some cases. For example, we introduced 'chatter baskets': we filled a basket with items and then sat with the children while they pulled each item out, talked about it and, when appropriate, staff interjected to support their thinking and learning. One child, Jack, had had some difficulty settling into nursery. He often played alone. After talking to Jack's parents we noted that Jack was very interested in sea creatures. We placed a ticket from a visit to an aquarium in the basket along with some models and pictures of creatures. Jack became more animated than we have previously seen. He was able to go into great detail, using language we had not previously observed. He told the other children about his fish at home and the places he had visited. This opportunity for dialogue helped Jack to forge new relationships.*

Discovering what children know and their misconceptions requires good communication skills, language skills and empathy. Rather than a practitioner's questions eliciting brief responses from children, we can see that dialogic talk is a type of interaction where practitioners and children have the potential to make substantial and significant contributions. Planning for these opportunities is a good way of ensuring there are frequent opportunities for children to engage in dialogue and help to build dialogic practice.

## 5 Language development and wider considerations

## 5.1 The development of phonological awareness

Phonological awareness has been much studied, partly because of its link with learning to read. As far as language acquisition is concerned, there are some understandings and skills that have to be acquired before those which are beneficial for learning to read and write. Following on from this line of thinking, Shankweiler and Fowler (2004: 483) argue that there are stages of phonological awareness that children must go through in relation to language development before they are ready to receive specific, discrete phonics instruction in the classroom. A focus in the early years on listening to and being able to discriminate sounds, for example in the child's environment, supports this argument.

Phonological activity begins from birth; babies are encouraged to use their voices to make sounds and babbling noises, for example. They will also listen to the intonations and sounds of the voices of their adult carers, thus supporting their potential from the outset to discriminate with regard to the sounds, rhythms and patterns of their native language. Children need to be encouraged to experiment with sound. As language develops, they will learn to control their vocal cords. The sound and air flow which pass from the vocal cords is obstructed in various ways in order to form sounds which eventually become words. The place of articulation involves use of the teeth, lips, tongue, mouth and glottis. The manner of articulation involves obstructing the air flow to varying degrees, such as completely stopping it or allowing some to pass through the nose. As they grow, children have the ability to communicate meaningfully using, by varying degrees, approximations, single, and eventually combinations of words. These spoken words can then be broken down into various constituents or phonological units in different ways. It follows that sensitivity to larger phonological units including words, rhymes and syllables occurs earlier and probably more naturally than awareness of individual phonemes (Goswami and Bryant, 1989; Shankweiler and Fowler, 2004). This is an important phase of a child's life in relation to future phonics instruction and learning to read through a focus on paying attention to the sounds of individual phonemes when decoding text. Children will be taught to use the strategy of blending phonemes in order from left to right, from the beginning of a word to the end. They will need to become experts at distinguishing sounds or phonemes so that they can reproduce these orally, recognize them on the page, and use them confidently and appropriately in order to spell correctly when writing. Children therefore need to be exposed to sounds, rhymes, poems, stories, and songs from birth so that the important underpinnings of phonological awareness are embedded within their growing repertoire of language skills (see Schmidt, Reading 12.6).

## 5.2 Language skills and fluent reading

Prosodic reading, or reading with expression, is considered one of the hallmarks of fluent reading. The study by Schwanenflugel, Hamilton, Kuhn, Wisenbaker and Stahl (2004) highlights the key role of word decoding speed in reading prosodically. When a child is reading prosodically, oral reading sounds much like speech with appropriate phrasing, pause structures, stress, rise and fall patterns, and general expressiveness. To read in this way, children must be able to do more than decode the text and translate punctuation into speech. They must also incorporate the ordinary rise and fall of pitch in ordinary conversation. Without appropriate language skills, there will therefore be a negative impact on reading ability. However, it is important to note that in the early years young readers begin with an emerging decoding speed. They will read with lengthy, sporadic pauses between sentences, marked with a hesitant start–stop quality. Young readers may also read with unnecessarily long pauses in the middle of sentences where none are needed. They are developing their skills, however. It is important that the reflective early years practitioner understands the trajectory children are on in relation to becoming a so-called skilled reader (see Harrison, Reading 12.5). A key question for reflection is: 'what opportunities can I provide to support such a trajectory?', in addition to giving children time and awarding appropriate encouragement and praise for new achievements.

## 5.3 Language and role-play

The early years practitioner must focus on language development as a priority to ensure that children know how to communicate successfully. Social interactions should be an embedded element of practice in the early years and beyond. Role-play areas provide good opportunities for children to learn how to communicate together in a range of situations. Learning through play in this way provides a 'no risk' environment in which children learn to express themselves, alongside others, through language. Role-play areas can be the province of children only – and sometimes it is important for the children to play alone. However, there are times when the practitioner could enter the fantasy situation and play alongside them – for example, having their hair done at the hairdresser's. Knowing when and how to intervene constructively without the children feeling that the practitioner is intruding takes sensitivity and watchfulness.

# 5.4 The bilingual learner

Kuhl (2004) argues that young children usually learn their mother tongue rapidly and effortlessly, following the same developmental path regardless of culture. Bilingual children are hearing two languages – or two distinct systems – which they have to internalize and respond to. At an early age, neither language is likely to interfere with the other, so young children can learn two languages easily. Reese et al.'s (2000) research showed that bilingual pupils' success in learning to read in English does not rest exclusively on primary language input and development. The most significant finding was that parents' engagement with reading using the second language is beneficial for their children's reading in the first language, and their education more generally. Time spent on literacy activity in a child's native language – whether at home or at school – is therefore not time lost with respect to English reading acquisition. These findings also support our earlier claims that working with families of all children can enhance their learning. Working with families whose first language differs from our own may present challenges, and efforts need to be made to ensure that appropriate communication is reached, whether through an interpreter or through efforts to decode practice language (see Reading 12.4).

It has already been pointed out in this chapter (and indeed throughout this book) that the social and cultural aspects of language development are important as children learn, through talk, to place themselves within a specific social context. In this way the development of language and identity are closely linked. The quality of social experience and interaction will vary greatly between children, and, during the early years, practitioners need to be aware that some children will arrive at the setting appearing to be confident, articulate users of the English language, whereas others seem less comfortable language users. However, practitioners should beware of deficit models and remember that it is too easy to label a child's spoken language as 'poor', or even to say that they have 'no language', without sufficient thought.

It is important, then, that practitioners understand about language diversity and the ways in which judgements are made about speakers in the setting. From this perspective, it is equally important that practitioners recognize their own histories and status as language users, and resist the temptation to impose their own social criteria on the child's ongoing language development. As Bearne argues:

Language diversity is ... deeply involved with social and cultural judgements about what is valuable or worthy ... Judgements are often made about intelligence, social status, trustworthiness and potential for future employment on the basis of how people speak – not the content of what they say, but their pronunciation, choice of vocabulary and tone of voice. Such attitudes can have an impact on later learning. (1983: 155)

For the reflective early years practitioner there are a number of ways to support bilingual learners within the language environment you create in your setting or classroom. Encourage children's use of their first language; if your knowledge of the language is poor, learn simple key phrases such as 'hello' and 'goodbye', 'please' and 'thank you'. Always create a focus for speaking and listening activities. Include the child in activities and lessons right from the start and build bilingual learners' needs into the overall language and literacy objectives for the whole class. It is a good idea to integrate language learning within the lesson content of subjects other than literacy. Model speaking the English language (young monolingual learners will also benefit from this strategy). Consider the use of visual aids such as pictures, photographs and real objects to support language learning, such as those used in Makaton. Finally, involve parents in their children's learning if you can. Encourage them to record stories in the child's home language that you can use in the setting or classroom, for example. Additional ideas for inclusion are approached in Chapter 15.

## Conclusion

Communication begins at birth and can be both verbal and non-verbal. Language develops over a long period of time; it is a gradual process that must be appropriately supported in order to optimize future outcomes. The early years practitioner must therefore model and scaffold language and communication skills. Language acquisition is likely to be stronger if children are encouraged to become active participants in conversation – if they are encouraged to be questioning, to hypothesize, imagine and wonder. The development of language and identity are closely linked. In order to develop and consolidate their communication skills, young children need:

- to feel safe and secure in their early years environment.
- to build relationships of trust and understanding with the practitioner.
- to have access to a wide variety of resources and activities to encourage, develop and support language skills.
- to have constancy and consistency in terms of opportunities and situations in which to develop their language skills. Repetition in routines needs to involve repetition with words and phrases so that language has meaning and familiarity, for example.

Language development should be a fundamental goal of all early years curricula for two reasons: 1) the early childhood years are a critical period in the development of linguistic competence; and 2), language development provides access to future learning, equips the child with an essential communication tool, and enables future access to economic and civic participation in society. Language has to be learnt. The reflective early years practitioner will understand the necessity of clear planning to support the development of effective communication skills from an early age, because, without oral language, children will be unable to pursue an academic career successfully; neither will they be equipped for life.

## Key readings

For more on how children's language develops and how this can be supported, see:

Baker, C. (2011) *Foundations of Bilingual Education and Bilingualism.* Bristol: Multilingual Matters.

Bradford, H. (2009) *Communication, Language and Literacy in the Early Years Foundation Stage.* London: Routledge.

Bruner, J. S. (1983) *Child's Talk: Learning to Use Language.* Oxford: Oxford University Press.

Dukes, C. and Smith, M. (2007) *Developing Pre-school Communication and Language.* London: Sage Publications Ltd.

Kuhl, P. (2004) 'Early language acquisition: cracking the speech code', *Neuroscience,* 5, 831–43.

Peccei, J. S. (ed.) (2006) *Child Language: A Resource Book for Students.* London: Routledge.

To delve more deeply into why language development is so important for learning, see:

Mercer, N. (2000) *Words and Minds: How We Use Language to Think Together.* London: Routledge.

Wells, G. (1986) *The Meaning Makers: Children Learning Language and Using Language to Learn.* London: Hodder and Stoughton.

For a more specific focus on how babies communicate, the following article by Parker-Rees is essential reading:

Parker-Rees, R. (2007) 'Liking to be liked: imitation, familiarity and pedagogy in the first years of life', *Early Years,* 27 (1), 3–17.

The associated website, **reflectiveteaching.co.uk**, offers a wealth of supplementary resources including reflective activities, research briefings, advice on further reading and downloadable diagrams, figures and checklists from the book. It also features a compendium of educational terms, links to useful websites, policy and curriculum documents, and showcases examples of excellent research and practice.

# Assessment
## How can assessment enhance learning?

**13**

# Introduction

Assessment has a profound influence on learning. While the term *assessment* is one which can feel at odds with early years practice, it *is* an essential aspect of teaching. In this chapter we will consider the ways in which assessment supports and enhances learning in the early years – for assessment does not just measure or find out what has been learnt, it also affects what is learnt, how children come to view themselves as learners, and as such possibly their futures (see Nutbrown, Reading 13.6). If these seem startling claims, think about your own experience: perhaps you did well in one subject because it was clear what was required of you and each step was manageable; alternatively you might have disliked another subject and dropped it as soon as possible because everything seemed so confusing and difficult. Maybe you were motivated by the encouragement, support and kindness of one teacher, or humiliated by the comments from another. Possibly you know one of the many people who consider themselves failures because they did not pass formal exams or got lower exam grades than they hoped for. You yourself might be one of the people who thinks that they cannot do maths, or sing, or draw. More positively, you might have achieved something you never thought possible, and become confident that, given effort and the right support, you are able to succeed in many fields. Perhaps you are reading this book as you plan to gain new qualifications and progress in your career. You have undoubtedly helped others to learn and achieve, in formal and informal settings, and across a range of subjects, topics and tasks. Assessment is at the heart of all these scenarios (see Broadfoot, Reading 13.2).

Assessment is much more than testing, although tests and examinations are an important aspect. We will focus upon types of assessment and how we capture what has been learned in Chapter 14, which considers outcomes and how to monitor children's learning achievements. In this chapter we will consider how assessment in itself supports learning. The word 'assessment' comes from the Latin 'assidere' meaning 'to sit besides', and this broadens the conception of assessment to include collaborative activities, bringing to mind two people in dialogue, looking at something together, one person seeking to understand another's work and making comments and suggestions.

## TLRP principles

Two principles are of particular relevance to this chapter on assessment for learning:

**Principle 5: Effective teaching and learning needs assessment to be congruent with learning.** Assessment should help to advance learning as well as determine whether learning has taken place. It should be designed and carried out so that it measures learning outcomes in a dependable way and also provides feedback for future learning.

**Principle 6: Effective teaching and learning promotes the active engagement of the learner.** A chief goal of teaching and learning should be the promotion of learners' independence and autonomy. This involves acquiring a repertoire of learning strategies and practices, developing positive attitudes towards learning, and confidence in oneself as a good learner.

There are three main sections to this chapter: 'assessment, learning and teaching', 'strategies for supporting learning through assessment', and 'family involvement in assessment'. In the first section, key issues, definitions and principles that concern the interrelationships among assessment, learning and teaching are introduced and discussed, including Assessment for Learning (AfL). In the second section, ways of including children and understanding their perspectives are considered. The final section affirms an understanding of assessment for learning and considers the role of parents in assessment.

# 1 Assessment, learning and teaching

Education Scotland identifies the 'Key messages' about assessment as being:

- Assessment is an integral part of learning and teaching, and planning high-quality learning activities for all children.

- Assessment provides an emerging picture of the child and their achievements, and can be a motivation for the child to do better and progress further in their learning.

- Assessment relates to the engagement of staff, children and parents, carers and the wider community in sharing and using a range of information to improve learning and development.

  (Education Scotland, n.d.; see Reading 13.4)

For us these statements affirm the role of assessment in ECEC practice.
Broadfoot states that assessment:

… is arguably the most powerful policy tool in education. Not only can it be used to *identify* strengths and weaknesses of individuals, institutions and indeed whole systems

Table 13.1 Assumptions about assessment [adapted from Carr, 2001: 3]

|  | Assumption | Alternative |
|---|---|---|
| **Purpose** | To check progress against specific criteria | To enhance learning |
| **Outcomes** | Are fragmented and context free<br>Based upon school oriented criteria | Positive dispositions to learning |
| **Focus** | To identify deficits and fill gaps | To acknowledge achievements |
| **Validity** | Objective observations | Observations interpreted through discussions with others |
| **Value to practitioner** | To report to other agencies | For communicating with families, children and staff<br>To inform own practice |

of education; it can also be used as a powerful source of *leverage* to bring about change. (1996: 21)

The tension that exists is fundamentally around what is considered to be good early years practice and what assessment is seen to be. Is assessment about achievements and data or about promoting learning? In her review of assessment, Carr (2001: 3) identified some of the assumptions made about assessment and the alternative viewpoints. This is summarized in **Table 13.1**.

Based upon the *alternative* view, assessment can indeed be seen as a valuable part of early years practice. It can enhance relationships between practitioners, children and families, support children's learning, and help them develop positive dispositions toward education.

## 1.1 Assessment for learning

Assessment that supports learning is referred to as 'Assessment for Learning' (AfL), a term that is often used interchangeably with 'Formative Assessment', which we discuss in Chapter 14. In brief, AfL is a whole way of working involving learners and teachers that integrates assessment, learning and teaching. Activities associated with AfL not only provide information to be used for formative purposes but rather – and probably even more importantly – they are learning processes in themselves. Not only does AfL support the learning of whatever is being studied at the time, it also promotes learning how to learn. AfL is underpinned by a set of beliefs about learning, which, when enacted, establish a learning culture and helps develop learners' metacognitive skills and sense of responsibility. The dialogue which takes place during episodes of sustained shared thinking (Siraj-Blatchford, 2002) would be an example of how a practitioner can sit with a child, engage in dialogue, ask questions to support the child's thinking and promote positive dispositions to learning. By taking time to understand the child and assess their current knowledge, the practitioner is able to guide their progress in a conversation which values exploration and gives credit to new ideas.

### Case study 13.1 AfL in Sunny Days Nursery

After reviewing AfL in relation to their practice, the staff at Sunny Days Nursery reflected that while this fitted well with their practice, it also allowed them to identify areas which could be improved upon. One particular area was identified as requiring improvement following a period of reflection. This related to *making learning intentions explicit*. As the team favoured notions of free play and exploration, finding ways of make learning intentions explicit seemed challenging to many of the practitioners and unnecessary to others. After discussing the issue, the team decided to put the following mechanisms into place.

They developed a *We Are Learning To …* (WALT) wall, which explained some of the things the children are learning, at the entrance to the nursery. The staff drew both children's and families' attention to the wall and discussed the topics with them. The wall included photographs of the children with written descriptions of what the children were learning, which had been dictated to the practitioners by the children. This included age-appropriate tasks – for example, crawling, feeding myself, recognizing numbers, writing my name, and so on.

They sent a WALT newsletter home with the children. It explained both what the children were learning and how the children could be supported to develop the same knowledge and skills at home – for example, reading everyday things to children: cereal boxes, adverts on trains, etc.; talking about floating and sinking when bathing; allowing children time to feed themselves so they refine their skills.

The team continues to review this process but agrees that this has helped staff, families and children to develop a clearer understanding of what is being learned and how the children are being supported.

In summary, AfL is a useful way of conceptualizing early years practice. The purpose of AfL is to:

- support children to learn;
- make learning aims explicit;
- develop children's confidence, independency and autonomy;
- ensure children's individual needs are met;
- create a culture of risk-taking where investigating and 'having a go' are valued as much as, or more than, achievement;
- support children to be resilient.

## 1.2 Guiding principles for assessment

Three key principles about AfL were generated through TLRP's *Learning How to Learn* project (James et al., 2007):

- making learning explicit;
- promoting autonomous learning;
- focusing on learning (as opposed to performance).

These principles provide a useful way of considering assessment. 'Making learning explicit' involves opening up and making very clear all phases and aspects of learning: what precisely is to be learnt, how it will be judged and what counts as quality. A setting in which learning is made explicit features rich dialogue, dialogue between practitioners and children and practitioners and families. Such exchanges go far beyond closed questions and very short answers, to open questions eliciting extensive responses, with in-depth probing leading to detailed explanation and considered reflection. When practitioners engage with children about learning, they do not just use praise, but rather they identify particular strengths and build upon ideas and extend thinking. This becomes possible when a practitioner comes to understand what a child knows and how they think about things.

'Autonomous learning' refers to children taking responsibility for their learning and exercising some measure of independence. While this can be seen to be challenging when working with the youngest children, the beginnings of autonomous learning can be fostered. Practitioners can support children to develop the skills and confidence to make decisions about learning and help them to learn to evaluate their own work and progress. In one setting we have worked with, they encouraged the children to look back on their learning journeys and comment on the recorded work and milestones and how they had progressed. As time went on, the children gained the skills to be able to look back and see the progress they had made. Self-regulating learning is not age- or stage-dependent, but is a learnt process: children become more autonomous learners with guidance and through practice.

The third principle, 'focusing on learning' (as opposed to performance) draws attention to the nature of the learning that is promoted and valued. It is learning with understanding at its core, and learning for its intrinsic worth and long-lasting value, rather than a mechanistic and utilitarian approach to getting things done and recording the evidence. Focusing on learning includes focusing on the process of learning. This principle aligns well with the views promoted by many early years practitioners.

## 1.3 Key ideas

Lying beneath any principles and practices are sets of beliefs, values, theories and ideas that, whether or not we acknowledge or are even conscious of them, shape our actions. Mary Jane Drummond (2008: 3) highlighted the 'close and necessary relationship' between assessment and values, arguing that through the practice of assessment educators make 'value-driven choices about children, about learning and achievements'. She reminded us that over the years children have been conceptualized in different ways – for  example, as empty vessels or blank sheets (John Locke), or as passing through stages of development (Jean-Jacques Rousseau and Jean Piaget; see Reading 2.2). Some conceptualizations are essentially deficit models, where children are viewed as lacking or yet to develop the characteristics of a competent learner on the way to adulthood. By contrast, the image of pre-school children held by educators in Reggio Emilia, Italy, is of children as 'rich, strong and powerful' (quoted in Drummond, 2008: 9, see Nutkins, McDonald and  Stephen, Reading 9.2).

Earlier we noted that assessment could be seen to be at odds with effective early years practice. In part this is because the construction of curricula, learning activities and recording mechanisms based on pre-specified goals, sequenced steps and checklists reflect a view of children's learning as standardized, linear and predictable, rather than unique, complex and divergent. It is possible, though, to take the alternative perspective of assessment and apply more appropriate tools to capture learning. There may still be specific requirements such as profiles, but learning can be captured in more holistic ways. One example of this can be seen in the 'Learning Stories' approach to assessment and recording developed in New Zealand (Carr, 2001, 2008; Carr and Lee, 2012) which uses

narrative to document children's learning not only for recording purposes but, more importantly, as a learning process in itself, shared with friends, teachers, families and others.
Mary James (1998, 2012) has explored the implications for assessment of three theories
of learning (behaviourist, constructivist and socio-cultural; see Chapters 2 and 14), noting
that beliefs about learning are often out of kilter with assessment practices. She advocated
reviewing the methods we use for assessment to see the extent to which they align with
beliefs and understandings about learning.

What practitioners give attention to and what they say indicates to children what is
valued. If feedback and comments are predominantly about presentation and quantity,
being good and conforming, rather than efforts, working with others or the testing of
new ideas, these aspects will be seen as the most important (see Burrell and Bubb,
Reading 13.3). Crucially, if the highest attainment in the group – being the first to read or
write their name – is valued more than the greatest achievement by an individual, and if
'correct answers' appear to be more important than 'having a go', then most of the group
will feel they can never succeed and will probably disengage and the rich learning that
comes through effort and risk-taking will be rare. They will already be forming identities
of themselves as learners and what they can achieve (see Dweck, 2006; Reading 2.5). The
idea of a 'growth' mindset as opposed to a 'fixed' mindset has been referred to above and
in Chapter 2. The characteristics of each are summarized in **Table 13.2**.

Whichever mindset is held has far-reaching repercussions for the disposition of both
practitioners and children. Practitioners who ascribe to a fixed mindset try to ascertain a
child's abilities and then match their expectations to this supposed stable and constant
entity. Children in their turn are concerned how they appear to their peers and practitioners, are anxious to look clever not stupid, and believe that effort and challenges reveal
inadequacies. By contrast, a growth mindset fosters effort, engagement, a willingness to
tackle new and challenging tasks, and to view failure as part of a learning journey. When
growth mindsets characterize a classroom, expectations are high, everyone tries and efforts
are valued whatever the outcome.

The roles and relationships of, and among, children and practitioners are closely
connected with the prevalent conceptions of children, learning and ability. It makes
a huge difference whether children are regarded as rich, strong and powerful, with
unlimited possibilities for growth in diverse and complex ways, or of fixed potential

Table 13.2 Fixed and growth mindsets

| Fixed mindset | Growth mindset |
| --- | --- |
| Intelligence is static | Intelligence is expandable |
| 'I must look clever!' | 'I want to learn more' |
| Avoids challenge | Embraces challenge |
| Gives up easily | Persists in the face of setbacks |
| Sees effort as pointless | Sees effort as the way |
| Ignores useful criticism | Learns from criticism |

with deficiencies yet to be remedied by the gaining of the knowledge necessary to succeed in tests. Further, if young children are seen as incomplete or not yet capable, the opportunities given to them and the expectations placed upon them are narrowed. The interrelationships between assessment practices on the one hand, and roles, relationships, autonomy, agency and identity formation on the other have been explored by a number of researchers (Pollard and Filer, 1999 – see Reading 13.5; Carr, 2001, 2008; Drummond, 2008, 2012). The essential argument is that the way assessment is practised shapes how learners view themselves (which has far-reaching consequences), has a strong influence on their development as successful learners (or not), and determines the culture and interactions of the classroom – and that this is also shaped by practitioners' views of children.

---

### Reflective activity 13.1

*Aim:* To reflect upon the impact of practitioner views of children.

*Evidence and reflection:* Thinking about your own practice, do you think that you hold a *fixed* or *growth* mindset in relation to children? Do you think this changes depending on the child or their family? What impact might this have on your practice? The opportunities given to the child? Have you seen others behave in a way which suggests that they have a fixed mindset? What are the consequences of this?

*Extension:* Reflect on the influence you may have on the developing identities of young children. Consider how the opinions you hold of them and thus what you say and how you respond to them may have influence. Does this impact on the opportunities they have and, in turn, on the chances they have to demonstrate their knowledge and skills? Does this have consequences for assessment?

---

## 2 Strategies for supporting learning through assessment

## 2.1 Involving children in discussions and decision-making

Mary Alice White wrote that adults might comprehend what the experience of education is like for learners if they imagine being:

> … on a ship sailing across an unknown sea, to an unknown destination. An adult would be desperate to know where he is going. But a child only knows he is going to school … The chart is neither available nor understandable to him … Very quickly, the daily life on board ship becomes all-important … The daily chores, the demands, the inspections, become the reality, not the voyage, nor the destination. (White, 1971: 340)

White is reminding us of the importance of helping children see the bigger picture and knowing how what they are learning through play, through routines, through behaviour management today fits in with what they have learnt previously and will do in the future. Not only does this support constructivist learning (see Chapter 2), but it can also capture children's interest and increase motivation to learn. If we listen to children, we can gain great insight into their perspectives.

Involving children in decision-making does, though, involve more than asking their opinion or listening to them. Waller (2009) suggests that a modern view of the child acknowledges agency – that is, children's capacity to understand and act upon their world. It acknowledges that children demonstrate extraordinary competence from birth and are perceived as actively involved in the co-construction of their own lives. From this perspective, children are viewed as active agents who construct their own cultures (Corsaro, 2005), have their own activities, their own time and their own space (Qvortrup et al., 1994). This perspective, therefore, sees the child as actively participating in her own childhood in accordance with Malaguzzi's (1993) concept of the 'rich child': the child who is 'rich in potential, strong, powerful and competent' (1993: 10). The fact that children can express their feelings and emotions in their surroundings confirms their ability to act as competently. Nevertheless, the term 'agency' embeds a more active role (Mayall, 2002). Children as agents can express not only their desires and wishes but also they can negotiate and interact within their environment, causing change. However, Wyness (1999) states that in practice the school system has failed to recognize the child either as competent actor or as agent. Children must be given the opportunity to enter into debates and discussions. Often they are '… denied the right to speak for themselves either because they are held incompetent in making judgements or because they are thought of as unreliable witnesses about their own lives' (Qvortrup et al., 1994: 2). Thomas (2001) suggests that if there is presumption of competence, rather than incompetence, children often turn out to be more capable and sophisticated than they are given credit for.

---

## Reflective activity 13.2

*Aim:* To reflect upon how you involve children in decision-making on issues which affect their lives.

*Evidence and reflection:* With a peer or colleague, think about how you view children and whether your practice gives the impression that you view them as competent actors. In what ways do you involve them? Are there additional ways they could be included?

*Extension:* Consider the skills you believe the children in your care have at this point in terms of participating in decision-making processes. Think about how you will, first, provide them with opportunities to demonstrate their capabilities, and second, how you will support them to develop and practise the skills required to engage in such discussions.

Two studies have recently been carried out in England that have helped to inform us of children's perspectives and how we may seek them in the early years setting.

## Study 1: Children's experiences of the Early Years Foundation Stage

This study, conducted by Garrick et al. (2010), aimed to gather examples of children's perspectives on their experiences in a range of early years settings, and to consider what these perspectives tell us about the effectiveness of the Early Years Foundation Stage (EYFS) in England (DCSF, 2008). Particular consideration was given to play-based learning, outdoor provision and children's participation. Researchers worked with 146 children aged between 3 and 5 years in different types of early years settings across four local authorities in England. The sample comprised 16 settings, including one Steiner setting. Research questions included:

- To what extent and in what manner are children's experiences in early years settings based around play and how enjoyable are those experiences?
- How well do children's experiences in early years settings meet individual children's needs and interests?
- To what extent do children's experiences in early years settings include physical activity, including physical activity outdoors?
- To what extent do children's views inform planning and delivery of the Early Years Foundation Stage by practitioners?

The researchers spent time with children, talking to them and sharing in activities. They then focused on the things that seemed to be most important to the children – for example, the kinds of play they were keen to show and/or talk about. Further analysis involved identifying appropriate ways of connecting children's talk with the abstract concepts, language and assumptions of the EYFS and early years professionals.

The findings of the study showed, among other things, that:

- children especially appreciated social play opportunities, social occasions and opportunities to care for others in their settings;
- children's views reflected their need for parents, carers and siblings to be welcomed into settings;
- children talked about variations in how far adults get to know them as individuals. Children's comments suggested that in smaller settings, they were more likely to feel that adults knew them as individuals;
- children demonstrated great interest in the rules, boundaries and routines of their settings. Some children seemed to find this structure helpful; others seemed to want more freedom;
- children were often keen to understand why particular rules and routines were needed;

- most, though not all, children talked about their enjoyment of physical activities, particularly outdoors. The extent of these opportunities varied from setting to setting;

- some children commented positively on being free to choose when to play outside. In several settings, children described feeling unhappy about waiting for particular times of day for outdoor activity;

- children often see themselves as capable of being involved in planning their activities. They preferred less organized spaces which provided them the freedom to select their tasks.

  (Garrick et al., 2010)

Such findings can be used both to provide ideas for practice but also to demonstrate how children are able to provide unique insights into their experiences in ECEC and, thus, be actively involved in assessment processes.

## Study 2: Listening to children's perspectives: Improving the quality of provision in early years settings

This study was conducted by Coleyshaw et al. (2012) as part of the Longitudinal Study of Early Years Professional Status (see Hadfield et al., 2012) and investigated how Early Years Professionals (EYPs) in England consulted with children in their setting. The study found that effectively integrating children's perspectives requires practitioners who have:

- the depth of understanding of children's perspectives to develop it as part of a setting's overall pedagogical approach;

- the leadership skills to develop a common understanding of children's perspectives among staff in order to ensure that it does not become tokenistic or contrived;

- the ability to link children's perspectives with the learning and developmental stages … in order to create a phased programme that can support children in acquiring the required skills, understandings and attitudes, including the ability to be critical of provision, throughout their time in a setting;

- the capacity to deal with conflicts and tensions between children's, colleagues' and parents' views of quality provision.

  (Coleyshaw et al., 2012: 25)

This study provides a useful insight into how best to begin to, or increase, children's participation in ECEC settings and how staff teams need to engage with this process. In terms of assessment, this study demonstrates how, when provided with opportunities by staff, children are capable – perhaps more capable than is recorded in environments where opportunities for children to express themselves and demonstrate the ability to think and to negotiate are few. There is a need for pedagogic practice to be such that it encourages and supports children to be active agents in their worlds.

## 2.2 Evaluating dispositions to learn

Lilian Katz (1993) suggested that early years practitioners need to consider four types of learning goals: 'those related to knowledge, skills, dispositions and feelings' (1993: 1). We have noted that assessment, particularly in ECEC, involves developing dispositions to learn. But how do we evaluate children's disposition to learn? Katz defines dispositions as 'habits of mind' or 'tendencies to respond to certain situations in certain ways' (1999: 2). These include friendliness, curiosity, willingness to take risks and tenacity. Katz reminds us that not all dispositions are positive and suggests that practitioners need to attend to the dispositions they want to encourage in the children in their settings – making developing such skills a part of the planned activities.

Carr and Claxton (2002) have identified three positive learning dispositions that it may be particularly valuable to strengthen in early years children: resilience, playfulness and reciprocity. Resilience is the disposition to persist with a task even after a setback, to tackle a learning challenge where the outcome may be uncertain and to persist, even when this is hard work. Playfulness involves the inclination to be creative in response to situations: to tend to notice, imagine and explore alternative possibilities. Reciprocity is the willingness to engage with others, ask questions, communicate ideas and listen to and take on board the views of others (Carr and Claxton, 2002). This provides a useful way to frame observations and/or assessments and judgements about children's dispositions to learn.

In addition to these dispositions, it is also argued that a child's general well-being is a crucial indicator of their disposition to learn. Laevers (2000: 24) argues that we can gain an insight into how children are progressing and achieving by considering the linked dimensions of 'well-being' and 'involvement' that children display when engaged in activity (as discussed in Chapter 7). He contends that children experiencing the highest levels of involvement demonstrate their well-being and are disposed to engage in 'deep-level learning' (Laevers, 2000: 20); thus, being aware of dispositions to learn and supporting the development of positive dispositions to learn is likely to contribute to a child's well-being and future academic successes and their enjoyment of education.

## 2.3 Encouraging children to reflect upon their progress and achievements

'All young people need to become their own best self-assessors' (Earl and Katz, 2008: 90). The logic behind this is that everyone needs to be continually learning and adapting, becoming more autonomous, self-regulating, self-monitoring learners. The strategies discussed in the sections above help children to become more self-regulating learners – in particular, understanding the objectives. Self-assessment, as with so many other aspects of AfL, needs support and practice, so to begin with the practitioner initiates the activity. However, the aim is for the learner to take control so that they initiate repeated moments of self-assessment, integrating the practice into the continual process of working on a task and furthering skills and knowledge. This is where the real power of self-assessment lies.

Similarly, peer assessment is becoming to be seen as 'co-operative improvement' (Clarke, 2011). If we return to the findings of the SPRinG research (see Chapter 4), we considered how young children can be supported to develop the skills to recognize their contributions to the group, their strengths, areas they could seek to improve and generally build self-awareness. Where this has been achieved and children feel 'safe and secure', they are able to help each other and ask each other for help. These are the beginnings of being able to become involved in self and peer assessment. Again, children need to be supported to develop and practise these skills. You may be concerned that the children in your care are not able to assess their own progress, but many of them never will be if they aren't supported to develop these skills. We have had many experiences of students working towards their degrees who have struggled with the idea of self and peer assessment, as they did not see the value, they had never experienced the process and they did not have the skills. If peers look at and discuss work together, whether it be a track they have built or a painting they have made, they can enter into a dialogue together and extend each other's thinking.

Putting the focus on improvement also reduces the emphasis on judgement, and thus lessens some of the more sensitive aspects of self and peer assessment, including possible threats to self-esteem and opportunities for bullying. Cooperating with a peer in order to make work even better helps learners to appreciate others' strengths and the value of another point of view, and can enhance learning autonomy by assisting the realization that it can be very useful to seek another person's perspective. Peer assessment should be focused, with the owner of the work indicating which particular aspect he or she is seeking help to improve.

---

## Reflective activity 13.3

*Aim:* To reflect upon how children in your setting are supported to develop and practise the skills of self and peer assessment.

*Evidence and reflection:* Consider the opportunities that children already have in your setting to improve their learning through self and peer assessment. Do they have the skills to do this? Do you invest time in supporting these skills to develop and grow?

*Extension:* Work with a colleague to plan age-appropriate activities to support the development of self and peer assessment skills. There are additional resources to help you at **reflectiveteaching.co.uk.**

## 3 Family involvement in assessment

We have consistently reiterated that families – by which we mean parents, carers and all those who care for the child: grandparents, aunts and uncles, siblings – must be involved in their children's education. One of the starting points of this is how we communicate with families. There is a need to develop a shared language so the communication is meaningful. Since parents are not a homogeneous group they will all have different needs and different starting points. They will want to get involved in

their children's early years settings in different ways (Whalley, 1997: 17; see Reading 13.1). As such, communication will have to be reflected upon on a family-by-family basis. While there will be overlaps, there will also be differences, and a 'one size fits all' approach will not succeed, particularly with the 'hard to reach' group. Guidance on how to work with families is available; the work of the Pen Green Centre offers a good example.

Parents Involved in their Children's Learning (PICL) is an approach and a way of working that has been developed across the Pen Green Centre for Children and Families over the last 28 years (see Whalley, 2007). Pen Green describes PICL as a way of working rather than a parenting programme.

The PICL approach encourages families and practitioners to support children's learning and development using the cycle shown in the 'Pen Green Learning Loop' (**Figure 13.1**). This involves the flow of knowledge, through dialogue between parents and workers, from the home into the setting. Correspondingly, knowledge flows from the setting to the home and enables the parents to support their child more effectively within the home learning environment.

Video clips from both the home and the setting can be shared between parents and practitioners to support dialogue about children's learning. Parents and practitioners notice

**Figure 13.1**
Pen Green
Learning Loop

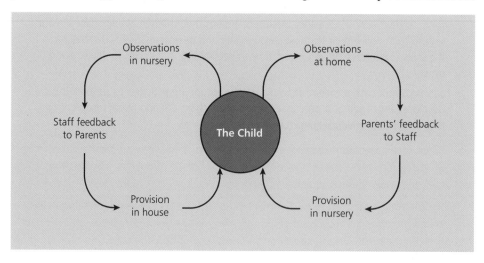

what is significant in the video and discuss what the child is doing and how it relates to prior learning and experiences. They discuss how they can support the child's learning at home and in the setting.

One of the core aims of the PICL approach is to increase parents' and practitioners' understanding of children's learning and development using video reflection and sharing key concepts for understanding and analysing children's learning and development. By engaging with parents and developing strong and equal partnerships, the PICL approach helps parents and practitioners to support children both at home and in the setting and embark on assessment processes together. It is an approach underpinned by a strong ethos which respects parents as co-educators of their children, redressing the imbalance of power between families and professionals. It emphasizes the importance of achieving an equal relationship between families and practitioners, where family members are acknowledged as knowing their children best and wanting the best for them.

PICL is different from a content-led parenting programme. It is a way of working that aims to:

- challenge and support practitioners to find ways of involving families and to develop effective family–practitioner relationships.

- share knowledge about the child in an ongoing dialogue.

- increase parents' enjoyment and confidence in being with their child.

- increase parents' knowledge about their child's interests and how to support their child's learning and their ability to be an advocate for their child.

- increase practitioner knowledge about the child's interests and prior learning experiences.

- promote an effective home learning environment.

- support the child's learning and development over time and improve outcomes for children.

Some of the tools used within the approach include:

- Involvement (Laevers, 1997) – this concept is used to establish when a child is involved in what they are doing, with deeper-level involvement showing deep-level learning as discussed – see Chapter 7.

- Well-being (Laevers, 1997) – the concept of well-being is central to a child's educational development, where low well-being can prevent a child from learning – see Chapter 7.

- Schemas (Athey, 2007) – these are repeated patterns of action which children show when they are exploring the world around them. These repeated patterns help them to develop theories about how things work and to develop an understanding of concepts (see Nutbrown, Reading 13.6).

- 'Adult pedagogic strategies' (Pen Green, 2005) are also shared – these strategies enable families and practitioners to reflect on how they interact with children and how their approach can support and impact on a child's learning.

The use of these tools allows families and practitioners to develop a shared language about learning. The PICL approach also uses several key models of engagement, which are opportunities for professionals to initiate, maintain and reflect on dialogue with parents. These contribute to developing ongoing relationships between children, families and practitioners to foster an equal partnership, enriching both parties' understanding of the child's learning and interests.

These tools and the approach are used at various key points to develop the relationship and shared communication; these include:

- Key concept sessions – these sessions are a way for parents/carers to learn about some of the key concepts that underpin the PICL approach.

- A sustained settling in period in a setting – giving practitioners the opportunity to discuss the key concepts that are shared with parents in order to be able to analyse the child's learning. A settling-in period also allows workers to get to know all the important adults in the child's life.

- Informal chats – communication with families is maintained through 'daily chats', either during home visits or when the child is being dropped off or picked up from the setting. This is also seen as an opportunity to share information on their children's learning and it develops a stronger partnership.

- Home visits – practitioners carry out visits to the home of each child and share video and documentation on the child's learning.

- Home/setting exchange – families and practitioners exchange videos of children learning at a deep level at home and in the setting. They also share information through the portfolios that are developed on each child by families and practitioners.

- Attendance at an event – a range of events and sessions are held which can be used for families and practitioners to support the child's learning.

- Supporting children on trips – families join practitioners in supporting their children's learning on trips.

- Families and practitioners share information to make assessment judgements about the child three times in the year. They look at progress between the first and second assessment and discuss the child's strengths and how best to support the child's learning.

These opportunities for dialogue promote the processes that parents say have been significant in supporting their learning and enabling them to support their children to make good progress. Thus, the assessment process is firmly rooted in a cycle of improving outcomes for children through support which is based upon knowing the child, their lives and their prior experiences. Do you use any of these tools? May some of them offer a way for you to extend and develop your interactions with families?

# Conclusion

By focusing on assessment to support learning in this chapter we have sought to acknowledge the complexity of the relationship between assessment and learning and demonstrate that assessment is a valuable and important aspect of teaching in the early years. We have highlighted the profound influence of assessment practices not only on the content of what is being learned, but, even more importantly, on the process of learning and on the child's sense of self.

# Key readings

For a comprehensive review of assessment and learning in the early years, see:

Dubiel, J. (2014) *Effective Assessment in the Early Years Foundation Stage*. London: Sage Publications Ltd.

Whitebread, D. and Coltman, P. (2008) *Teaching and Learning in the Early Years*. Oxon: Routledge.

For support with developing observation, see:

Barber, J. and Paul-Smith, S. (2012) *Early Years Observation and Planning in Practice*. London: Practical Pre-School.

Brodie, K. (2013) *Observation, Assessment and Planning in the Early Years: Bringing It All Together*. Maidenhead: Open University Press.

Kamen, T. (2013) *Observation and Assessment for the EYFS*. London: Hodder.

Broadfoot's book is a very clearly written excellent overview covering many aspects of assessment and drawing on a wealth of material:

Broadfoot, P. (2007) *An Introduction to Assessment*. London: Continuum.

In an eye-opening book, Drummond provides an important critical alternative to mechanistic approaches to assessment:

Drummond, M. (2012) *Assessing Children's Learning*. London: David Fulton.

Black and Wiliam's influential review of research is summarized in:

Black, P. and Wiliam, D. (1998) *Inside the Black Box: Raising Standards through Classroom Assessment*. London: King's College.

An innovative and internationally acclaimed approach particularly for younger children links assessment practice with the formation of learning dispositions:

Carr, M. and Claxton G. L. (2002) 'Tracking the development of learning dispositions', *Assessment in Education*, 9, 9–37.

Carr, M. and Lee, W. (2012) *Learning Stories: Constructing Learner Identities in Early Education.* London: Sage Publications Ltd.

The associated website, **reflectiveteaching.co.uk**, offers a wealth of supplementary resources including reflective activities, research briefings, advice on further reading and downloadable diagrams, figures and checklists from the book. It also features a compendium of educational terms, links to useful websites, policy and curriculum documents, and showcases examples of excellent research and practice.

# part four

# Reflecting on consequences

Part Four draws attention to the consequences of what we do in ECEC. Chapter 14 reviews big issues in assessment, with particular attention to how we need to work with parents when we are assessing children's needs and progress. 'Inclusion' (Chapter 15) asks us to consider various dimensions of difference and also the ways in which routine processes differentiate between people. The emphasis is on accepting difference as part of the human condition and on how to build more inclusive communities within settings, which in turn will contribute to the development of a more inclusive society.

# Outcomes
## How do we capture learning achievements?

**14**

# Introduction

Assessment is a natural feature of interaction with others; when meeting someone for the first time an assessment is made of their dress, their demeanour and their language. Inevitably these assessments are embedded within our own values, experiences and preconceptions. Therefore, they often contain stereotyped assessments or evaluations that may not always be founded on fact. Hence, interactions with others can just as often be about miscommunication and misunderstandings as they can about effective communication and shared understandings. It is important to note that assessments of children are also influenced by these same values and preconceptions (Drummond, 2003). As we have discussed previously (see for example Chapter 3), it is easy to hold preconceptions of children and their families. As such, assessments are value-laden and can only ever provide an incomplete picture of a child (Bruce, 2011). This limitation is compounded when working with the youngest children in our care, who may not be able to express themselves through verbal language or the written word. Thus, in order to assess young children's development, progress and achievements, we believe that a *holistic* approach is needed – that is, that such assessments need to be founded on data collected from a range of sources including children's families, our colleagues and the children themselves (Bruce, 2011). Such detailed assessments, if utilized in planning, are key to ensuring children's safety, inclusion and individual rights, as we have seen in a number of case studies in this book – for example **Case studies 9.1** and **11.2**.

Ultimately, as discussed in the previous chapter we recognize that 'assessment plays an important part in helping parents, carers and practitioners to recognize children's progress, understand their needs, and to plan activities and support' (DfE, 2012: 10). We need to understand where a child is in order to support them to move forward. This may be in terms of cognitive activities but, crucially, this also applies to a child's personal, social and emotional, and physical development.

The purpose of any given assessment will affect the type of assessment used and how and when it is carried out. The assessment type to be used is also inextricably linked to political and economic systems (Drummond, 2003) as well as local systems within settings, local schools and local authorities (LAs). Political systems decide which curricula are to be used and often the pedagogic approach taken and subsequently assessment processes (Fleer, 2002); a recent example of this is the introduction of phonics testing in England at the end of Year 1, with children who are around 6 years of age. Within this chapter we will extend our discussions from Chapter 13 to consider types of assessment, the theoretical and political positions behind these assessments, and how assessments can be useful for different stakeholders. We will then move on to consider how we collect evidence, understand that evidence and then use it to feed forward into our work with children.

> ## TLRP principles
>
> Two principles are of particular relevance to this chapter on assessment:
>
> **Principle 5: Effective teaching and learning needs assessment to be congruent with learning.** Assessment should help to advance learning as well as determine whether learning has taken place. It should be designed and carried out so that it measures learning outcomes in a dependable way and also provides feedback for future learning
>
> **Principle 6: Effective teaching and learning promotes the active engagement of the learner.** A chief goal of teaching and learning should be the promotion of learners' independence and autonomy. This involves acquiring a repertoire of learning strategies and practices, developing positive attitudes towards learning, and confidence in oneself as a good learner.

The four nations of the United Kingdom have different statutory arrangements for assessing pupils' learning outcomes, and there is a continuing history of change. For specific information on the current summative assessment requirements in Scotland, Wales, Northern Ireland and England respectively, please visit:

- **educationscotland.gov.uk**
- **learning.wales.gov.uk**
- **deni.gov.uk**
- **education.gov.uk**

This chapter reviews issues and principles to assist the reflective teacher whatever the jurisdiction or context they work in.

## 1 Perspectives on assessment

In this section we explore the relationship between pedagogy and assessment. To do this we consider approaches to assessment from three positions: *behaviourism*, *constructivism* and *social constructivism*.

## 1.1 A behaviourist approach to assessment

Broadly speaking, behaviourist approaches consider learning to be a permanent change in behaviour (Hergenbahn and Olson, 2001). In the field of education this change in behaviour is attributed to the actions of others – for example, the practitioner. Viewing learning in this way, as a transmission approach whereby the teacher delivers lesson content to the child who, as an empty vessel, tabula rosa (blank slate) or sponge, absorbs this information – or not, as the case may be – has particular implications for assessment. Such assessment focuses upon capturing the change or, indeed, how much or how little the child has absorbed. This usually involves a straightforward recall of the knowledge through some form of verbal or written test. We see this approach taken in many forms of assessment as children enter statutory schooling – for example, GCSEs, A Levels and Highers. Glazzard et al. (2010) refer to this philosophy as the conformist approach which assesses *what* is known as opposed to *how* it has come to be known. This is known as the *summative approach* to assessment.

Within ECEC provision (for example, the EYFS [DfE, 2012]), while such an approach may influence practice – after all, these same children will enter a culture where summative assessment is frequently used – assessment is based on a much more holistic view of the child, with practitioners focusing on how children are learning and what their interests are. Behaviourist approaches to assessment thus have little place in most ECEC settings.

Assessing children in a holistic manner does, however, present its own issues. As we have discussed in Chapter 9, many countries now have a prescribed early years curriculum; in addition, schools feel under pressure to ensure children are achieving 'expected levels' as the results of such assessments are placed in league tables. Such issues can impact upon ECEC practice as issues of 'school readiness' come into play. The first curriculum for the early years in England, the Curriculum Guidance for the Foundation Stage (CGFS), had a focus on ensuring preparedness for school (QCA, 2000) and emphasized the role of the practitioner in supporting children's learning. In the foreword to the CGFS (2000) Margaret Hodge MP states: '[the CGFS's] principal aim is to help practitioners to plan how their work will contribute to the achievement of the early learning goals' (2000: 2). Such a statement highlights the focus placed upon outcomes in this curriculum. The CGFS was heavily criticized for taking this approach, as many practitioners working within the sector were focused on facilitating children's learning rather than directing it (Bertram and Pascal, 2002). The replacement of the CGFS, the EYFS, placed an increased emphasis on facilitating learning. While some guidance on levels of expected development are provided to support practitioners, the guidance material for the revised 2012 curriculum (Early Education, 2012: 6) states:

> Children develop at their own rates, and in their own ways. The development statements and their order should not be taken as necessary steps for individual children. They should not be used as checklists. The age/stage bands overlap because these are not fixed age boundaries but suggest a typical range of development.

This reminds us that normative scales, which provide expected levels, are to be used as a guide rather than a checklist of progress. As a society and as early years practitioners working with young children, it is important to reflect upon the continued use of a binary system that reinforces terms such as 'normal' and 'not normal' without giving consideration to the complexities and how humans demonstrate such diversity within those categories. In addition, such categories are devised at particular times within particular cultures, as the following case study related to physical development demonstrates.

## Case study 14.1 Using normative scales for assessing children

In the earliest years of a child's life, multiple phases of assessment are carried out. These assessments begin while the child is in the womb and focus on physical growth and health. After birth, the infant's growth is measured and plotted against a normative scale: what the expected rate of growth is and where the baby is placed upon the scale. It is worth taking a moment to think about this scale. The scale was developed in the 1970s and was based on the average weight trajectory of bottle-fed babies. The issue here is that while this scale provided a useful way for health practitioners to follow children's weight, breast-fed babies were, in the main, assessed as underweight. To address this anomaly the chart has been revised by the World Health Organisation (2006) and now reflects the 'average growth' of a breast-fed baby, resulting in bottle-fed babies being assessed as being towards the heavier end of the scale, though within the 'normal' range.

This case highlights that comparing children to a normative scale leads the parent/carer away from recognizing their baby as the unique individual they are – they may have a genetic pattern inherited from great aunt Louise who was 2m tall and 70kg, or 1.2m tall and 50kg; normative scales may lead parents, carers and professionals alike to focus on an average pattern rather than the individual's uniqueness. Such comparisons can lead to a range of, usually, unfounded anxieties. All babies are different and their growth and development is affected by a range of factors: genetic, social and emotional. Thus, assessments based solely on normative scales may not be helpful.

Any scaled approach to development, as seen by the growth scales for new-borns, will not reflect the uniqueness of each child; they represent an imaginary child. Some children's growth, development and/or learning may correspond to these patterns, but many do not. As with the anxiety induced by a baby assessed as 'underweight' or 'overweight', the early years practitioner may also inadvertently cause anxiety in parents/carers through an assessment of a child as achieving 'below expected levels' or 'below levels appropriate to their age'. We are often presented with scales which provide a range within which a child may be placed – charts provided to map children's height are a good example of this. While such scales can be helpful in alerting families and practitioners to potential developmental issues for which a child needs care and support, they can also induce unnecessary stress and, at times, lead to increased competition between children and families.

In relation to a child's cognitive development, assessment of that development by a practitioner can carry similar issues. One must be aware that a judgement made solely through normative scales (summative) obscures the fact that this skill may not yet have been witnessed in the setting. This may be because it has been overlooked; because practitioners have not provided the necessary opportunities or environment which allowed the child to demonstrate the specified target; because the practitioner does not know what to look for; or, simply, because the child has yet to develop this skill but, given the development of many other skills, this is not a particular cause for concern. An assessment which records a child as lacking in one or more criteria can lead to further limitations in the curriculum, that is, practitioners may feel under pressure (due to the expectation of reporting achievements) to tailor activities, strategies or general provision to ensure the child meets that specific criterios. This may narrow the curriculum on offer as practitioners work to fill the gaps in children's achievements rather than giving children access to the curriculum upon the needs and interests of the children (Bruce, 2011). Reception class teachers, teaching children ages 4 to 5 years, confirmed to the Cambridge Primary review that the pressures placed upon them to demonstrate improvements in outcomes tended to skew the curriculum they delivered (Alexander, 2010: 165). Katz (2011: 124) reminds us of the importance of providing a 'developmentally appropriate curriculum that helps children to make better, fuller and deeper sense of their own experience'; no mention here of the reaching of targets. A key role of a reflective early years practitioner will therefore be to consider assessments and their impact and be prepared to justify their work as being in the best interests of the child (see Claxton, **Reading 14.1**).

While we have been somewhat critical of summative assessment, we are not suggesting that tests or scales ought to be abandoned. Indeed, such scales can be very useful in highlighting physical or developmental disabilities or delays which require support from expert practitioners. What we would suggest is that how the scales are applied and explained to families and children needs careful consideration. This will be considered further in section 3 and in Chapter 15.

---

### Reflective activity 14.1

*Aim:* To consider your practice in relation to assessment criteria and levels.

*Evidence and Reflection:* Write your own personal reflection; the following questions may support your writing:

- Do you ever feel pressure from colleagues, schools or families to ensure children reach particular targets?
- Where does this pressure stem from?
- Do you ever feel under pressure to 'fill the gaps' and so narrow a child's experience?
- Could this be avoided?

*Extension:* As you have highlighted pressures from particular sources, think about how you could work with others to alleviate this pressure. For example, would a parent feel less anxious if they understand the thinking behind the unique child and children's unique development? Discuss your ideas with a colleague.

---

## 1.2 A constructivist approach to assessment

The constructivist approach views the child as an *active constructor of knowledge* receiving information from the environment and interpreting this in the light of previous experience, knowledge and interests. As noted in Chapter 2 the most influential constructivist theorist was Piaget (see for example 1926, 1950, 1961; see also **Reading 2.2**). To recap on our earlier summary, Piaget states that when children encounter a new experience they both 'accommodate' their existing thinking to it and 'assimilate' aspects of the experience. In so doing they move beyond one state of mental 'equilibration' and restructure their thoughts to create another. Piaget proposed that there are characteristic stages in the successive development of these mental structures, stages in which children's learning and understanding grow. His thinking has influenced the development of curricula around the world, particularly in the UK.

In relation to assessment there are some potential problems attributed with this approach, particularly as learning can be viewed as a series of sequenced stages: B cannot be achieved until A is in place. This view of learning lends itself well to the use of a curriculum and the type of normative scales discussed in the previous section, as it stresses the importance of planning and recording which stages have been reached in order to support progress to the next stage. To this end, the constructivist approach recognizes the need to watch children at play, observing their interests and threads of thinking (Nutbrown, 2006). Evidence from these observations is used to inform planning and provide a stimulating and appropriate environment for children. In this process, assessment is used to encourage children 'to *produce* knowledge rather than to *reproduce* knowledge' (Wortham, 2008: 108, emphasis added). In this way it is distinct from the summative testing we considered in the previous section. Thus, the emphasis is placed on the early years practitioner understanding *how* children are learning in addition to *what* they are learning so that learning can be supported. This is achieved through observation of the child in their environment and through gathering evidence from a range of sources. As we have noted in various sections, particularly in Chapter 10, such observations are ongoing and are carried out across a range of activities and interactions in order to interpret the meaning the child assigns to their experiences overtime. This process is known as *formative* assessment and 'provide[s] a rich picture of the ways in which children act, think and learn' (Dunphy, 2008: 6) over time, unlike the 'snapshot' feature of the summative assessment approach.

Thus far we have discussed two seemingly different forms of assessment: *summative* – a snapshot of children's achievements through a test or overview of achievements compared with a normative scale; and *formative* – a process of discovering how children are engaging with learning over time. However we may be presenting a false dichotomy (Hargreaves, 2005) as these forms of assessment are not necessarily incompatible or opposite ends of a scale. In many instances formative assessment is used as evidence of what children know and for meeting the standards or curriculum levels (what has passed) and not as a means to inform future learning (or to feed forward into future planning) (Fleer, 2002). Thus both may be considered to be simply the reproduction of knowledge, depending on how they are used. As with so many things, the tool is only as skilled as the user. In the following discussion we highlight how assessments in the early years can be used to support the child's potential and work towards the *production* of knowledge as opposed to the *reproduction* of knowledge.

# 1.3 A social constructivist approach to assessment

Vygotsky (1978) and Bruner (1960) are the forerunners in this approach. In brief, this approach concurs with the constructivist approach in that the child is viewed as an active participant in their learning (Carr, 2001, 2012). In addition to this, the interactions the child has with others, both peers and adults, are seen as central to learning and development. In this transformative approach, learning is recognized as taking place within a social and cultural context which therefore highlights the importance of developing effective partnerships within and beyond the setting – to involve all in the discourse of what constitutes teaching and learning. Such an approach acknowledges power relations between practitioners and children, practitioners and families and between children. As with the constructivist approach, in this approach assessment is carried out through observation of the child, in a range of contexts, with input from multiple stakeholders and with recognition of the environment. Therefore assessment needs to take place on what Rogoff (1995) refers to as the:

- *personal plane* – in which skills are practised with others.
- *interpersonal plane* – in which partners communicate and participate in structured collective activities.
- *community/institutional plane* – in which individuals develop their understandings through their own participation.

Thus, the focus of the assessment is no longer placed exclusively on the individual's abilities to absorb and recall knowledge, but on the context in which learning takes place; it has 'shifted from internal structures and representations in the mind to meaning-making, intention and relationships in the experienced world' (Carr, 2011: 5). It requires the participant to look through different lenses (Rogoff, 1998).

The term 'Formative Assessment' was, and continues to be, used interchangeably with 'Assessment for Learning' (AfL), defined as '… children and practitioners working together to decide where the learners are in their learning, where they need to go and how best to get there' (ARG, 2002) – an approach which complements the social constructivist position. This statement recognizes both the importance of children's voice in determining their own learning and that learning is a social process created through dialogue with others. AfL is discussed in greater detail in Chapter 13.

## 2 Purpose and values of assessment

As we have discussed, there are different approaches to assessment which produce different data (or information) and meet different needs. We have also noted that the early years practitioner can face conflicting expectations in terms of what stakeholders expect children to achieve while in ECEC. We will now turn our focus to consider the purposes and values of assessment for different groups.

## 2.1 Purpose and value of assessment for government, local authorities and schools

As we have noted, there has been an increase in the attention given to ECEC and the role it plays in children's lives. This focus has resulted in an increase in the funding available to support ECEC provision which (inevitably) led to increased accountability and the need for evidence that the funding was making a difference to children's futures (Staggs, 2012). This, along with curriculum developments, has led to an increase in the use of and attention given to assessment tools in ECEC. For example, in England, the Labour administration of 1997–2010 transformed the early years curricula (*Birth to Three Matters* and *Curriculum Guidance for the Foundations Stage*) into one coherent framework which provided for all children from birth to 5 years in England. Subsequently the point of assessment shifted from entry to reception class to the end of the reception year. This shift transformed the use of specified Early Learning Goals from *aspiration recommendations* for 5-year-olds to being *assessment instruments* which seek to capture both the level of a child's attainment *and* the effectiveness of early years settings and local authorities (Staggs, 2012). This is then used for comparison with future achievement in further tests as the child progresses through school.

This form of assessment is used to provide a baseline of the child's ability which can then be measured at regular points. These measurements also serve as indicators for both the child's achievements and the effectiveness of teachers and schools, though it is not used in all countries. For example, the Welsh Assembly introduced a similar measure in 2011 which outlined 114 key skills, behaviours and knowledge against which children were to be tested. This was, however, withdrawn five months later due to it being considered 'unwieldy' by teaching unions and ECEC experts such as Siraj-Blatchford (Evans, 2012). In addition to such schemes being considered to be unmanageable by some, they are also questioned from the standpoint of testing children's skills and knowledge at such a young age. Wolfendale (1995) argues how such practices 'label' children, for example, as *high achievers* or *low ability*, which then becomes a self-fulfilling process impacting upon children's educational experiences. Equally, the demand for summative assessments for young children is critiqued by a number of educationalists and early years specialists who, together under the Open EYE campaign, discuss issues pertinent to good practice in the early years, including why and how testing in the early years can potentially damage young children's progress. Specifically, in an open letter to *The Times* in 2008, the group argued for all compulsory guidance contained within the EYFS to become voluntary, for it to be extended to the school year when children turn 6, and for no achievement targets to be required until this point (cited in Alexander, 2010: 165).

Despite such concerns, summative assessment continues to be used and required by schools, governments and local authorities. Reasons for this include a perceived need to:

- ascertain levels of pupils achievement on a standardized basis;
- hold schools and teachers to account;
- assess the quality of education available to children across the country.

Alexander, in the Cambridge Review (2010), agrees that achievement may well be addressed through the administration of tests or completion of summative profiles, but questions whether this information provides enough data to inform accountability or the standardization of provision.

## 2.2 Purpose and value of assessment for practitioners

As we established in Chapter 13, we believe that both summative and formative assessments fulfil a range of purposes for the ECEC practitioner. We also advocate, in line with established ECEC practice, that all assessments begin with observation and, in the process of watching children engaged in play, practitioners are in a privileged position of gaining insight into the wonders of children's worlds (Nutbrown, 2006). It is through observation the practitioner can come to appreciate the child's 'level of achievement, interests and learning styles' and, in using this information, can 'shape learning experiences for each child reflecting those observations' (DfE, 2012: 10). As we have reiterated, these observations support effective planning (see Chapter 10). Observation reveals events that take place, but practitioners need to interpret and analyse what the behaviours may mean (Drummond, 2003). (Some of the tools available to practitioners to shape observations and the interpretations of these observations are discussed in section 3 of this chapter.)

There are multiple meanings associated with both children's capabilities and practitioners' perceptions of them and, for this reason, reflection plays a key role in 'making multiple meanings visible and ... considering subjectivity' (Karlsdottir and Gardarsdottir, 2010: 264). Such reflection needs to be carried out both as an individual and with others: families, colleagues, other professionals and the children themselves (Fook, 2010), in addition to an analysis of how the environment may be impacting on children's behaviours. Reflection upon and analysis of these factors is known as *evaluative assessment*, which provides a holistic view of the child. This view of the child can then be used as *informative assessment* as it feeds into planning (see **Figure 14.1**), ensuring the child is supported in their learning in a way which is appealing to them.

A further purpose of assessment for practitioners is to support liaison with families. The sharing of observations opens up dialogue and invites families to share their observations, which are essential if the practitioner is to build a holistic picture of the child. Family involvement in all assessments, especially diagnostic, is essential for developing respect and trust in the partnership. (See Chapter 13 for a more detailed discussion on parental involvement in assessment; see also Glazzard, Reading 14.5).

While the focus thus far has been on the benefits of formative assessments, summative assessments can also serve a purpose for the ECEC practitioner. Through performance data gathered from profiles and test scores, settings, schools and local authorities can identify patterns of performance of large cohorts of children. Such information may highlight areas where children are not achieving as would perhaps be expected and therefore indicates where further training of staff or allocation of resources may be needed.

**Figure 14.1** The purpose and value of assessment for practitioners

---

### Case study 14.2 Recognizing gaps in practitioner understanding

Mary, a manager at Tinytots pre-school, was critical of the curriculum. She had noted that children of 30–50 months consistently failed to reach one of the criteria related to mathematics. Upon reflection of the assessment statistics, Mary realized that she and her colleagues were possibly not identifying children's progress in this area due to the fact that they were not wholly confident with what the outcome actually meant, and lacked confidence with maths generally. Upon further reflection of the findings and discussions with colleagues, Mary concluded that this gap in practitioner understanding and their lack of confidence in this area meant that they were failing to plan effectively and thus failing to support the children to demonstrate this skill.

As a result of these findings, Mary arranged for staff training from an outside facilitator. She is pleased with the progress they have made and is continuing to monitor the assessment statistics.

---

It is now standard practice for teaching and learning to encompass both summative and formative forms of assessment (Black and Wiliam, 1998) in what is referred to as the 'interactive' approach to assessment (Bruce, 2005: 210). However, as previously discussed, when summative assessments are used for accountability and indicators of children's progress, practitioners experience an uncomfortable tension.

---

### Reflective activity 14.2

*Aim:* To consider the use of assessment in your setting.

*Evidence and reflection:* Review your assessment processes. Identify those which are formative and those, if any, which are summative. Consider their purpose and how they are used, specifically whether they are used to:

- provide an overview of all children in the setting.
- identify the needs of particular children.
- identify which children haven't yet completed a task.
- as part of an audit, for example to assess equalities.

*Extension:* Reflect on whether these assessment methods are fit-for-purpose – whether they provide the information you need, whether the information is useful to practitioners, children and families and/or local authorities and government bodies. Consider whether any of these assessments would benefit from being adapted following your reading and reflection.

---

# 2.3 Purpose and value of assessment for families

Parents, carers and families want to know that children are happy, settled and progressing through the education system. The nature and extent of the information expected or desired will vary from family to family and is closely connected to the social and cultural expectations of the community, family culture, society, and each government's political agenda. In addition to using formative and summative assessments to inform discussions with families, the information can also be used to support the establishment of and/or consolidate family–practitioner partnerships through the sharing of information. As we have noted in previous chapters, since families are the child's first educators and therefore have first-hand knowledge of the child's interests abilities and dispositions to learning, they are also a valuable source of information for the practitioner. How practitioners capture this knowledge can be a challenge. Many early years settings have 'interests sheets' which ask parents/carers to record what their child is enjoying or involved in at home; some settings recognize that time constraints can restrict parent engagement and provide a board for parents to scribble notes, while others use communication books and pictures.

---

## Reflective activity 14.3

*Aim:* To reflect upon whether and/or how information from parents is used as part of the assessment process in your setting.

*Evidence and reflection:* Take some additional time to review your assessment processes, this time with respect to your relationship with parents and how you share information. Consider:

- the methods you use to communicate with parents.
- do these methods work for all parents? Are some excluded?
- whether the information gathered is useful.
- how the information is used to supported the child both inside and outside of the setting.

*Extension:* Discuss your reflections with a colleague or peer. Consider whether there are alternative forms of communication you can try, particularly if you feel that communication with some parents is poor. Enter into discussions with families about ways they would like to share information about their child.

---

Through engaging in information-sharing with families, details from both practitioners in settings and families in homes can be shared, and thus both parties can potentially benefit from gaining an insight into how they can best support the child in their next stage of learning. This is especially important in demonstrating to families how you value the child as a unique individual and the valuable contribution each child makes to the setting.

# 3 Assessment in action

**Expert question**

**Development:** Does formative feedback and support enable children to reflect on their own achievements?

This question contributes to a conceptual framework representing enduring issues and practitioner expertise (see Chapter 16).

As we have noted, evidence of children's learning is gathered from a variety of sources and in a variety of ways. The need to collect information from parents, colleagues, other professionals and children has been discussed and the need to reflect upon and analyse this information noted. As has also been mentioned, all assessment in ECEC should begin with observation. Observations can take a variety of forms: some are *planned* and take place over a relatively long period of time when compared with those which provide snapshots, which are often *spontaneous*. We propose that a mixture of both is needed to identify patterns of learning (Nutbrown, 2006).

Examples of long-term observations include:

- **Target observations or narrative observations** – this involves observing a particular child or situation and recording, verbatim, what happens, without judgement or analysis.

- **Time sampling** – involves observing a child at regular intervals over a set period to ascertain patterns of behaviour (can take place over a day, week or month).

- **Tracking** – recording a child's movements within a defined period of time (reveals interests, levels of concentration, interactions).

- **Frequency sampling** – observing and recording a particular behaviour/event each time it occurs (when, where and how often it occurs and possibly what the triggers are). This type of observation is particularly useful if there are behaviour management issues.

Examples of snapshots observations include:

- **Photographs** – which capture a behaviour or moment of activity.

- **A sample of a child's work** – which captures a skill or experience, for example mark-making or a child's representation of a visit.

- **Maps** – which capture a snapshot of the setting; these can be useful for developing understandings of social groupings and/or the activities being undertaken by children.

- **Practitioner notes** – which record a behaviour, action or success at a particular point in time.

Drummond (2003) identifies three stages to observation, shown in **Figure 14.2**:

**Figure 14.2**
The three cyclical
stages of the
observation
process

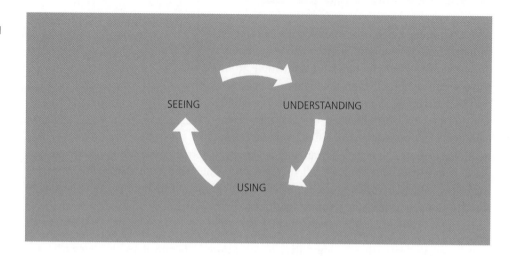

This process echoes the teaching/planning cycle and AfL outlined in Chapter 13. It is worth considering these aspects of observation in relation to assessment.

## 3.1 Seeing

There are a number of ways that a practitioner can 'see' what a child is doing, demonstrating, sharing and working towards. There are the different types of observations we noted above, but there are also tools which have been devised to help practitioners capture information. These are well tested and, as such, can be of great support when you are trying to measure particular things. Examples of the tools available would include the Laevers (2005) emotional well-being and involvement scales that we discussed in Chapter 7 on behaviour. Other scales which can support and help target observations are tools used to measure quality, such as the Early Childhood Environment Rating Scale (ECERS) (Harms and Clifford, 1980) and the revised version ECERS-R (Harms, Clifford and Cryer, 1998); the Infant Toddler Environmental Rating Scale (ITERS-R) (Harms, Cryer and Clifford, 2006), and ECERS-E (Sylva et al., 2010). More on these can be found in Chapter 5.

Observation must be conducted with an open mind and an awareness of the observer's own ideals, experiences and interests. It is well documented within the research world that when conducting observations, one often sees what one is looking for, sometimes at the expense of what else is happening (see Willan, **Reading 14.2**).

## Reflective activity 14.4

*Aim:* To reflect upon the accuracy of observations.

*Evidence and reflection:* Access Test Your Awareness: Do The Test video on YouTube
(see link at **reflectiveteaching.co.uk**) and follow the instructions. The exercise will
take just over a minute after you have located the source.

Think about what you have learned about your skills of observation. Did you answer
the question correctly? Does this make you think about the ways in which you observe
and how your preconceptions may shape what you see? And what you may miss?

*Extension:* You may have demonstrated excellent observation skills during the task
or you may have seen it before. Regardless, it makes a powerful point about us
seeing what we look for in the world. Ask a colleague to carry out an observation
of an area at the same time as you. Later, compare the observations and look at the
differences and similarities.

# 3.2 Understanding

After conducting an observation, the information needs to be interpreted. Observations
become useful when one is able to gain an understanding from the information collected
about where a child is with their understanding, their interests, and their dispositions to
learning, for example. John Dewey stated that: 'Observation alone is not enough. We have
to understand the significance of what we see, hear, and touch. This significance consists
of the consequences that will result when what is seen is acted upon' (1938: 68; see Carr
and Claxton, **Reading 14.3**). If observations are not reviewed or analysed then their worth is
diminished, but it is often a complex task. It involves the practitioner providing a professional opinion as to what has been observed and reviewing the information in light of their
reading, their knowledge of child development and of the child in question, discussions
with family members, discussion with the child, and discussions with other professionals.
Particularly where observations have been carried out with a specific purpose – for
example, to note how a child interacts with others or where a particular scale has been
used – there will also be prompts and information on how to analyse the data, to interpret
it, to give events meaning. Not all of these sources would be consulted for every observation – there isn't time – but when building an overall picture of a child or building an
understanding of a particular need or skill, each of these sources will need to be consulted
at some point to achieve the holistic view we noted was desirable at the beginning of this
chapter. It is not enough to think that a behaviour was seen; to interpret one must consider
the why, what and how. Some questions you may wish to consider are:

- What skills did the child demonstrate?

- What is the child interested in?

- What concepts was the child exploring?

- Did any factors impact upon what was observed? (*Analysis of an observation in a Reception class on a snowy day in the South of England revealed it was not a typical day and did not record typical behaviours!*)

- How does this compare with the data collected in previous observations?
- Do I need to discuss my findings with others – professionals or parents?

Examples of observations and how they were interpreted can be found at **reflectiveteaching.co.uk**.

## 3.3 Using and sharing

Following the analysis and interpretation of the information gathered, this must now be used in some way (see Emilson and Pramling Samuelsson, **Reading 14.4**). This can include: updating a child's record, profile or learning journey; consulting with parents; planning which activities, strategies and approaches are to be taken to extend progress (see Chapter 10); whether there is a need to conduct further observations or seek other opinions.

Assessments may identify concerns practitioners and/or families may have and alert the need for a diagnostic assessment. Such assessments are carried out by specialists working within a specific field: these could include speech and language therapists, educational psychologists and hearing impairment specialists, for example. A specialized service will have an extensive range of strategies – again, formative and summative assessment tools – to support them in their diagnosis and plans to support the children and their family moving forward. They can be a great source of support for practitioners, sometimes to help with a developmental delay, a disability, or to allay a fear and offer advice on suitable activities. Families must *always* be partners in this process.

Central to this process is an appreciation, as in the social constructivist approach, that children's learning is 'rapid, episodic and holistic. It is also highly influenced by the extent of support available' (DfES, 2007: 1).

## Conclusion

It is important for practitioners to understand what assessment is and the purposes it serves, along with how it can be used to benefit children and families, rather than to focus on techniques of assessment alone (Garnder, 2008, cited in Blandford and Knowles, 2012). An aspect of the role of the reflective early years practitioner is to create a culture which supports children both to develop and learn and to become confident and curious learners. An aspect of this is to be a part of internal, national and international debates. As early years practitioners, we have to make the case for what is to be assessed and how it is to be done. After all, it is the practitioners who will have the responsibility to conduct these assessments and who also have the experience of working day-to-day with children and their families and therefore make detailed informed comments on their suitability.

# Key readings

A good start to reading more about AfL in the early years is provided by:

Blandford, S. and Knowles, C. (2012) 'Assessment for learning: a model for the development of a child's self-competence in the early years of education', *Education 3–13*, 40 (5), 487–99.

To further develop your understanding of learning stories and how to use them, see:

Carr, M. (2001) *Assessment in Early Childhood Settings: Learning Stories.* London: Paul Chapman, Early Childhood Australia (ECA).

Carr, M. and Lee, W. (2012) *Learning Stories: Constructing Learner Identities in Early Education*. London: Paul Chapman.

For more on the theory of assessment, see:

Fleer, M. (2002) 'Sociocultural assessment in early years education – myth or reality?', *International Journal of Early Years Education*, 10 (2), 105–20.

Katz, L. (2011), 'Current Perspectives on the Early childhood Curriculum'. In R. House (ed.) *Too Much Too Soon*. London: Hawthorn Press.

Nutbrown, C. (2006) *Threads of Thinking*. 3rd edn. London: Sage Publications Ltd.

Wortham, S. (2008) *Assessment in Early Childhood Education*. New Jersey: Pearson.

The associated website, **reflectiveteaching.co.uk**, offers a wealth of supplementary resources including reflective activities, research briefings, advice on further reading and downloadable diagrams, figures and checklists from the book. It also features a compendium of educational terms, links to useful websites, policy and curriculum documents, and showcases examples of excellent research and practice.

# Inclusion

## How are we enabling learning opportunities?

**15**

## Introduction

In this chapter we consider inclusion, inclusive pedagogy and the consequences of such practices. As part of the research for the development of this chapter we held a multi-agency meeting to discuss issues around inclusion. We have included some of the statements made at this meeting within the chapter as they offer some insight into practice within different settings. The full transcript from that meeting can be accessed at **reflectiveteaching.co.uk.**

**www. C**

The chapter is structured into three sections. The first section outlines a series of brief discussions of some of the dimensions of difference, which inform how we think about the identities of others and ourselves. This helps to establish how diversity is associated with being human, and the ways in which the concept of inclusion can be expected to relate to this. The second section considers the practice and processes which support inclusive practices and for children to accept diversity as a part of being human. We might well pose the question – what is diversity? If we use ourselves as the exemplar, then anything that is not within our world is diverse – or different. How, then, do we include and tolerate other people's viewpoints? Examples of early years provision are used to illustrate the key themes and challenges for those of us who want to ensure that both the process of participation and educational outcomes are recognizable as inclusive. The final section focuses on why these practices are so vital and how inclusive pedagogy can support children to reach their potential and lead fulfilling lives.

The chapter is informed by two key assumptions:

- all children have the capacity to learn.
- diversity is to be expected and welcomed.

These assumptions are embedded in enduring, global concerns of social justice and equity. In 1948, Article 26 of the Universal Declaration of Human Rights stated that education 'shall promote understanding, tolerance and friendship among all nations, racial or religious groups'. Nearly 50 years later, the Salamanca Statement (UNESCO, 1994) declared that schools with an 'inclusive orientation are the most effective means of combating discriminatory attitudes, creating welcoming communities, building an inclusive society and achieving education for all'. The countries of the UK are signatories to this Statement and it is embedded in national legislation on inclusion and human rights. Florian (2007: 8) discusses how inclusive education can be understood 'both as a human right and a means of achieving human rights'. (See also the discussion in Chapter 17.)

---

## TLRP principles

Three principles are of particular relevance to this chapter on social differences, opportunities and inclusion:

**Principle 1: Effective teaching and learning equips learners for life in its broadest sense.** Learning should aim to help people to develop the intellectual, personal and social resources that will enable them to participate as active citizens, contribute to economic development and flourish as individuals in a diverse and changing society. This implies adopting a broad view of learning outcomes and ensuring that equity and social justice are taken seriously.

**Principle 7: Effective teaching and learning fosters both individual and social processes and outcomes.** Learning is a social activity. Learners should be encouraged and helped to work with others, to share ideas and to build knowledge together. Consulting learners about their learning and giving them a voice is both an expectation and a right.

**Principle 8: Effective teaching and learning recognizes the significance of informal learning.** Informal learning, such as learning out of school, should be recognized as at least as significant as formal learning and should therefore be valued and used appropriately in formal processes.

This chapter makes reference to many key issues, and the resources at **reflectiveteaching.co.uk** will help you to consider them more deeply. There is also commonality between this chapter and others in the book, such as Chapter 6 on relationships.

## 1 Dimensions of difference

We are familiar with the idea that 'everybody is different'. Indeed, the curriculum in England highlights 'every child is unique' at the bottom of each page (DfE, 2013). But we live in societies where difference is accepted to varying degrees. There are limitless dimensions of difference; we will consider eight of those most commonly noted as impacting upon education in the UK in this chapter.

When working with young children, the dimensions of difference that may come to affect them as learners may be influenced by the ways in which their family is perceived and understood as much as they are as individuals. Early years practitioners must be aware of the significance of building relationships with parents and carers as part of the process of educating and caring for their children. Indeed, within ECEC, inclusion is as much about how ECEC is perceived by the community and their beliefs as it is about the need for, and benefits of, attending any form of education and/or care prior to statutory schooling. Others may feel that ECEC is useful for childcare, perhaps when working or caring for other members of the family, but not that it is a valuable educational experience. A parent commented to us recently that 'it doesn't matter what your child does before the age of 11. I will worry then about what school he goes to, but I don't think it makes any difference where they are at this age, so long as they're safe.'

# 1.1 Social class

Inequalities of wealth, income and material opportunities remain highly significant in determining life-chances (Feinstein et al., 2008; see also Chapter 2). For the last 20 years, there has been a consistent trend for the gap between the highest and lowest incomes to widen each year. One consequence was the fact that in 2011 there were four million children living in families on or below the 'poverty line' (Office for National Statistics, 2012). A UNICEF report (2012) compares children's material well-being in the UK with other 'economically advanced' nations and warns that child poverty is worsening.

Not all definitions of class are based on income, wealth or economic capital, and some focus more on status and level of education. The concepts of 'cultural capital' (Bourdieu and Passeron, 1977) and 'social capital' (Coleman, 1988) were developed to describe the knowledge, attitudes and experiences which socialization within a 'higher-class' family may offer, and which complement material wealth. One of their major insights on educational inequality is that those with social and cultural capital are likely to fare better in education than their peers with less valuable social and cultural capital. For example, parents may deploy their economic, cultural, social and emotional capital by ensuring their child attends a favoured setting or school. In addition, families with such capital may have more choice about types of care, whether they take time out of work to care for children or select part-time care. Such strategies are manifestations of the process of 'social reproduction', in which one generation seeks to pass on the advantages of its social position to another (see for instance Connell et al., 1982).

We thus face the challenge of, on the one hand, understanding the economic, social and cultural advantages and disadvantages of particular children and, on the other, affirming and building on the diverse backgrounds and cultural resources within families and communities. Recent research in the early years has documented that high-quality early years experience can help to overcome such disadvantage based upon family background (e.g. HighScope and EPPE). With inclusion and outcomes in mind, this has implications for the reflective ECEC practitioner to consider the provision children are able to access, the children they welcome into the setting, and whether their setting is selective. It is also important to be aware that children who do not have access to this social and cultural capital may succeed and indeed thrive in the education system.

# 1.2 Ethnicity

The term 'ethnicity' is used to describe ancestry, heritage, religion, culture, nationality, language and religion. As such, we all have ethnic identities. Globalization and changing patterns of migration have challenged the idea that ethnicities are fixed. Cultures and social structures, compounded by differences of historical development, can make a considerable difference to people's experience, leading to much variation among ethnic groups. Definitions of what constitutes an ethnic group or ethnic minority are commonly based on a combination of categories including 'race', skin colour, national origins and language (e.g. White British), and information about our ethnicity is routinely collected to understand many current social and economic trends.

The population of the UK is, increasingly, ethnically diverse. Alibhai-Brown (2000) claimed that Britain should adopt an approach which accepts the diverse contributions of different cultures and groups, past and present – including those White communities, rich or poor, which also feel excluded from significant aspects of modern society and which may harbour racism (see also Gay, 2010).

Racism is the term that describes processes in society that affect people according to their identification as members of one ethnic group or another. Racism has a long history in the UK, going back to the imperial past and beyond, and it has taken root in the discourse and structure of society. Gillborn's (2006) recent analysis of research in the UK using Critical Race Theory offers, in his words, 'a damning critique of the racist nature of the education system'. Such prejudices may be further amplified by the social, cultural, legal and political structures that have developed over time. Tackling such issues with children at a young age, encouraging them to celebrate and accept diversity and all we have to offer, as unique individuals, may go some way to changing futures.

## 1.3 Gender

There is an accepted scientific basis for recognizing two sexes: there are differences within the reproductive process and there is also evidence of genetic and neurobiological differences affecting innate behaviours and brain functioning (Greenfield, 1997). The term 'gender', on the other hand, describes the *social definition of sex roles* rather than the biological distinction itself. Indeed, masculinity and femininity should not be considered to be inherent, biological properties, but as socially constructed products of society. They arise from, and condition, social processes (Money, 1995).

'Sexism' is the operation of forces in society by which members of one sex obtain advantages over the other, because of and through their gender. Patterns of discrimination prompt us to ask questions such as how school life contributes to restrictive or enabling socialization. For example, in the last 20 years researchers have asked why it is that girls tend to perform better than boys when in school (see for example Younger et al., 2005; Warrington et al., 2006) and research suggests that this begins in pre-school (see for example Miller et al., 2009). The assumption of such research is that, because such patterns in performance are not inevitable, the underlying processes that give rise to them should be challenged (Murphy, 2001). This is a complex task, because it is important not to inadvertently disadvantage one group in the act of trying to improve the achievements of another.

## 1.4 Sexuality

There is still considerable social stigma associated with open expressions of sexuality and some practitioners may be hesitant about addressing such issues, particularly with young children. Yet the recognition and acceptance of such differences may be important to the provision of equal opportunities for some children, young people, teachers or parents. Not only in terms of how they may define themselves, both now and in the future, but also as the number of same-sex parents rises, children need to feel that their family structure is one which is as accepted and supported as any other.

## 1.5 Age

The Universal Declaration of Children's Rights establishes the principle that children and young people should not be discriminated against because of their age. Indeed, we have promoted the notion that children are complete beings and ought not be seen as inadequate or incapable. Research in the philosophy, history, psychology and sociology of childhood has repeatedly demonstrated how children's perspectives, activities and rights are structured, ignored or constrained by adults (Archard and MacLeod, 2002; James and James, 2004; Johnson, Hart and Colwell, 2014). Indeed, there is a discernible tension around whether the purpose of education is the protection or correction of children during childhood (Linklater, 2010).

One aspect of school experience that has received particular attention in the UK and USA is how the accident of birth date combined with the start of the school year produces age effects on academic attainment that can be traced throughout primary and secondary school (see for example Crawford, Dearden and Maghir, 2007). In particular, children who are young in their year group can be disadvantaged when immaturity is misinterpreted as a lack of ability, producing an exclusionary effect. In the past, practitioners have been accused of constraining children's education because of a misplaced adherence to Piaget's conception of 'stages of development' (Walkerdine, 1984). Indeed, there remains a risk that linear assumptions of progress or achievement though curricula could have a similarly limiting effect (Hart et al., 2004). Early years practitioners must therefore continue to see children as unique and support them through transitions into school as best they can. In addition, with these issues of age in mind, having precise ages when children move from one 'room' or 'group' within the setting may also be misplaced. If we believe children are progressing at different rates, then we must provide for them in the way which is most appropriate to their needs.

## 1.6 Physical appearance

Physical appearance and perceptions of physical attractiveness have been found to have an important influence on our identities, behaviour and experiences, both in terms of what we expect for ourselves and how others respond to us. In the 1960s and 1970s social and psychological research focused on understanding teachers' expectations of pupils. Findings showed that children's attractiveness was significantly associated with how intelligent a teacher expected a child to be, how interested in education their parents were expected to be, how far the child was likely to progress in school and how popular they would be with their peers (Clifford and Walster, 1973; also Seligman, Tucker and Lambert, 1972).

Recent research by Wakako (2013) found that at aged 5, children selected friends based upon similarity to self, which included how similar they looked to themselves. This has implications for children avoiding those who look different based upon race, gender, disability, or for any other reason.

In Chapter 2 we considered physical disability and how a person may have a physical impairment, and that is the context which leads to the person being identified as disabled (see Thomas and Loxley, Reading 15.3). This perspective is crucial for how we perceive inclusion in ECEC settings: remove barriers and ensure children can be included. The Children Act (1989) states:

> A child is disabled if he is blind, deaf or dumb or suffers from a mental disorder of any kind or is substantially and permanently handicapped by illness, injury or congenital deformity or such other disability as may be prescribed. (Section 17 (11), Children Act, 1989)

In addition to physical disabilites, Special Educational Needs (SEN) are often considered alongside diability, although distinct (see Laisidou, Reading 15.1). The Education Act (1996) states:

> Children have special educational needs if they have a learning difficulty which calls for special educational provision to be made for them.

Children have a learning difficulty if they:

> (a) have a significantly greater difficulty in learning than the majority of children of the same age; or

> (b) have a disability which prevents or hinders them from making use of educational facilities of a kind generally provided for children of the same age in schools within the area of the local education authority.

> (c) are under compulsory school age and fall within the definition at (a) or (b) above or would so do if special educational provision was not made for them. Children must not be regarded as having a learning difficulty solely because the language or form of language of their home is different from the language in which they will be taught.

Special educational provision means:

> (a) for children of two or over, educational provision which is additional to, or otherwise different from, the educational provision made generally for children of their age in schools maintained by the LEA, other than special schools, in the area.

> (b) for children under two, educational provision of any kind.

> (Section 312, Education Act, 1996)

Such definitions can be useful to consult as you reflect upon the practice and provision in your setting. It may be that a young child you meet is currently being assessed for an impairment or SEN or that a family are not yet aware that the child has a particular need. Practitioners will play an important role in helping the child and the family to weave their way through the systems of diagnosis and support, helping all to come to terms with any diagnosis and making plans for the future.

## 1.7 Learning

For some, learning is said to 'come easily', while for others, the acquisition of the knowledge, concepts, skills and attitudes in the school curriculum or beyond is much more difficult. Psychologists, neuroscientists and geneticists study differences in the learning capabilities of individuals, and such abilities are likely to have very significant effects throughout a child's life. For most of us, too, there are variations in relation to particular topics; we tend to find it easier to learn things which are of intrinsic, personal interest. One can readily see then how the factors we have reviewed above such as social class, ethnicity or gender can create conditions which may enable or constrain the particular types of learning. Some children may readily display an interest in reading as they come from a home where reading is a key part of family life; perhaps their parent's job relates to reading and writing and this it is seen as a part of life. Others may wish to be outdoors; perhaps they are more interested in helping family members in the garden, or participating in sports, for example. Social, economic and cultural circumstances often have educational consequences.

Understanding of differences and variations in the self-confidence and disposition and attitudes of children to learning is essential knowledge for planning provision. It enables targeted preparation to match children's interests and needs. Indeed, practitioners tend to be very aware of 'quick' or 'slower' learners and many gradations in between. While such thinking may have a practical purpose in fine-tuning provision, it is potentially dangerous if it leads to a reduction in expectations for some and very high expectations of others (Hart et al., 2004).

Why are all these dimensions so important? These dimensions interact in creating our individual identities. They are a reflection of the society in which we live. As early years practitioners, our job is to create a diverse environment and model how we accept and learn from each other's differences. One of the great motivators for working in early years is that it's the age group with the most opportunity. We can aim to lay the foundations by creating a world for children in which you want them to continue to live, and equipping them with an appropriate skill set.

## 1.8 What needs?

There are many categories or conditions of special or additional needs and disabilities, about which specific information will be helpful. Fortunately, there is a huge range of commercially published books that focus on such issues and also many websites that include advice specifically for practitioners in early years settings. Some are run by national governments; additionally, many charities and organizations provide guidance, advice and materials via their websites. The following links represent just a very small sample of those that are available:

- Autism – **autism.org.uk**
- Down's syndrome – **downs-syndrome.org.uk**
- Dyslexia – **bdadyslexia.org.uk**
- Language development – **ican.org.uk**
- Hearing impairment – **elizabeth-foundation.org/default.asp**
- Social, Emotional, Behavioural difficulties – **sebda.org**
- Visual impairment – **rnib.org.uk**

Many adults in and beyond settings will have a particular role in helping to support the learning of children identified as having special or additional needs, and they can be an invaluable source of professional information and advice for practitioners.

It is not in the remit of this chapter to give a detailed analysis of legislation around children and young people's special or additional needs. However, there are two key themes across the UK that are worth noting, because they are currently shaping legislation on children and young people identified as having special or additional needs. These are first, a strengthening of the role of parents/carers in deciding the educational provision for their children, and second, a continuing concern to ensure consistency across education, health and social services. Both these developments are to be welcomed, because they acknowledge the holistic nature of the lives of learners and their families.

---

### Reflective activity 15.1

*Aim:* To reflect upon what is meant by inclusion.

*Evidence and reflection:* Think about the dimension of difference discussed above. Take two dimensions which are relevant to your practice and one which you feel is less relevant. What does inclusion mean in your setting? – think about those three dimensions. What do you do to ensure inclusion for those children? What could you do?

---

## 2 Practices and processes

As human beings, our need to be included as equals is important to our well-being and mental health; it has ramifications for our whole lives (and those around us). Translating this need to early childhood scenarios, we can see the importance of the acceptance of diversity as a positive thing. Difference is not an opinion, it is a fact of life, and therefore its interrogation in our daily practice ought to be positive (see Borkett, Reading 15.2). This has been recognized in the United Nations Convention on the Rights of the Child – a valuable framework and ideal for us to work to. For a child-friendly and accessible version, see *For Every Child: The Rights of the Child in Words and Pictures* (UNICEF/ Random House, 2000).

Key to the element of acceptance of others as unique individuals is also recognizing and embracing our similarities. However, this does not mean we need to create a 'neutral environment' (Brown, 1998: 53) in which we treat everyone the same. This could generate a denial of the individual's differences, ultimately affecting their sense of 'identity and self worth' (1998: 54). Thus, positive discrimination encourages 'children to learn about and value each other's cultures, languages, abilities and life styles and draw strength from their own' (1998: 55).

We recognize that inclusion is not simple. We acknowledge that challenges of time, resource and expertise can make inclusive practices difficult. At times you may be concerned that some children are being included at the expense of others – for example, when levels of disruption are high. This is a challenge for the reflective practitioner: what is suitable? when is additional support required? Staff teams will need to work together to develop and review inclusive practices. The follow excerpt is from our inclusion meeting.

> When somebody feels or finds it difficult to include a child or a member of staff, then it's usually something to do with their personal experience in the past or recently or whatever, then that's where I think really good reflective practice can help because being able to look at where that's come from and understand it, and make that person feel aware and able to deal with that is really important because otherwise it can become very much just, oh, y'know, I've obviously got the wrong attitude.
>
> Just bringing it into the open.
>
> In a non-judgemental way, I think that's the thing, it's not – we can all have different views and maybe prejudices that we're not even aware of ourselves and so some … and so airing that and talking it through with colleagues in a sort of very safe environment and not – where you're not gonna feel judged but you can discuss it, move forward with it, maybe have a couple of steps back, but you know what I mean, I think it's a whole process and then …
>
> Because if you can't say how you feel, then how are you ever going to move forward with it …
>
> … I mean we had a brief conversation a couple of weeks ago about understanding that sometimes, that people have a real fear or a real unhappiness about these things … [We] just really have to try and understand what it is that's going on for them cos actually it can be, very emotional and very, very difficult for them actually.
>
> … it can really affirm or help to affirm a staff group as well …
>
> Oh absolutely.

## 2.1 Principles of inclusive pedagogy

To have an inclusive pedagogy is to recognize and encompass the needs of all the children within the setting. It is about meeting the needs of diverse groups and being concerned about the experience and choices we enable children to have through our positive interactions. In early years we see a 'patchwork of diverse forms of provision … matched with an equally diverse workforce' (Sylva et al., 1992; Siraj-Blatchford, 1995). As individual practitioners and parents we each develop a unique pedagogy. Our group ethos, our environment, and our interactions with children, families and each other all help to make up our pedagogical approach to inclusive practice. By ensuring inclusive practice is something we do and reflect on all the time, not something additional or different done occasionally which highlights a particular individual or group, then we are able to provide rich and diverse opportunities for all to access. Carl Rogers suggests we need an honest transparency where we should be willing to offer an openness about ourselves to encourage reciprocation; an acceptance of the other person as a separate being with 'value in his [sic] own right' and a 'deep empathetic understanding' (2004: 34). Rogers termed this as 'unconditional positive regard' (ibid.).

Inclusive pedagogy focuses on the needs of *all* learners working together as an inclusive community. This requires a subtle but crucial shift in practitioners' thinking (Florian et al., 2010). Using this approach to conceptualizing practice is reflected in the TLRP Principles of Effective Teaching and Learning. Most notable, in terms of developing inclusive communities, is Principle 7. This concerns the importance of fostering 'both individual and social processes and outcomes' because 'learning is a social activity. It demands inter-action with other minds.' Kershner (2009) reiterates this focus on the collective experience of inclusive practices for *all* learners (and therefore not only *some*). As we have discussed that children learn through dialogue with others, it seems reasonable to suggest that they ought to be supported and able to interact with others and not just those most similar to themselves if we are to increase learning opportunities. This would then require us to move *away* from traditional approaches to inclusion based on making provision for *most* learners, and then something 'special' or 'additional' for *some* who experience difficulties, *towards* enriching and extending the learning opportunities that are ordinarily available for everyone, so that *all* learners are able to participate in setting life. This reiterates the need for good relationships to be formed.

Having already noted that diversity is a fact of life and that the exploration of this should be positive, however scary this may seem at times, what better way to model the imagined future than by living it in the present? By noting and exploring, not hiding or running away from, difference and diversity, we open up opportunities that actively enable children

---

### Reflective activity 15.2

*Aim:* To consider how you and your staff team approach inclusion.

*Evidence and reflection:* Consider two children: one who has a particular physical disability or emotional need and one who is from a minority group within your setting – perhaps based on race or culture. Observe these children in play. Are these children supported to access all of the opportunities in the setting? Do the other children acknowledge their needs and 'get on with the business of the task' or is the child excluded? How do staff approach this? Is the child identified as different and so therefore unable to participate, or are children supported to see everybody brings something to the group?

*Extension:* Work with a partner to plan for adopting or developing an inclusive pedagogy. This may be a process of working with staff initially. Consider the needs of the staff, children and families in your setting.

to negotiate who they are and who they can become. Children should be around people who role-model a positive attitude towards diversity, who celebrate difference and enjoy learning about the world in which we live. We should embrace our own cultural identity while accepting that of others. 'It is important to highlight the complexity of identity formation in children. To ignore it is to ignore the child's individuality' (Siraj-Blatchford and Clarke, 2000: 5). Thus, principles for inclusive pedagogy require a particular mindset and for practitioners to be comfortable with this and themselves.

## 2.2 Responding to learner diversity

As established in section 1, there are many ways in which people are diverse from each other. It is generally acknowledged that this diversity should be thought of as positive – to be recognized and celebrated. Certainly, for many practitioners, one of the most rewarding aspects of the work is getting to know children and the ways in which they are so individual and unique. However, this needs to be reconciled with the fact that human difference can also produce discomfort, even fear, especially when it is unfamiliar or considered abnormal. Thomas and Loxley (2007) explore these tensions in schools, arguing that: 'Whether difference is seen positively, as diversity, or negatively as deviance or deficit depends on the mindset of the person or group of people who observe that difference' (2007: 93). Perhaps, the key questions are, as Minow (1990) has asked: What counts as difference? And what difference does difference make?

About half-way through their course, a group of trainee teachers were asked to reflect on how they felt about 'teaching a diversity of learners' in relation to a class. They were then asked to think of a metaphor to express their feelings and to explain their choice. The results were varied and interesting. Three of their metaphors are shown below, selected because they present a range of different ideas. While the children they are working with may be older than those you are working with, the feelings are likely to be similar.

---

### Thinking metaphorically, teaching a diversity of learners is ...

1   ... a sea of complexity! Because ... all so different. It feels like you need years of experience and expertise in order to understand and provide for the needs.
2   ...keeping a garden. Because ... every plant needs to be nurtured with food, water and warmth, but every plant needs slightly different care. Every plant grows at its own rate and responds differently to the environment it is in and therefore needs caring for.
3   ... discovering buried treasure. Because ... often the children you are teaching are categorized by their diversity and are sometimes simply reduced to this label. I think no matter how informed you are, it is always exciting and surprising to discover the potential, then achievement, of children with diverse needs.

---

**Reflective activity 15.3**

*Aim:* To reflect upon understandings of learner diversity.

*Evidence and reflection:* Think about the four metaphors for teaching diverse learners in terms of similarities and variations. Are there any that particularly resonate with your own experiences, or that interested, or even surprised you?

Then think about a group of children you know well and reflect on your feelings about working with the diversity of learners in it. What would your metaphor be and why?

*Extension:* Reflect on what your metaphor expresses about: a) 'sameness', b) 'difference', and c) 'belonging'.

The significance of these metaphors (those of the trainee teachers and your own) is in how they illustrate the relationship between learners and the adult responsible for their education and care. The trainee teachers articulated varying levels of confidence in how they might respond to encountering diversity. However, they all reflected a general acceptance that their practice would need to respond to the needs of the children (rather than remaining fixed), and that they might even delight in being surprised. In this way their ideas reflect the ideas that children are co-agent, interactive and diverse in the process of teaching and learning. Also, the metaphors and explanations suggest that confidence is likely to come with experience. Levels of experience and experience of working with children with diverse needs will differ between practitioners. This is a good example of when reflecting in a team could be very useful for early years practitioners (see Rix, **Reading 15.4**).

# 2.3 Putting inclusive principles into practice

This section considers what we can do as part of our everyday routines and practices to develop our settings as more inclusive learning communities. Inclusive principles in practice ought to enable all children to:

- make progress in their learning.
- feel accepted and valued for who they are.
- have opportunities to participate in a full range of activities.

The following excerpt, taken from our inclusion meeting, demonstrates how one practitioner reflected upon her own inclusive pedagogy.

## Multi-agency discussion

**How do we professionally work inclusively with families when you may personally disagree with aspects of their lifestyle?**

It depends what aspects doesn't it.

Maybe establish the relationship first.

I think you need to develop the trusting relationship and build connections first.

… it depends what you're finding difficult, is it on a personal level or, is it … I mean I'll just say that personally I don't like boxing for example, which is a very big part [of life] for some traditional Traveller children and parents, and I've had quite a few discussions [with them] about that but I certainly wouldn't have had those conversations when I was first meeting a family, I'd have them later …

The thing is [to have] a discussion about your opinions rather than what you think and how they should change.

Yes, otherwise you're being – you patronize people don't you, you've got to be honest with people, you can't say, I just think all your culture's brilliant, because I mean, in the same way I've had conversations with Traveller families who say, well I just think a lot of you gorgers, which is a term for non-Travellers, which is a bit of an overgeneralization, but a lot of gorgers, say why are your families so spread out, why aren't you with your families, where are your parents? why do they live up there and you live down here? how do you see each other? how do you connect when you live so far away?

We had [the Traveller family] grandma [visit], and we were able to sit and have a great conversation with her, she sat with us for ages and gave us some real insights, and one of the things she said was I never thought that I would allow my babies to come to a nursery and be looked after by someone who wasn't family, and she said, I just don't understand that culture, and she said, I'm loving it and it's great, but she said, I never thought that would happen because we look after our own …

… it must be very hard if they arrive and you have to have a difficult conversation on the first day, but sometimes, if it's not about opinions about lifestyles when the relationship's further down the line that sometimes might come up, but if it's dealing with something like safeguarding and – but sometimes actually, not always, but sometimes actually, if it's dealt with honestly and in …

… in a supportive way, as non-judgemental as you can possibly be, then actually you can be stronger because the relationship's more honest afterwards isn't it.

And I think this is where you can lean on your policies and procedures, that's where you have that transparency …

Yeah, this is sort of like, this isn't about me as a person and you as a person, this is about me as a setting and responding to you as a parent, carer or whatever your relationship with the child is.

I think you have to be forgiving as well, I know when I've suddenly reacted to something and then wished that I hadn't or I've been shocked by something and then thought, well I shouldn't, I wish I hadn't presented like that, so you need to – which is hard as well, particularly if it's you who feels the brunt of that, but actually to be forgiving of people because sometimes people react and then go away and think about it and wish they'd behaved differently …

The key to how we put our inclusive pedagogy into practice is cyclical. It is developing the skill to reflect both *on* action and *in* action (see Schon, Chapter 2). Inclusive practice should be at the core of everything we do. Anybody walking into your settling should instantly be able to see and feel your approach to inclusivity and diversity. From images you have on your walls, the books you have, the resources and language you use with children and adults alike – all stemming from the initial smile and welcome everybody receives. There should be a transparency and openness to inclusivity, which is there for all to see, challenge, question, celebrate and reflect on. In reflecting on the complexity of how to contribute to inclusive environments for learning, it is helpful to remember the two principles outlined in the introduction of this chapter: first, that all children are capable of learning; second, that difference is part of the human condition – so diversity among a group of learners is to be expected and welcomed. As practitioners, we have both the responsibility and *possibility* to mitigate adverse or limiting effects.

---

## Case study 15.1 Whole team approaches to a child's learning

A child with identified special needs who would require periods of 1:1 work was about to start at a setting. A staff meeting discussion around this was facilitated by the manager for all practitioners to discuss initial positive ways forward. Given the short timescale involved and the length of time it would take to employ a specific 1:1 worker, it was decided to initially move forward by using the funds available for this work to employ cover staff for the session the child was attending, freeing up a permanent member of staff to undertake the 1:1 work. This had the added advantage of the setting being able to revolve the 1:1 role through the whole staff team, ensuring all practitioners were known to the child and gained an insight into the child's needs and uniqueness. This also allowed the child to form his own relationships with all practitioners and meant that other children within the setting didn't see him as having his own separate worker.

Initially, a daily diary was kept sharing observations and noting points of interest, strengths, areas for support and development, all of which led to the formation of 1:1 working guidelines for the setting and informed the child's Individual Education Plan (IEP). The diary was a shared document between the setting and home, thereby embedding the partnership process.

Completing the 'triangle of care' (Siraj-Blatchford et al., 2003; Ball, 1992) was the involvement of an identified Special Educational Needs worker from an outside agency who visited the child both in the setting and at home for 1:1 activities.

The strength of relationships the child built with individual practitioners supported the child to develop the skill needed to form lasting and meaningful relationships and friendships with peers and ensured their full inclusion within the cohort.

The child's development exceeded the expectations of the team of professionals built around them; this proved to be an enabling and positive learning experience for all involved.

---

As the proverb states, 'It takes a village to raise a child'. The concept of individuals or groups working in partnership to realize a far greater outcome together than could be achieved alone is not new. In order to present an inclusive pedagogy, it is important to draw on the expertise of the whole team working around the child, and this team should significantly involve parent/carers. As practitioners and individuals we cannot pretend to know everything there is to know about every child and their unique way of being. Through multi-agency working and sharing knowledge and experience, we are most likely to meet the needs of individuals as well as learn how we can enable them to have choice and a voice both within our settings and their home environment. It would make sense to suggest that the more diverse the team is, the more inclusive the outcome will be. However, it should be recognized that this seemingly perfect paradigm takes skill, commitment and sensitivity, not only to set up a partnership but also to keep it going.

## 3 Consequences

In this final section we consider the outcomes of inclusive practice, or lack thereof. A participant at the inclusion meeting we held stated: 'The children are going to grow up to be adults and have the attitudes that they had when they were little, if prejudice has never been worked with … that will just continue [and] the problems that are currently existing in our society which could otherwise have been worked with [will continue].'

This is a key concern. We are a part of an education system and children's lives. We want them to thrive. We have established that for this to happen, they need to have high self-esteem, self-confidence and resilience. Being comfortable with oneself is a crucial aspect of this. Being accepted by the community we live in is another. This is complex, but at the heart of each of us is the recognition and celebration of diversity. The Peace Initiatives Institute (cited in Nutbrown and Clough, 2010) has an aim to teach young children the value of respecting and including those who are different, as they believe this will 'impact on their beliefs and behaviours in adulthood'. Nutbrown and Clough (2010), drawing on work by Cook and Nutbrown (2006, p. 153), state:

> … education for peace is an essential part of citizenship, creating communities where young children can live and learn together peacefully and respectfully, respecting and celebrating the differences which make them each unique.

As we will outline in Chapter 17, reflective practice on issues such as these can help to contribute to society.

In addition to inclusive pedagogy having the potential to contribute to society, it is also a fundamental aspect of educational opportunity and supporting individual children to reach their potential. In section 1 we noted a number of dimensions of difference which could lead to a child being *disadvantaged* within the education system. Such disadvantage – for example, within social and cultural capital – can lead to children living in cycles of poverty; poverty which has been shown (see Chapter 2) to impact upon children's educational and life chances. Thus, it impacts upon everything we have established as a desirable contribution of early years practice.

# Conclusion

This chapter has explored how practitioners in a range of early years settings can support the inclusion of all children and young people. Inclusion is concerned with understandings of, and attitudes towards, all children and young people in relationship to their age, gender, ethnicity, sexuality, social class, physical appearance, disability and performance at school. Discrimination can be subtle and complex, sometimes unintended, and rarely straightforward. However, the marginalization or stigmatization of anyone, for whatever reason, forms a barrier to inclusion. The challenge we face recognizes that diversity is to be expected and welcomed in a setting, and that every learner has the right to achieve. For a reflective practitioner, the challenge is how to manage these processes so that divisive consequences on the lives of children and young people are limited, rather than the possibilities for children's learning.

Finally, the promotion of inclusion and social justice must also be actively pursued beyond the early years setting. Education may not be able to change society (Bernstein, 1970), but practitioners should, if possible, try to remove its most divisive effects. These are difficult goals, but working towards them nevertheless remains a continuing responsibility.

There is no one simple answer on how to be inclusive, but lots of small steps to take. It should continue to be an ongoing process for individuals and settings. This chapter provides some thoughts to provoke and support reflective practice. As with all areas of early years work, there are challenges in working inclusively, because celebrating diversity within an inclusive and anti-discriminatory framework calls for flexibility, sensitivity, and a willingness to try new ideas and to make mistakes.

# Key readings

There is an enormous literature on topics such as diversity, opportunity, inclusion and special educational needs, and the list below is indicative only.

For practical support we would highly recommend:

Brown, B. (2004) *Celebrating Diversity: Inclusion in the Early Years*. Maidenhead: Open University Press (video and book).

—(1998) 'Learning the Anti-discriminatory Way'. In *Unlearning Discrimination in the Early Years*. Stoke-on-Trent: Trentham Books, 49–68.

For an overview of key issues of inclusion in the early years, see:

Nutbrown, C., Clough, P. and Atherton, C. (2013) *Inclusion in the Early Years: Cultural Analyses and Enabling Narratives*. London: Sage Publications Ltd.

Siraj-Blatchford, I. and Clarke, P. (2000) *Supporting Identity, Diversity and Language in the Early Years*. Buckingham: Open University Press.

Specific treatment of particular issues with regard to dimensions of difference is provided in many books. Examples include:

Connolly, P. (1998) *Racism, Gender and Identities of Young Children: Social Relations in a Multi-ethnic, Inner-city Primary School*. London: Routledge.

Feinstein, L., Duckworth, K. and Sabates, R. (2008) *Education and the Family: Passing Success Across the Generations*. Abingdon: Routledge.

Jackson, P. and Marsden, D. (1962) *Education and the Working Class*. London: Ark.

Siraj-Blatchford, I. (2010) 'Learning in the home and at school: how working-class children succeed against the odds', *British Educational Research Journal*, 36 (3), 463–82.

For ideas on ways to work with very able children in the early years, see:

Sutherland, M. (2005) *Gifted and Talented in the Early Years*. London: Sage Publications Ltd.

—(2008) *Developing the Young Gifted and Talented Learner*. London: Sage Publications Ltd.

For an international overview of inclusion, see:

Florian, L. (ed.) (2007) *The Handbook of Special Education*. London: Sage Publications Ltd.

On disability and special educational needs, innovative perspectives are provided by:

Lewis, A. and Norwich, B. (2004) *Special Teaching for Special Children? Pedagogies for Inclusion*. Maidenhead: Open University Press.

Thomas, G. and Loxley, A. (2007) *Deconstructing Special Education and Constructing Inclusion*. Buckingham: Open University Press.

On the conceptualization of inclusive education, see:

Hick, P., Kershner, R. and Farrell, P. (eds) (2008) *Psychology for Inclusive Education: New Directions in Theory and Practice*. Abingdon: Routledge.

Mitchell, D. (ed.) (2005) *Contextualizing Inclusive Education: Evaluating Old and New International Perspectives*. London: Routledge.

**www.C**

The associated website, **reflectiveteaching.co.uk**, offers a wealth of supplementary resources including reflective activities, research briefings, advice on further reading and downloadable diagrams, figures and checklists from the book. It also features a compendium of educational terms, links to useful websites, policy and curriculum documents, and showcases examples of excellent research and practice.

# part five

# Deepening understanding

This is the final and synoptic part of the book. It integrates major themes though discussion of practitioner expertise and professionalism. Chapter 16 harvests and integrates powerful ideas from previous chapters into a holistic conceptual framework of enduring issues in teaching and learning in ECEC. The chapter constructs a framework describing dimensions of expert thinking. In Chapter 17, we consider the role of the early years provision in our societies and suggest how reflective practitioners can contribute to democratic processes.

# Expertise
## Conceptual tools for career-long fascination?

**16**

## Introduction: A conceptual framework for deepening expertise

The contemporary world is complex, challenging and rapidly developing. As Collarbone (2009, Reading 16.1) argues, we have to get used to change itself. And there will certainly be pressure on all educators.

As we saw in Chapter 4, it is now internationally recognized – more than ever before – that educators (OECD, 2005; Sahlberg, 2012; Hattie, 2009) and the earliest years of children's care and education are crucial to their future life chances. Jane Osgood (2006) notes that the early years workforce has received unprecedented attention from policy-makers in recent years.

The influence of recent analyses of the potential for ECEC to impact upon a child's education and future are found throughout this book. Such findings offer wonderful insights into high-quality provision and its impact. However, specific findings also need to be integrated more holistically into practitioners' routine practices and ways of thinking. For some, this may be relatively easy, where staff are highly qualified and time for training, staff development and reflection are built into routines. For others, this may not be straightforward. Many in the sector have little time to converse, and arranging meetings and training can be challenging where funds are scarce and practitioners are 'in ratio' so therefore need to be with the children. This brings us to a discussion of the progressive development, and deepening, of practitioner expertise (see Eaude, Reading 16.2 and Happo and Määttä, Reading 16.4).

---

### TLRP principles

One principle is of particular relevance to this chapter on expertise:

**Principle 9: Effective teaching and learning depends on teacher learning.**
The need for teachers to learn continuously in order to develop their knowledge and skills, and adapt and develop their roles, especially through classroom inquiry, should be recognized and supported.

---

The development of practitioner expertise has been the focus of much research within the ECEC field in recent years. Glaser (1999) identified three key 'cognitive stages' in the development of expertise, thereby highlighting a transition from dependent to independent ways of thinking about practice:

Externally supported → Transitional → Self-regulatory

Glaser notes that we start with support, followed by a stage of transition, of gradually reduced external support, which ultimately leads to increased expertise and confidence and decreased reliance on external sources. While this progression makes considerable sense, a further element of expertise lies in developing appropriate judgement in the environment in which one works. In other words, it is not enough simply to accumulate a 'box of tricks' or, as we discussed in Chapter 7, taught skills which, recipe-like, can be produced and applied to a variety of situations – valuable though these may be. The key capability is to understand when and how to deploy such capabilities. Berliner (2004) picked out the significance of contextual judgement and of practice itself in his elaboration of five stages of teacher development (originally proposed by Dreyfus and Dreyfus, 1986). This is summarized by Eaude (2012) in Table 16.1.

Table 16.1 Stages in the development of expertise [Eaude, 2012, after Alexander, 2010: 416–7]

| Stage | Strategies | Overall approach | Characteristic |
|---|---|---|---|
| Novice | Context-free rules and guidelines | Relatively inflexible, limited skill | Deliberate |
| Advanced beginner | Practical case knowledge | Use of rules qualified by greater understanding of conditions | Insightful |
| Competent | Discrimination of what matters or not | Conscious choices, but not yet fast, fluid or flexible | Rational |

Here we see the rationale for the notion of 'deepening expertise'. As a 'novice' starting out in the field, following rules and guidelines provides boundaries, support and helps us to make justifiable decisions. While this is useful, and often very necessary, it does not support flexible ways of working to support the families and children with whom we work. As time progresses – and we must acknowledge that this will take different lengths of time for different people working within different circumstances – we begin to consider what will work well in specific circumstances, at particular points in time. For example, one of us recalls how, when a Traveller family joined a pre-school setting, the children brought food into the setting, which was actively discouraged. Given that the head of this family had had several long conversations with the staff about how attending pre-school was a major step and change for the family, one which she had never thought would have occurred, it was decided that being critical of diet was not a basis for beginning the relationship and thus this 'agreed rule and setting policy' was 'put aside'. Having the confidence, experience and being able to justify decisions to others with ease requires advanced forms of expertise.

The need for contextual understanding and for experience over many years helps to explain the common scepticism of many educators working across sectors to the 'latest fad' or to a 'new policy', which may emerge from the media, government or elsewhere. Hargreaves describes such 'presentism' as a conservative force (2008) but also recognizes it as a foundational form of professional knowledge and security, from which new practices can only develop through work *with* teachers and in ways which authentically respect their agency, values, vision and expertise.

In summary, the development of expertise occurs over time and is, in essence, concerned with acquiring more sophisticated ways of thinking about teaching and learning as well as the refinement of practical skills and knowledge (Winch, 2012). From a reliance on generic rules for challenges, such as behaviour management, the expert practitioner is able to 'read' a situation and draw intuitively on his or her repertoire of responses (see

Osborne, et al. Reading 16.3). As indicated in **Table 16.1**, this appears 'almost effortless', but it is also possible to 'fall back on a deliberate, analytical approach'.

This book has progressed, section by section, through the principles of educational intentions, conditions for learning, teaching processes and outcomes. Each chapter has focused on practical challenges, but has also been written with an eye to the cumulative development of practitioner expertise alongside and acknowledgement that 'being a professional working with young children is not just about meeting standards; it's about attitude, ideology and passion' (Brock, n.d.). To that end, powerful concepts and expert questions for analysing teaching and learning in ECEC have been seeded through the chapters.

We are now thus able, in this chapter, to harvest cumulatively from across the book and to offer an integrated, conceptual foundation for deepening expertise.

## Deepening expertise: A framework of concepts and expert questions

We have provided (see **Table 16.2**) a slightly amended version of the conceptual framework for teacher expertise, which was developed in collaboration between TLRP and colleagues from the General Teaching Council for England (Pollard, 2010). This framework is based on the proposition that, in one way or another, educators inevitably face issues concerning **educational aims, learning contexts, processes** and **outcomes** (the rows) and they do so in relation to **curriculum, pedagogy** and **assessment** (the columns). While there may be a different emphasis in early years settings than in schools – for example, what is considered to be appropriate and excellent pedagogy may have a greater emphasis on elements of care – these issues are present and enduring and provide a useful framework for capturing the key points made within this book.

The expert questions in each cell highlight the enduring issues which reflective practitioners need to consider and, as we have noted throughout this book, this calls for evidence-informed professional judgement. However, the analytic capacity of the concepts which are used to think about and discuss such evidence is also absolutely vital. Without this, neither enquiry nor discussion with colleagues will build sustainable professional understandings nor lead to agreed ways of working. As we established in Chapter 6, communicating with colleagues is vital for excellent pedagogy and provision.

There is an important assumption behind the way this representation of conceptual tools has been developed, which we need to make explicit. It is that we are concerned with the provision of some form of 'high-quality education and care'. In other words, the ideas in the framework are informed by particular educational values and by available evidence about 'high-quality education and care'. The specific meaning and usage of the identified concepts can thus certainly be challenged. The framework is simply an analytical device for representing practitioner expertise. It could certainly be compiled and re-presented in different ways. Indeed, we have made adjustments to ensure that the relevance for those working within ECEC is clear.

Review of the *columns* of curriculum, pedagogy and assessment are an important way of using the framework. For example, a practitioner, staff team or any other group of stakeholders in a setting might want to focus on curriculum provision alone, in which case the 'expert questions' in that column would be effective probes for this, enabling considerations of aims, contexts, processes and outcomes (Chapters 8, 9 and 10 cover this ground, too). Pedagogy could be similarly reviewed using the set of expert questions in its column (and Chapters 5, 6, 7, 11, 12 and 15 also focus on these issues). Assessment is the subject of the third column (which articulates directly with Chapters 13 and 14).

But it is also worthwhile to think of the *rows*. If this is done, the interrelationship of provision for curriculum, pedagogy and assessment is reviewed in relation to each of the enduring issues concerned with aims, contexts, processes and outcomes. This is the approach taken in the remainder of this chapter.

Alternatively, it is often insightful to explore connections between the concepts and questions in different parts of the framework. The framework is simply a tool for thinking and for discussion, to be used as readers see fit.

For more information on how the original conceptual framework was created, see the supplementary material for Chapter 16 and Deepening Expertise section at **reflectiveteaching.co.uk**.

| ENDURING ISSUES | | Curricular concepts |
|---|---|---|
| **1** EDUCATIONAL AIMS | **1. Society's educational goals** What vision of 'education and care' is the provision designed to achieve? | **Breadth:** does the curriculum represent society's educational aspirations for its citizens? Does it support children to develop secure curious dispositions? |
| | **2. Elements of learning** What knowledge, concepts, skills, values and attitudes are to be learned? | **Balance:** does the curriculum-as-experienced offer everything which each child has a right to expect? |
| **2** SOCIAL CONTEXTS | **3. Community context** Is the educational experience valued and endorsed by parents, community and civil society? | **Connection:** does the curriculum engage with the cultural resources and funds-of-knowledge of families and the community? |
| | **4. Institutional context** Does the setting promote a common vision to extend educational experiences and inspire children? | **Coherence:** is there clarity in the purposes, content and organisation of the curriculum and does it provide holistic learning experiences? |
| **3** PROCESSES | **5. Processes for children's social needs** Does the educational experience build on social relationships, cultural understandings and children's identities? | **Personalization:** does the curriculum resonate with the social and cultural needs of diverse children and provide appropriate learning opportunities? |
| | **6. Processes for children's affective needs** Does the educational experience take due account of children's views, feelings and characteristics? | **Relevance:** is the curriculum presented in ways which are meaningful to children so that it can excite their imagination? |
| | **7. Processes for children's cognitive needs** Does the educational experience match the children's cognitive needs and provide appropriate challenge? | **Differentiation:** are curriculum tasks and activities structured appropriately to match the needs and interests of children? |
| **4** LEARNING OUTCOMES | **8. Outcomes for continuing improvement in learning** Does the educational experience lead to *development* in knowledge, concepts, skills and attitudes? | **Progression:** does the curriculum-as-delivered provide an appropriate sequence and depth of learning experiences and activities? |
| | **9. Outcomes for certification and the lifecourse** Does the educational experience equip children for an unknown future? | **Effectiveness:** are children supported to achieve and thus does our provision support the meeting of society's educational goals? |

[Adapted from *A Framework for Teacher Expertise* (Pollard, 2010)]

| Pedagogic concepts | Assessment concepts |
|---|---|
| **Principle**: is our pedagogy consistent with established principles for effective teaching and learning? | **Congruence**: is observation and dialogue with families widely used to inform understanding of the child, their needs and their next steps for learning? |
| **Repertoire**: is our pedagogic expertise sufficiently creative, skilled and wide-ranging to support all elements of learning? | **Validity**: are the forms of assessment used to identify next steps based upon individual children's needs and interests? |
| **Warrant**: are our teaching strategies evidence-informed, convincing and justifiable? | **Dependability**: are assessment processes understood by children and families? How do we ensure young children understand them? |
| **Culture**: does the setting support expansive learning by affirming children's contributions, engaging partners and providing attractive opportunities? | **Expectation**: do we have high expectations of all children? Are they realistic and achievable? How do we ensure children are aware of the expectations we have of them? |
| **Relationships**: are relationships nurtured as the foundation of mutual well-being? | **Inclusion**: are all children and their families treated respectfully and fairly in both formal and informal interaction? Is information made available and accessible? |
| **Engagement**: do our teaching strategies and the organization of the environment allow for planned and unplanned learning experiences both indoors and outdoors? | **Authenticity**: are children allowed to develop at their own rate and in their own time? Are they respected as unique individuals each with their own needs and interests? |
| **Dialogue**: does practitioner-child talk scaffold understanding, build on existing knowledge and strengthen dispositions towards learning to allow children to become active learners? | **Feeding-back**: is there a routine flow of formative feedback to support children's learning and development? Are routines flexible to meet the needs of all children? |
| **Reflection**: is our practice based on incremental, evidence-informed and collaborative improvement strategies? | **Development**: does formative feedback and support enable children to reflect on their own achievements? |
| **Empowerment**: is our pedagogic repertoire successful in enhancing wellbeing, learning dispositions, capabilities and agency? | **Consequence**: do children develop a confident sense of personal identity? And grow to be curious independent learners? |

Table 16.2
A Framework
for Practitioner
Expertise: powerful
concepts and
expert questions

## 1. EDUCATIONAL AIMS

### 1.1 Society's goals

| What vision of 'education and care' is the provision designed to achieve? | **Breadth:** does the curriculum represent society's educational aspirations for its citizens? Does it support children to develop secure curious dispositions? | **Principle:** is our pedagogy consistent with established principles for effective teaching and learning? | **Congruence:** is observation widely used to inform understanding of the child, their needs and their next steps for learning? |
| --- | --- | --- | --- |

**Society's educational goals**

Education connects our past to the future – but exactly what happens is worked out through debate and action in the present.

Children and young people are our most precious asset. They come to embody our culture and their values and capabilities will determine the ways in which our economy and society will evolve over the twenty-first century. Education both reflects society and contributes to it. Issues such as whether education reproduces social differences or provides new opportunities thus become very important. As we have noted throughout this book, the earliest years of development play an unparalleled role in this. What vision of education and care should we adopt?

The law now formally enshrines ECEC provision in many countries through the introduction of a curriculum – a relatively new development. However, a focus on school readiness and the reaching of goals could impact upon the breadth of experience and limit children's opportunities for exploration and free play. The consequences of this may narrow provision and impact on children's opportunities to become curious, secure and confident learners.

**Breadth**

There are now a variety of statutory early years curricula which are usually built upon the premise that children benefit from exposure to a range of experiences, from 1:1 time with a practitioner through to practitioner-led group sessions and child-led sessions (Bowman et al., 2001), with lone play also being recognized as having a potentially important developmental role (Henniger, 1994; Lloyd and Howe, 2003).

**Principle**

This challenge concerns the extent to which practitioners' pedagogic judgement is informed by deep understanding of learning and teaching and of the factors involved. TLRP's Ten Principles (see Chapter 4) is one way of representing these factors holistically so that their interconnectedness is emphasized.

TLRP's principles form four groups. The first concerns the goals and moral purpose of education, knowledge to be learned and the prior experience of the learner. Three aspects of practitioner expertise, in 'scaffolding' learning, assessment for learning and active engagement, form another. The role of social processes and informal learning feature next. Finally, the principles emphasize the significance of practitioner learning and the need for consistent policy frameworks.

**Congruence**

Assessment activity should support children's learning – hence 'assessment for learning' (Chapter 13). Evidence from observations is used to inform planning a stimulating and appropriate environment for learning. Assessment is used to increase our understandings of the child and their needs while also encouraging children 'to produce knowledge rather than to reproduce knowledge' (Wortham, 2008: 108).

## Reflective activity 16.1

*Aim:* To reflect upon enduring educational issues.

*Evidence and reflection:* Take two or three of the questions above. Work alone initially and then with a colleague to discuss your responses to the questions.

## 1. EDUCATIONAL AIMS

### 1.2 Elements of learning

| What knowledge, concepts, skills, values and attitudes are to be learned? | **Balance:** does the curriculum-as-experienced offer everything which each child has a right to expect? | **Repertoire:** is our pedagogic expertise sufficiently creative, skilled and wide-ranging to support all elements of learning and unique children? | **Validity:** are the forms of assessment used to identify next steps based upon individual children's needs and interests? |
|---|---|---|---|

### Elements of learning

Throughout their educational experience children acquire knowledge, concepts, skills, values and attitudes.

Knowledge and concepts to be learned are often suggested by national curriculum frameworks, and, particularly in the early years, these are complemented by a requirement to support the skills and dispositions of 'learning-how-to-learn'. While particular values may be advocated and made explicit by the curriculum, the tacit messages that go out from the 'hidden curriculum' of everyday experience will also have an influence. As we noted in Chapters 2 and 6, children learn a great deal from their observations of, and interactions with, adults and their peers in pre-schools. The messages transmitted to children in these ways are every bit as powerful (and often more so) than those contained in any official curriculum.

Practitioners thus have enormous responsibilities not just for the content of what children may learn, and how this may impact upon a young child's development, but in contributing to the values and attitudes of our future citizens. This responsibility cannot be declined, for children will develop values and attitudes in any event.

### Balance

Overemphasis on knowledge or skills in the early years would be considered by many educationalists to be inappropriate, not least as this may hinder children's free play and exploration. Yet, we are also increasingly aware of the impact of the potential benefits of a high-quality ECEC experience. Supporting the development of each child in a flexible way is clearly dependent on having an appropriate pedagogic repertoire.

### Repertoire

Educational objectives are wide-ranging so that a range of teaching approaches is required. Practitioners can select from these having considered the needs of the child, the intended outcomes and other circumstances. The SPEEL framework (discussed in Chapter 11), provides an overview of the key components of effective pedagogy, this includes that practitioners:

- play alongside children, scaffolding and extending children's learning;
- communicate with children at their level, listen to and talk with children, valuing what they say;
- engage and direct children's attention, interest and motivation in focused teaching activities;
- teach and model language and communication skills, thinking skills, collaborative working, and positive attitudes;
- know when (and when not) to intervene in children's learning experiences;
- actively seek opportunities to give positive feedback to children, and celebrating children's genuine successes;
- clarify and convey to children learning expectations, intentions, outcomes and targets;
- use children's experiences and theories and share own experiences and learning with children.

[Adapted from Moyles, Adams and Musgrove, 2002: 52]

As this list, which is by no means exhaustive, demonstrates practitioners need to be confident users of a range of pedagogic approaches to ensure there are opportunities for play (indoors and outdoors), dialogue with peers and dialogue with practitioners.

### Validity

Assessment is a complex activity. It requires observations to be conducted over time, in a variety of ways and in consultation with the child and their families to ensure that an understanding of the child's current development and interests is gained. This knowledge can then be used to plan for the child's future learning.

## Elements of learning

**What knowledge, concepts, skills and attitudes are to be learned in formal education?**

How we understand children and their learning affects the choices that we make when planning, facilitating, encouraging and supporting learning. The agendas of politicians, the needs of society, and the needs and desires of parents and families also impacts upon what is expected from early years provision.

We have reiterated through this book that supporting children to develop dispositions for learning which allow them to be curious and approach learning with a willingness to try, will support them to learn across the life-course.

Within this section we consider what the child has the right to expect from education, specifically early years provision. With this in mind – and considering what children may learn, both implicitly and explicitly, through education – it is useful to consider the United Nations Convention on the Rights of the Child. Of particular relevance are:

**Article 2 (Non-discrimination)**: No child should be treated unfairly on any basis. It doesn't matter where children live, what language they speak, what their parents do, whether they are boys or girls, what their culture is, whether they have a disability or whether they are rich or poor.

**Article 3 (Best interests of the child):** The best interests of children must be the primary concern in making decisions that may affect them. All adults should do what is best for children. When adults make decisions, they should think about how their decisions will affect children.

**Article 12 (Respect for the views of the child):** When adults are making decisions that affect children, children have the right to say what they think should happen and have their opinions taken into account.

**Article 28: (Right to education):** All children have the right to a primary education, which should be free.

**Article 29 (Goals of education):** Children's education should develop each child's personality, talents and abilities to the fullest. It should encourage children to respect others, human rights and their own and other cultures.

**Article 30 (Children of minorities/indigenous groups):** Minority or indigenous children have the right to learn about and practise their own culture, language and religion.

**Article 31 (Leisure, play and culture):** Children have the right to relax and play, and to join in a wide range of cultural, artistic and other recreational activities.

Almost all countries have signed up to the UNCRC, including the United Kingdom, making the articles law, therefore relevant to us all, particularly those with working with children. More about the UNCRC can be found at **reflectiveteaching.co.uk**.

WWW.C

## 2. SOCIAL CONTEXTS

### 2.1 Community context

| Is the educational experience valued and endorsed by parents, community and civil society? | **Connection:** does the curriculum engage with the cultural resources and funds-of-knowledge of families and the community? | **Warrant:** are our teaching strategies evidence-informed, convincing and justifiable? | **Dependability:** are assessment processes understood by children and families? How do we ensure young children understand them? |
| --- | --- | --- | --- |

**Community**

'Community' is associated with social relationships, cultures and histories, and with a collective sense of place and identity (Chapter 5).

Some people and families may feel deeply embedded in their communities and benefit from extensive social networks; such social capital often brings status and advantage. Others, perhaps minority groups, may feel more marginal or even excluded. Such diversity is a very strong feature of contemporary life.

TLRP's research has consistently shown the significance of informal, out-of-school learning: what happens within education is enriched by an understanding of what happens outside education. Families and others in the community can thus help considerably, if constructive and trusting connections are made.

However, families, children and the community as a whole are also positioned as consumers. Families expect children to receive high-quality education and care, and inspectors and the media are quick to condemn when they feel standards fall short. For this reason, forms of pedagogy increasingly have to be justified.

**Connection**

There are many ways in which practitioners can engage with families and communities. We have mentioned many of them in this book and **Case study 16.1** provides an example of this.

The underlying theme here is about the contextual meaningfulness of the curriculum. While national frameworks exist in Wales, Scotland, Northern Ireland and England, local adaption and adaption for unique children in age-appropriate ways is likely to enhance both the perceived value of education and the quality of learning.

**Warrant**

In relation to pedagogy, the concept of warrant challenges us to justify our practice to stakeholders such as families, employers and children themselves. We defined pedagogy as the skilful interplay of practitioners' craft knowledge and their creative responsiveness to specific situations and thus, given this complex interplay, that reflective practice can support continuing improvement in the quality of professional judgements.

**Dependability**

Young children's understanding and development often changes rapidly in the early years. Consistent, dependable forms of observation and dialogue will be required to ensure that any assessment processes are useful for understanding the child's current needs. In addition, it will be important that families and, where appropriate, children have an understanding of the process, procedures and 'judgements' made. It is also important to ensure that this is shared in an appropriate way, in accessible language (perhaps translated) and that dialogue is possible. The *We Are Learning To…* (WALT) wall example we provided (see Chapter 13) offers a way in which this could be achieved.

## 2. SOCIAL CONTEXTS

### 2.2 Setting and sector context

| Does the setting promote a common vision to extend educational experiences and inspire children? | **Coherence**: is there clarity in the purposes, content and organization of the curriculum and does it provide holistic learning experiences? | **Culture**: does the setting support expansive learning by affirming children's contributions, engaging partners and providing attractive child-led and adult-led opportunities? | **Expectation**: do we have high expectations of all children? Are they realistic and achievable? How do we ensure children are aware of these expectations? |
| --- | --- | --- | --- |

### Setting and sector context

In the UK understandings of the attributes of high-quality provision are largely informed by the findings of 14 detailed case studies of pre-schools identified as providing 'excellent' quality in the aforementioned EPPE project. These settings were identified by the EPPE research team using ECERS-E in addition to other measures, including quality of care and pedagogical practice (which encompasses the relationships between child and practitioner and the environment) (Siraj-Blatchford et al., 2003). The main conclusions drawn from this study (Sylva et al., 2004) include that pre-schools providing high-quality or 'excellent' provision:

- hold the view that cognitive and social development are not compartmentalized, they are linked;
- offer a mix of planned practitioner-initiated group work and learning through freely chosen play;
- engage children in adult–child interactions that involve sustained shared thinking (SST) and open-ended questioning; provide formative feedback to extend children's thinking;
- provide children with support to rationalize their conflicts.

Such understandings can help to guide practice. However we must also remember, as we have established throughout this book, that children's learning can be significantly enhanced by practitioner learning.

### Coherence

Coherence and progression within areas of learning enable children to build their understanding cumulatively. In Scotland, the Curriculum for Excellence states that: 'all children and young people have an entitlement to a curriculum which they experience as a coherent whole, with smooth and well-paced progression through the **experiences and outcome's** (Education Scotland, 2013).

### Culture

Setting culture can be a major influence on teaching and learning. In ideal circumstances, a culture of collaboration would exist among all members of the staff team, in which the values, commitments and identities of individuals are perfectly aligned with the teaching and learning strategies and aspirations of the setting. Things are usually more complicated – but the ways in which such complexity is handled is crucial.

TLRP's studies of workplace cultures contrasted 'expansive' and 'restrictive' learning environments (Fuller and Unwin, 2003). In the former, staff were engaged in meaningful work, with supportive leadership and opportunities for personal learning and progression. Another TLRP project showed how teachers' sense of well-being and job satisfaction is a key factor in their effectiveness, finding that 'pupils of teachers who are committed and resilient are likely to attain more than pupils whose teachers are not' (Day et al., 2007).

Nivala and Hujala (2002) argue that collaboration and improvement will only happen within settings if there is interaction between leaders and staff teams. It has been widely accepted that such management is crucial if high-quality provision is to be available for children (see for example Nupponen, 2006a, 2006b).

### Expectations

Learners benefit when significant others in their lives believe in them. Parental and practitioner expectations are particularly significant for children and are often based on judgements about capability and potential. Expectations are thus pervasively embedded in perception, relationships and everyday life. As such, although tacit, they may be particularly meaningful to learners and influential in the formation of self-belief (Dweck, 1986; Reading 2.6).

Reflective early years practitioners must ensure that the expectations they hold are appropriate, realistic and are understood by parents and children. Our discussions around fixed and growth mindsets in Chapters 2 and 13 is useful to consider in relation to this.

# Social contexts: a case study

*Building effective partnerships – the 'Letters and Sounds' project, Kirklees*

The Kirklees Parents as Partners in Early Learning (PPEL) project addressed two fundamental questions:

- How do you create better communication between home and school settings?
- What skills and knowledge can we give parents to help them understand and support their children's language development?

Groups of practitioners from three economically deprived areas were invited to chart the planning and impact of the different bridge-building processes. The research also aimed to identify and record lessons learned about how early years settings might make effective links between children's home life and activities taking place within settings.

To understand how they could improve their practice, practitioners considered the barriers to parental involvement. One thoughtful response was expressed by a Children's Centre coordinator: 'It has always been my feeling that the majority of parents want the best for their children, and it is the professional's responsibility to raise the parents' consciousness about what they already do as a starting point.'

Picnics were the central focus of the PPEL project, based on the premise that sharing food is an ideal ice-breaker. Careful thought was given to making these gatherings as easy for parents to attend as possible. Another key consideration was how to communicate with families about the events.

The picnics provided a great opportunity for practitioners to dispel parents' doubts about the educational value of play and the need to forge links between school activities and family life. Each picnic showcased imaginative and fun Letters and Sounds activities. Among the most popular of these were:

- sing-alongs – parents were then given recordings of the music to help them practise singing with their children at home.
- a box game, which helped children match a phoneme (sound) on the top with an object inside.
- listening diaries in which parents and children could discuss and catalogue all the sounds they hear in and around their homes.

At the picnic, parents and children were able to try out a wide range of Letters and Sounds activities, including writing the first letters of their names in henna hand-decorations, playing musical instruments, and making noisy jewellery and rain-shakers.

At each event detailed notes were taken, recording parents' views – an exercise that enriched practitioners' understanding of how the resources might be adapted – and also measuring parents' willingness to try out at home what they had seen and done at the event. At one picnic, the value of older siblings helping their younger brothers' and sisters' learning was highlighted.

One mother's view of learning was greatly altered: 'Now I know that he doesn't have to just get it right or wrong. We can do this together at home … There should be more meetings like this.'

The PPEL work in Kirklees has confirmed the importance of practitioners developing a more collaborative model of working with parents, despite apparent barriers to such engagement.

Key findings of the project include:

- The need to challenge perceived barriers to parental involvement.
- Breaking down these barriers can be achieved with imagination, flexibility, and the careful timing and promotion of events.
- Recognizing the parents' desire to participate in their children's learning, even if they do not normally.
- How activities can achieve the transition to home if adjusted for accessibility.
- The impact of listening diaries as a way of encouraging active listening at home.
- The potential of family learning and extended schools provision in making links with parents, as well as the traditional school routes.
- Practitioners must discover and value what parents actually do at home and use it in the setting.

## 3. PROCESSES

### 3.1 Process for children's social needs

| Does the educational experience build on social relationships, cultural understandings and children's identities? | **Personalization:** does the curriculum resonate with the social and cultural needs of the unique child and provide appropriate learning opportunities? | **Relationships:** are relationships nurtured as the foundation of mutual well-being? | **Inclusion:** are all children and their families treated respectfully and fairly in both formal and informal interaction? Is information made available and accessible? |
|---|---|---|---|

**Processes for children's social needs**

Relationships are of such significance for children's well-being and learning that reflective practitioners are likely to almost constantly have their development in mind, working to ensure that the children are being supported to gain the greatest enjoyment and potential from their time in the ECEC setting. This involves considering the building of relationships with and between the adults and the children in the setting, with communities and families, and supporting children in their relationships with their peers.

**Personalization**

Through the building of such relationships it is possible to come to know the child, their interests and their needs. Without open communication and positive relationships, being able to plan for children as unique individuals becomes an impossible task. Personalizing children's experience while providing for a number of children of different ages and/or abilities requires expert judgement.

**Relationships**

'Good relationships' between practitioners and children, children and their peers, practitioners and their peers and practitioners and families are at the heart of pedagogic effectiveness. But what does it really mean?

Good relationships are founded on mutual respect and acceptance of ways of getting on together – described technically as a 'working consensus' (Pollard, 1985). We identified in Chapter 6 how this requires the development of skills for listening and talking to each other.

**Inclusion**

As identified in Chapter 15, we believe that inclusion is much more than supporting children with specific learning needs. Accepting and celebrating diversity in all its forms is likely to be crucial for supporting children to succeed in the world as they move through the education and employment systems. Particularly, as we have noted in a number of chapters, an enduring problem for education systems is that some groups tend to under-perform. That said, as we believe that every child does matter and that we need to ensure that no one is 'left behind', early years practitioners must be able to identify when children *may* need support and engage in careful and sensitive diagnostic work with families and other professionals. Children with special educational needs require particular attention to ensure that potential barriers to their learning are removed as far as is possible. In the case of a physical impairment this may require a practical form of provision.

# Processes for children's social needs: a case study

Does the educational experience build on social relationships, cultural understandings and learner identities?

### *Removing barriers to learning: Dean's School Language Development Programme*

Sarah, a reception class teacher, was becoming increasingly concerned about the number of children entering her class with a substantial language delay. She feared that these children could not access the curriculum as she would like. Sarah provided increased opportunities for language development within her school, but felt that these children were at a disadvantage from their first day.

Sarah raised her concerns with the local authority and, with support, was able to secure external funding to start a language development programme. This involved health visitors carrying out a simple language and communication assessment as they visited children. The families of children identified as being at risk of language delay were offered home visits by a speech and language therapist who offered simple tips to families, including games such as sock matching and reading to the child and talking them through their actions as they completed tasks.

Sarah also supported the opening of a pre-school which focused on providing language support to children who would move into the school the following year.

Sarah noted a substantial decrease in the number of children entering her class with language delay, and also the severity of any delay.

## 3. PROCESSES

### 3.2 Processes for children's emotional needs

| Does the educational experience take due account of children's views, feelings and characteristics? | **Relevance**: is the curriculum presented in ways which are meaningful to children so that it can excite their imagination? | **Engagement:** do our teaching strategies and the organization of the environment allow for planned and unplanned learning experiences both indoors and outdoors? | **Authenticity:** are children allowed to develop at their own rate and in their own time? Are they respected as unique individuals each with their own needs and interests? |
|---|---|---|---|

### Processes for children's emotional needs

We all, at any age, value our dignity and appreciate it when our individuality is recognized. And we also, as part of our personal development, have to learn to appreciate the needs of others. Goleman (1996) called this 'emotional intelligence' – an idea which combines social empathy and skills with personal awareness, motivation and capacity to manage one's own feelings. Early years practitioners have always worked hard to support such development though provision such as PSED.

Creating conditions for learning through the building of secure relationships was noted in Chapter 6 as the basis of high-quality provision. Provision must provide opportunities for children to engage in meaningful learning indoors and out; if children can support each other, much greater learning potential is available to them.

Feelings about learning itself are also of enormous significance and as we seek to support children to become lifelong learners, we need to instil curiosity and confidence.

### Relevance

It is vital that children are observed and that their interests are discussed with both the child and their family to ensure that engaging and relevant activities can be provided for the child. In addition, the child and their family need to feel that the learning activities are relevant to their lives, that they take into account their cultures and values. While part of providing an inclusive environment, this is also an aspect of providing a relevant curriculum which recognizes children's diverse needs.

### Engagement

TLRP research on pupil consultation (see Rudduck and McIntyre, 2007; Reading 1.3) and learner identities (see Pollard and Filer, 2007) showed that if pupils feel that they matter in school and are respected, then they feel more positive about themselves as learners. The underlying driver here is termed 'agency' – the opportunity for self-directed action and fulfilment. In Chapter 8 on spaces, we discussed how this is equally relevant for children in the early years, and we noted how there is a need to provide democratic spaces for children and for children to be included in decision-making processes.

We also noted how we must ensure that children are provided with a range of learning opportunities both indoors and outdoors to support engagement. This includes consideration of both *what* is provided for children and the *way* it is provided (Moyles, Adams and Musgrove, 2002).

### Authenticity

Perhaps the most important aspect of authenticity in learning for young children is to ensure there are opportunities to learn through play while also ensuring that learning can resonate with the child's experiences outside of the setting. One way of ensuring this is to engage with families and communities taking note of children's prior learning.

## 3. PROCESSES

### 3.3 Processes for children's cognitive needs

| Does the educational experience match children's cognitive needs and provide appropriate challenge? | **Differentiation**: are curriculum tasks and activities structured appropriately to match the needs and interests of children? | **Dialogue**: does practitioner–child talk scaffold understanding, build on existing knowledge, strengthen dispositions towards learning and allow children to become active learners? | **Feeding-back**: is there a routine flow of formative feedback to support children's learning and development? Are routines flexible to meet the needs of all children? |
| --- | --- | --- | --- |

**Processes for children's cognitive needs**

The brilliance of Vygotsky's psychology derives from his insight in relating cognitive, social and cultural factors together. So we meet each child's cognitive needs through social processes of teaching and learning, and the understanding that is developed relates to culturally embedded knowledge. Crucially, the educator *mediates* between knowledge and learner. A practitioner's explanation, questions, discussion or structured task provides another type of scaffolding – but must be expertly framed. In these cases, the practitioner combines challenge and support, most often through discussion, so that the child is encouraged to extend their understanding.

**Differentiation**

The curriculum content must be converted to tasks and activities and then presented to children in ways to which they can relate. Too difficult, and frustration often follows; too easy, and boredom may result. Too many adult-led activities may take children away from their play-based learning experiences and diminish their power. The goal is to ensure that there are activities available which are relevant to the child's interests and support them to learn, in a way in which they feel appropriately challenged. But since all children are different, there is considerable skill in achieving a differentiated match. Overall, children ought to experience a combination of child-led and adult-led activities. How these are planned and structured will be dependent on what the reflective early years practitioner identifies as being most appropriate for the children in their care.

**Dialogue**

In Chapter 2 we noted the term 'early childhood error' to describe the folly of practitioners laying out stimulating play environments but not supporting children in play and therefore their learning (Bredekamp and Rosegrant, 1992). In such instances the potential of the learning in that situation is lost. Practitioners must, at times, engage with children in their child-led activities using open-ended questioning to scaffold and support the child's learning. This takes practice to ensure that the adult does not begin to lead the 'investigation' or 'conversation' and yet they must use dialogue to support the child, through questioning, to reach new understandings.

**Feedback**

Providing appropriate feedback to children has one of the largest measurable effects of any teaching strategy (Hattie, 2009). This fact underlies assessment for learning (Black and Wiliam, 1998). Such formative assessment is an integral part of pedagogy and is designed to help children grow their capacity to manage their own learning.

One of the ways described for providing children with feedback is through the use of learning journals. These can document the child's learning over time. Indeed, reflecting with children on the content can support them to see how their capabilities and understanding have developed over time, giving them a sense of achievement and progress.

## 4. LEARNING OUTCOMES

### 4.1 Outcomes for continuing improvement in learning

| Does the educational experience lead to *development* in knowledge, concepts, skills and attitudes? | **Progression:** does the curriculum-as-delivered provide an appropriate sequence and depth of learning experiences and activities? | **Reflection:** is our practice based on incremental, evidence-informed and collaborative improvement strategies? | **Development:** does formative feedback and support enable children to reflect on their own achievements? |
|---|---|---|---|

**Learning outcomes**

Education is always, in a sense, about the tension between 'what is' and 'what might be'. The expert practitioner supports children to move forward in their learning. Ensuring progression in the educational experiences provided for children is therefore vital. Only through new challenges can they deepen and broaden their knowledge. However, the ultimate educational goal is to support the development of self-motivated and resilient learners who are not only knowledgeable but capable of taking control of their own learning, who are curious and confident enough to 'have a go'. Through encouragement to achieve personal learning goals, we sow the seeds of commitment to lifelong learning.

Reflective processes provide ways of marrying such ambitions, of reconciling what is and what might be. They enable practitioners to monitor their own performance, both reflexively and in collaboration with others, and thus to stimulate their own continuing professional development.

**Progression**

While we have noted the need to focus on building the skills for lifelong learning, there is also a need to provide children with opportunities to gain subject-specific knowledge, to build the foundations of numeracy and literacy. In addition, we have advocated that the basis for this must come from the child's interests, as noted through observations and discussions with families. The role of the expert practitioner is to ensure that these learning experiences are sequenced, that there is a degree of learning happening across areas (i.e. physical, social and cognitive development) and that that basic concepts and skills are developing – all this within a recognition of that child's current level of understanding!

**Reflection**

This concept represents a commitment to continuing and principled professional improvement. Reflective practice is based on open-minded enquiry and a willingness to use evidence to challenge one's own provision (see Chapter 3). This might be based on external evidence of performance, on reading research findings, on small-scale personal enquiries, on observations, on discussions or collaborative activities with colleagues. There are many possibilities but, in all cases, evidence is used to generate reappraisal. In this way, taken-for-granted thinking is challenged and professional judgement is refined (see Heilbronn, 2010).

Reflective enquiry may be focused on particular problems or issues and is best carried out in systematic ways and for specific purposes. Understanding then becomes embedded in practitioner expertise and enables decision-making at other times.

There are additional chapters and resources to support professional enquiry at **reflectiveteaching.co.uk**.

**Development**

Physical, cognitive, social and emotional development all influence and are influenced by educational experiences. This, we know, is an enduring process (see for instance Blyth, 1984). Resilient and resourceful learners develop when teaching combines appropriate challenge and support – 'building learning power', as Claxton (2002) puts it.

Assessment for Learning (Chapter 13) promotes child involvement in assessment so that learners can reflect on where they are, where they need to go next and how to get there (Assessment Reform Group, 2002). This requires an understanding of desired outcomes and of appropriate processes of learning. Such self-regulated approaches to learning can be nurtured by encouraging and helping children to see their achievements. Long-term developmental outcomes concern children's beliefs in themselves as learners, their skills in diagnosing learning challenges and their capacity for personal development in the future.

## Outcomes for continuing improvement in learning

Does the educational experience lead to *development* in knowledge, concepts, skills and attitudes?

A number of studies have provided us with insight into the ways in which experiences in the early years can support children's learning and development – for example, the HighScope Perry Pre-school Study (Schweinhart et al., 1985), the Carolina Abecedarian Project (Campbell et al., 2002) and the Effective Pre-school and Primary Education project (EPPE) (Sylva et al., 2004) see Reading 4.2.

The follow excerpt is taken from TLRP Briefing 24: Effective pre-school and primary education: Findings from the pre-school period.

### What makes an effective pre-school?

EPPE conducted case studies in 'effective' settings (where children made more progress than expected) to see what these centres did, on a day-to-day basis, that helped children. This has important implications for all early years staff who are concerned with promoting good outcomes for children. Five areas are particularly important when working with pre-school children. They are:

- the quality of adult–child verbal interactions;
- staff knowledge and understanding of the curriculum;
- knowledge of how young children learn;
- adults' skills in supporting children in resolving conflicts;
- helping parents to support children's learning in the home.

## 4. LEARNING OUTCOMES

### 4.2 Outcomes for the life-course

| Does the educational experience equip children for an unknown future? | **Effectiveness**: are children supported to achieve and thus does our provision support the meeting of society's educational goals? | **Empowerment**: is our pedagogic repertoire successful in enhancing well-being, learning disposition, capabilities and agency? | **Consequence**: do children develop a confident sense of personal identity? And grow to be curious independent learners? |
|---|---|---|---|

### Outcomes for certification and the life-course

What outcomes do we want from education?

We certainly need people who can contribute effectively in economic terms within the labour market. We also need citizens with social and global awareness in response to growing cultural diversity and the ecological challenge. We need those who will become 'good' parents and contribute to their communities and civil society. And then there is the need for future technologists, artists, entrepreneurs, and so on.

While there is relative continuity in general priorities, specific needs and circumstances do change over time. An enduring priority is that children should have self-confidence and a positive learning disposition. After all, we do not know what world children will face in 20, 30, 50 years' time. Early years practitioners are at the start of an educative process which helps children to develop a personal capacity to adapt to circumstances throughout the life-course.

### Effectiveness

Educational performance is a major public issue and will always be a concern for parents, local authorities, media and politicians. This sits alongside the issue of the provision of appropriate care. The quality of teaching is the single most important factor in realizing pupil potential through pre-school and into statutory education, a concept that is now internationally recognized (Ofsted, 2014; OECD, 2005).

What must be resisted is for the goals of governments to be placed upon young children at the expense of their right to play, have recreation and be supported to develop the skills of a lifelong learner. Too much pressure to achieve particular goals may lead the child to disengage from education, lose motivation and fail to reach their potential.

As far as the inspection of pre-school provision is concerned there appears to be an increasing focus on the quality of teaching and learning itself and on children's outcomes. Significantly, the professional judgement of inspectors has the potential to tackle issues which numeric data cannot reach.

### Empowerment

The first of TLRP's ten principles states that: 'Learning should aim to help people to develop the intellectual, personal and social resources that will enable them to participate as active citizens and workers and to flourish as individuals in a diverse and changing society' (see Chapter 4). So empowerment is the very stuff of 'education' in its broadest sense. But what does this mean in the early years?

Dweck (2000; Reading 2.5) differentiated pupils with a 'mastery' orientation from those who develop 'learned helplessness' in school. The conditions and experiences of setting life contribute to such self-beliefs. By creating opportunities for children to take independent action and experience success, practitioners support the development of self-confidence and positive learning dispositions.

TLRP researched learning at many stages of life and found that agency and self-belief were crucial at every age and in nursery, school, college, workplace, family and home settings (see: **tlrp.org/projects**).

### Consequence

In taking stock of their work as a whole, practitioners need to consider whether or not they have been able to enrich the lives of the children in their care and increased children's life chances (see Chapter 15). Are they better able to engage with learning? Are they prepared to enter statutory schooling? Have they developed self-confidence and a strong sense of personal identity? Education has sometimes been characterized as the process of 'becoming' a person, and it is certainly important to affirm the role of practitioners in facilitating the emergence of confident individuals and future citizens (see TLRP's Learning Lives project: Biesta et al., 2010) – after all, these early years are formative.

# Outcomes for the life-course: a case study

Does the educational experience equip children for an unknown future?

### 'Here's the keys, you're free now'

Tony Wilf was in his fifties, adjusting to the death of his wife, and had two young teenagers still at home. He wanted to look after them properly, and thought it would be nice to make home-made fish and chips. 'I couldn't remember how to do batter so I asked one of the old ladies next door, and she gave me this book', he told researchers, 'but I could not read.' Tony ended up going to the chip shop because he felt too humiliated to ask the neighbour, or his children, to read the recipe out to him.

Tony had been unfortunate in his schooling. 'I was told time and time again by teachers, "you're thick, you don't understand". If somebody had said, "right, what's the problem?"... that would have been fine.'

Tony had worked as an unskilled labourer for most of his life, and enjoyed learning from the older craftsmen, but he knew his literacy problems had stopped him from advancing.

It was 40 years after leaving school that Tony was finally diagnosed with dyslexia. In fact, this came about because he was trying to help his daughter, Clare, with her own literacy. Clare had trouble with her handwriting, so Tony decided to get a home computer to print out her work. 'So I went to "Computers for the Terrified". And it worked. I got into it, I really enjoyed that, and then something came up about "insert so and so after the third paragraph" and I thought, "what's a paragraph?" ... so that's why I started coming back to doing the English ...'

Tony's first English class didn't work out because he and the tutor got into arguments about his use of block capitals to write letters. His school experiences had left him unable to deal with not being listened to. Fortunately he tried again, and this time the tutor dealt with students as individuals. The use of coloured overlays designed for dyslexics led to a big improvement in his reading. Apart from improving his basic skills, the courses provided a focus for his life: 'What I like about it, you know, everybody works as a group; nobody takes the mickey out of anybody.'

Tony became interested in local history and started writing. 'It's as though I've been locked away for years and somebody's said, "well here you go, here's the keys, you're free now",' he said.

## 5 Using the conceptual framework

The conceptual framework has been developed based upon a wealth of educational research, its strength is that it is based upon a robust evidence base. The framework represents the moral and professional issues that practitioners face on a day-to-day basis. It is offered as a tool to support reflection and deepen expertise. It is a reference point for many of the major questions that must be faced when practical judgements are made.

---

### Reflective activity 16.2

*Aim:* To explore using the conceptual framework to reflect on professional expertise.

*Evidence and reflection:* Select one of the components of the framework provided above and identify a particular issue which has challenged you or that you see as particularly relevant to the practice in your setting. Does the framework help in reviewing this?

*Extension:* Use the framework when discussing a significant shared issue with a group of colleagues. Does it provoke new lines of discussion?

---

## Conclusion

This chapter has presented a conceptual framework which holistically represents the major dimensions of practitioner expertise. The framework is organized around nine enduring issues associated with educational aims, learning contexts, processes and learning outcomes. Each issue is explored in relation to curriculum, pedagogy and assessment. Links are also made back to chapters within the book.

The conceptual framework is offered as a contribution to the development of a shared professional language. It is a support for professional thinking and discussion.

However, the framework also *celebrates* practitioner expertise, for the truth is that, while it may seem complex, practitioners work and succeed within this terrain all the time. Indeed, during a career, a great deal of professional fulfilment is derived from exploring the issues which the framework highlights.

The contemporary challenge is to identify this expertise more explicitly and to find ways of representing it more clearly. If this can be done, the profession may become more self-confident as well as more effective. The public may become even more appreciative of the skills, knowledge, understanding and moral commitment which all educators embody.

## Key readings

Many of the readings suggested for Chapter 3 on reflective practice are very relevant for this chapter, including, for example, Schon (**Reading 3.5**). Readings for Chapter 4, on the principles of effective teaching and learning, are also highly pertinent to the enduring issues which have been identified.

Developmental accounts of how expertise evolves through the interaction of practice and analysis are provided by:

> Eraut, M. (1994) *Developing Professional Knowledge and Competence*. London: Routledge.
>
> Flook, J., Ryan, M. and Hawkins, L. (2010) *Professional Expertise: Practice, Theory and Education for Working in Uncertainty*. London: Whiting and Birch.

Two books which analyse and apply teacher expertise in primary school contexts are:

> Eaude, T. (2012) *How Do Expert Primary Classteachers Really Work? A Critical Guide for Teachers, Headteachers and Teacher Educators*. Northwich: Critical Publishing.
>
> Sangster, M. (2012) *Developing Teacher Expertise: Exploring Key Issues in Primary Practice*. London: Bloomsbury Academic.

For early years practitioner expertise, see:

> Anning, A. and Edwards, A. (2006) *Promoting Learning from Birth to Five: Developing Professional Practice in the Pre-school*. 2nd edn. Buckingham: Open University Press.
>
> Osgood, J. (2012) *Narratives from the Nursery: Negotiating Professional Identities in Early Childhood*. London: Routledge.

Tony's case is adapted from Hodkinson et al. (2007). It is available, with much more, from **tlrp.org/proj/phase111/biesta.htm**. An accessible book of the project is: Biesta, Field, Goodson, Hodkinson and Macleod (2010). A comprehensive case for lifelong learning has been made by Schuller and Watson (2009).

The Deepening Expertise section of **reflectiveteaching.co.uk** also offers useful links to a rich range of internet resources.

For an excellent guide to the use of the internet for education, see:

> Houghton, E. (ed.) (2012) *Education on the Web: A Tool-kit to Help You Search Effectively for Information on Education*. Slough: NFER.

The associated website, **reflectiveteaching.co.uk**, offers a wealth of supplementary resources including reflective activities, research briefings, advice on further reading and downloadable diagrams, figures and checklists from the book. It also features a compendium of educational terms, links to useful websites, policy and curriculum documents, and showcases examples of excellent research and practice.

# Professionalism
## How does reflective teaching contribute to society?

**17**

## 3 Early years teaching and society: The practitioner role (p. 394)

**3.1** Working with a moral purpose (p. 394)

**3.2** Working with early years curriculum frameworks (p. 394)

**3.3** Early years professionalism (p. 395)

**3.4** What practical approaches can be taken? (p. 395)

## 4 Reflective early years practice and the democratic process (p. 397)

**4.1** Demystifying the democratic process (p. 398)

**4.2** Identifying decision-makers (p. 398)

**4.3** Preparing the case (p. 398)

**4.4** Forming alliances (p. 399)

**4.5** Managing the media (p. 399)

**4.6** Lobbying decision-makers (p. 400)

**4.7** Current campaigns (p. 400)

**4.8** Campaigning organizations in the ECEC sector (p. 400)

## Conclusion (p. 401)

## Introduction

There are four sections to this chapter. The first considers professionalism as applicable to ECEC, which is characterized by diversity in types of provision and in the qualifications and career paths of practitioners. We outline a model of 'restricted' and 'extended' professionalism, and highlight some of the wider concerns that an extended professional may consider. We draw attention to a range of professional associations in the sector, relevant for practitioners in maintained and non-maintained contexts. The second section considers matters of theory and practice relating to the wider issues of ECEC and society, with the third section linking this to early years pedagogy. The fourth section looks at the actions that a reflective practitioner could take as a citizen in trying to influence democratic processes of decision-making, including at the level of local, regional and national government. We argue for the important and empowering role of reflective practitioners working in this phase of early education to promote the sector itself, underpinned by a broad and strong ethical commitment to equity and social justice.

> ## TLRP principles
>
> **The following principles are of particular relevance to this chapter on professionalism:**
>
> **Principle 1: Effective teaching and learning equips learners for life in its broadest sense.** Learning should aim to help people to develop the intellectual, personal and social resources that will enable them to participate as active citizens, contribute to economic development and flourish as individuals in a diverse and changing society. This implies adopting a broad view of learning outcomes and ensuring that equity and social justice are taken seriously.
>
> **Principle 7: Effective teaching and learning fosters both individual and social processes and outcomes.** Learning is a social activity. Learners should be encouraged and helped to work with others, to share ideas and build knowledge together. Consulting learners about their learning and giving them a voice is both an expectation and a right.
>
> **Principle 10: Effective teaching and learning demands consistent policy frameworks with support for teaching and learning as their primary focus.** Policies at national, local and institutional levels need to recognize the fundamental importance of teaching and learning. They should be designed to create effective learning environments in which all learners can thrive.

# 1 Professionalism and society

## 1.1 Professionalism in the ECEC sector

The public regard for an area of work, and the esteem with which it is held, has a powerful impact on the relationship of that sector to professionalism. Discussion of professionalism in ECEC is affected by culture-specific beliefs about early childhood, parenting and mothering. In the UK, childcare is overwhelmingly seen as women's work, which is reflected in the female-dominated composition of the ECEC workforce; the percentage of men working in the non-statutory sector remains at about 2 per cent (Nutbrown, **Reading 17.1**)

The non-statutory sector is characterized by low levels of formal qualifications, and wages are considerably lower than in the maintained education sector. Combined with a view of the care of very young children as largely practical, and an enduring distinction between education and care professions, the early years sector – particularly those working in contexts other than schools – has a problematic relationship with the public perception of professionalism.

A profession implies 'a group of people who work in a defined way and for an explicit purpose' (Whalley, 2008: 140). The term 'professional' is often linked to a path of accredited training within a field, giving access to specific languages and practices, which clearly includes or excludes those with or without the training. The training paths in ECEC are complex and changing, as identified by Tickell (2012) and Nutbrown (2012, 2013).

Maintained school-based early years classes and stand-alone nursery schools have, to date, been staffed by qualified teachers and nursery nurses drawing on a model of complementary expertise and training with distinct but clear career routes and traditions. To date, early years teachers have been part of the main teaching body, with a well-established identity as a profession, the same route to QTS via an initial degree or postgraduate qualification, the same pay and conditions, a shared language, career opportunities, specific trade unions or professional associations and the shared purpose of raising the educational standards of children, whatever their age group.

Although nursery nurses in maintained schools receive less favourable pay and conditions and are less likely to be part of a professional association or trade union than teachers, qualified nursery nurses have traditionally been employed as part of the early years nursery team. Although superseded by vocational Level 3 qualification pathways during the last 20 years, the Nursery Nursing Examination Board nursery nurse training is still regarded by many as the 'gold standard' nursery nursing qualification. This college-based, full-time two-year training was comprehensive, covering all aspects of children's physical and cognitive development from birth. The professional nursery nurse qualification was highly regarded within the sector and gave practitioners access to a complementary professional body, with a shared professional language. The replacement of the NNEB by vocational childcare training coincided with government funding for early education in the private, voluntary and independent sectors. There was no requirement for these settings to employ qualified teachers, and the Level 3 requirement, which applied to the manager or supervisor of the setting, could be achieved via a vocational route.

Nutbrown's extensive review of qualifications and training (2012) responded to long-standing concerns about the 'competence' model of initial training. Vocational qualifications had been extensively critiqued for prioritizing imitation and performance over understanding and theoretical awareness, with an emphasis on 'looking the part'. Nutbrown acknowledged widespread agreement that the turn away from taught, college-based initial training towards competence-based vocational qualifications had severely reduced the opportunities for students to access the concepts, language and dialogue necessary for reflective practice. Nutbrown's call for renewed academic rigour in initial training for early years practitioners raised enduring issues linked to the public perception of the ECEC sector.

> ## Expert question
>
> **Breadth:** Does the curriculum represent society's educational aspirations for its citizens? Does it support children to develop secure curious dispositions?
>
> This question contributes to a conceptual framework representing enduring issues and practitioner expertise (see Chapter 16).

## Reflective activity 17.1

*Aim:* To reflect upon the role of the early years practitioner and the need for specialist training.

*Evidence and reflection:* Take some time to think about the following:

It has been argued that the role of the childcare practitioner is largely based on personal qualities, such as empathy with children, which are unrelated to qualifications and training. To what extent is this true? How does this relate to assumptions about the gender and social class of the workforce? What current campaigns are you aware of to counteract these assumptions? How does this relate to the potential removal of qualified teacher status requirements in schools? What parallels may be made with other sectors and professions?

*Extension:* Discuss your thoughts with a colleague.

# 1.2 Graduate qualifications: Early Years Professionals and Early Years Teachers

The early years Foundation Stage in England, introduced in 2000, promoted the use of the term 'practitioner'. The term was applied to all workers in the sector, regardless of qualifications. The EPPE research report (Siraj-Blatchford et al., 2004) highlighted a correlation between high staff qualifications, high-quality educational provision and enduring cognitive benefits for children. The government-backed Children's Workforce Development Council (CWDC) launched the graduate-level Early Years Professional Status accreditation route in 2007. The Status was awarded once a number of standards were met, which included elements of practice and leadership across the full age-range from birth to 5, as well as a standard on reflective practice. These Early Years Professionals were identified by the government and CWDC as early years leaders, and money was made available for local networks. However, the promised publicity campaigns to inform parents and the wider community about the status failed to materialize and the term EYP remains only partially understood even within the sector.

The Coalition government dissolved the CWDC in 2012. Responsibility for graduate-level early years qualifications was given to the National College for Teaching and Leadership, who currently lead the Early Years Teacher initiative. This award does not give practitioners Qualified Teacher Status. The validity of the award in maintained schools is unclear. In the current context of ECEC in the private, voluntary and independent sector and the growth of academies and free schools in the maintained sector, there are threats to pay and conditions of all practitioners, including those with graduate qualifications and qualified teachers.

The use of the term 'professional' as related to the ECEC sector is, then, complex. However, we assume that the reader of this book will regard themselves as a professional, taking an ethical and moral stance towards the role and working to raise the public awareness of their vital work as educators, carers and advocates for the sector.

The following chapter discusses in more detail how professionals in the sector can develop as individuals and as a community to engage with the wider context of the work of the early years sector and how it relates to society, locally, nationally and internationally.

## 1.3 Restricted and extended professionalism

Many writers on early years practice and leadership have called for engagement in the wider socio-political context as an integral part of the role of an ethical early years professional (see for example Whalley, 2008). Rodd has written about the persistence of a limited model of professional leadership internationally, with a reluctance to look to a broad conceptualization of the professional role (2006). However, the extensive changes and threats to many long-established principles and practices within early years may be reawakening a feeling among practitioners that 'when you become a nursery teacher you also become a campaigner – the two roles go together' (Edgington, 2004: 236; see also Archer, Reading 17.2).

The wider role of a professional is explored further through the model of 'restricted' or 'extended' teacher professionalism suggested by Hoyle. His definitions take individual professionalism as assumed, but move beyond this to the wider context, where an individual is situated in a collaborative context. Particular account is taken of the moral purpose of the work, to a high level of commitment, responsibility and collective accountability. His definitions are as follows:

> *Restricted professionalism* describes the competence underpinning core effectiveness. Skills and perspectives are derived from immediate experience; and workplace learning occurs gradually, but largely passively. Consideration of teaching methods tends to be private and personal autonomy may be protected. Reading of professional literature or involvement in professional development activity is infrequent.

> *Extended professionalism* envisages that skills and understanding are developed from the interaction of practical experience and analysis, including theory; there is an awareness of social, economic and political contexts which impinge on education; and workplace events are considered in relation to policies and overall educational purposes. Teaching methods are shared with colleagues and reviewed in terms of research-informed principles. High value is placed on professional collaboration and on networking in sectoral or subject associations. Pedagogic repertoire and subject knowledge are kept up to date in active, committed and open-minded ways. (Hoyle, 2005)

The reflective early years practitioner, as defined in this book and linked materials, is envisaged as an extended professional. The following sections suggest ways that this can be applied and embedded within the ECEC sector.

> ## Reflective activity 17.2
>
> *Aim:* To consider the features of a professional practitioner.
>
> *Evidence and reflection:* Consider an ECEC practitioner you currently work with, or who you have worked with in the past, who you consider to be an inspirational professional. What characteristics do they have?
>
> *Extension:* How does this colleague link with other professionals, within the setting and beyond? How do they work as an advocate for the ECEC sector?

# 1.4 Professional and union organizations within ECEC

It is our firm belief that professional collaboration, networking, a wider contextual awareness of ECEC and a role as campaigner and advocate for the sector are features of an extended professional awareness. The following organizations, listed in alphabetical order, provide excellent information and opportunities for these qualities and activities to be developed.

## Early Education (British Association for Early Childhood Education)

This association grew from the National Society of Day Nurseries, founded early in the last century. The roots in the maintained sector continue, although all practitioners are welcome. It runs local branches, run and managed by volunteers, has a core London-based staff and associated trainers and consultants, and publishes a range of books and pamphlets. Early Education published the influential Development Matters document.

## Daycare Trust

A national childcare campaigning charity with a high-profile presence at national events. Its main remit is 'to promote high quality, affordable childcare'.

## National Day Nurseries Association

An active, sector-led organisation with its roots in the private daycare sector. The NDNA provides a range of accredited training, holds local branch meetings and national conferences. It has been very active in campaigning against proposed changes to ratios, and has an active online community.

## National Association of Schoolmasters Union of Women Teachers (NASUWT)

A long-established TUC-affiliated union for teachers.

## National Union of Teachers (NUT)

The largest TUC-affiliated union for teachers and related education professionals.

## Pre-School Learning Alliance

A leading, national charity supporting and campaigning for the voluntary pre-school movement. It provides training, a wealth of materials and locally based support for committee-run pre-school groups.

## Professional Association for Childcare and Early Years (PACEY)

This organisation developed from the National Childminding Association, and provides training and materials, a presence at conferences and a campaigning voice. Membership includes childminders, nannies and nursery workers.

## The Association of Professionals in Education and Children's Trusts (Aspect)

A TUC-affiliated professional organisation. Membership includes staff in maintained and non-maintained settings. The organisation has a specific section for Early Years Professionals.

## UNISON

The largest union for those other than teachers working in education in the UK. UNISON is TUC affiliated.

## 2 How early childhood education and care relates to society

The role of early years practitioners within schools and settings is shaped by the context in which they work. The setting or school is 'nested' within a broader community and locality, which are themselves seen as part of a wider national and international picture, in a way similar to Bronfenbrenner's ecological model of the child (Bronfenbrenner, 1979). (See Chapter 8.)

In many parts of this book we have considered the internal workings of early years settings and schools with occasional references to the social, economic, cultural and political contexts within which they are located. While this may be a necessary bias for a practice-oriented book, as identified above a reflective early years practitioner with an extended outlook will be aware of the ways in which educational processes are influenced by, and contribute to, wider social forces, processes and relationships.

In earlier chapters we introduced the idea of social development being based on a dialectical process, as individuals respond to and act within the situations in which they find themselves. Actions in the present are thus influenced by the past, but they also contribute to new social arrangements for the future. All practitioners, as professionals and as individual citizens, are members of society and we hope that reflective early years professionals will be well placed to act in society to foster morally and ethically sound developments.

This section discusses the relationship between ECEC and society with reference to the theoretical framework referred to in earlier chapters. This can be broadly characterized as a socio-constructivist perspective. We explore how ECEC relates to the social, economic, cultural and political context within which it is located, how it is influenced by these contexts and how it may contribute to wider social forces, processes and relationships.

## 2.1 The role of early childhood education and care in society

Two major questions or assumptions inform our understanding of the current and possible roles of early education in society. The first considers the policymakers' perspective, asking: 'What is it hoped that an early childhood education and care system will do?' The second considers the work in practice, considering: 'What can actually be achieved through early childhood education and care?' We will address these in turn and draw out the implications for reflective and professional practitioners. Where the discussion refers only to statutory or non-statutory elements of the sector, this will be made clear.

Young children and their families in the UK are accessing non-statutory pre-school early education and childcare for longer periods than at any time in the past. Globally, the extent of government funding for the education of young children prior to statutory school age varies enormously (Economist Intelligence Unit, 2012). The high state funding of ECEC in Nordic countries stands at one end of the spectrum. Funding in most countries in the cohort is through a combination of private and public funding of varying proportions. In some countries, such as South Africa and China, there is a limited state role. These statistics sit alongside globally varied pictures of variations in statutory school age, and of access to education itself.

Despite this disparity, there is a growing international consensus by policymakers, educationalists and campaigners on the potential contribution of ECEC to global development (Economist Intelligence Unit, 2012; UNICEF, 2013; Gammage, 2008).

We have identified three broad areas which have shaped debate in the past and that remain at the heart of contemporary discussion and policy on ECEC. These are:

- Economic benefits
- Cultural benefits
- The enhancement of individual rights

Each section will consider in turn how the ECEC provision is seen by policymakers as benefiting:

- babies and young children
- adults

# Benefits to the economy

This section discusses the perceived economic benefits of ECEC. We consider how these are felt to impact on the lives of children and adults, and refer to selected international examples to contextualize the arguments.

The perceived impact to the economy of children who have received ECEC is generally discussed as having wealth-creating and money-saving elements. Commentators focus on:

- the increased likelihood that these children will attain high educational standards and are prepared for employment, forming a productive, wealth-creating and adaptable workforce.
- the potential money saved on interventions later in the children's lives, summarized as 'cost benefit analysis of investment' (Pascal and Bertram, 2013: 26).

A summary of these economic benefits, with further research links, is given by UNICEF (2013).

For parents, and for women in particular, ECEC is seen as enabling them to enter or re-enter the paid workforce. This is seen as positive, in that it:

- retains and broadens the skills of the workforce.
- increases the numbers of those available for paid work.
- reduces the need for welfare benefits.

These arguments continue to be prominent in policy and debate in England. Related research and critical perspectives on these assertions as they relate to the economy will be considered here. The social and cultural implications will be discussed in the section below.

# 2.2 A highly educated future workforce

An important part of the argument for the establishment of an elementary school system in Britain was that it should provide a workforce which was more skilled and thus more economically productive. The idea became the linchpin of 'human capital' theory from the 1960s (Schultz, 1971). Influenced by models such as Rostow's *The Stages of Economic Growth* (1962), governments have continued to highlight a link between education systems and economic prosperity.

The link between pre-school education and future education and employment is a flourishing area of policy and research. In England, the influential EPPE and EPPSE research reported the enduring and significant positive effect of high-quality pre-school provision on future educational attainment (Sylva et al., 2012).

International data comparisons in educational attainment and standards are key indicators used by governments and other stakeholders to shape the strategic direction of policy. Where unfavourable comparisons are made with other countries, policymakers and governments are increasingly scrutinizing the ECEC alongside other phases of education.

---

### Reflective activity 17.3

*Aim:* To reflect upon data used to inform ECEC policy, how this is arrived at and what it shows.

*Evidence and reflection:* Locate a table of data related to ECEC and critically reflect on what it shows. How has the data been arrived at? What factors may not have been taken into consideration?

*Extension:* Access articles and blogs commenting on the above – for example, Pascal and Bertram, 2013; See link at **reflectiveteaching.co.uk**.

---

In recent years two elements have been a particular focus and have shaped early years education policy. These have been the overall standards of achievement by children, particularly in literacy, mathematics and ICT, and the gap between the highest and lowest achievers.

Earlier chapters have discussed the debates surrounding appropriate and effective teaching and learning of early literacy, particularly the politically charged and contested area of early reading and phonics (Evangelou, 2009). International comparisons are regularly cited which draw attention to the paradox whereby the UK has an early introduction to compulsory schooling but a lower standard of literacy among the older pupil population.

---

### Reflective activity 17.4

*Aim:* To consider the teaching of reading.

*Evidence and reflection:* Fierce debate continues on the appropriate start to the teaching of reading. In England it has been placed as a 'specific' area of learning within the 'literacy' area of learning in the EYFS. This is in recognition of the need for an earlier focus on children's Communication and Language. The placing does, however, sit alongside a phonics test introduced for children in Year 1 in 2012, and the Teachers' Standards requirements for a particular approach, where 'if teaching early reading, [teachers must] demonstrate a clear understanding of systematic synthetic phonics' (education.gov.uk).

Critics of the synthetic phonics approach, including previous Children's Laureate Michael Rosen, firmly contest the validity of the focus on this sole approach to reading (**michaelrosenblog.blogspot.co.uk**).

Reflect on the emotive language used by both advocates and opponents of synthetic phonics. Why and how has this debate become politically charged?

---

## 2.3 A highly educated future workforce throughout society

International data tables also raise questions about the consistency of educational standards across the population. A pattern of equitable attainment without marked differences between groups of children is associated with a society's economic prosperity, as well as with high indicators of wellbeing.

In the UK there has been concern among educationalists, politicians and policymakers about the wide spread of educational attainment within the population, and in particular the very strong links between family income and educational achievement. The report by Frank Field (2010) argued clearly for the powerful role of ECEC in addressing this problem:

> By the age of three, a baby's brain is 80% formed and his or her experiences before then shape the way the brain has grown and developed. That is not to say, of course, it is all over by then, but ability profiles at that age are highly predictive of profiles at school entry. By school age, there are very wide variations in children's abilities and the evidence is clear that children from poorer backgrounds do worse cognitively and behaviourally than those from more affluent homes. Schools do not effectively close that gap; children who arrive in the bottom range of ability tend to stay there. (2010: 5)

Field firmly argues that very early intervention should be put into place in the years prior to statutory school age in the UK. Both the Field and Allen reports (2011; see Field, Reading 17.3) link the educational attainment of children with their future potential as employees.

> It is (early intervention) which offers the prospect of preventing poor children from becoming poor adults. The evidence about the importance of the pre-school years to children's life chances as adults points strongly to an alternative approach that focuses on directing government policy and spending to developing children's capabilities in the early years. A shift of focus is needed towards providing high quality, integrated services aimed at supporting parents and improving the abilities of our poorest children during the period when it is most effective to do so. Their prospects of going on to gain better qualifications and sustainable employment will be greatly enhanced. The aim is to change the distribution of income by changing the position which children from poor backgrounds will be able to gain on merit in the income hierarchy. (Field, 2010: 6).

The Early Years section of the National Strategy reported to the government on the impact of a number of pioneering teaching and learning initiatives on reducing attainment differences, looking in detail at vulnerable groups of children who achieved a lower level than average in the national Early Years Foundation Stage Profile. Although the National Strategies were disbanded in 2011, maintained schools and funded settings in England have a statutory duty to report outcomes of the Profile, and to scrutinize this data as evidence of how vulnerable groups of children achieve in the early years, with regard to pupil characteristics such as gender, ethnicity, free school meal eligibility, SEN and English as an additional language.

## 2.4 A wealth-generating, adaptable future workforce

Alongside well-established educational objectives, the impact of new technologies and innovations raises continual questions about the skills and knowledge required by future workers. Research into brain development in babies and very young children has provided a wealth of evidence that early experiences and relationships play a significant role in shaping the intellectual capacities of the brain, along with genetic factors (Gammage, 2008). A future workforce is likely to be required to be highly adaptable and flexible, and open to new ways of thinking and working. It is suggested that a style of pedagogy in early childhood that prioritizes process-based approaches is best suited to developing 'life skills' and a readiness for the future changing world (Pascal and Bertram, 2013; Stewart, 2011).

The emphasis on 'being' as well as 'becoming' is echoed in a number of international early years curriculum frameworks, as discussed in earlier chapters. The English Early Years Foundation Stage upholds many principles found in international guidance documents, and has a particular emphasis on the 'characteristics of effective early learning', which includes the requirement for practitioners to provide opportunities to observe children 'playing and exploring, being active learners and creating and thinking critically' (DfE, 2012).

## 2.5 Economic benefits of ECEC: Cost benefits and reductions in later educational and social intervention

Increasing research evidence supports the claims of positive and long-standing educational and social benefits of early educational intervention. This clearly appeals to politicians. Allen cites Barack Obama:

> What you see consistently are children at a very early age starting school already behind. That's why I've said that I'm going to put billions of dollars into early childhood education … Every dollar that we spend in early childhood education, we get $10 back in reduced dropout rates, improved reading scores. That's the kind of commitment we have to make early on. (cited in Allen, 2011: 24)

A particularly compelling and profound impact of early intervention has been linked to reduced criminality, which has clear economic as well as social benefits (Allen, 2011; HighScope cited in Gammage, 2008). Pascal and Bertram (2013) provide a detailed review of effective early intervention programmes.

Gammage and others have discussed the potential difficulty in verifying outcomes of publicly funded early intervention projects, and the potential tendency to structure projects in a way that lends them to more readily evaluated data. Small-scale qualitative case study evaluations are published in journals and accessible online via organizations such as Pen Green and the Early Childhood Unit of the National Children's Bureau.

---

**Reflective activity 17.5**

*Aim:* To consider ways of evaluating projects in ECEC.

*Evidence and reflection:* Consider a project involving early communication interventions with a child and their family. How is this being evaluated? What quantitative and qualitative measures are being taken?

*Extension:* Locate similar projects, for example via Pen Green, NCB, the Communication Trust, the National Literacy Trust.

---

## 2.6 Economic benefits of ECEC for adults: Facilitating greater female participation in the workforce

The perceived economic benefits of ECEC for parents, particularly women, should be read in conjunction with the section below, which considers feminist perspectives and the implications for human rights and social justice. The entry of women into the labour market is seen internationally as an indicator of economic development and sustainability. For OECD countries the female workforce is seen as an integral part of 'welfare to work' policies, although the nature of the employment has been critiqued (Kenway, 2008).

Of the most affluent OECD countries, Sweden and the Nordic countries are frequently cited as having particularly high rates of female employment. The link between ECEC provision and the possibilities this gives to women to enter or retain paid work has been a cornerstone of policy in the UK for the last 20 years, allied to the Sure Start initiative. In many cases the opportunities this has given for women and for communities to rejuvenate and enrich their lives have been profound and positive.

---

**Case study 17.1 Pen Green Nursery and Children's Centre**

The Pen Green Nursery and Children's Centre now has an international reputation for excellence in the provision for care and learning and is a leading centre for sector-led research. The centre has always worked with the local community, and has pioneered ways of working with parents. Testimonies from individual mothers – and fathers – have regularly been included in accounts of practice at conferences and seminars, and are generously available online and in a range of publications [pengreen.org].

---

Critical analysis of the perceived economic benefits of women's paid employment in more affluent countries has scrutinized the type of work undertaken by low-paid women, which has often been characterized by poor conditions and long hours. Critics note that mothers in these circumstances often face more challenges to their parenting, and are less likely to be able to follow parenting advice that Ofsted and others expect to be given by ECEC settings, particularly those linked with the Sure Start programme (Ball and Vincent, 2005).

The needs of babies and very young children have been highlighted by advances in scientific research on the brain. Physiological evidence of the reactions of the brain to stress encountered during sessions at some daycare settings has problematized young children's attendance at ECEC. The work of Gerhardt on attachment has been particularly influential here (Gerhardt, 2004). The psychological effects on babies and young children of ECEC placements, how they relate to the need for attachment and consistency and how this has influenced the key person system are discussed in Chapter 6.

# 2.7 Cultural benefits

Alongside the relationship of ECEC to economic conditions of societies comes a debate on the way that it relates to the wider culture. Questions concern the reproduction and production of the values of society, as they relate to the lived experience of children, families and practitioners within the system of ECEC. For the purpose of this section, cultural reproduction will be taken to mean the continuation of existing – usually dominant – values and mores of a society, often defined by governments and policymakers. Cultural production will refer to the creation of new values and patterns of living, possibly by the combining of several distinct cultures.

There is an established literature exploring sociological perspectives on education in relation to statutory schooling and education systems, as detailed in Pollard et al. (2008). Within the non-statutory early years sector, analysis has focused on projects such as the Sure Start initiative in England and the *Every Child Matters* agenda. The role of the reflective practitioner will be considered further in section 3 below.

# 2.8 The child in society

Bronfenbrenner's model places ECEC in a continually interactive relationship with the child, 'nested' within the relationships of family and community. The complex interplay between the cultures and values surrounding the child, and the child's active role in constructing and co-constructing their beliefs, is highlighted by some national early years curriculum frameworks, in particular that of New Zealand.

The following themes are highlighted as key features of the values prioritized by international non-governmental organizations, such as the United Nations.

## Community cohesion

The ethical and moral values of citizenship and community cohesion resonate with the UN Declaration of Human Rights and Rights of the Child. Concern for shared values, feelings of togetherness and belonging, and concern for similarities as well as respect for differences are long-established themes in early childhood education and in young children's literature. Indeed, a focus on attachment and key persons, as detailed in Chapter 6 cited above, are highly compatible with these themes.

Materials produced by international organizations such as Oxfam and UNICEF as well as those published by independent UK consultancies and Department of Education materials on related themes are readily available in the UK to support these areas of the curriculum. Further ways that the reflective practitioner can work practically to promote these themes are included in the section 3 of this chapter.

## National identity

The child's right to a national identity appears in Articles 7 and 8 of the UN Convention on the Rights of the Child. In many global contexts, the promotion of national identity in all contexts, and particularly with young children, is a very high priority, especially where the identity has been forged in the aftermath of war and conflict. Religion and language are often prime aspects of this identity. Organizations such as UNICEF and Oxfam as well as Amnesty International have valuable links and materials to support practitioners for whom this is relevant.

In England, the requirement of teachers to adhere to 'fundamental British values' is now specified in the Teaching Standards. This phrase is taken from the definition of extremism as articulated in the Coalition government's Prevent Strategy, which was launched in June 2011. It includes 'democracy, the rule of law, individual liberty and mutual respect and tolerance of different faiths and beliefs' (DfE Teachers Standards, 2012).

Articles 12 and 29 of the UN Convention on the Rights of the Child are especially relevant here. In particular, with reference to Article 12, many reflective practitioners in ECEC settings have embraced a 'listening pedagogy', where the voices of children are sought and valued, and where 'Every child has the right to say what they think in all matters affecting them, and to have their views taken seriously'.

Definitions of nationality, where culture is linked to patterns of everyday family life and shared experiences including the media, and awareness of the 'canon' of literature, including children's literature, are further 'hidden' elements that can work to include or exclude children and families from a setting or community. These powerful but implicit elements of everyday culture should be considered carefully by the reflective practitioner, ensuring that children and families are included rather than excluded.

### Reflective activity 17.6

*Aim:* To consider and reflect on practical ways that you hope to develop respect and tolerance for others in your early years context.

*Evidence and reflection:* Article 29 of the UN Convention on the Rights of the Child calls for mutual respect and tolerance of different faiths and beliefs. Collate examples from your own setting where practitioners have planned activities and interventions which encourage children to respect their own and other cultures, and to accept and value diverse identities within the one setting. Which activities and approaches have been successful? How can you tell?

*Extension/follow up:* How can all practitioners at your setting develop their awareness of this aspect of practice?

Further discussion of practical strategies are included in section 3 below.

## Regional and national identity

The above points as discussed from the children's perspective are also relevant to the extended adult community linked to ECEC settings. From adult perspectives, the maintenance of established but threatened regional and national identities may be a fundamental aim of ECEC. For example, traditional regional celebrations, foods and dialects may be highly valued at the setting. The people of Wales preserve an important part of their culture through the teaching of Welsh in schools.

## Parenting

The ECEC setting may be central in a community as a source of advice on parenting. Societal and cultural expectations about child-rearing will be clearly relayed in these instances, particularly where informal networks of families or neighbourhoods are missing or inaccessible to certain families.

The Sure Start initiative in England formalized the role of many settings as sources of parenting advice, with this role expected to continue as outlined in the 2013 Ofsted Evaluation Schedule (Ofsted, 2013).

For many families, an early education setting is the site of the first enduring involvement with a formally organized group outside the family. The setting will hold and promote strong cultural expectations and norms, both explicitly and implicitly. For some families, this is a threatening and uneasy context. They may face prejudice from other families attending the setting, and may feel threatened by norms of child-rearing which are not compatible with their own views and practices. Reflective practitioners have a duty to recognize these tensions and support all families to feel included and valued by the setting.

## 2.9 Cultural production

International thinkers within the ECEC field have argued that early education is a potentially powerful site of socio-cultural production and meaning-making. When given conditions for creativity to flourish, children give meaning to the world as they interact with other children, practitioners and the environment. The ECEC setting can enable adults to encounter new people and create new ideas, as seen on the Pen Green website.

For many early educationalists inspired by pioneering thinkers and movements such as the Reggio Emilia nurseries in Italy, children's early years are viewed as a time of flourishing creativity, when children should have the opportunities to express themselves in a 'hundred languages'. Practice that celebrates and documents children's cultural creativity is shared on a number of national and international websites, including one based in Reggio Emilia itself (reggiochildren.it).

## New cultural identities

Some settings will be working in areas of conflict and tension. In many cases harmonious relationships have been forged when families come together to support the children, as seen in Northern Ireland. For some families, such as asylum seekers and refugees, the ECEC setting will be a core source of induction into a new community, and plays a vital role in the development of social cohesion with the wider network of adults as well as the children.

## New international identities

The UN Declaration of Human Rights is the key foundation practice here, both stated and implied, with many resources available to support the principles such as those produced by UNESCO and NGOs working to support international development projects

## 2.10 Cultural resistance and challenge

Several dominant economic and cultural structures within society are placed sharply in focus in the ECEC sector across all countries, in particular socio-economic factors, sometimes linked to cultural groups and the inclusion of people with additional needs.

In common with all sectors in education, ECEC systems are located within existing power structures and socio-economic conditions. The picture of government funding varies internationally, but the non-statutory early education sector is always funded at least partially, and in some cases almost entirely, by private investment and business. In many cases the access to ECEC is very limited and is only affordable by affluent families, with others excluded (*Economist,* 2012). The perception is that this phase of education and care is not appropriate for all families and children, and is only for an elite. Alongside financial exclusion, in many countries ECEC is associated with particular cultural, religious or ethnic groups. In this way Aboriginal people in Australia have limited access to ECEC (Gammage, 2008). Children and families affected by disability and other forms of special needs often face numerous factors that restrict full access to ECEC prior to statutory school age, which continue for many into later phases of education.

As mentioned above, the workforce in ECEC is overwhelmingly female. Dominant cultural assumptions about gender roles in relation to the care and education of young children are perpetuated by this workforce composition.

## 2.11 ECEC and social justice

Many providers of ECEC, and many practitioners working in the sector, are aware of these factors and others, have a firm and explicit moral purpose to work for social justice, and prioritize an inclusive agenda and pedagogy as a core aim. For the purpose of this overview we will highlight two broad definitions from the sociology of education and consider and how reflective practitioners in ECEC can work creatively on both levels to effect meaningful change.

Definitions of social justice can place particular emphasis on the individual level or on the wider socio-cultural structures. In this way:

- Social justice is concerned with promoting individual human rights and the rights of the child to personal, social and educational fulfilment.
- Social justice is concerned with challenging existing structures of society.

An international commitment to human rights has informed ECEC for many years. A very clear exposition of these issues is contained in the Universal Declaration of Human Rights (United Nations, 1948). Article 1 of the Declaration states that:

All human beings are born free and equal in dignity and rights. They are endowed with reason and conscience.

These rights are to be enjoyed, according to Article 2:

… without distinction of any kind, such as race, colour, sex, language, religion, political or other opinion, national or social origin, property, birth or other status.

Article 26 deals with education and asserts that:

Education shall be directed to the full development of the human personality and the strengthening of respect for human rights and fundamental freedoms. It shall promote understanding, tolerance and friendship among all nations, racial and religious groups.

As discussed above, the UN Convention on the Rights of the Child is used highly effectively in educational contexts and is referenced in a range of documentation and materials, as well as being promoted extensively by UNICEF.

International comparative data of population access to ECEC draws attention to global disparities in sufficiency, affordability and cultural norms (Economic Intelligence Unit, 2012). Sufficiency raising access to ECEC was given high priority in England from the start of the government funding scheme under New Labour in the 1990s. The increasing evidence of the impact of early intervention in countering the attainment gap in educational attainment across the socio-economic spectrum reinforced the initial push for sufficient places to be available in all parts of the country, including less affluent areas. This agenda has been given a high priority by Ofsted, whose commissioned research paper within the Access and Achievement review looked in more detail at the impact of specific programmes, moving beyond the sufficiency agenda and taking account of the long-standing call for quality in the early years to be given more attention (Pascal and Bertram, 2013).

## 2.12 Feminist perspectives: Women's rights and ECEC

The international women's movement has a well-established history of calling for accessible, affordable daycare to enable mothers to access education and paid work. Earlier feminist critiques of women's unpaid and often unrecognized labour in the home can be drawn on to remind us that data on ECEC across the globe excludes informal and family-based childcare networks (*Economist*, 2012).

The dynamics of socio-economic status, whereby women are employed by other women as childcarers, are complex and potentially divisive. Some childcare practitioners in a study on daycare in England expressed feelings of childcarers that they were placed in an inferior social position in relation to the working parents of the children:

> You feel a bit like a servant … you 'just look after the children' whilst they pursue their career. (Szanto, 2003: 38)

A concern for social justice through the highly gendered sector of ECEC needs to take the sensitivities of relationships between different groups of women seriously, and question assumed roles, if all are to benefit.

## 2.13 Social justice as a challenge to existing structures of society

There is, of course, a long tradition of writing on radical and politically active education. The work of Brazilian educator and activist Paulo Freire has inspired teachers and educationalists since the 1970s. Freire advocated an education for social justice (see Irwin, Reading 17.4), described as a 'pedagogy of the oppressed'. He argued that while individuals were potentially empowered through education, this was only meaningful when confronting the existing structural inequalities of wealth, status and power. He felt that if such issues were ignored then the promotion of social justice through education was very unlikely to be successful (Freire, 1996).

The UK ECEC sector draws inspiration from a powerful legacy of work by early socialists, anti-poverty campaigners and philanthropists (Gammage, 2008). Political activism embedded in ECEC continues to flourish in many traditional and non-traditional locations. The Pen Green Centre has worked over many years in a context of unemployment and economic hardship to become a centre for adult and community regeneration as well as for children's care and education, and is now a world-renowned education and training centre (Whalley, 2006).

Political oppression has been responded to by educationalists on other ways. For many early years educators, the founding father of the Reggio Emilia ethos, Loris Malaguzzi, has been an inspirational teacher. Devised as a response to Italian fascism, the approach explicitly promotes attention to children's individual voices, promoting original thought and free expression in an arts-based, community setting where adults work creatively alongside children. Malaguzzi and those who continue his work are clear of the specific context of their work, and call for individual interpretation (Rinaldi, 2006).

## 2.14 From vision to reality: What can realistically be achieved by ECEC?

So, how much can ECEC achieve? Can the vision of radical thinkers and of those with moral purpose effect meaningful change? Authors such as Bowles and Gintis, writing in the 1970s, argued that education could make little difference to the class structure of society, and that education should be seen as a part of the dominant social system which reproduced existing relations, rather than as an autonomous force within it (1976). Writers such as Petrie have suggested that although cultures and values might be altered and individuals may improve their economic circumstances, the 'socio-economic roots of poverty rest on economic structures that cannot be wholly remedied by education' (Petrie, 2003: 77).

Pascal and Bertram's more recent report notes the enduring patterns of low social mobility in the UK compared with other G20 nations, significant inequality of educational achievement and a wide gap in 'school readiness' found in the UK, which broadly echo patterns in income, social class and race (Pascal and Bertram, 2013; see Bertram and Pascal, Reading 17.5). Yet the intention of their report is to be 'realists but not defeatists'. The report goes on to detail programmes that have been shown to be particularly effective in countering socio-economic disadvantage.

Pascal and Bertram warn against limited ways of evaluating programmes, and call for value and impact to be noted in alternative ways, particularly where the work involves broader notions of social justice and reducing inequality. Many other educationalists and theorists argue that, since our sense of reality is socially constructed by people as they interact together, there is real scope for individuals to make an independent, powerful and profound impact on the course of future social development (Gammage, 2008). Examples of tangible developments where individuals, communities and wider societies have been proactively transformed through education are found throughout this series of books and linked materials.

The authors of this book firmly believe that there *is* potential for early education to influence change. We have discussed how ECEC is thought of by many policymakers and practitioners as well placed to develop society economically and culturally. However, we have recognized that major structural features of societies are extremely resistant to change. What is needed, then, is a theoretical position which recognizes the importance of action and of constraint. Such a position would accept that education has a degree of relative autonomy and would thus legitimate action by individuals to contribute to future social development.

A theoretical framework is provided by a dialectic model of the individual and society. As summarized by Berlak and Berlak, 'Conscious creative activity is limited by prevailing social arrangements, but human actions and institutional forms are not mere reflections of them' (1981: 121)

The clear implication is that people can make their own impact and history but must do so in whatever circumstances they find themselves. If this theoretical framework is adopted, social developments can be seen as the product of processes of struggle and contest between different individuals and groups in society. Such processes are ones in which ECEC must, inevitably, play a part.

Our answer to the question of what early years education can actually achieve must thus be based on a guarded and realistic optimism. The dialectical model of the influence of individuals and social structures recognizes constraints but asserts that action remains possible. This places a considerable responsibility on a reflective practitioner whose professional work is both shaped by, and contributes to, society.

## 3 Early years teaching and society: The practitioner role

## 3.1 Working with a moral purpose

In earlier chapters we raised this issue with the assertion that 'reflective teaching implies an active concern with aims and consequences as well as with technical efficiency', and we pick up the themes again here. One of the most important issues concerns the influence of a reflective practitioner's own value commitments, or moral purpose.

We believe that reflective practitioners should accept democratically determined decisions but should act both as responsible professionals and as autonomous citizens to contribute to such decision-making processes. We also suggest that attitudes of 'open-mindedness' and 'responsibility' are essential attributes. Open-mindedness involves a willingness to consider evidence and argument from whatever source it comes. It is thus the antithesis of closure and of habituated or ideological thinking. For example, we would suggest that there is a link between these attributes and the renewed emphasis on 'creating and thinking critically' in the Early Years Foundation Stage (2012).

## 3.2 Working with early years curriculum frameworks

The United Nations Declaration is accepted as a worldwide moral standard. Since 1998, the principles underlying these declarations have been incorporated into the UK's Human Rights Act. These are seen as being fundamental to democratic societies and all schools, including those for young children, are encouraged to introduce them to their pupils and to develop their understanding (Osler and Starkey, 2007). Europe-wide citizenship education for children of statutory school age is universal, although varied, as detailed in Eurydice, 2012 (eacea.ec.europa.eu/education/eurydice/index_en.php).

Appropriate broad principles and themes for children in early years contexts are integrated within national programmes: an outline of international curriculum frameworks for ECEC is found in earlier chapters. In the UK, the UN Convention on the Rights of the Child (1989), as highlighted earlier in this chapter, has set core principles for policy and practice in ECEC, including the *Every Child Matters* framework which has been influential across the range of statutory children's services, including health and social care (education.gov.uk).

Bowe and Ball with Gold (1992) argue that policy is not formed solely through political struggles and through the construction of legislation and official documents. Its operational reality is formed in the 'context of practice' – where it is often re-formulated and 'mediated' through the application of professional judgement (see Osborn, McNess, Broadfoot, Pollard and Triggs, 2000, see Reading 16.3). This is particularly relevant for English ECEC, where the emphasis could be seen as being on the unique child rather than on the child within a community. It will be for the practitioner to extend children's pro-social behaviour (Colwell, 2012).

## 3.3 Early years professionalism

Reflective practitioners are able to consider how their practice supports and develops the principles of ECEC in whatever context they are working. These include questions of individual dignity, equality and freedom, and the influence of sexism, racism and other forms of discrimination based on social class, age, disability or sexual orientation. These are issues upon which, we would argue, children have rights that socially responsible practitioners should not compromise. We take this to constitute a value commitment to the fundamental rights of citizens in a democratic society and a necessary underpinning for reflective professionalism. Reflective practitioners will adapt and enhance practice accordingly to ensure ethical practice forms the core of their work with children and families.

## 3.4 What practical approaches can be taken?

UNICEF and related organizations have developed curriculum materials that support themes which children will encounter later as citizenship, particularly focusing on the principles of 'justice, equality, freedom, peace, dignity, rights and democracy' (unicef.org.uk/Education).

The following sites detail practical, appropriate and robust ideas and best practice case studies to develop these themes with children. Many include ideas suitable for working with parents and the wider community.

### Listening, developing a voice and working together

A listening pedagogy and the 'Mosaic' approach: **ncb.org.uk/ycvn/resources/mosaic-approach**

The 'Listening to Young Children' resource and further related materials: literacytrust.org.uk/resources/external_resources/2276_listening_to_children. Working With Others: **workingwithothers.org.**

## Inclusion and anti-bias

Persona dolls: reducing social exclusion and anti-bias work: **persona-doll-training.org.** Special Educational Needs and inclusion: The Department of Education site holds an extensive archive of support materials, such as the Inclusion Development Programme, plus additional case studies: **webarchive.nationalarchives.gov.uk.**

## Support to counter disadvantage in early language and communication

The Communication Trust: an extensive website resource for practitioners and parents: **thecommunicationtrust.org.uk**

## Supporting parenting

National Children's Bureau materials to support work with parents, such as those focusing on literacy Home Learning Environment: **ncb.org.uk/areas-of-activity/early-childhood/ projects-and-programmes/making-it-real.**

Pen Green, sources through the Centre For Excellence in Outcomes for Children and Young People's Services (C4EO): pioneering and successful approaches to working with parents: **c4eo.org.uk/themes/earlyyears/vlpdetails.aspx?lpeid=414.**

## Working with other adults: modelling social justice within the workplace

Workplace relationships between adults in ECEC contexts have important resonance both for the individuals involved as well as the impact this has on the children attending the setting. Relationships are likely to vary according to a range of factors, particularly the ethos of the setting and the mode of leadership adopted by senior staff. Relationships may be characterized by a high level of agreement, shared approaches and mutual respect, arguably linked to the preference of women for collaborative and inclusive working models (Rodd, 2006; Siraj-Blatchford and Manni, 2007). However, the relationship between colleagues, such as teachers and nursery nurses in maintained schools, is set within a context of unequal pay and status. All must work to honestly and fairly address these differences, according to robust codes of conduct, supervision systems and ethical ways of working. Challenge to unfair or inappropriate treatment of an individual or team involves a high level of articulacy and critical dialogue within the team, and demands a high level of resilience by the practitioners involved and a readiness to articulate and communicate their views at all levels.

A number of consultancies can work with teams in practical ways to develop ethical and resilient workplace relationships. The *Working With Others* materials provide excellent practical ideas and ways of working to resolve conflict and embed a democratic approach (**workingwithothers.org**). For school-based staff, support can be drawn from mentors, school and local union representatives and professional associations.

## 4 Reflective early years practice and the democratic process

We suggest that, in addition to professional responsibilities to implement democratically determined decisions, early years practitioners as citizens also have a responsibility to act to influence the nature of such decisions. Practitioners have rights and it is perfectly reasonable that they should be active in contributing to the formation of public policy. In terms of Bowe, Ball and Gold's model (1992), this is about practitioner engagement in the 'context of influence'. The role, as Rodd (2006) suggests, is close to that of the activist and the methods to be utilized are those which have been well developed by a variety of pressure groups.

Writers in the field, such as Rodd, Whalley and Edgington, have called for those engaged with ECEC to become more politically engaged, as advocates for young children and for the sector itself. Successful and extensive lobbying and campaigns have been initiated by an increasing number of organizations and individuals in response to proposals and consultations by the Coalition government, often using social media.

Pressure-group activity and collective action by individuals can bring about new policy priorities and lead to a reappraisal of existing policies. This is an essential feature of democratic decision-making and we would suggest that reflective practitioners have both the right and responsibility to contribute to such processes.

There are seven basic elements of successful pressure group activity:

1 Demystifying the democratic process

2 Identifying decision-makers

3 Preparing the case

4 Forming alliances

5 Managing the media

6 Lobbying decision-makers

7 Following up

One of the most important aspects of this is to demystify the democratic process itself and we will make various suggestions on this and with regard to the seven elements of pressure-group activity which we have identified.

# 4.1 Demystifying the democratic process

There is a tendency to regard decision-making as something done by 'them' – an ill-defined, distant and amorphous body. In fact, decisions in democracies are taken by elected representatives. The connection between the ordinary citizen and decision-makers can thus be much more close, direct and personal.

Some possible ways to become aware of decision-makers and decision-making include attending a relevant meeting of your local council. Meetings are normally open to the public and attendance at an Education Committee meeting is likely to be very interesting to reflective practitioners. In addition, you could write to or make an appointment with your local elected representative to ask for their views on educational issues and to explain the constraints and pressures within which they serve.

Locally, and linked to the maintained sector, you could ask to attend a meeting of the governing body of the school, or a feeder school for your ECEC setting. Note who the governors are and enquire about their powers in relation to the affairs of the school. Consider the potential for partnership between practitioners and governors, and members of local non-maintained ECEC groups. For non-maintained settings, the meetings of trustees or committees of many settings are easily accessible.

# 4.2 Identifying decision-makers

Lists of MPs and Councillors are available on the internet and official offices. It is necessary to identify those who have a particular interest in education and those who have a particular degree of influence over decisions. A list of members of the Education Committee on a council or of members of the House of Commons with an interest in education will be helpful. The names of school governors, committee members and trustees will be available in your school or setting.

It is also often appropriate to identify the leaders of political groups and those who speak on education issues. In addition, the chair of the Finance Committee on a local council or Treasury Ministers in the House of Commons are likely to be worth identifying – depending, of course, on the issue under consideration.

A further group to identify is the education officers and civil servants who advise decision-makers and implement many decisions. Chief education officers, for instance, can be extremely influential.

# 4.3 Preparing the case

It is essential to prepare a case well. This requires at least three things:

- appropriate factual information about the issue.
- good educational arguments in support of whatever is being advocated.

- an understanding of the interests and concerns of those whom it is hoped to influence.

A great deal of factual information can be gathered from websites of national, regional or local government agencies, including DfE and Ofsted. Other sorts of information can be collected through discussion with those people who may be involved locally with the issue under consideration. Sources within the setting or school should be one starting point. Online blogs and newspapers also offer a regular source of reports and comment on educational developments and can be monitored for relevant material. If possible, it is worth checking key facts from a number of sources.

To develop coherent educational arguments, the research literature is an important resource. Almost all significant educational topics have been researched at some time, and there is much to learn from the experience of others. Of course, one would certainly wish to discuss the issues under consideration with colleagues, and to build a really secure understanding.

Regarding the interests of those whom one wishes to influence, a good place to start is with any published policy statements or manifestos. This could be followed up by discussion and by making judgements regarding the pressures and constraints that they face.

## 4.4 Forming alliances

Representative democracy is designed as a system which links decision-making with the views of a majority. It follows that the most successful type of campaigning is likely to be one which is broadly based – one which is produced by an alliance of interested parties bringing concerted pressure to bear on policymakers.

Reflective practitioners may thus wish to act with others if and when they wish to influence public policy. Obvious places to look for allies are other colleagues, perhaps through online links, professional associations, specific interest organizations or trade union links; parents and the importance of parental support cannot be overestimated; other workers in the public services if relevant; local community and interest groups who may be directly or indirectly affected by the issues under consideration; and existing national pressure groups such as those listed earlier in this section.

## 4.5 Managing the media

Important issues here include making your key message very clear; carrying out a review of the types of media which might be interested in educational issues (blogs, online and other press, radio, television); holding discussions with people who have had experience of managing publicity to learn from them; carrying out an analysis of the types of stories or news that each media outlet is likely to be interested in and, crucially, of the ways in which they are likely to handle educational issues; considering the timing constraints that appropriate media outlets face; holding discussions with selected journalists to get first-hand knowledge of their concerns; preparing press releases and considering suitable images for photographic or filming purposes; identifying and supporting a spokesperson for press follow-up.

## 4.6 Lobbying decision-makers

There are any number of possibilities here, ranging from discrete lobbying, discussion, letter writing by individuals, through to online petitions, media campaigns and demonstrations. However, it is important to remember that not many politicians enjoy being forced to change course, but most are open to persuasion if they have not previously taken up a hard public position.

## 4.7 Current campaigns

A reflective professional in the ECEC sector will be an advocate for the sector itself. The status of early years education within the broader educational sphere continues to be questioned both from within and in the wider public arena. The need for a strong campaigning voice for the sector, to put forward the case for the retention of services, for high quality at all levels and in all settings, and for the pay and conditions of the workforce continues to be essential.

> ### Case study 17.2 An effective campaign
>
> Changes to the ECEC Ofsted inspection schedule were causing consternation within the sector, who felt that their voices were not being heard. Little communication was evident between Ofsted, providers and local authorities. Using organizations such as the National Daycare Association, the London Early Years Federation, Nursery World magazine and an online blog, June O'Sullivan initiated a series of regional campaigning events. This led to constructive ways forward with Ofsted, new lines of communication and possible changes to processes and protocols. (**leyf.org.uk/blog/next-steps-in-the-ofstedbigconversation**)

## 4.8 Campaigning organizations in the ECEC sector

The following organizations are particularly active in the sector. Online social media sites enable quick responses to events by campaigners who can disseminate information to a wide audience. There are numerous examples of the use of blogs, Facebook and Twitter campaigns linked to the organizations and publications below, as well as the professional associations and unions above.

**National Children's Bureau, Early Childhood Unit**
Leading national charitable organization with strong campaigning role, including early years. A comprehensive summary of current research, consultations and campaigns is available fortnightly: **ncb.org.uk/ecu**. See also Early Childhood Forum: **ncb.org.uk/ecf**.

*Nursery World* **and online forum: forums.nurseryworld.co.uk.**
Comprehensive and current active website and publication including the maintained and non-maintained sector. A key reference for current campaigns, including online links.

*Times Education Supplement* **and online forum. Primarily for teachers and other staff in maintained schools and academies. Has links to campaigns including those linked to teachers' pay and conditions: **tes.co.uk/forums** and TES Subscriptions: **tes@email.tes. co.uk.**

**The National Campaign for Real Nursery Education**
Campaigning organization for state nursery provision. Active linked social media sites: **ncrne.squarespace.com**.

**Pen Green research base**
Pioneering setting, research and teaching centre, linked to a number of active campaigns and lobbies: **pengreen.org**.

**Association for the Professional Development of Early Years Educators**
Centre for research, publications and conferences, with associated campaigning links: **tactyc.org.uk**.

## Conclusion

This chapter has considered how an extended definition of professionalism can be applied in ECEC. Reflective practice, at the heart of this book, always takes place within a context: the society within which it is embedded, compatible with Bronfenbrenner's ecological model of the child 'nested' within the relationships of family, setting and neighbourhood. We have outlined how the relationship between early childhood settings, the economy of a society and the culture of a society are seen by policymakers, and we have considered what the contribution of ECEC may be to each, as they relate to children and parents. We have then considered the role played by ECEC in firmly promoting the rights of the individual, and have argued that the reflective practitioner has a crucial role to play in ensuring that concern for the individual is balanced with attention to the needs of the group and wider community. Practical strategies for the implementation of practice have been highlighted. We have detailed how practitioners can engage with the political process as an active citizen, and have concluded with a consideration of the campaigning role of ECEC.

Early education is inevitably concerned with being as well as becoming, and has an increasing profile on the policymaking agenda (Gammage, 2008). At the time of writing the global economy is facing a severe crisis. The need for a resilient workforce with the ability to rearticulate and assert the core moral and ethical principles of ECEC is as urgent as it has ever been.

We hope that this book will help practitioners and student-practitioners to develop not only the necessary skills of early years teaching but also the awareness and commitment to be this reflective future workforce who will make a vital contribution to early years education and the generations of children who will benefit from it.

## Key readings

The seminal work by Bronfenbrenner which endures as a model of the child 'nested' within the community is here:

> Bronfenbrenner, U. (1979) *The Ecology of Human Development: Experiments by Nature and Design.* London: Harvard University Press.

Powerful studies and summaries of research on the role of ECEC in countering disadvantage in the UK are here:

> National Children's Bureau (2013) *Greater Expectations. Raising Aspirations for Our Children.* London: NCB.
>
> Parker, I. (2013) *Early Developments. Bridging the Gap Between Evidence and Policy in Early Years Education.* London: Institute for Public Policy Research.
>
> Pascal, C. and Bertram, T. (2013) *The Impact of Early Education as a Strategy in Countering Socio-economic Disadvantage.* CREC, London: Ofsted. **ofsted.gov.uk/ accessandachievement**

The two most influential reports on early intervention, placing early years care and education in context of social issues in the UK, are essential reading:

> Allen, G. (2011) *Early Intervention: The Next Steps.* HM Government.
>
> Field, F. (2010) *The Foundation Years: Preventing Poor Children Becoming Poor Adults.* Report of the Independent Review on Poverty and Life Chances. HM Government.

The core references for work on human rights and the rights of children are here, followed by an excellent account of educational implications by Newell:

> Newell, P. (1991) *The UN Convention and Children's Rights in the UK.* London: National Children's Bureau.
>
> United Nations (1948) *Universal Declaration of Human Rights.*
>
> —(1989) *United Nations Declaration of the Rights of the Child.*

For guidance on Human Rights education, see:

> Osler, A. and Starkey, H. (2010) *Teachers and Human Rights Education.* Stoke-on-Trent: Trentham Books.

A useful and powerful overview of ECEC in a global context:

Gammage, P. (2008) 'The Social Agenda and Early Childhood Care and Education: Can we really help Create a better World?' Online Outreach Paper 4. The Hague, The Netherlands: Bernard Van Leer Foundation.

Margaret Edgington's straightforward and practical book on the role of the Foundation Stage teacher places them in a wider context:

Edgington, M. (2004) *The Foundation Stage Teacher in Action: Teaching 3, 4 and 5 Year Olds*. 3rd edn. London: Paul Chapman.

Jillian Rodd and Mary Whalley develop the practical strategies that a leader in early years can take:

Rodd, J. (2006) *Leadership in Early Childhood*. 3rd edn. Maidenhead: Open University Press.

Whalley, M. (2008) *Leading Practice in Early Years Settings*. Exeter: Learning Matters Ltd.

# Websites

Websites can provide a wealth of up-to-date information and support. We have listed those we refer to most frequently below.

International comparative data:

Economist Intelligence Unit 2012 *Starting Well: Benchmarking Early Education Around the World International Comparisons*. **lienfoundation.org/pdf/publications/ sw_report.pdf**

OECD PISA 2012 results: **oecd.org/pisa/keyfindings/pisa-2012-results.htm**

Resources for Human Rights and citizenship education:

UNICEF **unicef.org.uk/**

New Internationalist: **newint.org/**

Oxfam: **oxfam.org.uk/education/**

Working With Others: **workingwithothers.org/**

Campaign hubs, professional and other organizations and individuals:

Association for the Professional Development of Early Years Educators **tactyc.org.uk/**

Centre for research, publications and conferences, with associated campaigning links:

The Association of Professionals in Education and Children's Trusts (Aspect) **aspect. org.uk/**

The Communication Trust **thecommunicationtrust.org.uk**

Pen Green, sources through the Centre For Excellence in Outcomes for Children and Young People's Services, C4EO **c4eo.org.uk**

Early Education **early-education.org.uk/**
Daycare Trust **daycaretrust.org.uk/**
The National Literacy Trust **iteracytrust.org.uk**
Michael Rosen **michaelrosenblog.blogspot.co.uk/**
Mosaic' approach: **ncb.org.uk/ycvn/resources/mosaic-approach**
National Association of Schoolmasters Union of Women Teachers **nasuwt.org.uk/**
National Children's Bureau, Early Childhood Unit **ncb.org.uk/ecu**
National Day Nurseries Association **ndna.org.uk/**
Nursery World online forum **forums.nurseryworld.co.uk/**
The National Campaign for Real Nursery Education: **ncrne.squarespace.com/**
National Union of Teachers (NUT) **teachers.org.uk**
Pre-School Learning Alliance **pre-school.org.uk/**
Pen Green research base, linked to a number of active campaigns and lobbies:
   **pengreen.org/**
Persona Doll Training: **persona-doll-training.org**
Professional Association for Childcare and Early Years (PACEY) **pacey.org.uk/**
UNICEF **unicef.org.uk/**
UNISON **unison.org.uk/education/**

The associated website, **reflectiveteaching.co.uk**, offers a wealth of supplementary resources including reflective activities, research briefings, advice on further reading and downloadable diagrams, figures and checklists from the book. It also features a compendium of educational terms, links to useful websites, policy and curriculum documents, and showcases examples of excellent research and practice.

# List of reflective activities

**Part One: Becoming a Reflective Professional**

**1. Identity. Who are we and what do we stand for?**

1.1　To reflect upon your own decision to work in ECEC

1.2　To reflect upon perceptions of the characteristics of men, women and early years practitioners

1.3　To reflect upon whether your practice and your philosophy are always compatible

1.4　To reflect upon the ideas of 'school readiness' and 'school unreadiness'

1.5　To deepen your understanding of a child

1.6　To understand our perceptions of children and their families

1.7　To review the learning of a child in the light of Susan Hart's *Framework for Innovative Thinking*

**2. Learning. How can we understand learner development?**

2.1　To consider the application of behaviourist, constructivist and social constructivist psychology in practice

2.2　To consider the role of the early years practitioner's duty to identify potential developmental issues in babies and children

2.3　To consider the influence of culture on the development and the learning disposition of a child

2.4　To review your planning

**3. Reflection. How can we develop the quality of our practice?**

3.1　To review experienced dilemmas

3.2　To plan to conduct a small piece of research in your setting

3.3　To support critical engagement with policy documents

3.4　To explore how improvement can come from collecting evidence of our practice

**4. Principles. What are the foundations of effective teaching and learning?**

4.1　To review TLRP's principles on knowledge, prior learning, pedagogy and assessment

4.2　To review TLRP's principles on engagement, relationships and informal learning

4.3　To consider recent government policies on education

**Part Two: Creating Conditions For Learning**

**5. Contexts. What is, and what might be?**

5.1   To consider the current political and social climate and the impact this has had on the policies relevant to your practice

5.2   To review and explore the significance of ideology, culture, opportunity and accountability

5.3   To consider the meaning and significance of 'agency', both for practitioners and for learners

**6. Relationships. How are we getting on together?**

6.1   To consider the 'key person' role in your setting

6.2   To gather information on how children feel about activities which they undertake

6.3   To identify the traits practitioners need to support, care for and teach the children in your setting

6.4   To monitor and place in perspective your own feelings about staff relationships

6.5   To evaluate and understand the social and emotional climate of your setting

6.6   To evaluate progress towards an inclusive setting

**7. Engagement. How are we managing behaviour?**

7.1   To reflect on one child's behaviour and their needs

7.2   To consider a child's well-being in relation to their behaviour

7.3   To reflect upon how adults communicate with babies and/or young children

7.4   To reflect upon the impact practitioners have on children's lives

7.5   To reflect upon how you think children should behave and why

7.6   To reflect on how you convey to children the behaviours which are and are not acceptable in particular circumstances

**8. Spaces. How are we creating environments for learning?**

8.1   To reflect upon Case study 8.1 and what it tells you about values

8.2   To reflect upon how your values impact upon the provision the children in your care receive

8.3   To reflect upon the spaces provided within the indoor environment in your setting

8.4   To reflect upon how you plan the learning environment

8.5   To plan resources to support specific learning activities

8.6   To produce a room plan

8.7   To consider the plan for the day

8.8   To monitor an individual child to estimate active learning time and gain a sense of how they experience a typical day

8.9   To consider the opportunities the children in your care have to explore the outdoors

8.10  To review your own practice in relation to digital technologies

Part Three: Teaching For Learning

**9. Curriculum. What is taught in the early years?**

9.1    To deepen your understanding of the hidden curriculum operating in your setting

9.2    To deepen your understanding of the influences on your practice

9.3    To consider how practice in your setting supports the development of knowledge, concepts, skills and attitudes of the children in your care

**10. Planning. How are we implementing the curriculum?**

10.1   To consider the value of processes over product

10.2   To consider knowledge and the needs of children

10.3   To reflect upon the skills children require to participate in shared activities

10.4   To consider theory in relation to learning and practice

10.5   To reflect upon what children need to learn and when

10.6   To consider the learning needs of babies and toddlers

**11. Pedagogy. How can we develop effective strategies?**

11.1   To identify aspects of the craft, art and science of pedagogy in teaching

11.2   To reflect upon your pedagogic practice

11.3   To reflect from a learner's perspective on aspects of pedagogy

11.4   To explore how principles about pedagogy relate to our own planning and teaching

**12. Communication. How does language support learning?**

12.1   To analyse how listening and responding to children develops them as learners

12.2   To analyse a language episode in your setting or placement – for example, changing a baby's nappy, reading a story, or supporting child-initiated play

12.3   To investigate whether your setting or placement setting provides a stimulating, welcoming, language-rich environment

12.4   To investigate your use of questioning within your setting

12.5   To investigate whether your setting provides a participatory, active, language-rich environment

12.6   To reflect upon how you can use questioning to extend young children's thinking

**13. Assessment. How can assessment enhance learning?**

13.1   To reflect upon the impact of practitioner views of children

13.2   To reflect upon how you involve children in decision-making on issues which affect their lives

13.3   To reflect upon how children in your setting are supported to develop and practise the skills of self and peer assessment

Part Four: Reflecting On Consequences

**14. Outcomes. How do we capture learning achievements?**

14.1   To consider your practice in relation to assessment criteria and levels

14.2   To consider the use of assessment in your setting

14.3  To reflect upon whether and/or how information from parents is used as part of the assessment process in your setting

14.4  To reflect upon the accuracy of observations

**15. Inclusion. How are we enabling learning opportunities?**

15.1  To reflect upon what is meant by inclusion

15.2  To consider how you and your staff team approach inclusion

15.3  To reflect upon understandings of learner diversity

**Part Five: Deepening Understanding**

**16. Expertise. Conceptual tools for career-long fascination?**

16.1  To reflect upon enduring educational issues

16.2  To explore using the conceptual framework to reflect on professional expertise

**17. Professionalism. How does reflective teaching contribute to society?**

17.1  To reflect upon the role of the early years practitioner and the need for specialist training

17.2  To consider the features of a professional practitioner

17.3  To reflect upon data used to inform ECEC policy, how this is arrived at and what it shows

17.4  To consider the teaching of reading

17.5  To consider ways of evaluating projects in ECEC

17.6  To consider and reflect on practical ways that you hope to develop respect and tolerance for others in your early years context

# List of case studies, research briefings, figures and tables

# Acknowledgements

A number of people have contributed to Reflective Teaching in Early Education and the associated Readings book and website materials. In particular we would like to thank the staff and children at Oneworld Nursery and Phoenix nursery at the University of Brighton, for their contributions and expertise, Eileen Smith (QTS, EYPS) for her significant contributions and support, and Angela Coffey for her editorial support.

The staff at Bloomsbury have been extremely supportive throughout the process particularly Alison Baker, Miriam Davey and Kasia Figiel.

We would of course like to thank all those who have developed and contributed to the Reflective Teaching series, without whom we would not have had the opportunity to develop this book – Andrew Pollard, Amy Pollard, Paul Ashwin, Yvonne Hiller and Maggie Gregson.

# Bibliography

Adams, C. (2008) 'Intervention for Children with Pragmatic Language Impairments: Frameworks, Evidence and Diversity'. In C. F. Norbury, J. B. Tomblin and D. V. M. Bishop (eds) *Understanding Developmental Language Disorders in Children: From Theory to Practice*. London: Taylor & Francis.

Adams, S., Alexander, E., Drummond, M. J. and Moyles, J. (2004) 'Inside the Foundation Stage: Recreating the Reception Year'. Final Report. London: Association of Teachers and Lectures.

Adler, A. (1927) *The Practice and Theory of Individual Psychology*. New York: Harcourt.

Aileen, S. and Whalley, M. (2010) *Supporting Pedagogy and Practice in Early Years Settings*. Exeter: Learning Matters.

Ainscow, M., Booth, T. and Dyson, A. (2006) *Improving Schools, Developing Inclusion*. London: Routledge.

Alexander, R. J. (2000) *Culture and Pedagogy: International Comparisons in Primary Education*. Oxford: Blackwell.

—(2004) 'Still no pedagogy? principle, pragmatism and compliance in primary education', *Cambridge Journal of Education*, 34 (1), 7–34.

—(2008) *Essays on Pedagogy*. London: Routledge. (Reading 12.3)

—(ed.) (2010a) 'Children, their World, their Education'. Final report and recommendations of the Cambridge Primary Review. London: Routledge.

—(ed.) (2010b) 'Children, their World, their Education'. Final Report of the Cambridge Primary Review. London: Routledge.

Alibhai-Brown, Y. (2000) *Who Do We Think We Are?: Imagining the New Britain*. London: Allen Lane.

Allen, G. (2011) 'Early Intervention: The Next Steps. An Independent Report to Her Majesty's Government'. London: Cabinet Office.

Anderson, P. M. (2008) *Pedagogy Primer*. Peter Lang Primers. New York: Peter Lang International Academic Publishers.

Anning, A. (1991) *The First Years at School*. Milton Keynes: Open University Press.

Anning, A. and Edwards, A. (2006) *Promoting Learning from Birth to Five: Developing Professional Practice in the Pre-school*. 2nd edn. Buckingham: Open University Press.

Archard, D. and MacLeod, C. M. (2002) *The Moral and Political Status of Children*. Oxford: Oxford University Press.

Ardelt, M. (2000) 'Still stable after all these years? personality stability theory revisited', *Social Psychology Quarterly, Special Millennium Issue on The State of Sociological Social Psychology*, 63 (4), 392–405.

Arnett, J. (1989). 'Caregivers in day-care centres: does training matter?', *Journal of Applied Developmental Psychology*, 10, 541–52.

Assessment Reform Group (2002) *Testing, Motivation and Learning*. Cambridge: University of Cambridge Faculty of Education.

Athey, C. (2007) *Extending Thought in Young Children*. 2nd edn. London: PCP.

Atkinson, T. and Claxton, G. (eds) (2000) *The Intuitive Practitioner: On the Value of Not Always Knowing What One Is Doing*. Buckingham: Open University Press.

Aubrey, C. (1994) *The Role of Subject Knowledge in the Early Years of Schooling*. Lewes: Falmer Press.

Ausubel, D. P. (1968) *Educational Psychology: A Cognitive View*. New York: Holt, Rinehart and Winston.

Baker, C. (2011) *Foundations of Bilingual Education and Bilingualism*. Bristol: Multilingual Matters.

Baker, R. G. (1968) *Ecological Psychology. Concepts and Methods of Studying the Environment of Human Behaviour*. Stanford: Stanford University Press.

Baldock, P., Fitzgerald, D. and Kay, J. (2009) *Understanding Early Years Policy*. London: Paul Chapman Publishing.

Ball, D. (2002) *Playgrounds: Risks, benefits and choices*, Sudbury: Health and Safety Executive.

Ball, S. (1981) 'Initial Encounters in the Classroom and the Process of Establishment'. In P. F. Woods (ed.) *Pupil Strategies*. London: Croom Helm.

—(1994) *Education Reform: A Critical and Post Structural Approach*. Buckingham: Open University Press.

—(2003) 'The teacher's soul and the terrors of performativity', *Journal of Education Policy*, 18 (2), 215–28.

Ball, S. and Gold, A. (1992) *Reforming Education and Changing Schools*. London: Routledge.

Bandura, A. (1995) *Self-Efficacy in Changing Societies*. Cambridge: Cambridge University Press.

—(1997) *Self-efficacy: The Exercise of Control*. New York: Freeman.

—(1977) *Social Learning Theory*. New Jersey: Prentice Hall.

Banerjee, R., Bennett, M. and Luke, N. (2012) 'Children's reasoning about self-presentation following rule violations: the role of self-focused attention', *Child Development*, 83 (5), 1805–21.

Barber, J. and Paul-Smith, S. (2012) *Early Years Observation and Planning in Practice*. London: Practical Pre-School.

Barber, M. and Mourshead, M. (2007) *How the World's Best Performing School Systems Come Out on Top*. London: McKinsey and Company.

Barnes, D. (1971) 'Language in the Secondary Classroom'. In D. Barnes, J. Britton and H. Rosen (eds) *Language, the Learner and the School*. Harmondsworth: Penguin.

Barnett, W. S. (1993) 'Benefit-cost analysis of preschool education: findings from a 25-year follow-up', *American Journal of Ortho-Psychiatry*, 63, 25–50.

Barton, L. (2012) 'Response'. In *The Sociology of Disability and Inclusive Education: A Tribute to Len Barton*. London: Routledge.

Bearne, E. (1983). *Making Progress in English*. London: Routledge.

Beastall, L. (2008) 'Enchanting a disenchanted child: revolutionizing the means of education using information and communication technology and e-learning', *British Journal of Sociology in Education*, 27 (1), 97–110.

Beaumont, H. (2008) *How Practitioners in a Children's Centre Perceive and Articulate Pedagogy*. PhD Thesis, University of Brighton.

Beck, N. and Fetherston, T. (2003) 'Information technology', *Childhood Education Annual* (1), 139–61.

Brannen, J. and Moss, P. (2003) *Rethinking Children's Care*. Buckingham: Open University Press.

Bennett N. (1992) *Managing Learning in the Primary Classroom*. Stoke-on-Trent: Trentham Books.

Berger, P. and Luckmann, T. (1967) *The Social Construction of Reality*. New York: Doubleday.

Berlak, A. and Berlak, H. (1981) *Dilemmas of Schooling*. London: Methuen.

Berliner, D. C. (2004) 'Describing the behavior and documenting the accomplishments of expert teachers', *Bulletin of Science, Technology and Society*, 24 (3), 200–12.

Bernstein, B. (1970) 'Education cannot compensate for society', *New Society*, 387, 344–7.

—(1971a) 'On the Classification and Framing of Educational Knowledge'. In M. F. D. Young (ed.) *Knowledge and Control*. London: Collier-Macmillan.

—(1971b) *Class, Codes and Control: Theoretical Studies Towards a Sociology of Language*. Vol. 1. London: Routledge & Kegan Paul.

Bertram, T. and Pascal, C. (2002) 'Early Years Education: An International Perspective'. Research Report, Qualifications and Curriculum Authority (QCA), Centre for Research in Early Childhood, Birmingham.

Biesta, G., Field, J., Goodson, I., Hodkinson, P. and Macleod, F. (2010) *Improving Learning through the Lifecourse*. London: Routledge.

Black, P. and Wiliam, D. (1998a) 'Assessment and classroom learning', *Assessment in Education*, 5 (1), 7–74.

—(1998b) *Inside the Black Box: Raising Standards Through Classroom Assessment*. London: King's College.

Blanden, J., Gregg, P. and Machin, P. (2005) *Intergenerational Mobility in Europe and North America*. London: The Sutton Trust.

Blanden J. and Machin S. (2008) 'Up and down the generational income ladder in Britain: past changes and future prospects', *National Institute Economic Review*, 205 (1), 101–16.

Blandford, S. and Knowles, C. (2012) 'Assessment for learning: a model for the development of a child's self competence in the early years of education', *Education 3–13*, 40 (5), 487–99

Blatchford, P., Galton, M., Kutnick, P. and Baines, E. (2005) 'Improving the Effectiveness of Pupil Groups in Classrooms'. End of Award Report, ESRC Project Ref: L139 25 1046.

Blundell, D. (2012) *Education and Constructions of Childhood*. London: Continuum.

Bolster, A. (1983) 'Towards a more effective model of research on teaching', *Harvard Educational Review*, 53 (3), 294–308.

Bone, J. (2008) 'Creating relational spaces: everyday spirituality in early childhood settings', *European Early Childhood Education Research Journal [P]*, 16 (3). London: Taylor and Francis, 343–57.

Bourdieu, P. and Passeron, J. C. (1977) *Reproduction in Education, Society and Culture*. London: Sage Publications Ltd.

Bowe, R., Ball, S. and Gold, A. (1992) *Reforming Education and Changing Schools*. London: Routledge.

Bowles, S. and Gintis, H. (1976) *Schooling in Capitalist America*. London: Routledge.

Bowlby, J. (1944) 'Forty-four juvenile thieves: their characters and home life', *International Journal of Psychoanalysis*, 25, 1–57, 207–28.

Bowlby, J. (1951) 'Maternal Care and Mental Health'. World Health Organisation, Monograph Series No. 2.

—(1969b) *Attachment and Loss (vol. 1), Attachment*. New York: Basic Books. Penguin Books.

—(2005) *A Secure Base*. Oxon: Routledge.

Bowles, S. and Gintis, H. (1976) *Schooling in Capitalist America*. New York: Basic Books.

Bowman, B. T., Donovan, M. S. and Burns, M. S. (eds) (2001) *Eager to Learn: Educating Our Preschoolers*. Washington, DC: National Academies Press.

Bradford, H. (2009) *Communication, Language and Literacy in the Early Years Foundation Stage*. London: Routledge.

Bransford, J. D., Brown, A. I. and Cocking, R. R. (eds) (2000) *How People Learn: Brain, Mind, Experience and School*. Washington, DC: National Academy Press.

Bredekamp, S. and Rosegrant, T. (eds) (1992) *Reaching Potentials: Appropriate Curriculum and Assessment for Young Children*. Vol. 1. Washington, DC: National Association for the Education of Young Children.

Broadfoot, P. (2007) *An Introduction to Assessment*. London: Continuum.

—(1996) *Education, Assessment and Society: A Sociological Analysis*. Buckingham: Open University Press.

Brock, A. (n.d.) 'Dimensions of Early Years Professionalism—Attitudes Versus Competences?' Leads Metropolitan University. Available from http://tactyc.org.uk/pdfs/Reflection-brock.pdf (accessed 17 April 2012).

Bronfenbrenner, U. (1979) *The Ecology of Human Development: Experiments by Nature and Design*. London: Harvard University Press.

—(1993) 'Environments as Contexts of Development in "Ecological Models of Human Development"'. In M. Gauvain and M. Cole (eds) *Readings on the Development of Children*. New York: Freeman.

Brooker, E. and Siraj-Blatchford, J. (2002) '"Click on miaow!": how children of 3 and 4 experience the nursery computer', *Contemporary Issues in Early Education*, 3 (2), 251–73.

Brophy, J. (2004) *Motivating Students to Learn*. 2nd edn. Mahwah, NJ: Lawrence Erlbaum Associates.

Brophy, J. E. and Good, T. L. (1974) *Teacher–Student Relationships*. New York: Cassell.

Brown, B. (1998) *Unlearning Discrimination in the Early Years*. Stoke-on-Trent: Trentham Books Ltd.

—(2004) *Celebrating Diversity: Inclusion in Practice*. Stoke-on-Trent: Trentham Books Ltd/ Persona Doll Training.

Bruce, T. (1991) *Time to Play in Early Childhood Education*. London: Hodder & Stoughton.

—(1960) *The Process of Education*. Cambridge, MA: Harvard University Press.

—(1966) *Towards a Theory of Instruction*. Cambridge, MA: Harvard University Press.

—(1977) *The Process of Education*. Cambridge, MA: Harvard University Press.

—(1983) *Child's Talk: Learning to Use Language*. New York: W. W. Norton.

—(1990) *Acts of Meaning*. Cambridge, MA: Harvard University Press.

—(1996) *The Culture of Education*. Cambridge, MA: Harvard University Press.

—(2002) *Making Stories: Law, Literature, Life*. New York: Farrar, Straus and Giroux

—(2004) *Developing Learning in Early Childhood 0–8*. London: Sage Publications Ltd.

—(2005) *Early Childhood Education*. 3rd edn. London: Hodder Education.

—(2011) *Early Childhood Education*. 4th edn. London: Hodder Education.

Bullock, E. and Brownhill, S. (2011) *A Quick Guide to Behaviour Management in the Early Years*. London: Sage Publications Ltd.

Burke, C. (2005) 'Play in focus: children researching their own spaces and places for play', *Children, Youth and Environments*, 15 (1), 27–53.

Butt, G. (2011) *Making Assessment Matter*. London: Continuum.

Byron, T. (2008) 'Safer Children in a Digital World: The Report of the Byron Review'. Nottingham: DCSF publications.

Cable, C. and Miller, L. (eds) (2011) *Professionalization, Leadership and Management in the Early Years*. London: Sage Publications Ltd.

Calderhead, J. (ed.) (1987) *Exploring Teachers' Thinking*. London: Cassel Education.

—(1988) *Teachers' Professional Learning*. London: Falmer.

Cameron, C. (2001) 'Promise or problem? a review of the literature on men working in early childhood services', *Gender, Work and Organization*, 8 (4), 430–53.

—(2006) 'Male workers and professionalism', *Contemporary Issues in Early Childhood*, 7 (1), 68–79.

Campbell, J. and Neill, S. R. St J. (1992) *Teacher Time and Curriculum Manageability at Key Stage 1*. London: AMMA.

Campbell, F. A. and Ramey, C. T. (1995) 'Cognitive and school outcomes for high risk African American students at middle adolescence: positive effects of early intervention', *American Educational Research Journal*, 32, 743–72.

Campbell, F. A., Ramey, C. T., Pungello, E. P., Sparling, J. J. and Miller-Johnson, S. (2002) 'Early childhood education: young adult outcomes from the Abecedarian Project', *Applied Developmental Science*, 6, 42–57.

Carr, M. (2001) *Assessment in Early Childhood Settings: Learning Stories*. London: Sage Publications Ltd.

—(2008) 'Can Assessment Unlock and Open the Doors to Resourcefulness and Agency?'. In S. Swaffield (ed.) *Unlocking Assessment: Understanding for Reflection and Application*. Abingdon: Routledge, 36–54.

—(2011) 'Young children reflecting on their learning: teachers' conversation strategies', *Early Years,* 31 (3), 209–10.

Carr, M. and Claxton, G. (2002) 'Tracking the development of learning dispositions', *Assessment in Education*, 9, 9–37.

Carr, M. and Lee, W. (2012) *Learning Stories: Constructing Learner Identities in Early Education*. London: Sage Publications Ltd.

Carr, W. and Kemmis, S. (1986) *Becoming Critical: Knowing Through Action Research*. London: Falmer.

Central Advisory Council for Education (1967) *The Plowden Report: Children and Their Primary Schools*. A Report for the Central Advisory Council for Education, London: HMSO.

Chaplain, R. (2003) *Teaching Without Disruption in the Primary School*. London: Routledge.

Children Act 1989. London: HMSO.

Children Act 1991. London: HMSO.

Children in Europe Policy (2008) *Young Children and Their Services: Developing a European Approach*. A Children in Europe Policy paper.

The Children's Society (2007) 'When will we be heard? Advocacy provisions for disabled children and young people in England'. Leeds: The Children's Society.

The Children's Food Trust (n.d.) 'Eat Better, Start Better programme'. Available from http://www.childrensfoodtrust.org.uk/pre-school/eat-better-start-better (accessed 25 July 2014).

Chilvers, D. (2013) *Creating and Thinking Critically: Learning and Teaching in the Early Years*. London: Practical Pre-school Books.

Chomsky, N. (1971) *Chomsky: Selected Readings*, J. P. B. Allen and P. Van Buren (eds). London: Oxford University Press.

Chugani, H., Behen, M., Muzik, O., Juhasz, C, Nagi F. and Chugani, D. (2001) 'Local brain functional activity following early deprivation: a study of Romanian orphans', *Neuroimage*, 14, 1290–301. [Cited in Gerhardt, S. (2004) *Why Love Matters: How Affections Shapes a Baby's Brain*. Hove: Bruner-Routledge.]

Clark, A. (2010) *Transforming Childrens' Spaces: Children's and Adults' Participation in Designing Learning Environments*. London: Routledge.

Clark, A. (2005) 'Ways of Seeing: Using the Mosaic Approach to Listen to Young Children's Perspectives'. In A. Clark, A. Trine Kjrholt and P. Moss (eds) *Beyond Listening: Children's Perspectives on Early Childhood Services*. Bristol: Policy Press, 29–49.

Clark, A., Kjorholt, A. T. and Moss, P. (eds) (2005) *Beyond Listening: Children's Perspectives on Early Childhood Services*. Bristol: The Policy Press.

Clark A. and Moss, P. (2001) *Listening to Young Children: The Mosaic Approach*. London: National Children's Bureau.

Clarke, S. (2011) *The Power of Formative Assessment: Self-belief and Active Involvement in the Process of Learning* (DVD). Shirley Clarke Media Ltd.

Clarricoates, K. (1987) 'Child Culture at School: A Clash between Gendered Worlds?'. In A. Pollard (ed.) *Children and Their Primary Schools*. London: Falmer.

Claxton, G. (1999) *Wise Up: The Challenge of Lifelong Learning*. London: Bloomsbury.

Claxton, G. and Carr, M. (2002) 'Tracking the development of learning dispositions, assessment in education', *Principles, Policy and Practice*, 9 (1) 9–37.

—(2004) 'A framework for teaching learning: learning dispositions', *Early Years International Journal of Research and Development*, 24 (1), 87–97.

Clements, R. (2004) 'An investigation of the status of outdoor play', *Contemporary Issues in Early Childhood*, 5 (1), 68–80.

Clifford, M. M. and Walster, E. (1973) 'The effect of physical attractiveness on teacher expectations', *Sociology of Education*, 46 (2), 248–58.

Clifford, R. and Bryant, D. (2003) *Multi-state Study of Pre-kindergarten. National Center for Early Development & Learning*. Chapel Hill, NC: University of North Carolina.

Coffield, F., Mosley, D., Hall, E. and Ecclestone, K. (2004) *Learning Styles and Pedagogy in Post-16 Learning: A Systematic and Critical Review*. London: LSDA.

Coghlan, M., Bergeron, C., White, K., Sharp, C., Morris, M. and Wilson, R. (2010) *Narrowing the gap in Outcomes for Young Children through Effective Practices in the Early Years (C4EO Early Years Knowledge Review 1)*. London: Centre for Excellence and Outcomes in Children and Young People's Services.

Cole, M. (1996) *Cultural Psychology: A Once and Future Discipline*. Cambridge, MA: Harvard University Press.

Coleman, J. S. (1988) 'Social capital in the creation of human capital', *American Journal of Sociology*, 94 (Supplement), 95–120.

Coleyshaw, L., Whitmarsh, J. Jopling, M. and Hadfield, M. (2012) 'An Exploration of Progress, Leadership and Impact, as part of the Longitudinal Study of Early Years Professional Status': Final Report. Wolverhampton: University of Wolverhampton.

Collarbone, P. (2009) *Creating Tomorrow Planning, Developing and Sustaining Change in Education and Other Public Services*. London: Continuum.

Collins, A., Brown, J. S. and Newman, S. E. (1987) 'Cognitive Apprenticeship: Teaching the Craft of Reading, Writing and Mathematics'. Technical Report No. 403, BBN Laboratories, Cambridge, MA, Centre for the Study of Reading, University of Illinois at Urbana-Champaign.

Collins, J. (1996) *The Quiet Child*. London: Cassell.

Coltman, P., Anghileri, J. and Petyaeva, D. (2002) 'Scaffolding learning through meaningful tasks and adult interaction', *Early Years: Journal of International Research*, 22 (1), 39–49.

Colwell, J. (2012) *The Relational Approach to Group Work the Role of the Preschool Practitioner in the Development of Children's Social Competencies*. PhD Thesis, University of Brighton.

Connell, R. W., Ashden, D. J., Kessler, S. and Dowsett, G. W. (1982) *Making the Difference: Schools, Families and Social Division*. Sidney: Allen and Unwin.

Connolly, P. (1998) *Racism, Gender and Identities of Young Children: Social Relations in a Multi-ethnic, Inner-city Primary School*. London: Routledge.

Cook, T. and Nutbrown, C. (2006) cited in Clough, P. Nutbrown, C. and Cook, T. *Inclusion in the Early Years: Critical Analyses and Enabling Narratives*. London: Sage Publications Ltd.

Coolahan, K., Fantuzzo, J., Mendez, J. and McDermott, P. (2000) 'Preschool peer interactions and readiness to learn: relationships between classroom peer play and learning behaviors and conduct', *Journal of Educational Psychology*, 92 (3), 458–65.

Corsaro, W. A. (2005) *The Sociology of Childhood*. 2nd edn. Thousand Oaks, CA: Pine Forge Press.

—(2011) *The Sociology of Childhood*. 3rd edn. London: Sage Publications Ltd.

Costa, P. T. and McCrea, R. R. (1988) 'Personality in adulthood: a six year longitudinal study of self-reports and spouse ratings on the NEO personality inventory', *Journal of Personality and Social Psychology*, 54, 853–63.

Cowie, H. (2012) *From Birth to Sixteen: Children's Health, Social, Emotional and Linguistic Development*. London: Routledge.

Cowie, H. and Ruddock, J. (1990) 'Co-operative Group Work in the Multi-Ethnic Classroom'. In *Learning Together, Working Together*. Vol. 4. British Petroleum Service on behalf of the Co-operative Group Work Project, Division of Education, University of Sheffield: Sheffield.

Crawford, C., Dearden, L. and Meghir, C. (2007) *When You Are Born Matters: The Impact of Date of Birth on Child Cognitive Outcomes*. London: Institute for Fiscal Studies.

Crowe, B. (1983) *The Playgroup Movement*. 4th edn. London: Unwin.

Csikszentmihalyi, M. (1979) 'The Concept of Flow'. In B. Sutton-Smith (ed.) *Play and learning*. New York: Gardner Press, 257–74.

Curriculum Review Group (2004) 'A Curriculum for Excellence'. Edinburgh: Scottish Executive. Available from www.scotland.gov.uk/Resource/Doc/26800/0023690.pdf (accessed 17 July 2010).

Dadds, M. (1995) *Passionate Enquiry and School Development: A Story about Teacher Action Research*. London: Falmer.

Dahlberg, G. and Moss, P. (2005) *Ethics and Politics in Early Childhood Education*. Abingdon: Routledge

Daly, M., Byers, E. and Taylor, W. (2004) *Early Years Management in Practice – A Handbook for Early Years Managers*. London: Heinemann.

Damon, W. and Phelps, E. (1989) 'Critical distinctions among three approaches to peer education', *International Journal of Educational Research*, 58, 9–19.

Davies, B. (1982) *Life in the Classroom and Playground*. London: Routledge and Kegan Paul.

Day, C., Sammons, P., Stobart, G., Kington, A. and Gu, Q. (2007) *Teachers Matter: Connecting Work, Lives and Effectiveness*. Maidenhead: Open University Press.

Department for Children, Schools and Families (DCSF) (2008) 'Social and Emotional Aspects of Development: Guidance for Practitioners Working in the Early Years Foundation Stage'. Nottingham: DCSF Publications.

De Vries, R. (2000) 'Vygotsky, Piaget, and education: a reciprocal assimilation of theories and educational practices', *New Ideas in Psychology*, 18 (2–3), 187–213.

Denham, S. A., Caverly, S., Schmidt, M., Blair, K., DeMulder, E., Caal, S., Hamada, H. and Mason, T. (2002) 'Preschool understanding of emotions: contributions to classroom anger and aggression', *Journal of Child Psychology and Psychiatry*, 43 (7), 901–16.

Dennen, V. (2004) *Cognitive Apprenticeship in Educational Practice: Research on Scaffolding, Modelling, Mentoring, and Coaching as Instructional Strategies*. Florida: Florida State University.

Department for Children, Schools and Families (DCSF) (2007) *Social and Emotional Aspects of Learning for Secondary Schools*. Nottingham: DCSF Publications

—(2012) 'Statutory Framework for the Early Years Foundation Stage: Setting the Standards for Learning, Development and Care for Children from Birth to Five'. Nottingham: Crown copyright. Available from http://webarchive.nationalarchives.gov.uk/20110202093118/http:/nationalstrategies.standards.dcsf.gov.uk/node/157774 (accessed 11 August 2012).

Department for Education (2010) 'Review of Early Years Foundation Stage'. Available from www.education.gov.uk/news/news/eyfs- review (accessed 24 July 2010).

—(2011) *The Framework for the National Curriculum*. A Report by the Expert Panel for the National Curriculum Review, London.

Department for Education (2012) *Teachers' Standards*.Nottingham: Crown Copyright.

Department for Education and Employment (2001) *The National Standards for Under Eights Day Care and Child-minding*. Nottingham: DFEE.

Department for Education and Employment (DfEE)/Qualifications and Curriculum Authority (QCA) (2000) *Curriculum Guidance for the Foundation Stage*. London: QCA.

Department of Education for Northern Ireland (DENI) (2009) *Every School a Good School – The Way Forward for Special Educational Needs and Inclusion*. Bangor: DENI.

—(2012) *Review of Special Educational Needs*. Bangor: DENI.

—(2013) *Learning to Learn: A Framework for Early Years Education and Learning*. Bangor: DENI.

Department of Education and Science (DES) (1990) 'Rumbold Report: Starting with Quality'. London: Stationary office.

Department For Education and Skills (DfES) (2002) *Birth to Three Matters: A Framework for Supporting Children in their Earliest Years*. London: DfES.

—(2003) *Every Child Matters*. London: DfES.

—(2006) *Learning Outside the Classroom Manifesto*, Nottingham: Crown Copyright.

Department for Work and Pensions (DWP) (2011) *A New Approach to Child Poverty. Tackling the Causes of Disadvantage and Transforming Families' Lives*. London: DWP.

Dewey, J. (1933) *How We Think: A Restatement of the Relation of Reflective Thinking to the Educative Process*. Chicago: Henry Regnery.

Dixon, A., Drummond, M. J., Hart, S. and McIntyre, D. (2004) *Learning Without Limits*. Maidenhead: Open University Press.

Doddington, C. and Hilton, M. (2007) *Child-centred Education: Reviving the Creative Tradition*. London: Sage Publications Ltd.

Department for Education (2012) *Statutory Framework for the Early Years Foundation Stage*. Runcorn: Department for Education.

Doherty, J., and Hughes, M. (2009) *Child Development: Theory and Practice 0–11*. Harlow: Pearson Education Ltd.

Donaldson, M. (1978) *Children's Minds*. London: Fontana.

Dowling, M. (1992) *Education 3–5*. London: Paul Chapman.

—(1999) *Neurons and Networks: An Introduction to Behavioural Neuroscience*. Cambridge, MA: Harvard University Press.

—(2010) Y*oung Children's Personal, Social and Emotional Development*. 2nd edn. London: Paul Chapman Publishing.

Dreyfus, H. L. and Dreyfus, S. E. (1986) *Mind Over Machine*. New York: Free Press.

Drifte, C. (2001) *Encouraging Positive Behaviour in the Early Years: A Practical Guide*. London: Paul Chapman.

Drummond, M. J. (2008) 'Assessment and Values: A Close and Necessary Relationship'. In S. Swaffield (ed.) *Unlocking Assessment: Understanding for Reflection and Application*. Abingdon: Routledge.

—(2012) *Assessing Children's Learning*. London: Routledge.

Dukes, C. and Smith, M. (2007) *Developing Pre-school Communication and Language*. London: Sage Publications Ltd.

Dunn, J. (1988) *The Beginnings of Social Understanding*. Oxford: Blackwell.

Dunphy, E. (2008) 'Supporting Early Learning and Development through Formative Assesment, Aistear: The Early Childhood Curriculum Framework'. Research paper. Dublin: NCCA. Available from www.ncca.ie/earlylearning (accessed 7 January 2013).

Dweck, C. (1986) 'Motivational processes affecting learning', *American Psychology*, 41, 1040–8.

—(1999) *Self-Theories: Their Role in Motivation, Personality and Development*. Philadelphia: Psychology Press.

—(2006) *Mindset: The New Psychology of Success*. New York: Ballantine.

Earl, L. and Katz, S. (2008) 'Getting to the Core of Learning: Using Assessment for Self-monitoring and Self-regulation'. In S. Swaffield (ed.) *Unlocking Assessment: Understanding for Reflection and Application*. Abingdon: Routledge, 90–104.

Early Education (2012) *Development Matters in the Early Years Foundation Stage (EYFS)*. London: Early Education.

Eaude, T. (2012) *How Do Expert Primary Classteachers Really Work?: A Critical Guide for Teachers, Headteachers and Teacher Educators*. Northwich: Critical Publishing.

Economist Intelligence Unit (2012) 'Starting Well: Benchmarking Early Education Across the World'. A Report from the Economist Intelligence Unit, Lien Foundation. Available from http://www.lienfoundation.org/pdf/publications/sw_report.pdf (accessed 2 February 2013).

Edgington, M. (2004) *The Foundation Stage Teacher in Action: Teaching 3, 4 and 5 Year Olds*. 3rd edn. London: Paul Chapman.

Education Scotland (n.d.) 'Curriculum for Excellence: What can Learners Expect?'. Available from http://www.educationscotland.gov.uk/thecurriculum/whatcanlearnersexpect/ (accessed July 2014).

Education Act 1996. London: HMSO.

Edwards, C., Gandini, L. and Forman, G. (1993) *The Hundred Languages of Children: The Reggio Emilia Approach to Early Childhood Education*. Norwood, NJ: Ablex Publishing.

Egan, M. and Bunting, B. (1991) 'The effects of coaching on eleven-plus scores', *British Journal of Educational Psychology*, 61 (1), 85–91.

Ehrenreich, B. and English, D. (1979) *For her own Good: 150 Years of the Experts' Advice to Women*. London: Pluto.

Elfer, P., Goldschmied, E. and Selleck, D. (2003) *Key Persons in the Nursery*. London: David Fulton.

Elkind, D. (2007) *The Power of Play: How Spontaneous Imaginative Activities Lead to Happier, Healthier Children*. Cambridge, MA: Da Capo Press.

Eraut, M. (1994) *Developing Professional Knowledge and Competence*. London: Routledge.

Evangelou, M., Sylva, K. and Kyriacou, M. (2009) *Early Years Learning and Development: A Literature Review*. (Research Report no. DCSF-RR176). London: Department for Children, Schools and Families.

Evans, D. (2012) *Early Years 'Snapshot' Policy Falls at First Hurdle*. Times Educational Supplement.

Facer, K. (2011) *Learning Futures. Education, Technology and Social Change*. London: Routledge.

Feinstein, L. Duckworth, K. and Sabates, R. (2008) *Education and the Family: Passing Success Across the Generations*. Routledge: Abingdon.

Field, F. (2010) 'The Foundation Years: Preventing Poor Children Becoming Poor Adults'. The report of the Independent Review on Poverty and Life Chances. HM Government.

Filer, A. and Pollard, A. (2000) *The Social World of Pupil Assessment: Processes and Contexts of Primary Schooling*. London: Continuum.

Fjørtoft, I. (2004) 'Landscape as playscape: the effects of natural environments on children's play and motor development', *Children, Youth and Environments*, 14 (92), 21–44.

Flavell, J. H. (1970) 'Developmental Studies of Mediated Memory'. In H. W. Reese and L. P. Lipsett (eds) *Advances in Child Development and Behaviour*. New York: Academic Press.

—(1979) 'Metacognition and cognitive monitoring', *American Psychologist*, 34 (10), 906–11.

Fleer, M. (2006) 'Sociocultural Assessment in Early Years Education – Myth or Reality' In R. Parker-Rees and J. Willan (eds), *Early Years Education: Major Themes in Education*. Oxon: Routledge.

—(2002) 'Sociocultural assessment in early years education—myth or reality?', *International Journal of Early Years Education*, 10 (2), 105–20.

Flook, J., Ryan, M. and Hawkins, L. (2010) *Professional Expertise: Practice, Theory and Education for Working in Uncertainty*. London: Whiting and Birch.

Florian, L. (ed.) (2007) *The Handbook of Special Education*. London: Sage Publications Ltd.

Fook, J. (2010) 'Beyond Reflective Practice: Reworking the "Critical" in Critical Reflection'. In H. Bradbury, N. Frost, S. Kilminster and M. Zukas (eds) *Beyond Reflective Practice: New Approaches to Professional Lifelong Learning*. Abingdon: Routledge, 37–51.

Formby, S. (2014) *Practitioner Perspectives: Children's use of Technology in the Early Years*. London: National Literacy Trust.

Fraser, B. J. and Fisher, D. L. (1984) *Assessment of Classroom Psychosocial Environment: Workshop Manual*. Bentley: Western Australia Institute of Technology.

Freire, P. (1995) *Pedagogy of Hope. Reliving Pedagogy of the Oppressed*. New York: Continuum.

—(2000) *Pedagogy of the Oppressed*. London: Continuum.

Frieberg, H. J. (1999) *School Climate: Measuring, Improving and Sustaining Healthy Learning Environments*. London: Psychology Press.

Fuerst, J. S. and Fuerst, D. (1993) *Chicago Experience with an Early Childhood Program: The Special Case of the Child Parent Center Program.* URBAN EDUCATION 28 (1, April), 69–96. EJ 463 446.

Fuller, A. and Unwin, L. (2003) 'Learning as apprentices in the contemporary UK workplace: creating and managing expansive and restrictive participation', *Journal of Education and Work,* 16 (4), 407–26.

Furedi, F. (2002) *Culture of Fear: Risk Taking and the Morality of Low Expectation.* London: Continuum.

—(2005) *The Politics of Fear. Beyond Left and Right.* London: Continuum.

Galton, M., Simon, B. and Croll, P. (1980) *Inside the Primary Classroom.* London: Routledge & Kegan Paul.

Galton, M. and Williamson, J. (1992) *Group-work in the Primary School.* London: Routledge.

Gammage, P. (2006) 'Early childhood education and care: politics, policies and possibilities', *Early Years: An International Research Journal,* 26 (3), 235–48.

—(2008) *The Social Agenda and Early Childhood Care and Education: Can We Really Help Create a Better World?,* Online Outreach Paper 4. The Hague, The Netherlands: Bernard Van Leer Foundation.

Gandini, L. (1994) 'Not just anywhere: Making childcare centres into "particular" places', *Child Care Information Exchange,* 3, 48–51.

Garrick, R. (2009) *Playing Outdoors in the Early Years.* 2nd edn. London: Continuum.

Garrick, R., Bath, C., Dunn, K., Maconochie, H., Willis, B. and Wolstenholme, C. (2010) *Children's Experiences of the Early Years Foundation Stage.* Research Report DFE-RR071. London: Department of Education.

Gay, G. (2010) *Culturally Responsive Teaching: Theory, Research and Practice.* New York: Teachers College Press.

Gerhardt, S. (2004) *Why Love Matters: How Affection Shapes a Baby's Brain.* London: Routledge.

Gibson, E. J. (1977) 'The Theory of Affordances'. In R. Shaw and J. Bransford (eds) *Perceiving, Acting and Knowing.* Hillsdale, NJ: Lawrence Earlbaum.

Giddens, A. (1984) *The Constitution of Society: Outline of the Theory of Structuration.* Berkeley: University of California Press

Gilborn, P. (1995) *Racism and AntiRacism in Real Schools.* Buckingham: Open University Press.

Gillborn, David (2006) 'Critical race theory and education: racism and anti-racism in educational theory and praxis', *Discourse: Studies in the Cultural Politics of Education,* 27 (1), 11–32.

Gipps, C. and MacGilchrist, B. (1999) 'Primary School Learners'. In P. Mortimore (ed.) *Understanding Pedagogy and its Impact on Learning.* London: Paul Chapman.

Glaser, R. (1999) 'Expert Knowledge and Processes of Thinking' In R. McCormick and C. Paechter (eds) *Learning and Knowledge.* London: Paul Chapman Publishing, 88–102.

Glazzard, J., Chadwick, D., Webster, A. and Percival, J. (2010) *Assessment for Learning in the Early Years Foundation Stage.* London: Sage Pblications Ltd.

Goddard Blythe, S. A. (2005) 'Releasing educational potential through movement – a summary of individual studies carried out using The INPP Developmental Test Battery and Exercise Programme for use in Schools', *Child Care in Practice,* 11 (4), 415–32.

Goldschmied, E. and Jackson, S. (2004) *People Under Three: Young Children in Day Care.* 2nd edn. London: Routledge.

Goleman, D. (1998) *Working with Emotional Intelligence.* London: Bloomsbury.

Goodfellow, J. and Hedges, H (2007) 'Practitioner Research "Centre Stage": Contexts, Contributions and Challenges' In L. Keesing-Styles and H. Hedges (eds) *Theorizing Early Childhood Practice.* NSW: Pademelon Press.

Goouch, K. and Powell, S. (2013) 'Orchestrating professional development for baby room practitioners: raising the stakes in new dialogic encounters', *Journal of Early Childhood Research,* 11 (1), 78–92.

Gopnik, A., Meltzoff, A. N. and Kuhl, P. K. (1999) *The Scientist in the Crib: Minds, Brains, and how Children Learn*. New York: Morrow.

Gordon, D., Adelman, L., Ashworth, K., Bradshaw, J., Levitas, R., Middleton, S., Pantazis, C., Patsios, D., Payne, S., Townsend, P. and Williams, J. (2000) *Poverty and Social Exclusion in Britain*. York: Joseph Rowntree Foundation.

Goswami, U. (2008) *Cognitive Development. The Learning Brain*. Hove: Psychology Press.

Goswami, U. and Bryant P. E. (1989) 'The interpretation of studies using the reading level design', *Journal of Reading Behavior*, 21 (4), 413–24.

Gotts, E. E. (1989) *Hope, Preschool To Graduation: Contributions To Parenting And School-Family Relations Theory And Practice*. Charleston, WV: Appalachia Educational Laboratory. ED 305 146.

Green, A. and Janmaat, J. (2011) *Regimes of Social Cohesion: Societies and the Crisis of Globalization*. Basingstoke: Palgrave Macmillan.

Greenfield, S. (1997) *The Human Brain: A Guided Tour*. London: Weidenfeld and Nicolson.

Greig, L. (2001) *Supporting Development and Learning 3–5*. Learning Teaching Scotland: Early Education Support.

Grey, P. (2013) *Free to Learn: Why Unleashing the Instinct to Play Will Make Our Children Happier, More Self-Reliant, and Better Students for Life*. New York: Basic Books.

GTCE (2010) 'Pedagogy Matters'. In A. Pollard (ed.) *Professionalism and Pedagogy: A Contemporary Opportunity*. London: TLRP.

Gu, Q. (2007) *Teacher Development: Knowledge and Context*. London: Continuum.

Guimaraes, S. and McSherry, K. (2002) 'The curriculum experiences of pre-school children in Northern Ireland: classroom practices in terms of child-initiated play and adult-directed activities', *International Journal of Early Years Education*, 10 (2), 85–94.

Gura, P., Bruce, T. and the Froebel Blockplay Research Group (1992) *Exploring Learning: Young Children and Blockplay*. London: Paul Chapman Publishing.

Halpin, D. (2001) 'Hope, utopianism and educational management', *Cambridge Journal of Education*, 31 (1), 103–18.

Halsey, A. H. (1986) *Change in British Society*. Oxford: Oxford University Press.

Hamilton, L. and Corbett-Whittier, C. (2013) *Using Case Study in Education Research*. London: Sage Publications Ltd.

Hampson, S. E. (1988) *The Construction of Personality*. London: Routledge.

Handy, C. (1992) 'The Language of Leadership'. In M. Syrett and C. Hogg (eds) *Frontiers of Leadership*. Oxford: Blackwell.

Harden, J. (2000) 'There's no place like home', *Childhood*, 7 (1), 43–59.

Hadfield, M. and Jopling, M. (2012) 'How might better network theories support school leadership research?', *School Leadership & Management: Formerly School Organisation*, 32 (2), 109–21.

Hargreaves, A. 'The Emotions of Teaching and Educational Change'. In *Extending Educational Change*. Netherlands: Springer, 278–95.

Hargreaves, A. (2008) *The Persistence of Presentism and the Struggle for Lasting Improvement*. Inaugural Lecture. London: Institute of Education.

Harms, T. and Clifford, R. (1980) *Early Childhood Environment Rating Scale*. New York: Teachers College Press.

Harms, T., Cryer, D. and Clifford, R. M. (1998) *Early Childhood Environment Rating Scale*. Rev. edn. New York: Teachers College Press.

—(2006) *Infant/Toddler Environment Rating Scale, Revised Edition, Updated (ITERS-R)*. New York: Teachers College Press.

Harris, M. (1992) *Language Experience and Early Language Development: From Input to Uptake*. Hove: Lawrence Erlbaum Associates.

Hart, R. (1979) *Children's Experience of Place*. New York: Irvington.

Hart, S. (2000) *Thinking Through Teaching*. London: David Fulton Publishers.

Hart, S., Dixon, A., Drummond, M. J. and McIntyre, D. (2004) *Learning Without Limits*. Maidenhead: Open University Press.

Hattie, J. (2009) *Visible Learning: A Synthesis of Meta-analyses Relating to Achievement*. London: Routledge.

—(2012) *Visible Learning for Teachers: Maximising Impact on Learning*. London: Routledge.

Hayes, N. (ed.) (2006) *Contemporary Issues in Early Childhood Education and Care*. Proceedings of OMEP conference, UCC. Cork, Ireland: OMEP.

Heard, S. (2003) 'And so What did you do at Pre-school Today?'. *Nursery World* cited in L. Ang (ed.) (2014) *The Early Years Curriculum: The UK context and beyond*. Oxon: Routledge.

Hedges, H., Cullen, J. and Jordan, B. (2011) 'Early years curriculum: funds of knowledge as a conceptual framework for children's interests', *Journal of Curriculum Studies*, 43 (2), 185–205.

Heilbronn, R. (2010) 'The Nature of Practice-based Knowledge and Understanding'. In R. Heilbronn and J. Yandell, *Critical Practice in Teacher Education: A Study of Professional Learning*. London: Institute of Education.

Hellige, J. B. (1993) *Hemispheric Asymmetry: What's Right and What's Left*. Cambridge, MA: Harvard University Press.

Henderlong, J. and Lepper, M. R. (2002) 'The effects of praise on children's intrinsic motivation: a review and synthesis', *Psychological Bulletin*, 128 (5), 774–95.

Her Majesty's Inspectors (HMI) (1985) 'The Curriculum from 5 to 16', *Curriculum Matters 2*. An HMI Series. London: HMSO.

Hergenbahn B. R. and Olson M. H. (2001) *An Introduction to Theories of Learning*. New Jersey: Prentice Hall.

Hick, P., Kershner, R. and Farrell, P. (eds) (2008) *Psychology for Inclusive Education: New Directions in Theory and Practice*. Abingdon: Routledge.

Hirst, P. H. (1965) 'Liberal Education and the Nature of Knowledge'. In R. D. Archambault (ed.) *Philosophical Analysis and Education*. London: Routledge.

—(1973) 'What is Teaching' In R. S. Peters (ed.) *The Philosophy of Education*. London: Oxford University Press.

Ho, D., Campbell-Barr, V. and Leeson, C. (2010) 'Quality improvement in early years settings in Hong Kong and England', *International Journal of Early Years Education*, 18 (3), 241–56.

Hodkinson, P., Ford, G., Hawthorn, R.and Hodkinson, H. (2007) *Learning as Being*. Learning Lives Project, Working Paper 6. Available from www.learninglives.org (accessed 5 December 2012).

Hofkins, D. (2008) 'Gently Ranting for the sake of Children'. *The Guardian*, Tuesday 16 September. Available from http://www.guardian.co.uk/education/2008/sep/16/childrensservices (accessed 11 August 2011).

Holland, P. (2003) *We Don't Play with Guns Here: War, Weapon and Superhero Play in the Early Years*. Debating Play. Maidenhead: Open University Press.

Holloway, S., L. and Valentine, G. (2000) *Children's Geographies: Playing, Living and Learning*. London: Routledge.

Hornby, G. (1995) *Working with Parents of Children with Special Needs*. London: Cassell.

Houghton, E. (ed.) (2012) *Education on the Web: A Tool-kit to Help You Search Effectively for Information on Education*. Slough: NFER.

Howe, C. (2010) *Peer Groups and Children's Development*. Oxford: Blackwell

Howes, C. and Farver, J. (1987) 'Social pretend Play in 2-year-olds: effects of age of partner', *Early Childhood Research Quarterly*, 2, 305–14.

Howes, C., and Hamilton, C. E. (1993) 'The changing experience of child care: changes in teachers and in teacher-child relationships and children's social competence with peers', *Early Childhood Research Quarterly*, 8 (1), 15–32.

Howes, C. and Smith, E. W. (1995) 'Relations among child care quality, teacher behavior, children's play activities, emotional security and cognitive activity in child care', *Early Childhood Research Quarterly*, 10 (4), 381–404.

Hoyle, E. and Megarry, J. (2005) *World Yearbook of Education 1980: The Professional Development of Teachers*. Repr. London: Routledge.

Hunt, S., Virgo, S., Klett-Davies, M., Page, A. and Apps, J. (2011) 'Provider influence on the early home learning environment (EHLE)'. Report for the DfE. DFE-RBX-10-11.

Huotilainen, M. (2010) 'Building blocks of foetal cognition: emotion and language', *Infant and Child Development*, 19, 94–8.

Hutchin, V. (2007) *Supporting Every Child's Learning across the Early Years Foundation Stage*. London: Hodder Education.

—(2012) 'The EYFS: Effective Practice' In *The EYFS: An Essential Guide*. Maidenhead: Open University Press.

James, A. and James, A. L. (2004) *Constructing Childhood: Theory, Policy and Social Practice*. Hampshire: Palgrave Macmillan.

James, A. and Prout, A. (eds) (1997) *Constructing and Reconstructing Childhood*. London: Falmer.

James, M. (1998) *Using Assessment for School Improvement*. Oxford: Heinemann.

James, M. and Pollard, A. (2006) *Improving Teaching and Learning in Schools*. London: Teaching and Learning Research Programme (TLRP). Available from tlrp.org (accessed 17 March 2012).

—(2012) 'Principles for Effective Pedagogy: International responses to evidence from the UK's Teaching and Learning Research Programme'. Abingdon: Routledge. Available from www.tlrp.org (accessed 17 March 2012).

—(2012) *Principles for Effective Pedagogy: International Responses to Evidence from the UK Teaching and Learning Research Programme*. London: Routledge.

Janes, C. L., Hesselbrock, V. M., Meyers, D. G. and Penniman, J. H. (1979) 'Problem boys in young adulthood: teacher's ratings and twelve-year follow-up', *Journal of Youth and Adolescence*, 8, 453–72.

Jennings, P. and Greenberg, M. (2009) 'The prosocial classroom: teacher and emotional competence in relation to student and classroom outcomes', *Review of Educational Research*, 79, 491.

Jin, W., Joyce, R., Phillips, D and Sibieta, L. (2011) *Poverty and Inequality in the UK: 2011*. London: Institute for Fiscal Studies (IFS).

Johnson, V., Hart, R. and Colwell, J. (2014) 'Steps to Engaging Young Children in Research, Bernard Van Leer'. Available from http://www.bernardvanleer.org/steps-to-engaging-young-children-in-research (accessed 2 September 2014).

Johnson, M. H. and Morton, J. (1991) *Biology and Cognitive Development*. Oxford: Blackwell.

Jones, P. (2009) *Rethinking Childhood: Attitudes in Contemporary Society*. London: Continuum.

Joseph Rowntree Foundation (2000) *Poverty and Social Exclusion in Britain*. York: JRF.

Kamen, T. (2013) *Observation and Assessment for the EYFS*. London: Hodder.

Karlsdottir, K. and Gardarsdottir, B. (2010) 'Exploring children's learning stories as an assessment method for research and practice', *Early Years: An International Journal of Research and Development*, 30 (3), 255–66.

Karoly, L. A., Greenwood, P. W. and Everingham, S. (eds) (1998) *Investing in Our Children: What We Know and Don't Know about the Costs and Benefits of Early Childhood Intervention*. New York: RAND.

Katz, L. G. (1993) *Dispositions: Definitions and Implications for Early Childhood Practices*. Perspectives from ERIC Clearing House on ECCE.

—(1995) *Talks with Teachers of Young Children: A Collection*. Norwood, NJ: Ablex Publishing.

—(1998) 'A Development Approach to the Curriculum in the Early Years'. In S. Smidt *The Early Years: A Reader*. Routledge: London.

—(1999) *Confession of a Teacher Educator: Memorandum to the Department Chairman.* Revised. Report: ED428874.

—(2011) 'Current Perspectives on the Early Childhood Curriculum' in R. House (ed.) *Too Much too Soon.* London: Hawthorn Press

Kehily, M. J. (2002) *Sexuality, Gender and Schooling: Shifting Agendas in Social Learning.* London: Routledge.

Kelly, A. V. (1999) *The Curriculum: Theory and Practice.* 4th edn. London: Sage Publications Ltd. [Cited in M. Priestley and W. Humes (2010) 'The development of Scotland's curriculum for excellence: amnesia and déjà vu', *Oxford Review of Education*, 36 (3), 345–61.]

Kenway, P. (2008) *Addressing In-work Poverty.* York: Joseph Rowntree Foundation.

Kernan, M. (2010) 'Outdoor affordances in early childhood education and care settings: adults' and children's perspectives', *Youth and Environments,* 20 (1), 153.

Kershner, R. (2009) 'Learning in Inclusive Classrooms'. In P. Hick, R. Kershner and P. Farrell (eds) *Psychology for Inclusive Education: New Directions in Theory and Practice.* Abingdon: Routledge.

Kettle B. and Sellars N. (1996) 'The development of student teachers practical theory of teaching', *Teaching and Teacher Education*, 12 (1), 1–24.

Kincheloe, J. L. (2008) *Critical Pedagogy Primer.* New York: Peter Lang International Academic Publishers.

King, J. R. (1998) *Uncommon Caring: Learning from Men Who Teach Young Children.* New York: Teachers College Press.

Kingdon, Z. and Gourd, J. (2013) 'Part 2. Policy in Practice'. In *Early Years Policy.* Abingdon: Routledge.

Kinney, L. and Kjorholt, A. (2005) 'Small Voices, Powerful Messages'. In A. Clark, A. Kjorholt, and P. Moss (eds) *Beyond Listening: Children s Perspectives on Early Childhood Services.* Bristol: Policy Press.

Kline, P. (1991) *Intelligence: The Psychometric View.* London: Routledge.

Knight, S. (2010) 'Forest Schools: Playing on the Wild Side'. In J. Moyles (ed.) *The Excellence of Play.* 3rd edn. Maidenhead: Open University Press/McGraw-Hill.

Kotulak, R. (1996) *Inside the Brain.* Kansas City: Andrews and McMeel.

Krogh, S. and Slentz, K. (2010) *Early Childhood Education: Yesterday, Today, and Tomorrow.* 2nd edn. New York: Routledge.

Kuhl, P. (2004) 'Early language acquisition: cracking the speech code', *Nature Neuroscience*, 5, 831–43.

Kupersmidt, J. B. and Coie, J. D. (1990) 'Preadolescent peer status, aggression, and school adjustment as predictors of externalizing problems in adolescence', *Child Development*, 61, 1350–63.

Kutnick, P. and Brighi, A. with Avgitidou, S., Genta, M. L., Hannikainen, M., Karlsson-Lohmander, M. and Ortega Riuz, R. (2007) 'The role and practice of interpersonal relationships in European early education settings: sites for enhancing social inclusion, personal growth and learning?', *European Early Childhood Education Research Journal*, 15 (3), 379–406.

Kutnick, P. and Colwell, J. (2009) 'Relationships and Dialogue Enhancement: The Relational Approach'. In C. Howe and K. Littleton (eds) *Educational Dialogue: Understanding and Promoting Interaction.* London: Routledge.

Kutnick, P., Ota, C. and Berdondini, L. (2008) 'Improving the effects of classroom groupwork with young children: attainment, attitudes and behaviour', *Learning and Instruction*, 18 (1), 83–95.

Ladd, G. W. (2005) *Children's Peer Relations and Social Competence.* New Haven, CT: Yale University Press.

Laevers, F. (1991) 'The Innovative Project: Experiential Education and the Definition of Quality on Education' In *Defining and Assessing Quality in Early Childhood Education.* Lovaina: Leuven University Press.

—(2000) 'Forward to basics! deep-level-learning and the experiential approach', *Early Years*, 20 (2), 20–9.

—(2005) Deep *Level Learning and the Experiential Approach in Early Childhood and Primary Education: Experiential Education*. Leuven: Katholieke Universiteit.

Laming, W. (2003) *The Victoria Climbié Inquiry*. Inquiry by Lord Laming Great Britain: Department for Health and Home Office.

Lancaster, Y. P. and Kirby, P. on behalf of Coram (2010 [2003]) *Listening to Young Children*. 2nd edn. Buckinghamshire: Open University Press.

Lankshear, C. and Knobel, M. (2004) *A Handbook for Teacher Research: From Design to Implementation*. Maidenhead: Open University Press.

Lankshear, C. and Snyder, I. (2000) *Teachers and Technoliteracy*. Sydney: Allen & Unwin.

Lanyard, R. and Dunn, J. (2009) *A Good Childhood: Searching for Values in a Competitive age*. London: Penguin.

Lareau, A. (1989) *Home Advantage*. London: Falmer.

Larson, J. and Marsh, J. (2005) *Making Literacy Real: Theories and Practices for Learning and Teaching*. London: Sage Publications Ltd.

Lawn, M. and Grace, G. (1987) *Teachers: The Culture and Politics of Work*, London: Falmer.

Lawrence, D. (2006) *Enhancing Self-Esteem in the Classroom*. London: Paul Chapman.

Layzer, J., Goodson, B. and Moss, M. (1993) *Life in Preschool: Volume One of an Observational Study of Early Childhood Programs for Disadvantaged Four-year-olds*. Cambridge, MA: ABT Associates.

Leach, J. and Moon, B. (2008) *The Power of Pedagogy*. London: Sage Publications Ltd.

Leckie, G., Pillinger, R., Jenkins, J. and Rasbash, J. (2010) 'School, family, neighbourhood: which is most important to a child's education?', *Significance*, 7, 67–70.

Leeson, C (2007) 'In Praise of Reflective Practice'. In J. Willan, R. Parker-Rees and J. Savage (eds) *Early Childhood Studies*. 2nd edn. Exeter: Learning Matters.

Lefebvre, H. (2004) *Rhythmanalysis: Space, Time and Everyday Life*. London: Continuum.

Lenroot, R. K., Giedd, J. N. (2006) 'Brain development in children and adolescent: insights from anatomical magnetic resonance imaging', *Neuroscience & Biobehavioral Review*, 30, 718–29.

Lewis, A. and Norwich, B. (2004) *Special Teaching for Special Children? Pedagogies for Inclusion*. Maidenhead: Open University Press.

Light, P. and Littleton, K. (1999) *Social Processes in Children's Learning*. New York: Cambridge University Press.

Lindon, J. (2010) *Reflective Practice and Early Years Professionalism: Linking Theory and Practice*. Abingdon: Hodder Education.

—(2012a) *Parents as Partners (Positive Relationships in the Early Years)*. London: Practical Pre-school Books.

—(2012b) *Reflective Practice and Early Years Professionalism: Linking Theory and Practice*. London: Hodder Education.

Linklater, H. (2010) *Making Children Count? An Autoethnographic Exploration of Pedagogy*. PhD Thesis, University of Aberdeen, Scotland.

Little, H. (2006) 'Children's risk-taking behaviour: implications for early childhood policy and practice', *Journal of Early Years Education*, 14 (2), 141–54.

Little, H., Wyver, S. and Gibson, F. (2011) 'The influence of play context and adult Attitudes on young children's physical risk-taking during outdoor play', *European Early Childhood Education Research Journal*, 19 (1), 113–31.

Luke, C. (1999) 'What next? toddler netizens, playstation thumb, techno-literacies', *Contemporary Issues in Early Childhood* 1 (1), 95–100.

Lynn, A. (2013) *The Early Years Curriculum: The UK Context and Beyond*. Oxon: Routledge.

Mac an Ghaill, M. (2004) *Young Gifted and Black: Student-teacher Relations in the Schooling of Black Youth*. Milton Keynes: Open University Press.

MacNaughton, G. (2003) *Shaping Early Childhood: Learners, Curriculum And Contexts*. Maidenhead. Open University Press.

Magnuson, K. A., Meyers, M., Ruhm, C. and Waldfogel, J. (2004) 'Inequality in preschool education and school readiness', *American Educational Research Journal*, 41, 115–57.

Malguzzi, L. (1993a) 'History, Ideas, and Basic Philosophy'. In C. Edwards, L. Gandini and G. Forman (eds) *The Hundred Languages of Children: The Reggio Emilia Approach to Early Childhood Education*. Norwood, NJ: Ablex Publishing, 41–89.

—(1993b) 'For an education based on relationships', *Young Children*, 49 (1), 9–17.

Mallinckrodt, B. (2000) 'Attachment, social competencies, social support and interpersonal process in psychotherapy', *Psychotherapy Research*, 10, 239–66.

Malloch, S. (1997) 'Mothers and infants and communicative musicality', *Musicae Scientiae, Special Issue 1999–2000*, 29–57.

Manes, S. (1996) *Be a Perfect Person in Just Three Days!* New York: Yearling Books.

Marsh, J. (2004) (ed.) *Popular Culture, New Media and Digital Literacy in Early Childhood*. London: RoutledgeFalmer.

—(2007) 'icurricula, ipedagogies and outmoded ideologies: literacy teaching and learning in the digital era'. Paper presented at the 'Future Directions in Literacy' Conference, University of Sydney, September 2007.

Martin, J. (1983) 'What Should We Do with a Hidden Curriculum When We Find One?'. In H. Giroux and D. Purpel (eds) *The Hidden Curriculum and Moral Education*. Berkeley, CA: McCutchan Publishing Corporation, 122–39.

Maslow, A. H. (1954) *Motivation and Personality*. New York: Harper and Row.

Mathieson, K. (2005) *Social Skills in the Early Years: Supporting Social and Behavioural Learning*. London: Paul Chapman Publishing.

—(2012) *Understanding Young Children's Behaviour*. London: Practical Preschool.

Mayall, B. (2000) 'Conversations with Children: Working with Generational Issues'. In P. Christensen and A. James (eds) *Research with Children. Perspectives and Practices*. London and New York: Falmer Press.

—(2002) *Towards a Sociology for Childhood: Thinking from Children's Lives*. Milton Keynes: Open University Press.

Maynard, T. and Waters, J. (2007) 'Learning in the outdoor environment: a missed opportunity?', *Early Years: Journal of International Research and Development*, 27 (3), 255–65.

Maynard, T. (2007) 'Forest Schools in Great Britain: an initial exploration', *Contemporary Issues in Early Childhood*, 8 (4), 320–31.

McGillivray, G. (2008) 'Nannies, nursery nurses and early years professionals: constructions of professional identity in the early years workforce in England', *European Early Childhood Education Research Journal*, 16 (2), 242–54.

McIntyre, C. (2012) *Enhancing Learning Through Play – A Developmental Perspective for Early Years Settings*. London: Routledge.

McKey, R. H., Condelli, L., Ganson, H., Barrett, B. J., McConkey, C. and Plantz, M. C. (1985) *The Impact Of Head Start On Children, Families And Communities*. Washington, DC: CSR.ED 263 984.

McPake, J., Stephen, C., Plowman, L., Sime, D. and Downey, S. (2005) *Already at a Disadvantage? ICT in the Home and Children's Preparation for Primary School*. Coventry: British Educational Communications and Technology Agency.

Mead, G. H. (1934) *Mind Self and Society from the Standpoint of a Social Behaviorist*, C. W. Morris (ed.). Chicago: University of Chicago.

Mehrabian, A. (1971) *Silent Messages*. Wadsworth, CA: Belmont.

Mehrabian, A. and Diamond, S. G. (1971) 'The effects of furniture arrangement, props, and personality on social interaction', *Journal of Personality and Social Psychology*, 20, 18–30.

Meighan, R. and Siraj-Blatchford, I. (2007) *A Sociology of Education.* 5th edn. London: Continuum.

Melhuish, E. (2004) 'A Literature Review of the Impact of Early Years Provision on Young Children, with Emphasis Given to Children From Disadvantaged Backgrounds'. Birkbeck: University of London, Prepared for the National Audit Office.

Meltzoff, A. N. and Moore, M. K. (1983) 'Newborn infants imitate adult facial gestures', *Child Development,* 54, 702–809.

Menter, I., Elliot, D., Hall, J., Hulme, M., Lewin, J. and Lowden, K. (2010) *A Guide to Practitioner Research in Education.* Maidenhead: Open University Press.

Mercer, N. (1992) 'Culture, Context and the Appropriation of Knowledge'. In P. Light and G. Butterworth (eds) *Context and Cognition: Ways of Learning and Knowing.* Hemel Hempstead: Harvester Wheatsheaf.

—(2000) *Words and Minds: How we use Language to think Together.* London: Routledge.

Mercer, N. and Hodgkinson, S. (eds) (2008) *Exploring Talk in School: Inspired by the Work of Douglas Barnes.* London: Sage Publications Ltd.

Mercer, N. and Littleton, K. (2007) *Dialogue and the Development of Children's Thinking.* London: Routledge.

Merrett, F. and Wheldall, K. (1990) *Identifying Troublesome Classroom Behaviour.* London: Paul Chapman.

Millar, R., Leach, J., Osborne, J. and Ratcliffe, M. (2006) 'Improving Subject Teaching: Lessons from Research in Science'. In *Education.* London, Routledge.

Miller, C. F., Lurye, L. E., Zosuls, K. M. and Ruble, D. N. (2009) 'Accessibility of gender stereotype domains: developmental and gender differences in children', *Sex Roles,* 60, 870–81.

Miller, L., Cable, C. and Devereux, J. (2005) 'Reflection in Practice'. In *Developing Early Years Practice.* Oxon: David Fulton, 64–78.

Mills, C. W. (1959) *The Sociological Imagination.* Oxford: Oxford University Press.

Minow, M. (1990) *Making All the Difference: Inclusion, Exclusion and American Law.* Ithaca: Cornell University Press.

Mitchell, D. (ed.) (2005) *Contextualizing Inclusive Education: Evaluating Old and New International Perspectives.* London: Routledge.

Mitchell, N. and Pearson, J. (2012) *Inquiring in the Classroom: Asking the Questions That Matter About Teaching and Learning.* London: Continuum.

Money, J. (1985) *Gendermaps: Social Constructionism, Feminism, and Sexosophical History.* New York: Continuum.

Moore, A. (2004) *The Good Teacher: Dominant Discourses in Teaching and Teacher Education.* Abingdon: Routledge.

Mortimore, P., Sammons, P., Stoll, L., Lewis, D. and Ecob, R. (1988) *School Matters: The Junior Years.* Wells: Open Books.

Moss, P. (2008) 'What future for the relationship between early childhood education and care and compulsory schooling?', *Research in Comparative and International Education,* 3 (3), 224–34.

—(2005) 'Theoretical examinations of quality: making the narrative of quality stutter', *Early Education and Development,* 16 (4), 405–20.

—(2006) 'Structures, understandings and discourses: possibilities for re-envisioning the early childhood worker', *Contemporary Issues in Early Childhood,* 7 (1), 30–4.

—(2014) *Transformative Change and Real Utopias in Early Childhood Education: A Story of Democracy, Experimentation and Potentiality.* London: Routledge.

Moss, P. and Penn, H. (1996) *Transforming Nursery Education.* London: Sage Publications Ltd.

Moss, P. and Petrie, P. (2002) *From Children's Services to Children's Space.* London: RoutledgeFalmer.

Moyles, J. (ed.) (2005) *The Excellence of Play.* 2nd edn. Maidenhead: Open University Press.

Moyles, J., Adams, S. and Musgrove, A. (2002). 'SPEEL: Study of Pedagogical Effectiveness in Early Learning'. Research Report, Department for Education and Skills.

Mueller, C. M. and Dweck, C. S. (1998) 'Praise for intelligence can undermine children's motivation and performance', *Journal for Personality and Social Psychology,* 75 (1), 33–52.

Murphy, P. (2001) 'Gendered Learning and Achievement'. In J. Collins and D. Cook (eds) *Understanding Learning: Influences and Outcomes.* London: Paul Chapman.

Murray, R. (2003) 'Forest School Evaluation Project: A Study in Wales'. Report to the Forestry Commission, nef, London.

Musatti, T. and Mayer, S. (2011) 'EDUCARE in the Nidi: how to weave a tapestry from many threads', *Children in Europe,* 20, 6–7.

Mustard, J. F. (2006) 'Early child development and experience-based brain development—the scientific underpinnings of the importance of early child development in a globalized world', *Paediatrics & Child Health,* 11 (9), 571–2.

Nader, P. R., O'Brien, M., Houts, R., Bradley, R., Belsky, J., Crosnoe, R., Friedman, S. and Susman, E. J. (2012) 'Identifying risk for obesity in early childhood', *Pediatrics,* 118 (3), 594–601.

NAEYC (1993) *A Conceptual Framework for Early Childhood Professional Development.* Washington, DC: National Association for the Education of Young Children.

Nash, R. (1976) *Teacher Expectations and Pupil Learning.* London: Routledge.

National Children's Bureau (2013) *Greater Expectations: Raising Aspirations for Our Children.* London: NCB.

National Council for Curriculum and Assessment (2004) *Towards a Framework for Early Learning.* Dublin, NCCA.

Newell, P. (1991) *The UN Convention and Children's Rights in the UK.* London: National Children's Bureau.

Nieto, S. (2009) *The Light in their Eyes: Creating Multicultural Learning Communities.* New York: Teacher College Press.

Nivala, V. and Hujala, E. (eds) (2002) 'Leadership in Early Childhood Education: Cross-cultural Perspectives'. Finland: Department of Educational Sciences and Teacher Education, Early Childhood Education, University of Oulu. Available from http://herkules.oulu.fi/isbn9514268539/isbn9514268539.pdf (accessed 14 June 2009).

Northern Territory Government (2012) 'Play Based Learning. Available from http://www.education.nt.gov.au/__data/assets/pdf_file/0015/960/play-based_learning.pdf (accessed 5 June 2013).

Nowicki, S. Jr. and Duke, M. P. (2000) 'Interpersonal Sensitivity: The Diagnostic Analysis of Nonverbal Accuracy (DANVA): Assessment and Remediation'. In J. Hall and F. Bernieri (eds) *Interpersonal Sensitivity.* Mahwah, NJ: Lawrence Erlbaum Associates.

Nupponen, H. (2006a) 'Framework for developing leadership skills in child care centres in Queensland, Australia', *Contemporary Issues in Early Childhood,* 7 (2), 146–61.

—(2006b) 'Leadership concepts and theories: reflections for practice for early childhood directors', *Australian Journal of Early Childhood,* 31 (1), 43–50.

Nutbrown, C. (2006) *Threads of Thinking.* 3rd edn. London: Sage Publications Ltd.

—(2012) 'Foundations for Quality: The Independent Review of Early Education and Childcare Qualifications'. Final Report. Nutbrown Review London: DfE.

—(2013) 'Shaking the foundations of quality? Why childcare policy must not lead to poor-quality early education and care'. University of Sheffield. Available at from shef.ac.uk/polopoly_fs/1.263201!/file/Shakingthefoundationsofquality.pdf (accessed 12 December 2013).

Nutbrown, C. Clough, P. and Atherton, C. (2013) *Inclusion in the Early Years: Cultural Analyses and Enabling Narratives.* London: Sage Publications Ltd.

Nutbrown, C. and Clough, S. (2010) *Early Childhood Education: History, Philosophy and Experience.* London: Sage Publications Ltd.

—(2014) *Early Childhood Education: History, Philosophy and Experience*. 2nd edn. London: Sage Publications Ltd.

Nutkins, S., McDonald, C. and Stephen, M. (2013) *Early Childhood Education and Care*. London: Sage Publications Ltd.

Oberhuemer, P. (2005) 'Conceptualising the early childhood pedagogue: policy approaches and issues of professionalism', *European Early Childhood Education Research Journal*, 13 (1), 5–16.

Organisation for Economic Co-operation and Development (OECD) (2001) *Starting Strong: Early Childhood Education and Care*. Paris: OECD.

—(2004) *What makes School Systems Perform? Seeing School Systems through the Prism of PISA*. Paris: OECD: Paris.

—(2005) *Teachers Matter: Attracting, Developing and Retaining Effective Teachers*. Paris: OECD.

—(2006) *Starting Strong II: Early Childhood Education and Care*. Paris: OECD

Office for National Statistics (2012) *Britain: The Official Yearbook of the United Kingdom*. London: The Stationery Office.

Ofsted (2013) 'Conducting Early Years Inspections'. Available from http://www.ofsted.gov.uk/resources/conducting-early-years-inspections (accessed 6 Auguest 2014).

Opie, I. and Opie, P. (1959) *The Lore and Language of Schoolchildren*. Oxford: Oxford University Press.

Orme, M. E. J., McDonald, F. J. and Allen, D. W. (1966) 'The effects of modelling and feedback variables on the acquisition of a complex teaching strategy'. Paper presented at the American Education Research Association Chicago.

Osborn, M., McNess, E., Broadfoot, P., Pollard, A. and Triggs, P. (2000) *What Teachers Do: Changing Policy and Practice in Primary Education*. London and New York: Continuum.

Osgood, J. (2004) 'Time to get down to business? the responses of early years practitioners to entrepreneurial approaches to professionalism', *Journal of Early Childhood Research*, 2, 5–24.

—(2006) 'Editorial. rethinking "professionalism" in the early years: English perspectives', *Contemporary Issues in Early Childhood*, 7 (1), 1–4. Available from www.wwwords.co.uk/ciec/content/pdfs/7/issue7_1.asp (accessed 4 May 2012).

—(2012) *Narratives from the Nursery: Negotiating Professional Identities in Early Childhood*. London: Routledge.

Osler, A. and Starkey, H. (2007) 'Study on the advances in Civic Education in education systems: good practices in industrialized countries' [Chinese translation], *Journal of Information Center for Social Sciences*. Renmin: University of China.

—(2010) *Teachers and Human Rights Education*. Stoke-on-Trent: Trentham Books.

Ota, C. (n.d.) 'Working With Others: Canada'. Available from http://www.workingwithothers.org/international/canada/ (accessed 15 March 2012).

Paley, V. G. (1990) *The Boy Who Would Be a Helicopter: The Uses of Storytelling in the Classroom*. Cambridge, MA: Harvard University Press. Available from www.ofsted.gov.uk/accessandachievement (accessed 5 March 2013).

Palmer, S. (2006) *Toxic Childhood: How the Modern World is Damaging our Children and What we can do About it*. London: Orion.

Papatheodorou, T. (2009) 'Exploring Relational Pedagogy'. In T. Papatheodorou and J. R. Moyles (eds) *Learning Together in the Early Years: Exploring Relational Pedagogy*. Oxon: Routledge.

Papatheodorou, T. and Moyles, J. R. (eds) (2009) *Learning Together in the Early Years: Exploring Relational Pedagogy*. Oxon: Routledge.

Parker-Rees, R. (2007) 'Liking to be liked: imitation, familiarity and pedagogy in the first years of life', *Early Years*, 27 (1), 3–17.

—(2011) *Meeting the Child in Steiner Kindergartens: An Exploration of Beliefs, Values and Practices*. London: Routledge.

Parker-Rees, R., Leeson, C., Savage, J. and Willan, J. (eds) (2010) *Early Childhood Studies*. London: Sage Publications Ltd.

Parker, I. (2013) *Early Developments. Bridging the gap between Evidence and Policy in Early Years Education*. London: Institute for Public Policy Research.

Parkin, P. (2009) 'Need for more male role models', *Early Years Educator*, 10 (9), 6. [Cited in S. Bownhill 'The "brave" man in the early years (0–8): the ambiguities of the "role model"'. Paper presented at the British Educational Research Association Annual Conference, University of Warwick, 1–4 September 2010.]

Pascal, C. and Bertram, T. (2013) *The Impact of Early Education as a Strategy in Countering Socio-economic Disadvantage*. CREC. London: Ofsted.

Pascal, C., Bertram, A. D., Ramsden, F., Georgeson, J., Saunders, M. and Mould, C. (1998) *Effective Early Learning: Evaluating and Developing Quality in Early Childhood Settings*. Worcester: Amber Publications.

Pea, R. D. (2004) 'The social and technological dimensions of scaffolding and related theoretical concepts for learning, education and human activity', *Journal of the Learning Sciences*, 13, 423–51.

Peace Initiatives Institute. Available from http://www.pii-mifc.org/ (accessed 9 August 2014).

Peacock, P. and Robson, E. (2004) 'A Curriculum for Excellence Ministerial Response, SEED'. Available from http://www.scotland.gov.uk/Publications/2004/11/20175/45848 (accessed 17 April 2013).

Peccei, J. S. (ed.). (2006) *Child language: A Resource Book for Students*. London: Routledge.

Peeters, J. and Vandenbroeck, M. (2011) 'Childcare Practitioners and the Process of Professionalization'. In L. Miller and C. Cable *Professionalization, Leadership and Management in the Early Years*. London: Sage Publications Ltd.

Pellegrini, A. D. and Blatchford, P. (2000) *The Child at School: Interactions with Peers and Teachers*. London: Arnold.

Penn, H. (2011) *Quality in Early Education and Care: An International Perspective*. Maidenhead: Open University Press.

—(2008) *Understanding Early Childhood: Issues and Controversies*. Maidenhead: Open University Press/McGraw Hill.

Penn, H. and McQuail, S. (1997) 'Childcare as a Gendered Occupation'. Research Report No. 23. Nottingham: Department for Education and Employment.

Perry, B. and Szalavitz, M. (2011) *Born for Love: Why Empathy is Essential—and Endangered*. New York: Harper Taylor.

Peters, R .S. (1966) *Ethics and Education*. London: Allen and Unwin Ltd.

Petrie, S. (2003) 'Working with Families where there are Child Protection Concerns'. In M. Bell and K. Wilson (eds) *Practitioners Guide to Working With Families*. Basingstoke: Palgrave.

Piaget, J. (1926) *The Language and Thought of the Child*. New York: Basic Books.

—(1928) *Judgment and Reasoning in the Child*. London: Routledge & Kegan Paul.

—(1950) *The Psychology of Intelligence*. London: Routledge & Kegan Paul.

—(1951) *Play, Dreams and Imitation*. New York: W. W. Norton.

—(1961) 'A genetic approach to the psychology of thought', *Journal of Educational Psychology*, 52, 51–61.

Plowman, L. and Stephen, C. (2005) 'Children, play, and computers in pre-school education', *British Journal of Educational Technology*, 36 (2), 145–57.

—(2007) 'Guided interaction in pre-school settings'. *Journal of Computer Assisted Learning*, 23, 14–26.

Pollard, A. (1985) *The Social World of the Primary School*. London: Cassell.

—(1987) 'Social differentiation in primary schools', *Cambridge Journal of Education*, 17 (3), 158–61.

—(2007) 'Principles into practice: A teacher's guide to research evidence on teaching and learning'. Availabe from http://www.tlrp.org/pub/documents/Principles%20in%20Practice%20 Low%20Res.pdf (accessed 11 February 2010).

—(ed.) (2010) *Professionalism and Pedagogy: A Contemporary Opportunity*. London: Teaching and Learning Research Programme (TLRP).

Pollard, A. with Anderson, J., Maddock, M., Swaffield, S., Warin, J. and Warwick, P. (2008) *Reflective Teaching*. London: Continuum.

Pollard, A. with Filer, A. (1996) *The Social World of Children's Learning: Case Studies of Pupils from Four to Seven*. London: Cassell.

—(1999) *The Social World of Pupil Career: Strategic Biographies Through Primary School*. London: Cassell.

Pratt, D. (1980) *Curriculum Design and Development*. New York: Harcourt Brace Jovanovich.

Prenksy, M. (2001) 'Digital natives, digital immigrants, part II. do they really think differently?', *On the Horizon*, 9 (6), 1–6.

Prout, A. (2011) 'Taking a step away from modernity: reconsidering the new sociology of childhood', *Global Studies of Childhood*, 1 (1), 4–14.

Pugh, G. (2006) 'The Policy Agenda for Early Childhood Services'. In G. Pugh and B. Duffy (eds) *Contemporary Issues in the Early Years: Working Collaboratively for Children*. 4th edn. London: Sage Publications Ltd.

Pugh, G. and Duffy, B. (eds) (2009) *Contemporary Issues in The Early Years*. 5th edn. London: Sage Publications Ltd.

Qualifications and Curriculum Authority (QCA) (2007) *The Big Picture of the Curriculum*. London: QCA.

Qvortrup, J., Bardy, M., Sgritta, G and Wintersberger, H. (eds) (1994) *Childhood Matters: Social Theory, Practice and Politics*. Aldershot: Avebury.

Race Relations Amendment Act 2000. London: HMSO.

Rayna, S. and Laevers, F. (2011) 'Understanding children from 0–3 years of age and its implications for education. what's new on the babies' side? origins and evolutions', *European Early childhood Education Research Journal*, 19 (2), 161–72.

Reay, D. (2000) 'A useful extension of Bourdieu's conceptual framework?: emotional capital as a way of understanding mothers' involvement in their children's education?', *The Sociological Review*, 48, 568–85.

Reid, I. (1998) *Class in Britain*. Cambridge: Polity Press.

Reilly, J. J., Armstrong, J., Dorosty, A. R., Emmett, P. M., Ness, A., Rogers, I., Steer, C. and Sherriff, A. (2005) 'Early life risk factors for obesity in childhood: cohort study', *British Medical Journal*, 330 (7504), 1357–9.

Rinaldi, C. (1993) 'The Emergent Curriculum and Social Constructivism'. In C. Edwards, L. Gandini and G. Forman (eds) *The Hundred Languages of Children: The Reggio Emilia Approach to Early Childhood Education*. Norwood, NJ: Ablex Publishing, 101–11.

—(2005) 'Documentation and Assessment: What is the Relationship?'. In A. Clark, A. Kjorholt and P. Moss (eds) *Beyond Listening: Children's Perspectives on Early Childhood Services*. Bristol: Policy Press, 17–28.

—(2006) *In Dialogue with Reggio Emilia: Listening, Researching and Learning*. Abingdon: Routledge.

Robert-Holmes, G. and Brownhill, S. (2011) 'Where Are the Men? A Critical Discussion of Male Absence in the Early Years'. In L. Miller and C. Cable (eds) *Professionalization, Leadership and Management in the Early Years*. London: Sage Publications Ltd.

Roberts, M. (2002) *Self-Esteem and Early Learning: Key People from Birth to School*. 2nd edn. London: Paul Chapman Publishing.

Rodd, J. (1998) *Leadership in Early Childhood*. 2nd edn. Buckingham: Open University Press

—(2006) *Leadership in Early Childhood*. 3rd edn. Maidenhead: Open University Press.

Roffey, S. (2011) *Changing Behaviour in Schools: Promoting Positive Relationships and Wellbeing*. London: Sage Publications Ltd.

Roffey, S. and O'Reirdan, T. (1997) *Infant Classroom Behaviour: Needs, Perspectives and Strategies*. London: David Fulton Publishing.

Rogers, C. R. (1961) *On Becoming a Person-A Psychotherapists View of Psychotherapy*. Boston, NJ: Houghton Mifflin.

Rogers, C. (1969) *Freedom to Learn*. New York: Merrill.

—(1980) *A Way of Being*. Boston: Houghton Mifflin.

Rogers, B, (2011) *Classroom Behaviour: A Practical Guide to Effective Teaching, Behaviour Management and Colleague Support*. 3rd edn. London: Sage Publications Ltd.

Rogers, B. and McPherson, E. (2008) *Behaviour Management with Young Children: Crucial First Steps with Children 3–7 Years*. London: Sage Publications Ltd.

Rogoff, B. (1990) *Apprenticeship in Thinking: Cognitive Development in Social Context*. Oxford: Oxford University Press.

—(1995) 'Observing Sociocultural Activity on Three Planes: Participatory Appropriation, Guided Participation, and Apprenticeship'. In J. V. Wertsch, P. del Rio and A. Alvarez (eds) *Sociocultural Studies of Mind*. Cambridge: Cambridge University Press, 139–64. [Reprinted (2008) in K. Hall and P. Murphy (eds) *Pedagogy and practice: Culture and Identities*. London: Sage Publications Ltd.]

Rostow, W. W. (1960) *The Stages of Economic Growth: A Non-Communist Manifesto*. Cambridge: Cambridge University Press.

Rowe, N., Wilkin, A. and Wilson, R. (2012) *Mapping of Seminal Reports on Good Teaching*. Slough: NFER.

Rudduck, J. and McIntyre, D. (2007) *Improving Learning Through Consulting Pupils*. London: Routledge.

Rutanen, N. (2011) 'Space for Toddlers in Early Childhood Education and Care', *Nordic Early Childhood Education and Care (ECEC) – Effects and Challenges Research – Practice – Policy Making*, 18–20. May 2011, Oslo, Norway.

Rutter, M. and Madge, N. (1976) *Cycles of Disadvantage*. London: Heinemann.

Sachs, J. (2003) *The Activist Teaching Profession*. Buckingham: Open University Press.

Sahlberg, P. (2012) *Finnish Lessons: What the World Can Learn from Educational Change in Finland?*. Boston: Teachers' College Press.

Salmon, A. K. and Lucas, T. (2011) 'Exploring young children's conceptions about thinking', *Journal of Research in Childhood Education*, 25, 364–75.

Sammons, P., Elliot, K., Sylva, K., Melhuish, E. C., Siraj-Blatchford, I. and Taggart, B. (2004) 'The impact of pre-school on young children's cognitive attainments at entry to reception', *British Education Research Journal*, 30 (5), 691–712.

Sanefuji, W. (2013) 'Similar physical appearance affects friendship selection in preschoolers', *Psychology*, 4 (6), 8–13.

Sangster, M. (2012) *Developing Teacher Expertise: Exploring Key Issues in Primary Practice*. London: Bloomsbury Academic.

Schmidt, W. and Prawat, R. (2006) 'Curriculum coherence and national control of education: issue or non-issue?', *Journal of Curriculum Studies*, 38 (6), 641–58.

School Curriculum Assessment Authority (SCAA) (1996) *Nursery Education: Desirable Outcomes for Children's Learning on Entering Compulsory Education*. London: SCAA and Department for Education and Employment.

Schön, D. A. (1983a) *Educating the Reflective Practitioner: Toward a New Design for Teaching and Learning in the Professions*. New Jersey: Jossey-Bass.

—(1983b) *The Reflective Practitioner: How Professionals Think in Action*. London: Temple Smith. (Reading 3.3)

—(1987) *Educating the Reflective Practitioner*. San Francisco: Jossey-Bass.

Schuller, T. and Watson, D. (2009) *Learning through Life: Inquiry into the Future for Lifelong Learning*. Leicester: National Institute of Adult and Continuing Education.

Schultz, T. W. (1971) *Investment in Human Capital*. New York: Free Press.

Schunk, D. (1981) 'Modelling and attributional effects on children's achievement: a self-efficacy analysis', *Journal of Educational Psychology*, 73, 93–105.

Schwanenflugel, P. J., Hamiliton, A. M., Kuhn, M. R., Wisenbaker, J., and Stahl, S. A. (2004) 'Becoming a fluent reader: reading skill and prosodic features in the oral reading of young readers', *Journal of Educational Psychology*, 96, 119–29.

Schweinhart, L. J., Barnes, H. V. and Weikart, D. P. (1993) *Significant Benefits: The High/Scope Perry Preschool Study through Age 27*. (Monographs of the High/Scope Educational Research Foundation, 10), Ypsilanti, MI: High/Scope Press. PS 021 998.

Schweinhart, L. J., Berrueta-Clement, J. R., Barnett, W. S., Epstein, A. S. and Weikart, D. P. (1985) 'Effects of the Perry Preschool program on youths through age 19: a summary', *Topics in Early Childhood Special Education*, 5, 26–35.

Schweinhart, L. J., Montie, J., Xiang, Z., Barnett, W. S., Belfield, C. R. and Nores, M. (2005) 'Lifetime Effects: the High/Scope Perry Preschool study through age 40'. HighScope Educational Research Foundation. Online. Available from http://www.highscope.org/ (accessed 11 August 2012).

Scott-Baumann, A., Bloomfield, A. and Roughton, L. (1997) *Becoming a Secondary School Teacher*. London: Hodder and Stoughton.

Scottish Consultative Council on the Curriculum (SCCC) (1999) 'A Curriculum Framework for Children 3 to 5'. Dundee: Scottish Consultative Council on the Curriculum.

Scottish Executive (2009) 'Curriculum for Excellence'. Online. Available from http://www.educationscotland.gov.uk/thecurriculum/whatiscurriculumforexcellence/index.asp (accessed 19 January 2012).

Seligman, C. F., Tucker, G. R. and Lambert, W. E. (1972) 'The effects of speech style and other attributes on teachers' attitudes towards pupils', *Language in Society*, 1, 131–42.

Sfard, A. (1998) 'On two metaphors for learning and the dangers of choosing just one', *Educational Researcher*, 27 (2), 4–13.

Shankweiler, D. and Fowler, A. E. (2004) 'Questions people ask about the role of phonological processes in learning to read', *Reading and Writing: An Interdisciplinary Journal*, 17, 483–515.

Sharma, A. and Cockerill, H. (2014) *From Birth to Five Years: Practical Developmental Examination*. London: Routledge.

Sharp, R. (2004) 'Risk in Outdoor Education'. In P. Barnes and B. Sharp *Outdoor Education*. Lyme Regis: Russell House Publishing.

Sharp, R. and Green, A. (1975) *Education and Social Control*. London: Routledge.

Sheridan, S. (2001) 'Pedagogical Quality in Preschool: An Issue of Perspectives. Unpublished PhD Thesis, University Gothenburg.

—(2007) 'Dimensions of pedagogical quality in preschool', *International Journal of Early Years Education*, 15 (2), 197–217.

Siegler, R. S. (1996) *Emerging Minds: The Process of Change in Children's Thinking*. New York: Oxford University Press.

Sikes, P., Measor, L., Woods, P. (1985) *Teacher Careers: Crises and Continuities*. London and Philadelphia: The Falmer Press.

Silver, H. (1980) *Education and the Social Condition*. London: Methuan.

Siraj-Blatchford, I. and Sylva, K. (2004) 'Researching pedagogy in English pre-schools', *British Educational Research Journal*, 30 (5), 713–30.

Siraj-Blatchford, I. (1995) 'Expanding Combined Nursery Provision: Bridging the gap between Care and Education'. In P. Gammage and J. Meighan *The Early Years: The Way Forward*. Nottingham: Education New Books.

—(2008) 'Understanding the relationship between curriculum, pedagogy and progression in learning in early childhood', *Hong Kong Journal of Early Childhood Education*, 7 (2), 3–13.

—(2009) 'Conceptualising progression in the pedagogy of play and sustained shared thinking in early childhood education: a Vygotskian perspective', *Educational and Child Psychology*, 26 (2), 77–89.

Siraj-Blatchford, I. and Clarke, P. (2000) *Diversity and Language in the Early Years*. Buckingham: Open University Press.

Siraj-Blatchford, I. and Manni, L. (2007) *Effective Leadership in the Early Years Sector: The ELEYS Study*. London: University of London institute of Education

—(2008) *Early Years: An International Journal of Research and Development*. doi:10.1080/09575 146.2014.929362.

Siraj-Blatchford, I., Mayo, A., Melhuish, E., Taggart, B., Sammons, P. and Sylva, K. (2011) *Performing Against the Odds: Developmental Trajectories of Children in the EPPSE 3–16 Study*. London: Department for Education.

Siraj-Blatchford, I., Sylva, K., Taggart, B., Sammons, P., Melhuish, E. and Elliot, K. (2003) *The Effective Provision of Pre-school Education (EPPE) Project: Intensive Case Studies of Practice across the Foundation Stage*. London: DfEE/Institute of Education.

Siraj-Blatchford, I., Sylva, K., Laugharne, J., Milton, E. and Clarles, F. (2006) 'The Monitoring and Evaluation of the Effective Implementation of the Foundation Phase (MEEIFS) Project Across Wales'. Foundation Phase Pilot, Final Evaluation Report. Available from wales.gov.uk/ foundationphase (accessed 24 April 2013).

Siraj-Blatchford, J. and Siraj-Blatchford, I. (2002) 'Developmentally appropriate technology in early childhood: "video conferencing"—a limit case?', *Contemporary Issues in Early Education*, 3 (2), 216–25.

Skelton, C. (2001) *Schooling the Boys: Masculinities and Primary Education*. Buckingham: Open University Press.

Skinner, B. F. (1968) *The Technology of Teaching*. New York: Appleton.

Slyva, K. (1999). 'The Role of Research in Explaining the Past and Shaping the Future'. In L. Abbott and H. Moylett (eds) *Early Education Transformed New Millenium Series*. London: Falmer Press.

Smidt, S. (2011) *Introducing Bruner – A Guide for Practitioners and Students in Early Years Education*. London: Routledge.

Smith, A. (1998) *Accelerated Learning in Practice*. Stafford: Network, Educational Press.

Smith, L. A. H. (1985) *To Understand and to Help: the Life and Work of Susan Isaacs (1885–1948)*. Delaware: Associated University press.

Solar, J., Walsh, C. S., Craft, A., Rix, J. and Simmons, K. (2012) *Transforming Practice. Critical Issues in Equity, Diversity and Education*. Maidenhead: Open University Press.

Solomon, J. (1987) 'New thoughts on teacher education', *Oxford Review of Education*, 13 (3), 267–74.

Solvason, C. L. (2012) 'Research and the early years practitioner-researcher', *Early Years: An International Research Journal*, 33 (1), 90–7.

Southworth, G. Nias, J. and Campbell, P. (1992) 'Rethinking Collegiality: Teachers' Views'. Mimeo presented to the American Educational Research Association, New Orleans.

Staggs, L. (2012) 'The Rhetoric and Reality of a National Strategy for Early Education and Assessment. In L. Miller and D. Hevey (eds) *Policy and Issues in the Early Years*. London: Sage Publications Ltd..

Statistics for Wales (2014) 'Achievement and entitlement to free school meals in Wales, 2013'. Available from http://wales.gov.uk/docs/statistics/2014/140122-academic-achievement-free-school-meals-en.pdf (accessed 18 September 2014).

Stephen, C. (2010) 'Pedagogy: the silent partner in early years learning', *Early Years*, 30 (3), 28.

Stewart, N. (2011) *How Children Learn: The Characteristics of Effective Early Learning*. London: British Association for Early Childhood Education.

Stone, C. A. (1998) 'The metaphor of scaffolding: its utility for the field of learning disabilities', *Journal of Learning Disabilities*, 31, 344–64.

Sutherland, M. (2005) Gifted and Talented in the Early Years London: Sage Publishing Ltd.

Sutherland, R., Robertson, S. and John, P. (2008) *Improving Classroom Learning with ICT*. London: Routledge.

—(2009) *Improving Classroom Learning with ICT*. London: Routledge.

Swann, M., Peacock, A., Hart, S. and Drummond, M. J. (2012) *Creating Learning Without Limits*. Maidenhead: Open University Press.

Sylva, K. (1999) 'Linking quality processes to children's developmental outcomes'. Keynote Lecture, Warwick Conference, April.

Sylva, K., Melhushish, E., Sammons, P., Siraj-Blatchford, I. and Taggart B. (2004a) 'The Effective Provision of Pre-school Education (EPPE) Project: Findings from Pre-school to End of Key Stage 1'. Nottingham: DfES Publications.

—(2004b) 'The Effective Provision of Pre-School Education (EPPE) Project: Technical Paper 12 – The Final Report: Effective Pre-School Education'. London: DfES/Institute of Education, University of London.

—(2007) 'Effective Pre-school and Primary Education 3–11 Project (EPPE 3–11): Promoting Equality in the Early Years, Report to The Equalities Review'. London: Crown Copyright.

—(2008) 'Final Report from the Primary Phase: Pre-school, School and Family Influences on children's development during Key Stage 2 (7–11)'. Nottingham: DCSF.

—(2010) *Early Childhood Matters: Evidence from the Effective Pre-school and Primary Education Project*. London: Routledge.

—(2012) 'Effective Pre-school, Primary and Secondary Education Project (EPPSE 3–14)'. Final Report from the Key Stage 3 Phase: Influences on Students' Development from Age 11–14, DFE RB 202. London: Institute of Education, University of London.

Sylva, K., Sammons, P., Siraj-Blatchford, I. Melhuish, E. and Quinn, L. (2001) 'The Effective Provision of Pre-school Eduation (EPPE) Project, Symposium presented at the British Education Research Conference (BERA), Leeds.

Sylva, K., Siraj-Blatchford, I. and Johnson, S. (1992) 'The impact of the UK national curriculum on pre-school practice', *International Journal of Early Childhood*, 24, 41–51.

Sylva, K., Siraj-Blatchford, I., Melhuish, E. C., Sammons, P., Taggart, B., Evans, E., Dobson, A., Jeavons, M., Lewis, K., Morahan, M. and Sadler, S. (1999) 'The Effective Provision of Pre-School Education (EPPE) Project: Technical Paper 6A – Characteristics of Pre-School Environments'. London: DfEE/Institute of Education, University of London.

Sylvie, R. and Laevers, F. (2011) 'Understanding children from 0 to 3 years of age and its implications for education. What's new on the babies' side?', *Origins and Evolutions, European Early Childhood Education Research Journal*, 19 (2), 161–72.

Szanto, C., Banks, L., Gracethorne, C. and Balloch, S. (2003) *Research into the Childcare Workforce in Brighton and Hove*. Brighton: University of Brighton, Health and Social Policy Research Centre.

Tabachnick, R. and Zeichner, K. (eds) (1991) *Issues and Practices in Inquiry-Oriented Teacher Education*. London: Falmer.

Tancock, S .M. and Segedy, J. (2004) 'A comparison of young children's technology-Enhanced and traditional responses to texts: an action research project', *Journal of Research in Childhood Education,* 19 (1).

Tassoni, P. and Hucker, K. (2000) *Planning Play and the Early Years*. Oxford: Heinemann.

Tharp, R. and Gallimore, R. (1988) *Rousing Minds to Life: Teaching, Learning and Schooling in Social Context*. New York: Cambridge University Press.

The Royal Society (2011a) *Neuroscience, Society and Policy.* Brain Waves Module 1. London: The Royal Society.

—(2011b) *Neuroscience: Implications for Education and Lifelong Learning*. Brain Waves Module 2. London: The Royal Society.

Thomas, G. and Loxley, A. (2007) *Deconstructing Special Education and Constructing Inclusion*. Buckingham: Open University Press.

Thomas, N. (2001) 'Listening to Children'. In P. Foley, J. Roche and S. Tucker (eds) *Children in Society: Contemporary Theory, Policy and Practice*. Basingstoke: Palgrave.

Thomas, L. (2010) *The RSA Area Based Curriculum: Engaging the Local*. London: RSA.

Thompson, M. (1997) *Professional Ethics and the Teacher*. Stoke-on-Trent: Trentham Books.

Thorndike, E. L. (1911) *Human Learning*. New York: Prentice Hall.

Thorne, B. (1993) *Boys and Girls in School*. Michigan: Rutgers University Press.

Timperley, H., Wilson, A., Barrar, H. and Fung, I. (2007) *Teacher Professional Learning and Development: Best Evidence Synthesis Iteration (BES)*. New Zealand: Ministry of Education.

Titman, W. (1994) *Special Places, Special People. The Hidden Curriculum of School Grounds*. London: WWF UK (World Wide Fund for Nature)/Learning through Landscapes.

Tizard, B. and Hughes, M. (1984) *Young Children Learning*. London: Fontana.

Tomlinson, P. (1999) 'Conscious reflection and implicit learning in teacher preparation: implications for a balanced approach', *Oxford Review of Education*, 24 (4), 533–44.

Topping, K. and others 'Promoting social competence: detailed definition of "social competence"'. Available from http://www.dundee.ac.uk/eswce/research/projects/socialcompetence/definition/ (accessed May 2011).

Tovey, H. (2007) *Playing Outdoors: Spaces and Places, Risk and Challenge*. Maidenhead: Open University Press.

Tovey, H. and Waller, T. (2014) 'Outdoor Play and Learning'. In T. Waller and G. Davis (eds) *An Introduction to Early Childhood*. 3rd edn. London: Sage Publications Ltd.

Trevarthen, C. (2004) 'Brain Development'. In, R. L. Gregory (ed.) *Oxford Companion to the Mind*. 2nd edn. Oxford, and New York: Oxford University Press, 116–27.

Troyna, B. and Hatcher, R. (1992) *Racism in Children's Lives: A Study of Mainly White Primary Schools*. London: Routledge.

United Nations (1989) *Convention on the Rights of the Child*. New York: United Nations.

UNESCO (1994) *The Salamanca Statement on Principles, Policy and Practice in Special Needs Education*. Salamanca: UNESCO.

UNICEF (2002) *Every Child: The Rights of the Child in Words and Pictures*. London: Red Fox/ Random House.

UNICEF Office of Research (2013) 'Child Well-being in Rich Countries: A comparative overview'. Innocenti Report Card 11. UNICEF Office of Research, Florence.

United Nations (1948) *Universal Declaration of Human Rights*. New York: United Nations.

Van de Pol, J. Volan, M. and Beishuizen, J. (2012) 'Promoting teacher scaffolding in small group work: a contingency perspective', *Teaching and Teacher Education*, 28 (2), 193–205.

Vincent, C. (2000) *Including Parents? Education, Citizenship and Parental Agency*. Buckingham: Open University Press.

Vincent, C., Braun, A. and Ball, S. (2007) 'Childcare and social class: Caring for young children in the UK'. Centre for Critical Education Policy Studies. London: Institute of Education.

Vygotsky, L. S. (1962) *Thought and Language*. Cambridge, MA: Massachusetts Institute of Technology.

—(1978) *Mind in Society: The Development of Higher Psychological Processes*. Cambridge, MA: Harvard University Press.

Waite, S., Davis, B. and Brown, K. (2006) 'Final report: Current Practice and Aspirations for Outdoor Learning for 2–11 year olds in Devon, July 2006'. Report for funding body EYDCP (zero14plus) and participants.

Walkerdine, V. (1984) 'Developmental Psychology and the Child-centred Pedagogy'. In J. Henriques, W. Holloway, C. Unwin, C. Venn and V. Walderdine (eds) *Changing the Subject: Psychology, Social Regulation and Subjectivity*. London: Methuen.

Waller, T. (2006) 'Don't come too close to my octopus tree: recording and evaluating young children's perspectives on outdoor environments', *Children, Youth and Environments*, 16 (2), 75–104.

—(ed.) (2009) *An Introduction to Early Childhood: A Multi-disciplinary Approach*. 2nd edn. London: Sage Publications Ltd.

—(2010) 'Digital Play in the Classroom: A Twenty-first Century Pedagogy?'. In S. Rogers (ed.) *Rethinking Play and Pedagogy in Early Childhood Education: Concepts, Contexts and Cultures*. Abingdon: Routledge Falmer.

Waller, T. and Bitou, A. (2011) 'Research with children: three challenges for participatory research in early childhood', *European Early Childhood Education Research Association Journal*, 19 (1) (March), 129–47.

Warin, J. (2010) *Stories of Self: Tracking Children's Identity and Well-being through the School Years*. Stoke-on-Trent: Trentham Books.

Warrington, M., Younger, M. and Bearne, E. (2006) *Raising Boys' Achievements in Primary Schools: Towards a Holistic Approach*. Maidenhead: Open University Press.

Waters, J. and Begley, S. (2007) 'Supporting the development of risk taking behaviours in the early years: an exploratory study', *Education 3–13*, 35 (4), 365–77.

Wearmouth, J. (2011) *Special Educational Needs. The Basics*. London: Routledge.

Weiss, M. R. and Klint, K. A. (1987) 'Show and tell in the gymnasium', *Research Quarterly for Exercise and Sport*, 58, 234–41.

Wells, G. (1986) *The Meaning Makers: Children Learning Language and Using Language to Learn*. Portsmouth, NH: Heinemann.

Welsh Assembly (2002) *The Welsh Assembly Government Play Policy*. Cardiff: Welsh Assembly Government.

Welsh Assembly Government (2011) *Foundation Phase*. Available from http://wales.gov.uk/topics/educationandskills/earlyyearshome/foundation_phase/?lang=en (accessed 3 December 2011).

Wenger, E. (1998) *Communities of Practice: Learning, Meaning, and Identity*. Cambridge: Cambridge University Press.

—(1999) *Communities of Practice: Learning, Meaning and Identity*. Cambridge: Cambridge University Press.

Wertsch, J. V. (1985) *Vygotsky and the Social Formation of Mind*. Cambridge, MA: Harvard University Press.

—(1991) *Voices of the Mind: A Sociocultural Approach to Mediated Action*. Cambridge, MA: Harvard University Press.

West, A. and Pennell, H. (2003) *Underachievement in Schools*. London: RoutledgeFalmer.

Westcott, E. (2004) 'The early years workforce- towards professional status? An issues paper'. Unpublished paper presented at the Senior Practitioner Working group, DfES, 2004.

Whalley, M. (ed.) (1997) *Working with Parents*. Abingdon: Hodder & Stoughton.

—(2001) *Involving Parents in their Children's Learning*. London: Paul Chapman.

—(2006) 'Leadership in integrated centres and services for children and families—a community development approach: engaging with the struggle', *Children's Issues: Journal of the Children's Issues Centre*, 10 (2), 8–13. Available from http://www.ncsl.org/programmes/npqicl/index.cfm (accessed 10 August 2007).

—(2007) *Involving Parents in their Children's Learning*. London: Sage Publications Ltd.

—(2008) *Leading Practice in Early Years Settings*. Exeter: Learning Matters Ltd.

White, M. A. (1971) 'The View from the Pupil's Desk'. In M. Silberman (ed.) *The Experience of Schooling*. New York: Rinehart and Winston, 337–45.

White, J. (1978) 'The primary teacher as servant of the state', *Education 3–13*, 7 (2), 18–23.

Whitebread, D., Basilio, M., Kuvalja, M. and Verma, M. (2012) 'The importance of play'. Written for Toy Industries of Europe (TIE). Available from http://www.importanceofplay.eu/IMG/pdf/dr_david_whitebread_-_the_importance_of_play.pdf (accessed 13 June 2014).

Whitebread, D. and Bingham, S. (2011) 'School Readiness: A critical review of perspectives and evidence'. Association for the Professional Development of Early Years Educators: Occasional Paper 2. Available from http://tactyc.org.uk/occasional-paper/occasional-paper2.pdf (accessed 4 September 2012).

Whitebread, D. and Coltman, P. (2008) *Teaching and Learning in the Early Years*. Oxon: Routledge.

Wilcox-Herzog, A. and Kontos, S. (1998) 'The nature of teacher talk in early childhood classrooms and its relationship to children's play with objects and peers', *Journal of Genetic Psychology*, 159 (1), 30–44.

Wilkinson, R. and Pickett, K. (2010) *The Spirit Level: Why Equality Is Better for Everyone*. London: Penguin.

Wilshaw, M. (2014) 'Interview'. In *Today Show*, BBC Radio 4, 3 April 2014.

Winch, C. (2012) *Dimensions of Expertise: A Conceptual Exploration of Vocational Knowledge*. London: Continuum.

Wolfendale, S. (1996) 'The Relationship between Parental Involvement and Educational Achievement'. In C. Cullingford (ed.) *Parents, Education and the State*. Aldershot: Arena Books, 21–40.

Wood, D. (1988) *How Children Think and Learn*. Oxford: Blackwell.

Wood, D., Bruner, J. S. and Ross, G. (1976) 'The role of tutoring in problem solving', *Journal of Child Psychology and Psychiatry*, 17 (19), 89–100.

Woods, P. and Jeffery, B. (1996) *Teachable Moments: The art of Teaching in Primary Schools*. Buckingham: Open University Press.

World Health Organisation (2006) 'The WHO child Growth Standards'. Available from http://www.who.int/childgrowth/standards/en/ (accessed 10 August 2013).

—(2007) 'Early Childhood Development: A Powerful Equalizer'. Available from http://whqlibdoc.who.int/hq/2007/a91213.pdf (accessed 10 August 2013).

Wortham, S. (2008) *Assessment in Early Childhood Education*. New Jersey: Pearson.

Wragg E. C. and Brown, G. (2001) *Explaining in the Primary School*. London: Falmer.

Wright, C. (1992) *Race Relations in the Primary School*. London: David Fulton.

Wyness, M. G. (1999) 'Childhood, agency and education reform', *Childhood*, 6 (3), 353–68.

Yelland, N. J. (1999) 'Technology and play: new ways of discovery and learning', *Educating Young Children*, 5 (3), 32–4.

—(2007) *Shift to the Future: Rethinking Learning with new Technologies in Education*. New York: Routledge.

—(2009) 'What next for new Learning? Using new Technologies to Engage Learners in the 21st Century'. In F Sanjakdar (ed.) *Digital Portfolios: Reconceptualising Inquiry in Pre-service Teacher Education*. Frenchs Forrest: Pearson Education Australia, 117–25.

Young, M. F. D. (ed.) (1971) *Knowledge and Control*. London: Collier-Macmillan.

Younger, M., Warrington, M. and McLellan, R. (2005) *Raising Boys' Achievement in Secondary Schools: Issues, Dilemmas and Opportunities*. Maidenhead: Open University Press.

Zeedyk, S. (2006) 'From intersubjectivity to subjectivity: the transformative roles of emotional intimacy and imitation', *Infant and Child Development*, 15, 321–44.

Zeichner, K. and Liston, D. (1996) *Reflective Teaching: An Introduction*. Mahwah, NJ: Lawrence Erlbaum Associates.

Zevenbergen, R. (2007) 'Digital natives come to preschool: implications for early childhood practice', *Contemporary Issues in Early Childhood*, 8 (1), 19–29.

# Index

This index covers Chapters 1–17 and the Epilogue but not the Foreword, Introduction, summary pages at the start of each chapter or reading lists. Selected significant proper names are indexed. The index covers topics in case studies and reflective activities, though these are not specifically identified; an 'f' after a page number indicates a figure; an '(RA)' indicates a reflective activity (in boxed text); an '(RB)' indicates a figure in a research briefing; a '(CS)' indicates a case study; bold type indicates TLRP principles (in boxed text); italic type indicates framework concepts (in boxed text); underlined type indicates principal coverage of these principles and concepts (Chapters 4 and 16).

# Readings for Reflective Teaching in Early Education: Contents list

# The Reflective Teaching Series

**This book is one of the *Reflective Teaching Series* – applying principles of reflective practice in early, school, further, higher, adult and vocational education.** Developed over three decades, the series books, companion readers and website represent the accumulated understanding of generations of teachers and educationalists. Uniquely, they offer *two* levels of support in the development of teacher expertise:

- *Comprehensive, practical guidance* on key issues – including learning, relationships, curriculum, teaching, assessment and evaluation.

- *Evidence-informed principles* to support deeper understanding.

*The Reflective Teaching Series* thus supports both initial steps in teaching and the development of career-long professionalism.

The series is supported by a website, **reflectiveteaching.co.uk**. For each book, this site is being developed to offer a range of resources including reflective activities, research briefings, advice on further reading and additional chapters. The site also offers generic resources such as a compendium of educational terms, links to other useful websites, and a conceptual framework for 'deepening expertise'. The latter draws on and showcases some of the UK's best educational research.

Underlying these materials, there are three key messages.

- It *is* now possible to identify teaching strategies which are more effective than others in most circumstances. Whatever the age of the learners for whom we have responsibility, we now need to be able to develop, improve, promote and defend our expertise by marshalling such evidence and by embedding enquiry, evaluation and improvement within our routine practices.

- All evidence has to be interpreted – and we do this by 'making sense'. In other words, as well as deploying effective strategies, we need to be able to pick out the underlying principles of learning and teaching to which specific policies and practices relate. As well as being practically competent, we need to be able to *understand* what is going on.

- Finally, we need to remember that education has moral purposes and social consequences. The provision we make is connected to our future as societies and to the life-chances of those in our care. The issues require very careful consideration.

The series is coordinated through meetings of the volume and series editors: Paul Ashwin, Jennifer Colwell, Maggie Gregson, Yvonne Hillier, Amy Pollard and Andrew Pollard. Each volume has an editorial team of contributors whose collective expertise and experience enable research and practice to be reviewed and applied in relation to early, school, further, higher, adult and vocational education.

The series is the first product of the Pollard Partnership, a collaboration between Andrew and Amy Pollard to maximize the beneficial use of research and evidence on public life, policymaking and professional practice.

Andrew Pollard
Bristol, February 2015